Studies in the History of Medieval Religion

VOLUME XLVI

THE FRIARIES OF MEDIEVAL LONDON

Studies in the History of Medieval Religion

ISSN 0955–2480

Founding Editor
Christopher Harper-Bill

Series Editor
Frances Andrews

Previously published titles in the series
are listed at the back of this volume

THE FRIARIES OF MEDIEVAL LONDON

FROM FOUNDATION TO DISSOLUTION

Nick Holder

With contributions by Ian Betts, Jens Röhrkasten,
Mark Samuel and Christian Steer

THE BOYDELL PRESS

© Nick Holder 2017

All Rights Reserved. Except as permitted under current legislation
no part of this work may be photocopied, stored in a retrieval system,
published, performed in public, adapted, broadcast,
transmitted, recorded or reproduced in any form or by any means,
without the prior permission of the copyright owner

The right of Nick Holder to be identified
as the author of this work has been asserted in accordance with
sections 77 and 78 of the Copyright, Designs and Patents Act 1988

First published 2017
The Boydell Press, Woodbridge
Paperback edition 2019

ISBN 978-1-78327-224-2 hardback
ISBN 978-1-78327-431-4 paperback

The Boydell Press is an imprint of Boydell & Brewer Ltd
PO Box 9, Woodbridge, Suffolk IP12 3DF, UK
and of Boydell & Brewer Inc.
668 Mount Hope Ave, Rochester, NY 14620–2731, USA
website: www.boydellandbrewer.com

A CIP catalogue record for this book is available
from the British Library

The publisher has no responsibility for the continued existence or accuracy of URLs for external or third-party
internet websites referred to in this book, and does not guarantee that any content on such websites is, or will
remain, accurate or appropriate

Contents

List of Illustrations and Tables — vii
Contributors — xii
Acknowledgements — xiii
Abbreviations — xiv

Introduction — 1

Part I: The Nine London Friaries

1. The First Black Friars in Holborn, c. 1223–86 — 15
2. The Second Black Friars, 1275–1538 — 27
3. The Third Black Friars at St Bartholomew's, 1556–9 — 57
4. Grey Friars, 1225–1538 — 66
5. White Friars, c. 1247–1538 — 97
6. Austin Friars, c. 1265–1538 — 119
7. Crossed Friars, c. 1268–1538 — 142
8. Sack Friars, c. 1270–1305 — 160
9. Pied Friars, 1267–1317 — 167

Part II: The London Friars and their Friaries

10. Churches — 175
11. Precincts and the Use of Space — 191
12. Architecture and Architectural Fragments of the London Friaries — 211
    Mark Samuel
13. Floor Tiles and Building Materials from the London Friaries — 227
    Ian Betts

14. Water Supply 245

15. Economy 251

16. Spiritual Life and Education in the London Friaries 258
    Jens Röhrkasten

17. Burial and Commemoration in the London Friaries 272
    Christian Steer

18. London Friars and Londoners 293

19. Dissolution 305

Conclusions 313
Timeline 325
Bibliography 327
Index 352

Illustrations and Tables

Figures

1.	Map of medieval London showing the location of the friaries and other religious houses	2
2.	Illustration of the technique of digital map regression	8
3.	Map showing the location of the Holborn Black Friars precinct	16
4.	Map showing the approximate location of the tenements acquired by the Black friars for their Holborn priory	19
5.	Map showing the church and claustral wing(s) of the thirteenth-century Black Friars in Holborn	23
6.	Map showing the reconstructed precinct of the thirteenth-century Black Friars in Holborn	24
7.	Map showing the location of the medieval Black Friars precinct and archaeological excavations	30
8.	Map of the landscape of the future Blackfriars in the 1270s, indicating the probable parish boundaries of St Andrew, St Martin and St Bride	31
9.	Map showing the construction of the new city wall and the Black Friars priory beginning in 1278–9	33
10.	Map of the precinct of Black Friars in the sixteenth century	35
11.	Plan of the church of Black Friars	39
12.	Detail of Wyngaerde's view of the church of Black Friars in c. 1544 (© Ashmolean Museum, University of Oxford)	41
13.	Plan of the main cloister at Black Friars	44
14.	View of the remains of the main dormitory wing between the northern and southern cloisters of Black Friars, discovered in 1872 (by kind permission of the Society of Antiquaries of London)	46
15.	View of a window from the north wall of the undercroft of the late thirteenth-century chapter house, revealed in an excavation in 1988 (MOLA)	49
16.	Reconstructed detailed plan and sectional elevation of the late thirteenth-century chapter house of Black Friars	50
17.	Map showing the Black friars' precinct of 1556–9 within the former St Bartholomew's priory	62
18.	View of the gatehouse at St Bartholomew-the-Great	64

19.	Map showing the location of the Grey Friars and archaeological sites within its precinct	69
20.	Map showing the location of the tenements acquired by the Grey friars for their priory	74
21.	Map of the precinct of Grey Friars in the sixteenth century	75
22.	Plan of the western part of the former Grey Friars entitled 'The Plat of the Graye Friers', 1616 (© St Bartholomew's Hospital Archives)	79
23.	Detail of Wyngaerde's view of London showing the church of Grey Friars in c. 1544 (© Ashmolean Museum, University of Oxford)	80
24.	Detail of the 'copperplate' map-view of the 1550s showing Grey Friars shortly after the Dissolution (© Museum of London)	80
25.	Plan of the church of Grey Friars	81
26.	Plan of the eastern part of the former Grey Friars, surveyed in 1656 (by kind permission of Christ's Hospital Foundation)	87
27.	View of 1825 looking north in the former great cloister of Grey Friars (London Metropolitan Archives, City of London)	88
28.	Plan of the great cloister of Grey Friars	89
29.	Mid-seventeenth-century plan of the former friary infirmary	91
30.	Plan of the little cloister, including the infirmary wing on the west side	92
31.	Map showing the location of the White Friars and archaeological sites within its precinct	99
32.	The fourteenth-century vaulted undercroft of the Carmelite prior's house, on the move in 1991 (MOLA)	100
33.	Map showing the location of the tenements acquired by the White friars for their priory	102
34.	Map of the precinct of White Friars in the sixteenth century	106
35.	Plan of the medieval church of White Friars	107
36.	Early 'rescue archaeology' by Henry Hodge in 1882: the north-east corner of the White Friars nave (London Metropolitan Archives, City of London)	108
37.	Nineteenth-century copy of a survey of c. 1627 showing the area of the White Friars cloister (© The British Library Board)	111
38.	Map showing the medieval cloister of White Friars	112
39.	Photograph of the fourteenth-century vaulted cellar beneath the Carmelite prior's house (Andy Chopping/MOLA)	113
40.	Detail of the 'copperplate' map-view of the 1550s showing White Friars shortly after the Dissolution (© Museum of London)	116
41.	Map showing the location of the Austin Friars and archaeological sites within its precinct	122
42.	Map showing the area of Broad Street in the thirteenth century before the arrival of the Austin friars	123
43.	Map of the precinct of Austin Friars in the sixteenth century	127

ILLUSTRATIONS AND TABLES ix

44. View of the west end and north aisle of the Dutch Church, the former nave of Austin Friars, in 1823 (London Metropolitan Archives, City of London) 129
45. Plan of the church of Austin Friars 131
46. Montage of photographs of 1929 showing an arcade arch that once divided the choir of Austin Friars from the parish church of St Peter the Poor (reproduced by permission of Historic England Archive) 133
47. Detail of Wyngaerde's view of London showing the church of Austin Friars in c. 1544 (© Ashmolean Museum, University of Oxford) 134
48. Map of the two cloisters of Austin Friars: the late thirteenth-century main cloister and the late fourteenth-century inner or northern cloister 136
49. Reconstruction of the late thirteenth-century cloister at Austin Friars 137
50. Map showing the location of the Crossed Friars precinct and archaeological excavations on the site 144
51. Detail of Wyngaerde's view of London showing the church and precinct of Crossed Friars in c. 1544 (© Ashmolean Museum, University of Oxford) 145
52. Detail of Ogilby and Morgan's map of London of 1676, showing possible surviving buildings of Crossed Friars (reproduced by kind permission of Harry Margary in association with the London Metropolitan Archives) 145
53. Map showing the location of the tenements acquired by the Crossed friars for their priory 148
54. Map of the precinct of Crossed Friars in the sixteenth century 150
55. Plan of the church of Crossed Friars in 1320 151
56. Plan of the church of Crossed Friars showing the various phases of construction from the fourteenth to the sixteenth centuries 153
57. Tomb of Sir Richard Cholmeley and his wife Elizabeth, probably transferred from the church of Crossed Friars to St Peter ad Vincula (Christian Steer) 155
58. Map showing the location of the Sack Friars precinct 161
59. Map showing the approximate location of the tenements acquired by the Sack friars 164
60. Map showing the reconstructed precinct of Sack Friars 165
61. Map showing the location of the Pied Friars precinct 168
62. Map showing the plots and messuages acquired by the Pied friars 169
63. Map showing the arrangement of the Pied Friars precinct in the thirteenth century 171
64. Plans of the seven thirteenth-century friars' churches; the partly surviving churches of the Cambridge Dominicans and Norwich Sack friars are also shown 176
65. Photograph of the simple late thirteenth-century window arch from the chapter house of the second Black Friars 177
66. Plans of the five late medieval friars' churches 180
67. Chronology of construction campaigns at the friars' churches 181

x   ILLUSTRATIONS AND TABLES

68. Plan comparing the internal spaces of the four main London friary churches with other English mendicant churches — 186
69. Maps showing the foundation plots of the seven London friaries — 192
70. Maps showing the precincts of the seven friaries in the 1270s — 194
71. Chronology of construction campaigns at the friary precincts — 196
72. Plans showing the five friary precincts in the early sixteenth century — 197
73. Comparative plan of two late thirteenth- or early fourteenth-century cloisters: Grey Friars and Austin Friars — 199
74. The model for the London friaries? Two London monastic precincts of the thirteenth century: the Augustinian canons' houses of Holy Trinity and St Mary Spital — 201
75. Plan of Black Friars showing how friars, servants and visitors may have circulated — 208
76. A comparison of window mouldings used in the London friaries — 216
77. Pier base from the Black Friars church; 'sunk chamfer' tracery used in a window of the Grey Friars church (Richard Lea) — 217
78. Selected architectural mouldings (other than windows) from the London friaries — 218
79. Photograph of a column from the undercroft of the late thirteenth-century chapter house of Black Friars (Andy Chopping/MOLA) — 219
80. Floor tiles from Black Friars — 231
81. Floor tiles from Grey Friars — 233
82. Floor tiles from White Friars — 234
83. Floor tiles from Austin Friars — 237
84. Floor tiles from Crossed Friars — 238
85. Map showing the Grey Friars water supply — 247
86. Photograph of the Grey friars' fourteenth-century conduit-head in Bloomsbury, re-erected in 1927 (Andy Chopping/MOLA) — 248
87. The fourteenth-century missal owned by the London White Friars, detail showing Carmelite friars celebrating mass on Holy Saturday (© The British Library Board) — 260
88. Tombs of: a) William, Viscount Beaumont (d. 1507), Black Friars; b) Richard Beauchamp, Lord St Amand (d. 1508), Black Friars; c) Sir Stephen Jenyns (d. 1523), Grey Friars (© The British Library Board) — 274
89. Indents of memorial brasses from Austin Friars: a) a civilian with three wives, c. 1480; b) a civilian, c. 1480; c) a civilian kneeling at a prie-dieu, early sixteenth century (with permission from the Monumental Brass Society) — 278
90. Monumental brass of Gerard Danet (d. 1520), St Mary's church, Tilty, Essex (with permission from the Monumental Brass Society) — 282
91. Two rented tenements developed by the prior of Austin Friars in 1510 — 303

Tables

1.	The orders of friars in medieval England	xvi
2.	Quantitative summary of the documentary, archaeological, architectural and cartographic evidence used in this book	11
3.	List of the tenements acquired by the Black friars for their Holborn priory	18
4.	Royal grants towards the construction of the Holborn Black Friars, 1235–73	21
5.	List of the tenements acquired by the Grey friars for their friary	72
6.	Documentary information for the interior of Grey Friars church	83
7.	List of the tenements acquired by the White friars for their precinct	101
8.	Royal grants towards the construction of the White Friars, 1267–99	104
9.	List of the tenements acquired by the Austin friars for their friary	125
10.	Documentary evidence for chapels, altars and images in the church of Austin Friars	132
11.	List of the tenements acquired by the Crossed friars for their priory	147
12.	List of the tenements acquired by the Pied friars for their priory	170
13.	Size and date of the friars' churches and other London-area churches in the fourteenth century	183
14.	Summary of useful architectural fragments from London friary sites	212
15.	Types of floor tile correlated by friary and area of friary	228
16.	Explanation of the floor tile types used in the London friaries	229
17.	Documentary evidence for the use of lead as a roofing material in the London friaries	240
18.	Types of building stone identified at the London friaries	243
19.	Estimated annual income and expenditure at the London Austin Friars in the early sixteenth century	253
20.	The friars' rental income in the early sixteenth century	300

The authors and publishers are grateful to all the institutions and individuals listed for permission to reproduce the materials to which they hold copyright. Every effort has been made to trace the copyright holders; apologies are offered for any omission, and the publishers will be pleased to add any necessary acknowledgement in subsequent editions.

Contributors

The details of my fellow authors' contributions are given below, along with those who have provided illustrative material

Text

Ian Betts: Chapter 13: Floor Tiles and Building Materials from the London Friaries
Jens Röhrkasten: Chapter 16: Spiritual Life and Education in the London Friaries
Mark Samuel: Chapter 12: Architecture and Architectural Fragments of the London Friaries
Christian Steer: Chapter 17: Burial and Commemoration in the London Friaries

Graphics

Andy Chopping: photography (Figures 39, 79, 86)
Hannah Faux: tile drawings (Figures 80–4)
Carlos Lemos: maps, plans and other illustrations
Mark Samuel: architectural drawings (Figures 16, 49, 76, 78; reconstruction painting reproduced on front cover)
Christian Steer: photography (Figure 57)

Acknowledgements

Firstly, I would like to thank my fellow authors for their generous contributions to this book; their scholarship has also helped to shape it. The editorial team at Boydell & Brewer have carefully steered the work towards completion; I am very grateful for the guidance and help of Caroline Palmer, Robert Kinsey and others.

I am delighted to acknowledge the help and advice I have received from a large number of friends and colleagues; in particular, Caroline Barron, Roberta Gilchrist and Vanessa Harding gave me the initial idea for the book and have kindly commented on many aspects of the text. At, or formerly at, Museum of London Archaeology and the Museum of London, I thank David Bowsher, Sarah Jones, John Schofield, Roy Stephenson, Steve Tucker and Bruce Watson; at Royal Holloway (University of London) I am grateful for the advice of Clive Burgess; at Regent's University London may I acknowledge the support of Sophie Laws and Tom Villis. Many others have kindly answered queries, corrected errors or fed me useful information: I thank Charlotte Bolland, Ann Bowtell, Gary Brown, Nicola Clark, Justin Colson, Charlie Farris, Jessica Freeman, Dorian Gerhold, Alden Gregory, Peter Murray Jones, Jennifer Ledfors, Jessica Lutkin, David Moncur, Martin Ollé, Keith Pearshouse, the late Chris Phillpotts and Bob Wood.

No researcher can work without the help of archivists: I am always impressed by the welcome I receive in London, Swindon, Chester and elsewhere. I try to smile and say 'thank you' when visiting your institutions but I apologise if you caught me on a bad day.

Finally, may I thank my family Sophie, Leon and Bonnie for their patience with all this 'medieval stuff' (but this may not be the end of it).

The authors gratefully acknowledge the financial assistance received from the Arts and Humanities Research Council, the London and Middlesex Archaeological Society, the City of London Archaeological Trust, the Marc Fitch Fund and the Francis Coales Charitable Foundation.

Abbreviations

Bibliographic abbreviations

CChR	*Calendar of the Charter Rolls Preserved in the Public Record Office*, 6 vols (London: HMSO, 1903–20)
CCR	*Calendar of the Close Rolls Preserved in the Public Record Office*, 61 vols (London: HMSO, 1892–1975)
CLR	*Calendar of the Liberate Rolls Preserved in the Public Record Office*, ed. W.H. Stevenson, 6 vols (London: HMSO, 1916–64)
CPR	*Calendar of Patent Rolls Preserved in the Public Record Office*, 36 vols (various publishers, 1893–)
Letters and Papers	*Letters and Papers, Foreign and Domestic, of the Reign of Henry VIII*, ed. J.S. Brewer and others, 22 vols (London: Longman, 1862–1932)
Grey Friars	*Grey Friars of London: Their History, with the Register of Their Convent and an Appendix of Documents*, ed. Charles L. Kingsford (Aberdeen: British Society of Franciscan Studies, 1915)
Mills and Oliver	*The Survey of Building Sites in the City of London After the Great Fire of 1666*, P. Mills and J. Oliver, 5 vols, London Topographical Society, 97–9, 101, 103 (London: London Topographical Society, 1962–7)
ODNB	*Oxford Dictionary of National Biography* (Oxford: Oxford University Press), online edition, 2004 (with later updates)
PCC	Prerogative Court of Canterbury
VCH	Victoria County History (title abbreviated to *London*, *Kent*, etc)

Abbreviations of archives and other organisations

AOC	AOC Archaeology Ltd
BL	British Library
CC	Clothworkers' Company
CMH	Centre for Metropolitan History
CRO	Cheshire Record Office
DC	Drapers' Company

FSL	Folger Shakespeare Library
GL	Guildhall Library
LAA	London Archaeological Archive
LMA	London Metropolitan Archive
LTS	London Topographical Society
MOLA(S)	Museum of London Archaeology (formerly Museum of London Archaeology Service)
PCA	Pre-Construct Archaeology Ltd
RCHME	Royal Commission on Historical Monuments (England)
SBH	St Bartholomew's Hospital archive
SHC	Surrey History Centre
TNA	The National Archives

Abbreviations of measurements

ha	hectares
m	metres
ft	feet
in	inches

Note on spelling

The names of the friars and friaries are capitalised in this book as follows: the Black friars lived in their priory, Black Friars, which, after the Dissolution, was known as Blackfriars. The various English and Latin names of the friars are tabulated in Table 1. All quotations use the original spelling (with manuscript abbreviations silently expanded); most first names and street names are, however, given in modernised spelling.

Table 1 The orders of friars in medieval England.

Order	English name	Explanation of English name and other notes	Medieval Latin name	In London?
Dominican	Black friars	the black cloak the friars wore outside the friary	*fratres predicatorum*	Yes: Chapters 1–3
Franciscan	Grey friars	the grey hooded woollen habit	*fratres minorum*	Yes: Chapter 4
Observant Franciscan		the fifteenth-century 'observant' wing (not yet formally separate from the 'conventual' wing) had six houses in England	*fratres minorum de observantia*	near London in Greenwich and Richmond; see Introduction n. 5
Carmelite	White friars	the white cloak the friars wore outside the friary	*fratres de beatissime virginis Marie de monte Carmelo*	Yes: Chapter 5
Augustinian	Austin friars	spoken abbreviation of 'Augustine' to 'Austin'	*fratres sancti Augustini*	Yes: Chapter 6
Crossed	Crossed, Crutched or Crouched friars	the English translation (crossed) or pronunciation (crutched, crouched) of Latin *cruciferi*	*fratres cruciferi*	Yes: Chapter 7
Sack	Sack friars	sack-like cloth of their habit	*fratres de penitencia Jesu Christi*	Yes: Chapter 8
Pied	Pied friars	black outer scapular worn over a white mantle, hence pied (like a magpie)	*fratres beate Marie*; *fratres de Areno*	Yes: Chapter 9
Trinitarian	Trinitarian friars	friar-canons; referring to the doctrine of the trinity	*fratres sanctissime trinitatis*	near London in Hounslow; see Introduction n. 5

Introduction

THIS book takes one of the largest cities in northern Europe as its subject and examines in detail some of its most important medieval churches and landmarks: the friaries. The friars were a new religious group of the early thirteenth century. The young merchant Giovanni di Bernardone (better known as St Francis of Assisi) formed a band of poor lay preachers in Tuscany in the first decade of the century. At almost exactly the same time, the Castilian priest Domingo de Guzmán (later St Dominic) established a more organised group of anti-heretical preachers in the towns of southern France. These small groups were quickly embraced by the Church hierarchy who saw their potential as religious recruits to help spread the word of God in the ever-growing towns of Europe.

One can, perhaps, judge the size and significance of a medieval town or city by the number of its friaries: small towns in southern England like Ware or Maldon had a single friary, large regional centres such as Bristol had four friaries and the major administrative and mercantile centre of Norwich had five. London had a record-breaking seven friaries in the thirteenth century, nearly as many as the greatest city of the north, Paris, which had the full range of nine mendicant houses.[1]

Successive chapters of the book will consider the evidence for these London priories: Dominican, Franciscan, Carmelite, Augustinian, Crossed, Sack and Pied (Table 1; Figure 1).

---

[1] In addition to the seven mendicant orders present in London, Paris could boast (in the thirteenth century) Trinitarians and Williamites: Deirdre O'Sullivan, *In the Company of the Preachers: The Archaeology of Medieval Friaries in England and Wales*, Leicester Archaeology Monographs, 23 (University of Leicester, 2013), pp. 65–73, 235–7, 255–69, 331–3; Richard W. Emery, *The Friars in Medieval France: A Catalogue of French Mendicant Convents, 1200–1550* (New York: Columbia University Press, 1962), p. 109; Philippe Lorentz and Dany Sandron, *Atlas de Paris Au Moyen Âge: Éspace Urbain, Habitat, Société, Religion, Lieux de Pouvoir* (Paris: Parigramme, 2006), pp. 144–51. The idea of ranking a town based on the number of its friaries comes from the work of Jacques Le Goff: 'Apostolat Mendiant et Fait Urbain dans la France Médiévale: L'implantation des Ordres Mendiants', *Annales*, 23 (1968), 335–48; 'Ordres Mendiants et Urbanisation dans la France Médiévale', *Annales*, 25 (1970), 924–46.

Fig. 1. Map of medieval London showing the location of the friaries and other religious houses (scale 1:25,000).

From the thirteenth to the sixteenth century, medieval Londoners poured investment into these institutions in return for the spiritual services that the friars offered. The seven London friaries were reduced to five by the fourteenth century, once two orders – the Sack Friars and the Pied Friars – were closed down as part of the tidying up of the mendicant orders that followed the church council known as the Second Council of Lyon in 1274. Two and a half centuries later, English friars, like their religious colleagues the monks, nuns and (most) canons, had to 'change [their] coats' and seek work as ordinary secular priests with the Dissolution of the Monasteries in the late 1530s (Chapter 19: Dissolution).[2] A brief revival of a single London friary under Mary in 1556 lasted less than three years (Chapter 3: The Third Black Friars at St Bartholomew's). Nearly five centuries later, virtually no trace of these once great institutions survives in London, having been obliterated by the Dissolution, the Great Fire and wartime bombing.

[2] The London Franciscan guardian Thomas Chapman wrote to the archbishop of Canterbury's steward in August 1538 enthusing that 'we all long to change our coats'; three months later he and his friars did just that: *Letters and Papers*, xiii(2), no. 251.

Using a combination of documentary, cartographic, archaeological and architectural evidence, this book will attempt to reconstruct the layout of the churches, cloisters and precincts of these London monastic houses. It is divided into two parts. In Part I, successive chapters examine the evidence in detail for each of the seven friaries. The Dominican Black friars had three successive houses and so the seven orders are, in fact, dealt with in nine chapters, each dealing with a physical friary (Part I, Chapters 1 to 9).[3] In Part II the approach is more thematic, examining a range of historical and archaeological questions concerning the friars and their urban monastic houses. The spatial organisation and architecture of the friaries are examined in Chapters 10 to 14. Separate chapters examine the development of the friary churches (10) and precincts (11). Chapter 12 uses the evidence of archaeologically recovered architectural fragments to examine the architectural styles, dates and features of the friaries in more detail; the following chapter (13) takes a similar approach for the evidence of floor tiles and other building materials. The authors then address other themes including the friaries' water supplies (Chapter 14) and their economic arrangements (Chapter 15). We return to the friars themselves in Chapter 16, which considers their spiritual life and education. In the following two chapters we examine the relations between the friars and Londoners: the dead in Chapter 17 (which looks at the use of friaries for burial) and the living in Chapter 18. The end of the friaries with their Dissolution in 1538 is discussed in Chapter 19. The final chapter attempts to sketch some areas for future research and to draw some conclusions from this study.

The book does not deal with every mendicant house in the London region. For example, the Minoresses were a group of Franciscan nuns with a large and important priory just to the east of the walled city in Aldgate. They have been the subject of a detailed topographic study and, we suggest, they could profitably be re-examined as part of a comparative study of London's nunneries.[4] Five miles down the Thames to the east of London, the Observant Franciscans (a fifteenth-century reformed group within the Franciscan order) set up a priory by Henry VII's palace at Greenwich in the 1480s with, ten miles to the west of London and a decade later, a second house by Richmond Palace. The minor order of Trinitarian friar-canons had a priory a little further west in the small town of Hounslow.[5]

---

[3] The Franciscan Grey friars and the Sack friars also moved house but the lack of surviving evidence means that their early friaries do not warrant separate chapters in this book.

[4] Martha Carlin and Derek Keene, 'Historical Gazetteer of London before the Great Fire: St Botolph Aldgate: Minories, East Side; the Abbey of St Clare; Holy Trinity Minories' (unpublished typescript, London: University of London, Institute of Historical Research, 1987). Catherine Paxton's excellent doctoral thesis concentrates on the nuns rather than the nunneries: 'The Nunneries of London and its Environs in the Later Middle Ages' (unpublished D. Phil., University of Oxford, 1993).

[5] O'Sullivan, *In the Company of the Preachers*, pp. 152–4; VCH, *Kent*, ii, 194–8; Bruce Watson and Christopher Thomas, 'The Mendicant Houses of Medieval London: An Archaeological Review', in *The Friars in Medieval Britain*, ed. N. Rogers, Harlaxton Medieval Studies, 19 (Donington: Shaun Tyas, 2010), pp. 265–97 (pp. 285–8); Caroline M. Barron and Matthew Davies, eds, *The Religious Houses of London and Middlesex* (London: Centre for Metropolitan History, 2007), pp. 291–3;

Medieval friaries and medieval London in context

If we want to travel back in time and experience something of medieval London – an impossible task, of course – there is at least a published guidebook. In 1598 the Tudor merchant tailor and antiquary John Stow published his topographic and historical investigation of the city, the *Survey of London*.[6] Based around a guided walking tour of the city's twenty-five wards, Stow's book describes the buildings and streets, giving a remarkable flavour of the city and the customs of the citizens. And, in retrospect, we can be particularly grateful for his efforts in recording old London a couple of generations before the Great Fire of 1666. The city he describes was one of the largest in Europe: it had over a hundred parish churches and a cathedral pressed within its old Roman walls, with over a dozen monasteries clustered in and around the edges of the city. These churches were stone islands in a sea of timber-framed houses: London must have been rather dark at street level, with its many narrow lanes permanently in the shade of the sun thanks to the jettied houses on opposing sides of the lanes becoming closer together at every storey. London had its secular landmarks too, such as the city hall of Guildhall from where the Corporation's officers and aldermen governed, or Blackwell Hall where English and foreign cloth merchants came to sell and buy that most valuable English commodity, woollen cloth. Then there were the city markets where the citizens bought their provisions, such as the Stocks for meat and fish, and Leadenhall for poultry, cereal and dairy produce. When the first friars set foot in London in the 1220s, this city housed perhaps 40,000 people, and this number nearly doubled within a century. By the time that the friars melted away in the late 1530s, the population had still not quite recovered from the blows of fourteenth-century famine and plague. London was, however, gradually expanding beyond the walls with new houses forming straggling suburbs along the streets leading out of the city gates.[7]

In the generations after John Stow, subsequent historians of London have very much looked back to their illustrious predecessor but two relatively recent developments have opened up the range of evidence. Firstly, the creation of national and civic archives, respectively at the old Public Record Office and at the various predecessors and components of what is now the London Metropolitan Archives, gave historians access to a remarkable

---

Robert Cowie, 'The Priory and Manor of Hounslow: Excavations at Hounslow Police Station, Montague Road, Hounslow', *Transactions of the London and Middlesex Archaeological Society*, 46 (1995), 125–35.

[6] John Stow, *A Survey of London*, ed. C.L. Kingsford, 2 vols (Oxford: Clarendon, 1908). There are various more recent one-volume editions of this work; also of note is the 'British History Online' digital edition of the 1908 Kingsford edition: <http://www.british-history.ac.uk/no-series/survey-of-london-stow/1603> (accessed 10 July 2015).

[7] For detailed overviews of the medieval city, the first with a mercantile and administrative emphasis, the second more topographical, see Caroline M. Barron, *London in the Later Middle Ages: Government and People, 1200–1500* (Oxford: Oxford University Press, 2004); John Schofield, *London, 1100–1600: The Archaeology of a Capital City* (Sheffield: Equinox, 2011).

range of surviving documentation from the medieval city.[8] The nineteenth-century editors of Dugdale's earlier historical work, the *Monasticon*, and the twentieth-century historians of the Victoria County History of London made profitable use of this newly accessible documentary material.[9]

Secondly, in the twentieth century, a number of archaeologists and archaeological organisations began their search for buried evidence of the medieval city. There were pioneers during the early decades of the century such as Alfred Clapham and Philip Norman – names that will keep cropping up in the footnotes of this book – who carried out archaeological research including difficult 'rescue' excavations during major building projects like the construction of the new General Post Office building in 1905 (on the site of Grey Friars). By the 1970s and '80s, rescue archaeology had matured and was more closely integrated with the cycles of office redevelopment that were taking place in the City of London; the Museum of London's archaeological unit undertook a series of major excavations rediscovering lost landmarks of medieval London, for example the work at Leadenhall Market or Guildhall.[10]

These archaeologists of the twentieth and twenty-first century developed an integrated approach to the study of the churches and monastic houses of medieval London. A 1910 study of the White Friars and a monograph of a century later examining the Cistercian abbey of St Mary Graces share a number of important features: they combine documentary and archaeological evidence, and they illustrate the narrative with reconstructed plans of the whole monastic precinct.[11] The investigation of London's medieval monastic houses can be seen, therefore, as one of the success stories of British archaeology with monographs and articles on a dozen or more of these great churches and precincts.

For a variety of reasons the friars have received rather less historical and archaeological attention than their religious colleagues the monks and canons. Historians have, perhaps, been put off by the lack of friary archives: there is certainly a lot more to get your teeth into when studying a Benedictine abbey-cum-cathedral with a surviving medieval archive – Norwich or Peterborough, for example.[12] Several historians have,

---

[8] For an account of London's historians, see Caroline M. Barron and Vanessa Harding, 'London', in *English County Histories: A Guide. A Tribute to C.R. Elrington* (Stroud: Sutton, 1994), pp. 258–69.

[9] William Dugdale, *Monasticon Anglicanum: A History of the Abbies and Other Monasteries, Hospitals, Frieries, and Cathedral and Collegiate Churches, with their Dependencies, in England and Wales*, ed. J. Caley and others (London: Longman, 1817); VCH, *London*.

[10] Mark Samuel, 'The Fifteenth-Century Garner at Leadenhall', *Antiquaries Journal*, 69 (1989), 119–53; David Bowsher and others, *The London Guildhall: An Archaeological History of a Neighbourhood from Early Medieval to Modern Times*, MoLAS monograph, 36 (London: Museum of London Archaeology Service, 2007).

[11] Alfred Clapham, 'The Topography of the Carmelite Priory of London', *Journal of the British Archaeological Association*, 17 (1910), 15–31; Ian Grainger and Christopher Phillpotts, *The Cistercian Abbey of St Mary Graces, East Smithfield, London*, MOLA monograph, 44 (London: Museum of London Archaeology, 2011).

[12] See Chapter 15: Economy, n. 1.

however, looked at a particular 'product' of the friars – their sermons.[13] More recently historians have begun looking at other aspects of the friars; notable in this regard is the 2007 Harlaxton symposium 'The Friars in Medieval Britain'.[14] Archaeologists, or rather interdisciplinary teams led by archaeologists, have published some remarkable works on English friaries in Norwich and Coventry, for example, and have examined English friaries as a group.[15] The best work on the London friaries is undoubtedly a study of the five main orders of London friars, which squeezed from the (at first sight) limited documentary record a remarkable amount of detail of the lives and activities of these men.[16] This book aims to follow in the footsteps of these historians and archaeologists and to sketch out the landscape of London's friaries – powerhouses of prayer and preaching in the medieval capital.

The approach of this book

In this book I want to interpret the landscape of the London friaries, and the ways in which the friary spaces were used by friars and citizens. And in order to analyse, one first needs to map these urban landscapes. The plans and maps in this book are the product of a process of map reconstruction, one which combines the evidence of historic maps, documents such as charters and surveys, and archaeological evidence. In a few cases we can also make use of standing buildings, or of records of buildings which were once standing.[17] The history of London has not, however, been favourable to the survival of historic buildings: one can note the obvious destructive factors like the Great Fire of London of 1666 and wartime bombing (particularly from autumn 1940 to summer 1941) but one should also note that the wealth and economic success of London has had a role – Londoners have not, until recently, wanted to live or work in old and unfashionable buildings.

The technique of historic map reconstruction – often called map regression – is something of a tradition practised by generations of archaeologists and historical geographers, armed with maps, tracing paper and a large light-box.[18] Modern computer technology

---

[13] David L. D'Avray, *The Preaching of the Friars: Sermons Diffused from Paris before 1300* (Oxford: Clarendon Press, 1985).

[14] Nicholas Rogers, ed., *The Friars in Medieval Britain: Proceedings of the 2007 Harlaxton Symposium*, Harlaxton Medieval Studies, 19 (Donington: Shaun Tyas, 2010).

[15] O'Sullivan, *In the Company of the Preachers*; Phillip A. Emery and Elizabeth Rutledge, *Norwich Greyfriars: Pre-Conquest Town and Medieval Friary* (Dereham: Norfolk Museums and Archaeology Service, 2007); Charmian Woodfield, *The Church of Our Lady of Mount Carmel and Some Conventual Buildings at the Whitefriars, Coventry*, British Archaeological Reports, 389 (Oxford: Archaeopress, 2005).

[16] Jens Röhrkasten, *The Mendicant Houses of Medieval London, 1221–1539* (Münster: Verlag, 2004). Röhrkasten also examines the London Minoresses.

[17] See n. 25.

[18] For more detail on the author's approach to digital map regression, see 'Cartographic reconstruction' in Bowsher, *Guildhall*, pp. 416–17; Nick Holder, 'Mapping Medieval and Early Modern

has made this process easier thanks to the newer digital versions of the old techniques: scanners for creating digital images and software for processing and manipulating these images. The aim is to create an accurate reconstructed map: one which uses the modern Ordnance Survey grid and map co-ordinates (to ensure the compatibility of old and new data) but where the network of streets and boundaries is based on the evidence of historic maps. At its simplest, if you get the historic framework of roads and boundaries correct, once you add in the walls and other evidence from archaeology, and extend or add to these with measurements and descriptions from historic surveys, the maps more or less draw themselves.

The process is illustrated in Figure 2. It begins with a 100-metre-square sample of the modern digital Ordnance Survey map of the city of London, centred on the site of the former White Friars and showing the large purpose-built office blocks that replaced the earlier newspaper factories to the south of Fleet Street (Figure 2a). We then overlay a scanned version of the 1870s Ordnance Survey map, noting how some streets have hardly changed while others have been widened in the twentieth century (Figure 2b).[19] Earlier generations of historical geographers would have reached for the tracing paper and pencil at this point; we follow their example (Figure 2c) but trace the nineteenth-century streets using digital tracing paper – a process known as digitisation (and distinct from the photographic copying process of scanning). In Figure 2d we continue to work backwards in time, this time placing a scan of Ogilby and Morgan's map of 1676 over the digital tracing of the nineteenth-century streets.[20] This reveals a common problem with seventeenth-century maps: the representation of distance tends to be accurate but the depiction of angles much less so. This limitation – a reflection of seventeenth-century surveying practice – means that one cannot simply trace the roads and historic features on the Ogilby and Morgan map; instead we have to redraw it, making subjective inferences about which details of the road pattern should be 'retained' from the 1870s map and which details to trace or draw anew. The resulting digital version of Ogilby and Morgan's map, Figure 2e, is significantly more accurate than their original engraved map, Figure 2d: the seventeenth-century map has been imbued with the accuracy of twenty-first century surveying.

We can now start to bring in the evidence of earlier surveys, both drawn and descriptive. In Figure 2f dozens of surveys carried out in this area after the Great Fire of London

London: The Use of Cartographic, Documentary and Archaeological Evidence', in 'Hidden Histories and Records of Antiquity': Essays on Saxon and Medieval London for John Clark, Curator Emeritus, Museum of London, LAMAS Special Paper, 17 (London: London and Middlesex Archaeological Society, 2014), 26–32. The following paragraphs are largely based on the second article.

[19] A convenient source of these remarkable historic town maps is the Godfrey Edition series of printed reproductions. This figure uses the Ordnance Survey 1875 London sheet VII.64, reproduced in the Godfrey Edition series as *Fleet St & the Strand 1874* (Dunston, 1993).

[20] Ogilby and Morgan's map of 1676 reproduced as John Ogilby and William Morgan, *A Large and Accurate Map of the City of London* (Lympne Castle, Kent: Margary, 1976).

8   THE FRIARIES OF MEDIEVAL LONDON

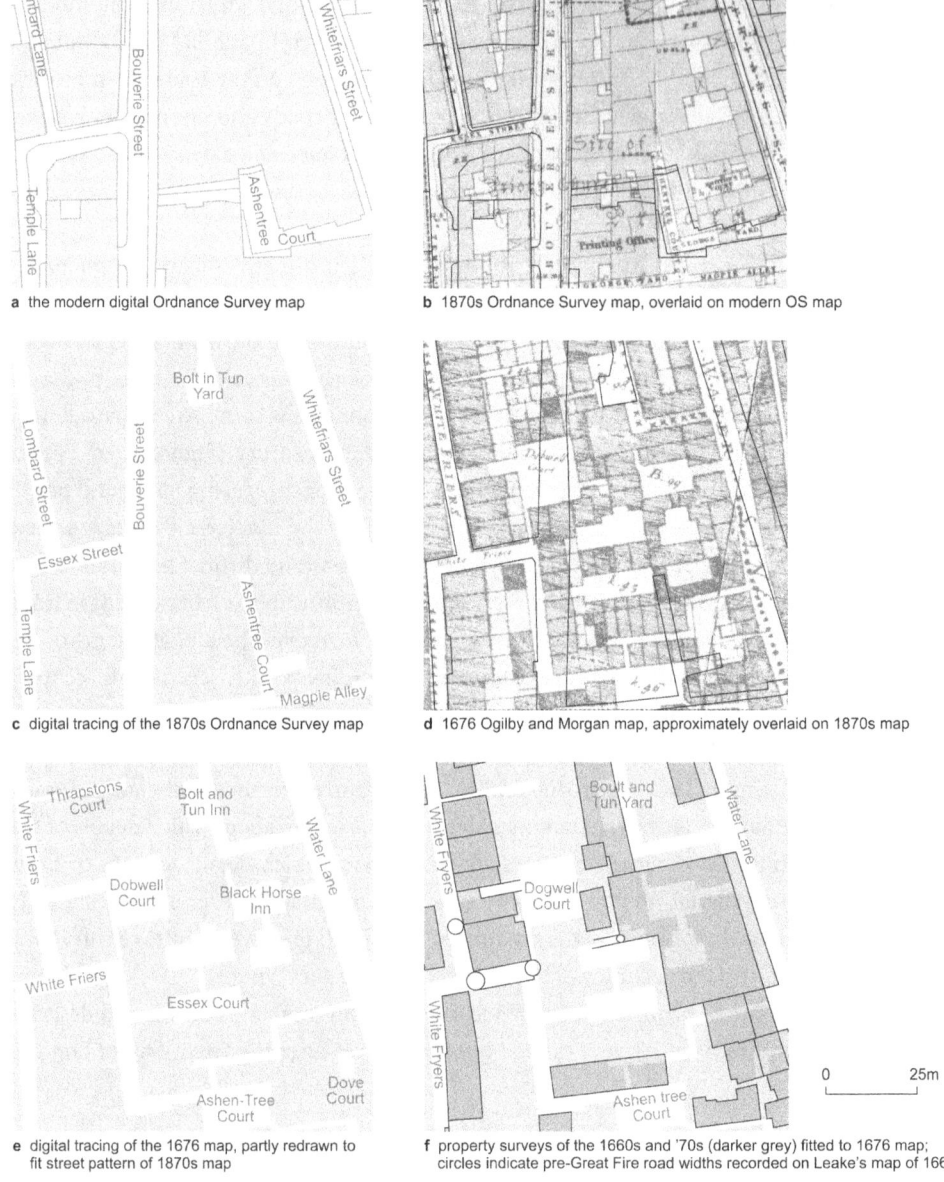

a the modern digital Ordnance Survey map

b 1870s Ordnance Survey map, overlaid on modern OS map

c digital tracing of the 1870s Ordnance Survey map

d 1676 Ogilby and Morgan map, approximately overlaid on 1870s map

e digital tracing of the 1676 map, partly redrawn to fit street pattern of 1870s map

f property surveys of the 1660s and '70s (darker grey) fitted to 1676 map; circles indicate pre-Great Fire road widths recorded on Leake's map of 1666

Fig. 2. Illustration of the technique of digital map regression, the process used to create the maps and plans in this book.

INTRODUCTION 9

g survey of c. 1630

h digital tracing of c. 1630 survey, overlaid and redrawn to fit 17th-c map

i properties sold in the 1540s after the Dissolution, overlaid on 17th-c mapping

j archaeological sites and areas of significant archaeological recording

k walls and significant archaeological features

l reconstructed map of part of White Friars precinct, integrating cartographic, documentary and archaeological evidence ('T' indicates rented tenement)

Fig. 2 (continued)

(by the surveyors Peter Mills and John Oliver) are pieced together as a partly completed jigsaw puzzle. Their measured sketches and notes record important details of the pre-Fire landscape such as walls and roads.[21] The other important source is the map of the Fire-

[21] Peter Mills and John Oliver, *The Survey of Building Sites in the City of London After the Great Fire of 1666*, 5 vols, London Topographical Society, 97–9, 101, 103 (London: LTS, 1962–7).

damaged city drawn by John Leake in 1666. The original manuscript version (although not that accurate in terms of its representation of distance and angle) has hundreds of annotations recording the pre-Fire widths of roads and lanes – unique evidence for the medieval and early modern layout of the city.[22] The relevant road widths are shown on Figure 2f as a series of circles whose diameters correspond to Leake's measurements and which can be used to map the pre-Fire lanes with their correct widths. There are few accurate drawn surveys of pre-Fire London: a rare surviving example is an estate survey of c. 1630 (Figure 2g) and this is also shown in Figure 2h, with the buildings redrawn and aligned to fit the more accurate later maps.[23] In Figure 2i simple outlines are shown of the written surveys carried out in the 1540s by surveyors from the Court of Augmentations (see below).

Having begun mapping the relevant documentary evidence, we can now turn to the archaeological evidence: Figure 2j shows the archaeological sites in the area with the (rather smaller) areas that were actually excavated; Figure 2k maps the various medieval walls and boundaries discovered in these excavations (and see below for further discussion of the archaeological evidence).

The last map detail in the series, Figure 2l, brings together the cartographic, documentary and archaeological evidence and this part of the medieval friary of White Friars is now revealed in some detail. The huge 75m-long (245ft) friary church can be seen, its dimensions indicated by archaeology but confirmed by various measurements given in the 1540s surveys. To the south lies the principal cloister (the main evidence for which is the survey of c. 1630) and to the north the cemetery and some rented tenements (recorded in Mills' and Oliver's surveys of the 1660s and '70s).

The most important documentary source for reconstructing the landscape of England's monastic houses (at least for the majority of houses which lack a surviving archive as good as, say, Westminster Abbey) is the archive of the Court of Augmentations. This largely administrative court was the government department set up in 1536 to administer the Dissolution of the Monasteries. As more and more houses were surrendered into the hands of the Crown in the late 1530s, teams of rent collectors began compiling lists of the monastic property assets. As attention turned in the 1540s to converting these assets into cash, Augmentations surveyors began drawing up 'particulars' for subsequent grants and leases: these written surveys contain extremely useful descriptions and measurements of the buildings of the newly closed religious houses and are, therefore, a vital source for understanding their medieval topography.[24] The more challenging aspect of the documen-

[22] British Library (BL), Add MS 5415.art.56.
[23] BL, Maps Crace Portfolio 8 104 is a nineteenth-century copy of the now-lost original. See also n. 26.
[24] The 'particulars for grant' (and lease) are mostly in the E 315 and E 318 series of The National Archives, with the subsequent grants in C 66. For a fuller exploration of the topographic value of the records of the Court of Augmentations, see Nick Holder, 'The Medieval Friaries of London: A Topographic and Archaeological History, before and after the Dissolution' (unpublished doctoral thesis, University of London, Royal Holloway, 2011), pp. 267–70. See also Joyce Youings,

Table 2 Quantitative summary of the documentary, archaeological, architectural and cartographic evidence used in this book.

	Holborn Black Friars	Black Friars	1550s Black Friars	Grey Friars	White Friars	Austin Friars	Crossed Friars	Sack Friars	Pied Friars	Totals
Documents	53	212	13	128	100	124	143	32	15	820
of which, pre-Dissolution documents	53	56		65	34	71	97	32	15	423
of which, pre-1500 documents	53	35		48	25	25	64	32	13	295
Archaeological sites[a]	2	43	0	12	13	19	5	1	0	95
of which, modern excavations	2	27		6	8	13	5	1		62
Standing buildings[b]	0	1	2	1	1	1	0	0	0	6
of which, recorded but now destroyed				1		1				2
Pre-1666 plans[c]	0	0	0	4	2	1	0	0	0	7

Notes:

[a] See n. 27.
[b] The standing buildings referred to here are the undercroft of the late thirteenth-century Dominican chapter house, partly dismantled in 1900 (Chapter 2: The Second Black Friars, 'The cloisters'), the church and gate-house of St Bartholomew's (Chapter 3: The Third Black Friars at St Bartholomew's), the north wing of the Franciscan cloister, which survived until the nineteenth century (Chapter 4: Grey Friars), the undercroft of the Carmelite prior's house (Chapter 5: White Friars, 'The cloister') and the former Dutch Church, destroyed in 1940 (Chapter 6: Austin Friars).
[c] Useful and what might be termed 'standard' historic maps of London like Ogilby and Morgan's map of 1676 are discussed above. The rarer pre-Great Fire plans referred to here are listed in Bibliography, 'Maps and plans'; four are reproduced as Figure 22, Figure 26, Figure 29 and Figure 37.

tary record, particularly for the friaries, is the lack of surviving medieval archives: it must be assumed that in most cases the material confiscated at Dissolution was simply discarded as it had no further use. In some cases there are runs of property charters (such as for the first Black Friars and for Crossed Friars) and in other cases there are a few surviving stray items from the medieval archive – some fifteenth- and sixteenth-century chantry agreements and other documents from Austin Friars, for example. The traditional historian's technique of combing indexes – whether online, card-index or printed – pays dividends: there are over four hundred pre-Dissolution documents relevant to the topography of the friaries, with nearly three hundred of these dating to before 1500 (Table 2).

There have been about ninety-five separate archaeological excavations within the friary

The Dissolution of the Monasteries (London: Allen and Unwin, 1971); Walter Cecil Richardson, 'Records of the Court of Augmentations', *Journal of the Society of Archivists*, 1.6 (1957), 159–68.

precincts. These range from limited observations of medieval walls made during Victorian construction works to full-scale late twentieth- or early twenty-first century excavations (Table 2). The records for the majority of these can be found at the Museum of London's archive, the London Archaeological Archive (LAA).[25] A comparison can be drawn here between archaeological and historical sources: the archaeological equivalents of the historian's 'primary source' documents are the context sheets and plans of the various excavated walls, pits, layers and other features. Depending on the complexity of the site, and the time and money available for what archaeologists term post-excavation work, the archaeologist will then draw up a stratigraphic matrix of the site (essentially a flow diagram expressing the excavated features as a sequence of events) together with interpretive plans and text, which will appear in an unpublished site report. This report (formerly termed an archive report, now generally called a post-excavation assessment) can be seen as the equivalent of the historian's interpretive printed primary text: it contains much of the original site 'document' but it has been filtered and interpreted by the archaeologist. The two elements – original records and site report – form the bulk of the primary archaeological evidence used for this book. In some cases, the archaeological evidence has been further interpreted and published in the form of an article or book – archaeological 'secondary sources', in other words.

On their own, archaeology, surviving buildings, maps or documents cannot reveal the medieval landscape, but when the sources are brought together, medieval and early modern London can be reconstructed in quite some detail. Let us turn now to a friary-by-friary investigation of this lost medieval landscape.

---

[25] The archaeological material is archived at the LAA and referred to in this book by alphanumeric Museum of London site-codes, for example, site WFT99. Excavations and archaeological observations from before the 'modern' period of archaeological excavation – before the 1970s – include Guildhall Museum sites (with a 'GM' prefix, catalogued in John Schofield and Catherine Maloney, *Archaeology in the City of London, 1907–1991: A Guide to Records of Excavations by the Museum of London and its Predecessors* (London: Museum of London, 1998)) and older 'Post-Roman Gazetteer' sites (with a 'PRG' prefix, catalogued in a typescript, three files and a card index compiled by C. Harding in the 1980s and stored at the LAA).

PART I

The Nine London Friaries

1

The First Black Friars in Holborn, c. 1223–86

THE Castilian priest Dominic of Caleruega (sometimes referred to with his probably aristocratic name of de Guzmán) founded a new religious order in the second decade of the thirteenth century. Dominic was an Augustinian canon and his new order grew out of his band of priests (which also included Cistercian monks) who were combating the Cathar heresy in the Languedoc. Dominic's way of dealing with the heresy was through itinerant, straightforward and organised preaching. This Dominican order of friars shared many characteristics with St Francis' new order founded in the same decade in Italy. The Dominicans quickly began to expand their order throughout Europe, moving from Toulouse to Paris and to Spain. They came to England in 1221 and the first friar to arrive in London was Gilbert de Fresnay in August. He began to look for a suitable site for a new priory, which was to be the second friary in England after the Oxford house.[1] De Fresnay quickly found a powerful supporter. Hubert de Burgh, earl of Kent, was the royal justiciar – senior minister to Henry III, who was still a minor. De Burgh purchased and then gave to the friars a parcel of land in suburban Holborn, just by the bridge over the Fleet river. The donation was confirmed with a quitclaim, datable to the mayoral term of October 1223 to October 1224, although the grant itself may well have been slightly earlier.[2] Although this was not a city-centre location, the site occupied a prominent position on the main approach to London from the west, and was only 320m from the Newgate entrance into the city (Figure 3, Figure 4).[3] Furthermore, the proximity to the bridge over the Fleet gave the friars a good opportunity to provide spiritual services to travellers and, potentially, receive alms in return.

---

[1] Röhrkasten, *Mendicant Houses*, p. 30; C.H. Lawrence, *The Friars: The Impact of the Mendicant Orders on Western Society* (London: Tauris, 2013), 2nd edn, pp. 65–88.

[2] The National Archives (TNA), DL 29/59; Elijah Williams, *Early Holborn and the Legal Quarter of London: A Topographical Survey of the Beginnings of the District Known as Holborn and of the Inns of Court and of Chancery*, 2 vols (London: Sweet & Maxwell, 1927), i, 696.

[3] Caroline M. Barron with Penelope Hunting and Jane Roscoe, *The Parish of St Andrew Holborn* (London: Diamond Trading Company, 1979), pp. 9–15.

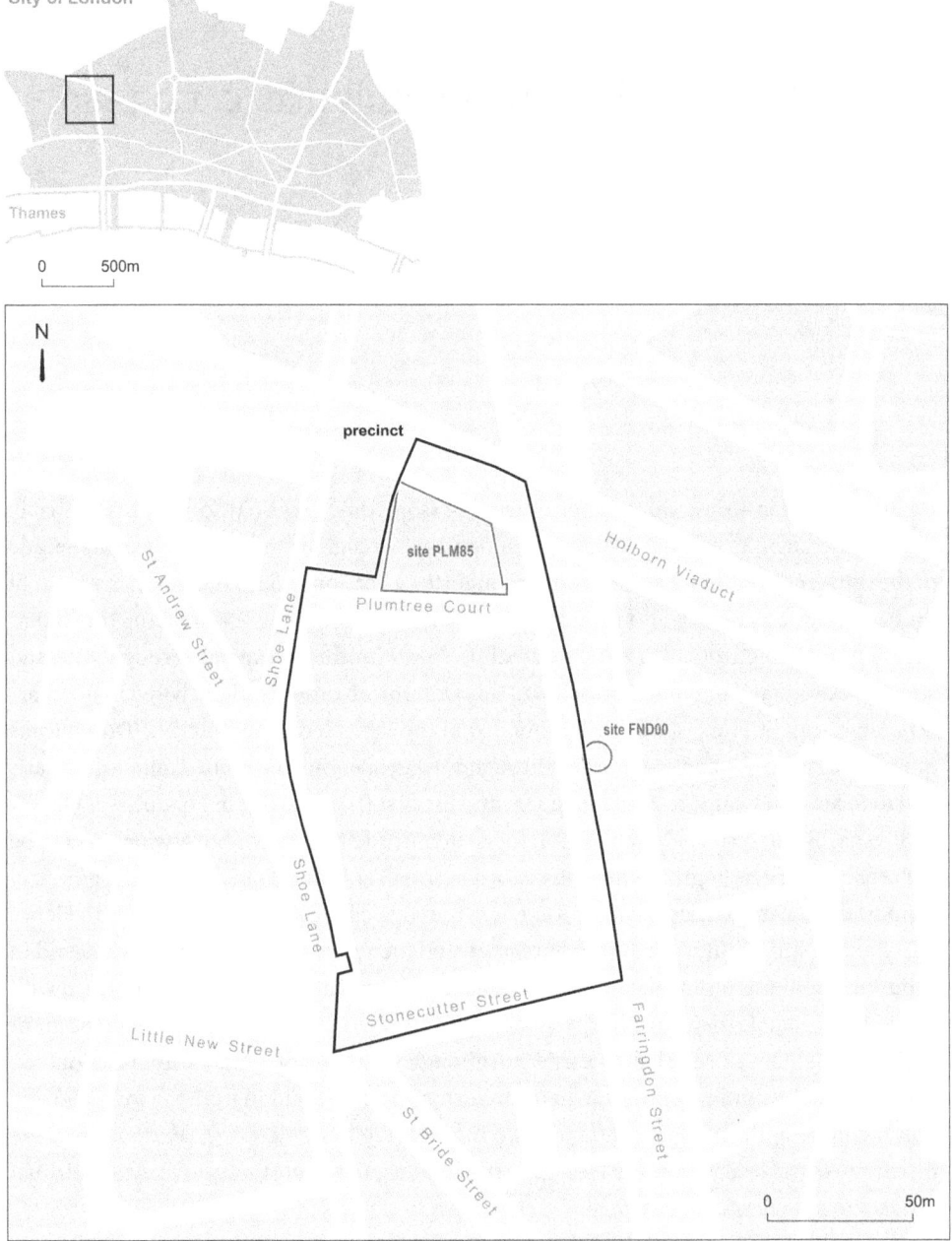

Fig. 3. Map showing the location of the Holborn Black Friars precinct and a 1985 archaeological site (scale 1:2500).

The Dominicans in England have long been known as Black friars, the colour referring to the cloak they wore outside the friary. The numbers of these London Black friars quickly increased in the period when the Holborn friary was being constructed and used. By 1243 there were about eighty Dominicans in London, although in 1278 numbers were down to sixty. When the Black friars left their Holborn friary in the 1280s, there may have been sixty-seven friars.[4] To these figures one should add novices and, of course, servants: the new religious house on Holborn must have been a busy place.

The next chapter examines the reasons why the Dominicans may have sought to move from their Holborn friary to a more central site (Chapter 2: The Second Black Friars, 1275–1538). As late as 1273 they were still planning construction work on the Holborn site (perhaps a second or third wing of the cloisters) but by about 1275 or 1276 the prior, John of Darlington, and the Dominican archbishop of Canterbury, Robert Kilwardby, were beginning the process of acquiring land in the south-west of the city for a new friary precinct.[5] The process of acquisition and initial construction took about a decade and in March 1286 the friars sold the Holborn site to Henry de Lacy, earl of Lincoln, for 550 marks.[6] It may be significant that de Lacy was married to Margaret (the daughter of Sir William Longespée) whose aunt Ela de Longespée, countess of Warwick, had been a benefactor of the friary in the 1260s.[7]

The sources available to us for understanding and reconstructing the first Black Friars in Holborn are largely documentary. In particular, there is a more or less complete collection of the friary's property charters, which ended up in the Duchy of Lancaster's records, now in The National Archives. One archaeological site on Holborn provides a little evidence for the location and size of the friary church.[8]

Acquiring and developing the friary

The friars acquired their monastic precinct over a period of forty years. Thanks to the survival of the friary's property archive, one can plot the various tenements that the friars purchased or were given (Table 3, Figure 4). The reconstructed map of the friary's tenements

---

[4] Röhrkasten, *Mendicant Houses*, pp. 74–5.
[5] Röhrkasten, *Mendicant Houses*, pp. 38–9.
[6] £366 13s 4d; TNA, DL 27/62; *CCR 1279–1288*, p. 428; Williams, *Early Holborn*, i, 717.
[7] J.S. Hamilton, 'Lacy, Henry de, Fifth Earl of Lincoln (1249–1311)', *ODNB*, <http://www.oxforddnb.com/view/article/15851> [accessed 20 December 2013]; Simon Lloyd, 'Longespée, Sir William (II) (c. 1209–1250)', *ODNB*, <http://www.oxforddnb.com/view/article/16984> [accessed 20 December 2013].
[8] There are nineteen property transaction documents in the DL 25 and DL 27 series at The National Archives; the majority of these have been translated and printed in Williams, *Early Holborn*. The archaeological excavation took place in 1985 at Morley House, 26–30 Holborn Viaduct. See Figure 3 and LAA, site PLM85. Archaeological work on the site of the large 1960s Fleet Building on Farringdon Street (the block to the south of the PLM85 site) showed that no archaeological remains survived on this site: MOLA, 'Fleet Building . . . and Plumtree Court . . . London EC4A: historic environment assessment', unpublished report, 2012.

Table 3 List of the tenements acquired by the Black friars for their Holborn priory.

Number on Figure 4	Date of acquisition	Grantor	Description	Reference
1	1221 × 1224, perhaps 1223?	Hubert de Burgh	long and narrow plot on Holborn (grant gives abutments and measurements)	TNA, DL 27/59
2	1220s?	William le Veill	little detail	TNA, DL 25/143
3	1231/2	Alice la Brune	next to cemetery of Black Friars	TNA, DL 25/131
4	1235/6	Richard Renger	by the Fleet (grant gives abutments and measurements)	TNA, DL 25/132 and /133
5	1231 × 1237	Adam le Cutiler	small tenement in Scholand (grant gives abutments and measurements)	TNA, DL 25/136
6	1230s, c. 1236?	Richer de Cruce	position uncertain (but abuts Black Friars to *south*)	TNA, DL 25/141
7	1230s, before 1237	Abbot of Nutley priory	on Scholand	TNA, DL 24/134, /148
8	1239/40	Ralph Eswy	on Soland, in parishes of St Andrew and St Bride	TNA, DL 25/135
9	late 1230s	Henry and Adam Tegularius and their wives	grant gives abutments	TNA, DL 25/140
10	1261/2	Ela, countess of Warwick, and Yvo de Mortelak	bundle of formerly separate tenements in parish of St Bride	TNA, DL 25/137
11	1261/2	Philip Bassett and Ela, countess of Warwick his wife	'by the bridge of the Flete'	TNA, DL 25/138

(Figure 4) uses measurements and abutments given in several grant documents and it also includes historic property boundaries, particularly the lanes, shown on Ogilby and Morgan's map of 1676. If the map is not a fully accurate topographic reconstruction, it should be a reliable *topological* plan.

In the 1220s, the friars acquired a second tenement, probably adjacent to the original de Burgh foundation grant (Tenement 2 on Table 3, Figure 4). By now they had the makings of a small religious precinct, although they were constrained by the shapes of the plots they had acquired, the site being perhaps only 20m (65ft) at its maximum east–west width. In the following decade a number of donors, both neighbours and more distant benefactors, gave the friars a series of tenements. With these they could enlarge their precinct, with the western edge defined by the lane known as Scholand (modern Shoe Lane) and the eastern edge by the Fleet river (Figure 4). The majority of these tenements appear to have been

Fig. 4. Map showing the approximate location of the tenements acquired by the Black friars for their Holborn priory; for tenement numbers, see Table 3 (scale 1:1500).

donations to the friars rather than sales (although medieval grant documents are often silent about any sums paid by the grantee). The exception is the friars' purchase of one tenement in the late 1230s; the purchase price is, unfortunately, not stated in the grant (Tenement 9 on Table 3, Figure 4).[9]

By 1240, then, the Black friars had a precinct that extended southwards from the Fleet bridge some 140m (155 yards) and was up to 95m (105 yards) wide along the southern edge. However, there was still an inconvenient gap in the precinct along the Holborn frontage, where land values would have been significantly higher and where it was perhaps harder to obtain the land. For this missing part, the friars had to wait another two decades until the early 1260s when Ela de Longespée, countess of Warwick, gave them the missing Holborn plot, which she may have inherited on the death of her brother in 1260. She also purchased a number of plots to the south of the friary and donated these to the friars, thus extending their precinct even further southwards (Tenements 10 and 11 on Table 3, Figure 4).[10] De Longespée was thus continuing the family tradition of generosity to religious houses: her mother and father had made a number of such gifts and had founded the Augustinian nunnery at Lacock, with her widowed mother becoming its prioress for twenty years. At the same time the friars were trying to reduce their annual quitrent payments due on several of their tenements by purchasing the quitrent from the owner (often another religious house): they made at least six such purchases between 1238 and 1263.[11] By 1262 the friars had thus obtained a sizeable precinct of 1.6ha (4 acres), most of which they owned outright, with an uninterrupted frontage along Holborn of some 40m (130ft) and situated in the prominent location of the approach to the Holborn bridge over the Fleet. This, surely, was the making of long-term spiritual and material investment in the area.

The Holborn friary

Of course, the acquisition of the parcels of land was only the initial stage in the process: the friary needed to be planned, money raised and a long construction campaign started. Fortunately, the friars – whose order was little over a decade old in the 1230s – enjoyed remarkable support from the English elite. In addition to the justiciar Hubert de Burgh, the young Henry III gave direct support to the friary, as is revealed in a succession of royal grants to the friars (Table 4).

The priory was enclosed, at least in part, by a precinct wall. A document of 1305 (two decades after the friars had sold this site) mentions repairs and alterations to 44 perches (242 yards; 221m) of boundary wall: this is approximately the length of wall running down

---

[9] TNA, DL 25/140; Williams, *Early Holborn*, i, 709; Röhrkasten, *Mendicant Houses*, pp. 31–3.
[10] TNA, DL 25/137 and /138; Williams, *Early Holborn*, i, 712–13.
[11] Jennifer C. Ward, 'Ela, suo jure Countess of Salisbury (b. in or after 1190, d. 1261)', *ODNB*, <http://www.oxforddnb.com/article/47205> [accessed 25 October 2013]; Matthew Strickland, 'Longespée, William (I), Third Earl of Salisbury (b. in or before 1167, d. 1226)', *ODNB*, <http://www.oxforddnb.com/article/16983> [accessed 25 October 2013]; Röhrkasten, *Mendicant Houses*, pp. 32–4.

Table 4 Royal grants towards the construction of the Holborn Black Friars, 1235–73.

Date	Royal grant	Purpose	Reference
April and June 1235	oaks for timber	(latter part of?) construction campaign on the friary church	*CCR 1234–1237*, pp. 71, 97
June 1237	200 quarters of lime		*CCR 1234–1237*, pp. 457, 459; *CLR 1226–1240*, pp. 275–6
January 1240 to Nov. 1241	four grants totalling £38	for the church of Black Friars	*CLR 1226–1240*, pp. 444, 501; *CLR 1240–1245*, pp. 48, 87
June 1250	six oaks for timber	timber-framed accommodation?	*CCR 1247–1251*, pp. 289–90
October 1256	lead-ash	uncertain	*CCR 1254–1256*, p. 366
March 1259 to March 1262	grants of fuel for lime kiln, money, building timber and freestone	first wing of the cloister, including a 'school' from February 1261	*CCR 1256–1259*, pp. 370, 378–9; *CCR 1259–1261*, pp. 244, 347, 372; *CCR 1261–1264*, p. 34; *CLR 1251–1260*, pp. 456–7; *CLR 1260–1267*, p. 50; WAA, Muniments 15999(b), 16000(b);
October 1259 to March 1261	grants of lead and lead-ash (litharge)	construction of a piped water supply: conduit-head, lead pipe, conduit-house and cistern?	*CLR 1251–1260*, p. 484; *CCR 1259–1261*, pp. 10, 130, 244, 359; *CLR 1260–1267*, p. 16; WAA, Muniment 15999(e, g); Muniment 16000(a, c)
January 1263 to April 1267	three grants of 47 oaks for timber	accommodation wing (first wing of cloister): dormitory	*CCR 1261–1264*, p. 194; *CCR 1264–1268*, pp. 168, 303
October 1273	permission to collect purchased oaks for timber from (now deceased) Bishop of London	planned second wing of cloister?	*CCR 1272–1279*, p. 32

the west side of the precinct from Holborn to Smallbridge Lane.[12] There were presumably one or two access gates to the friary; two passages on the Ogilby and Morgan map of 1676 suggest the location of gates on Holborn and Shoe Lane. Another gate was probably built at the junction of Shoe Lane and a small lane called Showell: in 1262 the friars received permission (after an *inquisition ad quod damnum*) to enclose the little lane on condition that they allowed access to a public well at the upper end.[13]

The first friars of the 1220s would have made use of the existing buildings on their new tenements, presumably the house or houses fronting onto Holborn; they may have kept these houses to provide rental income in later decades (Tenement 1 on Figure 4).

---

[12] smalebreggelan; TNA, DL 29/1/2, m. 15v.
[13] TNA, C 143/2/17; *CPR 1258–1266*, p. 225.

The building campaign on the friary church might have begun in the early 1230s, perhaps after the acquisition of Tenement 3 in 1231 or 1232: this plot now allowed the friars an east–west width of about 45m (140ft), enough to plan a church, small cloister and some access space. The royal grants of April 1235 to November 1241 – lime for the walls, oaks for the timber roof and cash to pay the builders – record this first construction campaign on the friary church. A medieval wall revealed in 1985 during archaeological excavation at 26–30 Holborn Viaduct can now be interpreted as the west wall of this church or chapel (site PLM85; Figure 3, Figure 5). The wall was built of irregularly coursed ragstone blocks, was bonded with a sandy mortar that presumably included the royal donations of lime, and was about 0.7m (2ft 4in) thick. Taking this wall, a fragment of medieval chalk foundation to the north and a building line on the 1676 Ogilby and Morgan map, it can be can surmised that the chapel had an external width of about 9m (30ft). There is no evidence for the east–west length of the building (perhaps about 22m or 75ft?).

The church was called 'St John the Evangelist of Holeburne' in the 1230s. Seventy years later (after the friars had moved) it was still described as a 'great chapel'.[14] The chapel contained a number of important noble burials and – perhaps – a royal burial. The earliest known burial was that of the founder Hubert de Burgh, earl of Kent, who died in 1243, soon after the completion of the chapel.[15] His wife Margaret, countess of Kent, was later buried with him (died 1259), as was her sister Isabel, countess of Norfolk (died after 1263). The chapel also contained at least two noble heart burials of the 1270s, of John and Margaret, the children of William de Valence, earl of Pembroke. It is possible that the heart of Edward I's ten-year-old son Alphonso – heir to the English throne until his early death in 1284 – was buried in this chapel. If the viscera burial was placed in *this* Black Friars chapel, the casket and memorial slab must have been moved within a couple of years to the refounded Black Friars church within the city walls.[16]

The friars may have begun construction work on an accommodation wing in 1259. Once again, the king granted many of the essential items for the project: stone and lime for the walls, oak for the floors and roof, and cash for the construction expenses (Table 4). For this phase of the works Henry may have been influenced by the London Dominican John of Darlington, who was both confessor to Henry and a member of the royal council.[17] The grants specifically mention a school in April 1261 and a dormitory in January 1263; the

---

[14] *magna capella*; TNA, DL 29/1/2, m. 15v; TNA, DL 25/131; Williams, *Early Holborn*, i, 697.
[15] F.J. West, 'Burgh, Hubert de, Earl of Kent (c. 1170–1243)', *ODNB*, <http://www.oxforddnb.com/view/article/3991> [accessed 12 May 2016].
[16] W.W. Scott, 'Margaret, Countess of Kent (1187×95–1259)', *ODNB*, <http://www.oxforddnb.com/view/article/49377> [accessed 19 December 2013]; Christian Steer, 'Royal and Noble Commemoration in the Mendicant Houses of London, c. 1240–1540', in *Memory and Commemoration in Medieval England*, eds C.M. Barron and C. Burgess, Harlaxton Medieval Studies, 20 (Donington: Shaun Tyas, 2010), pp. 117–42 (pp. 126, 131).
[17] Röhrkasten, *Mendicant Houses*, p. 35.

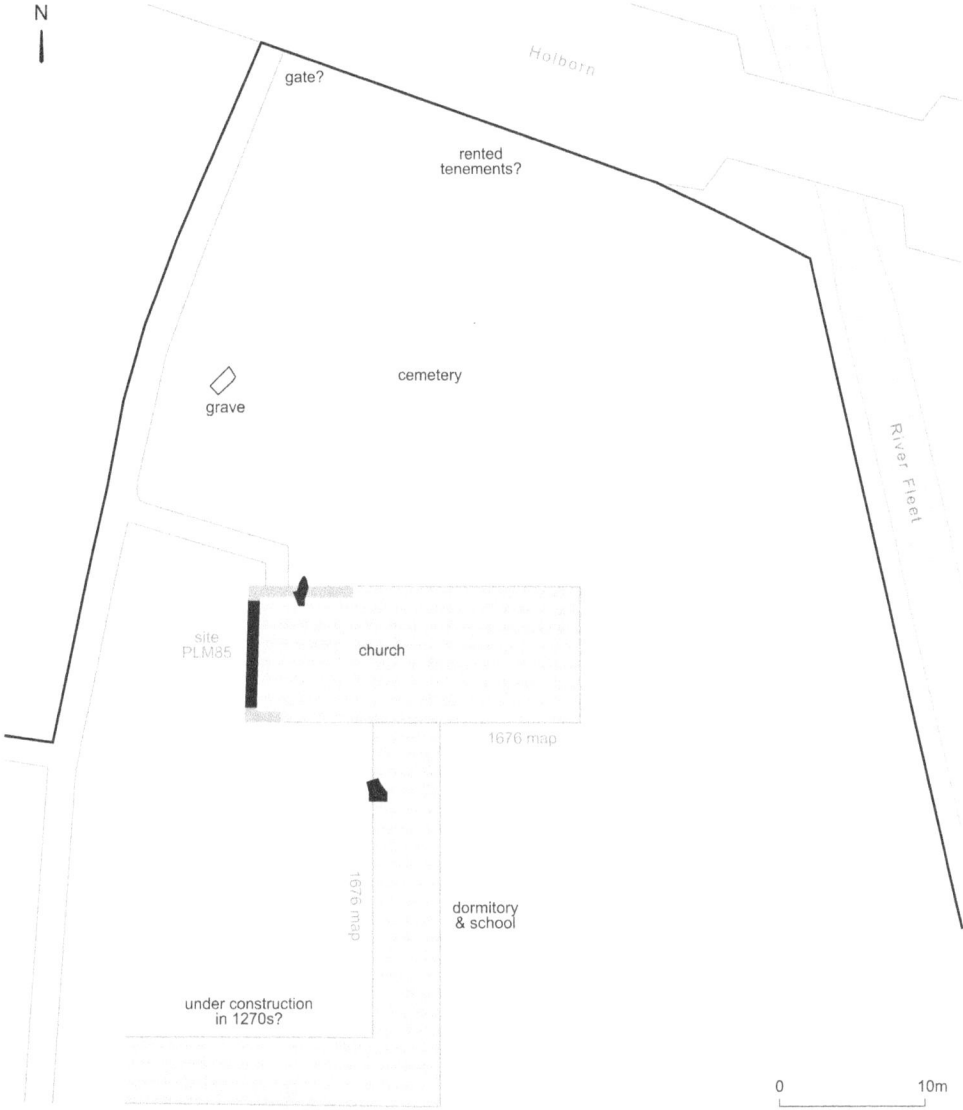

Fig. 5. Map showing the church and claustral wing(s) of the thirteenth-century Black Friars in Holborn (scale 1:500).

final grant of this phase of works is dated April 1267.[18] This wing may well have included a chapter house: a document (largely unrelated to the friary) was signed in the Dominican chapter house in December 1278.[19] A reasonable interpretation is that the friars may have been planning a whole or part-cloister to the south of their church, away from the main road, and began with an eastern wing. They may well have continued clockwise with the

---

[18] *CCR 1259–1261*, p. 372; *CCR 1261–1264*, p. 194; *CCR 1264–1268*, p. 303.
[19] WAA, Muniment 5779.

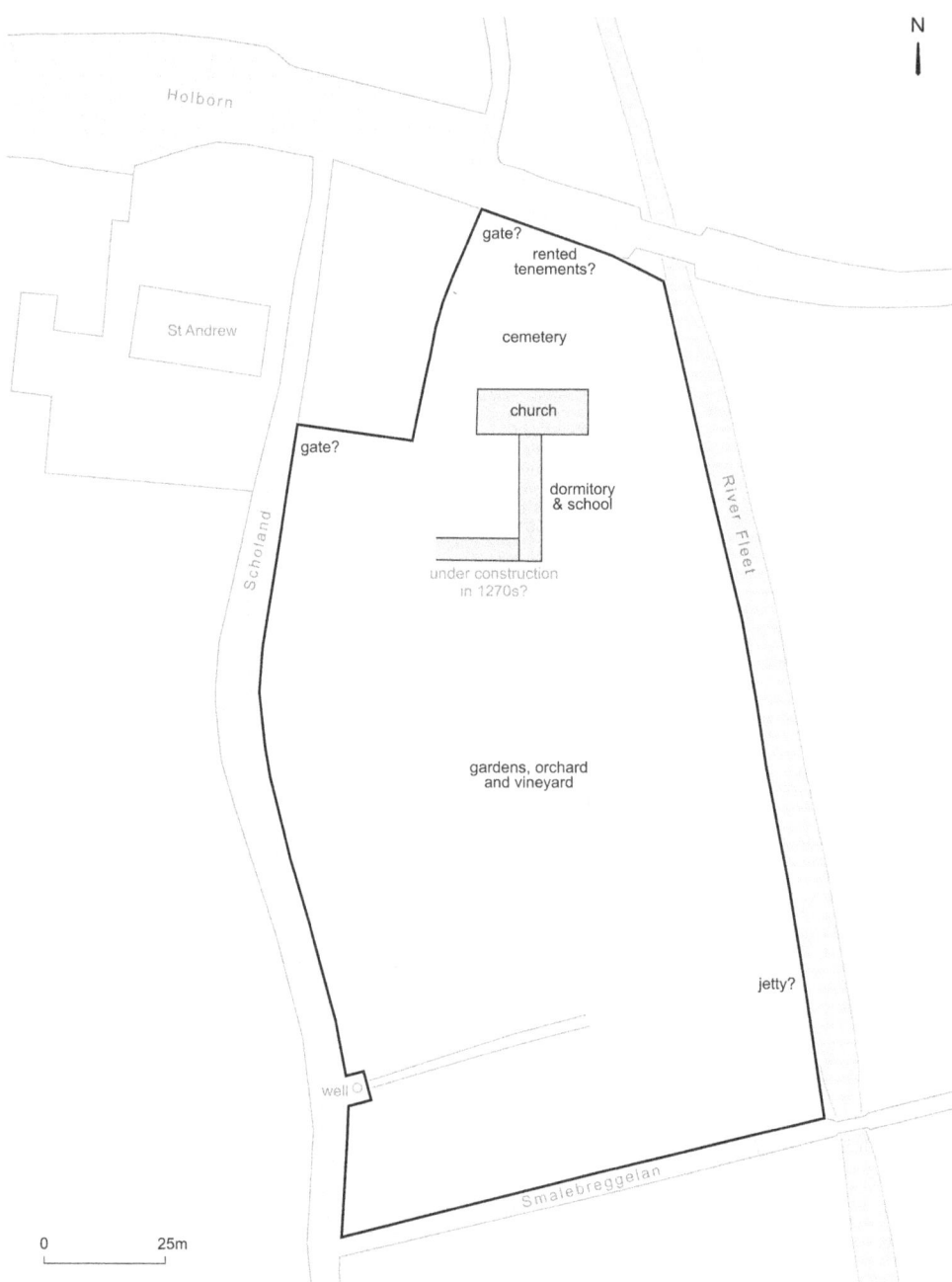

Fig. 6. Map showing the reconstructed precinct of the thirteenth-century Black Friars in Holborn (scale 1:1500).

southern wing. There is very little physical evidence for this cloister – a fragment of foundation discovered to the south of the church could have supported the western wall of the eastern wing – but the arrangement of later buildings in this area of the 1676 Ogilby and Morgan map is suggestive of at least two such wings of a putative early cloister. A document of October 1273 seems to be the latest evidence for construction on this site: royal permission was granted to collect timber purchased from the (now deceased) bishop of London. This could relate to the construction of a second wing of the cloister but specific evidence is lacking.

A few other details about the layout of this thirteenth-century friary are known. The cemetery was located between the main road and the church: when Alice la Brune gave her Holborn tenement to the friary in 1231/2 (Tenement 3 on Figure 4), the western abutment was the Dominicans' cemetery. The graveyard seems to have expanded westwards to include another Holborn tenement granted in the 1230s: a grave was observed on the 26–30 Holborn Viaduct archaeological site (Tenement 6 on Figure 4; grave on Figure 5). The friary had a piped water supply, built between 1259 and 1261, which carried water from a spring in Clerkenwell, half a mile (750m) to the north of the friary (Table 4).[20]

A little more information about the friary can be gleaned from a set of accounts of the subsequent owner of the site, Henry de Lacy, earl of Lincoln. His household accounts of the year ending November 1296 – just ten years after the friars sold the site (below) – reveal a number of unusual features of the property that may relate to the former friary.[21] Firstly, the friary site had a large garden, presumably located to the south of the cloister. The garden had a large ditch (*major fossat[us]*) that ran north–south; the use of the comparative adjective (*major*, greater) suggests that the garden was bounded by other lesser ditches. A fence connected the northern end of this ditch to a stable (although the latter could well have been built for de Lacy). The 1286 accounts record a number of annual crops (which need not relate to the friary) but they also note more established plants in an orchard including apple trees, pears, cherries and walnuts (*gross[e] nuc[es]*). The accounts also reveal the sale of greenwood fuel (*viridi[s] fuoco in foliis*, presumably faggots of brushwood and rods) and planks, suggesting that the gardens had a variety of trees including coppice or pollards and standards (of oak, ash or beech?). Is this suburban garden with trees the equivalent of a rural field with trees, a type of medieval woodland pasture found in eastern counties like Suffolk?[22] Significantly, there is also mention of the maintenance of a vineyard (*vine[a]*), the only documentary evidence for a London monastic vineyard known to this

---

[20] CLR 1251–1260, p. 484; C.J. Bond, 'Water Management in the Urban Monastery', in *Advances in Monastic Archaeology*, ed. R. Gilchrist and H.C. Mytum, British Archaeological Reports, 227 (Oxford: Tempus Reparatum, 1993), pp. 43–78 (p. 61). The evidence for the spring being situated in Clerkenwell is slightly later (1306) and it is possible that the first Black friars in Holborn used a different spring, although this seems unlikely: CPR 1301–1307, pp. 538–9.

[21] TNA, DL 29/1/1, m. 11v.

[22] Oliver Rackham, *The History of the Countryside: The Classic History of Britain's Landscape, Flora and Fauna* (London: Phoenix, 2000), p. 230, plate xvi; James Galloway, Derek Keene and Margaret

author. Finally, the accounts refer to the repair of a quay (*kay[um]*) to bring in materials to repair the fence. The repairs (costing 44s 4d) suggest the presence of a small ex-monastic jetty on the west bank of the river Fleet, thus giving the friars direct water access to the river Thames a little further to the south.

Conclusion

If the archaeological evidence for this friary is disappointing, the almost complete survival of the friary's property charters allows us a detailed look at the process of acquiring an urban monastic precinct in the thirteenth century. Over a fifty-year period beginning in the 1220s, the Dominicans gradually acquired the land and built a fair-sized urban priory. By the 1270s they had a 1.6ha site (4 acres) and they had built a church, a chapter house and one or two wings of accommodation. There was also room to expand: they could have begun work on a nave (although, depending on its intended size, this might have required the purchase of more tenements on the east side of the road called Scholand). They managed extensive gardens in their precinct, including an orchard and a vineyard. Their church, dedicated to St John the Evangelist, occupied a prominent position, set back from one of the main approach roads to London from the west, just before the bridge over the river Fleet that led on to Newgate. They enjoyed the support of several high-status benefactors, including Henry III and Edward I, the Dominican archbishop of Canterbury and a number of prominent families such as the Longespées and the earls of Pembroke. Perhaps surprisingly, just a half-century after their arrival in the kingdom and the establishment of their London house, they decided to move to a more prestigious site within the walls of the city – once those walls were rebuilt to accommodate the new friary, as we will see in the next chapter.

Murphy, 'Fuelling the City: Production and Distribution of Firewood and Fuel in London's Region, 1290–1400', *Economic History Review*, 49 (1996), 447–72 (pp. 451–5).

2

The Second Black Friars, 1275–1538

By the 1270s the Dominicans had acquired, planned and partly built a sizeable and convenient friary on one of the main approach roads to the walled city of London (Chapter 1: The First Black Friars in Holborn). However, between about autumn 1273 and summer 1275 the friars decided to move their priory into London itself. When royal permission was granted in October 1273 to obtain timber for building materials, the focus of the friars' plans was still very much the Holborn friary, but by June 1275 Robert Kilwardby, the Dominican archbishop of Canterbury, was beginning to acquire the properties for a new friary site on the west side of the walled city.[1] The project was particularly complex and ambitious: the large site comprised numerous properties and straddled the old Roman city wall. A remarkable planning meeting must have taken place in about 1274 to make the decision to move – a decision which would entail relocating a 225-yard stretch of the city wall of London![2] Complex negotiations must have taken place over the coming months between the prior, archbishop, mayor and king. The Dominicans certainly had a fortuitous combination of key personnel: John of Darlington, the prior or outgoing prior of the house, had been confessor to Henry III and was an experienced royal minister; the archbishop, Robert Kilwardby, had been the Dominican provincial prior and had plenty of experience of building new priories; and the mayor, Henry le Waleys, was a long-term friend to the mendicants and another favourite of the king with experience of urban building projects.[3] As will be seen, the acquisition and construction of the new friary, including the additional

---

[1] *CCR 1272–1279*, p. 32; *CPR 1272–1281*, pp. 96–7.
[2] Röhrkasten, *Mendicant Houses*, pp. 30–8; Barron and Davies, *Religious Houses*, pp. 117–18; Mary D. Lobel, *The City of London from Prehistoric Times to c. 1520* (Oxford: Oxford University Press and Historic Towns Trust, 1989), pp. 65, 81 and map 'City of London 1270'.
[3] C.H. Lawrence, 'Darlington, John of (d. 1284)', *ODNB*, <http://www.oxforddnb.com/view/article/7159> [accessed 9 June 2014]; Simon Tugwell, 'Kilwardby, Robert (c. 1215–1279)', *ODNB*, <http://www.oxforddnb.com/view/article/15546> [accessed 9 June 2014]; Frédérique Lachaud, 'Waleys, Henry le (d. 1302)', *ODNB*, <http://www.oxforddnb.com/view/article/28460> [accessed

requirement to build 565 yards (515m) of new city wall, was to take place in a remarkably short time.

The refounded Dominican friary was the largest, wealthiest and most politically significant of the English friaries. It housed nearly a hundred friars at the turn of the thirteenth and fourteenth centuries and still had about sixty in the late fourteenth century after the effects of the Black Death. The friary contained the order's *studium provinciale*, which trained English and some foreign Black friars and sent them on for higher study at Oxford, Cambridge and Continental universities. Together with the Franciscans, the Dominicans were the academic elite of London, ensuring the city's status as a European cultural and intellectual centre (Chapter 16: Spiritual Life and Education in the London Friaries). The friary – conveniently sited between Westminster and the city – retained its special links to the Crown, serving as a venue for council meetings and, on occasion, sittings of parliament.[4]

The friars also retained close links with Londoners who could come and hear friars preaching in the great nave or outdoors at a preaching cross in the churchyard.[5] The friars also attracted financial support from London's merchants and there seem to have been more bequests and more Londoners buried here than at the Austin and White Friars (Chapter 17: Burial and Commemoration in the London Friaries).

The friary was the setting for a number of nationally significant events including the church council held to condemn the teachings of John Wyclif in 1382, a meeting ominously interrupted by an earthquake.[6] A century and a half later another dramatic encounter took place here: the religious court of 1529 headed by Cardinals Wolsey and Campeggio held its inquiry into the 'great matter' of the marriage of Henry VIII and Catherine of Aragon.[7] In a chain of events leading on from the inevitable postponement of the court, Henry changed his advisors and began to listen to more heterodox views on religion. In a sense, those few days at Black Friars in 1529 were the crucial first steps on the road that

---

9 June 2014]. For a list of known priors of the London friary, see Barron and Davies, *Religious Houses*, pp. 120–1.

[4] Röhrkasten, *Mendicant Houses*, pp. 210–18, 239–41, 261, 270–3, 479, 518, 560–2; Jens Röhrkasten, 'Secular Uses of the Mendicant Priories of Medieval London', in *The Use and Abuse of Sacred Places in Late Medieval Towns*, ed. M. De Smet and P. Trio, Mediaevalia Lovaniensia, Series 1, 38 (Leuven: Leuven University Press, 2006), pp. 135–51 (pp. 140–1).

[5] The preaching pulpit is mentioned in a will of 1410: *Calendar of Wills Proved and Enrolled in the Court of Husting, 1258–1688*, ed. Reginald R. Sharpe, 2 vols (London: Corporation of London, 1889–90), ii, 391.

[6] Anne Hudson and Anthony Kenny, 'Wyclif, John (d. 1384)', *ODNB*, <http://www.oxforddnb.com/view/article/30122> [accessed 10 June 2014]; Henry Knighton, *Knighton's Chronicle, 1337–1396*, ed. Geoffrey H. Martin, Oxford Medieval Texts (Oxford: Clarendon, 1995), pp. 258–61.

[7] *Letters and Papers*, iv(3), no. 5613 (pp. 2483–4); George W. Bernard, *The King's Reformation: Henry VIII and the Remaking of the English Church* (New Haven and London: Yale University Press, 2005), pp. 13–14.

led to the royal supremacy, the Dissolution and, in the end, the English Reformation. In November 1538 the unfolding events caught up with the friary: prior John Hilsey (an active supporter of the 'new learning', now bishop of Rochester) and fifteen friars signed the surrender document.[8]

The Dominican friary has the widest range of sources of all the London friaries. The survival of a large archive of property documents and correspondence of the main post-Dissolution owner of the friary, Thomas Cawarden, provides much information on the layout of the medieval friary that he purchased.[9] This material is supplemented by a good range of documents drawn up by the Court of Augmentations after the Dissolution of the friary.[10] Numerous archaeological excavations have taken place in its precinct with, in particular, the excavations at 10 Friar Street (site FRI88) revealing parts of the medieval church and chapter house, and the large Fleet Valley project (VAL88) uncovering long stretches of the friary wall (Figure 7). There are even some (just about) visible remains of the friary: a large medieval window is preserved within the office building at 10 Friar Street and a rather forlorn stub of medieval wall stands in the old graveyard of St Anne's church in Ireland Yard. Finally, mention should be made of the extensive archaeological and documentary investigations of twentieth-century researchers, in particular Alfred Clapham and Irwin Smith.[11]

Acquiring and developing the friary

By the 1270s the area of the future Black Friars was partly built up, but, fortunately for the friars, there were several large properties rather than the dense pattern of small properties that characterised much of the city. There were two largely derelict Norman castles in this part of the south-west of the city, Montfitchet's Tower and Baynard's Castle (Figure 8). Ogbourne priory, a small Wiltshire monastery that belonged to Bec Abbey in Normandy, had a house to the south of Baynard's Castle and, beyond that, there was

---

[8] *Report of the Deputy Keeper of the Public Records*, 120 vols (London: HMSO), viii (1865), 28; S. Thompson, 'Hilsey, John (d. 1539)', *ODNB*, <http://www.oxforddnb.com/view/article/13325> [accessed 11 June 2014]. *Letters and Papers*, xiii(2), no. 809 (pp. 320–1).

[9] Cawarden's material is part of the Loseley archive which is now divided between Surrey History Centre (SHC) and Folger Shakespeare Library (FSL), Washington DC. Both archives have detailed catalogues of their respective Loseley holdings; most of the Folger material has been microfilmed and can be consulted at the Surrey History Centre (microfilm Z/407/2 and /3).

[10] Thanks to a Shakespearean connection – friary buildings were later used as an indoor Jacobean theatre – a large amount of the Cawarden and the Court of Augmentations documents have been printed: Irwin Smith, *Shakespeare's Blackfriars Playhouse: Its History and its Design* (London: Owen, 1966); *Blackfriars Records*, ed. Albert Feuillerat (Oxford: Malone Society, 1913).

[11] For Smith, see n. 10. Alfred W. Clapham, 'On the Topography of the Dominican Priory of London', *Archaeologia*, 63 (1911), 57–84.

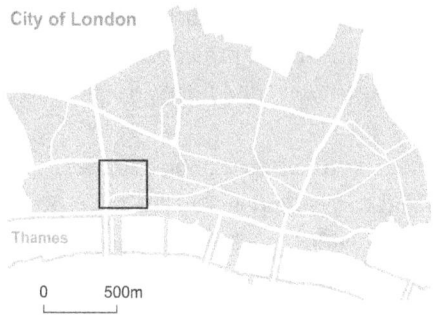

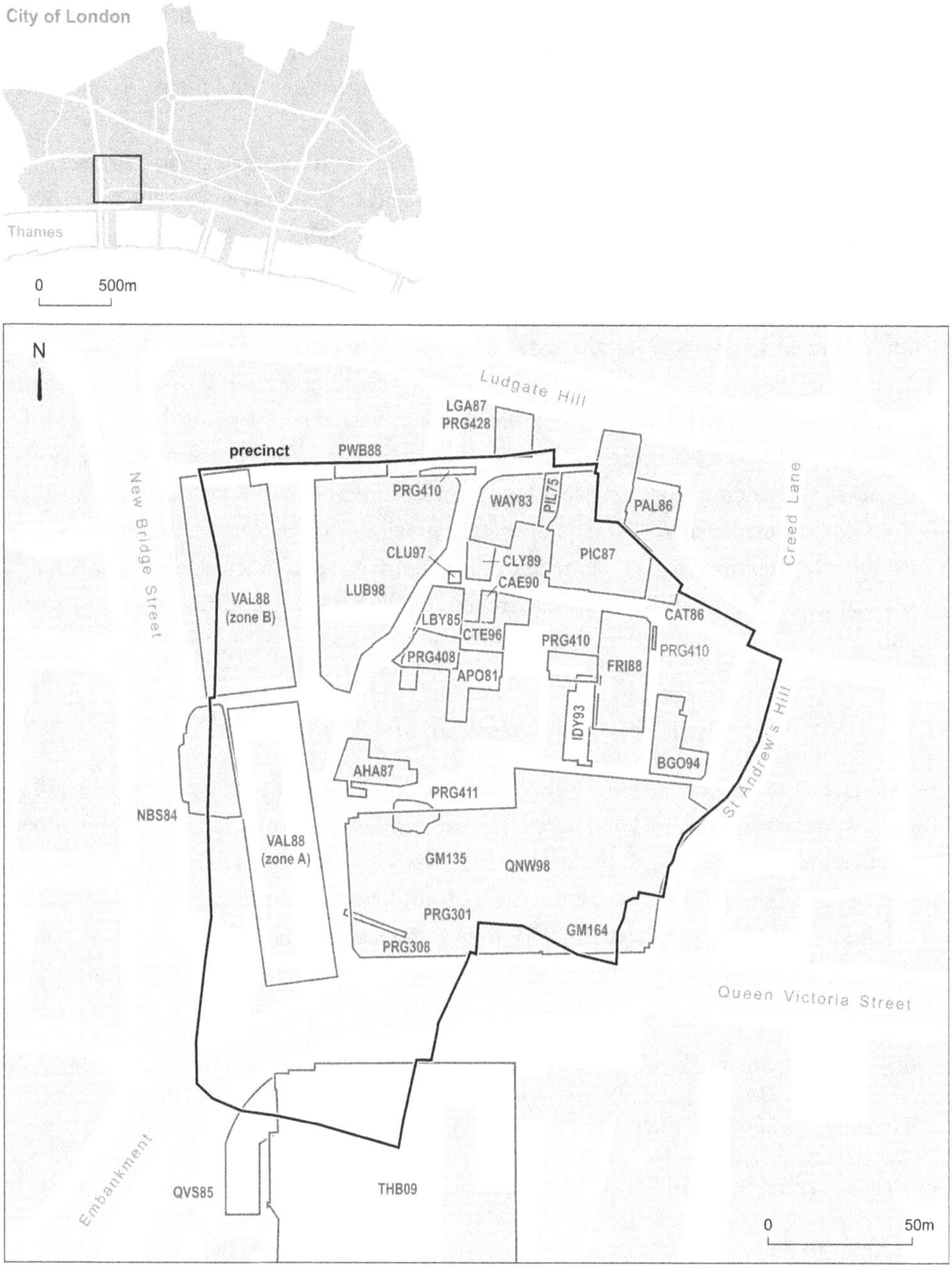

Fig. 7. Map showing the location of the medieval Black Friars precinct and archaeological excavations (scale 1:2500).

THE SECOND BLACK FRIARS, 1275–1538 31

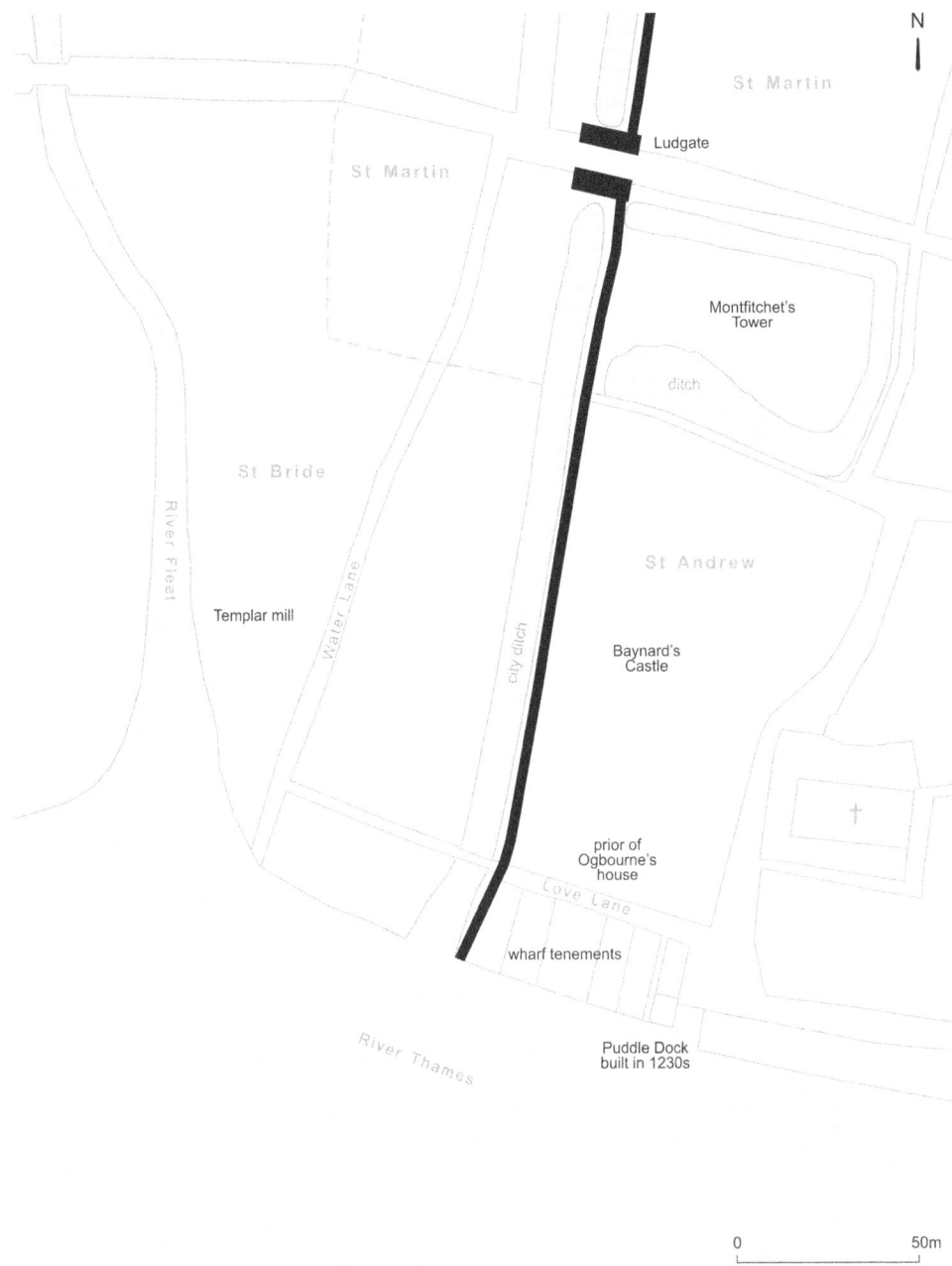

Fig. 8. Map of the landscape of the future Blackfriars in the 1270s, indicating the probable parish boundaries of St Andrew, St Martin and St Bride (scale 1:2000).

a cluster of wharf properties on the Thames.[12] On the external (west) side of the city wall the land sloped down to the river Fleet and seems to have been much less built up: there are few surviving pre-friary documentary records and, furthermore, archaeological excavations on this side of the wall have not revealed any significant pre-friary occupation. The one documented property is the Templar water mill which lay between the river Fleet and Water Lane.[13]

Between 1275 and 1277 the friars obtained, via their influential intermediary Robert Kilwardby, Baynard's Castle and part of Montfitchet's Tower, and the City granted them permission to close off the lanes in between the castles. In 1278 the king granted permission to begin demolition of the part of the city wall that lay to the south of the city gate known as Ludgate.[14] With these property acquisitions and permissions, prior John of Darlington could begin construction of the new church. The construction work may have begun as early as 1278 when the king granted additional alms to the friars but it should be noted that this gift was of an irregular royal fine (deodands) rather than a cash sum or regular tax payment. The earliest record of construction is from June 1280 and this may be a more reliable indication of when construction works started.[15]

Constructing a new church, cloister and other buildings was quite some task in itself but building the new friary also entailed first demolishing and then rebuilding the whole south-western section of the city wall. Work began by Ludgate in 1279 when Edward I granted the mayor the right to levy a special murage duty on incoming merchandise for three years (Figure 9). The construction of the new wall continued westwards, reaching the river Fleet by around 1284 and terminating in a tower. The work continued in an anti-clockwise direction around the new friary precinct, with a north–south stretch and another tower probably complete by 1286. Little further work was done until 1302 when a new murage grant was allowed and work began on the most difficult part, the extension of the wall into the Thames and then eastwards towards Puddle Dock. This stretch was probably complete by 1306. In 1308–9 the missing part of the wall by the old Templar mill could be completed, thanks to the confiscation of Templar property by

---

[12] Lobel, *City of London from Prehistoric Times to c. 1520*, pp. 65, 78, 81; Bruce Watson, 'The Norman Fortress on Ludgate Hill in the City of London, England, Recent Excavations 1986–1990', *Château Gaillard*, 15 (1992), 335–45; Marjorie B. Honeybourne, 'The Reconstructed Map of London under Richard II', *London Topographical Record*, 22 (1965), 29–66 (pp. 35–7). For the wharfside properties see LAA, Dyson and Taylor archive, parish of St Andrew Baynard's Castle, tenements A1, A2, A3, A4, A5, AX, AY, AZ and AA.

[13] Lobel, *City of London from Prehistoric Times to c. 1520*, p. 95. The two large archaeological excavations in this area to the west of the old city wall are sites VAL88 and LUB98: neither site produced significant evidence of pre-friary medieval occupation or buildings; Kieron Tyler, 'Changing the Landscape: Excavations at Black Friar's Court, Ludgate Broadway, London EC4', *Transactions of the London and Middlesex Archaeological Society*, 53 (2002), 25–51; LAA, VAL88, Bill McCann, 'Fleet Valley project, interim report' (unpublished Museum of London report, 1993).

[14] *CPR 1272–1281*, pp. 96–7, 98, 147–8, 258.

[15] *CPR 1272–1281*, p. 252; *CCR 1272–1279*, p. 515; *CCR 1279–1288*, p. 2; *CPR 1272–1281*, pp. 376, 399.

THE SECOND BLACK FRIARS, 1275–1538   33

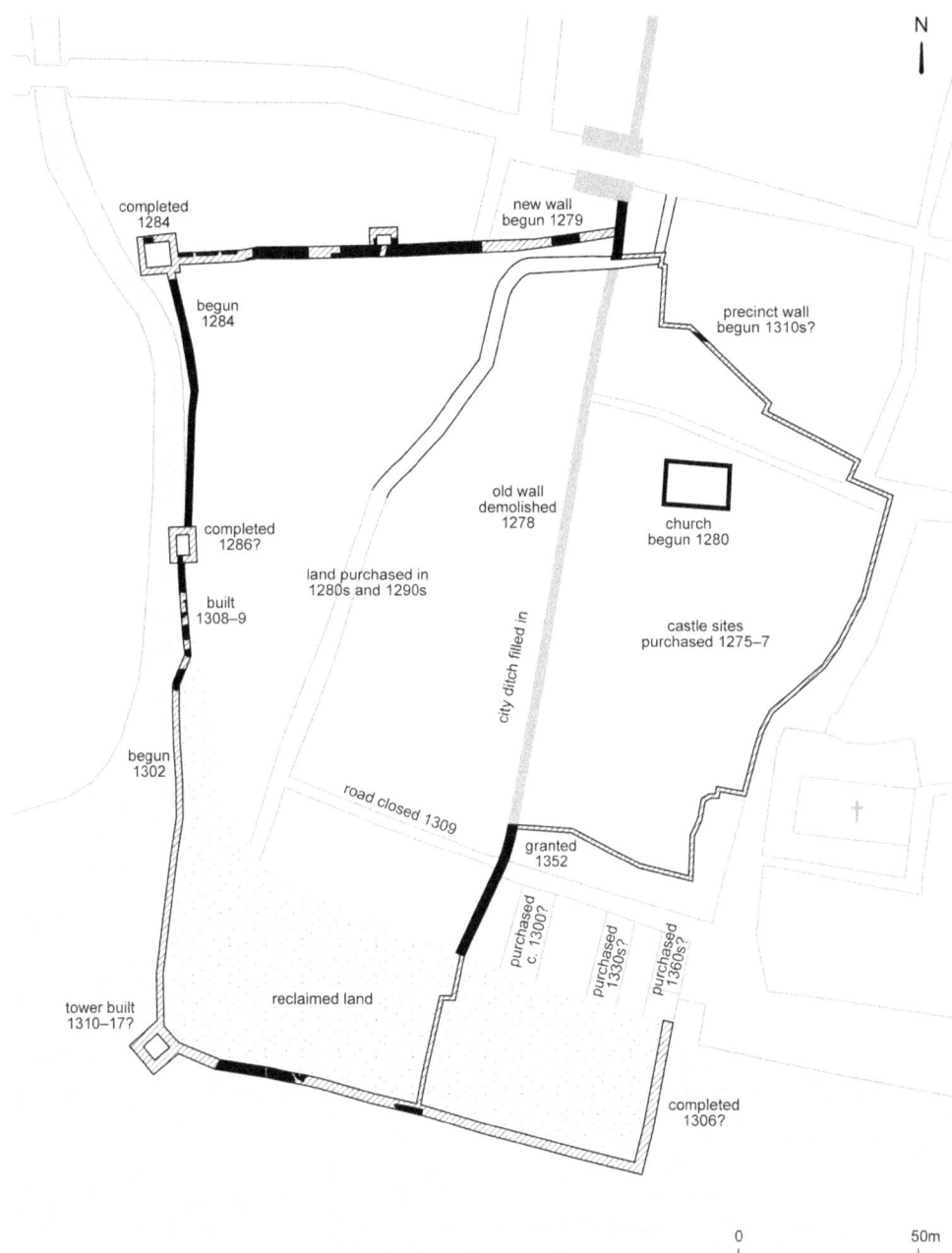

Fig. 9. Map showing the construction of the new city wall and the Black Friars priory beginning in 1278–9 (scale 1:2000).

Edward II. Finally, a new tower was built between 1310 and 1317, probably right on the south-west corner of the wall and thus strategically guarding the corner of the city.[16] Archaeological evidence shows that the wall was generally 6ft wide (1.8m) along the Fleet and 9ft wide (2.7m) along the Thames. The wall was built from Kentish ragstone and chalk, with the waterside face built in neat ashlar (almost certainly Hythe Beds stone from Kent). It was also 'battered' at angle of 5° on the water side (it was therefore thicker towards the base) in order to give greater strength.[17] The rebuilding of the city wall was thus used as an opportunity by the mayor and the friars to reclaim a large block of land from the Thames by building the wall out into the river, probably as far as the low tide mark, and filling in the foreshore between the new wall and the old river bank. In total, nearly 1¾ acres of land were reclaimed (6800m^2), eventually making a friary precinct of just over 8 acres (3.25 ha). The new wall therefore combined the functions of city defence, monastic precinct boundary and a huge engineering mechanism for land reclamation.

With the large city-wall works gradually encircling the new friary, prior John of Darlington or his successor John de Sevenehok began to plan a church and cloister. As has been stated, construction work on the new church probably began in 1280. By 1286 the church must have been just about usable – perhaps with two or three finished bays – since the friars completed the sale of the Holborn convent that year.[18] Work was still continuing in 1288, but in 1290 the king gave £22 6s 8d to pay for five windows at the west end of the church (at that stage only the choir), suggesting that the final stages of that part of the construction project had been reached. When Eleanor of Castile, consort of Edward I, died later that year, her heart was buried here and in 1291–2 payments were made for her tomb, including for the floor and ceiling of the chapel where she was buried.[19] The eastern part of the church, as yet without a nave, must have been largely complete.

By 1292 the prior's attention had turned to a cloister, to be situated to the south-west of the church so that it would connect with the planned nave (Figure 10). The friars received a licence to purchase £10 worth of timber from the forest of Essex that year, specifically for the new cloister.[20] At around this time they also began work on a beautiful

---

[16] This analysis of the construction sequence is based on unpublished documentary research by Colin Taylor carried out for the VAL88 archaeological excavation: LAA, VAL88, Colin Taylor, 'The building of the City wall at the Friars Preachers', in B. McCann, 'Fleet Valley project, interim report' (unpublished Museum of London report, 1993), pp. 87–92.

[17] Archaeological evidence for the wall is from LAA, sites APY82, LGA87, NBS84, PWB88, QVS85, THB09 and VAL88 (particularly the latter three sites). See also Ken Steedman, 'Queen Victoria Street Excavation', *Archaeology Today*, 8(11) (1987), 26–30.

[18] TNA, DL 27/62, printed in Williams, *Early Holborn*, i, 717.

[19] *Manners and Household Expenses of England in the Thirteenth and Fifteenth Centuries: Illustrated by Original Records*, ed. Beriah Botfield (London: Nicol, 1841), p. 103; Röhrkasten, *Mendicant Houses*, p. 503.

[20] *CPR 1281–1292*, p. 484.

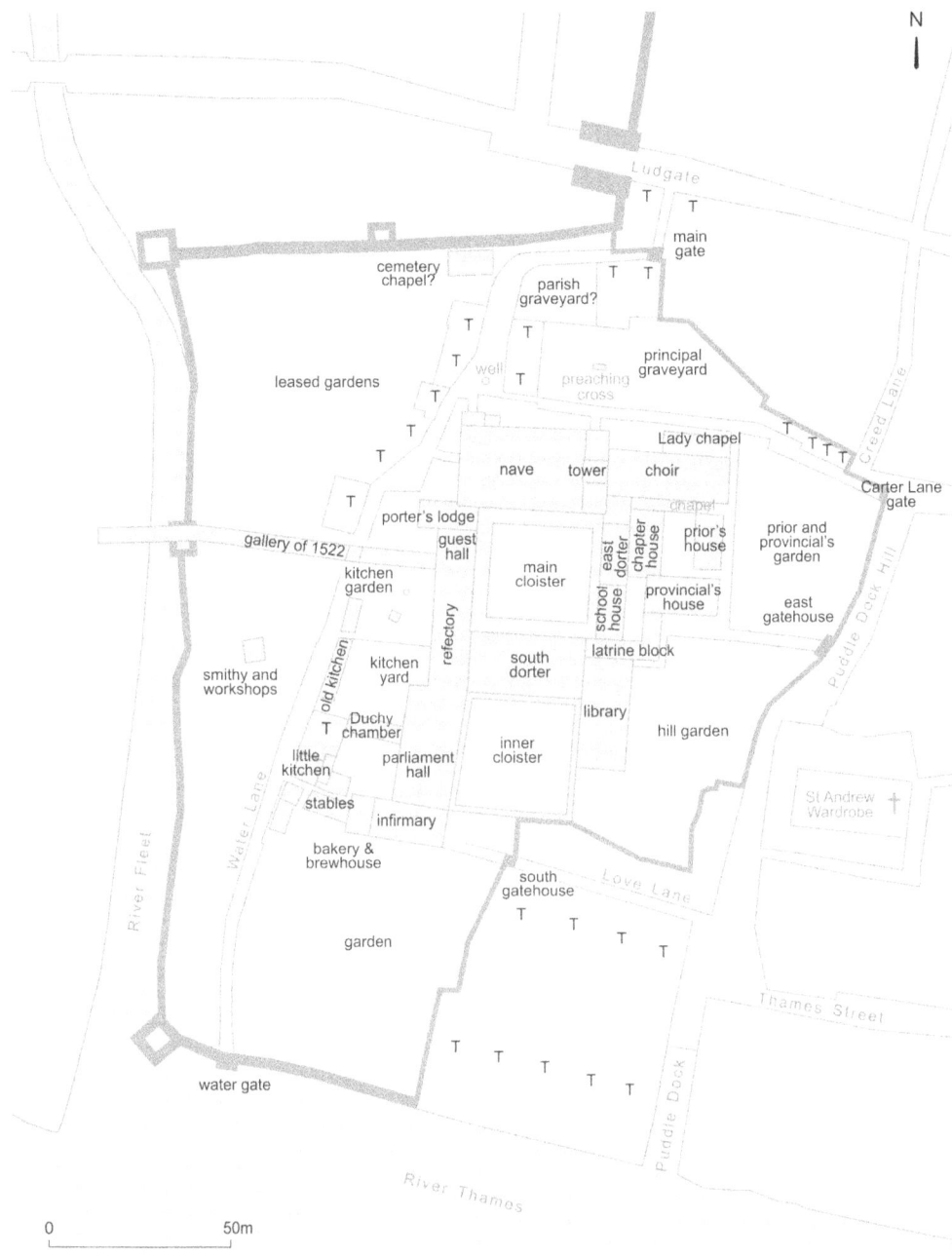

Fig. 10. Map of the precinct of Black Friars in the sixteenth century (scale 1:2000).

two-storey building just to the east of the cloister. By the sixteenth century this was the provincial prior's house but it must originally have been the chapter house. Funding for the chapter house had been set aside in 1281 when the novitiate friar Richard de Stratford bequeathed property whose rent was to pay for the project (it is not certain when he died).[21] The building survived, somewhat surprisingly, until the early twentieth century and the architectural details suggest a construction date in the last decade of the thirteenth century (below: 'The cloisters').

By 1312 the cloisters may have been more or less finished and the new prior, John de Wrotham, moved his attention back to the church. A team of twenty-four masons supervised by Michael Canterbury was working here in that year under royal patronage: master Michael had worked on St Stephen's chapel in the Palace of Westminster and he may now have been responsible for the design and execution of the Black Friars nave.[22] Architectural fragments including part of a pier and an external weather moulding point to a date for the nave in the first half, perhaps the first quarter, of the fourteenth century (Chapter 12: Architecture and Architectural Fragments of the London Friaries).

The final stage of the main Black Friars project was the construction of a second cloister to the south of and slightly downhill from the main cloister (Figure 10). There is, unfortunately, little direct documentary or archaeological evidence for the construction of these buildings. However, in 1371 the newly appointed chancellor of the exchequer is recorded as meeting in a room at Black Friars called the 'counseil house', situated beside the lower cloister (*inferior claustr*[*um*]): the term would seem to distinguish this cloister from the main claustral range to the north. In the same decade Merton College in Oxford was planning the enlargement of its library and the clerk of works and the mason went on a fact-finding mission, inspecting the library of the London Black Friars.[23] The library was on the east side of the second cloister and the evidence would therefore point to the construction of this cloister around the middle or the third quarter of the fourteenth century, perhaps after the nave was finished. A few fragments of mid- to late-fourteenth-century glazed and unglazed tracery were found on the PIC87 archaeological site and they may have been used in this stage of the construction campaign; the unglazed example is particularly characteristic of a cloister (Chapter 12: Architecture and Architectural Fragments of the London Friaries).

In summary, documentary and architectural evidence would suggest that the bulk of the precinct of the second Black Friars was planned and built in a remarkably short time – less than a century – beginning in 1280.

The church

The Dominicans' church was dedicated – like the first church in Holborn – to St John the Evangelist. With its thirteenth-century choir and generously proportioned fourteenth-century nave (designed by the great architect Michael Canterbury?), it was undoubtedly

---

[21] *Calendar of Wills Proved and Enrolled in the Court of Husting*, i, xlv, 52.
[22] Howard M. Colvin, *The History of the King's Works*, 6 vols (London: HMSO, 1963), i, 207; Barron and Davies, *Religious Houses*, p. 120.
[23] TNA, C 54/209, m. 35v; G.H. Martin and J.R.L. Highfield, *A History of Merton College, Oxford* (Oxford: Oxford University Press, 1997), pp. 88–91.

one of the finest churches of London.[24] Its splendour was evocatively described in the late fourteenth-century poem known as 'Pierce the Ploughman's Crede', even if the poet's intention was to satirise rather than glorify the architectural achievements of these rather wealthy mendicants. The poet-narrator enters the church and immediately notes the stone carvings with details picked out in gold:

> Thanne y munte [hurried] me forth the mynstre to knowen,
> And a-waytede [found it, i.e. the church] a woon wonderlie well y-beld
> With arches on everiche half & belliche y-corven,
> With crochetes on corners with knottes of golde.

He goes on to describe the windows – apparently forty-four (twice twenty-two) in number – noting the accompanying inscriptions and the arms of civic benefactors:

> Wyde wyndowes y-wrought y-written full thikke
> Schynen with schapen scheldes to schewen aboute
> With merkes of marchauntes y-medled bytwene,
> Mo than twenty and two twyes y-noumbred.

The narrator is also very impressed by the large number of colourful chest-tombs and other monuments commemorating lay men and women, comparing, in a rather daring metaphor, their occupants to saints:

> Tombes opon tabernacles tyld [raised] opon lofte,
> Housed in hirnes [placed in corners?] harde set abouten,
> Of armede alabaustre clad for the nones.
> Made upon marbel in many maner wyse
> Knyghtes in her conisantes [symbol or crest] clad for the nones.
> All it semed seyntes y-sacred opon erthe
> And lovely ladies y-wrought leyen by her sydes
> In many gay garmentes that weren gold-beten.[25]

---

[24] The dedication of the high altar is noted in a will of 1503 with that of the church recorded in a lease of 1536; for the will see Clapham, 'Topography of the Dominican Priory', p. 65. The lease is TNA, E 315/216, f. 52; E 326/12376; printed in Smith, *Shakespeare's Blackfriars Playhouse*, p. 426; *Blackfriars Records*, p. 104. For Canterbury, see n. 22; Christopher Wilson, 'Canterbury, Michael (fl. 1275–1321)', *ODNB*, <http://www.oxforddnb.com/view/article/37763> [accessed 11 June 2014].

[25] *Pierce the Ploughmans Crede, to which is Appended God Spede the Plough*, ed. Walter W. Skeat, Early English Text Society, 30 (London: Paul, 1867), pp. 7–8 (quotation includes variant lines); Smith, *Shakespeare's Blackfriars Playhouse*, pp. 547–50. It is possible that the satirical description refers to the Norwich Black Friars: Röhrkasten, *Mendicant Houses*, p. 504.

Our task is now to understand something of the size, layout and appearance of this great 'mynstre'. Fortunately several archaeological excavations have revealed stretches of wall and foundation, enough to piece together the basic plan of the church. Furthermore, the same excavations have produced a few architectural fragments (often unceremoniously recycled in sixteenth- or seventeenth-century wall foundations) that reveal something of the glory of these 'wyde wyndowes'. Beginning at the choir end of the church, the lines of the north and east walls are defined by a stub of wall and an east-facing buttress foundation (sites FRI88 and PRG410 on Figure 11). Moving clockwise around the church, the south walls of the choir and the nave are clearly defined (sites PRG410 and APO81); two more archaeological sites gave us most of the foundations of the west wall and the north-west corner (sites PRG408 and LBY85), with a few fragments of the north wall of the nave also recorded (site CTE96). The full external length of the church can now be understood to be 74.0m (243ft), with the width of the fourteenth-century nave 21.9m (72ft). The archaeological measurement of the internal width of the nave – 65ft – corresponds remarkably well with a dimension of 66ft recorded in a 1550 grant.[26] Several discontinuous foundations for the arcade piers and responds have also been discovered, thus revealing the aisle and bay structure of the nave. The nave had seven bays that were 15ft 3in wide (4.6m, measured centre to centre), with the crossing being a slightly wider eighth bay, about 20ft according to both the archaeological evidence and a lease of 1553.[27] The position of the crossing between nave and choir – sometimes referred to in sixteenth-century sources as a 'walking place' – is not certain but is likely to be defined by the narrow street still known as Church Entry.[28] The choir to the east probably had seven bays arranged in a single aisle (Figure 11).

The church was constructed using the traditional techniques of London masons: they dug a deep foundation trench with an arched (rather than flat) base and then carefully poured mortar, ragstone and chalk to form the foundation. The main walls were about 3ft 9in thick above ground (1.1m; the less certain evidence for the choir suggests the walls were slightly thinner) and were built of roughly coursed, quite small Kentish ragstone blocks, with Reigate stone used for quoins and architectural details. There is also some evidence for the use of other fine building stones including Caen stone and Purbeck marble. The arcades of the nave were supported on Purbeck marble piers, composed of four clustered shafts forming a quatrefoil moulding and resting on an octagonal base. At least one of the

---

[26] Corresponding internal measurements: length 72.0m (236ft); width of nave 19.7m (65ft). These reconstructed measurements ignore the additional thickness of the foundations and do not include the length of the buttresses. 1550 grant: TNA, C 66/831, mm. 32–3.

[27] The small parcel of land at the south end of the 'late belfry' was measured at 20ft wide (east–west): SHC, LM/346/37.

[28] This interpretation follows Clapham's reconstruction: Clapham, 'Topography of the Dominican Priory'. For an example of the term 'walking place', presumably describing the function of the bay that separated nave from choir and allowed circulation across the church, see BL, Harley MS 6033, ff. 31–2, printed in W.A. Cater, 'The Priory of Austin Friars, London', *Journal of the British Archaeological Association*, 18 (1912), 25–44, 57–82 (pp. 80–2).

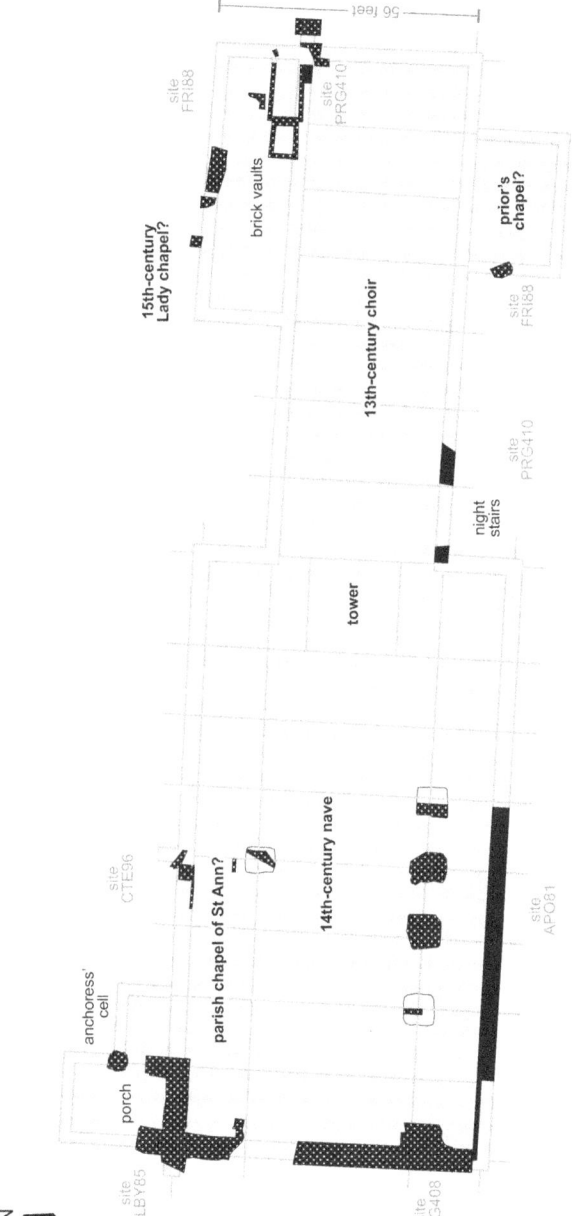

Fig. 11. Plan of the church of Black Friars (scale 1:500).

windows used imported Caen stone mullions and, given its early form and the location where it was found, this is more likely to be from the thirteenth-century choir than the fourteenth-century nave. Much of the church was tiled: a 1550 grant and survey does not list any paving stones from the church (in contrast to the cloister) and a patch of *in situ* 'plain red tiling' was observed at the west end of the nave in an early archaeological excavation (site PRG408). The evidence from stray tiles found during more recent excavations here would suggest that the thirteenth-century choir used 'Westminster' floor tiles with the fourteenth-century nave using decorated Penn tiles and a few plain Eltham Palace tiles (Chapter 13: Floor Tiles and Building Materials from the London Friaries).

A few other features of the church can be identified, largely from documentary sources. There was a central tower over the crossing between the nave and choir. Wyngaerde's view of c. 1544 (drawn about a year before the steeple was demolished) seems to show a large polygonal tower with a relatively squat spire. Lay visitors to the friary would have entered the church through a porch in the north-west corner, described in 1554 as the 'greate porch or gatehouse of sand stone covered with lead' and later as 'the Square Tower sometyme called the Church portch & the little gaterome thereunto adjoyninge'.[29] One should probably picture a two-storey porch, decorated with statues, which would have guided visitors to the friary who were walking down the lane from Ludgate.

Next to the porch was an anchoress's cell.[30] The Black Friars anchoress was one of about twenty London anchorites living in cells by parish churches, religious houses or against the city wall. Her cell was probably built up against the second and third buttresses of the church and it almost certainly had a 'squint' or small window into the corresponding chapel in the north aisle. In the 1470s Katherine Foster was the anchoress, living with her maid; in 1521 Margaret Elyote became anchoress (after winning an unusual case at the Court of Chancery in which she promised not to be a financial burden on the friary, seeking alms instead from the mayor and City); at the time of the Dissolution Katherine Man occupied the cell.[31]

The conventual church had numerous chapels, some within the main footprint, some added on to the outside. Archaeological evidence shows that the most prominent of these chapels lay on the north side of the choir (Figure 11). At the Carter Lane archaeological site (FRI88) a pair of late medieval brick-lined burial vaults were discovered (the bodies had

---

[29] SHC, LM/347/10 [1554 lease]; *Blackfriars Records*, p. 108 [1592 lease].

[30] The clearest source that gives its location is a lease of 1570 where the 'tenemente sometime called the Ancres howse' abuts the gate-room (porch) to the west and the way leading from Carter Lane to the north: Loseley MS printed in *Blackfriars Records*, pp. 112–13. It is mentioned in several other leases.

[31] TNA, C 1/538/13 (the Chancery document is very faded and hard to read: the information therefore derives from the catalogue entry); Barron and Davies, *Religious Houses*, p. 238; Ann K. Warren, *Anchorites and their Patrons in Medieval England* (Berkeley: University of California Press, 1985), pp. 288–9; Rotha M. Clay, *The Hermits and Anchorites of England* (London: Methuen, 1914), pp. 96, 230–1.

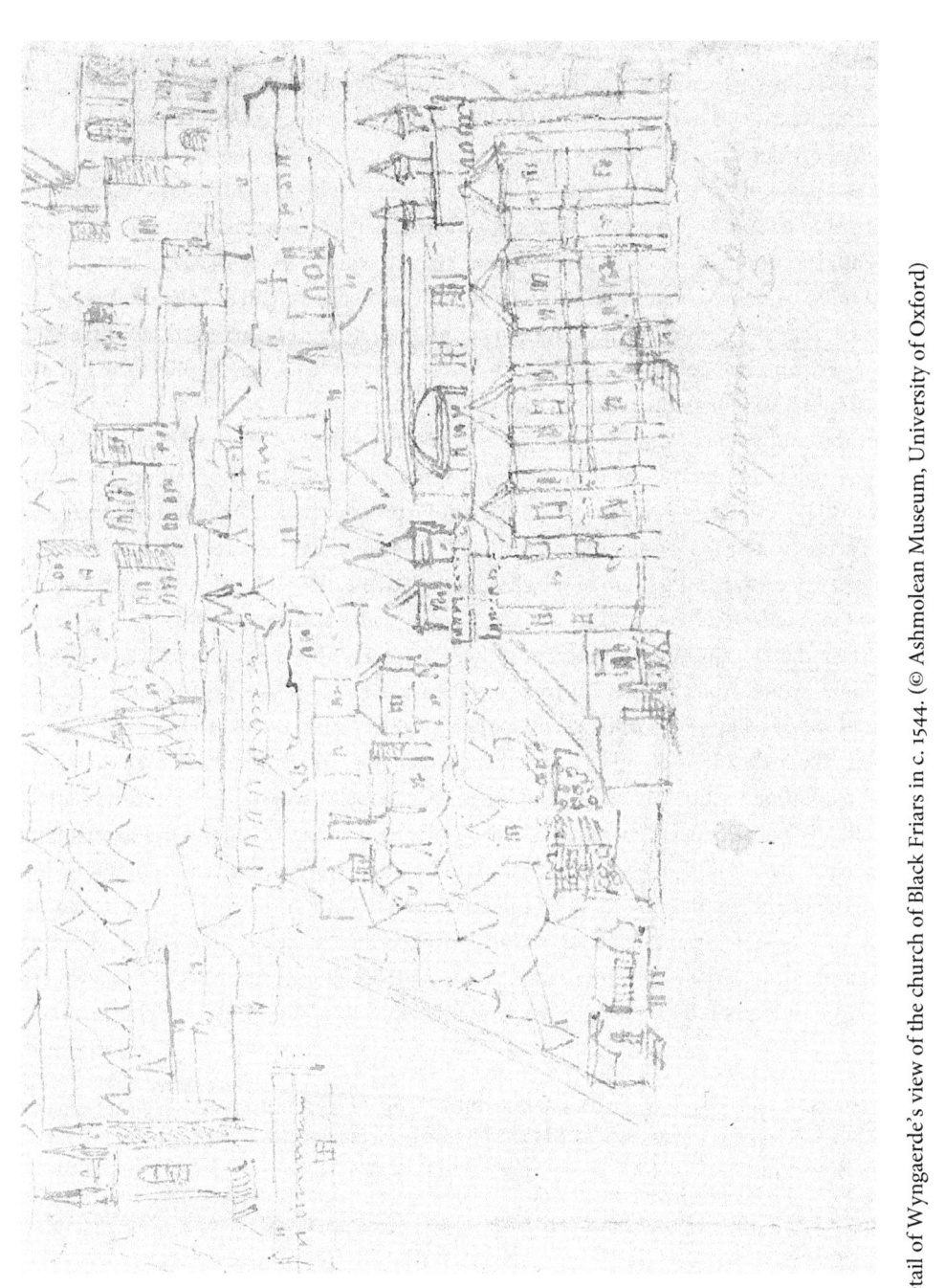

Fig. 12. Detail of Wyngaerde's view of the church of Black Friars in c. 1544. (© Ashmolean Museum, University of Oxford)

probably been transferred to another location by family members at the Dissolution) and several fragments of wall foundation define an east–west wall further north of the main wall of the choir. This wall seems to be slightly out of alignment with the main church wall, presumably influenced by the adjacent lane and graveyard. The authors reconstruct this part of the church, therefore, as a distinct chapel of three or four bays, not a complete aisle extending westwards to meet the nave (Figure 11). It is tempting to identify a chapel in this prominent position by the choir as a Lady chapel and there are several documentary references to images of the Virgin in chapels at the friary; the problem is distinguishing between images of Mary and a 'standalone' large Lady chapel. Between the late fourteenth and early sixteenth century there are at least seven references in wills to altars, images and statues of Mary, but only one that refers to a specific chapel.[32] In the 1470s Joan de Ingaldesthorp paid for a new chapel dedicated to the Virgin to commemorate her brother John Tiptoft, earl of Worcester, who had been executed in October 1470 when his ardent support for Edward IV cost him his life with the return of Henry VI.[33]

On the south side of the church there was another smaller chapel abutting the choir: in a post-Dissolution grant of 1548 it forms part of the prior's suite of buildings (below: The cloisters) and it may well have been the prior's private chapel giving him physical and visual access to the choir stalls and high altar.[34] The chapel has been reconstructed here as occupying two bays to the south of the choir, its western extent defined by the archaeological evidence (admittedly very slim) of a south-west-facing buttress (Figure 11; site FRI88).

Within the Dominican nave and choir there must have been dozens of statues, images and altars, which friars and lay visitors (or at least *some* lay people) could have accessed through a maze-like series of painted wooden screens, walls, doors, arches and separate chapels. The dedications of only a few of these are known, largely thanks to the evidence of wills. In addition to the Lady chapel and the prior's chapel there were at least three distinct chapels: a Pardon chapel (referred to in a will of 1464), a chapel of St John the Baptist built in the early sixteenth century (will of 1509) and a chapel of St Anne (first mentioned in 1502). The chapel of St Anne must be the quasi-parish church referred to in a parish tax survey of 1535–6. In 1520 this parish chapel was described as being 'within and adjoining the church of the Friars Preachers' and it may have occupied a few bays of the northern aisle, close to the porch entrance for lay worshippers.[35] In addition to these chapels, there

---

[32] Clapham, 'Topography of the Dominican Priory', pp. 64–5; Röhrkasten, *Mendicant Houses*, pp. 503–4. Clapham tentatively located the Lady chapel in the north-western corner of the nave.

[33] Röhrkasten, *Mendicant Houses*, pp. 503–4; Benjamin G. Kohl, 'Tiptoft, John, First Earl of Worcester (1427–1470)', *ODNB*, <http://www.oxforddnb.com/view/article/27471> [accessed 11 June 2014].

[34] TNA, C 66/814, m. 10; printed in Smith, *Shakespeare's Blackfriars Playhouse*, pp. 433–4; *Blackfriars Records*, pp. 103–4.

[35] Clapham, 'Topography of the Dominican Priory', pp. 65–67; Röhrkasten, *Mendicant Houses*, pp. 503–4. For the dating and identification of the tax survey of 1535–6 (TNA, SP 1/25, ff. 35–6, nos 222–3) see John Oldland, 'The Allocation of Merchant Capital in Early Tudor London', *Economic History Review*, 63.4 (2010), 1058–80 (p. 1060).

are several further references in late fifteenth- and early sixteenth-century wills to altars, most of which would have been sited in chapel-like bays of the aisles. Six altars are attested, dedicated to our Lady of Grace, St Michael the Archangel, St Peter, St Thomas Aquinas, St Zita and to the founder of the Dominican order, St Dominic. Finally, other testators requested burial near to a particular image (whether a statue or a painting) and many of these images would also have had altars: St Peter of Milan (in the north aisle, presumably the Dominican martyr Peter of Verona), St Erasmus (also in north aisle), our Lady of Pity, St Michael and St Patrick.[36]

A few fragmentary remains of these one-time splendours of the church were noted down by surveyors after the closure in 1538, including just over seventy pounds of church plate.[37] An inventory of the church drawn up soon afterwards lists some surviving fixtures including pews and screens in the nave, two organs in the rood-loft, the stalls in the choir and the table of the high altar. Even at this time, probably weeks after the friars had departed, a few sad reminders of the friars' liturgical cycle remained, left standing on the altar: 'iiij candelstykes of latten & an sylver & the Images aboth sydes the alter'.[38]

The cloisters

The friars enjoyed the use of two complete, or nearly complete, cloisters (Figure 10). The main cloister seems to have been built at the turn of the thirteenth and fourteenth centuries, with a second cloister added to the south half a century or so later. This southern cloister is described in several sixteenth-century documents as the inner cloister, being further from the church and cemetery and more secluded, therefore, from lay visitors.[39] Most of the evidence for the description and identification of the various buildings in the two cloisters comes from a very useful series of post-Dissolution grants and their accompanying 'particulars for grant', prepared in the 1540s by surveyors from the Court of Augmentations. Particularly important are the 1548 lease and subsequent 1550 grant of much of the main and inner cloisters to Thomas Cawarden, and grants to further purchasers or lessees made in 1540, 1544 and 1545.[40] Rather more is known, therefore, about the

---

[36] For altars of St Thomas Aquinas and St Zita see *Calendar of Papal Letters*, 20 vols (various publishers, 1893–), *1513–1521*, pp. 558 (no. 1245), 578 (fn. 109).

[37] John Williams, *Account of the Monastic Treasures Confiscated at the Dissolution of the Various Houses in England*, ed. W. Turnbull (Edinburgh: Abbotsford Club, 1836), p. 19.

[38] TNA, E 117/14/202.

[39] For example 'le inner cloyster *modo gardinum*' in 1540: TNA, E 315/212, ff. 134v–135 printed in Smith, *Shakespeare's Blackfriars Playhouse*, p. 426; *Blackfriars Records*, p. 104.

[40] Lease of much of the cloisters and precinct to Thomas Cawarden in 1548: TNA, E 315/219, ff. 20v–21; accompanying particulars for lease: E 310/3/18, no. 61, a Loseley copy of which is printed in Smith, *Shakespeare's Blackfriars Playhouse*, pp. 431–2; *Blackfriars Records*, pp. 6–8. Subsequent grant to Cawarden in 1550: TNA, C 66/831, mm. 32–3; accompanying particulars for grant printed in Smith, *Shakespeare's Blackfriars Playhouse*, pp. 435–8; *Blackfriars Records*, pp. 8–12. Further details of the buildings appear in the earlier 1540 lease of the inner cloister to Henry Kingston:

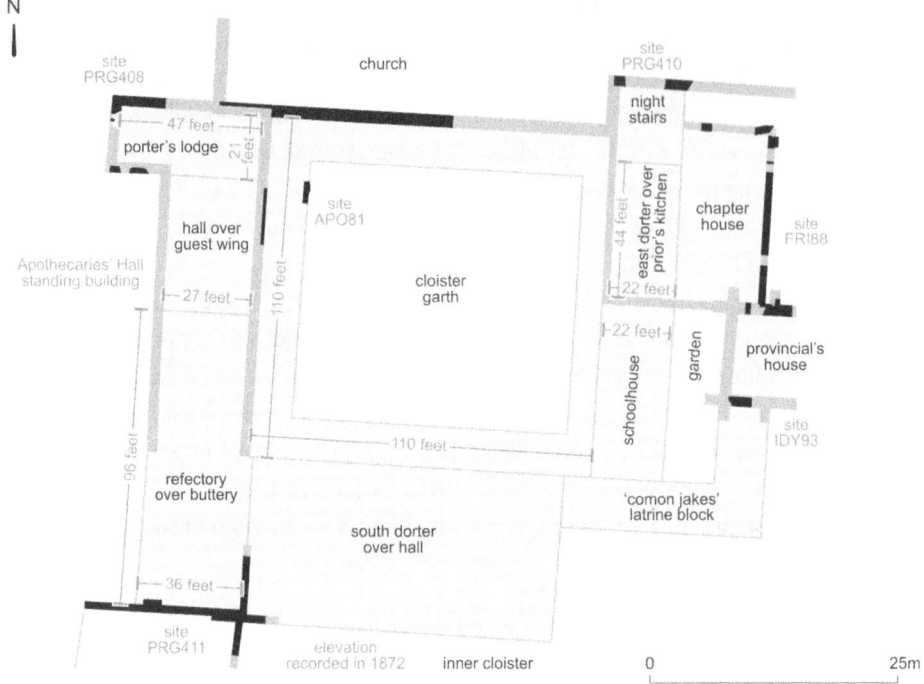

Fig. 13. Plan of the main cloister at Black Friars (scale 1:750).

use of the various cloister buildings in the early sixteenth century than in the fourteenth century: the inevitable problem is that some buildings undoubtedly changed function over time, for example, the chapter house. A little archaeological evidence locates key walls of the cloisters: for example, what seems to be the south-west corner of the main cloister buildings can be located thanks to archaeological observation of medieval walls during works at *The Times* printing house in 1928 (PRG411 on Figure 13). With these fixed points, measurements recorded in the various surveys and grants (such as the dimensions of the main cloister: 110ft square) can be added to the plan – and the buildings begin to map themselves.

The main cloister was built as three wings of buildings around a single-storey cloister

TNA, E 315/212, ff. 134v–135, printed in Smith, *Shakespeare's Blackfriars Playhouse*, p. 426; *Blackfriars Records*, p. 104; accompanying particulars: TNA, E 315/191, f. 57. 1544 grant of east side of main cloister to Paul Gresham and Francis Boldero: TNA, E 315/191, f. 58; C 66/749, mm. 22–3; accompanying particulars: E 318/11/524, Loseley copy of which is printed in Smith, *Shakespeare's Blackfriars Playhouse*, p. 428; *Blackfriars Records*, p. 106. Grant of inner cloister property to Lady Mary Kingston in 1545: C 66/768, mm. 23–4; accompanying particulars: TNA, E 318/14/662; SC 12/11/18, Loseley copy printed in Smith, *Shakespeare's Blackfriars Playhouse*, p. 427; *Blackfriars Records*, p. 105. For a plan showing which part of the precinct was granted to which grantee or lessee, see Holder, 'Medieval Friaries of London', fig. 16, p. 380.

walk, the latter having a fourth side to the north beside the nave of the church. In 'Pierce the Ploughman's Crede' the narrator enters the cloister and notes the carved tracery, the painted walls and the low lead roof of the single-storey cloister:

Thanne kam I to that cloister & gaped abouten
Whough it was pilered and peynt & portred [carved] well clene
All y-hyled with leed lowe to the stones.

The main cloister had a laver for the friars to wash their hands before services and meals, described as 'a fayre lavytery' in 1540. This feature also caught our poet-narrator's eye and he notes the engraved brass laver basin and its tin (or lead?) conduit tank:

With kundites of clene tyn closed all aboute
With lavoures of latun lovelyche y-greithed.[41]

Moving clockwise from the north-east corner of the cloister, the various post-Dissolution grants identify the buildings in the east wing as the prior's kitchen and cellars (his mansion lay just to the east) and the friary school ('le Scolehouse' in the 1544 grant), the *studium provinciale* that trained Dominican friars for further study at Oxford, Cambridge or Paris. Above these was the first-floor dormitory, complete with night-stairs to allow the friars to walk down to the choir for Lauds.

On the south side of the cloister lay the principal dormitory wing or dorter: it faced both northwards onto the main cloister (according to the evidence of the 1550 grant) and southwards onto the inner cloister (according to the 1540 lease). The latter evidence shows that the dormitory itself was on the first floor with 'lodgynges' underneath, and a separate hall, buttery and cellar. Part of what must be the southern wall of this building was discovered during construction work at *The Times* printing house in 1872: a painting shows four or five bays of a hall, the bays separated by south-facing buttresses (Figure 14). There are two ground-level doorways (the painting shows the below-ground foundation exposed beneath the door openings) and two plain two-light windows (only the right-hand window has its surviving mullion; Figure 14). It is not possible to fix the location of this wall with absolute precision but the evidence suggests a very substantial building running between the two cloisters, about 102ft long and 54ft wide (31m × 16m).[42]

---

[41] TNA, E 117/14/202; *Pierce the Ploughmans Crede*, p. 8.

[42] The painting is reproduced in Clapham, 'Topography of the Dominican Priory', p. 78, plate xiii. Clapham identifies the building as a parochial chapel of St Anne; however, the two door openings and the square windows suggest that this is a claustral building not a chapel. The approximate location of this substantial piece of walling is shown in a later plan produced by *The Times* when further medieval walls were discovered just to the west (site PRG411): William Martin, 'Blackfriars and *The Times*', *Transactions of the London and Middlesex Archaeological Society*, 6 (1929), 205–7. The painting is described as being in the Guildhall Museum but it no longer appears to exist in

Fig. 14. View of the remains of the main dormitory wing between the northern and southern cloisters of Black Friars, discovered in 1872 (from Clapham, 'Topography of the Dominican Priory', plate xiii; by kind permission of the Society of Antiquaries of London).

Part of the western claustral wing survives today as Apothecaries' Hall, a historic seventeenth-century building built on the base of the medieval building. Just less than a metre of medieval wall survives in the elevation of the east wall of the hall and it is of an unusual construction, employing a technique known as galetting in which slivers of black flint were pressed into the white lime mortar joints in order to create a decorative dotted effect.[43] The southern part of this wing can be identified as the refectory hall, with a buttery and stores below. The 1548 lease describes: 'an owlde buttery and an entrye or passage with a greate stayre therein with Sellers therunder with a hall place at the upper ende of the stayre and an entere there to the frater over the same buttery'.

Moving northwards along this western wing, it is likely that the next building was the friary's guest hall. It is consistently described in post-Dissolution grants and leases as a hall or *magna aula* and it is probably where Emperor Charles V stayed on his visit to London in 1522 (with Henry VIII staying the other side of the Fleet river in Bridewell Palace, the two having been linked by an extraordinary bridge-cum-gallery).[44] At the very north end of this wing was the porter's lodge, controlling lay access to the guest hall and the rest of the cloister. A surviving medieval ground-floor window was discovered in the fabric of Apothecaries' Hall during works in the early twentieth century (site PRG408) and documentary sources describe another window as a 'closet wyndowe' looking into the south aisle of the church.[45]

To the east of the main cloister lay the chapter houses and the priors' halls (both, confusingly, in the plural). We argue elsewhere that a remarkable thirteenth-century undercroft that survived until the early twentieth century was the original chapter house of the friary.[46] During an impressive rescue excavation here in 1900 a vaulted undercroft was

---

the collections of the Guildhall Museum's successors (the Museum of London, the Guildhall Art Gallery and the London Metropolitan Archive). I am grateful to Francis Marshall (MoL), Vivien Knight (GAG) and Jeremy Smith (LMA) for their assistance in trying to track down this painting.

[43] This medieval part of the wall elevation was recorded when an adjacent building was being redeveloped; the majority of the hall is now covered with render. LAA, site APO81, D. Bluer and P. Allen, 'A watching brief at Apothecaries Hall, 20–26 Blackfriars Lane, EC4' (unpublished Museum of London report, 1985). It has been suggested that much of the north wall of the hall, some 30ft in elevation, is surviving medieval masonry, with the implication that other parts of the hall could preserve similar amounts of medieval fabric: Simon Bradley and Nikolaus Pevsner, *London 1: The City of London*, The Buildings of England (New Haven and London: Yale University Press, 2002), p. 376. However, this statement was based on an erroneous interpretation of the archaeological evidence of site APO81 by the Apothecaries' Company archivist, Charles O'Leary, in a letter to Bradley: Apothecaries' Company, 'secondary sources' file, 'Hall redevelopment', letter of 6 April 1995 from O'Leary to Bradley. The archaeological evidence does, however, suggest that the *plan* of Apothecaries' Hall follows the medieval plan.

[44] Colvin, *King's Works*, iv (2), 55–6.

[45] *Blackfriars Records*, p. 115.

[46] Mark Samuel and Nick Holder, 'The Thirteenth-Century Chapter House of Black Friars, London', forthcoming. This first chapter house is labelled 'provincial's house' on Figure 10 and Figure 13, referring to its use in the sixteenth century; see below).

discovered, complete with a surviving window, an *in situ* pier, several responds and a complete arch spanning the undercroft (site PRG407).[47] Ninety years later, other surviving parts of the same building were recorded by the Museum of London (sites FRI88 and IDY93). The window has been preserved in the modern office block at 10 Friar Street (Figure 15) and the south-west corner of the chapter house survives as a short stub of wall in the old St Anne's churchyard on Ireland Yard. Furthermore, the authors were able to track down some relocated parts of this building: a column in the new Dominican friary in Belsize Park, London (Figure 79) and an arch in the former garden of the nineteenth-century Surrey palace of the bishop of Rochester (Figure 65; now the Selsdon Park Hotel). The position of this building to the east of the cloister, its form and the stylistic date, late thirteenth-century, strongly suggest that this is the chapter house for which funding was being arranged in the 1280s. In June 1281 the novice friar Richard de Stratford walked into Guildhall to enrol and prove his own will at the Court of Husting (unusually he was still very much alive for the probate process), bequeathing tenements to be sold to raise money for a chapter house.[48] The finished building had two storeys. At ground level there was a well-lit five-bay undercroft with a complex quadripartite vault rising from responds and Purbeck marble piers (Figure 16). Above, there would have been a large hall, measuring some 56ft by 28ft (17.3m × 8.5m). This building seems to have been a gem of the London Decorated style, perhaps designed by Robert of Beverley, the king's master mason from 1260. If the 'Pierce the Ploughman's Crede' poet is to be believed, the main hall had painted walls and carved decoration:

Thanne was the chaptire-hous wrought as a greet chirche,
Corven and covered and queyntliche entayled.
With semlich selure [ceiling] y-set on lofte,
As a Parlement-hous y-peynted aboute.[49]

By the sixteenth century, however, this building seems to have been used as the provincial prior's hall. The precise arrangement of the buildings in this area is, it should be admitted, surprisingly hard to understand in the post-Dissolution grants: the warren of medieval chambers to the east of the main cloister was divided between three grantees in 1544, 1548 and 1550. But by this date the former chapter house seems to have become the building that housed the 'provincyalls chamber', situated by a garden and including three rooms (apparently in addition to the chamber itself) with two fireplaces.[50] Before turning to the new chapter house one must mention the separate prior's house – 'le Priors

---

[47] A detailed drawn record was made and was deposited in the Victoria and Albert Museum: Department of Prints Drawings and Paintings, D.1291–1907.
[48] See n. 21.
[49] *Pierce the Ploughmans Crede*, p. 8.
[50] TNA, E 315/191, f. 58.

Fig. 15. View of a window from the north wall of the undercroft of the late thirteenth-century chapter house, revealed in an excavation in 1988. (MOLA)

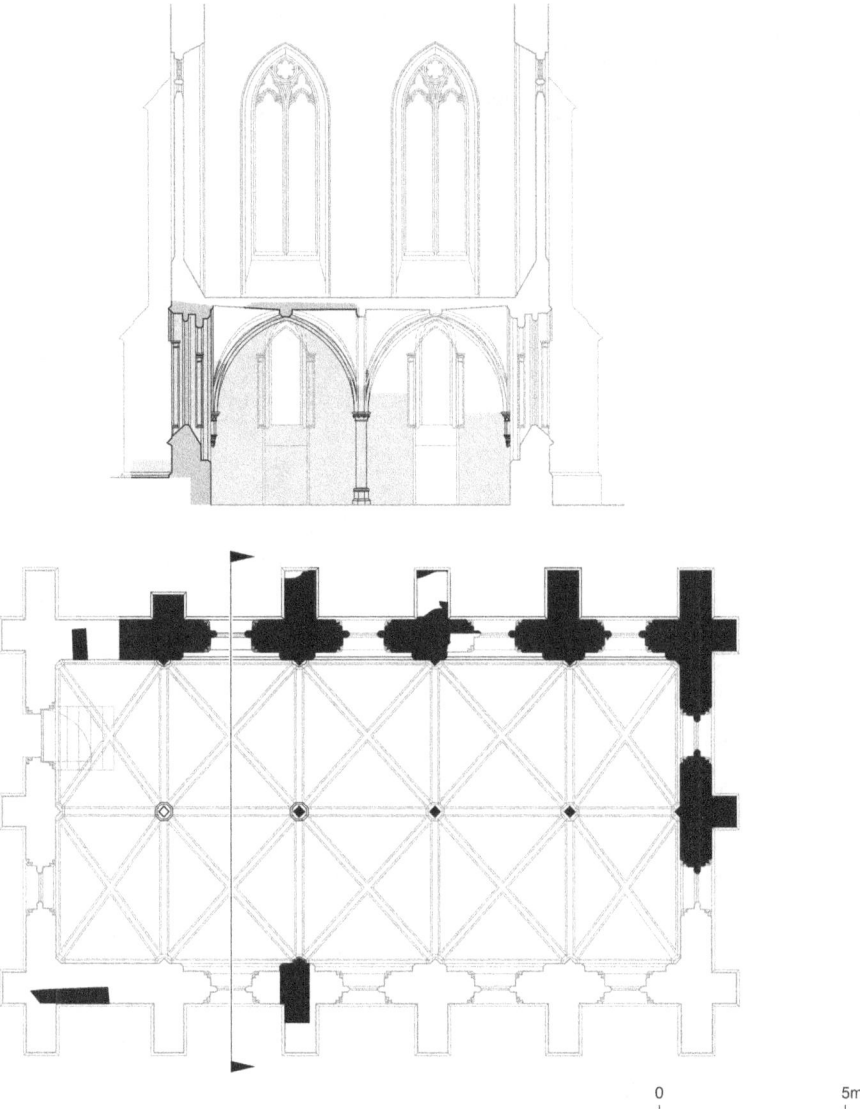

Fig. 16. Reconstructed detailed plan and sectional elevation of the late thirteenth-century chapter house of Black Friars (scale 1:200; Mark Samuel).

lodgynge' – between the provincial prior's house and the church. The 1548 grant describes the house in some detail: on the ground floor it had a 'greate dynynge Chamber' at one end and, moving north, a 'bedde Chambre' followed by a 'parler' (the latter adjacent to the prior's chapel by the church choir). On the first floor there was a large chamber with two galleries, and a small chamber on the west side: archaeological evidence of a privy pit suggests that this refers to a small garderobe wing on the south-west corner of the building. The prior also had the use of a separate kitchen, larder and cellar-buttery which, perhaps surprisingly, seem to have been sited underneath the east dormitory in the cloister. The 1548 grant implies that access between the prior's kitchen and the house was along the south side of the choir, passing through a 'little chamber adjacent to the south side of the church', presumably under the night-stairs.

There is no direct evidence for when the friars built a new chapter house but various building works were taking place at the friary in 1489 ('towards the reparacion of thair churche and place') and in 1505–6 (in the cloister): these might have included a new chapter house.[51] The location of the late medieval chapter house is known: it was converted, in the late sixteenth century, into the parish church of St Anne and there is a simple drawn survey of the building after its damage in the Great Fire of 1666.[52] The east and north walls of the building were recorded in excavations at site FRI88, including the position of two doors and a window, and the evidence suggests a large chamber on a north–south axis, immediately east of the cloister and just to the north of the thirteenth-century chapter house (Figure 13).

The southern or inner cloister was built around the mid-fourteenth century. As has been stated, the 1545 and 1550 post-Dissolution grants allow the identification of the function of most of the buildings in the sixteenth century. But there is very little other information apart from a few measurements and one or two fragments of walls found in archaeological excavations. Parts of the cloister walk survived as late as 1671: the annotation 'cloysters' (and a useful measurement of width) appear on one of the post-Great Fire surveys, thus helping to fix the location of the northern walkway. The overall north–south length of the cloister is about 107ft, although this measurement is an internal length of the western wing, not necessarily corresponding exactly to the length of the cloister. On the east side of the inner cloister lay the library. The 1545 grant notes that there was a main library room over a lower floor known as 'le under lybrarye'. The building has been mapped here using a width recorded in a post-Great Fire survey and with the assumption that it extended southwards as far as the south-east corner of the seventeenth-century Printing-House Yard (not illustrated in detail; see Figure 10).[53] On the opposite side of the cloister lay a large building described in the 1548 lease to Thomas Cawarden as the 'upper frater' and measuring 107ft by 52ft. A document of 1562 makes clear that this was the large hall known as 'the parlyament chamber', the room in which parliament sat on several occasions in the fifteenth and sixteenth centuries and which was also the setting for the 1529 inquiry into the marriage of Henry VIII and Catherine of Aragon.[54] In a herald's drawing of the Blackfriars parliament in 1523 – in effect a

---

[51] Röhrkasten, *Mendicant Houses*, p. 503.

[52] Mills and Oliver, v, 133; Clapham, 'Topography of the Dominican Priory', pp. 73–4.

[53] Mills and Oliver, ii, 45. The recorded width is 43½ft (13.3m) with a reconstructed external length of 100ft (30.4m).

[54] Loseley MS printed in Smith, *Shakespeare's Blackfriars Playhouse*, pp. 457–8; *Blackfriars Records*, pp. 105–6. The earliest sitting of parliament at Black Friars seems to have been in 1311 and it was intermittently used until the Dissolution: J. Enoch Powell and Keith Wallis, *The House of*

seating plan – there is little architectural detail apart from the chequered floor, perhaps contrasting slabs of dark Purbeck marble and paler limestone or sandstone paving.[55] No other details are shown in the illustration but this large space could have been divided into two aisles by a central line of columns, like the Franciscan refectory building in Paris.[56]

According to the 1545 grant, the infirmary and adjacent bakery and brew-house lay in the south-west corner of the inner cloister. The infirmary had two floors: an upper floor 'which was a lodgyng for those that were syck', presumably a ward of beds, and a lower floor that would have had a separate kitchen and a pharmacy room. There was also a cellar or undercroft under part of the ground floor (the whole of the long west wing of the cloisters was built on a slope down towards the Thames and so the arrangement of storeys would have been complex).[57]

The precinct

The friary was bounded by a large precinct wall, much of which was also the new city wall, built between 1279 and 1317 (above: 'Acquiring and developing the friary'). On the east side of their convent the friars had a normal monastic boundary wall, about which rather less is known. It may well have been built in the second decade of the fourteenth century, once the bulk of the work on the city wall had been completed. The earliest mention of the precinct wall (not the portion which also served as city wall) seems to be in 1361, when the 'close of the Friars Preachers' is recorded as the western abutment of a property outside the precinct.[58] A short stretch of the inland wall was recorded in archaeological work in the north-east corner of the precinct where the wall was faced with Kentish ragstone and

---

Lords in the Middle Ages: A History of the English House of Lords to 1540 (London: Weidenfeld and Nicolson, 1968), p. 276; John S. Roskell, Carole Rawcliffe and Linda S. Clark, *The History of Parliament: The House of Commons 1386–1421*, 4 vols (Stroud: History of Parliament Trust and Alan Sutton, 1992), i, 150; Röhrkasten, 'Secular Uses', pp. 140–1. For the 1529 inquiry, see n. 7.

[55] David Dean, 'Image and Ritual in the Tudor Parliaments', in *Tudor Political Culture*, ed. D. Hoak (Cambridge: Cambridge University Press, 1995), pp. 243–71 (p. 250, plate 57). For archaeological evidence for limestone and sandstone floor slabs, see Chapter 13: Floor Tiles and Building Materials from the London Friaries.

[56] The 1596 sale document of this building has an unusual description of the upper hall, partitioned but with the original large space somehow still apparent: 'seaven greate upper Romes as they are nowe devided being all upon one flower and sometyme beinge one greate and entire rome with the roufe over the same covered with Leade'; Loseley MS printed in Smith, *Shakespeare's Blackfriars Playhouse*, pp. 471–5; *Blackfriars Records*, pp. 60–9 (60–1). For the Franciscan refectory in Paris, see Lorentz and Sandron, *Atlas de Paris Au Moyen Âge*, pp. 145–6. The refectory of the Cluniac Saint-Martin-des-Champs in Paris is broadly similar (pp. 137–8).

[57] FSL, Loseley MS L.b.426 (2).

[58] LAA, Dyson and Taylor archive, parish of St Andrew Baynard's Castle, record card for Tenement A1, quoting Husting Roll 89/27.

was 4ft (1.2m) wide (sites CAT86 and PAL86), rather less substantial than the city and river wall to the south. A number of gates gave access in and out of the friary. The main gate was in the north of the precinct, close to the city gate at Ludgate; up to three other gates lay on the eastern side of the precinct, with a water-gate giving access to and from the Thames.[59]

The bulk of the precinct consisted of gardens and other open spaces: the friary must have been the greenest space in the whole of the walled city. There were two large half-acre gardens on the east of the friary, the prior's garden and the 'hill garden' (so named because the land sloped down to the river), with a larger 1-acre garden to the south of the infirmary (Figure 10). In the north-west of the precinct lay more garden space, much of which was leased to tenants by the sixteenth century.[60]

Between the main gate of the friary and the church lay the large cemetery. By the late medieval period this seems to have been divided into two areas by a brick wall, perhaps separating the parish burial ground from the monastic cemetery, and several rented tenements clustered around the edge of the graveyards (Figure 10).[61] The cemetery contained a pulpit cross, the setting for outdoor sermons by the friars.[62] Sixty burials were archaeologically excavated from the southern (monastic) part of the cemetery and this is the best archaeological assemblage of burials from a London friary (site PIC87).[63] Not surprisingly, men outnumbered women in the excavated group of burials (2.8 male:1 female) and there was a relatively low proportion of children and adolescents compared to adults (13%; low compared to a parish graveyard). Thirteen of the burials had been interred in a trench, a form of mass burial characteristic of the Black Death.[64] Over half the normal burials were interred in wooden coffins, a rather higher proportion than in most monastic cemeteries, and a few had other special treatment such as having a layer of ash at the

---

[59] Main or northern gate, *borial[is] port[a]*, mentioned in 1540: TNA, SC 6/HenVIII/2396, m. 54v; Carter Lane gate at east end of churchyard mentioned in 1553: SHC, LM/346/37; 'wattergate' mentioned in 1559: FSL, Loseley MS L.b.416. There is no direct documentary evidence for the east and south gatehouses on Figure 10 but slight topographic evidence for them can be seen in Ogilby and Morgan's map of 1676.

[60] For the hill garden, see n. 40 (leases and grants to Kingstons). For the rented gardens, see TNA, SC 6/HenVIII/2396, mm. 54–6; the earliest surviving pre-Dissolution lease of a garden is from 1523: Röhrkasten, *Mendicant Houses*, p. 240.

[61] The boundaries and walls are described in a grant of 1550 and a lease of 1553: TNA, C 66/831, mm. 32–3; SHC, LM/346/37.

[62] See n. 5.

[63] LAA, site PIC87; Roberta Gilchrist and Barney Sloane, *Requiem: The Medieval Monastic Cemetery in Britain* (London: Museum of London Archaeology Service, 2005), p. 241.

[64] Black Death trenches, admittedly much longer ones, have been excavated at the City's eastern Black Death cemetery: Ian Grainger and others, *The Black Death Cemetery, East Smithfield, London*, MOLA monograph, 43 (London: Museum of London Archaeology Service, 2008), pp. 12–13, 120–3. In contrast, mass graves of the thirteenth and early fourteenth century excavated at the priory and hospital of St Mary Spital, containing victims of other catastrophes including famines, tend to be 6ft square pits rather than trenches.

base of the coffin (evoking the Cistercian tradition of burial in sackcloth and ashes), or having their coffins lined with lime. Apart from the higher status of burial suggested by the prevalence of coffins (ordinary lay people were generally buried in shrouds without a coffin), this group of burials is in many ways typical of a London monastic house: there are relatively high numbers of men interred as one would expect in a friary, but with enough women and children to show that the burial space was 'mixed', that is used for both religious and lay burials. Using the excavated graves as a guide, it can be estimated that the graveyard once held between 500 and 1000 graves. Some lay people were buried in the cloister or claustral walk: in his will of 1411 the fishmonger John Gayton asked to join his late wife here.[65]

There is slim but intriguing evidence for a small chapel situated opposite the cemetery on the lane leading into the precinct: a grave and part of a wall arcade were recorded in the late nineteenth century by the reliable Victorian archaeologist Henry Hodge (site PRG431). It is difficult to interpret the fragmentary remains Hodge found but it is a distinct possibility that he recorded part of a cemetery chapel, conceivably one with a charnel crypt for the appropriate storage of disturbed human remains. This may be the fifteenth-century chapel of St Mary, founded by John Cornewall, Baron Fanhope, in his will of 1437 and in which he was later buried. The chapel is specifically referred to as located in the friars' churchyard.[66]

There is evidence for a few other buildings scattered around the precinct. There was a kitchen with attached yard and garden, complete with conduit and latrine, situated immediately west of the refectory wing. Further down the road leading to the Thames was the friary stable. On the other side of the road there was a smithy (according to archaeological evidence of site VAL88) and, most probably, some other workshop buildings as well.[67] Another building lay along this lane, described as 'le Dutchie Chamber', and it housed meetings of the important council that managed the king's revenues deriving from the huge estate of the duchy of Lancaster. Administrative meetings of the council seem to have been held here before the annexation of the duchy's estates to the Crown in 1399 but the

---

[65] *Calendar of Wills Proved and Enrolled in the Court of Husting*, ii, 399–400.

[66] Steer, 'Royal and Noble Commemoration', p. 120; *Testamenta Vetusta: Being Illustrations from Wills, of Manners, Customs, &c. as Well as of the Descents and Possessions of Many Distinguished Families*, ed. Nicholas H. Nicolas, 2 vols (London: Nichols, 1826), i, 246; Simon J. Payling, 'Cornewall, John, Baron Fanhope (d. 1443)', *ODNB*, <http://www.oxforddnb.com/view/article/54423> [accessed 22 May 2015]; *The Parliament Rolls of Medieval England, 1275–1504*, ed. C. Given-Wilson and others, 16 vols (Woodbridge: Boydell, 2005), xi, 205. There is some ambiguity about the location of this chapel: the will describes it as in the cemetery, the Parliament Rolls entry as in the church.

[67] For the kitchen complex, see TNA, E 315/219, ff. 20v–21; E 310/3/18 (no. 61), Loseley copy printed in Smith, *Shakespeare's Blackfriars Playhouse*, pp. 431–2; *Blackfriars Records*, pp. 6–8. Evidence for the latrine comes from LAA, site AHA87. For the stable, see TNA, E 315/212, ff. 134v–135, printed in Smith, *Shakespeare's Blackfriars Playhouse*, p. 426; *Blackfriars Records*, p. 104.

building may not have become the main administrative base for the council until after this date.[68]

The final component of the precinct to consider is the Dominican's fairly numerous rented tenements. In the first half of the fourteenth century the friars owned only two shops, just outside the precinct near the city gate on Ludgate. Rented tenements *inside* the precinct crop up in the surviving records from 1373. By the sixteenth century the friars rented out about twenty-two tenements in the precinct, most of which were sited along the lane leading south from the main gate, and these brought in an annual income of £64 10s 8d, a figure increasing to £68 14s including the ten rented gardens. To these figures one should add the income from properties lying outside the precinct: the shops and a tenement by Ludgate, and nine riverside tenements to the east of the precinct. The friars' total rental income was therefore about £95 – a substantial sum for a mendicant house (Table 20 in Chapter 18).

Conclusion

The London Dominicans made a bold decision in about 1274 to move from their first convent in Holborn to a more central site. Luckily for the friars, they received the support of the archbishop of Canterbury, the mayor and the king. The former gained a more prestigious site for his own religious order; the latter two brought about the enhancement of the capital's defences and the 'upgrading' of the under-used land in and beyond the south-west corner of the walled city. This risky and expensive gamble was successful: with the exception of St Paul's cathedral, the friars ended up with the largest religious precinct in London, some 8 acres (3.25 ha). The friars' great preaching church was designed and built (at least the nave) by the king's mason, the celebrated Michael Canterbury. In less than a century they had acquired, planned and built a whole urban monastery, with a church, two cloisters and extensive gardens, and the process was largely complete by the third quarter of the fourteenth century. The Dominicans were the most economically secure friary in London, with nearly £100 of rental income, an annual royal grant of £20, nearly £80 of annual chantry and anniversary funeral payments, and further income from the funeral fees and bequests of Londoners.

In this chapter we have used the extensive range of documentary and archaeological sources to map and understand the whole friary, building on the work of earlier historians and archaeologists. Notable buildings rediscovered here include the friars' chapter house of c. 1290 and a fifteenth-century cemetery chapel. The landscape of the late medieval friary can now be glimpsed in its entirety for the first time, and it must have been a striking combination of grand architecture in the Decorated style and secluded open spaces. A painting of the friary by Mark Samuel appears on the front cover of this book: the reconstruction is

---

[68] TNA, SC 6/HenVIII/2396, m. 54v; R. Somerville, 'The Duchy of Lancaster Council and Court of Duchy Chamber', *Transactions of the Royal Historical Society*, 23 (1941), 159–77 (p. 172).

based on the evidence presented in this chapter. In addition to fifty or so friars, and perhaps twice that number of servants, by the early sixteenth century it was home to perhaps a hundred lay residents living in the twenty or so buildings that the friary rented out. On occasion the priory even became a royal palace like Bridewell or Westminster in which the business of Crown and parliament could be conducted, within the city walls but physically and spiritually separated from the bustle of urban life.

3

The Third Black Friars at St Bartholomew's, 1556–9

IN August 1553 England's experiment with religious reform and the country's uneasy shift to Protestantism came to an end with the entry of Queen Mary into London. It would only be a matter of time, surely, before the largely unwelcomed changes of the previous two decades – the break with Rome, the stripping of church decoration, the introduction of the vernacular common prayer book and the Dissolution of the Monasteries – would all be undone. The efforts of Mary, her husband Philip of Spain, the Privy Council and the new archbishop of Canterbury Reginald Pole successfully reversed some of those Protestant reforms in 1553 and 1554, bringing back traditional worship in churches and reuniting the English church with Rome.[1] However, the Dissolution of the Monasteries could not be undone quite so quickly: too many powerful people – including many traditional Catholics – had paid good money for ex-monastic property and were not about to hand it back to the various monastic orders, although this was what Mary and Pole had originally intended.[2] Mary and Pole therefore began the slow process of refounding monastic houses, beginning in London and the south-east of England. In 1555 they were able to endow and renew the house of Observant Franciscans at Greenwich and that of the London Carthusians, now moved to Sheen. The next year saw the re-establishment of the Black Friars at St Bartholomew's (the subject of this chapter) and the return of Benedictines to Westminster, followed by, in 1557, Dominican nuns returning to Dartford (initially to Kings Langley) and the Bridgettines to Syon.[3] There was some discussion about the re-establishment of the London Grey Friars – in their old home – but it was not thought possible or desirable to close down the newly founded school and orphanage of Christ's Hospital, which had opened in 1552 in the old

---

[1] Eamon Duffy, *The Stripping of the Altars: Traditional Religion in England, c. 1400–c. 1580* (New Haven and London: Yale University Press, 2005), 2nd edn, pp. 524–37.
[2] Richard Rex, *The Tudors* (Stroud: Tempus, 2006), pp. 190–6.
[3] David Knowles, *The Religious Orders in England*, 3 vols (Cambridge: Cambridge University Press, 1948–59), iii, 438–40; C.S. Knighton, 'Westminster Abbey Restored', in *The Church of Mary Tudor*, ed. E. Duffy and D. Loades (Aldershot: Ashgate, 2006), pp. 77–123.

friary.[4] The London Dominicans were, therefore, a significant part of a remarkably small group of religious men and women who returned to their vocation when the opportunity arose in Mary's reign, a very brief opportunity as it turned out.

The Dominican friars refounded their London house in 1556, not at their old cloister at the eponymous Blackfriars but 500 yards to the north-east in the former Augustinian canons' house at St Bartholomew's. The best authority for the exact date for the refoundation comes from Charles Wriothesley's chronicle: 'This yeare at Easter [5 April 1556] the churche of Great St Bartlemewes, in Smythfeilde, was sett up with black friers; Fryer Perwyn beinge head thereof.'[5]

The preparation for the refoundation had, however, begun two or three years earlier. Richard Rich, who had been ennobled as Baron Rich at the beginning of Edward VI's reign, was one of those religious conservatives who had benefited from the booming property market that flourished in the 1540s after the Dissolution of the Monasteries. Among the many properties that he bought after the Dissolution was the former Augustinian canons' priory of St Bartholomew. He lived there from early 1540 and purchased the majority of the precinct in May 1544. He paid £1064 11s 3d, a large sum indeed but one which included all the precinct's rental properties and the valuable rights to the annual fair. The total price was calculated at the rather favourable rate (to Rich) of only nine times the annual rental value.[6] A decade later (having already changed his political allegiance from Edward Seymour, duke of Somerset, to John Dudley, duke of Northumberland), Rich signed the 'device' that altered the succession to the gravely ill Edward VI from Mary to Lady Jane Grey. Following Edward's death in July 1553, Rich promptly declared his support for Mary. It would seem that one of the conditions of Mary's acceptance of the inconstant Rich as a privy councillor was an undertaking to restore some of the ex-monastic lands he had acquired over the previous decade.[7] Rich, having agreed to hand back the St Bartholomew's estate (in a private agreement with Mary in 1553 or 1554?), may originally have been intending to give the precinct back to the Augustinian canons but by the 1550s – a decade and

---

[4] John Howes, *John Howes' MS., 1582: Being 'a Brief Note of the Order and Manner of the Proceedings in the First Erection of the Three Royal Hospitals of Christ, Bridewell & St Thomas the Apostle*, ed. William Lempriere (London: privately printed, 1904), pp. 64–70.

[5] Charles Wriothesley, *A Chronicle of England during the Reigns of the Tudors, from A.D. 1485 to 1559*, ed. William D. Hamilton, 2 vols, Camden Society, new series, 11, 20 (London: Camden Society, 1875), ii, 134.

[6] This figure is for the whole value of the precinct, including the numerous rented tenements (bringing in over £66 in annual rent) and the rights to the annual Bartholomew's Fair (over £65 in annual income). The built-up monastic core of the precinct was valued at an annual rental sum of £6, clearly an undervaluation, making the price paid for this part of the precinct just £54: *The Records of St Bartholomew's Priory and of the Church and Parish of St Bartholomew the Great, West Smithfield*, ed. E.A. Webb, 2 vols (Oxford: Oxford University Press, 1921), i, 264–73, 502–18 (p. 507).

[7] P.R.N. Carter, 'Rich, Richard, First Baron Rich (1496/7–1567)', *ODNB*, <http://www.oxforddnb.com/view/article/23491> [accessed 28 May 2014].

a half after the Dissolution – the international orders such as the mendicants still had the necessary organisational structure and manpower to re-establish their friaries; the decentralised and dispersed Augustinian canons did not. In December 1555 Rich gave the priory back to the Crown, retaining only the old prior's house for his personal use.[8] Was this refoundation simply a matter of political expediency for Rich, securing his position in Mary's administration, or was it something deeper, perhaps expiating his sins (as many religious conservatives would have seen them) in assisting in the conviction of Thomas More, or in administering the Dissolution of the Monasteries as chancellor of the Court of Augmentations? Whatever Rich's motivation, his endowment allowed the first refoundation of a Dominican house in England. Less than four months later, prior William Peryn and perhaps a dozen friars came to London from Louvain and Brussels and entered their new priory.[9]

The first prior, William Peryn, was English, as was his successor, Richard Hargrave, and both had spent the previous decade or more in exile in the Low Countries. The name of just one other friar of the house is known: the Spanish friar John of Vilagrassa. Richard Hargrave records that his friars came from Spain, *Germania inferiore* (Flanders and the Low Countries) and England.[10] In their short time in London the friars seem to have settled back into a pattern of preaching and providing spiritual services to Londoners, particularly the traditional *post mortem* services such as processions, commemorative masses and anniversary funeral services. The Londoner Henry Machyn records a number of occasions when prior Peryn gave public sermons, for example at St Paul's cross in 1556 on the occasion of the public penance of a married (in fact bigamously married) priest, Thomas Samsun. In 1558 Machyn describes what might be termed the 'house style' of the Black friars at the burial of Cecily Mansel, one of Mary's gentlewomen: the funeral service was elaborate but the actual interment was plain. Mansel's body was brought in procession to the Black Friars church at St Bartholomew, where there were:

> iiij baners of santes and a ij dosen torchys, and ij grett whytt branchys, and iiij gylt candylstykes and armes on them, and many clarkes syngyng, and mony morners: and my lade Peter cheyff morner, and odur lades and gentyll-women and knyghtes and gentyllmen; and her servandes bare my lade, and bare the torchys all in blake cottes; and bered a-for the he [high?] auter at the hed of the old pryar Boltun; and the chyrche and the qwer and the raylles hangyd with blake and armes; *and the frers song durge after ther songe, and bered her after ther fasyon, with-owt clarkes or prestes.*[11]

---

[8] *Records of St Bartholomew*, i, 277–9, 521–3.

[9] Mary C. Erler, *Reading and Writing during the Dissolution: Monks, Friars, and Nuns 1530–1558* (Cambridge: Cambridge University Press, 2013), pp. 113–17.

[10] G.M. Pio, *Delle Vite de gli Huomini Illustri de S. Domenico* (Bologna: Bellagamba, 1607), p. 379.

[11] Henry Machyn, *The Diary of Henry Machyn: Citizen and Merchant-Taylor of London, from A.D. 1550 to A.D. 1563*, ed. John G. Nichols, Camden Society, old series, 42 (London: Camden Society, 1848), pp. 100, 174.

The year 1558 marked the beginning of the end of the revived Black friars' short spell in London. Firstly, their prior, William Peryn, died in August and he was buried (like Cecily Mansel) by the high altar near the Augustinian priors Rahere and William Bolton.[12] The newly elected prior, Richard Hargrave, did not even have time to take up formally his new position because, in November, Mary and her archbishop, Reginald Pole, died on the same day. With the religious tide turning again under Mary's half-sister Elizabeth, the friars finally received confirmation from Rome of their new prior in March 1559 but friar John of Vilagrassa nervously handed in the official letter to the Privy Council. Hargrave went into hiding and left the country: he wrote in October to the head of his order explaining 'I went into exile – my life was in grave danger'. Some of the remaining friars struggled on until July, when just three friars and a novice remained, presumably all English and intending to remain in the country.[13]

Under Elizabeth the monastic choir became the parish church once again and Richard Rich got back the inner precinct, although he had to pay for it a second time. This time, the annual rental value of the precinct was reckoned at £6 13s 4d, with this amount converted to a freehold value by multiplying by twenty-three (compared to a rental value of £6 and a nine-times multiplier used in 1544). So, the inner precinct this time cost Rich £153 8s 3d, rather more than the £54 he had paid in 1544.[14]

This chapter is very reliant on the work done by Edward and Aston Webb in the late nineteenth and early twentieth centuries. The former carried out extensive archival research into the history of the priory of St Bartholomew while the latter led the long restoration campaign and recorded many historic architectural details; both were parishioners. The results of their efforts were fully published in 1921 and the work includes numerous printed primary sources including the various grants to and from Richard Rich around the time of the Dissolution and selected wills.[15]

The church and cloister

The Crown granted the friars much, but not all, of the former Augustinian priory's precinct (Figure 17). There does not appear to be an extant foundation grant for the friary but a good sense of the friary property can be obtained by examining the 1560 grant (when the now-closed friary was sold back to Richard Rich). In particular, one needs to be aware of the parts of the old St Bartholomew's priory which are *not* included in this document:

---

[12] Machyn, *Diary*, pp. 171–2.
[13] 'io fui discacciato, e fui in gran pericolo della vita': Pio, *Delle Vite de gli Huomini Illustri*, p. 379; Machyn, *Diary*, p. 204.
[14] Calculations based on *Records of St Bartholomew*, i, 277–9, 286–8, 521–6. See also the 'Acte to annexe to the Crowne certayne Religious Howses and Monasteries and to refourme certayne Abuses in Chantreis', clause 16: *The Statutes of the Realm: From Original Records, etc. (1101–1713)*, ed. A. Luders and others, 11 vols (London, 1810–28), iv, 397–400.
[15] *Records of St Bartholomew*.

these can be identified by comparing the 1560 grant with the original 1544 post-Dissolution grant to Richard Rich (and with Rich's re-grant back to the Crown in 1555).[16] When the friars returned to London in April 1556, Richard Rich kept his London house – the former prior's house and garden situated to the east of the built-up core of the precinct. Rich also kept the rights to the fair ground in the north of the precinct, most of the rented tenements that surrounded the close in the south, and the former service yard and buildings in the north-east of the precinct (latter not illustrated on Figure 17). The friars thus obtained most of the built-up area of the inner precinct including the cloister and an adjacent part-cloister or close of buildings to the south-east, housing the old dormitory and infirmary complex. The friars were also given the surviving parts of the former Augustinian church, but these came with the obligation to provide a parish church and facilities to the newly formalised parish of St Bartholomew. The friars may have used the large southern close of the precinct as their monastic garden, although it is likely that the tenants of the surrounding properties had access rights.

Having received much of St Bartholomew's, what might have been prior Peryn's plans to redevelop the priory? He had most of the cloister buildings, as well as the kitchen wings, so his priorities would surely have been to recreate a monastic choir, to rebuild the nave of the church to provide an indoor preaching space and to construct a new prior's apartment. However, to achieve all this he would also have had to build or rebuild a new parochial chapel for the parishioners of St Bartholomew. In the first half of the 1540s the Augustinians' choir had been converted into the new parish church (parishioners had previously used a chapel on the north side of the nave), and the nave had been demolished and turned into the new parochial burial ground (the earlier burial ground lay to the north of the Lady chapel). Peryn thus faced a rather difficult challenge, to rebuild a religious house while negotiating between three sets of interests: those of the friars, the rector and his parishioners, and the former landowner Rich, still living next door. There is, unfortunately, little information about the refurbishment and rebuilding campaign. Peryn and the rector, John Deane, must have begun work on a replacement parish chapel – in order to free up the old monastic choir for the friars – and they would probably have selected for the task the pre-Dissolution parish chapel (on the north side of the choir) or the Lady chapel (east of the choir). It is not clear to what degree these chapels had been dismantled or demolished by 1556. In January 1557 the St Bartholomew's parishioner Richard Bartlett bequeathed his worsted gown to the rector and £1 to the parish church, 'towardes the makynge of the churche wall', with a further sum (at the discretion of his executors) 'towardes the makynge of a Soller in the parish church'.[17] These works sound like just the sort of refurbishment that would be required to make good the parish chapel or Lady chapel, including, it would seem, some sort of rebuilt upper storey such as a rood loft or screen (the 'soller').

---

[16] *Records of St Bartholomew*, i, 261–79, 286–8, 502–18, 521–6.
[17] *Records of St Bartholomew*, i, 282, 544–5.

Fig. 17. Map showing the Black friars' precinct of 1556–9 within the former St Bartholomew's priory; the church choir was reclaimed by the friars while the parishioners used the old parish chapel or Lady chapel as their church (scale 1:1500).

The only indication that Peryn began work on a new nave for the church comes from a note in the eighteenth-century compendium *Notitia Monastica*: '[the] Black or Preaching friers ..., under father Person [Peryn], began to rebuild the nave of the church, which had been pulled down'.[18] Peryn presumably carried out refurbishment works in the choir, perhaps spending some of the £6 bequeathed in Richard Bartlett's will, or the £3 6s 8d left by another parishioner, Robert Urmestone, in 1558, or the 12s left by John Garatt in 1556. A little architectural evidence for the friars' works was recorded during refurbishment in 1905: a doorway had been built, probably around 1556, to re-open access between the church and the east wing of the cloister (the opening had been closed with a stone wall in or soon after 1539). Finally, the evidence of a written survey of 1616 suggests that the chapter house had two storeys by this date; it has been plausibly suggested that the second storey was inserted in or soon after 1556 to create a prior's apartment.[19]

There is one other construction project that the friars may have undertaken: the creation of a new western gateway for the friary. The main monastery gatehouse had been to the south-west and the friars probably retained this, although it may now have been shared with tenants of the close. The friars may also have had an eastern gate leading to a passage on Aldersgate (Figure 17). However, with the changes that had taken place since the Dissolution, the friars lacked convenient access to and from West Smithfield. There was another gate to the north of the church on West Smithfield but this now must have formed the entrance for parishioners, lying beyond the friars' area which was exclusively to the south of the church. It is likely, therefore, that the friars created a new gate on West Smithfield from the south-western door of the old church. This gate survives today (in a restored form) with its thirteenth-century ground floor and late sixteenth-century upper floors, but some fabric of the mid 1550s may be preserved inside (Figure 18). In a Chancery case in 1596, the rector of St Bartholomew was in dispute with Philip Scudamore, who occupied the gatehouse and had just rebuilt its upper storeys. The court papers describe the former house, before rebuilding, as 'certayne chambers or roomes one over another *auncyently edified* builded and standing over and upon the same gate on an arche of stone and two greate mayne pillers of stone bering upp the saide arche chambers and roomes'. Furthermore, during renovation work in 1915 it was noted that the majority of timbers showed signs of having been previously used in a different setting, probably the result of dismantling and re-modelling an existing timber frame in the 1590s.[20] Given that the need for this gatehouse only came about in 1556 with the arrival of the friars, it seems quite possible that it was prior Peryn who was responsible for the conversion of this end of the largely demolished nave into a gatehouse building and tenement.

---

[18] Thomas Tanner, *Notitia Monastica: Or, an Account of all the Abbies, Priories and Houses of Friers, Heretofore in England and Wales* (London: William Bowyer, 1744), p. 306. Tanner cites 'Stow MS' as his source for this.

[19] *Records of St Bartholomew*, i, 282, 544–5; ii, 141, 144–5, plate 49.

[20] *Records of St Bartholomew*, ii, 67–70; TNA, C 2/Eliz/D9/54, m. 10. Webb argues that the tenement over the gatehouse was built before the Dissolution.

Fig. 18. View of the gatehouse at St Bartholomew-the-Great: although the ground floor is thirteenth-century and the upper floors late sixteenth-century, the conversion of the south-west corner of the church into a gatehouse was probably carried out by the Dominicans in about 1556.

Conclusion

The Dominicans' first spell in London lasted over three centuries, their second stay just three years and three months. It is, of course, difficult to evaluate the achievements of the friars of the 1550s with that knowledge; the limited evidence suggests that they quickly regained the trust of some Londoners and rediscovered some of their core roles in London, preaching and offering *post mortem* spiritual services to Londoners. Unsurprisingly, they made rather less of a physical impression on their new priory during their short stay. In this chapter we have tried to map out the friars' precinct for the first time and guess at some of the plans (however unrealised) of their prior, William Peryn. The only visible reminder of the friars' few years in St Bartholomew's may be their new gatehouse on West Smithfield, happily surviving (albeit rebuilt in the late sixteenth century) some four and a half centuries later.

4

Grey Friars, 1225–1538

In the first decade of the thirteenth century a young man in his twenties called Giovanni, the son of a wealthy Italian silk merchant, Pietro di Bernardone, renounced military service, his friends, his family and even his inheritance. Under his family name of Francesco and with a toponymic surname recording the Umbrian town of his upbringing, Francis of Assisi began a career of simple popular preaching. Recognised by Pope Innocent III in 1210 and in 1215, and with a Rule approved by Honorius III in 1223, Francis' informal group of poor itinerant preachers quickly grew into an international religious order. Francis termed his preachers *fratres minores*, lesser brothers, with the term 'minor' alluding to an exhortation to poverty and humility in the Rule: *et sint minores* – 'let [the friars] be the lowest'.[1] The first Franciscans – a party of nine – arrived in England in September 1224, during the lifetime of their founder. Four of them quickly made their way to London, staying initially with the newly established Dominicans and then at a house in Cornhill. The following year they moved to newly granted premises in the parish of St Nicholas Shambles, near Newgate in the west of the city.[2] In England the friars quickly became known as Grey friars, a reference to the colour of their hooded woollen habits or cowls.

The numbers of London Franciscans quickly increased from that first group of the 1220s, reaching a peak of about ninety in the early fourteenth century. After this, numbers seem to have declined for the rest of the house's existence, with fewer than fifty residents by the late fourteenth century and thirty-five in 1460 (including the guardian and provincial prior). Twenty-seven friars remained in 1538 to sign the dissolution agreement. Of all the London mendicants, the Franciscans had the least secure finances and the greatest reliance on alms: they had a church and buildings second only to the Dominicans in terms

---

[1] Lawrence, *The Friars*, pp. 26–42; John Moorman, *A History of the Franciscan Order from its Origins to the Year 1517* (Oxford: Clarendon, 1968), p. 17
[2] Röhrkasten, *Mendicant Houses*, pp. 43–51.

of grandeur and extent, but they lacked their counterparts' regular royal income and large rental portfolio. They would have struggled to meet the annual living costs of some £50, just for feeding the friars, let alone paying for servants, repairs and the house's contribution to the province and prior general in Rome.[3]

The friary housed the English province's *studium generale*, training English and visiting students for higher education at Oxford, Cambridge or Paris. Although it did not receive this formal designation until the fifteenth century, it was already functioning as an important study centre in the thirteenth century, thanks to the efforts of its *lector* and chronicler Thomas of Eccleston (Chapter 16: Spiritual Life and Education in the London Friaries).

The friars seem to have enjoyed consistently good relations with Londoners, receiving land donations in the early days of the friary and, later, attracting bequests and anniversary payments. Furthermore, to a greater extent than the Dominicans, their benefactors included ordinary Londoners as well as the civic elite. At the very end of the thirteenth century the friary attracted a different level of support, with Edward I's new queen, Margaret, contributing large sums to the rebuilding campaign, and a generation later Edward II's consort, Isabella, continued this high level of queenly support (Chapter 17: Burial and Commemoration in the London Friaries).[4]

In the 1520s and '30s the friary's officers aligned the house with Crown policy, largely supporting the religious changes, in marked contrast to the opposition shown by their Observant brethren in Greenwich (the Observant Franciscans were a fifteenth-century splinter group within the Franciscan order who placed greater emphasis on poverty). The last two guardians, Thomas Cudnor and Thomas Chapman, were supporters of Thomas Cromwell and there is surviving correspondence from Chapman denouncing the Observant friar John Forest and planning the closure of the London house.[5] The suppression document was duly signed by Chapman and twenty-six friars on 12 November 1538. Parcels of the convent were sold off to investors (and some of the existing tenants) in the 1540s, with the friary church granted by the Crown to serve as the centre of a newly created parish, Christ Church, and the cloisters given over for a new secular orphanage and school, Christ's Hospital.

The Franciscan friary is the best documented of the London friaries, thanks to an account of the convent's early history and the remarkable survival of their Register, a late medieval document that was used and maintained by the friars right up to the Dissolution. The latter book contains a calendar of their property deeds (which would probably have acted as a summary of a now lost cartulary) and notes on the building history of the friary (recording which donors gave what and when).[6] There are also some excellent visual

---

[3] Röhrkasten, *Mendicant Houses*, pp. 74, 79–80, 227–8, 245–7.

[4] Röhrkasten, *Mendicant Houses*, pp. 44–8, 265–76, 449–50; Steer, 'Royal and Noble Commemoration', pp. 119–20, 127–30.

[5] Röhrkasten, *Mendicant Houses*, pp. 568–9; Barron and Davies, *Religious Houses*, p. 126.

[6] Thomas of Eccleston, *Tractatus de Adventu Fratrum Minorum in Angliam*, ed. A.G. Little (Manchester: Manchester University Press, 1951); translated as: *The Coming of the Friars Minor*

sources for understanding the layout of the friary including two seventeenth-century pre-Great Fire plans that between them map virtually the entire precinct area.[7] Conversely, the archaeological evidence for the Grey Friars is disappointing: in 1905 the archaeologists Philip Norman and Francis Reader made valiant efforts to record what they could during the rapid demolition of the old Christ's Hospital buildings and the construction of the new General Post Office but they met with little success (site PRG414 on Figure 19).[8] When, in turn, the General Post Office buildings were pulled down nearly a century later, very little of the friary survived for the later generation of archaeologists to discover (site KEW98).

Acquiring and developing the friary

The founder of the Franciscan friary was a London mercer called John Iwyn who in 1225 joined the order as a lay friar and donated a tenement in the parish of St Nicholas. The exact position of this foundation donation cannot be determined but it presumably lay on the west side of Stinking Lane, just north of Newgate Street – the location of the friars' first church.[9] The Grey Friars Register contains a list of the numerous donations and purchases with which the friars created their friary precinct, beginning with Iwyn's gift in 1225 and ending with a donation by Queen Isabella a century and a quarter later in 1352.[10] Although the Register lacks detailed descriptions of these properties (including the vital abutments), by using the streets and parishes named in the Register entries it is possible to sketch the process of the friars' acquisition of tenements (Figure 20, Table 5).[11] At least twenty-seven separate donations of property were made to the Franciscans and the majority of these were paid for by the city authorities, although from the early

to England & Germany. Being the Chronicles of . . . Thomas of Eccleston and . . . Jordan of Giano, ed. E. Gurney Salter (London and Toronto: Dent, 1926); BL, Cotton Vitellius F xii, printed in *The Grey Friars of London: Their History, with the Register of Their Convent and an Appendix of Documents*, ed. Charles L. Kingsford, (Aberdeen: British Society of Franciscan Studies, 1915), pp. 70–177. Another example of an English monastic register is Bodleian, MS Laud misc. 625, the register of the Augustinian canons of Leicester Abbey, compiled by the prior, William Charite, in 1477. Were many of these registers compiled in lesser monasteries and friaries at this time?

[7] St Bartholomew's Hospital (SBH), HC 19, f. 59; LMA, COLLAGE 21718; reproduced here as Figure 22 and Figure 26.

[8] Philip Norman and Francis W. Reader, 'Further Discoveries Relating to Roman London, 1906–12', *Archaeologia*, 63 (1912), 257–344 (pp. 274–6).

[9] Eccleston, *Tractatus*, p. 21; Eccleston, *Coming of the Friars Minor*, pp. 29–30; Röhrkasten, *Mendicant Houses*, p. 44.

[10] BL, Cotton Vitellius F xii, ff. 317–22, printed in *Grey Friars*, pp. 146–57.

[11] The process is hampered by the fact that the exact boundaries of the parishes of St Nicholas Shambles, St Audoen and St Sepulchre are not known: the former two parishes ceased to exist and the boundaries of the latter changed at the Dissolution with the closure of the friary and the creation of the new parish of Christ Church Newgate Street; Derek Keene and Vanessa Harding, *A Survey of Documentary Sources for Property Holding in London before the Great Fire* (London:

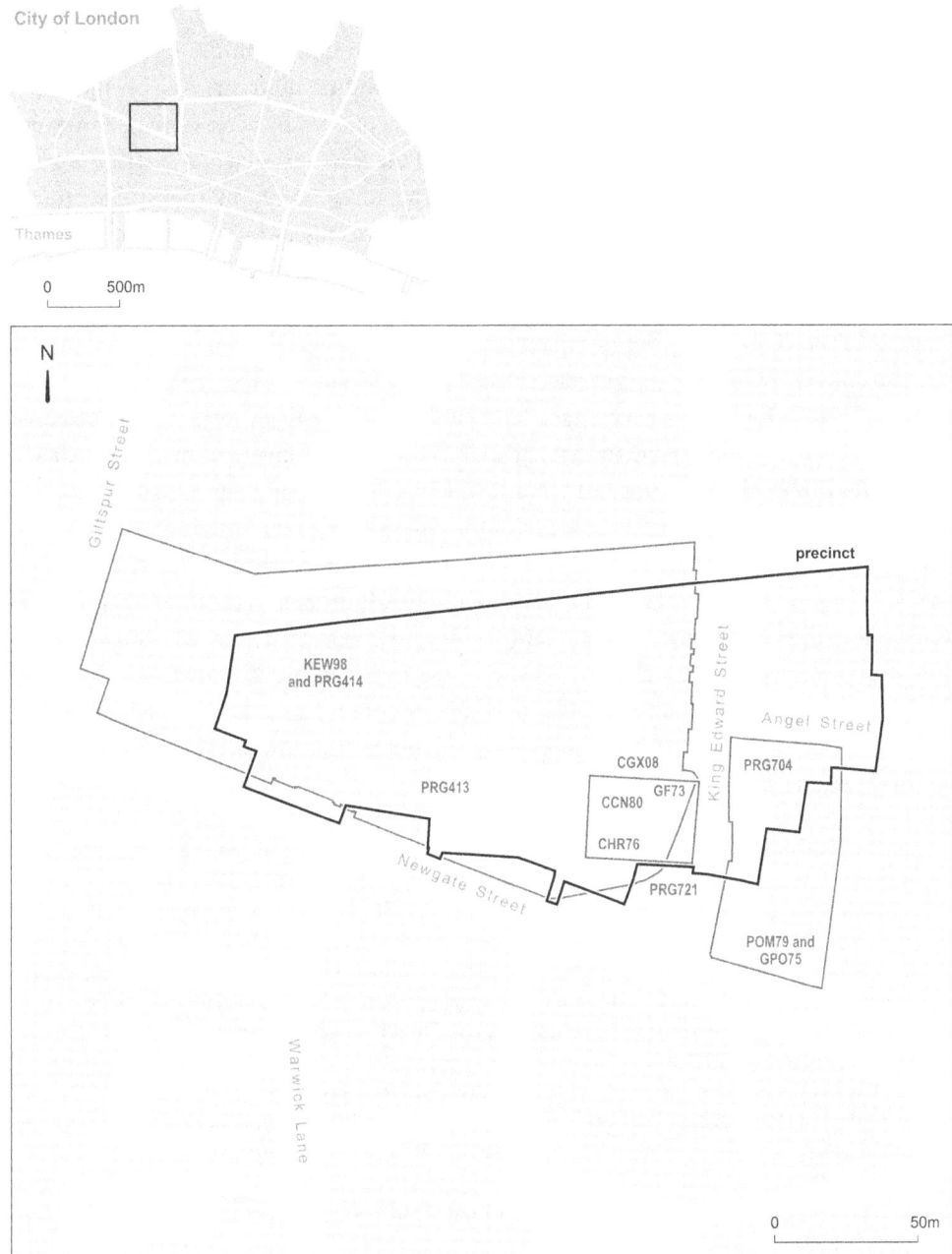

Fig. 19. Map showing the location of the Grey Friars and archaeological sites within its precinct (scale 1:2500)

fourteenth century Queens Margaret and Isabella bore the financial burden. The cost of the tenements purchased directly for the friars came to £130, with the city, queen and friars spending a further £20 or so redeeming outstanding quitrents due on the tenements. By the 1350s the friars ended up with a precinct of over 4½ acres (1.9ha). However, in the second half of the century (in 1368 and 1398) the friary gave back two strips of land along its Newgate Street frontage to the city, to be administered by the Bridge House estate that looked after London Bridge. The financial details of this transaction are not recorded but the friary would, presumably, have expected some reward for this valuable land along the busy main road between Newgate and the meat shambles.[12] The final, slightly reduced, precinct thus occupied just less than 4½ acres (1.8ha).

The immediate task for the guardian Henry de Treviso in 1225 was the construction of a first chapel.[13] The London merchant (and later mayor) William Joyner began making donations towards this chapel in 1228, giving £200 in his lifetime, and the king donated an oak for timber the following year. Work on non-religious buildings probably began as early as the 1240s (following completion of the chapel?): funding for an infirmary building – perhaps part of a small accommodation wing – was provided by a bequest from Peter de Helyland (or Elinant) who died in the late 1230s. A little later William of Nottingham, the head of the English Franciscan order (died 1254), ordered that excessive decoration be removed from the London cloister; his use of the term 'cloister' (*claustr[um]*) may well indicate a wing or two of accommodation buildings rather than a fully formed four-sided cloister at this early date.[14] A water supply was also built at this time, in the 1250s or slightly earlier (Chapter 14: Water Supply).[15]

> London Record Society, 1985), pp. xvi–xix. Even the position of 'St Nicholas Lane' is uncertain since it was erased by the creation of the friary precinct; in Figure 20 it is assumed that the lane lay to the west of the church of St Nicholas (which was on Stinking Lane), implying that the parish of St Nicholas extended much further westwards in the thirteenth century. This hypothesis has the advantage that it 'spaces out' the various bequests more evenly across the area of the eventual precinct. An indication of the extent of the original parish of St Nicholas Shambles can be seen in the extra-mural part of the post-Dissolution Christ Church parish: this was presumably part of the pre-friary parish of St Nicholas.

[12] BL, Cotton Vitellius F xii, ff. 327–9v, printed in *Grey Friars*, pp. 171–7.

[13] The following discussion of the early works at the London Franciscan house incorporates ideas and suggestions of Martin Ollé (Charles University, Prague) who is researching the early history of the order in England; I gratefully acknowledge his help and look forward to his published account of the church and friary. For a list of Franciscan priors, see Barron and Davies, *Religious Houses*, p. 127.

[14] BL, Cotton Vitellius F xii, f. 322, printed in *Grey Friars*, pp. 157–8; Eccleston, *Tractatus*, p. 45 (see below, 'Conclusion' and n. 60, for a discussion of this decoration); Eccleston, *Coming of the Friars Minor*, p. 63; *CCR 1227–1231*, p. 169 (the royal donation of oak is not specified as being for the chapel); A.R. Martin, *Franciscan Architecture in England* (Manchester: Manchester University Press, 1937), p. 177; C.H. Lawrence, 'Nottingham, William of (d. 1254)', *ODNB*, <http://www.oxforddnb.com/view/article/20373> [accessed 26 June 2014].

[15] BL, Cotton Vitellius F xii, f. 322, printed in *Grey Friars*, pp. 158–9; Eccleston, *Tractatus*, p. 21; Eccleston, *Coming of the Friars Minor*, pp. 29–30; Röhrkasten, *Mendicant Houses*, pp. 414–17.

Further work was taking place on the friars' chapel in the 1260s, with carts bringing in building stone for the church in 1269.[16] It seems likely that these works were enlarging Joyner's earlier chapel, although it could be argued that the 1260s works were on a new chapel building. Either way, this chapel of the 1260s (whether newly built or enlarged) formed the core of the much larger later church (below: 'The church').

The planning and construction of a full cloister may well have taken decades, as the acquisition of tenements and additional funding allowed, and as the ambitions of the friars increased. The friars acquired a series of tenements on St Nicholas Lane in the 1270s, '80s and '90s and it may be these that permitted the construction of the actual cloister (tenements 14–18 in Table 5 and on Figure 20). Further work on the east wing seems to have been taking place in the 1270s or '80s: the Register records the financial support of Walter le Potter for the chapter house and kitchen (he was sheriff in 1272–3 and died in 1280) and of Gregory de Rokesle for the first-floor dormitory (he was mayor in the 1270s and '80s and died in 1291). Construction of the cloister continued, it can be surmised, in an anticlockwise direction with the north wing. The west wing housed the refectory, funded by donations from Bartholomew de Castro. Again, the dates are not certain but he was politically active in a long career spanning the last four decades of the century.[17] The windows of the north wing of the cloisters (Figure 27) are in a Geometric style of the late thirteenth or early fourteenth century. Broadly similar windows survive at St Mary, Rickinghall Inferior (Suffolk; end of thirteenth century), St Margaret, Stoke Golding (Leicestershire; late thirteenth or early fourteenth century) and St Andrew, Trowse with Newton (Norfolk; late thirteenth century).[18]

The next project was the largest undertaken by the London Franciscans: the conversion of their chapel into a great abbatial church with choir and nave. The precise chronology of the project or projects is not completely understood but construction seems to have begun in the 1280s or 1290s, thanks to financial (and quite probably logistical) support from royal servant and mayor Henry le Waleys. In 1299 the works received a welcome boost when Edward I's new queen, Margaret of France, arrived in London: bringing her own Capetian enthusiasm for the Franciscans, she 'scaled up' the project, providing generous sponsorship, as well as arranging further donations of land to the friars. At least ten masons were working on the project in 1310, when they were diverted to assist Edward II's military works in Scotland.[19]

---

[16] CPR 1266–1272, p. 339.

[17] BL, Cotton Vitellius F xii, f. 322; *Grey Friars*, pp. 34–5, 42–6, 158; Röhrkasten, *Mendicant Houses*, pp. 417–23. For dates of these and other city officers, see Barron, *London in the Later Middle Ages*, pp. 308–55.

[18] Stephen Hart, *Medieval Church Window Tracery in England* (Woodbridge: Boydell, 2010), pp. 50, 53, plates 25c, 25d, 29a; Historic England, listed buildings online, <http://historicengland.org.uk/listing/the-list/list-entry/1097030> [Rickinghall], <.../1074214> [Stoke Golding], <.../1050444> [Trowse] (accessed 12 February 2016).

[19] Henry Summerson, 'Seen through the Eyes of the Law: Judicial Records as Evidence for London's Physical Environment, 1272–1327', *London Topographical Record*, 31 (2015), 1–13 (p. 9).

Table 5 List of the tenements acquired by the Grey friars for their friary (source: Grey Friars register).

Number on Figure 20	Date of acquisition	Grantor	Description	Price
1	1225	John Iwyn, mercer	built-up land in parish of St Nicholas	donation
2	1227–8	Joce fitz-Peter, former sheriff	land in Stynkynglane, extending north to city wall	donation
3	1238–9	Peter de Gruncestre	land in parish of St Audoen	6 marks
4	1242–3	Arnulphus the monk and John his son	land in parish of St Sepulchre, extending north to city wall	30 marks
5	1242–3	Adam Garston, Emma his wife and Isabelle, daughter of Ralph Stanmor	land in parish of St Sepulchre, extending north to city wall	20 marks
6	1251–2	John Coferrer, goldsmith	built-up land in Stynkynglane	10 marks
7	1252–3	Galfridus son of Nicholas de Norwich	land in parish of St Audoen	5 marks
8	1260–1 and 1283–4	St Mary Clerkenwell	land and houses in Stynkynglane in parish of St Nicholas	5 marks 40 shillings
9	1260–1 and 1283–4	Holywell priory	rents in St Nicholas Lane	19 marks
10	1260–1	Bartholomew, canon of St Bartholomew the Less	rent on a tenement in Stynkynglane in parish of St Nicholas	donation?
11	1260–1	St Bartholomew	rent on two tenements in parish of St Audeon	donation?
12	1261–2	Hugo de Turre and Theophania his wife	land in Stynkynglane in parish of St Nicholas	15 marks
13	1266–7 and 1281–3	Ela, countess of Warwick	built-up land on Stynkynglane in parish of St Nicholas	donation
14	1278–9	John Colchister	messuage in St Nicholas lane	donation
15	1281–2	Thomas de Storteforde, clerk	tenement in St Nicholas lane	donation
16	1284–5	Philip le Taillour, former sheriff	built-up land in St Nicholas lane, within the wall of the city to north	donation
17	1290–1	Galfridus de Bocham	built-up land in parish of St Nicholas	16 marks
18	1291–2	Adam de Fulham, citizen	built-up land in St Nicholas Lane	donation
19	1292–3	Rector of St Nicholas	rented tenement in the parish	40 shillings
20	1301–2	Egidius de Auderuco (paid by Queen Margaret)	land with houses in parish of St Nicholas	60 marks
21	1301–2	Lady Denise, daughter of William de Munchensi	tenement in parish of St Nicholas	donation

Table 5 (continued)

Number on Figure 20	Date of acquisition	Grantor	Description	Price
22	1303–4	Eleanor de Ewelle	built-up tenement in parish of St Nicholas	donation
23	1305–6	William Moday, goldsmith	tenement in parish of St Nicholas	donation
24	1313–14	William de Melton, dean of St Martin	a piece of land 30ft by 22ft in parish of St Anne, with?adjoining tenement in parish of St Nicholas	3 marks
25	1316–17	Hospital of St James	rented tenement next to Newgate and king's highway on south	donation
26	1328–9	Queen Isabella	two messuages in parish of St Nicholas, city wall to north	donation
27	1353–4	Queen Isabella, John de Reffham and Edmund de Norwich	tenement in parish of St Nicholas	donation
			subtotal	£130
			paying off quitrent obligations	c. £20
			total	**c. £150**

The substantial programme of works continued until the 1350s, with Edward II's consort Queen Isabella taking over Margaret's role (below: 'The church').

The next construction campaign must have been on the second cloister, the 'little cloister' that lay on the west side of the great cloister. The friars may have had to wait until they obtained land to the west of the great cloister: the donation of Queen Isabella in 1328 or the following year may be the significant land parcel (tenement 26 in Table 5 and on Figure 20). The evidence of the sponsorship of one part of that cloister – a new infirmary and guest house by the friars Richard Knotte and William Albon – suggests construction in the first half of the fourteenth century, perhaps in the third or fourth decade and quite possibly coterminous with work on the nave.[20]

By about 1360 the Franciscan priory was largely complete. In a century and a quarter successive guardians had built their choir, cloisters and a large preaching nave, the second largest church in London (Figure 21). In the fifteenth century, therefore, the friars turned their attention to improvements rather than new construction, adding various chapels and altars to their church. The grandest of their projects was the rebuilding of the library in the north wing of the cloister: the wealthy City merchant and mayor Richard Whittington contributed £400 and he laid the foundation stone in October 1411 (below: 'The cloisters').

---

[20] BL, Cotton Vitellius F xii, f. 323, printed in *Grey Friars*, pp. 161–2.

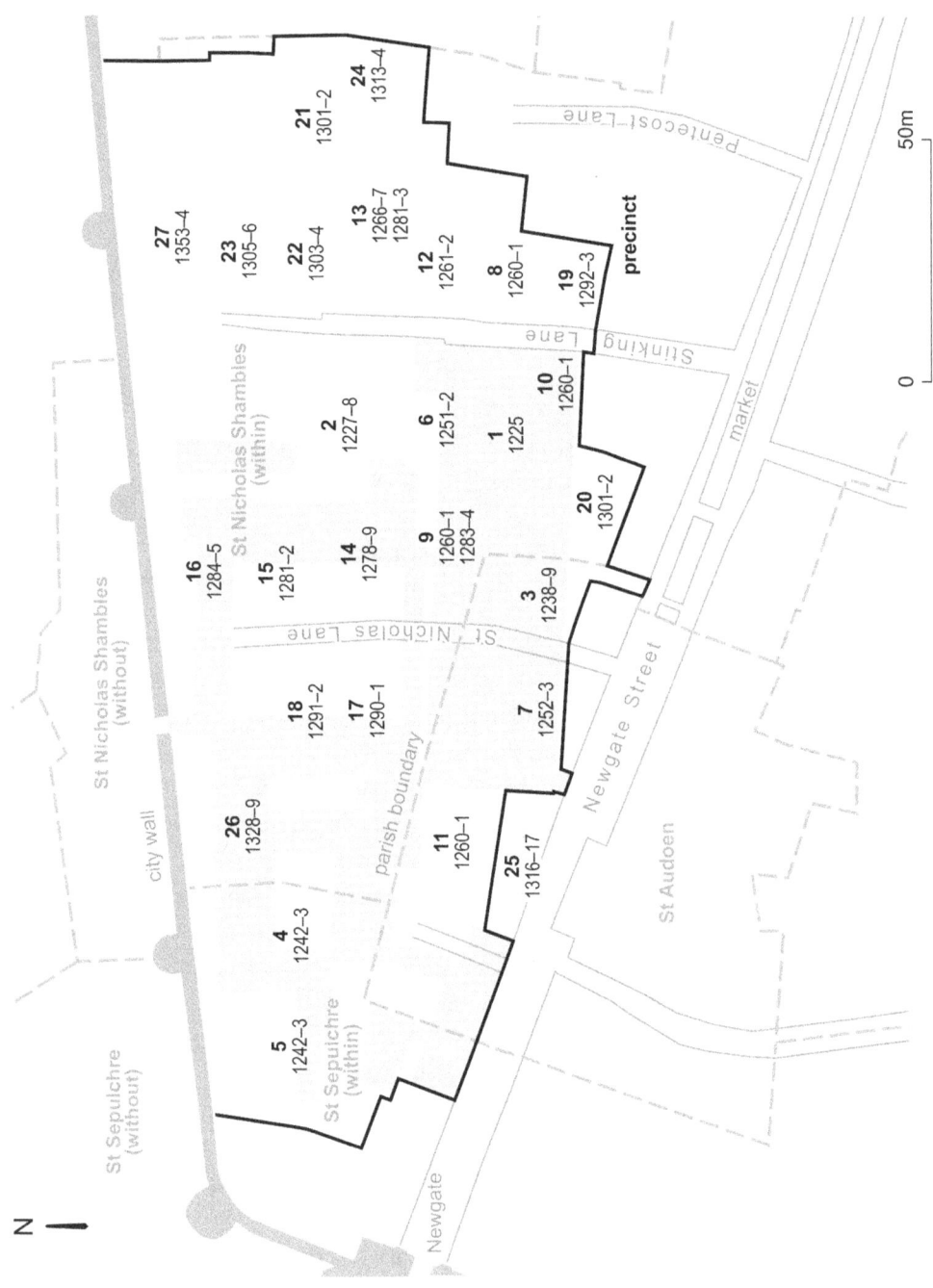

Fig. 20. Map showing the location of the tenements acquired by the Grey friars for their priory; for tenement numbers, see Table 5 (scale 1:1500).

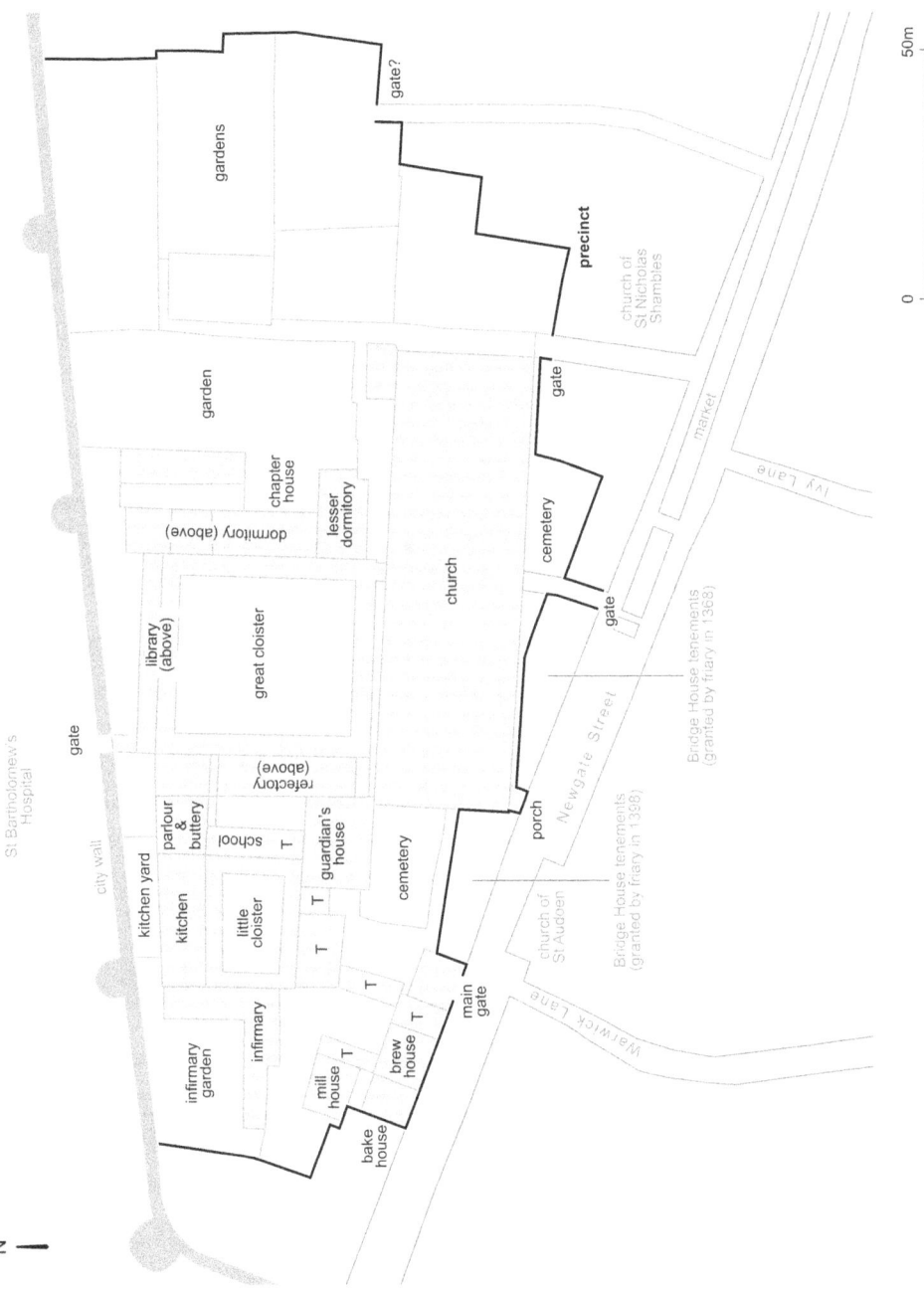

Fig. 21. Map of the precinct of Grey Friars in the sixteenth century (scale 1:1500).

The church

The church of Grey Friars was the second largest in the walled city of London, after St Paul's cathedral. With much of the building sponsored by Edward I's consort Queen Margaret and built by a team of royal masons including master Walter de Hereford, it must have been a marvel of the Decorated style. As has been stated, the first chapel was begun in the late 1220s and probably completed in the 1230s or '40s; further work on it took place in the 1260s. The Grey Friars Register gives us some useful information on the location of this early chapel, noting that it was 'afterwards the great part of the choir' (*que postmodum facta est magna pars chori*), presumably indicating that the thirteenth-century church was incorporated in and formed a sizeable part of the fourteenth-century choir. As early as the 1250s (so before the 1260s works), the Franciscan writer Thomas of Eccleston describes the chapel as *ecclesia* rather than *capella*, implying it was quite substantial.[21] There is a little archaeological evidence for this early church: two sets of excavations within Christ Church Newgate Street (Christopher Wren's rebuilding of the original medieval friary choir, now a walled garden following bomb damage in the Second World War) revealed evidence for chalk wall foundations that were clearly earlier than the fourteenth-century choir. The evidence is far from conclusive but suggests an early church occupying part or all of the central vessel of the later choir.[22]

The mayor Henry le Waleys and Queens Margaret and Isabella were certainly involved in building campaigns on the friary church in the very late thirteenth and fourteenth centuries but it is the precise chronology of and relationship between these campaigns that is difficult to interpret.[23] By the 1290s le Waleys – with his experience as mayor, merchant and project manager of large construction projects including the city's Guildhall – initiated the new construction campaign on the Franciscans' nave.[24] The Grey Friars Register records the tomb of Henry Frowike (died 1286) in the nave and this could have been one of the first

---

[21] BL, Cotton Vitellius F xii, f. 322, printed in *Grey Friars*, p. 157; Eccleston, *Tractatus*, p. 45; Eccleston, *Coming of the Friars Minor*, p. 63.

[22] Sites GF73 and CHR76; see Figure 19.

[23] Scholars place different emphases on the various parts of the construction campaigns: Charles Kingsford argued that le Waleys built the nave and Margaret then rebuilt the choir: *Grey Friars*, p. 35. A.R. Martin argued instead that Margaret's project involved extending or even demolishing le Waleys' nave: *Franciscan Architecture*, pp. 178–9. Hilda Johnstone showed that Margaret's involvement in the project probably overlapped with that of le Waleys at the turn of the thirteenth and fourteenth centuries: 'The Chapel of St Louis, Greyfriars, London', *English Historical Review*, 56 (1941), 447–50. More recently Laura Slater convincingly demonstrated the connections between the roles of Queens Margaret and Isabella and the civic sponsorship of le Waleys and other leading merchants: 'Defining Queenship at Greyfriars London, c. 1300–1358', *Gender and History*, 27.1 (2015), 53–76.

[24] BL, Cotton Vitellius F xii, f. 322, printed in *Grey Friars*, pp. 157–8. For le Waleys and his experience, see Bowsher, *Guildhall*, i, 139; ii, 359; Lachaud, 'Waleys'.

monuments placed there.²⁵ Did the arrival of Queen Margaret in 1299 raise the already high ambitions of the Franciscan guardian Henry de Sutton? The guardian, mayor le Waleys and now the queen then set out to build a nave of the finest quality, with funding for a generation of building works. Le Waleys – during his life and in his will – gave the Franciscans property and Queen Margaret, Queen Isabella and other donors gave huge sums to the project: those recorded in the Register add up to about £2700.²⁶

It seems likely that the early works paid for by le Waleys in his life were one or two new bays of a nave, with construction moving westwards from the friars' enlarged chapel of the 1260s. Margaret's works began with a chapel dedicated to her canonised grandfather St Louis, built between 1299 and 1301. The accounts refer to enlarging existing windows: did this chapel form part of a new aisle added on to the choir, requiring both conversion works and new construction?²⁷ The foundation stone for the new work on the nave was laid in 1306, and a twenty-one-year phase of works drew to a close in 1327. Queen Philippa, Edward III's consort from 1328, continued the queenly tradition and gave money to pay for the roof of the church. Henry of Lancaster (who died in 1345) and the former sheriff Walter Mordon (died 1351) made donations for windows at the west end of the nave, suggesting that the works were drawing to a close in the 1340s. Some works resumed in the 1350s after the Black Death and the church had apparently not been re-dedicated in 1358 when Queen Isabella (consort of Edward II) was buried there. The church was, however, completed and, one assumes, dedicated soon afterwards because in 1363 the main west window had to be repaired after a storm (with a gift from Edward III): this is the only window donation described as a *repair* and the west end of the nave must therefore have been finished before this date.²⁸

Alterations and improvements to the church continued to be made in the following two centuries. In about 1380 Margaret Brotherton, duchess of Norfolk (and granddaughter of Edward I and Queen Margaret), gave 350 marks for some choir stalls (and, like many

---

[25] One could, however, argue that Frowike was originally buried in the churchyard and later moved to the nave by a family member, once construction work had finished.

[26] BL, Cotton Vitellius F xii, ff. 321–4, printed in *Grey Friars*, pp. 154–65. The total donations listed on f. 324 (pp. 163–5) come to £2647 (this figure does not include a separate donation of £10 specified as 'for the convent', from a donor who also gave £40 specifically for the church). The donations listed from le Waleys and later his executors (ff. 321–3; pp. 154–5, 157, 162) were rents and are therefore recorded as annual rental values rather than freehold values: these donations (rents of 6s, 8s 6d, 15s 2d, 2 marks) would be worth about £56 using a 'multiplier' of 20 × rental value.

[27] TNA, E 101/507/5, printed in *Grey Friars*, pp. 202–3; *et pro fenestris eiusdem capelle elongandis*: BL, Additional MS 7966A, f. 40v, printed in Johnstone, 'Chapel of St Louis, Greyfriars'.

[28] In June 1350 the friars were seeking stone and timber for works in the church and other parts of the friary: TNA, C 66/230, m. 4. The church is described as *nondum dedicata* at the time of Isabella's burial in November 1358: *Chronicon Angliae, Ab Anno Domini 1328 Usque ad Annum 1388, Auctore Monacho Quodam Sancti Albani*, Rolls series, 44 (London: Longman, 1874), p. 38. The window donors are named in the Register and analysed by Kingsford: BL, Cotton Vitellius F xii, ff. 325–6; *Grey Friars*, pp. 165–9.

benefactors, she later chose the friary as her place of burial). Friar Thomas Wynchelsey then gave 200 marks towards decorative stonework or woodwork in the choir in 1420 (with another donation of 50 marks spent on painting), and further works including new chapels were paid for in the second half of the fifteenth century.[29]

The best evidence for the late medieval church is a remarkable illustration in a plan drawn in the early seventeenth century, 'The Plat of the Graye Friers' (Figure 22).[30] The building is shown in a combined plan-elevation: the end windows seem at first sight to be tall, fifteenth-century Perpendicular windows (rather than the fourteenth-century Decorated windows one might expect), although the artist may be indicating a Decorated rose design in the upper part of the main west window with mouldings in the spandrels on either side of the rose (the repaired window paid for by Edward III in c. 1363; see above). The gables of the two end windows are each capped with an iron or timber cross and the aisle windows are shown with pairs of lights, matched by the shorter clerestory windows above. A large fragment of one of these windows was discovered in archaeological excavation within the medieval church: an unusual form of sunk chamfer moulding is datable to the third or fourth decade of the fourteenth century and it suggests a continuing link with Hereford masons, even after the death of master Walter of Hereford in 1309 (Chapter 12: Architecture and Architectural Fragments of the London Friaries). On Wyngaerde's view of c. 1544, the choir has three aisles of the same height whereas the nave is shown slightly taller, with a lower south aisle visible in the foreground (Figure 23). The small porch in the south-west corner is just visible, as is a long and slender south transept (for which there is no other evidence). The squat tower has two stages, with the upper considerably smaller than the lower. The overall breadth of the tower is almost certainly exaggerated and the 'copperplate' view of the 1550s shows instead a smaller tower with a short spire or fleche capped with a cross (Figure 24).

The seventeenth-century plan of the medieval church can be securely 'tied down' with limited but useful archaeological evidence. The western end of the nave, including the line of the southern arcade, can be fixed from deep chalk and ragstone foundations discovered on site KEW98. At the other end of the church, three buttresses and three pier foundations define the eastern bays of the choir (sites CHR76 and GF73 on Figure 25). Combining the pictorial evidence with the archaeological evidence, and making use of the Register's

---

[29] *Grey Friars*, pp. 208–11, 238; Charles L. Kingsford, 'Additional Material for the History of the Grey Friars, London', in *Collectanea Franciscana II*, British Society of Franciscan Studies, 10 (Manchester: Manchester University Press, 1922), pp. 61–156 (pp. 104–5, 145–7).

[30] The plan of the friary – by 1616 the school and orphanage known as Christ's Hospital – was drawn by Edward Mansell and Martin Llewellyn, commissioned by St Bartholomew's Hospital. Its function was probably to resolve ownership disputes between the latter hospital and other parties concerning buildings in Newgate Street, disputes that required a plan of the friary (not the hospitals) in order to clarify the meaning of grants made in the 1540s shortly after the Dissolution; Dorian Gerhold, *London Plotted: Plans of London Buildings c. 1450–1720*, London Topographical Society, 178 (London: LTS, 2016), pp. 69–71, plan 20, fig. 63. The plan contains, therefore, elements of reconstruction and is not necessarily a fully accurate portrayal of the late medieval friary.

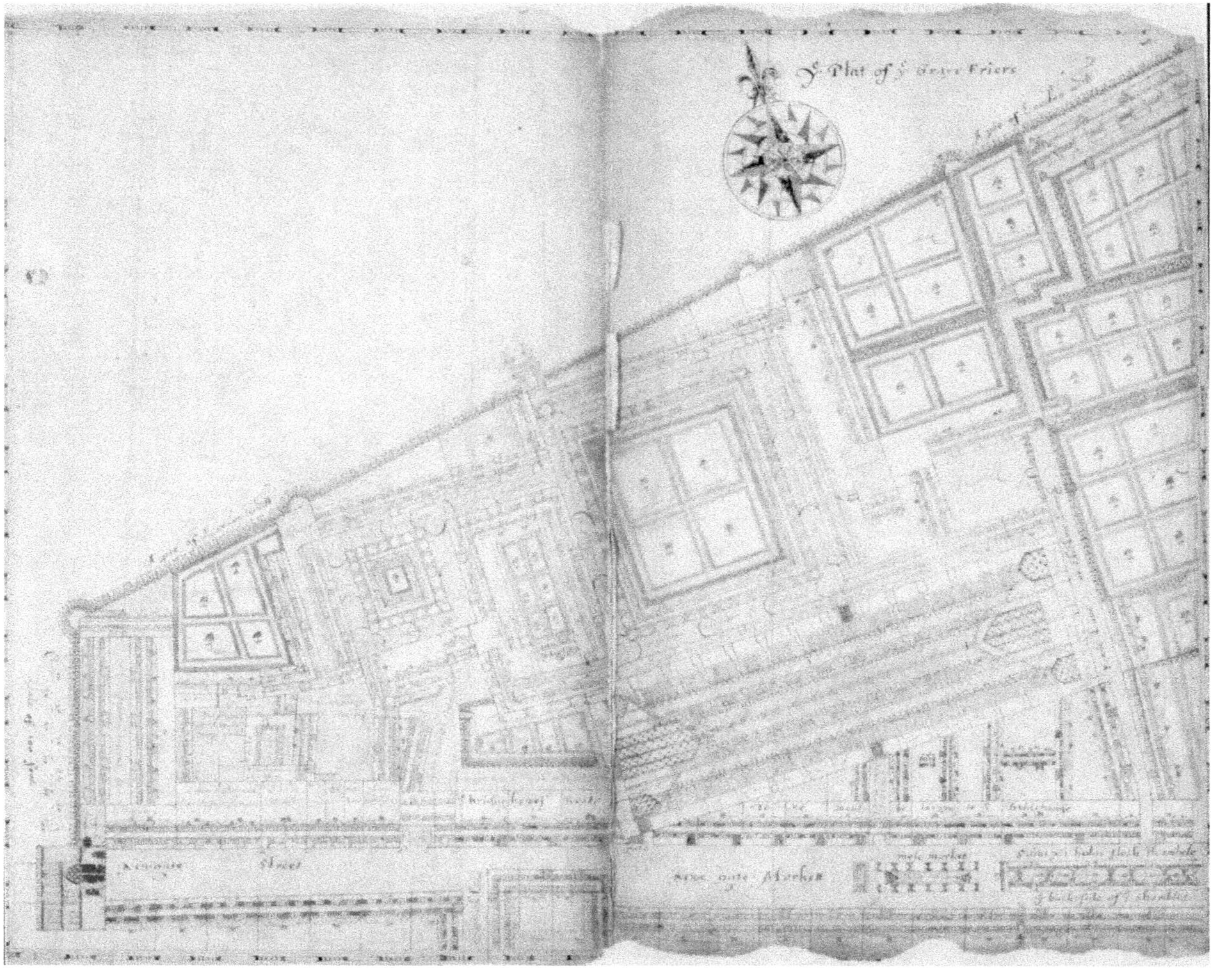

Fig. 22. Plan of the western part of the former Grey Friars entitled 'The Plat of the Graye Friers', 1616. (© St Bartholomew's Hospital Archives, HC 19, f. 59)

Fig. 23. Detail of Wyngaerde's view of London showing the church of Grey Friars in c. 1544. (© Ashmolean Museum, University of Oxford)

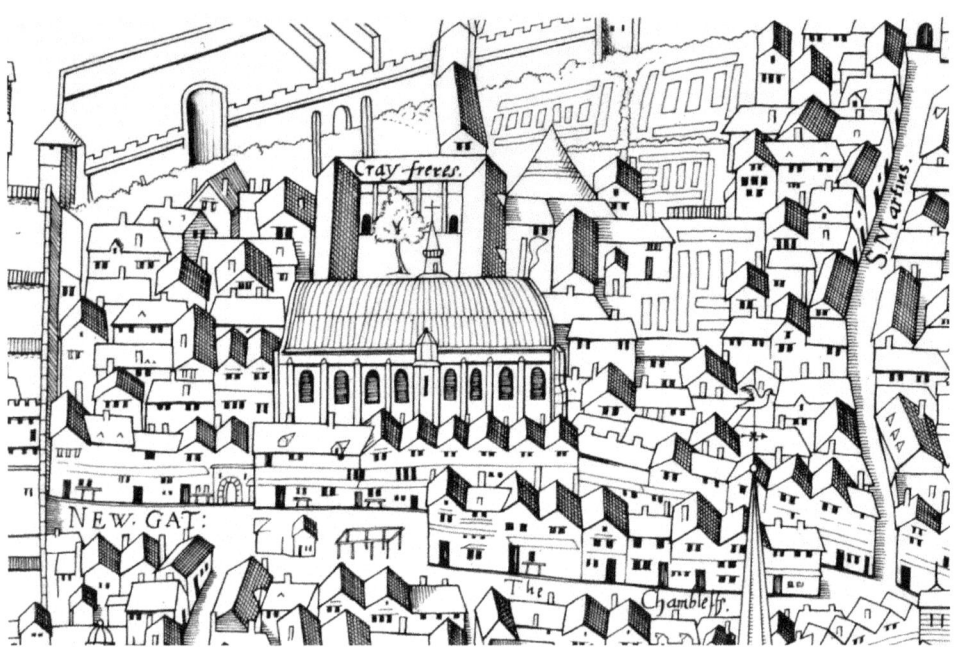

Fig. 24. Detail of the 'copperplate' map-view of the 1550s showing Grey Friars shortly after the Dissolution. (© Museum of London drawing from plate in Anhalt Art Gallery, Dessau)

description of the windows, it can be seen that the choir had seven bays and three aisles, and was separated from a nave of similar proportions by a bay or corridor giving access to the great cloister. Our reconstruction reveals that the church measured an astonishing 299ft feet in length and was 90ft wide (91.1m by 27.4m), dimensions which correspond

Fig. 25. Plan of the church of Grey Friars, showing archaeological and documentary evidence for the internal arrangements (scale 1:500).

closely to the measurements recorded in the early sixteenth-century Register (300ft by 89ft) and in a post-Dissolution survey (280ft by 90ft).[31] The Register also gives the height of the church as measuring 64ft from floor to roof, presumably an internal measurement up to the underside of the timber roof.[32] The bays of the medieval nave are approximately 20ft wide (6.1m; measured centre-to-centre), with those of the choir having the slightly smaller module of 19ft (5.8m). The 'walking place' – separating nave from choir and allowing communication between cloister and street – is thus a fifteenth bay (also about 20ft wide).

Inside, the church must have been an impressive space and its huge (but heavily partitioned) nave would have seemed particularly striking to contemporaries. A rare description of the interior is given in the post-Dissolution 'particulars' that were drawn up in 1546 prior to its sale.[33] The document describes the nave as 'all covered with leade & paved with stoun' and even records the rather sad remains of '4 olde frontes of Awters with Imagery gyltted and one tumbe envyronned with strakes of iron'. The choir was similarly roofed and had 'dyvers paretycions of tymber worke, two payre of olde Organs, one deske and 2 greate candelstyckes of latten'. The Grey Friars Register contains a detailed description of the tombs and graves in the church (this list will be further examined in Chapter 17: Burial and Commemoration in the London Friaries) and the description also provides a valuable record of the dedication and location of many chapels and altars, whose positions are shown in Figure 25.[34] To this evidence can be added several wills requesting burial in the church, thus piecing together a remarkable amount of detail about the interior of this vanished church (Table 6).

The cloisters

The Franciscan friars had two cloisters that included the majority of their monastic buildings. They are described as the 'great cloister' and the 'little cloister' in several post-Dissolution documents of the 1540s; it is very likely that these terms were also used by the friars.[35] As has been suggested, the great cloister next to the church was largely built in the late thirteenth and early fourteenth century (perhaps incorporating parts of the mid-thirteenth-century buildings in the east wing). The little cloister was added in the first half of the fourteenth century, perhaps in the 1330s (above: 'Acquiring and developing the friary'). The cloisters can be mapped with some confidence: in addition to the 'The Plat of the Graye Friers' (Figure 22), there is a rather plainer seventeenth-century survey that records the

---

[31] BL, Cotton Vitellius F xii, f. 326v, printed in *Grey Friars*, pp. 169–70; SBH, HC 19, f. 5v. The archaeological internal measurements are 293ft by 84ft or 89.3m by 25.6m.

[32] John Stow specifies the remarkably precise height of 64ft 2in: Stow, *Survey of London*, i, 318.

[33] SBH, HC 19, f. 5v.

[34] See also E.B.S. Shepherd, 'The Church of the Friars Minors in London', *Archaeological Journal*, 59 (1902), 238–87.

[35] For example, the 1546 survey of the property of Grey Friars 'in on and aboughte the great cloyster and lytle cloyster'; SBH, HC 3, m. 4.

Table 6 Documentary information for the interior of Grey Friars church (points of compass abbreviated to N, E, S, W; C for century).

Place	Evidence	Earliest mention	Source	Citation
Chapels				
St Louis (south aisle of choir?)	account of construction	c. 1300	TNA, E 101/507/5; BL, Additional MS 7966A (f. 40v)	
St Bernadine of Siena	Thomas Battell requested burial *in capella ex parte boriali chori . . . coram ymagine sancti Bernardini*; later will specifies that this is a separate 'chapell of S. Barnadyne within the covent church'	1468 and 1492	Commissary Court and PCC will	Röhrkasten, *Mendicant Houses*, p. 506
St Mary	description of burial location	1526	Grey Friars Register	*Grey Friars*, p. 80
Apostles	description of burial location	1526	Grey Friars Register	*Grey Friars*, p. 88
St Francis	John Baldewyne requested burial in chapel of St Francis	1469	PCC will	Kingsford, 'Additional material', p. 104
All Hallows, also known as 'Vestry Chapell'	Richard Hastings, lord Willoughby, requested burial 'within the qwere or within the Vestry Chapell'; he was buried in All Hallows Chapel	1510	PCC will	Kingsford, 'Additional material', p. 128
Altars				
Holy Cross (at E end of nave)	will of Nicholas Uske specifies burial 'under the cross' before the altar of the Holy Cross	1403	PCC will	Kingsford, 'Additional material', p. 83
Hatton altar (in chapel of St Francis in choir)	will of John Bailley requested burial *coram altari vocato Hatton Aweter*; he was buried two bays from Thomas Hatton's tomb in chapel of St Francis	1420	PCC will	Kingsford, 'Additional material', p. 90
St Clement (at E of nave, perhaps N side or N aisle)	John Lethum requested burial 'afore the aulter of Saint Clement'; he was buried by altar of St Mary (Kingsford suggests that this was an altar used by the confraternity of bakers)	1478	PCC will	Kingsford, 'Additional material', pp. 66 and 109
'the Common Awter' (at E end of nave)	William Brereton requested burial by 'the Common Awter'	1488	Commissary Court will	Kingsford, 'Additional material', pp. 111–12

Table 6 (continued)

Place	Evidence	Earliest mention	Source	Citation
'altar of Jesus' (at E end of nave)	*altare Jhesu*	16th C	Grey Friars Register	*Grey Friars*, p. 105
altar of the Blessed Mary, with adjacent *sedilia* (at E end of nave)	*altaris . . . Beate Marie*	16th C	Grey Friars Register	*Grey Friars*, p. 107
St Michael	William Kebyll requested burial 'bifore the aulter of seynt Michell on the south side of the same covent church within the parclose there redy made of tymber and pyked with yron pykes'; Edward Assheley's will of 1518 describes it as 'Saint Mighell awter, otherwise called the Comyn awter'	1509 and 1518	PCC wills	Kingsford, 'Additional material', pp. 124–5 and 129
'morow messe aulter'	Alice Lewcas requested burial to the right of the 'morow messe aulter'; she was buried in the second bay of the N aisle of the nave	1524	Commissary Court will	Kingsford, 'Additional material', p. 133
Images				
St Louis	Marie de Seintpol bequeaths image of St Louis for the high altar	1377	Court of Husting will	*Calendar of Wills*, ii, 195
St Christopher (painted window in N aisle of nave)	will of Richard Covyntre, skinner, requests burial by the '*ymaginem sancti Christofori*'. The image may be the window of the fifth bay of N aisle of nave: Richard Hallam, buried there, had requested burial *ex opposito fenestre Sancti Christofori ex parte boriali*	1405 and 1419	Archdeaconry Court will; PCC will	Kingsford, 'Additional material', pp. 85 and 89
St Mary (in screen between nave and S aisle, at E end)	David Bardevyle requested burial *coram imagine beate Marie in parte australi dicte ecclesie*; it was later described as 'the ymage of our Lady within the valens of the said church' in Margaret Yonge's will	1411 and 1497	Archdeaconry Court and PCC wills	Kingsford, 'Additional material', pp. 87 and 119–20
statue of St Mary (in chapel of St Mary in choir)	in her will Joan Elveden bequeathed a necklace to adorn the Virgin	1421	PCC will	Kingsford, 'Additional material', p. 90

Table 6 (continued)

Place	Evidence	Earliest mention	Source	Citation
St Mary and St James (in N aisle of nave)	William Hoton requested burial *in Aleya Boreali nave ejusdem ecclesie coram ymaginibus beate Marie et sancti Jacobi*; he was buried in third bay. The image of Mary was later described as 'our Lady of Pitie' in Gilbert Belamy's will, and as a painted window in Register	1445 and 1498	Commissary Court and PCC wills; Grey Friars Register	Kingsford, 'Additional material', pp. 96–7 and 118; *Grey Friars*, p. 119
St Erasmus (W end of N aisle of nave): alabaster tablet?	Thomas Dagworthe requested burial 'on the north syde... affore the ymage off Seint Erasmus'; Thomas Hewett requested burial 'where as is a table hangyng of Saincte Erasmus in the north syde as you come oute of the west doore'	1474 and 1532	Commissary Court and PCC wills	Kingsford, 'Additional material', pp. 107–8 and 139–40
St Mary Magdalene (in chapel of St Francis)	Hugh Acton requested burial 'before the pyctour of Seint Mary Magdaleyn standyng in the South Ile of the quere'; he was buried in the chapel of St Francis	1530	PCC will	Kingsford, 'Additional material', p. 138
St Francis (by high altar in choir)	Eleanor Stafford, duchess of Buckingham, requested burial 'before the image of Saint Frauncis'; she was buried by the high altar of the choir	1528	PCC will	Kingsford, 'Additional material', p. 139
Other details				
screen or 'bars'	will of William Asshe mentions 'bars' (a screen?), apparently separating nave and S aisle: he requests burial *in ecclesia Fratrum Minorum ex parte australi extra barras*	1406	Archdeaconry Court will	Kingsford, 'Additional material', p. 85
high cross (in N aisle of nave)	Walter Potter, goldsmith, requested burial *coram alta cruce ibidem*; he was buried in third bay of N aisle	1459	Commissary Court will	Kingsford, 'Additional material', p. 101
organs	Nicholas Pembyrton requested burial 'on the north syde of the quere yn the lytyll chapell cawlyd our lady chapell by the organs'	1519	Commissary Court will	Kingsford, 'Additional material', pp. 129–30
pulpit (N of nave between second and third bays)	Thomas Roos requested burial 'nyh unto the pulpytt'; he was buried in the nave near the column separating second and third bays	1529	PCC will	Kingsford, 'Additional material', p. 136

Table 6 (continued)

Place	Evidence	Earliest mention	Source	Citation
lectern (in middle of choir)		16th C	Grey Friars Register	*Grey Friars*, p. 73
piscina (on S side of chapel of All Saints)		16th C	Grey Friars Register	*Grey Friars*, p. 76
stalls (in choir)		16th C	Grey Friars Register	*Grey Friars*, pp 74–5

great cloister in remarkable detail, including every pillar and doorway (Figure 26).[36] Parts of the great cloister survived into the nineteenth century and an engraving of 1825 shows that the cloister walk was lit by three-light Geometric windows separated by buttresses (Figure 27; the upper floors of the west (left) side had been rebuilt by the date of the engraving). The windows would suggest a completion date for the cloister in the first half, perhaps the first quarter, of the fourteenth century.[37] The cloister was of the 'covered' type, with the main buildings sailing over the walk. The south cloister walk had no claustral building behind, although it was itself a narrow two-storey building with 'eight lyttle roomes . . . above' (Figure 28).[38]

The function of the various claustral buildings and rooms in the early sixteenth century can be identified thanks to a detailed 'particulars for grant' that accompanied the sale of much of the former friary to the city in 1546.[39] Fortunately, the document contains a number of measurements that enable the listed rooms to be correlated with those illustrated on the 1656 survey. The eastern wing accommodated the chapter house on the ground floor with two separate dormitories above (Figure 28). The rooms of the 'greater dormitory' are described in the 1546 particulars as 'dyvers lytle romes above in the Dorter', presumably indicating that the once-open upper dormitory had been partitioned off into a number of private cells for the friars.

The library occupied the main part of the north wing of the cloister and it is one of the best known buildings of the friary thanks to its well-known benefactor (mayor 'Dick' Whittington) and its survival into the nineteenth century (Figure 28). In the early fifteenth century it was extensively rebuilt. The wealthy City merchant and mayor Richard Whittington contributed £400 and friar Thomas Wynchelsey paid the remaining costs

[36] Gerhold, *London Plotted*, pp. 85–6, plan 26, fig. 86.
[37] See n. 18.
[38] SBH, HC 19, f. 5.
[39] SBH, HC 3, m. 4; the missing parts at the bottom of the original particulars for grant document can be found in a late sixteenth-century copy: SBH, HC 19, ff. 4v–5v. The document was brought to my attention by Frances Maggs, 'Londoners and the London House of the Greyfriars' (unpublished MA dissertation, Royal Holloway, University of London, 1996) [Guildhall Library].

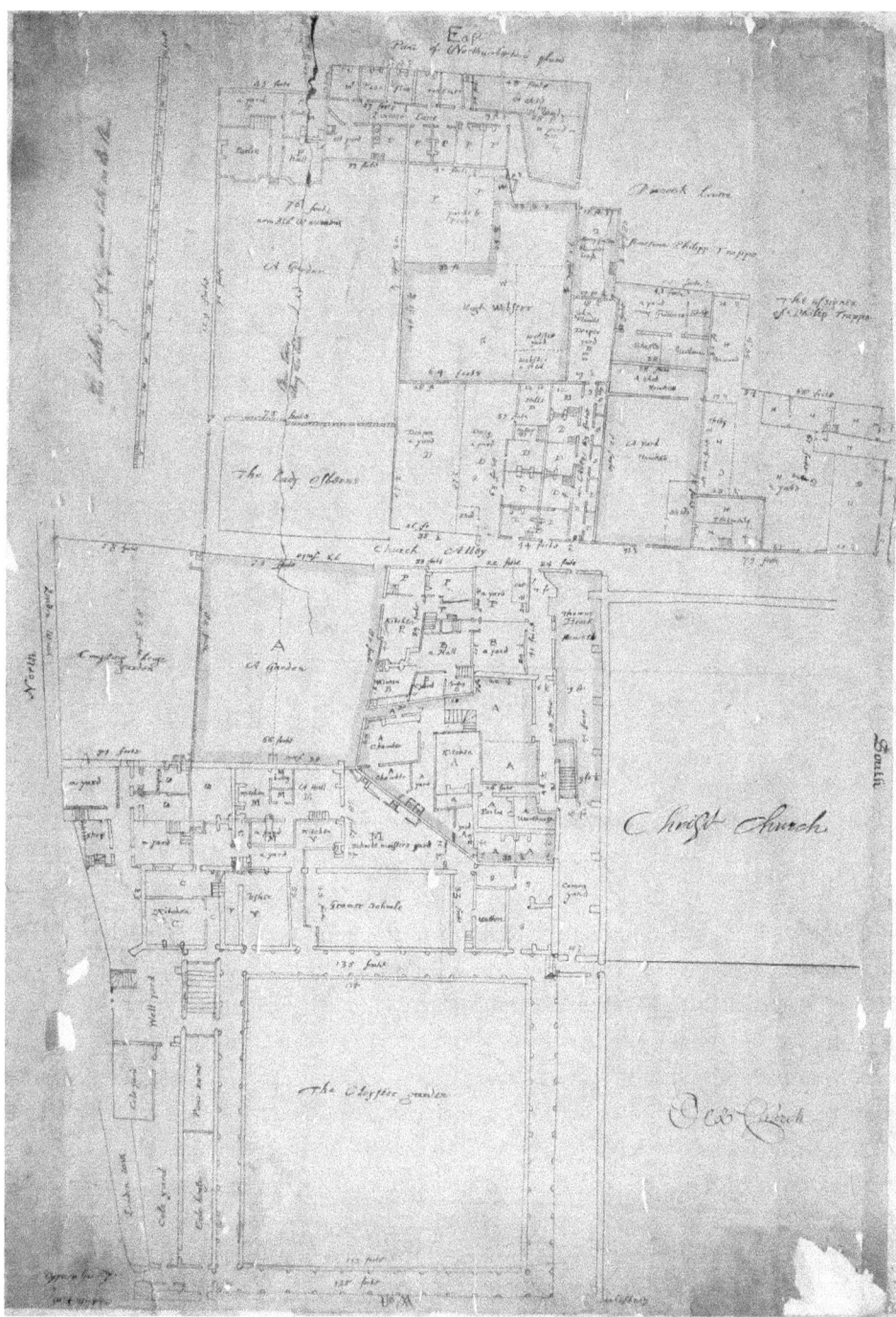

Fig. 26. Plan of the eastern part of the former Grey Friars, surveyed in 1656; note the detailed illustration of the buildings of the great cloister, lower left (north is to the left). (London Metropolitan Archives, CLC/210/H/049/MS 22637/001; by kind permission of Christ's Hospital Foundation)

Fig. 27. View of 1825 looking north in the former great cloister of Grey Friars: the medieval library is on the second floor on the far side of the cloister (note that the cloister may in fact have had eleven visible bays at ground level, not ten: see Fig. 26). (London Metropolitan Archives, COLLAGE 1332)

of £56 16s 8d. Whittington laid the foundation stone in October 1411. The structure of the building was finished at the end of the following year and over the next three years it was 'rendered, plastered, glazed, decorated with galleries, benches and carved woodwork, and stocked with books' (*fuit terrata dealbata vitriata ambulacionibus scannis et celatura ornata et libris instaurata*).[40] It was a three-storey building. On the ground floor was the cloister walk with narrow undercroft rooms behind. On the first floor lay study rooms, described in 1546 as '12 lettle romes on either side with partycions as muche as lettell studies, nowe beynge decayed': this presumably means two rows of small carrels either side of a corridor (the lancet windows lighting the cloister-side rooms can be seen on Figure 27). The grand library itself – some 128ft (39.0m) long – occupied the second floor and was lit by twelve tall Perpendicular windows on each side.[41] Whittington probably

---

[40] BL, Cotton Vitellius F xii, ff. 326v–7, printed in *Grey Friars*, pp. 170–1.

[41] This internal measurement is based on the reconstructed mapping, in particular the 'best fit' of the 1656 survey of Christ's Hospital (Figure 26; LMA, COLLAGE 21718); the 1546 'particulars' give the length as 129ft and the breadth as 21ft.

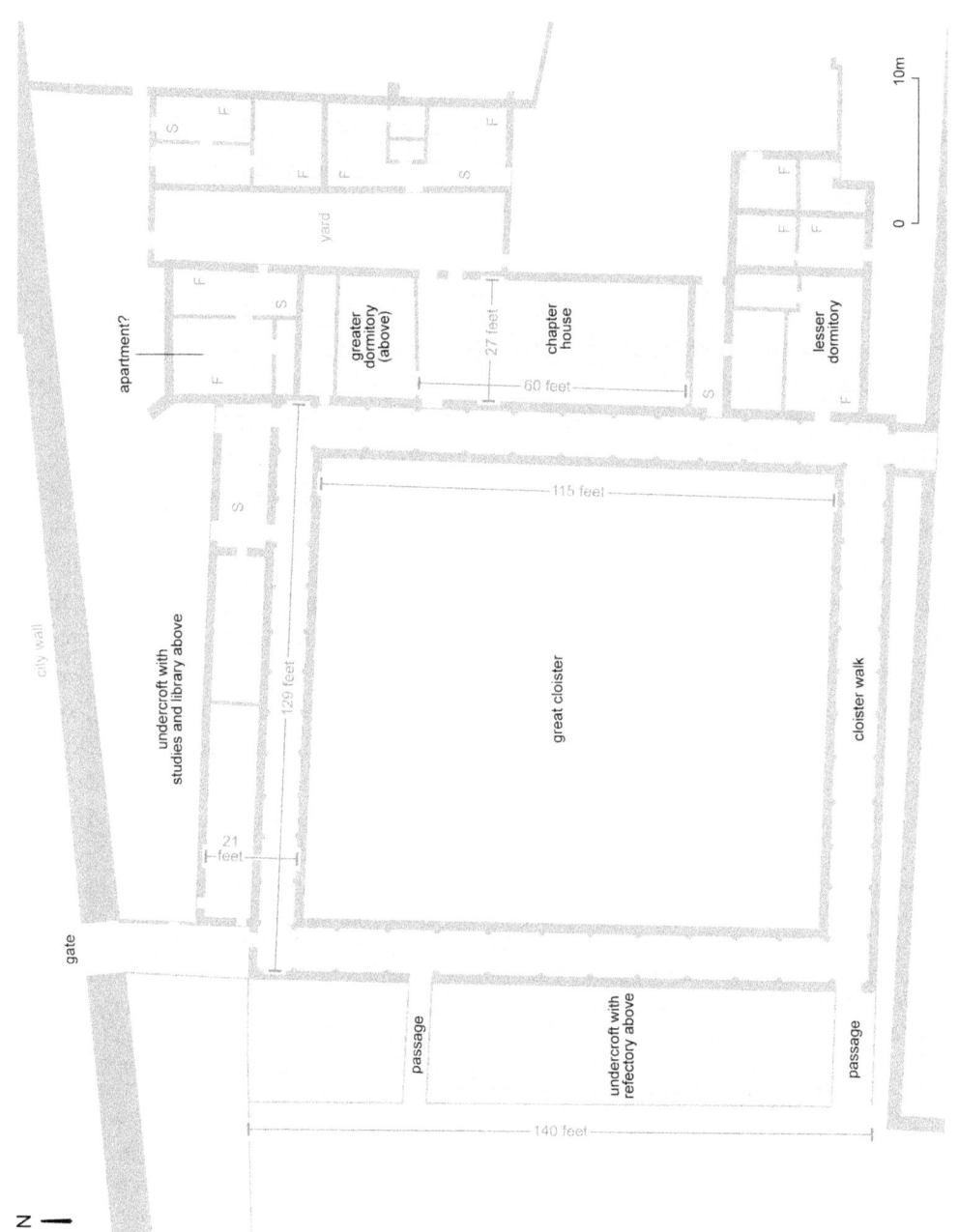

Fig. 28. Plan of the great cloister of Grey Friars ('S' indicates stairs; 'F' fireplace; scale 1:500).

only rebuilt the actual library floor: the module of the library storey (twelve bays of about 8ft 8in width, plus one unlit bay at each end behind the west and east sides of the cloister) does not match the module of the cloister walk below.[42] The 1546 survey records the internal arrangements: '28 deskes and 28 doble settels all of wanscote', presumably laid out with one desk on each side of the fourteen (twelve plus two) bays. When John Leland visited the library in the 1530s, he recorded forty-four books and there would presumably have been several others on loan to individual friars. In addition to books by English Franciscans and Dominicans, there were two chronicles and a copy of Aristotle's *Rhetorica*.[43] By the time of the 1546 survey, the remaining contents of this one-time centre of London's intellectual life could be dismissed with the following note: 'And also there be certayn olde bookes upon the saide deskes.'

On the west side of the cloister lay the refectory hall, situated over the cloister walk and some long, narrow, ground-floor rooms. The refectory must have been the largest room in the friary (excepting the church): it was some 140ft long and 36ft wide and in 1546 it still had several 'settels and 9 tables all of wanscote & of joynours worke'. The lower part of the medieval fabric survived into the nineteenth century: the medieval window openings of the ground-floor cloister walk can be seen on the left of Figure 27, partly bricked and barred by this time.[44]

The arrangement of the little cloister buildings to the west is less clearly expressed in the 1546 particulars and other Dissolution surveys but several rooms can be indentified. On the north side lay the kitchen wing, with an adjacent buttery and dining parlour, probably situated at the junction of the little and great cloisters (Figure 21). On the west side was the infirmary, with a second wing extending beyond the little cloister. By a stroke of good fortune, a seventeenth-century drawn survey of the building survives (once attached to a lease), which includes details such as windows, fireplaces and doors, and whose annotations describe a two-storey building (Figure 29, Figure 30).[45] The large mullions and the

[42] Although the nineteenth-century engraver of Figure 27 shows ten bays on the ground floor, the two seventeenth-century surveys (Figure 22, Figure 26) clearly show *eleven* bays (plus corner bays) on each side; see Chapter 11: Precincts and the Use of Space, n. 5.

[43] Röhrkasten, *Mendicant Houses*, pp. 481–2; Kenneth W. Humphreys, *The Friars' Libraries* (London: British Library in assoc. with British Academy, 1990), pp. 217–23. In addition to Leland's forty-four books, four others are known from other sources. Nine surviving library books have been traced, only one of which seems to occur on Leland's list; Neil R. Ker, *Medieval Libraries of Great Britain: A List of Surviving Books* (London: Royal Historical Society, 1964), p. 123.

[44] The post-Dissolution 'old hall' of Christ's Hospital almost certainly incorporated much of the fabric of the medieval refectory: William Trollope, *A History of the Royal Foundation of Christ's Hospital: With an Account of the Plan of Education, the Internal Economy of the Institution, and Memoirs of Eminent Blues* (London: Pickering, 1834), p. 347; Ernest H. Pearce, *Annals of Christ's Hospital* (London: Methuen, 1901), plate between pp. 50–1.

[45] Nomura, loose plan in private collection; Gerhold, *London Plotted*, pp. 213–14, plan 125, fig. 256. In 2010 the plan was framed and on display on the ninth floor of the bank's European headquarters at Nomura House, London, EC1A 4NP. The lease to which it would once have been attached has not been securely identified but may be LMA, GL MS 39246 (dated 1639), which was donated to the library

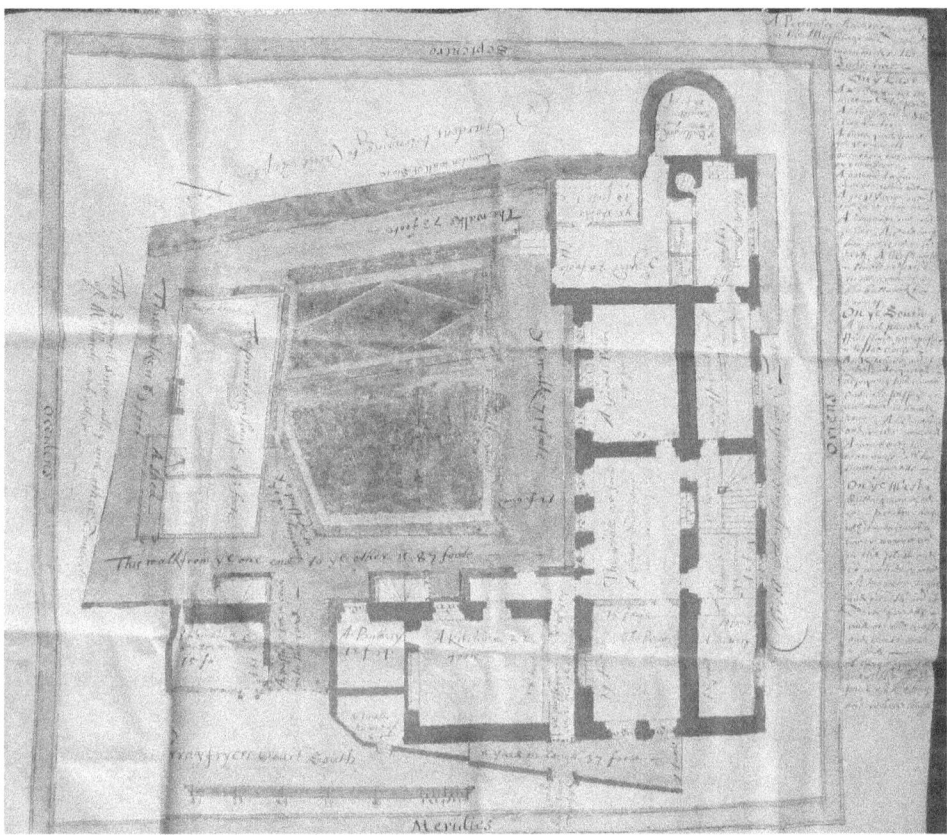

Fig. 29. Mid-seventeenth-century plan of the former friary infirmary (north is at the top; Nomura, unnumbered loose plan).

thick walls shown in the plan strongly suggest that the building is medieval but dating the illustrated elements is problematic. It *could* be argued that this infirmary was built in the thirteenth century: Peter de Helyland gave money in the 1230s towards the construction of the original infirmary, with further sums given by Walter le Potter around the 1270s. Furthermore, this corner of the friary was acquired by the friars very early on, in the 1240s (tenements 4 and 5 in Table 5 and on Figure 20). However, it would have taken a bold Franciscan guardian to build an infirmary here in 1245, over 90 yards (85m) from the church, with the two buildings separated by at least three tenements then in private hands. A more plausible interpretation is that the original infirmary was a building to the north of the first church (quite possibly later incorporated in the east side of the great cloister); the infirmary in the little cloister is therefore likely to be the *hospicium* paid for by friar Richard

by Nomura. The building can be identified as the infirmary thanks to the caption 'Boltons Garden now Mallowes' in this location on the early seventeenth-century 'Plat of the Graye Friers'; in a lease of 1539 William Bolton receives the buildings (plural) called 'le farmorye': TNA, E 315/233, ff. 338v–9.

Fig. 30. Plan of the little cloister, including the infirmary wing on the west side (scale 1:500).

Knotte in c. 1330. The east wing of the little cloister may well have been the school. It was situated opposite the infirmary in the fourteenth century, although by the early sixteenth century this building was leased to the Playsterers' company.[46]

[46] BL, Cotton Vitellius F xii, f. 323, printed in *Grey Friars*, pp. 161–2. 'A hall called the playsterers hall': TNA, E 315/191, f. 60.

On the south side of the little cloister was a series of separate buildings rather than a formal cloister walk and wing. The large house in the south-east corner had its own small chapel and altar, and this is probably the guardian's house. The interior is described in a legal case of the 1540s: it had a 'kychyn, entre, parlar, with the aulter there, the old garett above the said parlar, a Chamber called a study with the lead above, and the stayers lying within the precincte of the Grey frieres agaynst the second cloyster'.[47]

The precinct

The early and still evolving friary of the mid thirteenth century was unenclosed: when questioned about this shortcoming, the English provincial prior, brother William, replied tartly, 'I did not join the order to build walls.'[48] Most of the precinct was probably enclosed in the ensuing half century and the final parts of the boundary wall would have been completed in the mid fourteenth century after the last land donation. The precinct wall was built of stone and so the new late fourteenth-century stretch of wall (necessitated by the friars' grant of land on Newgate Street to the Bridge House estate in 1398) was similarly to be in stone and was to be built 11ft (3.4m) high.[49] By the sixteenth century parts of the boundary wall were, however, in brick, for example on the south side of the small churchyard behind Newgate Street.[50]

Access to and from the precinct was via a series of gates. The main gate was rebuilt in c. 1400 (after the same 1398 land deal with the city), although it may have incorporated elements of an earlier gatehouse. According to the elevation on the 'Plat of the Graye Friers', it had three storeys with battlements on the top: the double-height arched gateway itself was offset to the west (Figure 22). Post-Dissolution leases indicate that there was a small room on each of the ground and first floors, with three rooms across the larger second floor over the arch: a 'greate hall' and 'two chambers . . . with a chimney, a glasse wyndowe and a dore into the saide chambers'.[51] Five other gates and porches allowed access to different parts of the friary; access would have been controlled by doors and gates, and in some cases supervised. For example, lay people would have been allowed largely unrestricted access to the nave of the church via a porch on Newgate Street, its peculiar shape created by the oblique angle of church and street. Most other gates would have been reserved for friars and servants, for example the next entrance east along Newgate Street which led into the 'walking place' between the nave and choir and into the great cloister (Figure 21).

In addition to the church and cloisters, the precinct contained one other essential group of buildings: the service court. This lay in the west of the precinct and included a

[47] TNA, E 321/37/18.
[48] Eccleston, *Tractatus*, p. 45; Eccleston, *Coming of the Friars Minor*, p. 63.
[49] BL, Cotton Vitellius F xii, ff. 327–9v, printed in *Grey Friars*, pp. 171–7. A grant of 1436 mentions the muru[s] lapideu[s] gardini fratrum minorum as an abutment: TNA, C 66/439, m. 15.
[50] TNA, E 315/214, ff. 111–12, printed in *Grey Friars*, p. 212.
[51] SBH, HC 1/3903 [1584]; HC 1/3905 [1608].

bake-house, brew-house and mill-house; all are shown on the 'Plat of the Graye Friers' and can be identified in various post-Dissolution grants. The bake-house is first documented in 1421, when it was the subject of legal action in the Mayor's Court: 'all the sheds in front of the bake-house of Grey Friars' were said to be causing a public nuisance.[52] The brew-house was next door, a timber-framed building on Newgate Street (viewers' certificates of 1547 and 1549 refer to the repair of the 'principalls' or main structural timbers). An investigation into alleged slander at the friary just before the Dissolution reveals, incidentally, the name of the brewer, William Pykering, 'bruer servant to the house or companye of grae friers in London'.[53] The mill-house is described as a *domu[s] molendinari[a] vocata a milhowse* and it was presumably a horse-powered mill, although there were a number of post-type windmills on the fringes of the walled city by the sixteenth century.[54]

The friary had two small churchyards, one to the south of the church behind Newgate Street and a second to the west (Figure 34). One of the churchyards had an external statue or shrine of St Francis (*ymagin[a] sancti Francisci*) next to which a testator requested burial in the early fifteenth century.[55] Like brethren in all London's urban monasteries, the Grey friars had privileged access to a series of gardens, occupying an acre and a half (0.6ha), about a third of the whole precinct (Figure 21). The infirmary garden lay on the west of the precinct but the largest area was a series of garden plots on the east side of Stinking Lane: these presumably included a kitchen garden, orchards, enclosures for poultry and perhaps a vineyard. The name of one of the friar-gardeners is known: in a court case of 1550, a former friar gave evidence and recalled that 'one Walter Roben beyng a fryer of the seid hows was keper of the seid garden duryng the seid 30 yeres' (i.e. the thirty years prior to the Dissolution).[56]

The Franciscans had the smallest rental portfolio of all the London friaries: in the sixteenth century they rented out just five tenements on the edge of the precinct and two sets of rooms, one in the little cloister and one in the gatehouse. To this £10 2s 8d of income can be added ten shillings from two rented gardens, making a total of £10 12s 8d. Some of the tenements probably began as servants' houses: in 1440 one Elizabeth washed the friary's altar cloths and in return she and her husband William lived rent-free in the upper

---

[52] 'toutz les scheddes devant la pestrine dez freres menours': LMA, CLA/024/01/02/51 (Plea and Memoranda roll A 50), m. 6, calendared in *Calendar of Plea and Memoranda Rolls Preserved among the Archives of the Corporation of the City of London at the Guildhall*, ed. Arthur H. Thomas and P.E. Jones, 6 vols (Cambridge: Cambridge University Press, 1926–61), iv, 129.

[53] *London Viewers and Their Certificates, 1508–1558: Certificates of the Sworn Viewers of the City of London*, ed. Janet S. Loengard, London Record Society, 26 (London: London Record Society, 1989), pp. 85–6, 98 (nos 206, 244); TNA, E 36/120, f. 42.

[54] TNA, E 315/22, ff. 91v–92. Windmills are shown on the 'copperplate' and 'Agas' map-views of the 1550s and '60s: *A Collection of Early Maps of London, 1553–1667* (Lympne Castle: Margary in assoc. with Guildhall Library London, 1981).

[55] Will of 1406 cited by Kingsford, 'Additional Material', p. 85.

[56] TNA, E 321/46/51.

rooms of the main gatehouse.⁵⁷ By the sixteenth century the friary had one or two fairly high-status tenants including Lady Rose Wallop, probably a member of the Wallop family of Hampshire gentry, at least two of whom served in Henry VIII's administration. She rented rooms in the little cloister in the 1530s.⁵⁸ This small reliance on rental income would suggest that the Franciscans of all the London friars retained their devotion to poverty. In the fourteenth century the friars gave their Newgate Street tenements to the city's Bridge House Estates: the financial details of these two transactions are not clear but it seems likely that the Dominicans or the Carmelites, had they owned these tenements, would have kept them for their valuable rental income.⁵⁹

Conclusion

Of all the London friars, the Grey friars had the longest-lived friary: over three centuries passed from its foundation in 1225 to its closure in 1538. The friars began their stay in London guided and inspired by their founder Francis. They built a small chapel and some modest accommodation buildings and even altered these in the middle of the thirteenth century when the head of the English order decided that the decoration was too elaborate for mendicants: provincial prior William of Nottingham ordered that the church roof be 'rearranged' (*tectum ecclesie Londonie fecit disponi*) and that the embellishments (bosses or vaults?) be removed from the claustral wing (*incastraturas claustri iussit abradi*).⁶⁰ Unlike the Dominicans, the Franciscans did not move to a different site half a century after their arrival. However, something in their approach did change and they may have been influenced by the Dominicans. From about the 1270s or '80s – just when the Black friars were planning and building their new church and cloister – the Grey friars changed their friary as well. With the support of several mayors and leading city merchants the friars began to build a more elaborate (and therefore more conventionally monastic) urban priory with a large dormitory, chapter house, library and refectory forming a grand cloister. By the end of the thirteenth century mayor Henry le Waleys was sponsoring and co-ordinating the construction of a new preaching nave to attract ordinary Londoners to the friary. Then at the turn of the thirteenth and fourteenth centuries the friars raised their ambitions once again with the arrival of Edward I's new consort, Queen Margaret of France.

Queen Margaret brought her personal enthusiasm for the Franciscans – their church of

---

⁵⁷ TNA, C 146/1479, printed in *Grey Friars*, pp. 207–8. The numbers and value of the friary's tenements given here do not include precinct buildings that were probably only rented around the time of the Dissolution – the infirmary, brew-house, vestry and guardian's house: TNA, SC 6/HenVIII/2396, m. 62; Chapter 18: London Friars and Londoners, Table 20.
⁵⁸ TNA, E 315/191, f. 60 (particulars for grant of 1542 or 1543 but apparently referring to pre-Dissolution lease); Alan Bryson, 'Wallop, Sir John (b. before 1492, d. 1551)', *ODNB*, <http://www.oxforddnb.com/view/article/28581> [accessed 12 May 2016].
⁵⁹ BL, Cotton Vitellius F xii, ff. 327–9v, printed in *Grey Friars*, pp. 171–7.
⁶⁰ Eccleston, *Tractatus*, p. 45; Eccleston, *Coming of the Friars Minor*, p. 63.

Les Cordeliers in Paris was a Capetian mausoleum – and she joined le Waleys' project to build the new Franciscan church in London. Instead of merely extending the chapel westwards by adding a nave and thus creating a choir from the old chapel, Margaret's involvement allowed a complete redesign. Within fifty or sixty years the friars and their royal and civic sponsors had built a fifteen-bay church that was 299ft feet long and 90ft wide (91.1m by 27.4m), not as large as the cathedral of St Paul's or the abbey of Westminster, but the largest 'ordinary' church in London. And this was a church that cost at least £2700, a huge sum. Like the Dominicans' new priory, the Grey Friars church can be seen as a grand design of the very end of the thirteenth century, a co-operative project between friary, city and Crown that was executed over the following half century.

But royal patronage was relatively short-lived: after the deaths of Queens Margaret (1318), Isabella (1358) and Philippa (1369), there were no more royal sponsors (with the exception of Margaret's granddaughter Margaret of Brotherton) and the Franciscans did not even secure the royal payment of £20 that the Dominicans received every year. They would surely have needed to beg for alms just to meet their annual running costs. The Grey friars did, however, enjoy the support of Londoners and the evidence of the Register makes clear that a sizeable minority of Londoners came to the friary, in life and in death. By the time of the Dissolution at least 790 people were buried and commemorated in the church, probably well over a thousand allowing for earlier burials that were not listed in the Register (Chapter 17: Burial and Commemoration in the London Friaries).

In a century and a half these poor mendicant friars had built a grand church, a great cloister and a second smaller cloister, and had a 4½-acre precinct with gardens and a cemetery. In this chapter we have mapped out that precinct and charted the chronology of the friars' works. Thanks to the good documentary and visual evidence (rather than the virtually non-existent archaeological evidence), the layout of the friary can be better understood (particularly its gardens and the rather small cemetery), and more detail has been revealed about individual buildings such as the infirmary and the library.

5

White Friars, c. 1247–1538

THE Carmelites or White friars began as a group of hermits living on Mount Carmel in Palestine in the late twelfth or early thirteenth century. The Arab reconquest of the Holy Land in the thirteenth century pushed these hermits back towards Europe, and they established Carmelite provinces in Cyprus, Sicily and England, the latter in 1242. This change of location gradually brought about a change in purpose as the hermits became friars, with a new mendicant Rule authorised by Pope Innocent IV in 1247. The early Carmelites brought their eremitic lifestyle with them to Europe, setting up small rural monasteries, for example, at Hulne in Northumberland and Aylesford in Kent. But the change of status from hermit to friar soon brought about a move from country to town and most Carmelite houses from the second half of the thirteenth century onwards were urban friaries.[1] The Carmelite friars became known as White friars in England thanks to the colour of their cloak, the main distinguishing feature when meeting a Carmelite outside his friary.

The English White friars probably established their London house in the late 1240s, although the evidence is not as clear as one would like. The late sixteenth-century historian John Stow, citing the early sixteenth-century Carmelite historian John Bale, says that the London White Friars was founded by the returning crusader Richard de Grey in 1241, and de Grey is also credited in a papal bull of 1254. Modern scholars have, however, suggested that his foundation could well post-date the order's new mendicant Rule of September 1247, which encouraged the new friars to look to the towns.[2] Other evidence shows that the papal authorities were negotiating with the bishop of London in 1246 about the establishment of a friary; furthermore, Carmelite lists of houses place London chronologically before Cambridge, the latter given formal permission in November 1247.[3] Our best guess

---

[1] Frances Andrews, *The Other Friars: The Carmelite, Augustinian, Sack and Pied Friars in the Middle Ages* (Woodbridge: Boydell, 2006), pp. 14–15.

[2] Stow, *Survey of London*, ii, 46; Röhrkasten, *Mendicant Houses*, pp. 51–2.

[3] Richard Copsey, 'The Medieval Carmelite Priory at London, a Chronology' (unpublished

is therefore to say that de Grey gave the friars their first plot of land for the London friary in about 1247.

The friary became a successful urban institution, housing sixty to eighty friars in the first half of the fourteenth century. Unusually among London's monastic houses, the numbers seem to have recovered quickly after the Black Death with seventy-eight friars identified here at the end of the century. By the fifteenth century the priory may even have overtaken the Dominican, Franciscan and Augustinian houses in terms of the numbers of brethren (although not in income). Even though the numbers had dropped to twenty-nine friars by the early sixteenth century, this is still a fairly respectable figure compared to the other London convents at that time.

The London house was, in effect, the senior house of the English Carmelite province as it housed the provincial prior and the principal school or *studium generale*, which sent Carmelite students to the universities of Oxford, Cambridge and Paris, and received visiting friars from the Continent (with foreign friars probably accounting for over a quarter of the London house).[4] The intellectual and spiritual importance of the house is reflected in its large library, with sixty-six books recorded in three late medieval lists and another dozen or more surviving manuscripts. And, given that the surviving medieval library catalogue from the smaller rural Carmelite house at Hulne lists ninety-seven volumes, the London house probably had well over a hundred.[5]

The London White friars never quite achieved the political or popular status of their more important Dominican and Franciscan neighbours. Senior Carmelites sometimes crop up in London or even in national politics: the London Carmelite John Latimer played a strange role in a plot against John of Gaunt in 1384; two White friars were involved in the theological clash of the fifteenth century between the London mendicants and the secular church concerning poverty and the payment of tithes (Chapter 16: Spiritual Life and Education in the London Friaries).[6] The Carmelites certainly maintained a level of popular support from Londoners, hearing confession and providing spiritual services at funerals and afterwards, with townsmen and women purchasing the usual range of commemorative masses and anniversary funeral services. Even in this regard, the available evidence suggests Londoners looked more frequently to Franciscans than to Carmelites, at least in their choice of final resting place (Chapter 17: Burial and Commemoration in the London Friaries).

The end of the White Friars came in November 1538 when the prior, John Gybbes, and the twelve remaining friars signed the surrender document in the presence of the royal

typescript, 2008), pp. 3–4, available online at 'British Province of Carmelite Friars' <http://www.carmelite.org/> [accessed 13 May 2015].

[4] Röhrkasten, *Mendicant Houses*, pp. 484, 536.

[5] Humphreys, *Friars' Libraries*, pp. 167–88; Ker, *Medieval Libraries*, pp. 124–5; Andrew G. Watson and Neil R. Ker, *Medieval Libraries of Great Britain: A List of Surviving Books. Supplement to the Second Edition*, Royal Historical Society Guides and Handbooks, 15 (London: Royal Historical Society, 1987), p. 48.

[6] Röhrkasten, *Mendicant Houses*, pp. 310–13, 538–9.

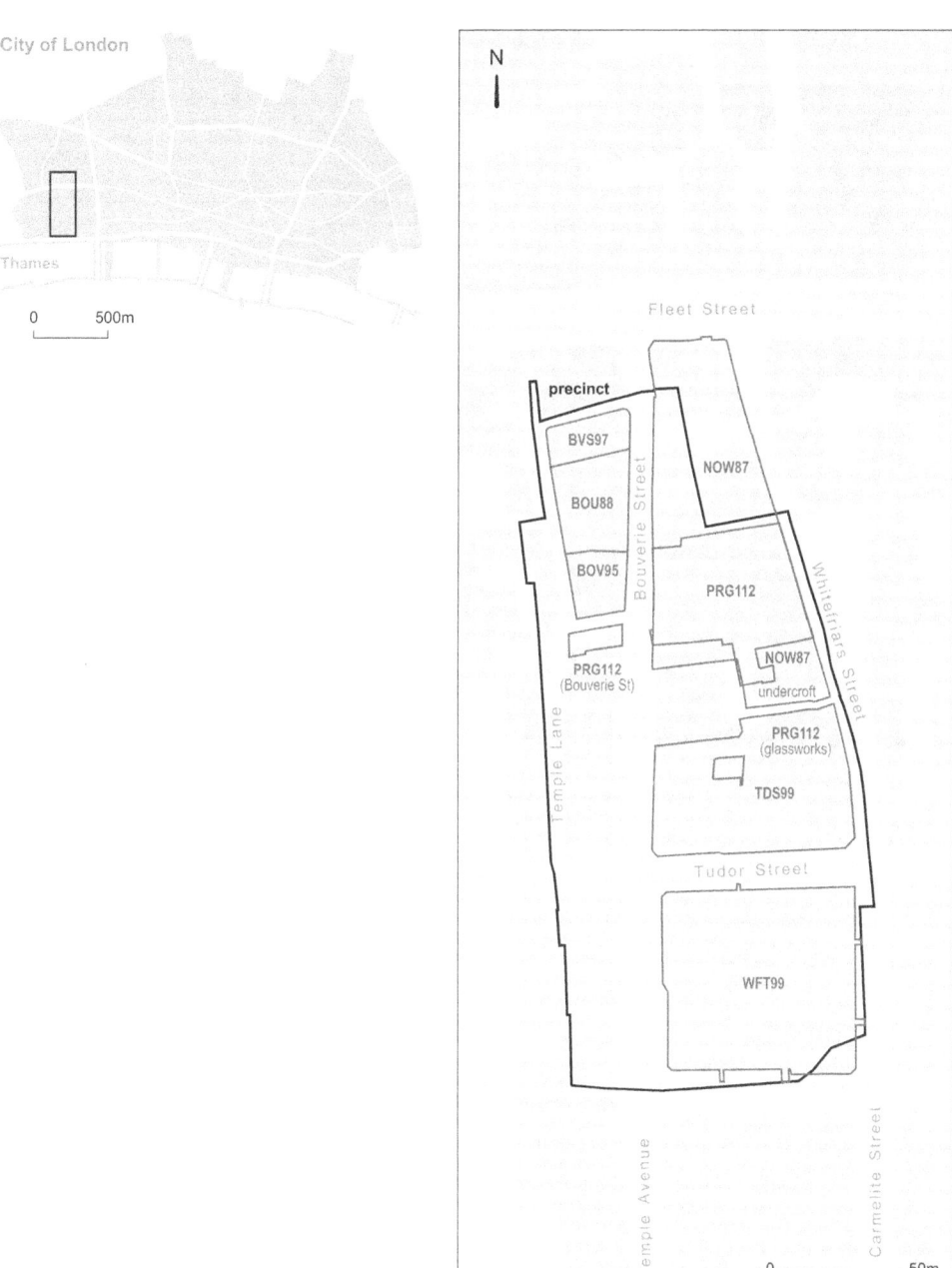

Fig. 31. Map showing the location of the White Friars and archaeological sites within its precinct (scale 1:2500)

commissioner, Thomas Legh.[7] The church, cloisters and precinct were divided into thirteen blocks of land and royal sales commenced in 1540, with the bulk of the plots sold in 1544–5.[8]

[7] *Letters and Papers*, xiii(2), no. 788.
[8] Holder, 'Medieval Friaries of London', pp. 128–38.

Fig. 32. The fourteenth-century vaulted undercroft of the Carmelite prior's house, on the move in 1991 (MOLA)

There is a good range of surviving sources for this friary: in addition to the excellent survey and sale records kept by the Court of Augmentations in the 1540s there is an early seventeenth-century map of the central part of the convent, probably drawn for the Morrison-Capel family who had previously bought the two largest property blocks of the friary in the 1540s (Figure 37). A good number of archaeological excavations have taken place in the area of the medieval precinct, throwing light on the arrangement of the church and cloister (Figure 31). Much of this work was carried out at the beginning of the twentieth century by the prominent London archaeologist Alfred Clapham and his interpretation of the archaeological and documentary evidence was inspired.[9] Of particular note is the surviving vaulted undercroft of the prior's house – discovered in the nineteenth century, investigated in the twentieth and (in 1991) physically lifted up on a crane and put back during construction of the large 65 Fleet Street building (Figure 32).

Acquiring and developing the friary

It is possible to reconstruct the basic pattern of the various plots of land with which the White friars created and then enlarged their precinct, although without a surviving 'register' (like that of the London Franciscans), or surviving property archives (such as for

---

[9] Clapham, 'Topography of the Carmelite Priory', 15–31.

Table 7 List of the tenements acquired by the White friars for their precinct.

Number on Figure 33	Date of acquisition	Grantor	Description	Reference
1	1247	Richard de Grey	a field or close south of Fleet Street?	Stow, *Survey of London*, ii, 46
2	1310		messuage and meadow in Lymbrennereslan	TNA, C 143/83/16
3	after 1317	Adam de Brom	messuage in Fleet Street?	*CPR 1317–1321*, 61
4	1348	Thomas de Fencotes	messuage in Fleet Street to east of friary	*CPR 1348–1350*, 298, 420; *Cal. Inquis. Misc. 1348–1377*, no. 42, p. 17
5	1349	Edward III and city of London	'Crokkereslane' running down west side of precinct	*CPR 1348–1350*, 298
6	1350	Hugh de Courtenay	long plot on the west side of Crokers Lane	*CPR 1348–1350*, 512
7	mid 14th century	Edward III	land reclaimed from Thames	site WFT99
8	1358	Ralph de Hull	messuage with shops in Fleet Street	*CPR 1358–1361*, 65
9	1396	Richard II	land reclaimed from Thames	*CPR 1391–1396*, 658
10	1411	John Cokayn and other Grocers	messuage with shops in Fleet Street	*CPR 1408–1413*. 276
11	1442	John, bishop of Bath and Wells	tenement called 'le Boreshede'	*CPR 1441–1446*, 182

the Crossed friars or early Black friars), a certain amount of conjecture has to be accepted (Table 7, Figure 33). Richard de Grey's foundation bequest of c. 1247 was a large property to the south of Fleet Street, the road leading westwards out of London to Westminster. Although no contemporary evidence for the size and location of the plot survives, its shape can be reconstructed from later and better known boundaries (the eastern edge of the precinct, a lane to the west and the fourteenth-century river bank): it must have been a small field, surviving on the fringe of the built up area of the city ('1' on Figure 33). Thanks to its location on the edge of town, this field was rather larger than the foundation bequests of the other friaries, occupying about 1.3ha (3¼ acres). The Carmelite priors of the thirteenth century – unlike their Dominican and Franciscan colleagues – seem to have been quite satisfied with their precinct and they made little effort to enlarge their property.

Efforts to acquire more land began in the fourteenth century with the acquisition of a messuage on Limeburners lane (Lymbrennereslan). The precise location of this vanished lane is unclear but the messuage included a meadow and a quay on the waterfront. Was prior John de Lacok trying to 'tidy up' the south-east corner of his precinct (Figure 33)?[10]

[10] Röhrkasten, *Mendicant Houses*, p. 54; TNA, C 143/83/16. The lane might be a now-lost part of the small modern lane Primrose Hill that runs southwards on the east side of Whitefriars Street and

Fig. 33. Map showing the location of the tenements acquired by the White friars for their priory; for tenement numbers, see Table 7 (scale 1:2000).

Later priors of the fourteenth century adopted two strategies for their precinct. Firstly, they began to accept donations of property on Fleet Street, not to enlarge their precinct but rather to provide a small annual rental income from shops and houses that backed onto the friary (tenements 3, 4, 8, 10 and 11 in Table 7 and on Figure 33). Secondly, they sought to enlarge the precinct westwards as far as the former Temple precinct and southwards into the Thames. In the mid fourteenth century the Carmelite prior (probably John Elm)

then turns west towards the former precinct. This lane does not appear in Lobel, *City of London from Prehistoric Times to c. 1520*, map 2 and gazetteer, p. 80.

acquired Crokers Lane on the west side of the friary, having obtained permission from the king and city, and an adjacent strip of land given by Hugh de Courtenay, earl of Devon (5 and 6 in Table 7 and on Figure 33).[11] There was undoubtedly an additional motivation for acquiring this lane: three years earlier the prior had appealed to Edward III to get the city authorities to do something about the prostitutes who lived and worked along it.[12]

The large archaeological site on Tudor and Carmelite Streets produced evidence of two phases of land reclamation at the south of the precinct, carried out, respectively, in the middle and end of the mid fourteenth century (site WFT99 on Figure 31; nos 7 and 9 in Table 7 and on Figure 33). In both cases the friars employed medieval engineering techniques, building a new stone river wall out on the foreshore and then dumping large amounts of earth and refuse between the old and new waterfronts to create the newly reclaimed land. The first phase of works could have been carried out under prior John Elm (the archaeological pottery evidence points to a date in the mid fourteenth century). The second and larger of these works must be that for which Richard II gave permission, probably to prior John French, in January 1396, allowing the friars to reclaim 100ft into the river; the archaeological evidence shows that they in fact managed to reclaim about 150ft (40–50m).[13]

By the mid fifteenth century the friars had thus enlarged their original 3¼-acre field to create a precinct of 5 acres (2.1ha), with an adjacent quarter-acre parcel of revenue-raising shops, houses and inns on Fleet Street (0.1ha).

Having obtained a field around the year 1247 on which to create a friary, the first prior (his name is unknown) must have turned his attention to building a church. Documentary evidence for the construction of this first church can be found in a series of grants by Henry III and Edward I (Table 8). The earliest royal grant is for oaks for timber in July 1267, followed by a burst of royal gifts between 1269 and 1275, several of which specify the works on the church. However, it seems likely that our first prior began work on the church much earlier than 1267, quite possibly in the early 1250s. The White friars must surely have had a chapel or oratory by 1254 when the general chapter was first held here: one assumes that even if they used another London building for the actual meeting and accommodation, the new prior would have wanted to show his English and Continental colleagues the works taking place on his new site.[14] The White friars may simply have had to 'wait their turn' for royal grants as there were other local demands: the first phase of construction works at the Black Friars finished in about April 1267, just when Henry III turned his attention to the London Carmelites (Chapter 1: The First Black Friars in Holborn). The royal grant of Purbeck marble for the new altar suggests that the initial construction was finishing off in the first half of the 1270s, with the church probably a single-aisled chapel of three or four bays.

---

[11] CPR 1348–1350, pp. 298, 512; for priors see lists in Barron and Davies, *Religious Houses*, pp. 131–2; Copsey, 'Carmelite Priory at London', pp. 60–1.
[12] CCR 1346–1349, p. 37.
[13] CPR 1391–1396, p. 658; LAA, site WFT99, D. Killock, 'An archaeological excavation at Whitefriars, City of London' (unpublished Pre-Construct Archaeology report, 2002).
[14] Copsey, 'Carmelite Priory at London', p. 4.

Table 8 Royal grants towards the construction of the White Friars, 1267–99.

Date	Royal grant	Purpose	Reference
July 1267	seven oaks		*CCR 1264–1268*, pp. 321–2
April 1269	firewood for lime-kiln		*CCR 1268–1272*, p. 39
January 1270	100s	works on church	*CLR 1267–1272*, p. 113
July 1270	fifteen oaks	works on church	*CCR 1268–1272*, p. 206
May 1271	ten oaks		*CCR 1268–1272*, p. 340
May 1272	twelve oaks		*CCR 1268–1272*, p. 482
June 1272	200s	works on church	*CLR 1267–1272*, p. 220
May 1273	Purbeck marble	altar	TNA, C 62/49, m. 4
December 1275	twelve oaks	works on church	*CCR 1272–1279*, p. 261
October 1293	at least seven trees for timber	cloisters?	*Cal. Inquis. Misc.*, i, 457 (no. 1628)
May 1299	thirteen oaks		*CCR 1296–1302*, p. 249

There is, unfortunately, little information about the order of construction of the rest of the friary. Royal gifts of timber in the 1290s (Table 8), along with a papal indulgence from the same decade, could well have been providing for works on the roof on an accommodation block – the first wing or two of the cloisters – but specific evidence is lacking.[15]

The next documented construction campaign at the friary is on the church in the fourteenth century. Again, the evidence is not as clear as one would like but the sixteenth-century historian John Stow records works paid for by Hugh de Courtenay, earl of Devon, Sir Robert Knolles, the celebrated soldier of the Hundred Years War, and Robert Mascall, bishop of Hereford. The de Courtenay works were on a new choir and began in about 1349 (when the works were noted in an inquisition), around the same time as his donation of the parcel of the land to enlarge the priory westwards.[16] The documentary evidence suggests that work on the new choir continued in the third quarter of the century: a new window, quite possibly one of several, was added to the church in the 1360s or '70s, suggesting that at least part of the new choir may have been completed, and a testator in 1369 referred to the 'new church' of the London White friars.[17] The earliest identifiable burial in the new choir (according to an early sixteenth-century list) was that of Elizabeth Malewyn, countess of Atholl, in 1375.[18]

The Knolles works are undated but he was certainly investing heavily in other religious and public building campaigns in the 1380s. A will of 1386 mention the 'new works' taking place in the church and another testator sponsored a new window here in 1390.[19] Did these works relate to the nave of the church? The earliest recorded tomb in the nave is that of

---

[15] *Calendar of Papal Letters*, i, 513.
[16] *Calendar of Inquisitions Miscellaneous, Chancery, Preserved in the Public Record Office*, 7 vols (London: HMSO, 1916–68), iii (1348–1377), p. 17 (no. 42).
[17] Stow, *Survey of London*, ii, 46; Copsey, 'Carmelite Priory at London', pp. 24, 26.
[18] Stow, *Survey of London*, ii, 46.
[19] Röhrkasten, *Mendicant Houses*, p. 508; *Calendar of Wills Proved and Enrolled in the Court of Husting*, ii, 300–1.

Robert Knolles, who died in 1407 (Chapter 17: Burial and Commemoration in the London Friaries, 'Military knights and their tombs'). Robert Mascall (or Marshall), a Carmelite himself, died in 1416 and may have been buried here; the works that he paid for in life or death included additional work on the choir and presbytery, and the construction (or repair) of the church tower.[20] These works could have taken place in the first decade or two of the fifteenth century. The evidence therefore suggests a sixty- or seventy-year construction campaign on the church and, rather unusually for the mendicants, this campaign was for a complete new church, situated immediately to the north of the old church.

No other major campaign of works on the friary is documented. The friars probably renovated or completed their cloisters in the fourteenth century; they were certainly building within the service court in the south of the precinct in the following century. Was the friary simply more or less 'complete' (apart from the evolving service court) in the early fifteenth century (Figure 34)?

The church

The documentary evidence suggests that the original friars' church – a humble building of the third quarter of the thirteenth century – was superseded by a much grander nave and choir of the fourteenth and early fifteenth century. In order to understand the rather unusual layout of this church or churches, we must turn to the archaeological evidence for the later White Friars church.

The basic shape of the late medieval church can be understood thanks to some fortuitously located archaeological evidence. The south-west and north-east parts of the nave are defined by two excavations in Bouverie Street (BOV95 and PRG114 on Figure 31 and Figure 35). At the former, remains of the below-ground chalk piers for a typical medieval arched foundation were discovered in the 1990s. At the latter, the remarkable London rescue archaeologist Henry Hodge recorded in 1882 the north-east corner of the nave, exposed during the demolition of a more recent building and standing some 40ft high (Figure 36).[21] If one 'joins the dots' and assume that the church only extended westwards as far as the newly acquired Crokers Lane, the dimensions of the reconstructed nave match those recorded in a 1544 survey by an official of the Court of Augmentations.[22] The latter document records the internal dimensions as 44 yards by 18 yards (40.2m × 16.5m), which correspond nicely with the archaeologically derived reconstructed measurements (40.5m × 16.5m; Figure 35).

A similar process can be carried out for the choir of the late medieval church. Parts of

---

[20] Stow, *Survey of London*, ii, 46; R.G. Davies, 'Mascall, Robert (d. 1416)', *ODNB*, <http://www.oxforddnb.com/view/article/18257> [accessed 14 May 2015].

[21] LAA, BOV95, '10 Bouverie Street, London EC4, an archaeological excavation and watching brief', B. Barber (unpublished Museum of London report, 1997), pp. 10–11, 19; Clapham, 'Topography of the Carmelite Priory', pp. 20–1. I am grateful to Keith Pearshouse for drawing my attention to this uncatalogued Henry Hodge drawing in the London Metropolitan Archives.

[22] TNA, E 314/54 [piece indexed as 'London and Middlesex: Whitefriars, lead at'].

Fig. 34. Map of the precinct of White Friars in the sixteenth century (scale 1:1500)

the north and east walls were recorded during an early rescue excavation carried out in the late 1920s when the large *Daily News* building in Bouverie Street was being redeveloped (PRG112 on Figure 31 and Figure 35). The north wall of the choir was still standing after the Great Fire of London: a surveyor noted the (presumably still impressive) stone wall

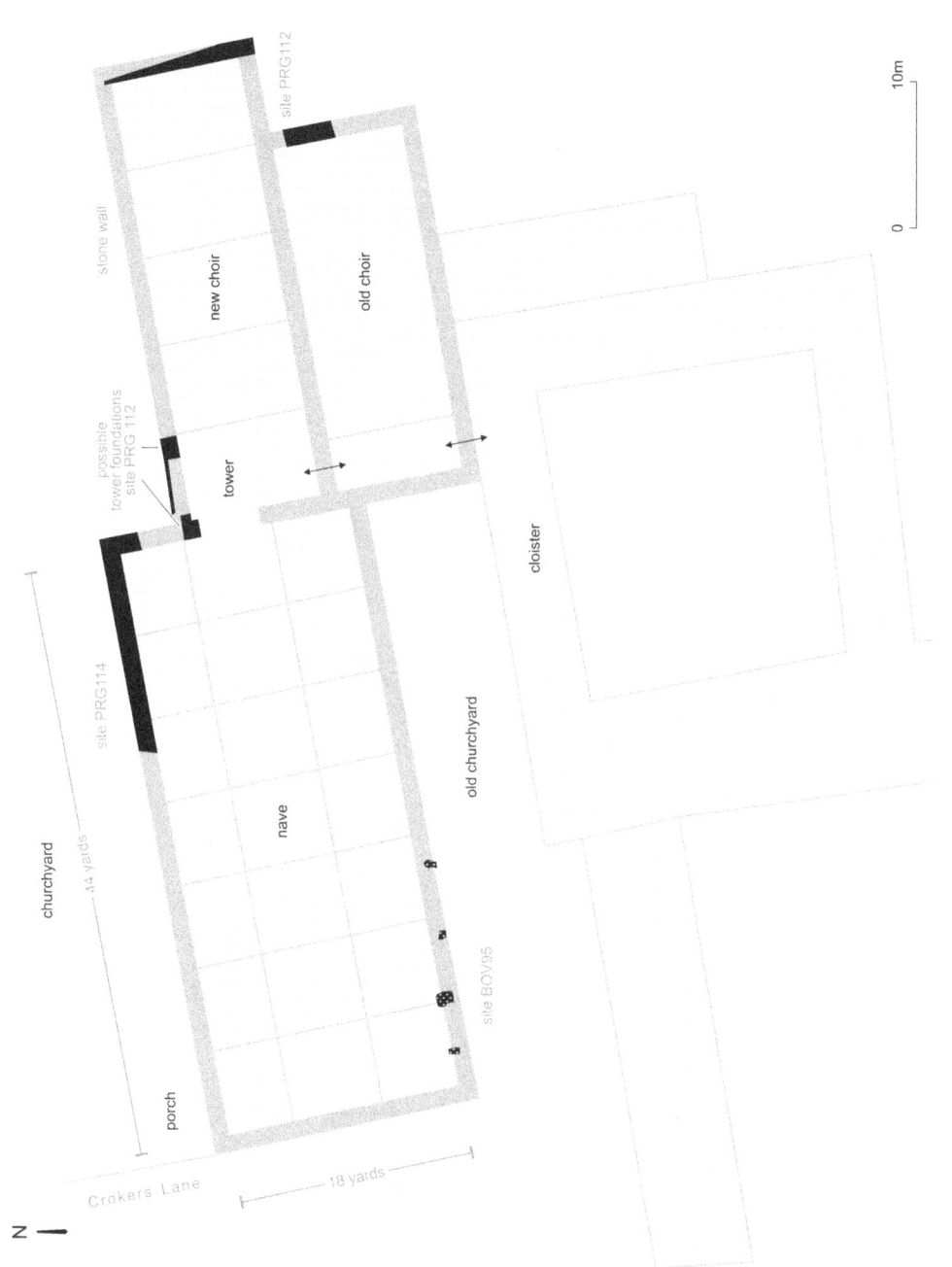

Fig. 35. Plan of the medieval church of White Friars (scale 1:500).

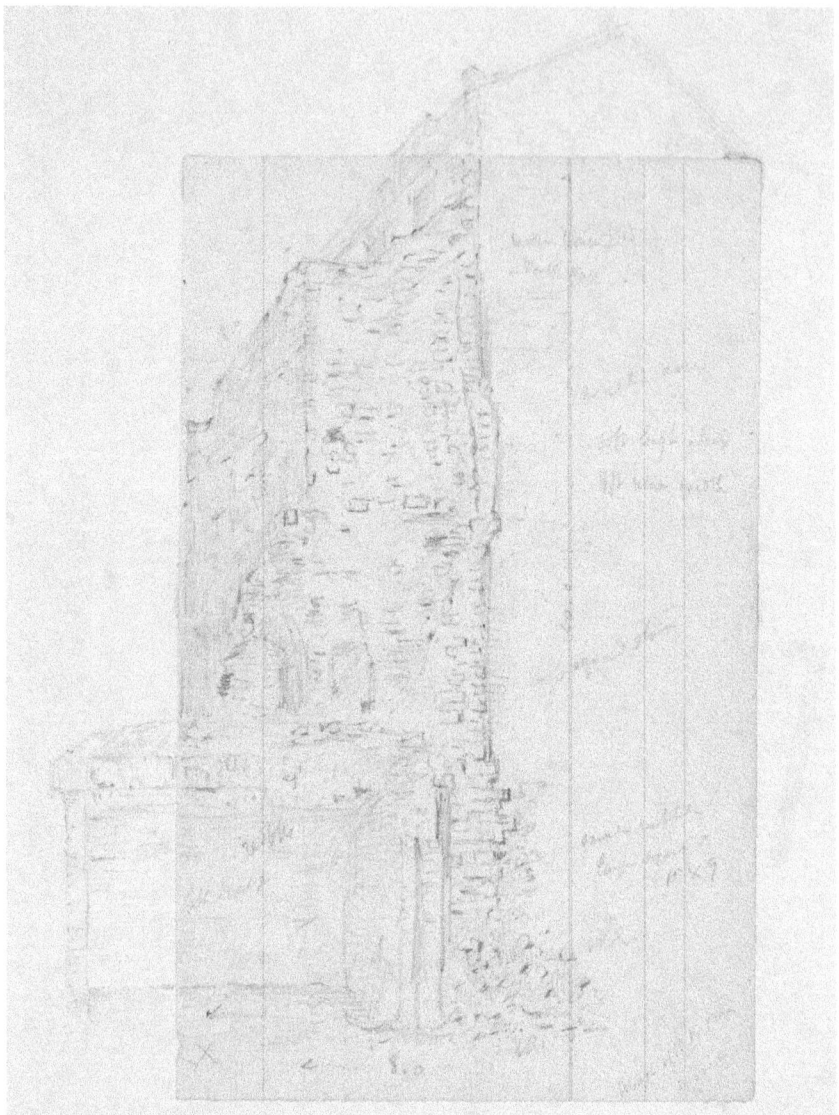

Fig. 36. Early 'rescue archaeology' by Henry Hodge in 1882: the north-east corner of the White Friars nave stands some 40ft high, exposed after demolition of a building; note the brick burial vault (bottom left). (London Metropolitan Archives, SC/PD/UNCAT/01)

marking the northern extent of a ruined property in 1669.[23] At the western end of the choir the substantial foundations encountered by the 1920s archaeologists might well be for the northern piers of a tower.[24] There is no documentary evidence for the size of the choir but

---

[23] Mills and Oliver, iii, 105v.

[24] W. Martin, 'The Excavation at Whitefriars, Fleet Street, 1927–8: Report of Committee', *Journal of the British Archaeological Association*, 30 (1927), 293–320 (p. 299).

the archaeological evidence suggests that it had internal dimensions of about 30.5m by 9.3m (100ft × 30ft).

Now we must turn to the original friars' church of the thirteenth century. The pattern at the other London friaries is that their original chapel or choir was the nucleus for the later choir, with the church simply expanding westwards or eastwards out from the first chapel and enveloping it. This does not appear to be the case at the White Friars. Here, an early sixteenth-century survey of the burial monuments in the church distinguished 'the ould quyre' and 'the New quire'. Furthermore, a post-Dissolution grant of 1540 (granting the area to the east of the cloister and south of the church) includes a yard described as being between the church and the old choir.[25] The impression of two separate choirs is reinforced when considering the relationship of the new church to the cloister (both have good evidence for their location): there is an unusual gap of about 8m (27ft) between nave and cloister. The original friars' church – the 'ould quyre' – must lie between the cloister and the new choir, and its east end is probably indicated by a wall discovered in the 1920s excavation (PRG112 on Figure 35). The western end of the old choir remains unknown but a reasonable guess is to align it with the offset between new choir and nave, imagining that the fourteenth-century builders, having been instructed to keep the old choir, simply worked around it (Figure 35). The resulting reconstruction suggests a double-aisled choir, with the old and the new builds side by side, probably linked by doors or a partly open arcade.[26] The west end of the old choir must have been screened to create a passage connecting the cloisters and the main church. The old choir thus formed a substantial side chapel to the newer choir, and functioned as a mausoleum to the early benefactors of the friary. A similar choice seems to have been made by the Carmelites of Norwich and Paris, who retained their old chapel by the cloister when they constructed a larger (and adjacent) church in the fourteenth century.[27]

Having established the basic outline of the old and new churches, the documentary evidence can elucidate something of their use and layout. In 1507 the judge Sir Robert Rede paid for renovations to the tower, described as worn out and old (although it can hardly

---

[25] BL, Harley MS 6033, ff. 9–10; TNA, C 66/700, m. 34.

[26] Clapham's and Martin's reconstructions of the church both have a narrow passage between old and new choirs: Clapham, 'Topography of the Carmelite Priory', plan between pp. 16–17; Martin, 'Excavation at Whitefriars', sheet 1. It is quite possible that such a passage existed but the model of a twin-aisled contiguous choir used here (Figure 35) creates a wider and more liturgically useful space, allowing more room for side altars and lay monuments (in both choirs). Both Clapham and Martin were influenced by the 1540 mention of a yard between church and old choir (cited in n. 25); this yard is, however, simply described as a parcel of vacant land in this location, not the dark and narrow alley some 6ft wide shown in Martin's plan.

[27] O'Sullivan, *In the Company of the Preachers*, pp. 71–3, 257–60; Lorentz and Sandron, *Atlas de Paris Au Moyen Âge*, pp. 150–1; Rachel Clarke, ed., *Norwich White Friars*, East Anglian Archaeology monograph (Chelmsford: East Anglian Archaeology, forthcoming). The Bristol Franciscans also kept their original chapel.

have been more than a century old).²⁸ Rede was paying for masses and anniversary services to be performed for his wife, his parents and (in the future) for himself. His advance payment of 120 marks perhaps funded a steeple and some new bells for the church (as well as repairs to the library and west window of the church). A 1545 survey of the church lead specifies that the tower was capped by a steeple – covered with an estimated five fothers of lead – but neither tower nor steeple survived by the time of the 'copperplate' map of the 1550s.²⁹ The survey also mentions a porch and 'lytle tower' (distinct from the steeple), presumably at the north-west end of the nave giving access to lay people walking to the friary church from Fleet Street.

The inside of the church with its large nave and double aisle must have been a complex space, with parts of the aisles subdivided by screens, altars and statues. There were distinct chapels dedicated to Saints Mary, Fabian and Sebastian. Several altars are attested in wills, such as those dedicated to Mary, the Trinity, St Anne and St Catherine, and testators also referred to other artworks inside the church including statues of the Virgin, St Anne, St Anthony, St Gratian and an unidentified 'seynt Gastayne', as well as a wall painting of St Christopher.³⁰ In 1544 the carpenter William Collyng was commissioned by the Court of Augmentations to give a valuation of the timberwork left in the main church (the old choir had been sold by then) and he noted several items including a rood screen with its upper crucifix: 'the particion in the bodie of the churche [rood screen], two pewes, 4 deskes, the stalles in the quere and the cros over the same, and 2 dores'.³¹ In addition to the screens and statues, visitors would have noticed the many monuments to patrons and benefactors of the priory, as well as the occasional and less ostentatious monument to former priors and other friars: about eighty burial monuments were recorded around this time by John Bale, John Stow and other early antiquarians.³² In addition to Rede's funding of a new west window for the nave, another testator paid for the restoration of the east window of the new choir.³³

The cloister

Work on the cloisters might have commenced in the 1290s (above: 'Acquiring and developing the friary'; Table 8). The cloisters appear to be mentioned for the first time in 1334 when a testator requested burial there. The chapter house is also first mentioned in the second quarter of the fourteenth century when the friary was used on occasion by the royal Chancery.³⁴ If the cloister is poorly documented in terms of written evidence, there is,

---

²⁸ TNA, E 328/274; J.H. Baker, 'Rede, Sir Robert (d. 1519)', *ODNB*, <http://www.oxforddnb.com/view/article/23247> [accessed 14 May 2015].
²⁹ TNA, E 314/54 [piece indexed as 'London and Middlesex: Whitefriars, lead at'].
³⁰ Evidence from wills collated in Röhrkasten, *Mendicant Houses*, pp. 508–9.
³¹ TNA, E 314/69, no. 29.
³² Steer, 'Royal and Noble Commemoration', p. 127.
³³ TNA, E 328/274; Röhrkasten, *Mendicant Houses*, p. 509.
³⁴ *Calendar of Wills Proved in the Court of Husting*, i, 410; Röhrkasten, 'Secular Uses', pp. 143–4.

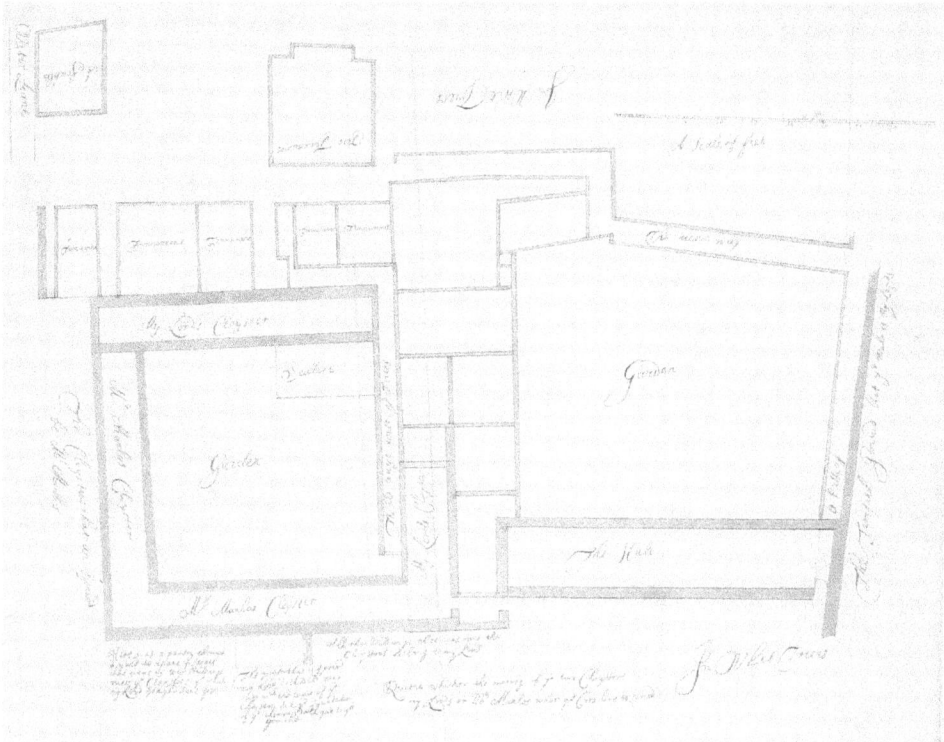

Fig. 37. Nineteenth-century copy of a survey of c. 1627 showing the area of the White Friars cloister. (© The British Library Board, Department of Maps, Crace, Portfolio 8, no. 104)

happily, some remarkable cartographic and archaeological evidence. A detailed survey of the seventeenth-century property was drawn, probably commissioned by the then owner Arthur Capel soon after 1627 (Figure 37). The majority of the four sides of the cloister walk still survived at that time, along with parts of the adjoining west and east building ranges. And in the 1920s, and again in the 1980s, parts of the eastern cloister range were archaeologically excavated. Although rather less of the medieval fabric survived in the twentieth century than in the seventeenth, the two sets of evidence, archaeological and cartographic, can be married quite easily (Figure 38; sites PRG112 and NOW87).[35] Most of the cloister range was two storeys high, with the upper floor oversailing the cloister walk (an annotation on the survey refers to 'all the buildings that was over the Cloysters'), but the northern cloister walk was presumably a single storey. Archaeological evidence shows that the cloister walks were paved with plain red tiles (site PRG112) and the seventeenth-century plan details a single quadripartite roof vault on an 11ft module (measured along the cloister walk), presumably indicating that all four cloister walks were similarly vaulted.

[35] The seventeenth-century plan (Figure 37) appears to survive only in a nineteenth-century copy: BL, Department of Maps, Crace, Portfolio 8, no. 104. The archaeological site PRG112 (see Figure 31) is reported in Martin, 'Excavation at Whitefriars'.

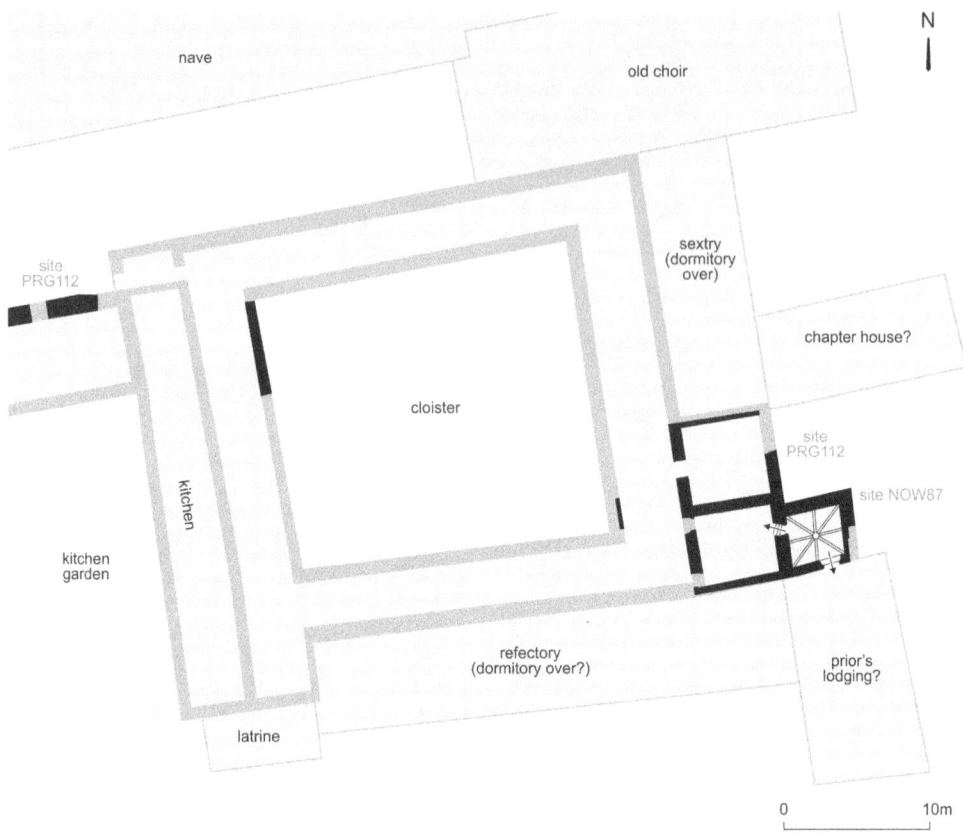

Fig. 38. Map showing the medieval cloister of White Friars (scale 1:500).

The evidence of post-Dissolution grants allows us to identify most of the components of the cloister, or at least how the friars used them in the sixteenth century. The northern wing was simply a cloister walk, without an attached or upper wing. Moving clockwise around the cloister, the eastern range housed the sextry (sacrist's office) with a dormitory above; the chapter house was also accessed through the east wing. There is little evidence for the shape and size of the chapter house: it is reconstructed here as if its southern wall was reused in a later building, surveyed after the Great Fire.[36] The south and west wings housed the refectory, another dormitory, a latrine and the kitchen: although the precise locations are not specified, the refectory and second dormitory probably occupied the south wing with the kitchen in the west.[37] Several friars had separate chambers by the early fourteenth century. According to the colourful evidence of the London eyre (circuit court) of 1321, the friar William Portehors carried out an audacious robbery in 1305 by concealing co-conspirators in his chamber and then knocking on the doors of other friars' chambers, tying them up and

---

[36] TNA, C 66/700, m. 34; Mills and Oliver, iii, 65v; v, 77.
[37] TNA, C 66/700, m. 11.

Fig. 39. Photograph of the fourteenth-century vaulted cellar beneath the Carmelite prior's house (compare Fig. 32). (Andy Chopping/MOLA)

locking them in his own (rather spacious) room while the gang robbed the friary treasury (which was temporarily flush with the money of a west country landowner who had deposited £300 for safekeeping)![38] Focusing on the architectural rather than the criminal details of this report, it would suggest that these individual chambers – not necessarily for all friars – were part of the original cloister design of the late thirteenth century (Table 8).

The friary building that has received most attention from archaeologists and architectural historians is a vaulted cellar adjacent to the south-east corner of the cloister. This was almost certainly part of the prior's house: 'le Priours lodging' was included in the post-Dissolution grant of the eastern claustral wing. A rather rare medieval survival in London, its existence was reported in *The Builder* in 1895, and the cellar was archaeologically investigated in 1928 and 1987.[39] After being lifted up on a crane and moved slightly in 1991 (Figure 32), it can now

---

[38] Summerson, 'Seen through the Eyes of the Law', p. 10.
[39] *The Builder*, Nov. 1895, p. 356; Clapham, 'Topography of the Carmelite Priory', p. 30; Martin,

be seen within the large 65 Fleet Street building complex (from Magpie Alley; Figure 39). The room is a vaulted chamber about 12ft square (3.5m × 3.8m), with eight limestone ribs that support a chalk or clunch vault: a late fourteenth-century date is the most likely. The ribs spring from the sides and corners and meet at a central boss decorated with a figure enclosed by a rose. A doorway with chamfered moulding in the south wall led to a second chamber, which has not survived. There was also a short set of spiral stairs rising to the west, which connected with the east range of the cloisters. The connecting door and chamber to the south suggest that the prior's house above was on a north–south axis and so the outline of the house has been reconstructed here using post-Great Fire survey evidence (Figure 38).[40]

The precinct

The Carmelites' 5-acre (2.1ha) precinct was bounded by a wall that was pierced by three gates and a Thames-side water-gate (Figure 34, Figure 40). The main gate lay on Fleet Street and it was still known as 'whitefryers gate' in the seventeenth century.[41] There was also 'Sergeanntes Ingate' in the north-west (adjacent to Serjeants' Inn), 'le estgate' on Water Lane and a water-gate or stairs giving access to the Thames.[42]

In the thirteenth century the friary's cemetery lay to the west of the old choir: archaeological excavation in Bouverie Street found graves that had been disturbed by the construction of the nave in the fourteenth century.[43] The construction of the new church must have pushed the cemetery further north, beyond the nave, so that visitors to the friary entering from Fleet Street walked southwards through or beside the cemetery (Figure 34). To the west of the cloister there lay a courtyard of buildings, nearly, but not quite, arranged as a second cloister. The open space may have formed a kitchen garden, to the west of the kitchen wing of the cloister proper. The most important building here was the library (Figure 34). This appears on the seventeenth-century survey (annotated as 'the hale') and several of its walls were discovered in the *Daily News* building excavations of the 1920s. The library lay to the west of the cloister (it is included in the post-Dissolution grant of this area) and the mapped and excavated dimensions of 'the hall' match those in a 1545

'Excavation at Whitefriars', pp. 308, 315; Sidney Toy, 'The Crypt at Whitefriars, London', *Journal of the British Archaeological Association*, 37 (1932), 334–6; Sidney Toy, *Building Report by Mr. Sidney Toy, F.S.A., F.R.I.B.A., on the Excavations at Whitefriars, Fleet Street, 1927–8, London* (London: News of the World, no date [1930s?]); RCHME, *Inventory of the Historical Monuments in London*, 5 vols (London: HMSO, 1924–30), iv (*The City*), 160–1. Architectural recording (photographs and drawings by A. Wittrick) in LAA, NOW87; Historic England London office, registered file AA 053413/2.

[40] Only the properties immediately to the east and south of the prior's house can be traced in the post-Fire surveys: Mills and Oliver, v, 101, 124.

[41] Mills and Oliver, iii, 98v.

[42] TNA, SC 6/Hen VIII/2396, ff. 57–9; C 66/708, m. 35.

[43] LAA, BOV95, '10 Bouverie Street, London EC4, an archaeological excavation and watching brief', B. Barber (unpublished Museum of London report, 1997), pp. 10, 19.

document referring to the library (the length of the building in the seventeenth-century drawn survey is 29.6m; the length stated in the 1545 document is 32 yards (29.3m)).[44] This long fourteenth-century library with study desks and a hundred or more books was perhaps lit by high south- and north-facing windows (above).

Continuing our imagined tour of the friary, southwards from the library and across the kitchen garden there was probably another chapel, named as St Nicholas' chapel in documents of the 1530s and '40s.[45] It cannot be located with certainty but the seventeenth-century survey shows a lane to the west of the cloister and south of the library ('the newe way') with a noticeable 'dog-leg', as though it went around a large building in this location (Figure 37). Continuing down the slope towards the Thames, the next building is the infirmary (Figure 34). There is a fortuitous combination of evidence for this building: its location is known thanks to abutments recorded in a 1536 lease; the building is then described in a lease of 1577 and it was surveyed in a plan of c. 1658; finally, parts of the building were excavated in 1923. The building had three storeys: a ground floor consisting of a large infirmary hall and a kitchen and larder; a first floor containing at least two chambers; and an upper storey of garret rooms. There was also a cellar, a yard with a privy and shed, and an infirmary garden with a water pump.[46] To the south of the infirmary, the Clothworkers' Company (with the agreement of the friary and in partnership with the enterprising and upwardly mobile sponsor Margaret, countess of Kent) built a late addition to the friary in 1536: a row of almshouses for poor widows of the company. The almshouses were close by an earlier friary building, the Carmelite school or *studium generale* that prepared friars for university study: the 1536 almshouses were erected in the 'place sometyme called the skollers gardeyne' (Chapter 16: Spiritual Life and Education in the London Friaries).[47] The school may therefore be the large building to the east that was surveyed after the Great Fire.[48]

The south-east corner of the precinct was the service court of the friary. The brew-house

---

[44] TNA, C 66/700, m. 11 [1541 grant]; TNA, E 314/54 ('London and Middlesex: Whitefriars, lead at') [1545 written survey]; annotation 'the hale' on BL, Department of Maps, Crace, Portfolio 8, no. 104 (Figure 37).

[45] The chapel formed part of the property block leased in 1538 and then purchased in 1545 by Thomas West, Baron de la Warr: TNA, E 303/9 no. 175; C 66/740, mm. 29–30; Holder, 'Medieval Friaries of London', pp. 136–7.

[46] Aspects of the cited arrangements of the rooms or garden could of course be sixteenth- or seventeenth-century rather than medieval: Gerhold, *London Plotted*, pp. 86–8, plan 27, fig. 88; Clothworkers' Company (CC), CL/A/4/4 (Book of Deeds and Wills), pp. 51–2 [1536 lease]; CL/G/7/1 (Plan Book), f. 42 [plan of c. 1658; alternative numbering: f. 59]; Martin, 'Excavation at Whitefriars', p. 317. A parliamentary survey of 1653 may also describe the former infirmary: TNA, E 317/Middx/15.

[47] Holder, 'Medieval Friaries of London', pp. 128–9. The foundation lease is dated 15 October 28 Henry VIII [1536] and refers to 'all houses & buyldynges lately sett buylt and edyfied upon the same': CC, MS CL/A/4/4 (Book of Deeds and Wills), pp. 51–4; John Schofield, *The London Surveys of Ralph Treswell* (London: London Topographical Society, 1987), pp. 129–30, no. 44.

[48] Mills and Oliver, ii, 85.

Fig. 40. Detail of the 'copperplate' map-view of the 1550s showing White Friars shortly after the Dissolution. (© Museum of London, drawing from plate in Anhalt Art Gallery, Dessau)

was there by the early sixteenth century: in 1522 it was leased to Hilary Warner, brewer, and the lease names Anthony Kyngynge and Michael Buck, also brewers, as Warner's predecessors. Warner seems to have enlarged the brewery at this time: a later grant notes 'the houses and buildings that Hilary [Warner] built' near the brewery and these may be the houses around a large yard surveyed after the Great Fire (Figure 34).[49] Was one of these buildings a bake-house? There was also a mill next to the brewery and its Thames-side location rather implies that this was a tide-mill rather than a horse-mill or windmill. Two sixteenth-century buildings and other features discovered here in the Tudor Street excavation may

[49] TNA, E 315/191, no. 63 (second item); C 66/708, m. 35 [grant of 1541]; Mills and Oliver, ii, 58v; iii, 10v, 158v.

be associated with the mill, although the dating evidence is not precise enough to be sure that they are *pre*-Dissolution (Figure 34; site WFT99 on Figure 31).[50] The inlet at the south-east of the precinct (known in the early seventeenth century as 'the dock at waterlane'; Figure 34) could therefore have originated as a millpond, perhaps created at the end of the fourteenth century as part of the new river wall and land reclamation scheme?[51] The mill and the brewery complex are illustrated in their post-Dissolution state in the 'copperplate' map-view of the 1550s, which shows three north–south aligned gabled buildings near the waterfront, with two smaller buildings to the north (Figure 40). The inlet is also suggested in this view, where Water Lane seems to merge with the Thames.

The south-west corner of the precinct must have been a calmer place for the friars because it was the site of the friary's extensive gardens. These included the main friary garden ('le covent garden'), subdivided into smaller rented gardens by the time of the Dissolution. By 1527 the friars even had their own summer-house or 'pleasure house' (to use a seventeenth-century term), down by the banks of the Thames: 'a littell house made upon the waters syde used for the recreacion and comfort of the freers'. The 'Cookes gardine' lay just to the east, probably between the convent garden and the brew-house, according to a 1541 document.[52]

The friars owned a quarter-acre (0.1ha) block of property on Fleet Street next to their precinct that they rented out as shops and houses. They began to acquire and develop this in the fourteenth century and by the sixteenth century it was worth £29 10s in annual rents. By the sixteenth century, perhaps earlier, the friars had begun renting out tenements and gardens within the precinct as well: these were worth another £46 11s 8d, making a substantial total rental income of £76 1s 8d (Chapter 18: London Friars and Londoners).[53]

Conclusion

In many ways the Carmelites had an easier job building a London friary than the other mendicants; rather than beginning with one or two small urban tenements, the White friars had a whole field on the western edge of London. Once the Black friars moved within the city walls in the late thirteenth century (Chapter 2: The Second Black Friars), the White friars were the only mendicants left outside. Furthermore, they were able to enlarge their (former) field over the fourteenth century, not so much through the usual method of

---

[50] The mill is described as 'a certain house above a mill leading to the entrance to the brew-house': *quadam dom[us] supra molendum ducentem iuxta introitum sive le entre abinde ducentem usque le brewhouse*; see n. 49 [1541 grant]; archaeological evidence discussed in Killock, 'An archaeological excavation at Whitefriars'.

[51] For land reclamation, see above, 'Acquiring and developing the friary'; for the 'dock at waterlane', see LMA, CLA/008/EM/02/01/001 (City Lands grant book 1), f. 125v.

[52] TNA, SC 6/Hen VIII/2396, f. 58v; BL, Harley charters 79.F.32; TNA, E 315/191, no. 63 (second item).

[53] Holder, 'Medieval Friaries of London', pp. 262–3, table 18.

persuading sponsors to donate adjacent tenements, but through reclaiming land from the Thames. In one huge engineering operation of 1396 the friars enlarged their precinct by a quarter, increasing their land holding from 4 to 5 acres (1.6ha to 2.1ha).

The Carmelites' church also seems to have been slightly unusual. Like their fellow friars, they began in the thirteenth century with a small church or chapel. But whereas the other mendicants quickly enlarged their first church, extending it in length, breadth and height, the White friars kept their simple chapel, then built themselves a 'proper' monastic church next door in the fourteenth century, a church some 245ft (75m) long. This may be something of a Carmelite tradition: the White friars of Norwich and Paris seem to have done something similar. Is this some sort of practical combination of the mendicant ideal of the small hermitage with the urban reality of the large preaching church filled with the tombs and altars of lay sponsors? Rather than compromising on their monastic ideals, the Carmelites were, so to speak, having their cake and eating it.

As has been seen, in order to understand the core of the friary precinct we are still reliant on the impressive work of the early twentieth-century archaeologist and historian Alfred Clapham, in particular, his archaeological analysis of the church and his discovery of a seventeenth-century plan of the cloister. This chapter has drawn a little more of the picture of the rest of the friary, including buildings beyond the cloister such as the library, infirmary and school. And in the service court at the south of the precinct, the friars' brewer and tenant Hilary Warner may have redeveloped the area in the early sixteenth century: perhaps in a joint venture with the friary he seems to have created a part-private commercial zone, one that included a brewery and a mill (quite possibly a tide-mill), all with separate access via the river.

It is possible to picture the friars walking in contemplation around their gardens and vaulted cloister walks, or looking out at the lighters and cargo boats on the Thames from their riverside summer-house, built 'for the recreacion and comfort of the freers'. Of course, the friars' work and leisure (not to mention their buildings) were mostly paid for by Londoners, whether from the £76 of rental income that the friars received in the sixteenth century, or the £10 to £20 they received each year in bequests.[54] On top of this there would have been all the other contracts for what might be termed spiritual services, such as funeral processions and anniversary masses. In the absence of a surviving friary archive we can only guess at the amounts these raised each year but, on occasion, these were substantial sums, for example in 1507 when the judge Sir Robert Rede bequeathed 120 marks (£80).[55]

[54] Röhrkasten, *Mendicant Houses*, pp. 270–3.
[55] TNA, E 328/274.

6

Austin Friars, c. 1265–1538

IN the second quarter of the thirteenth century groups of Tuscan hermits were forming, a generation after St Francis' band of poor itinerant preachers and St Dominic's group of anti-heretical preachers.[1] Agreeing to follow the rule of St Augustine, the hermits came together and became a new mendicant order of friars in 1256, the Order of Augustinian Hermits. With this background, the interests and the inclinations of the brothers faced in different directions: the hermit tradition demanded isolation and favoured rural settings; the newer mendicant movement emphasised preaching and therefore lived more happily in towns. The hermits had reached England before their formal unification, probably establishing their first English house on the edge of the small Suffolk wool town of Clare by 1249. From this base the order spread to numerous English towns in the second half of the century, and the order and its houses became known as the Augustinian or Austin friars.[2]

The Augustinian friars probably established their London house in the 1260s, slightly later than the date of 1253 given by the Tudor historian John Stow. Significantly, the Augustine friars – unlike the other mendicant orders – are *not* included in a list of recipients of royal alms given in Lent 1260. The first definite mention of this order of friars in London comes in 1271.[3] Stow names Humphrey de Bohun, earl of Hereford and Essex, as the founder of the friary and de Bohun also made substantial gifts of land to other religious houses in England and Wales. Perhaps he founded the London house in or soon after 1265

---

[1] Some of the material in this chapter has been previously published in Nick Holder, Mark Samuel and Ian Betts, 'The Church and Cloisters of Austin Friars', *Transactions of the London and Middlesex Archaeological Society*, 64 (2013), 143–62.

[2] Francis Roth, *The English Austin Friars, 1249–1538*, 2 vols (New York: Augustinian Historical Institute, 1961) i, 18–22, 259–60; Andrews, *The Other Friars*, pp. 101–2.

[3] The suggestion was made by Röhrkasten, *Mendicant Houses*, pp. 54–5; *CCR 1259–1261*, pp. 238–9. The 1271 document is LMA, GL MS 25121/1590, printed in Roth, *English Austin Friars*, ii, 42.

when he was the royalist keeper of the city of London, guarding against a potential attack by Simon de Montfort (another friary founder!) and the barons.[4]

The friary housed about sixty friars by the end of the thirteenth century. Although fluctuating and temporarily declining as a result of the Black Death, the numbers were broadly maintained throughout the fourteenth century but then fell in the fifteenth century. The friary was probably reasonably financially stable, having a rental income of nearly £60 by the sixteenth century, and receiving good support in the bequests given by Londoners in their wills.[5] Unique among the London friaries, there is a surviving page of sixteenth-century accounts listing the money given by the province to the order's prior general in Rome; this source will be examined in a later chapter (Chapter 15: Economy).

The friary was used by Londoners in a variety of ways, in addition to its valuable function as a place of burial and commemoration. As well as coming to the friary to hear preaching, groups of Londoners used it for guild and fraternity meetings, including the Pewterers' Company and Pouchmakers' Company (both in the late fifteenth century).[6] The friary had particularly close relations with some of London's alien populations, especially the Italians (most of whom lived in the north-east of the city) and, to a lesser extent, the Germans. The fact that alien friars came to England to study was key because such native speakers often stayed in London and acted as confessors and preachers to their own countrymen. In 1427 John Frederici was given permission by the prior general to leave Oxford (where he was studying) and go to London to preach to and hear confession from Germans and Flemings.[7]

If the Dominican friary housed one of the crucial stages on which the English Reformation began (the setting for the cardinals' hearing into the proposed divorce of Henry and Catherine in 1529; Chapter 2: The Second Black Friars), Austin Friars was the location for act two of the drama. From the 1520s the friary was the London home of Wolsey's and then Henry's rising administrator Thomas Cromwell. In a sense, therefore, draft bills for the Reformation Parliament of 1529–36 had their origin in Austin Friars, as did the emerging plans for the Dissolution of the Monasteries in the second half of the decade. The prior George Brown (later provincial prior) was an ally of Cromwell and he

---

[4] Stow, *Survey of London*, i, 177; Röhrkasten, *Mendicant Houses*, pp. 54–5; Barron and Davies, *Religious Houses*, pp. 133–6; Nicholas Vincent, 'Bohun, Humphrey (IV) de, Second Earl of Hereford and Seventh Earl of Essex (d. 1275)', *ODNB*, <http://www.oxforddnb.com/view/article/2775> [accessed 12 May 2016].

[5] Röhrkasten, *Mendicant Houses*, pp. 80–2, 257–78; Roth, *English Austin Friars*, i, 289; Virginia Davis, 'Mendicants in London in the Reign of Richard II', *London Journal*, 25.2 (2000), 1–12 (pp. 8–9).

[6] TNA, LR 15/12; Roth, *English Austin Friars*, ii, no. 948.

[7] For Italians, see Helen L. Bradley, 'Italian Merchants in London 1350–1450' (unpublished doctoral dissertation, University of London, 1992), pp. 17–20, 30, 43–4, 54–5. For the German connections see Roth, *English Austin Friars*, ii, no. 747; another example is a 1496 agreement between the prior and an 'alman' fraternity called the 'brethern and susters of the fraternite of seint Sebastian'; TNA, LR 15/13.

was one of the commissioners appointed to visit the English mendicant houses in 1534.[8] Two leading Reformers of the order spent time in the London house in the 1520s and 1530s: Robert Barnes and Miles Coverdale.[9] The house surrendered in November 1538: prior Thomas Hamond and twelve friars signed the document and left the friary to find employment as priests or clerks (only Hamond could claim a pension).[10] The precinct was divided into various plots for lease and sale in the late 1530s and '40s: Thomas Cromwell and the courtier William Paulet acquired the two largest parts of the friary.

There is a very good range of sources to help us understand this London friary. Most notably, the nave of the church survived into the twentieth century as the Dutch Church, only to be destroyed by a parachute mine in October 1940. Although the loss is regrettable, there is fortunately a body of published and unpublished architectural studies on the church (below: 'The church'). A wide range of documentary records survive, including the order's archives in Rome, which have been combed for information relating to the medieval friars in England.[11] A handful of the friary's medieval property records survive in the archive of the Drapers' Company, who purchased part of the friary in 1543. Finally, a number of twentieth-century archaeological excavations allow us to understand the arrangement of the friary's cloisters and choir (Figure 41).

Acquiring and developing the friary

The foundation grant of Humphrey de Bohun must have been a large piece of land on the west side of Broad Street and he may also have granted the friars the small parish church of St Olave Broad Street. Both church and parish were soon to vanish from the records of London: the church was taken over by the friars and the parish was subsumed into the neighbouring parish of St Peter. In order to understand the early history of the friary we need briefly to examine the evidence for the two parishes and churches.

Before the friars came to the area there were two parish churches along Broad Street: St Peter and St Olave, both described with the suffix 'Broad Street' (Figure 42). St Peter is first mentioned in a late twelfth-century inventory when it was one of twenty parish churches belonging to St Paul's cathedral.[12] The evidence discussed below ('The church') suggests

---

[8] Roth, *English Austin Friars*, ii, no. 1090; *Letters and Papers*, vii(1), no. 587 (18).
[9] Cater, 'Priory of Austin Friars', 62–7; Susan Brigden, *London and the Reformation* (Oxford: Clarendon Press, 1989), p. 159.
[10] *Letters and Papers*, xiii(2), no. 806 (p. 320).
[11] Roth, *English Austin Friars*.
[12] LMA, GL MS 25504, f. 87 ('Liber L'), printed in W. Sparrow Simpson, 'Visitations of Certain Churches in the City of London in the Patronage of St Paul's Cathedral Church, between the Years 1138 and 1250', *Archaeologia*, 55 (1897), 283–300 (p. 295). The church's later dedication to St Peter *the Poor* is not entirely clear, although this early inventory does indeed suggest that it was one of the London diocese's most poorly furnished and equipped churches: there were few books, only four altar palls and not even one chalice (cf the other inventoried London churches in the table on p. 290).

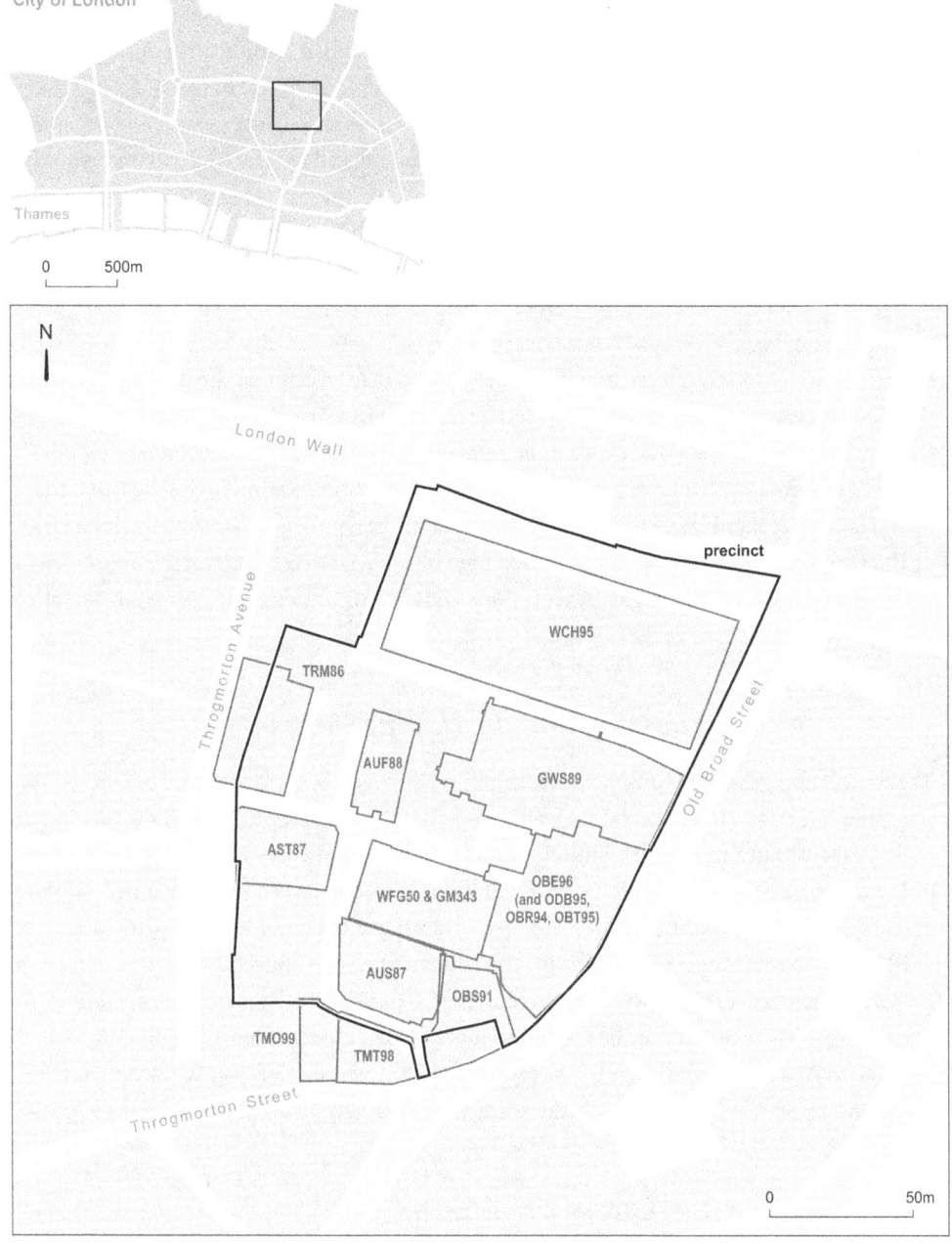

Fig. 41. Map showing the location of the Austin Friars and archaeological sites within its precinct (scale 1:2500).

that the medieval church of St Peter later formed the south aisle of the choir of Austin Friars; it is also likely to have occupied this approximate position before the friary was built (Figure 42). St Olave Broad Street is harder to locate: unlike St Peter it is not included in the c. 1181 document but both churches appear in a mid-thirteenth-century list stating

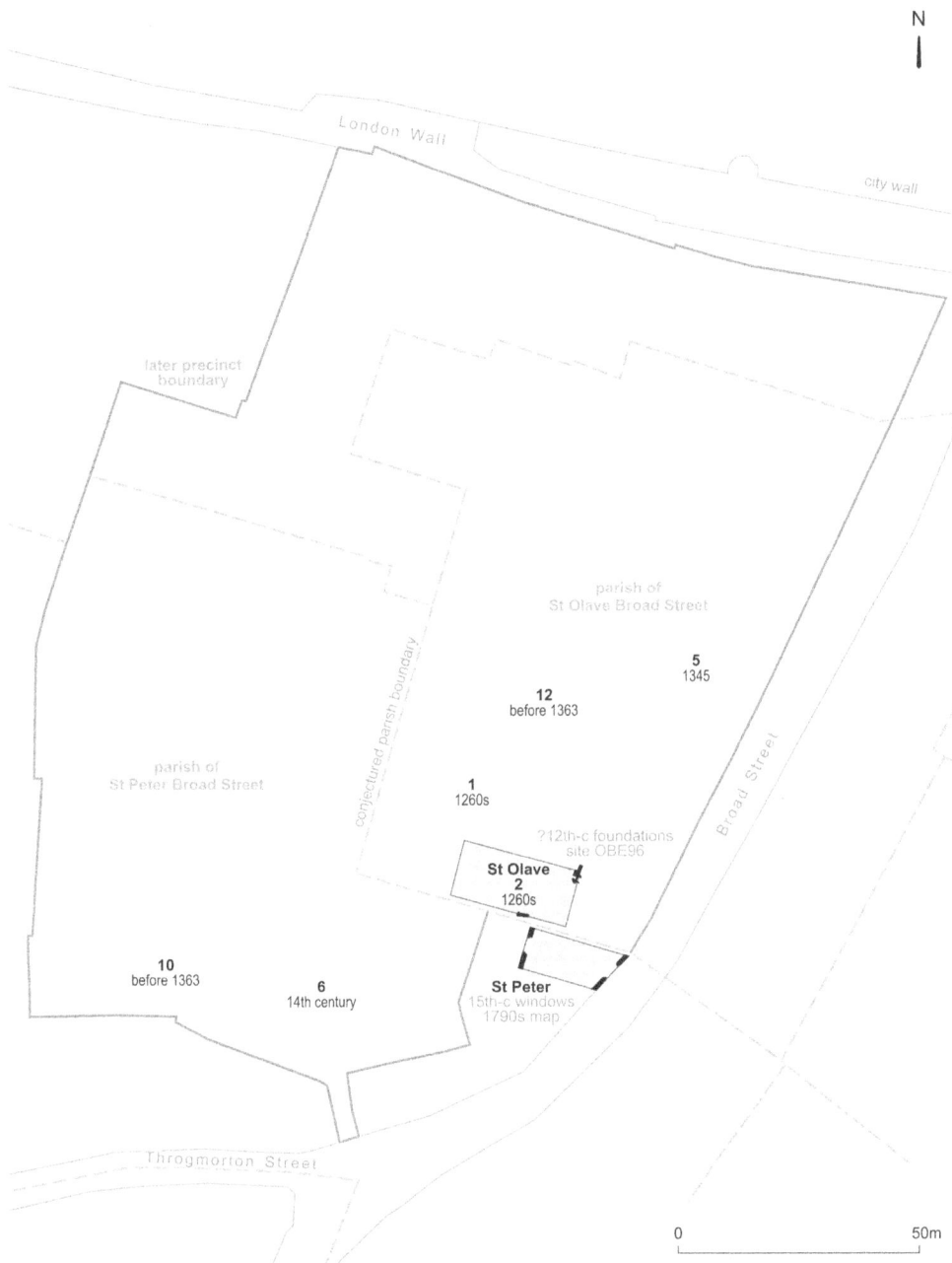

Fig. 42. Map showing the area of Broad Street in the thirteenth century before the arrival of the Austin friars. Note the evidence for the two parishes and churches of St Peter and St Olave. Locations of some tenements acquired by the friary are also shown (see Table 9 for tenement numbers) (scale 1:1500).

the financial obligations of parish churches to St Paul's.[13] The arrival of the Austin friars seems to have brought about the demise of St Olave's because a document of 1271 records the annual payment of 3s by the friars to the archdeacon of St Paul's as compensation 'for the land and appurtenances where the parish church of St Olave Broad Street, which had been granted to us [i.e. to St Paul's], used to be'.[14] It seems likely, therefore, that the church was converted into the friars' first chapel and it is quite possible that it lay on the site later occupied by the main body of the friary choir. Archaeological excavations on Broad Street provide a little evidence to back up this hypothesis: two fragments of medieval chalk foundation predate the northern aisle of the friary choir (site OBE96). The dating evidence for these two fragments of foundation is limited but one of them was dug through a layer containing twelfth- or early thirteenth-century pottery, suggesting that the foundations were not dug until the late twelfth or thirteenth century.[15] Might they be the remains of the original parish church of St Olave? If the church was taken by the friars in the 1260s, the parish was presumably amalgamated with the adjacent parish of St Peter, thus forming one of the largest parishes within the city walls (the evidence for the church and the suggested parish boundary are illustrated on Figure 42).

After Humphrey de Bohun's foundation grant of land on Broad Street, only another ten or so donations can be traced in the surviving records (Table 9). This low number must surely reflect the lack of surviving sources rather than be a true reflection of the tenements that the friars acquired since, to achieve a similarly sized precinct, the Grey friars required twenty-seven tenements (Chapter 4: Grey Friars). It was St Paul's that granted the church of St Olave to the friars and it is likely that de Bohun (or another sponsor) compensated the cathedral for this loss to its endowed estate. Very few of the remaining ten known gifts of land can be located: most seem to be tenements on the west side of Broad Street or land north of Throgmorton Street (Figure 42). By the mid fourteenth century the friars had used these urban plots (and no doubt others) to create a precinct of over 5½ acres (2.3ha).[16]

The early priors of the London house came from the order's first priory in Suffolk, and William de Clare (documented in 1279, perhaps the first London prior) and Richard de Clare (documented in 1310) must have had a difficult job gathering the expensive London

---

[13] LMA, GL MS 25509, f. 49v [*sancti Olavi de bradestrat*]; f. 52 [*sancti petri de Bradestrete*].

[14] *pro area & pertinentiis, ubi consuevit esse parochialis ecclesia sancti Olavi in Bradestrete nobis concesa*: LMA, GL MS 25121/1590, printed in Roth, *English Austin Friars*, ii, no. 42.

[15] LAA, site OBE96, G. Bruce, 'An archaeological excavation and watching brief on the site of 109–118 Old Broad Street, City of London EC2' (unpublished AOC Archaeology report, 1997). The archaeological evidence is reinterpreted in Holder, 'Church and Cloisters of Austin Friars'.

[16] The precinct boundary can be traced on Ogilby and Morgan's map of 1676 (the north-western part of the precinct) and on a mid-seventeenth-century Drapers' Company plan (south-west of precinct); Drapers' Company (DC), A XII 121. See also Marjorie B. Honeybourne, 'The Extent and Value of the Property in London and Southwark Occupied by the Religious Houses' (unpublished MA dissertation, University of London, 1929), pp. 191–205.

Table 9 List of the tenements acquired by the Austin friars for their friary.

Number on Figure 42	Date of acquisition	Grantor	Description	Reference
1	1260s	Humphrey de Bohun	land to west of Broad Street	Stow, *Survey of London*, i, 177
2	1260s	Humphrey de Bohun and St Paul's cathedral?	church of St Olave Broad Street	GL, MS 25121/1590
3	1281 or 1282	Robert Burnell, bishop of Bath and Wells	land in London	TNA, LR 14/583
4	1334	John de Haudlo[a]	land in parish of St Peter	TNA, LR 14/85; DC, A I 34; *CPR 1334–1338*, p. 31
5	1345	Reginald de Cobham	three tenements on Broad Street	DC, A I 44, 45; *CPR 1343–1345*, p. 458; Röhrkasten, *Mendicant* Houses, p. 56
6	14th century	William de Yorke, farrier of London	'garden with trees' in parish of St Peter	DC, A I 40
7	1310s or '20s	prior of St Mary Bishopsgate[b]	tenement formerly of Isabelle, daughter of Gerard Bat	TNA, C 66/267, m. 20; *CPR 1361–1364*, pp. 329–30
8	1330s	prior of St Mary Bishopsgate[c]	tenement formerly of Arnold le Tanner	TNA, C 66/267, m. 20
9	before 1363 (before 1349?)	unknown, perhaps St Mary Bishopsgate	tenement formerly of Hugh Moton	TNA, C 66/267, m. 20; *Cal. Inquis. Misc. 1348–1377*, p. 17, no. 42
10		unknown, perhaps St Mary Bishopsgate	tenement formerly of Peter le Coefrer	
11		John de Hereford, citizen of London	tenement formerly of William de Parys	
12		John de Bradeford and Isabelle his wife	tenements in Froggemerestrete in St Olave's Lane	

Notes:

[a] The grant refers to the grantor as 'de Haudlo' rather than 'de Handlo': the writer used distinct letter forms for 'u' and 'n': TNA, LR 14/85

[b] This mortmain certificate names the prior of St Mary Bishopsgate as William de Heston: other sources name him as prior in c. 1317 and 1327; Christopher Thomas, Barney Sloane and Christopher Phillpotts, *Excavations at the Priory and Hospital of St Mary Spital, London*, MoLAS monograph, 1 (London: Museum of London Archaeology Service, 1997), pp. 180–1.

[c] Prior named as John de Abiton, occurs c. 1335 and 1337; see n. b.

tenements to create their friary and paying for the construction of the first buildings.[17] However, William de Clare may have had it easier than the other London priors when it came to building the first friary church: as has been stated, he seems to have taken over and adapted the existing parish church of St Olave. Construction works continued into the 1270s: in 1277 the king granted six oaks from Windsor Forest, quite possibly for the roof of an enlarged church.[18] The next project seems to have been the cloisters. There is no specific documentary evidence but architectural fragments from the first cloister suggest a date of construction around the turn of the thirteenth and fourteenth centuries (below: 'The cloister').

Having a church to house the friars at prayer and a cloister to give them food and shelter, the prior – perhaps Thomas de Dunolm or John de Ardern – now turned his attention to a preaching nave to attract lay Londoners to the friary. The building campaign on the nave must have begun by the second quarter of the fourteenth century: a testator of 1343 bequeathed money in his will for 'the works on the church of Austin Friars' and six years later a financial agreement was made with the rector of the local parish of St Peter concerning tithes. The friars were presumably attending to the spiritual needs of local lay people and had reached an agreement with the local parish; this would suggest that the friars now had a functioning nave and burial ground. The works on the nave restarted after the Black Death and continued into the early 1370s: a descendant of the original founder Humphrey de Bohun made a generous bequest of 300 marks to the friary in 1361 (and was duly buried here), and wills of 1369, 1370 and 1371 record donations to pay for windows, suggesting that the nave was finally being completed.[19]

The final component of the friars' ambitious plans for their precinct was a second cloister, situated in a more secluded position to the north of the first cloister. The evidence of architectural fragments discovered in recent excavations suggests that this was begun in the last quarter of the fourteenth century, after the completion of the nave, and there is also evidence that the first cloister was modernised at this time (Chapter 12: Architecture and Architectural Fragments of the London Friaries). Work on this second cloister continued into the fifteenth century and in 1419 permission for the construction of a new infirmary was granted by the order's prior general. The northern cloister was probably completed by the middle of the century: construction works on the library were taking place at this time and a new set of rules for the library was agreed in 1456.[20] By the middle of the fifteenth century the friary was complete, the culmination of a two-century building campaign (Figure 43).

---

[17] Barron and Davies, *Religious Houses*, pp. 133–6.; see list of priors on p. 136.
[18] TNA, C 54/94, m. 6.
[19] Röhrkasten, *Mendicant Houses*, p. 510; Roth, *English Austin Friars*, ii, 381; Barron and Davies, *Religious Houses*, p. 134; *Calendar of Wills Proved and Enrolled in the Court of Husting*, ii, 134.
[20] TNA, LR 14/86; Roth, *English Austin Friars*, i, 106–7, 289, 374; ii, nos 713, 839.

AUSTIN FRIARS, C. 1265–1538   127

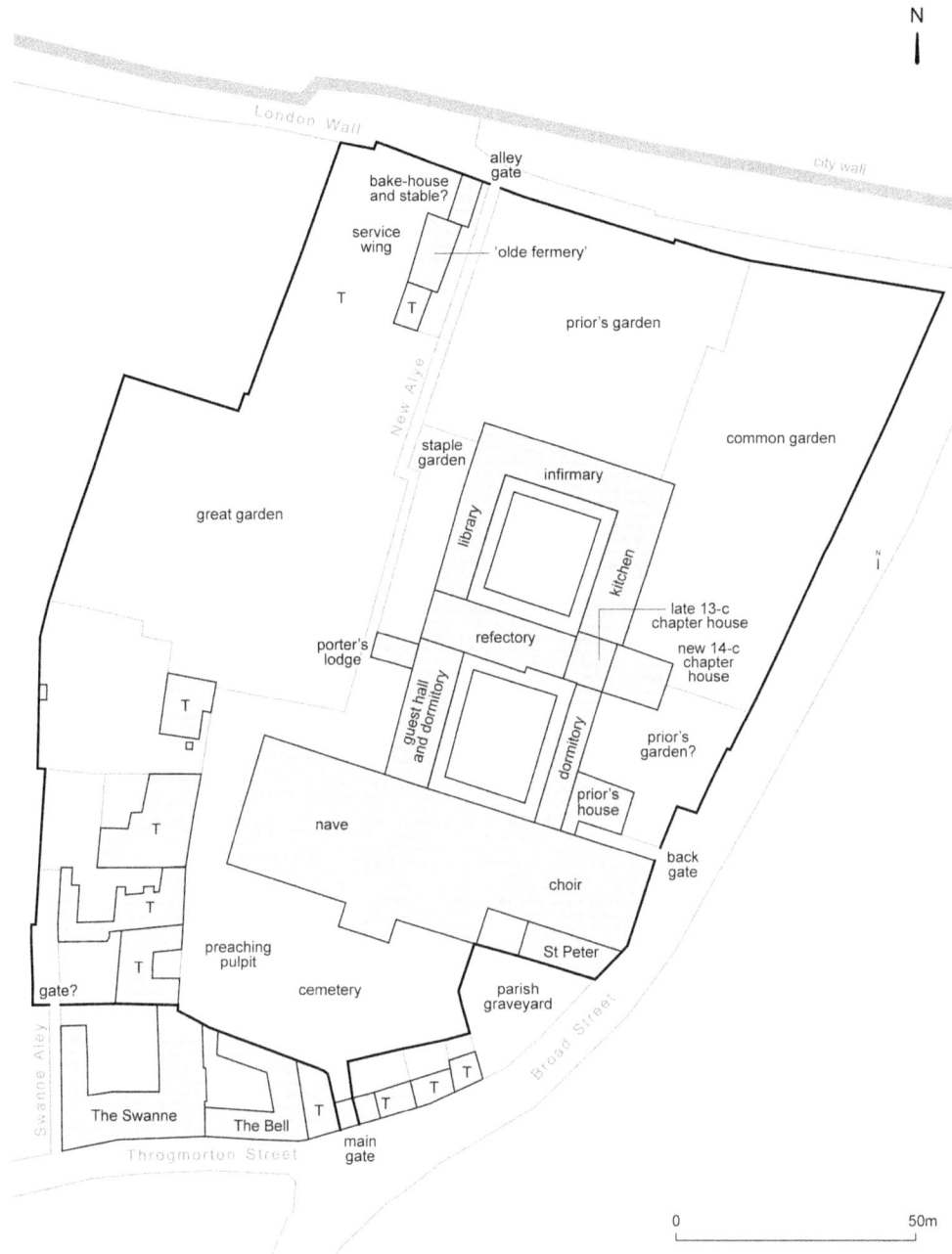

Fig. 43. Map of the precinct of Austin Friars in the sixteenth century (scale 1:1500).

The church

The documentary evidence just discussed suggests that the friars' church contained a thirteenth-century core that was enlarged to form the choir in the 1270s, with the nave added in the fourteenth century. To understand the church in more detail we need to start by examining it in two halves – nave and choir – with rather different sets of evidence.

After the Dissolution of the Monasteries, the Protestant government of Edward VI granted the nave of the friary church to a congregation of Reformed aliens, many of whom were religious refugees from the German-speaking areas of the Holy Roman Empire. This 'Temple of the Lord Jesus' of 1550 became known as the Dutch Church thanks to the links of its first pastor, John à Lasco, with Frisia (an area that spans the modern German/Dutch border). By the twentieth century the church was one of the few surviving treasures of medieval London, until, that is, the night of 15/16 October 1940 when an enemy parachute mine detonated and destroyed virtually all the fabric of the building.[21] Fortunately, the church had been extensively studied before its destruction, including an important description of the building before its renovation in the 1860s and a detailed architectural study by the Royal Commission on the Historical Monuments of England.[22] And, following its destruction, the pioneering post-war rescue archaeologist W.F. 'Peter' Grimes excavated the footprint of the building before its reconstruction.[23]

The architectural, archaeological and documentary evidence can be brought together to give an impression of what the nave of the church looked like. It was built from Kentish ragstone with occasional decorative flint courses; Reigate stone (or a similar Upper Greensand stone) was used for the window and door mouldings. The west window was a seven-light window with a six-petal rose below the apex of the arch, and the aisle windows had four lights terminating in a two-centred arch filled with complex tracery (Figure 44). In the complicated architectural vocabularies of the Gothic style, the windows are Curvilinear but also belong to the First Perpendicular style of 1330–60.[24] As has been discussed, the documentary

---

[21] TNA, C 66/830, m. 42; Diarmaid MacCulloch, *Reformation: Europe's House Divided 1490–1700* (London: Penguin, 2004), pp. 257–8; Johannes Lindeboom, *Austin Friars: History of the Dutch Reformed Church in London, 1550–1950*, trans. D. de Iongh (The Hague: Nijhoff, 1950), pp. 191–2.

[22] Thomas Hugo, 'Austin Friars', *Transactions of the London and Middlesex Archaeological Society*, 2 (1864), 1–24; Edward I'Anson, 'Account of the Restoration of the Dutch Church, Austin Friars', *Papers Read at the Royal Institute of British Architects*, 1866, 67–75; RCHME, *Inventory of the Historical Monuments in London*, iv (*The City*), 32–4, plate 217.

[23] LAA, site WFG50; William F. Grimes, *The Excavation of Roman and Mediaeval London* (New York: Praeger, 1968), pp. 124–7; Bruce Watson, 'Excavations and Observations on the Site of the Dutch Church, Austin Friars, in the City of London', *Transactions of the London and Middlesex Archaeological Society*, 45 (1994), 13–22. Two further important sources of information are the field notes written by the architectural historians compiling the 1929 RCHME volume and a survey drawn by the architects of the post-war reconstructed Dutch Church: Historic England Archive, RCHME investigators' field notes; LAA, site WFG50, copy of architects' survey of 1950.

[24] John Harvey, *The Perpendicular Style, 1330–1485* (London: Batsford, 1978), pp. 75–96 (p. 91).

Fig. 44. View of the west end and north aisle of the Dutch Church, the former nave of Austin Friars, in 1823. (Lithograph by Charles Burton; London Metropolitan Archives, COLLAGE 563)

evidence suggests a date at the very end of this range. The piers of the arcades were formed of four engaged shafts, whose moulding is also stylistically compatible with a mid-fourteenth-century date. Much of the floor was in Purbeck marble rather than tiles. The nave had nine bays and it thus formed a very large London church (ignoring, for now, the friars' choir), measuring 149ft by 83ft internally (Figure 45; 45.3 × 25.2m). Lay people entered the church through a two-bay porch on the south aisle, with the main western door probably reserved for processions.[25] The plan of the nave gives the impression of a great open preaching space but to a lay person going through the porch, walking into the south aisle and turning left or right into the nave, the church must have seemed long, narrow and dark. The nave had no clerestory and the timber screens along the arcades would have allowed glimpses of the aisle chapels while leading the eye towards the rood screen and altars at the east end. The evidence of wills, chantries and religious fraternity agreements tell us the dedications of a few of the aisle chapels with their own altars and statues: Saints Catherine, Mary, James,

[25] TNA, C 66/727, m. 18; DC, charter X.

Roche, Nicholas and Sebastian (Table 10; in one or two cases these dedications could refer to chapels or altars in the choir). The church itself was dedicated to St Augustine of Hippo.[26]

Much less is known about the choir of Austin Friars than the nave. In 1546, the Crown converted it into a state warehouse and four years later sold it to William Paulet, one of Henry VIII's inner circle of courtiers. His son John began stripping the old choir in the 1570s, selling the paving stone, monuments and lead; most of the building was demolished at the turn of the sixteenth and seventeenth centuries.[27] The key to understanding the layout of the choir is in its relationship with the neighbouring parish church of St Peter. In John Rocque's map of 1746 the parish church is illustrated immediately to the east of the Dutch Church and, like the Dutch Church, looks like it was once part of the old friary. A 1790s survey of St Peter (before its demolition) confirms its location, as does a row of foundations discovered on the archaeological site of 109–118 Old Broad Street (site OBE96). In summary, the medieval parish church must have formed the southern aisle of the choir of the Austin Friars church (Figure 45).[28] The fact that the parish church had medieval windows at its *west* end (as well as at the east end) shows that this aisle was discontinuous and did not reach the nave. There is also intriguing evidence for the internal wall that once separated this parish chapel from the friars' choir. Remarkably, one of the arcade arches survived both the demolition of the choir (at the turn of the sixteenth and seventeenth centuries) and the subsequent demolition of the parish church of St Peter (in the 1790s). The arch was bricked up and reused in the wall of the Georgian house that was built after the demolition of the parish church. When, in turn, this house was about to be taken down in 1929, various parts of the medieval arch were recorded in a series of photographs shot in three different rooms. Using modern photographic software one can, as it were, go back in time and change the photographer's perspective so that he is standing directly opposite the arch fragments in each room. By scaling each photograph to the same size (using the bricks as the common scale) and pasting the three adjusted images in their original medieval positions, one can create a partial photographic elevation of the arcade (Figure 46).[29]

---

[26] Roth, *English Austin Friars*, ii, no. 877; *Calendar of Papal Letters*, xi, 651.

[27] The account for the conversion works is dated 1545–8 (TNA, E 351/3329) but a refund to the Court of Augmentations official Hugh Losse was made in early 1547, suggesting that the works had taken place in 1546; E 315/254, f. 93. Alum was being stored here in 1547: C 66/802, rear of mm. 27–8. The 1550 grant to Paulet is TNA, C 66/834, mm. 24–5. John Stow records the stripping of the former choir, probably in the 1570s after the death of William Paulet in 1572 but before his son John's death in 1576: Stow, *Survey of London*, i, 176–7.

[28] The argument is explained in more detail in Holder, 'Church and Cloisters of Austin Friars'. The 1790s survey is LMA, COLLAGE 5470; the 1746 map is John Rocque, *A Plan of the Cities of London and Westminster, and Borough of Southwark with the Contiguous Buildings* (Lympne Castle, Kent: Margary in assoc. with Guildhall Library, 1971).

[29] A number of photographs were taken of medieval arches and wall fabric, exposed in several rooms on two floors of the Georgian house during building works in 1929. The precise details of this remarkable exercise of architectural recording (by the photographer W. Ingle) are not clear but the photographs are now preserved in Historic England Archive: OP 15755–15760.

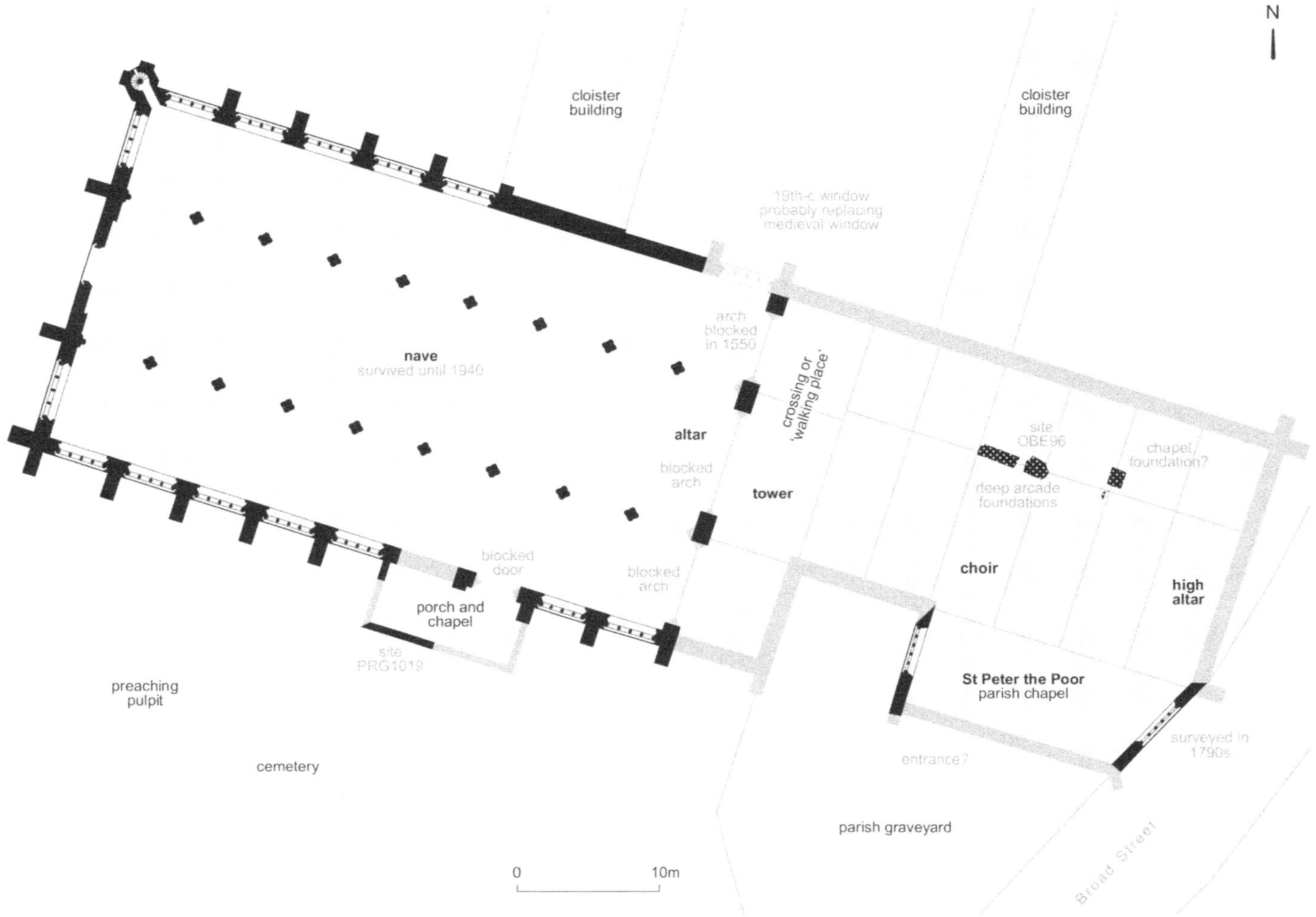

Fig. 45. Plan of the church of Austin Friars (scale 1:500).

Table 10 Documentary evidence for chapels, altars and images in the church of Austin Friars (points of compass abbreviated to N, E, S, W; C for century).

Saint	Evidence	Date	Reference
Chapels			
Thomas	herald's visitation; probably in N aisle of choir	early 16th C	BL, Harley MS 6033, ff. 31–2
John the Baptist	herald's visitation; probably in N aisle of choir	early 16th C	BL, Harley MS 6033, ff. 31–2
Catherine (on S of church)	will in Archdeacon's Court	early 15th C	Bradley, 'Italian Merchants', p. 19
Mary	chantry agreement of 1490 describes location of adjacent altars of our Lady and St James; herald's visitation fixes location; altar of Virgin mentioned in PCC will of 1378.	1490 (1378?)	Röhrkasten, *Mendicant Houses*, p. 510; TNA, LR 14/87
duke's	post-Dissolution grant	by 1538	TNA, C 66/797, m. 23
Altars			
James	wills in Husting and PCC	1472	Röhrkasten, *Mendicant Houses*, p. 510
Nicholas/Sebastian	agreement with fraternity of St Sebastian, changing dedication of existing altar of St Nicholas	1496	TNA, LR 15/13
Roche	will in PCC	1492	Röhrkasten, *Mendicant Houses*, p. 511
(Pouchmakers' altar)	agreement with Pouchmakers' guild to maintain altar by a tomb (the tomb can be located in the herald's visitation)	1482	TNA, LR 15/12
Images			
Mary (in nave)	'greatt image' in Husting will	1498	Röhrkasten, *Mendicant Houses*, p. 511; Bradley, 'Italian Merchants', p. 19

The opening of the arch is about 14ft or 15ft across, which fits nicely into the reconstructed bay width of the choir of 16ft (4.9m, centre to centre). The combined evidence therefore suggests that the choir of Austin Friars was 95ft (29.1m) long and designed with six bays and two aisles, with the parish church of St Peter the Poor forming a third aisle to the south (Figure 45).

A few other features of the friary church deserve mention. Separating the nave and the choir was a wide bay described as 'le cross Ile' in a post-Dissolution document: this bay allowed the friars to walk through the church from their cloister to the cemetery.[30] This bay also formed the base of the most visible part of the church: a landmark spire rising from

---

[30] TNA, C 66/834, mm. 24–5.

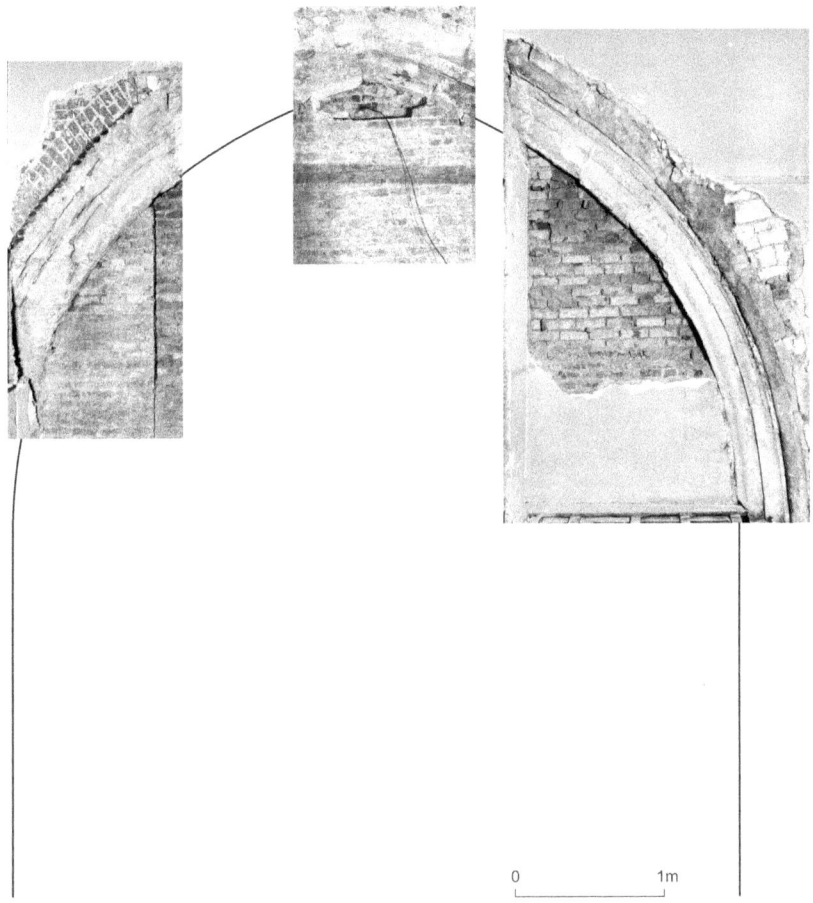

Fig. 46. Montage of photographs of 1929 (with adjusted perspectives) showing an arcade arch that once divided the choir of Austin Friars from the parish church of St Peter the Poor, looking south towards St Peter (scale c. 1:50). (reproduced by permission of Historic England Archive, OP 15755, 15758 and 15760)

a polygonal tower. It was built in or shortly after 1362 (following the destruction of the original spire in a storm), and John Stow described it as 'a most fine spired steeple, small, high, and streight, I have not seene the like' (Figure 47).[31] Virtually the whole church was used as a burial ground for important lay people (including several executed aristocrats), with their burial fees and payments for spiritual services such as chantry masses providing an important source of income for the friary. An early sixteenth-century herald recorded eighty-eight people buried in seventy-seven tombs here, with John Stow noting another eight names (Chapter 17: Burial and Commemoration in the London Friaries).[32]

---

[31] Stow, *Survey of London*, i, 177.
[32] BL, Harley MS 6033, ff. 31–2; Stow, *Survey of London*, i, 177–9; Cater, 'Priory of Austin Friars', pp. 80–2; Steer, 'Royal and Noble Commemoration', pp. 121, 123, table 1. The figure of eighty-eight excludes two burials in the chapter house, presumably of priors or senior friars.

Fig. 47. Detail of Wyngaerde's view of London showing the church of Austin Friars in c. 1544. (© Ashmolean Museum, University of Oxford)

The cloister

The friary had two cloisters, a main cloister that lay immediately north of the choir and an inner cloister further north (Figure 43). Two archaeological excavations permit a partial reconstruction of the pair of cloisters. In 1909 a building site in Great Winchester Street was archaeologically recorded (in an early rescue excavation) by an architect from the London County Council and, some eighty years later, the same site was re-excavated by the Museum of London, although with rather less surviving the second time round (sites PRG1020 and GWS89 on Figure 41).[33] It is worth remarking that the Great Fire of London did not quite reach this far north and so further information about the layout can be gleaned from Ogilby and Morgan's map of 1676, particularly the illustration of Pinners' Hall (the partly surviving northern cloister of the friary).

There appears to be no surviving documentary evidence for the date of construction of the first cloister. Archaeological evidence suggests that it was enlarged when the second

---

[33] For site PRG1020 see Cater, 'Priory of Austin Friars'; W. A. Cater, 'Further Notes on the Austin Friary of London', *Journal of the British Archaeological Association*, 21 (1915), 205–30; for GWS89 see LAA, site GWS89, C. Rosborough, 'Archaeological excavations at Pinners' Hall, 105–108 Old Broad Street and 8 Austin Friars Square' (unpublished Museum of London report, 1990).

cloister was being built in the late fourteenth or fifteenth century, and during this process the masons broke up part of the original arcade and recycled the fragments as a foundation for the second cloister. These architectural fragments were then discovered in the 1989 excavation and give us a good idea of the design of the first cloister.[34] Several fragments of the coupled colonnade of the cloister were discovered, together with a Purbeck marble base and capital of the original arcade. By using the moulding and geometry of a fragment of arch, the tracery and the probable spacing of the paired shafts can be reconstructed (Figure 49). When was this cloister arcade built? It displays moulding features which variously suggest dates between c. 1250 and c. 1325. The most reliable clue is the 'concave fillet' moulding on the capital which can be paralleled in the chapter house at Wells Cathedral, which is dated to the 1290s.[35] As has been stated, the works on the first chapel at Austin Friars were drawing to a close in the 1270s so it is entirely possible that work on the cloister began soon after this in the late thirteenth century. The Austin Friars cloister can therefore be seen as a late example of the open, unglazed, columnar cloister in England.

The function of most of the components of the main cloister can be identified using a post-Dissolution grant of 1546, although it is quite possible that some functions changed over the two centuries of use.[36] By the sixteenth century the east wing housed the main dormitory on the upper floor and a vestry in one of the lower rooms by the church. To the north there was both a great and a small chapter house (*magn[a] domus capitularis*; *parv[a] domus capitularis*) and it seems likely that the small chapter house was the one built in the north-east corner of the original late thirteenth-century cloister, with a newer and larger chapter house added next door in the works a century later (Figure 48). Further evidence for the appearance of the original chapter house comes from a number of floor tiles of a type known as 'Westminster' tiles, made in Farringdon in the second half of the thirteenth century (with production perhaps continuing in the early fourteenth century). A number of decorated 'Westminster' floor tiles were found at Austin Friars and the majority came from an archaeological context probably dating to shortly after the Dissolution, whose location just east of the main cloister suggests that the tiles were originally used in the chapter house (Chapter 13: Floor Tiles and Building Materials from the London Friaries; site GWS89). The northern wing is not identified in any grant but it probably housed the friars' refectory (which is not mentioned in any other wing) and the west wing was the 'hostry', the guest hall (Figure 48).

The documentary evidence for the construction of the infirmary and library in the fifteenth century has already been noted, with permission to build the former given in 1419 and the completion of the latter probably in 1456. Some architectural fragments of the new cloister (demolished after the Dissolution) include a fragment of an arcade

---

[34] Holder, 'Church and Cloisters of Austin Friars'. See also Chapter 12: Architecture and Architectural Fragments of the London Friaries.

[35] Richard K. Morris, 'The Development of Later Gothic Mouldings in England c. 1250–1400: Part I', *Architectural History*, 21 (1978), 21–57 (figure c).

[36] TNA, C 66/797, m. 23; C 66/686, m. 11; E 318/13/577. The latter document, the particulars for grant, describes the guest hall as 'thostrye'.

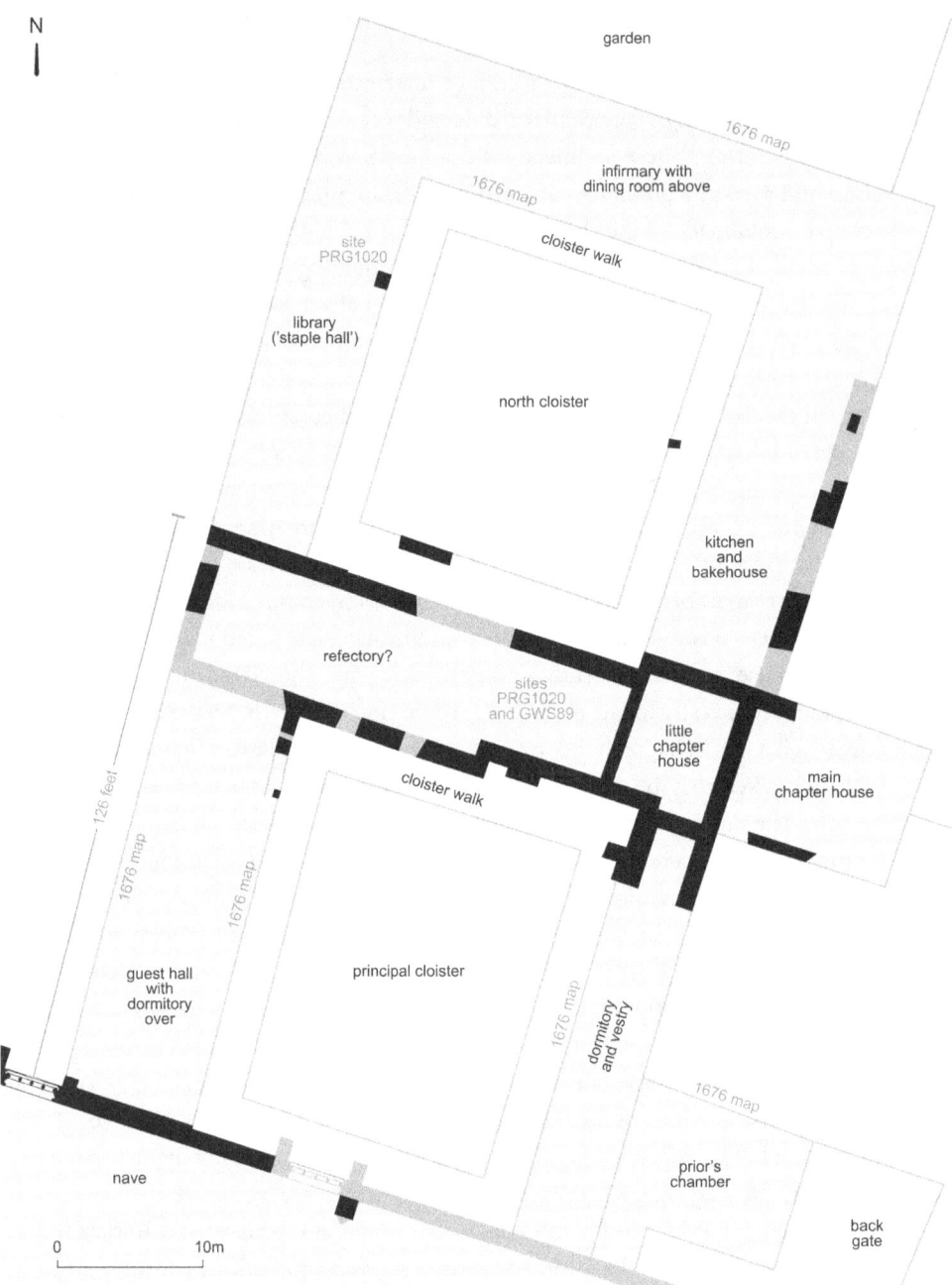

Fig. 48. Map of the two cloisters of Austin Friars: the late thirteenth-century main cloister and the late fourteenth-century inner or northern cloister (scale 1:500).

shaft in Northamptonshire Barnack stone, a piece of window tracery, a mullion and a sill. The arcade fragment is similar to designs used in the south and west cloisters of Westminster Abbey in the mid fourteenth century, and the hollow-chamfered mouldings of the mullion and tracery pieces are typical of designs employed in the London

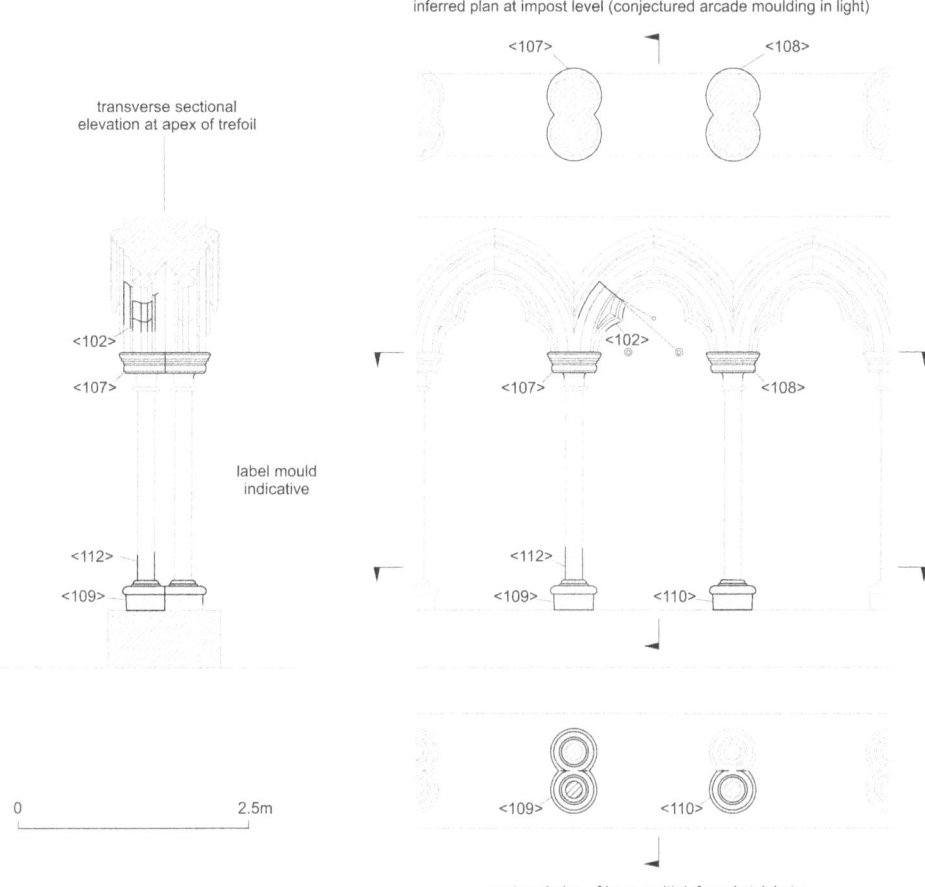

Fig. 49. Reconstruction of the late thirteenth-century cloister at Austin Friars, based on architectural fragments discovered at site GWS89 (scale 1:80). (Mark Samuel)

area in the second half of the century.[37] With the friars' building campaign on the nave ending in the 1370s, they may have begun work on the new inner cloister (and the remodelled main cloister) in the fourth quarter of the century. On the east side they built a new kitchen (it is not clear where its predecessor was sited), with the infirmary wing and a large first-floor dining room – 'the brade dynyng chamber' – in the north wing.[38] The latter hall had a distinct advantage over the refectory in that it did not have the near-vegetarian dietary requirements specified in the original Rule of St Benedict; by applying a little flexibility of interpretation, these strict dining regulations only applied

[37] Harvey, *Perpendicular Style*, p. 263, fig. 30; Holder, 'Church and Cloisters of Austin Friars'.
[38] TNA, C 66/686, m. 11; E 315/103, ff. 27–28v; LR 14/86 [north and east wings]; C 66/690, m. 8 [west wing]; see also documents cited in n. 39, which describe the west wing of the northern cloister as an abutment.

to the actual refectory.³⁹ The original function of the western wing is not specified but it was most probably the new library.

The precinct

The friary, like virtually every urban monastery, was surrounded by precinct walls to ensure privacy and security. Its boundary can be traced with reasonable confidence: it fronted or ran just behind London Wall to the north, Broad Street to the east and Throgmorton Street to the south (Figure 43). The south-east corner of the precinct skirted round the small church and churchyard of St Peter and the western boundary can be traced on Ogilby and Morgan's map of 1676 and on a mid-seventeenth-century Drapers' Company plan.⁴⁰ The large-scale construction of the precinct wall seems to have taken place in the first two decades of the fourteenth century. The London eyre (circuit court) of 1321 recorded encroachments made by the friary in 1306 and 1315: in the former instance the disputed portion of wall was 200ft long and in the latter 150ft. The case must have gone against the friars because they quickly had to muster royal support, obtaining, in July 1321, an injunction that the city sheriffs should stop the demolition of the new walls.⁴¹ Most of the wall was built of stone although the stretch behind Throgmorton Street was in brick and may have been newer.⁴²

There were at least three gates to the priory, the principal gate being located to the south on Throgmorton Street and giving direct access to the church through the churchyard (Figure 43). The carriageway of the 'wide gate called the Augustine Friars gate' (*lat[a] port[a] vocat the augustyne friers gate*) was 12ft wide. Along Broad Street there was a back gate ('le Bakegate') to the north of the choir, probably reserved for the prior and his servants, with a small gate known as the 'alley gate' to the north on London Wall. Finally, there may have been a small postern gate right in the south-west corner of the precinct, at the end of Swan Alley and linking the tenements there to Throgmorton Street.⁴³

The friary's cemetery lay on the south side of the church, set back from Throgmorton

---

³⁹ Barbara F. Harvey, *Living and Dying in England, 1100–1540: The Monastic Experience* (Oxford: Clarendon, 1993), pp. 38–44.

⁴⁰ DC, A XII 121; Honeybourne, 'Extent and Value of the Property in London', pp. 192–200.

⁴¹ TNA, JUST 1/547A, m. 34; C 54/138, m. 1.

⁴² Along Broad Street it was a *muru[s] lapiden[s]*, along London Wall it was 'the stone walle on the north' and along the western boundary it was the 'Stone Wall': TNA, C 66/704, m. 1; LR 14/86; will of William Cony, printed in *Records of the Worshipful Company of Carpenters*, ed. Bower Marsh, 7 vols (Oxford: Oxford University Press, 1913–68), ii, 256–7; between the church and Throgmorton Street it was 'the Brekewall whiche encloseth the churchyard or close lyeng on the South syde of the said churche', with the wall by the main gate on Throgmorton Street described as 'le brikewall': TNA, LR 14/129; C 66/727, mm. 18–19; DC, charter X.

⁴³ Main gate: DC, charter X; back gate: TNA, E 318/13/577; E 318/16/755, m. 18 (note that 'le Bakegate' is translated as *posteri[or] port[a]*, not the bake-house gate); 'aylye gate': TNA, E 318/16/772; 'Swanne Aley': TNA, SP 2/L, ff. 205–210, nos 183–8; DC, A I 61.

Street behind the rented tenements. The cemetery had a cross and preaching pulpit on the west side, a spiritual and physical landmark noted in two early fifteenth-century wills.[44] Like the other London friaries, the Austin Friars had a mansion for its prior that was situated immediately north of the church choir and with its own garden and entrance on Broad Street. In 1546 this was described as 'the prior's chamber and garden, formerly of Doctor Bolland', a reference to the former prior of the 1510s and '20s, Edmund Bellond. The house is presumably the building drawn in this location on Ogilby and Morgan's map of 1676. There may, at times, have been two prior's houses, in cases when the occupant remained in the house after his term as prior, as occurred in 1433 when John Lowe had permission from the order to remain there. In a newly built house of the second decade of the sixteenth century, right opposite the western door of the church, there was a room known as 'Mr Pryors chamber', presumably a reference to its one-time use by the prior or provincial prior.[45]

The friary's service court lay in the north of the precinct with its own entrance on London Wall (the road running inside the actual city wall). A conventual lease of 1533 describes a bake-house and stables in this location and a 1546 post-Dissolution grant of this area also includes a brew-house. In addition to a rented tenement, the cluster of buildings included the old infirmary, a building planned in the 1350s and repaired in 1391 (and replaced by the new infirmary in the fifteenth-century inner cloister).[46] The majority of these buildings remained standing in the seventeenth century and are illustrated on Ogilby and Morgan's map of 1676.

There is evidence for a few other buildings scattered around the precinct. There was a friary prison, the only recorded prison among the London friaries and the scene of an unfortunate death in 1525 that resulted in the subsequent arrest of several friars, a penitential procession and a stern statement from the prior general.[47] A number of guilds and religious fraternities made use of the friary: the fraternity of Pouchmakers rented 'a convenient place within the said hous of freres Augustines, that is to say [a] parlor kechen and Botery'. The Pewterers' Company also rented space in the friary and used the friars' dining hall for their annual feast (until the completion of their company hall in 1486). Other fraternities such as the 'maisters of the brethern and susters of the fraternite of seint

---

[44] Archdeaconry Court wills; information kindly provided by Robert Wood from his database, part of his doctoral thesis: 'Life and Death: A Study of the Wills and Testaments of Men and Women in London and Bury St Edmunds in the late Fourteenth and early Fifteenth Centuries' (University of London, Royal Holloway, 2013); TNA, C 1/1515/25; SP2/L, f. 205, no. 183; DC, A I 61.

[45] 1546 particulars and grant: TNA, E 318/13/577; C 66/797, m. 23; 1433 permission: Roth, *English Austin Friars*, ii, no. 768; prior's chamber: TNA, SP 1/42, ff. 104–16, nos 101–13), printed in *Letters and Papers*, iv(2), no. 3197 (pp. 1454–7).

[46] 1533 lease and 'olde fermery': TNA, LR 14/787; 1546 grant: C 66/787, m. 17; construction and repairs of original infirmary: Roth, *English Austin Friars*, ii, no. 438; *Calendar of Plea and Memoranda Rolls*, iii, 178.

[47] *Monumenta Franciscana*, ed. John S. Brewer, 2 vols, Rolls series, 4 (London: Longman, 1858), ii, 191; Roth, *English Austin Friars*, ii, no. 1058.

Sebastian', a German fraternity, had arrangements with the friary to use parts of the church (made, in their case, in 1496) and they too may have had designated buildings or rooms for their feasts or meetings.[48]

Much of the precinct consisted of open gardens including a great garden in the west, the prior's garden in the north and the common garden in the east. The latter garden probably included areas reserved for medicinal plants for the infirmary and a kitchen garden; a conventual lease of 1537 mentions the right to enter and 'gether fruet' from an orchard.[49]

Like all London's monastic houses, the Augustinian friars owned and rented out London property, including several tenements within their precinct. This seems to have been the case quite soon after their arrival in London: at an inquisition in the early fourteenth century they were found to have acquired a messuage in the parish of St Benet Fink before the Statutes of Mortmain, presumably therefore in the 1260s or 1270s in the very early days of the friary.[50] Compared to most monastic houses they had a rather small property portfolio but they owned a similar group of properties to the other London friaries, with a few tenements within the precinct and others on the adjacent main street. By 1533 they received £22 9s 4d from six tenements within the precinct, including a group of three grand mansions built in the second decade of the century, one of which was occupied by Thomas Cromwell in the 1520s and '30s (Chapter 18: London Friars and Londoners).[51] They also received £14 13s 4d from six tenements by the gate on Throgmorton Street, including the Swan and the Bell inns, and another £21 18s 8d from their other rents in London. Their total rental income was a useful £59 1s 4d (Chapter 18: London Friars and Londoners).

Conclusion

The friary was one of the landmarks of medieval London with its tall prominent spire described by John Stow in the late sixteenth century. The nave of the church was one of the few buildings of medieval London to survive the Great Fire and, until its destruction in the Second World War, it was one of the best preserved friary churches in England, probably second only to the Norwich Black Friars. In this chapter we have restored the church to its

---

[48] Pouchmakers: TNA, LR 15/12. The fraternity had apparently moved from St Mary Bethlehem and St Paul's, where they were based in the fourteenth century: Caroline M. Barron and Laura Wright, 'The London Middle English Guild Certificates of 1388–9', *Nottingham Medieval Studies*, 39 (1995), 108–45 (p. 140). Pewterers: Roth, *English Austin Friars*, ii, no. 948. Fraternity of St Sebastian: TNA, LR 15/13.

[49] 'Great garden' (*magnum gardinum*): TNA, C 66/704, m. 1; prior's garden: TNA, LR 14/86; 'the greate or comen Gardeyn': TNA, LR 14/708.

[50] Roth, *English Austin Friars*, ii, no. 40.

[51] For Cromwell's houses in Austin Friars, see also Gerhold, *London Plotted*, pp. 78–82, plan 24, figs 77, 82; Tracy Borman, *Thomas Cromwell: The Untold Story of Henry VIII's Most Faithful Servant* (London: Hodder & Stoughton, 2014), pp. 46–48, 135–9; Holder, 'Medieval Friaries of London', pp. 160–9, figs 65–70.

full size by reuniting the famous nave with its lost choir: the whole church was long and low, sixteen bays on the inside (with no upper clerestory) and 278ft (85m) on the outside. The plan of the church was unusual, with the parish church of St Peter forming a southern aisle of the choir. This is not, however, unique in London: the Benedictine nunnery of St Helen also had an attached parish church, as did the Franciscan nunnery of the Minoresses.[52] More light has been shed on the arrangement of the cloisters: a double-cloister consisting of the late thirteenth-century main cloister with its unglazed twin-column arcade, and a newer inner cloister further to the north.

---

[52] RCHME, *Inventory of the Historical Monuments in London*, v (*East London*), 19–24; Minnie Reddan and Alfred W. Clapham, *The Parish of St Helen, Bishopsgate*, Survey of London, 9 (London: Survey of London and LCC, 1924), pp. 31–5; Carlin and Keene, 'Historical Gazetteer of London before the Great Fire', pp. 17–18.

7

Crossed Friars, c. 1268–1538

THE early history of the religious order known today as Crosiers – the Canons Regular of the Holy Cross – is not at all clear due to a lack of surviving documentary evidence, particularly for the order in the thirteenth and fourteenth centuries.[1] There was almost certainly a small and mixed religious community of canons, laymen and laywomen in the early thirteenth century at Clairlieu in the diocese of Liège (modern Belgium). This group lived a communal religious life (including observation of a monastic daily liturgy); they would have offered hospitality, and they may also have preached and heard confession. As the group gradually solidified into a more formal religious order in the first half of the thirteenth century, they (like many other small religious orders) were not specifically identifiable as friars or canons. They broadly followed Dominican statutes but they did not adopt the strict mendicant ideal of poverty. The *fratres sancte crucis*, brethren of the Holy Cross, founded their first house in England in the 1240s at Whaplode in Lincolnshire, founding a second house in London about two decades later.[2] In England these friar-like preaching canons were generally assumed to be friars. Furthermore, the English pronunciation of their alternative name, *cruciferi*, caused them to be commonly known as Crutched or Crouched friars, rather than the more correct translation of Crossed friars; the limited evidence suggests that they themselves preferred the latter.[3] Given the English

---

[1] Aspects of the archaeological and documentary evidence presented in this chapter have previously been published in Antonietta Lerz and Nick Holder, 'Medieval Crossed Friars and its Roman to Post-Medieval Landscape: Excavations at Mariner House, in the City of London', *Transactions of the London and Middlesex Archaeological Society*, 66 (2015), 137–97.

[2] Michael Hayden, *Crutched Friars and Croisiers: The Canons Regular of the Order of the Holy Cross in England and France* (Rome: Crosier Generalate, 2013), pp. 15–59.

[3] For example, Londoners referred to the street on which the priory was situated as Crouchedfrerestrete in 1405: LMA, Husting Roll 136(11) (microfilm X109/416). In a letter of c. 1535 the prior referred to his own institution as 'the religious hows of crossid freers': TNA, E 314/76 [item labelled 'London: Crutched Friars'].

tendency to describe religious according to their clothes (White monks, Black friars . . .), the description of these friars as crutched or crouched rather than crossed might suggest that the English brethren did not in fact have as prominent an image of the crucifix on their scapular as their Continental counterparts.[4]

The Crossed friars were one of the smallest of the London friaries, although they were probably more numerous than the short-lived order of Pied friars in the thirteenth century (Chapter 9: Pied Friars, 1267–1317). In the late thirteenth century they numbered twenty-nine friars, half the number of London Carmelites and only a third of the number of London Dominicans. With the whole London population – religious and lay people – halved as a result of the Black Death, recruitment at the Crossed Friars seems to have been increasing by the end of the fourteenth century, with numbers restored to thirty or forty by the late fifteenth and early sixteenth century.[5] The house and the order never achieved the same degree of local, let alone national, prominence as the larger Grey Friars and Black Friars but Crossed Friars does seem to have attracted consistent support from Londoners. And, thanks to the order's origins in the Low Countries, the house had particular links with members of London's Flemish and Dutch communities. The Crossed friars could provide tailored spiritual services to these merchants: confession in their native tongues, a meeting place for several alien religious fraternities (such the Holy Blood of Jesus fraternity, for example) and a place of burial.[6]

The friary experienced something of a late revival as it went through a process of reform initiated by the order's leaders in the Low Countries in the late fifteenth century and carried out by the charismatic London prior William Bowry in the early sixteenth century. However, with one of the last priors, John Dryver, in trouble in 1532 (for satirically subverting the king's title of Defender of the Faith as 'destroyer of the faith') and a subsequent prior, probably Robert Ball, experiencing a different kind of problem three or four years later (a scandal with a mistress or prostitute and an accompanying blackmail attempt), the six remaining friars signed the deed of surrender on 12 November 1538.[7]

The priory of Crossed Friars has a relatively good range of sources to help us understand its history and layout. With the exception of the Holborn Black Friars, it is the

---

[4] The earliest evidence for Continental Crosiers wearing an image of the cross on their scapula is on late thirteenth-century wall paintings from the shrine of St Odilia at the Crosier priory at Huy (Belgium); Hayden, *Crutched Friars and Croisiers*, p. 75, illustration 4.

[5] Röhrkasten, *Mendicant Houses*, pp. 83–4; Davis, 'Mendicants in London', p. 7; Hayden, *Crutched Friars and Croisiers*, pp. 96–7.

[6] Röhrkasten, *Mendicant Houses*, pp. 470, 474–5; Justin Colson, 'Alien Communities and Alien Fraternities in Later Medieval London', *London Journal*, 35.2 (2010), 111–43; Christian Steer, '"Better in Remembrance": Medieval Commemoration at the Crutched Friars, London', *Journal of the Church Monuments Society*, 25 (2010), 36–57.

[7] *Letters and Papers*, vii, 665; ix, 1092; xiii(2), 807; *Three Chapters of Letters Relating to the Suppression of Monasteries*, ed. Thomas Wright (London: Camden Society, 1843), pp. 59–60; Barron and Davies, *Religious Houses*, pp. 141–2; Röhrkasten, *Mendicant Houses*, pp. 366–7, 407–8, 470–1, 555–9; Hayden, *Crutched Friars and Croisiers*, pp. 103–4, 112–13, 118–22, 127–41.

144 THE FRIARIES OF MEDIEVAL LONDON

Fig. 50. Map showing the location of the Crossed Friars precinct and archaeological excavations on the site (scale 1:2500).

only London friary to have a surviving property archive: a large group of charters and other medieval documents have been preserved in the Cholmondeley collection at Chester Record Office. Secondly, the site of the friary church was investigated in a relatively large-scale archaeological excavation in 2008, with other parts of the friary precinct excavated in smaller excavations (see site MCF06 and others on Figure 50).[8] There are also several useful visual sources for the friary including Anton van den Wyngaerde's view of c. 1544, which shows the church and some claustral buildings, and

[8] The relevant documents are in series DCH/O/, DCH/P/ and DCH/X/ in Cheshire Record Office (CRO), Chester. The archaeological archives for site MCF06 and the other sites shown on Figure 50 are in the Museum of London's LAA archive, under their respective alphanumeric site-codes.

CROSSED FRIARS, C. 1268–1538   145

Fig. 51. Detail of Wyngaerde's view of London showing the church and precinct of Crossed Friars in c. 1544. (© Ashmolean Museum, University of Oxford)

Fig. 52. Detail of Ogilby and Morgan's map of London of 1676, showing possible surviving friary buildings. (Reproduced by kind permission of Harry Margary in association with the London Metropolitan Archives)

Ogilby and Morgan's London map of 1676. The latter map is more useful for this friary than the other London friaries since this area by the Tower largely escaped the Great Fire of 1666.[9]

Acquiring and developing the friary

The Crossed friars acquired a large urban plot of land near the Tower of London over about two centuries. They were given, acquired leases on or purchased twelve tenements and a strip of land in the area lying to the north of the open space of Tower Hill, to the west of Woodruff Lane (modern Cooper's Row) and to the south of Hart Street (modern Crutched Friars; Table 11, Figure 50, Figure 53).[10] The foundation gift that enabled the friars to set up their priory came from two men, Ralph Hosiar and William Sabernes. The Tudor historian John Stow, who gave us the names of the founders, tells us that the priory was founded in 1298; other evidence suggests that the date of foundation was slightly earlier. The friary is, in fact, first mentioned in May 1269 when Henry III contributed to the construction costs of the friars' chapel; furthermore, this instruction came four years after a more general royal letter of protection was issued to the English order of Crossed friars.[11] The names of the founders, Hosiar and Sabernes, are probably correct: an earlier Ralph the Hosier was a landowner in this area in the late twelfth century and a later Ralph – perhaps the founder – was a witness to a London property transaction of c. 1240; a William Sabarn seems to have been active in London in the third quarter of the thirteenth century.[12] The evidence therefore points to the foundation of the priory in the second half of the 1260s (perhaps 1268 rather than John Stow's erroneous date of 1298?) by Ralph Hosiar and William Sabernes, who gave the friars a lease on four tenements on Hart Street (tenements 1–4 in Table 11 and on Figure 53). These properties were owned by a nearby and rather older London religious house, Holy Trinity priory, and the Crossed friars duly appear as lessees in the Holy Trinity cartulary.[13]

The friars then gradually enlarged their property with the help of sympathetic neighbours. In the fourth quarter of the thirteenth century Herildis, daughter of William Burgoine, granted them two tenements immediately west of the four original tenements, with another local landowner Adam Hunteman granting them the next tenement west in 1324 (tenements 5, 6 and 9 in Table 11 and on Figure 53). The friars were also able to

---

[9] *The Panorama of London by Antonis Van der Wyngaerde Circa 1544*, ed. H. Colvin and S. Foister, London Topographical Society, 151 (London: LTS, 1996); *A Large and Accurate Map of the City of London* (Lympne Castle, Kent: H. Margary in association with Guildhall Library, 1976).

[10] A fuller account of the various tenements can be found in Lerz and Holder, 'Medieval Crossed Friars'.

[11] *CPR 1258–1266*, p. 456; *CLR 1267–1272*, p. 81; Röhrkasten, *Mendicant Houses*, p. 62; Stow, *Survey of London*, i, 147.

[12] *The Cartulary of Holy Trinity Aldgate*, ed. Gerald A.J. Hodgett, London Record Society, 7 (London: LRS, 1971), p. 28; *Cartulary of St Bartholomew's Hospital, Founded 1123*, ed. Nellie J.M. Kerling (London: St Bartholomew's Hospital, 1973), pp. 20, 129.

[13] *Cartulary of Holy Trinity Aldgate*, pp. 25, 29–30, 234–35.

Table 11 List of the tenements acquired by the Crossed friars for their priory.

Number on Figure 53	Date of acquisition	Grantor	Description	Reference
1–4	1260s	Ralph Hosiar and William Sabernes	grant of lease on four tenements (owned by Holy Trinity Priory) to friars	*Cartulary of Holy Trinity Aldgate*, pp. 25, 29–30, 234–5
5	1276 or 1277	Herildis, daughter of William Burgoine	grant to friars	CRO, DCH/O/56/8
6	1295	Yerilda, daughter of William de Burgoingne [sic]	grant of 200-year lease to friars	CRO, DCH/O/56/1
7	early 14th C	Barking Abbey	friars rented this plot from Barking Abbey by the early 14th C	*The Eyre of London, 14 Edward II*, ii, 196–202; LMA, Husting Roll 56 (126)
8	by early 1320s	Lilleshall Abbey, Shropshire	friars rented the tenement from Lilleshall Abbey	*Cartulary of Lilleshall Abbey*, no. 302, p. 155
9	1324	Adam Hunteman	grant of two houses to the friars	LMA, Husting Roll 53 (5)
10	1387	Lilleshall Abbey, Shropshire	friars rented a garden plot from Lilleshall Abbey	CRO, DCH/O/56/5
11	15th C?	unknown	friars must have owned or leased this by early 16th C when they enlarged church	
12	15th C?	City of London Corporation	at Dissolution this plot was described as property of prior and City	TNA, E 40/12598
13	1521	City of London Corporation	City grants strip of Hart Street for the enlargement of the friars' church	LMA, COL/CA/01/01/004 (Repertory Book 4), f. 122v

negotiate with other religious houses, acquiring a lease on a large block of land behind Hart Street from the nuns at Barking Abbey and leases on two tenements fronting east onto Woodrove Lane from the Augustinian canons of rather more distant Lilleshall Abbey in Shropshire (tenements 7, 8 and 10). Within about half a century of their arrival in London, the Crossed friars had thus put together a sizeable urban precinct of 0.7ha (1¾ acres; the area of tenements 1–9 on Figure 53). The prior and friars must have faced real challenges: this was a long-term process of growth, achieved over more than one generation of personnel. Furthermore, the generosity of neighbours was not without limits: Herildis, daughter of William Burgoine, gave two tenements to the friars in the final quarter of the thirteenth

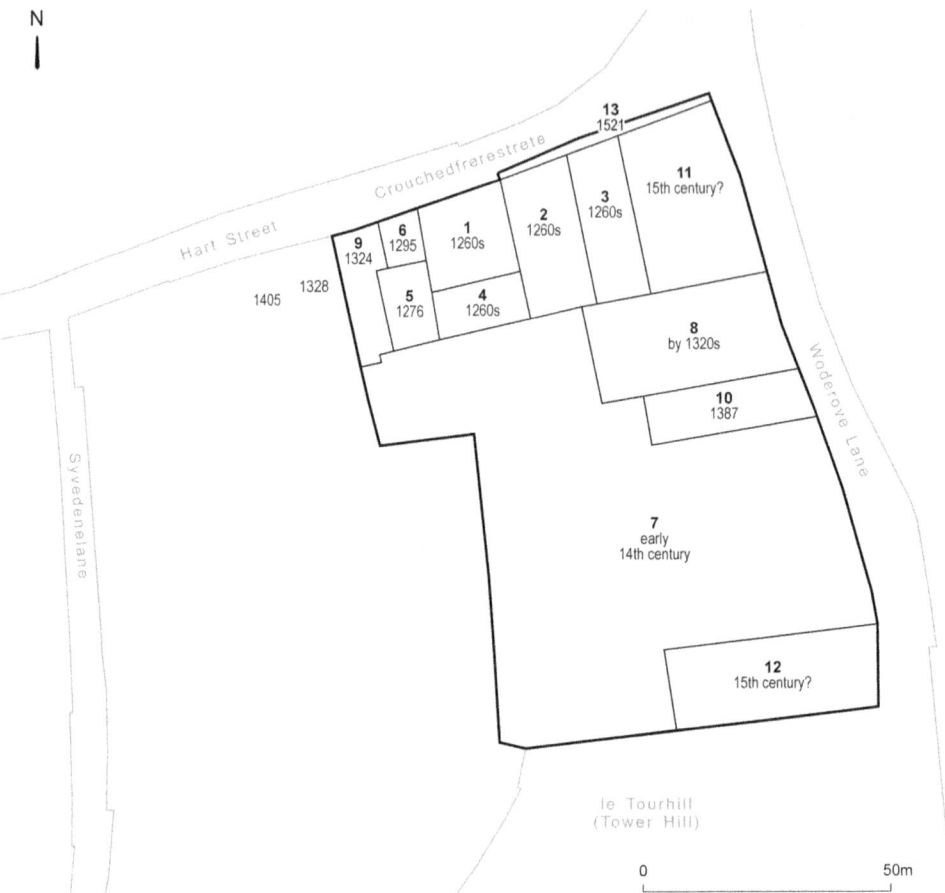

Fig. 53. Map showing the location of the tenements acquired by the Crossed friars for their priory (for tenement numbers, see Table 11) (scale 1:1500).

century but she sold a third tenement at this time in a normal property transaction to another purchaser; it was Adam Hunteman who eventually gave this tenement to the friars, twenty-five years after he had bought it from Herildis.[14] And the long-term financial security of the friars was not certain: they still owed annual rents and quitrents on the majority of their precinct, amounting to at least £1 13s 8d in the early fourteenth century, probably well over £2 including the unknown rent they paid to Barking Abbey and to Herildis.

The friars were subsequently able to enlarge their precinct further over the next century or so, acquiring the 'missing' tenements on their northern and eastern frontages (tenements 10–12 in Table 11 and on Figure 53) and, it can be assumed, buying the freehold title to some of their leased properties; there is rather less surviving documentary evidence for this process. Their final acquisition was a strip of land taken in from the northern street frontage and granted by the City in 1521 (tenement 13); this was ostensibly for a new eastern

[14] LMA, Husting Roll 28(33) (microfilm X109/403); 53(5) (microfilm X109/404).

extension to the church, but was in fact to build some rented and corrodians' houses (with these houses making a financial contribution to the works on the new church, just to the south).[15] By the sixteenth century, therefore, the friars had an urban precinct of 0.9ha (2¼ acres).

One additional point is worth making about the way that the various priors created their precinct: they acquired other tenements on Hart Street and so they had to make decisions about which properties to incorporate in the ever-growing precinct area. For example, the friars were granted the property immediately to the west of the precinct in 1328, and the tenement to the west of that in 1405; had they been able to acquire the large tenement to the south they might have chosen to enlarge the whole precinct area to the west. Perhaps because they could not acquire this tenement, they simply added the 1328 and 1405 tenements to their rent-earning property portfolio (which included several tenements in London and further afield), keeping them outside their religious precinct.[16]

The prior and obedientiaries would have planned the construction of a series of monastic buildings in tandem with and dependent on the acquisition of the various properties: at the very least they needed a continuous east–west width of about 100ft to fit in a church and a north–south dimension of about 150ft in order to allow for a churchyard on the road (northern) side of the church and a cloister on the private southern side. The first task for the friars was the construction of a chapel; the early friars were presumably temporarily accommodated in one of the houses granted by Hosiar and Sabernes in the 1260s. If the chapel was begun in about 1268, the initial phase of work seems to have been completed in the 1270s, with further work drawing to a close in the 1310s (below: 'The church'). The friars must also have been building monastic accommodation in a cloister at this time (Figure 54). A legal case of 1321 mentions the friary cloister and its refectory for the first time: the building or buildings must also have been completed in the late thirteenth or early fourteenth century.[17] There is little evidence for the dates of construction of other buildings in the precinct; the prior had a separate house by 1440 and further works were carried out in the church in the 1450s and '60s (below: 'The precinct' 'The church').

A final phase of construction works began in the late fifteenth century at the friary, prompted by a disastrous fire of 1490 or 1491. The prior was granted a licence to issue indulgences to those who donated to the rebuilding programme and the terms of the indulgence describe the earlier fire in graphic detail: 'the place of the seid Prioure and Covent Upon Mydsomer evyn last past by a sodeyne tempest of fyre savyng the Chirche was devoured and

---

[15] LMA, COL/CA/01/01/004 (Repertory book 4), f. 122v; Holder, 'Medieval Friaries of London', pp. 189, 266, 336–7.

[16] CRO, DCH/O/56/3; LMA, Husting Roll 136(11) (microfilm X109/416); for further discussion of the friars' properties beyond the actual precinct area, see Holder, 'Medieval Friaries of London', pp. 189–90, 266; Lerz and Holder, 'Medieval Crossed Friars'.

[17] *The Eyre of London, 14 Edward II, AD 1321*, ed. Helen M. Cam, 2 vols, Selden Society, vols 85–6 (London: Selden Society, 1968), ii, 196–202.

Fig. 54. Map of the precinct of Crossed Friars in the sixteenth century (scale 1:1500).

destroyed to there Utter enpoverysshyng'.[18] Although this document states that the church was spared by the fire, other evidence shows that the prior began extending the church to the east in the first or second decade of the sixteenth century (below: 'The church').

The church

When Ralph Hosiar and William Sabernes granted the Crossed friars their London plots of land in about 1268, the first prior (whose name is unknown) must have begun planning the construction of the first chapel. The location of what must be the east wall of the first church was revealed in archaeological excavations in 2008 in the form of a line of four deep foundation piers (site MCF06 on Figure 50). The masons building the church had employed the traditional building techniques of medieval London: they had dug a foundation trench about 3ft deep and 4ft wide (0.9m by 1.2m), and then dug a series of evenly spaced deeper

[18] BL, IA.55480 [incunable].

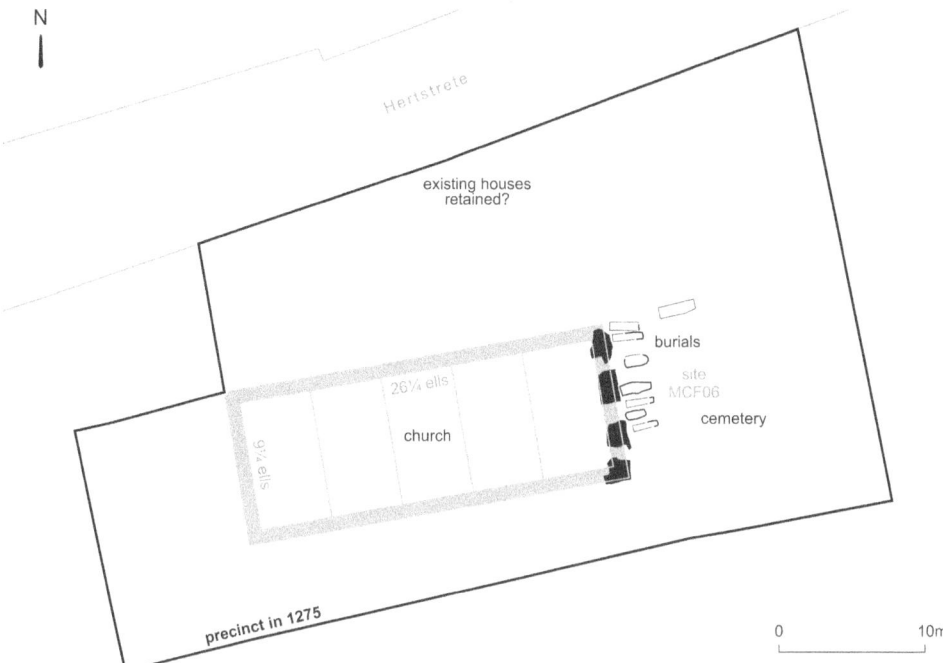

Fig. 55. Plan of the church of Crossed Friars in 1320 (scale 1:500).

holes in the base of the trench, with these 'pier' pits another 3ft deeper and spaced about 8ft to 10ft apart (centre to centre, 2.5 to 3m). The foundation trench thus ended up as a pattern or mould of earthen arches, which the masons then filled with chalk and mortar, gradually bringing the foundation up to ground level in irregular courses of masonry. Because of the effects of modern truncation (for example, deep Victorian cellars), the archaeologists of 2008 only found the deeper piers and not the shallower trench that formerly linked the piers (Figure 55). The first church seems to have been built remarkably quickly: 20 marks were given by the king in 1269, with a further donation of six oak trees for timber in 1270 and additional money granted in 1273.[19] The grant of timber suggests that the chapel was near completion and a roof was being constructed. This first chapel may have been quite small: perhaps only three bays of the church were roofed at this time as construction proceeded westwards. An agreement of 1320 between the friars and their main landlord, Holy Trinity priory, was drawn up as additional works on the church were drawing to a close: the document describes the location of the church in the Holy Trinity tenements and refers to the church as being 'as yet undedicated' (*nondum dedicata*), also noting 'that the Crossed friars intend the church [imminently?] to be dedicated' (*quam etiam ecclesiam dicti religiosi Sancte Crucis dedicari ... facere intendunt*').[20] The fifty-year gap following

---

[19] *CCR, 1268–1272*, p. 232; TNA, E 404/1/2, no. 1; Röhrkasten, *Mendicant Houses*, p. 62.
[20] TNA, E 40/2666; CRO, DCH/O/56/2; *Cartulary of Holy Trinity Aldgate*, pp. 29–30, 234–5.

the earlier phase of works on the church would surely suggest that this agreement refers to an enlarged church, extended to the west. The document also gives the dimensions of the church, 26¼ ells by 9¼ ells (24.0m x 8.5m), and the archaeological evidence of the foundations for the east wall suggests that these are internal not external measurements. By 1320, then, the church probably had five bays of about 16ft length (Figure 55).

A little other archaeological evidence for the 1320 church was found in the form of a number of late thirteenth- or early fourteenth-century floor tiles which, although no longer *in situ*, would once have decorated the floor of the church. These included seven designs of 'Westminster' tile (a type manufactured in the Farringdon area of London and named after a surviving tile floor) and six designs of the Eltham Palace/Lesnes Abbey type (manufactured somewhere in the London area and, again, named after surviving floors; below, Chapter 13: Floor Tiles and Building Materials from the London Friaries). A few surviving fragments of painted glass and an oyster shell paint palette with traces of red iron oxide hint at a decorative interior with stained glass and painted walls.[21]

The documentary and archaeological evidence shows that the friars continued to enlarge and adapt their church over the next two centuries. In 1350 and 1360 they were fundraising for a Lady chapel, perhaps as a venue for the performance of chantry masses and anniversary funeral services for the victims of the catastrophic Great Pestilence. A testator of 1364 mentions the chapel, suggesting that it was largely complete, while another testator of 1507 notes the statue or picture of the Virgin 'on the south side of the same [Lady] chapell next the south wall there'.[22] A second chapel may have been built in the second half of the fourteenth century. Sir Thomas Haseley, the under-marshal of England, requested burial in the chapel of St Anne in his will of 1449 and it is tempting to see the origin of this chapel in 'new work' on the church documented in the 1380s.[23] The precise arrangement of these chapels is uncertain but fragments of wall foundation discovered in the archaeological excavation show that the friars were enlarging the church eastwards at this time (Figure 56). Might the Lady chapel have been added to the east end of the original church, as happened at the nearby Augustinian priory of St Bartholomew, with a chapel of St Anne adjacent on the south or north side? Archaeological evidence showed that this possible Lady chapel was floored in mid to late fourteenth-century Penn tiles, with several broken fragments discovered as well as a single tile still *in situ* in its mortar bed.[24]

The liturgical arrangements may well have changed again in the fifteenth century. Work on a new choir began in the mid fifteenth century: a donation was made by a testator in 1455 with a second testator granting money for new choir stalls in 1469 ('to make it and Stalle it with tymbr and of Joynours Werk'), suggesting that the works were nearly complete.

[21] Lerz and Holder, 'Medieval Crossed Friars', p. 151.
[22] TNA, C 66/229, m. 3; C 66/258, m. 2; Röhrkasten, *Mendicant Houses*, p. 512.
[23] Bequests to pay for work at the friary in wills of 1385 and 1387: *Excerpta Historica: Or Illustrations of English History*, ed. Samuel Bentley (London: privately printed, 1831), pp. 136, 139; Röhrkasten, *Mendicant Houses*, p. 512.
[24] Lerz and Holder, 'Medieval Crossed Friars', pp. 167–8, fig 17.

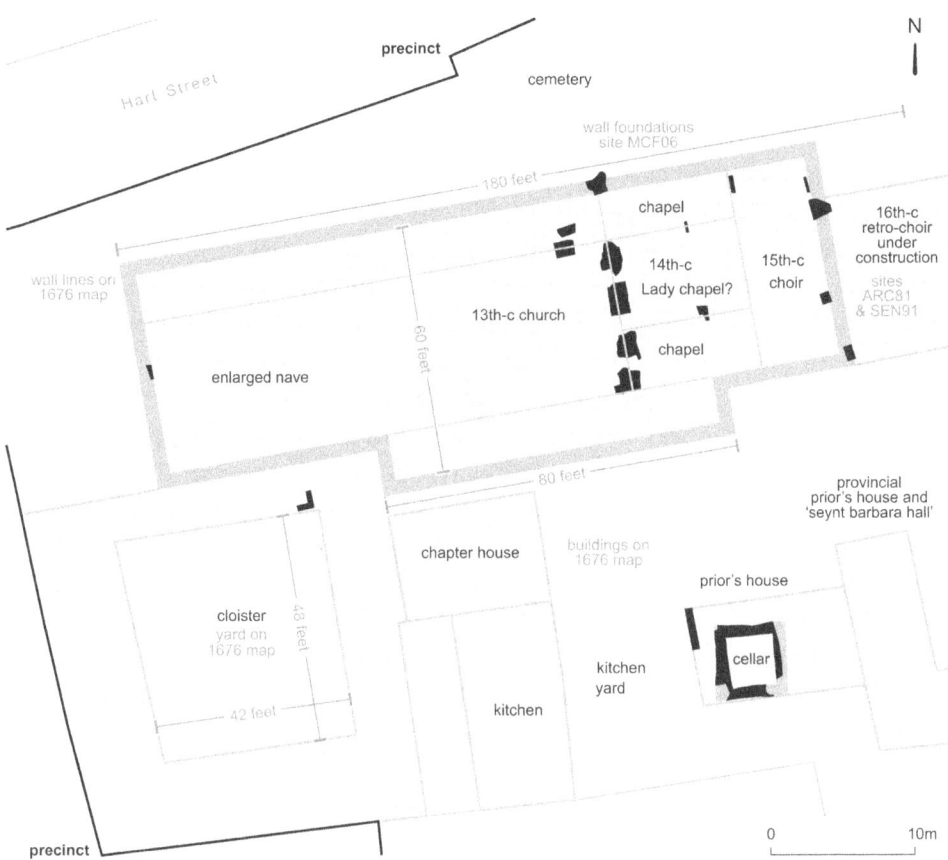

Fig. 56. Plan of the church of Crossed Friars showing the various phases of construction from the fourteenth to the sixteenth centuries (scale 1:500).

Wyngaerde's panorama of the 1540s shows a central church tower and this may also have been constructed in the fifteenth century.[25] By 1517 the friars had won the special privilege of having a chapel in which the pope had granted the right to perform *scala coeli* masses. The chapel and the special masses made reference to the church of S. Maria Scala Coeli in Rome where St Bernard had had a vision of souls climbing a ladder to heaven. These chapels – with the first English one established at Westminster in about 1476 – became popular sites for the prayers of the living and masses for the dead since they carried generous indulgences for the souls of those for whom the masses were performed.[26] There may also have been separate chapels in the church dedicated to St James and the Trinity: testa-

---

[25] Röhrkasten, *Mendicant Houses*, p. 512; Wyngaerde panorama; Roskell, *The History of Parliament. The House of Commons 1386–1421*, iv, 309.

[26] CRO, DCH/X/13/2; Duffy, *Stripping of the Altars*, pp. 375–6; Nigel Morgan, 'The Scala Coeli Indulgence and the Royal Chapels', in *The Reign of Henry VII*, ed. B. Thompson, Harlaxton Medieval Studies, 5 (Stamford: Paul Watkins, 1995), pp. 82–103 (p. 89).

tors make reference to images (whether carved, painted or in glass) of the saint and the Trinity.[27]

The Crossed friars began another ambitious programme of construction in the early sixteenth century, not knowing, of course, that the works were soon to be interrupted. A will of 1507 mentions 'the new quere' (apparently referring to an intended project rather than a completed building) and another will of 1518 refers to 'the new fabric' (*in nove fabrice*). Three years later the City Corporation granted the friars a strip of Hart Street 148½ft long and 5ft wide 'for the enlargement of their church' (*pro elargande ecclesie sue*). Further sums were spent in the 1520s and in about 1535 the prior wrote to the king to request royal support for the construction project; a draft reply by Thomas Cromwell apparently agrees to the request, although the amount to be given is not specified (nor is it known if the sum was ever paid).[28] Documentary evidence of 1534 suggests that the enlarged church reached nearly as far as Woodrove Lane: that year the friars sold a plot of land in the east of their precinct to the Drapers' Company for the construction of a set of almshouses and the boundary of the plot is described and measured from 'the southeast corner of the said Churche [Crossed Friars] along by the kynges highwey [Woodrove Lane]'.[29] The almshouses survived until the nineteenth century and their position can be securely established on modern Cooper's Row (historic Woodrove Lane). The building project must have been for a remarkable new choir or retro-choir, which, had it ever have been completed, would have brought the length of the church to about 70m (230ft). It is not clear how much of the project was completed by the time of the friary's closure in 1538: could this be a lost example of London late Perpendicular monastic architecture?

So, the documentary evidence would suggest a thirteenth-century church, with further construction campaigns in the fourteenth century (chapels to the Virgin and St Anne), fifteenth century (an enlarged choir) and sixteenth century (a retro-choir). Our next problem is therefore to map out these projects using the limited archaeological and documentary evidence. The best clue for the physical extent of the Crossed friars' church is from the sixteenth century, shortly before the Dissolution. By bringing in measurements of the church recorded by surveyors from the Court of Augmentations in 1549, the various phases of construction and the evolving layout of the friary church can be mapped (Figure 56). The measurements were made by the surveyors after the partial demolition of the church and it is not always apparent what they are referring to. They recorded the length of the 'North Isle' as a remarkable 180ft, presumably including the choir and part of the new retro-choir, whose construction had of course been abandoned by 1538. The length of the south aisle is

---

[27] Röhrkasten, *Mendicant Houses*, p. 512; Steer, 'Better in Remembrance', pp. 45–50; Michael Hayden, 'The Crutched Friars in England', *Clairlieu*, 47 (1989), 145–75 (p. 162).

[28] Röhrkasten, *Mendicant Houses*, p. 512. LMA, COL/CA/01/01/004 (Repertory book 4), f. 122v; COL/CA/01/01/005 (Repertory book 5), f. 52; TNA, C 1/534, no. 5; E 314/76 ('London: Crutched Friars'); SP 1/100, f. 57, no. 46.

[29] DC, A VII 48.

Fig. 57. Tomb of Sir Richard Cholmeley and his wife Elizabeth, probably transferred from the church of Crossed Friars to St Peter ad Vincula in the Tower of London at the Dissolution. (photograph: Christian Steer)

specified as 80ft, with its width given as 60ft, the latter dimension surely indicating the full width of the church.[30] These measurements, and the various fragments of wall foundation discovered on the archaeological excavation at site MCF06, are plotted on Figure 56.

The church had numerous tombs and monuments: twenty-six church burials with funerary monuments are listed in sixteenth-century heralds' visitations, and another one or two tombs are mentioned in wills. Just one of these tombs survives today, an alabaster tomb chest commemorating Sir Richard Cholmeley (Figure 57). Sir Richard's widow, Dame Elizabeth, seems to have moved her late husband's tomb to the chapel of St Peter ad Vincula in the Tower of London at the time of the Dissolution.[31] Archaeological excavation revealed the graves of two other men buried in a prominent location in what may have been the fourteenth-century Lady chapel, together with a charnel or ossuary pit in the northern chapel, which contained the disarticulated remains of at least twelve individuals (whose graves had probably been disturbed during the fourteenth-century construction work).[32]

---

[30] TNA, C 66/815, m. 16; WARD 2/58/215/8; CRO, DCH/O/56/9.
[31] Stow, *Survey of London*, i, 147; Steer, 'Royal and Noble Commemoration', table 1; Steer, 'Better in Remembrance', pp. 51–3.
[32] Lerz and Holder, 'Medieval Crossed Friars', pp. 169–70.

The cloister

There is, unfortunately, remarkably little information about the cloister of Crossed Friars. Measurements recorded in a 1549 survey record a rather modest cloister garth of 48ft by 42ft (14.6m × 12.8m); these dimensions concur with a yard to the south of the church shown on Ogilby and Morgan's 1676 map of the area (Burnt Yard).[33] One or two wings of the cloister must have been complete by 1321 for in that year bailiffs acting for one of the friary's landlords (the nunnery of Barking Abbey) came into the cloister and removed a large bell in lieu of five years of rent arrears.[34] The cloister may not have been fully completed until the early fifteenth century: a will of 1411 specifies funds 'for the work and construction of the cloister of the church' (*ad opus et edificationem claustri eiusdem ecclesie*).[35] The dormitory was presumably at first-floor level on the east side of the cloister to allow the friars night-time access to the choir for the service of Lauds.[36] The refectory may therefore have been on the south side of the cloister (the bailiffs of 1321 had to go through the church and then cross the cloister to get to the refectory: *et per medium claustri sui euntes usque refectorium ceperunt*), with space for a guest hall in the west wing. The northern arm of the cloister adjacent to the church would only have housed the cloister walk without any claustral buildings.

The precinct

Various buildings within the friary precinct can be mapped by archaeological discoveries or surmised from historic map evidence but the identification of these buildings is problematic. A building to the east of Burnt Yard shown on Ogilby and Morgan's map of 1676 is a good candidate for the medieval chapter house, which would then have been accessed from the east side of the cloister (Figure 54, Figure 56). An adjacent building to the south, shown on the same map, could be the monastic kitchen: the building itself was not archaeologically excavated but the yard to the east was and rubbish pits contained remains of shellfish (oyster and mussels), fish (cod) and meat (pork, mutton and goose), with another pit containing discarded tableware and copper-alloy cooking vessels.[37] Moving further east (Figure 54 Figure 56), there is archaeological evidence for a late medieval building with a square internal cellar. The superstructure was in Kentish ragstone masonry, with the relatively narrow surviving wall (0.5m or 1ft 8in wide) suggesting a timber-framed upper storey. The size of the building is not clear from the surviving evidence but it had

---

[33] TNA, C 66/815, m. 16; WARD 2/58/215/8; CRO, DCH/O/56/9; Honeybourne, 'Extent and Value of the Property in London', pp. 223–4.
[34] *The Eyre of London*, ii, 196–202.
[35] Röhrkasten, *Mendicant Houses*, p. 512.
[36] The dormitory wing is mentioned with the cloister in the post-Dissolution rent collector's accounts of 1539–40: TNA, SC 6/Hen VIII/2396, f. 63.
[37] Lerz and Holder, 'Medieval Crossed Friars', p. 172.

a cellar about 11ft square and at least 5ft deep (3.5m × 1.5m). The location of the building, to the south of the church and aligned with the choir, could suggest that it is the prior's mansion: the priors of the London Black and White Friars had similar houses. A lease of 1440 reinforces this hypothesis, describing 'a hall called the prior's chamber with a cellar below' (*una aula vocata le prioures chambre cum uno celario subtus*). This documented house had a parlour and four rooms in addition to the cellar, suggesting a two- or three-storey building, with an adjacent stable and garden. Unusually, the 1440 grant was a lease for life to Thomas Haseley, a royal administrator and member of Parliament who became a lay member of the friary, presumably a member of a confraternity based here; he was also buried at the priory.[38]

The Tudor historian John Stow mentions the 'Fryers hall' and the context (referring to the reuse of the building after the Dissolution as a glassworks) indicates that this hall cannot be the former dormitory or refectory in the cloister but must be another building further to the east or south. The post-Dissolution rent collector's accounts specify a 'seynt barbara hall' next to the 'pryours chambre' which may well refer to the same hall; the use of the saint's name would surely suggest that the hall was used by a lay religious fraternity. Two London fraternities with that dedication are known to have met at other religious houses and a number of fraternities were based at Crossed Friars including the Holy Blood of Jesus, a Flemish and Dutch fraternity active in the fifteenth century.[39] The rent collector's accounts mention another building, 'le pryncypalls chambre', and this must be the house which served as the accommodation for the provincial prior, the head of the Crossed friars' English province. The arrangement of these buildings is uncertain but they have been reconstructed in Figure 54 and Figure 56 following the lines of two rows of buildings on Ogilby and Morgan's map of 1676.

The original friary cemetery lay to the east of the church (Figure 55) but with the enlargement of the church in the fourteenth and fifteenth centuries, a new cemetery was laid out between the church and Hart Street (Figure 56). The 2008 archaeological excavations revealed two adult graves in this northern churchyard, with several more disturbed during late nineteenth-century building works on a house at 22 Crutched Friars (historic Hart Street).[40]

The friars had a large open area to the south of their buildings: this outer precinct with its gardens and orchards can be seen on Wyngaerde's view, immediately north of the open space of Tower Hill. The inner and outer precincts were enclosed with walls and the main

---

[38] TNA, C 54/290, m. 11v; Roskell, *The History of Parliament. The House of Commons 1386–1421*, iii, 307–10.

[39] TNA, SC 6/Hen VIII/2396, f. 63; Stow, *Survey of London*, i, 148; Caroline M. Barron, 'The Parish Fraternities of Medieval London', in *The Church in Pre-Reformation Society: Essays in Honour of F.R.H. Du Boulay*, ed. C.M. Barron and C. Harper-Bill (Woodbridge: Boydell, 1985), pp. 13–37; Colson, 'Alien Communities', pp. 112, 118.

[40] Richard Kemp, *Some Notes on the Ward of Aldgate, its Neighbourhood and its Ancient and Modern History* (London: Eden Fisher, 1935), 2nd edn, p. 100.

precinct wall was probably built of stone: a nineteenth-century view of the 1534 Drapers' Company almshouses on Cooper's Row (historic Woodrove Lane) shows that the builders reused part of the stone precinct wall for the ground-floor facade, building the upper storey in brick.[41] Further south by Tower Hill, the outer precinct was bounded by an earthen bank, described as a 'mud wall' on a map of 1597, with the south-western boundary (alongside an access road running northwards towards the cloister) built of brick by the sixteenth century.[42] The friary had at least three gates. The main gate was probably in the north-west, allowing lay people to enter the precinct via Hart Street and attend sermons in the nave of the church or walk into the churchyard (the evidence is a passage leading into Burnt Yard on Ogilby and Morgan's map of 1676). The Drapers' Company almshouses of 1534 had a small gatehouse and passage, probably incorporated in order to preserve access to the friary precinct from Woodrove Lane, and there was a third gate in the south-west corner of the precinct.[43]

Having created their precinct through the acquisition of numerous houses and tenements, the friars almost certainly retained a few of the houses to rent to lay tenants, particularly those fronting onto the two principal streets around the friary. There is a little evidence for how the prior and friars managed their rental portfolio in the sixteenth century. By the time of the Dissolution, the friars owned various tenements in their home parish of St Olave, others further afield in London and a manor in Suffolk, but their tenements within the precinct accounted for nearly a fifth of their total rental income (£6 18s 4d out of a total of £40 8s 8d). Setting aside three monastic buildings in the precinct which may only have been rented out from the 1530s (the prior's and provincial prior's houses and St Barbara hall), there were four tenements within the precinct, bringing in annual rent of £5 6s 8d.[44] One of the four tenements was a corrodian's house and was therefore rent-free: Peter and Margaret Johnson had granted sums of money (presumably substantial) in 1512 and 1518 and in return they received a newly built house for life and an annuity of £3 6s 8d (which was to continue after their death as 20s and 46s 8d due, respectively, to their son and daughter). The house was in the north-east corner of the precinct (in the former tenement 11 on Figure 53 and in Table 11), close to the construction site of the new church retro-choir. Indeed, it is quite likely that the financial arrangement for the corrody was part of prior William Bowry's fundraising for the new choir.[45]

---

[41] LMA, COLLAGE 1964.
[42] TNA, E 40/5521; *The Elizabethan Tower of London: The Haiward and Gascoyne Plan of 1597*, ed. Anna Keay, London Topographical Society, 158 (London: LTS, 2001).
[43] DC, Plan book ('A Survey of the several estates . . .'), f. 1; LMA, COLLAGE 1805; Keay, *Elizabethan Tower of London*.
[44] Holder, 'Medieval Friaries of London', pp. 189–90, 266.
[45] TNA, E 315/100, f. 123; SP 1/89, ff. 132, 134, nos 113–14.

Conclusion

The Crossed Friars has a good range of documentary, cartographic and archaeological evidence – a rare combination in London – allowing us to trace the creation of an urban monastic precinct over three centuries. The friary grew from a small church built in the 1270s on the founders' bequest of a bundle of urban plots occupying just a third of an acre (0.1ha). From these small beginnings successive priors were able to plan the expansion of the precinct and the construction of a fairly full range of conventual buildings, with the friary ending up as a moderately large urban precinct of 2¼ acres (0.9ha) by the sixteenth century. Unsurprisingly, the Crossed friars did not share the architectural splendour and variety of the wealthier Dominicans' or Franciscans' houses: the Crossed friars lacked the more formal second cloister that the wealthier friars built (typically housing a library and infirmary), and there is no evidence that the friars had a developed service wing with bake-house or brew-house. The evidence for the enlargement of the church in the sixteenth century is, however, tantalising: was this project for a retro-choir intended to form a grand architectural statement of the order's success and status, a lost work of late London Perpendicular style? Londoners certainly seem to have responded positively to the programme of fundraising and reform carried out by prior William Bowry in the sixteenth century: bequests to pay for *post mortem* spiritual services increased dramatically and, exceptionally rarely for London, one of those benefactor's tombs survives, that of Sir Richard Cholmeley, moved to the chapel of St Peter ad Vincula in the Tower (Figure 57).[46]

---

[46] For Bowry, see Röhrkasten, *Mendicant Houses*, pp. 556–8; Hayden, *Crutched Friars and Croisiers*, pp. 121–2, 128.

8

Sack Friars, c. 1270–1305

THE Friars of the Penitence of Jesus Christ, popularly known as the Sack Friars, were a mendicant movement formed in Provence in the 1240s, inspired by the teaching of Franciscans. Their official name hints at their connection to penitential groups of lay people such as Beguines, while their unofficial name in the vernacular must refer to the sack-like cloth they wore, and reveals the emphasis the friars placed on humility and poverty. In 1251 they received official approval from the pope and adopted a Dominican version of the monastic Rule of St Augustine. The movement spread rapidly and won high-ranking backers including Louis IX of France and Henry III of England. By the third quarter of the thirteenth century they were the third largest order of friars, behind the Dominicans and Franciscans, of course, but often more numerous in members and more popular with lay people than the Carmelites and Augustine friars. The Sack friars planned their move into England in 1256 and they arrived the following year.[1]

They set up their first English house in London, initially based in the parish of St Lawrence Jewry. They soon moved to a larger site just outside the city walls to the north, probably before 1259, funded by a donation of 100 marks (£66 13s 4d) from Henry III. This first priory was in the parish of St Botolph Aldersgate, although its precise location is not known.[2] In the 1260s the friars received continuing support from the king in the form of grants of food and fuel and, in 1266 and 1268, of timber for building projects and repairs. They received a donation of land in St Botolph from a lay benefactor with which to enlarge their priory and they owned at least one property in another parish.[3] However, by the

---

[1] Andrews, *The Other Friars*, pp. 175–203; *CPR 1247–1258*, p. 493; Matthew Paris, *Chronica Majora*, ed. H.R. Luard, Rolls series, 57, 7 vols (London: Longman, 1872), v, 612, 621; Richard Emery, 'The Friars of the Sack', *Speculum*, 18.3 (1943), 323–34.

[2] Röhrkasten, *Mendicant Houses*, p. 57.

[3] *CCR 1259–1261*, pp. 56, 238–9; *CCR 1261–1264*, pp. 5, 265; *CCR 1264–1268*, pp. 176, 433; *CCR 1268–1272*, p. 5; LMA, Husting Roll 2(96) (microfilm X109/399); *Cartulary of Holy Trinity Aldgate*, pp. 106–7, 535.

Fig. 58. Map showing the location of the Sack Friars precinct and a 2006 archaeological site (scale 1:2500).

end of the decade the friars had chosen to move to another site within the walls, perhaps because the Aldersgate friary was too close to the Grey Friars, or because they wanted a more central and prestigious location. The Sack friars received a royal licence to sell their Aldersgate friary in February 1270, presumably having acquired (and begun work on?) a new site in Colechurch Street, later known as Old Jewry (Figure 58).[4]

The London priory of Sack Friars remained quite small in terms of the numbers of religious: there may only have been ten friars here in 1278. And the sudden growth in numbers to thirty by 1289 may simply reflect the merger of the London house with the closed Cambridge house.[5] That merger was the result of a disaster in the history of the order, one

[4] Röhrkasten, *Mendicant Houses*, p. 58; *CPR 1266–1272*, p. 406.
[5] Röhrkasten, *Mendicant Houses*, p. 85.

which prevented the friary from continuing to develop and prosper like London's other mendicant houses. As part of the Church's great 'tidying up' of the mendicant orders in the 1270s, at the Second Council of Lyon in 1274 the pope and the council decided to close those mendicant orders that had been created since the Fourth Lateran Council of 1215. Although the Carmelites and Augustine Friars succeeded in creatively retelling the story of their origins, the Friars of the Penitence of Jesus Christ seem to have been caught by surprise and did not manage to secure an exception.[6] The London house, like the order's other houses, did not close overnight: the 1274 ruling allowed the suspended orders to continue but prevented the recruitment of any new friars, thus condemning the Sack friars and the other new mendicant orders to a gradual but inevitable decline. In 1282 John le Hurel, a descendant of Richard le Keu (the original grantor of one of the Sack Friars tenements), sensed an opportunity: he began a court case to recover the family land from the doomed friars, a case that was to last for two decades. In 1304 the City sheriffs were asked to hold an inquest *ad quod damnum*, to search for any potential hindrance before the friars could sell the priory. On 8 March the following year the friars received their royal licence to sell. Furthermore, John le Hurel had won his tenement back by that date (although this was later challenged by Bridge House) and sold it on to Robert Fitz Walter, who also bought most of the rest of the friary.[7] The buildings were used as a temporary prison for arrested knights Templar in 1310 and the former friary gradually faded from memory, erased by the evolving land ownership and development of this part of the City.[8]

Unfortunately, there are few surviving sources for this short-lived friary: the order no longer exists, its charters have not survived and there is only limited information from property transaction records in the City of London's Court of Husting. Nor is there any useful archaeological information on the friary: an archaeological watching brief was carried out on the One Lothbury site in 2006, but it simply demonstrated that virtually all archaeological deposits had been destroyed in the 1950s (Figure 58, site OLO06).[9]

Acquiring the Colechurch Street priory

The Sack friars built up their new Colechurch Street priory from three tenements. Between 1265 and 1271 Eleanor of Castile, wife of the future Edward I, acted as the warden of London

---

[6] Andrews, *The Other Friars*, p. 209.
[7] Röhrkasten, *Mendicant Houses*, pp. 59–60; TNA, C 143/45 no. 10; C 66/125, m. 16; *CPR 1301–1307*, pp. 316–17; LMA, Husting Roll 31(73) (microfilm X109/402); CLA/007/EM/02/B/069 (Bridge House deed B69); CLA/007/EM/04/1 (Bridge House Large Register of deeds), ff. 58v–59 (pp. 116–17).
[8] *CCR 1307–1313*, p. 285.
[9] The archaeological excavation took place during the construction of the elegant curved office then known as Bank Buildings, now the European headquarters of Bank of China; PCA, site OLO06, Barry Sudds, 'An Archaeological Watching Brief on a Geotechnical Investigation at One Lothbury, City of London, London EC4' (unpublished Pre-Construct Archaeology report, 2006).

Bridge and its valuable property portfolio (known as the Bridge House estate). During her tenure, presumably in the late 1260s before the couple departed for the Holy Land in summer 1270, she sold one of the estate's tenements on Colechurch Street to the Sack Friars for £40. The property came with a continuing obligation to pay for a chantry priest to perform commemorative masses for the soul of Richard le Keu, who had bequeathed the property to Bridge House in 1231.[10] The friars acquired a second property in or soon after 1272 when Henry III granted them the adjacent synagogue, although the Jews were allowed to retain their property until the completion of their new synagogue. The 'continuous wailing of the jews' (presumably a pejorative reference to the *chazzan* or cantor and his congregation) had allegedly been disturbing the friars and gave a pretext for the royal grant. This grant seems to have been given without any payment by the friars; twenty years earlier the nearby hospital of St Anthony had received a similar gift of a former synagogue from the king. The Colechurch Street synagogue had been owned before 1270 by Cresse, son of the leading London Jew Master Moses.[11] The friars seem to have acquired a third property, for which no contemporary document survives but which was later described as their 'great garden'.[12]

The approximate locations of the three tenements are shown in Figure 59.[13] The Bridge House part of the Sack Friars property was described as being on Colechurch Street but straddling the parishes of St Olave and St Margaret. The friary is mentioned in 1281 as the eastern abutment of a property fronting onto Colechurch Street, suggesting that the friars only had a small part of the street frontage.[14] The synagogue property seems to have been to the north of the Bridge House property: Stow describes it as lying at the north end of Colechurch Street/Old Jewry and he also notes that it was 'opening into Lothberie, of Saint Margarets parrish, and opening into the Old Jury of Saint Olaves parrish'. Stow also says that the synagogue building was still standing in the 1590s, by which time it was a tavern known as the Windmill. The alleys of Windmill Yard and Windmill Court thus define the locations of the two main Sack Friars tenements (Figure 59).[15] The third part of the Sack

---

[10] *Calendar of Letter-Books Preserved among the Archives of the Corporation of the City of London at the Guildhall*, ed. Reginald R. Sharpe, 11 vols (London: Francis, 1899), vol. C, 61–2; John C. Parsons, 'Eleanor (1241–1290)', *ODNB*, <http://www.oxforddnb.com/view/article/8619> [accessed 23 November 2012].

[11] *CCR 1268–1272*, p. 562; Barron and Davies, *Religious Houses*, p. 228; John Watney, *Some Account of the Hospital of St Thomas of Acon, in the Cheap, London, and of the Plate of the Mercer's Company* (London: privately printed, 1892), pp. 256–7; Joe Hillaby, 'London: The 13th-Century Jewry Revisited', *Jewish Historical Studies*, 32 (1990), 89–158 (pp. 101, 138, fig. 5).

[12] LMA, Husting Roll 157(8) (microfilm X109/418).

[13] Figure 59 is partly based on unpublished research carried out by the 'Social and Economic Study of Medieval London' in the 1980s, now archived at the Centre for Metropolitan History: CMH, SESML, St Margaret Lothbury 33.

[14] *Calendar of Letter-Books*, vol. C, 61–2; *CPR 1272–1281*, p. 435.

[15] Stow, *Survey of London*, i, 277; CMH, SESML, St Margaret Lothbury, reconstructed 'Fire Court' map of properties in 1666.

Fig. 59. Map showing the approximate location of the tenements acquired by the Sack friars for their Colechurch Street priory (scale 1:750).

Friars property, the 'great garden', was described as lying to the east of the built-up part of the friary (in a later transaction of 1426) and it must be the large tenement lying to the east of Windmill Court and south of Lothbury at the time of the Great Fire.[16]

The church and precinct

The friars' precinct occupied an area of about half an acre (0.2ha; Figure 60). Unfortunately, there is very little information on how the Sack friars laid out their friary. The original chapel was in the south-west of the precinct; the synagogue that they obtained in or soon after 1272 was adjacent.[17] The chapel and the converted synagogue were probably fairly austere: the order generally retained their early enthusiasm for poverty and humility.[18] The eastern part of their precinct was a garden with a separate entrance, enclosed by walls (*cum introitu eiusdem gardini & muris circumstantibus*).[19] The Sack friars probably

---

[16] LMA, Husting Roll 157(8) (microfilm X109/418); CMH, SESML, St Margaret Lothbury, reconstructed 'Fire Court' map.
[17] *CCR 1268–1272*, p. 522.
[18] Andrews, *The Other Friars*, pp. 187–9.
[19] LMA, Husting Roll 31(69) (microfilm X109/402).

Fig. 60. Map showing the reconstructed precinct of Sack Friars (scale 1:750).

allowed lay people to be buried in their cemetery: the friars had paid 40s a year to the vicar of St Botolph as compensation for lost revenue when they were in their Aldersgate friary and they may well have had a similar arrangement with the parish of St Olave and/or St Margaret.[20] Building works were taking place at the friary in early 1272 when the king granted five oaks for structural timbers; the synagogue presumably became the friary church at the end of that year.[21]

Conclusion

John Stow, writing at the end of the sixteenth century, neatly summarised the medieval history of the Sack Friars site: 'And thus much for this house, sometime the Jewes Synagogue, since a house of Fryers, then a Noble mans house, after that a Marchauntes house, wherein Mayoralties have beene kept, and now a Wine Taverne.'[22]

The 1274 decision of Pope Gregory X and the Council of Lyon consigned the Friars of the Penitence of Jesus Christ to a short existence in medieval London: just over three decades in their principal English priory. This short lifespan and the consequent dearth of

---

[20] LMA, GL MS 25121/592; Röhrkasten, *Mendicant Houses*, p. 58.
[21] *CCR 1268–1272*, pp. 456, 522.
[22] Stow, *Survey of London*, i, 277.

documentary records, not to mention the lack of archaeological evidence from the 1950s redevelopment of the site, mean that there is little evidence for the house of the London Sack friars. In this chapter, however, the limited sources have at least permitted us to locate the friary with more precision and estimate the size of its half-acre precinct for the first time.

9

Pied Friars, 1267–1317

THE final London friary to consider is that of the Friars of the Blessed Mary (*fratres beate Marie*), also known as the Pied friars. The order began in Marseilles in the mid thirteenth century and the bishop soon granted them a chapel in the area of the city known as Aren in 1259, thus giving the order one of their (many) Latin names of *fratres de Areno*.[1] These friars were the least successful of the thirteenth-century mendicant orders, ending up with about seven houses in France and another half dozen elsewhere in Europe. They arrived in England in 1267 where they became known as the Pied friars (*fratres de pica*), a playful reference to their magpie-like appearance with a black outer scapular over their white mantle. After founding their first English house in London, they had established a second house in Norwich by 1274.[2] The London friary housed about twenty friars in the 1270s and '80s: the order was clearly quite successful in its early days in England. However, like the Sack friars, the Pied friars were in effect killed off at the Second Council of Lyon in 1274, which prevented the lesser mendicant orders from recruiting new members. The number of friars, unsurprisingly, declined, with twelve living at the London friary in 1297 and a sole survivor, Hugh of York, collecting his royal alms in April 1317.[3]

The main source for the London house is an order recorded on the Close rolls and resulting from an inquisition into the former house after the death of Hugh in August 1317.[4]

---

[1] François-Xavier de Belsunce, *L'Antiquité de l'Église de Marseille et la Succession de ses Évêques*, 3 vols (Marseilles: Brébion, 1747), ii, 229–34.

[2] Richard Emery, 'The Friars of the Blessed Mary and the Pied Friars', *Speculum*, 24.2 (1949), 228–38.

[3] Röhrkasten, *Mendicant Houses*, p. 84. In the revised edition of the Victoria County History article on this friary (Barron and Davies, *Religious Houses*, pp. 143–4), Röhrkasten corrects the erroneous *two* articles on the house in the 1909 edition, which had separate entries for the Pied Friars and the Friars de Areno; VCH, *London*, i, 516.

[4] *Calendar of Inquisitions Miscellaneous*, ii (1307–1349), 70–1; *CCR 1313–1318*, p. 503. There is a copy of the royal order in Westminster Abbey Muniments (WAM), Muniment book 11 (Domesday cartulary), f. 112.

168   THE FRIARIES OF MEDIEVAL LONDON

Fig. 61. Map showing the location of the Pied Friars precinct (1:2500).

The royal order – which recounts the history of the house – returned the property to the original owners, Westminster Abbey, and it became part of the abbey estate that supported the sacrist; the sacrist's accounts and leases therefore contain a number of useful references to the former friary.[5] No archaeological work has been carried out within the area of the friary, which lies between Covent Garden and the Strand (Figure 61).

The friary

Henry III granted the newly arrived Pied friars the right to establish an English friary in October 1267. This royal permission was granted around the time that the founder of the

---

[5]   F.H.W Sheppard, *Covent Garden*, Survey of London, 36 (London: Athlone Press, 1970), pp. 21–2.

Fig. 62. Map showing the plots and messuages acquired by the Pied friars for their precinct (1:1500).

friary, the knight William Arnald, granted them their first plot of land along the road leading from the city of London to the royal palace and abbey at Westminster; the plot lay in between the two, just under a mile from both city and palace (Table 12, Figure 62).[6] There is some uncertainty about the identity of the founder. In a document of 1268 he is described as William Arnald, a landowner in Middlesex; in fourteenth-century documents he is identified as a knight, with his surname spelt as the more French-sounding Arnaud.[7] The fact that in the 1268 document he is recognising a 15-mark debt to William de Plumpton (a second founder or benefactor of the priory) would suggest that this is the more reliable identification: the founder is therefore more likely to be this Middlesex knight than a French knight.[8] The following year, in February 1268, William de Plumpton, a royal servant (the 'king's clerk'), granted a pair of messuages to the king for the use of the friars.[9] The two messuages were presumably adjacent to the earlier Arnald gift and the new gift also contained a chapel dedicated to St Margaret the Virgin (Table 12, Figure 62). However, this existing chapel may have been quite small because the grant allowed the friars to build

---

[6] *CPR 1266–1272*, p. 122.
[7] *CCR 1264–1268*, p. 519; see n. 4 for the fourteenth-century documents.
[8] For French and Aquitaine knights named William or Guillaume Arnaud, see *CPR 1266–1272*, pp. 492, 498; TNA, SC 1/3/168 [catalogue]); SC 8/89/4404 [catalogue].
[9] *CChR 1257–1300*, p. 89; TNA, C 53/57, m. 10 [1268 grant]. William de Plumpton crops up in various other documents of the 1260s, where he is named as the king's clerk; for example *CCR 1264–1268*, p. 519.

Table 12 List of the tenements acquired by the Pied friars for their priory.

Number on Figure 62	Date of acquisition	Grantor	Description	Reference
1	c. October 1267	William Arnald (Arnaud?)		*CCR 1313–1318*, p. 503
2 & 3	February 1268	William de Plumpton	two messuages and a chapel in parish of Holy Innocents	TNA, C 53/57, m. 10
4	July 1270	Henry III	plot of land in parish of Holy Innocents	*CPR 1266–1272*, p. 447
	Before November 1272	Henry III and William de Aldenham	tenement in Westminster	Röhrkasten, *Mendicant Houses*, p. 61

a new chapel (or enlarge the old one?). Two years later the friars were granted a fourth plot along the street frontage and to the west of the chapel (Table 12, Figure 62).[10] In 1280 the royal Chancery was examining the king's earlier donation to the friars of a tenement in Westminster of William de Aldenham; this might reveal the source of Henry III's 1270 donation to the friars, or it could have been a separate grant.[11]

The Pied Friars precinct can be located with some confidence thanks to long-lasting historic boundaries. Two out of the three grants specify that the messuages were in the parish of Holy Innocents (the present-day St Mary le Strand), between the cities of London and Westminster.[12] Furthermore, the western limit of the Pied Friars precinct is shared with part of the historic boundary of Westminster Abbey's convent garden estate, the latter fossilised as the new parish of St Paul Covent Garden after the seventeenth-century development of the estate.[13] Starting with this western edge of the Pied Friars precinct (a line just to the west of modern Southampton Street), one can bring in measurements recorded in an abbey lease of 'le fryer pys' of 1524, where the dimensions of the old precinct are given as 329ft along the main road (Strand, running between Westminster and London) and up to 184ft deep (Figure 63).[14]

A little more detail of the Pied friars' church and precinct can be pieced together. Their church must have been towards the east end of their precinct: when the friars acquired their fourth plot in 1270, the dimensions of this additional parcel were specified as 13½ perches 2 feet (224ft 9in; 68.5m), running westwards from the friars' church (Figure 63).[15] A second measurement of this additional plot, 2 perches 4 feet (37ft; 11.3m), probably gives

[10] *CPR 1266–1272*, p. 447.
[11] Röhrkasten, *Mendicant Houses*, p. 61.
[12] The parish of the William Arnald plot of land is not specified.
[13] Sheppard, *Covent Garden*, pp. 19–22, 53–63.
[14] WAM, Register book 2, f. 209v. The location of the 'fryer pys' property has been analysed in some detail in Sheppard, *Covent Garden*, pp. 21–2.
[15] *CPR 1266–1272*, p. 447; TNA, C 66/88, m. 8.

Fig. 63. Map showing the arrangement of the Pied Friars precinct in the thirteenth century (1:1500).

the distance between the church and the main road. This space between church and road might have formed a small friary graveyard, through which visitors could have passed in order to enter the church, perhaps by a porch in the south-west corner.

The friars' old church and churchyard are mentioned in chronicles recounting the murder of Walter Stapeldon, bishop of Exeter, in 1326. Stapeldon had been a prominent figure in the losing side in the civil war between, on the one hand, Edward II and the Despensers, and, on the other, Edward's estranged wife Isabella and Roger Mortimer. Stapeldon – unpopular in London – was killed by a crowd in Cheapside in October 1326 after Isabella's successful invasion of England; his decapitated corpse was temporarily buried in the Pied Friars graveyard. The friary church was named in one of these chronicles as 'Le Laweles Chirche', although this may simply refer to the abandoned church in the fourteenth century. The choice of the friars' old churchyard as Stapeldon's initial burial site was felt by one chronicler to be particularly appropriate: in the bishop's lifetime he had ordered his men to take stone from the abandoned friary church to reuse in his London mansion.[16]

Very little else is known about the friary. The friars' accommodation might have been

[16] M.C. Buck, 'Stapeldon, Walter (b. in or before 1265, d. 1326)', *ODNB*, <http://www.oxforddnb.com/view/article/26296> [accessed 11 May 2015]; Thomas Walsingham, *Historia Anglicana: Thomæ Walsingham, Quondam Monachi S. Albani*, ed. Henry T. Riley, Rolls series, 28, 2 vols (London: Longman, 1863), i, 182; BL, Cotton MS Tiberius A VI, ff. 121–9; John Leland, *Antiquarii de Rebus Britannicis Collectanea*, ed. Thomas Hearne, 6 vols (London, 1770), i, 467–8 [reuse of

in a wing behind the church, perhaps running north or north-west (Figure 63). Had events turned out more favourably for the friars this could have developed into a normal monastic cloister. Much of the precinct may have been a garden: a 1354 Westminster Abbey lease describes the old precinct plot as 'a garden with appurtenances formerly called the garden of the Pied Friars'.[17]

Conclusion

The small friary of the Pied friars lay on the then rural road between London and Westminster and lasted for just fifty years between 1267 and 1317, its history cut short by the decision of the Second Council of Lyon to close down the minor orders of friars. Remarkably little is known about the friary but, using the evidence of a sixteenth-century lease, we argue that the friars' precinct occupied an area of 0.5ha (1¼ acres) and some tentative suggestions can be made for the layout of this precinct (Figure 63). On the positive side, the basic outline of the friary's history was recorded in a Chancery inquisition and Close roll. Less positively, any archaeological evidence for the friary was probably destroyed in 1907–9 during the construction of the Strand Palace Hotel, although some evidence may survive beneath modern Exeter Street (Figure 61).

stone]; Arnold Fitz-Thedmar, *Chronicles of the Mayors and Sheriffs of London: A.D. 1188 to A.D. 1274*, ed. Henry T. Riley (London: Trübner, 1863), p. 263 [le laweles chirche].

[17] *Unum gardinum suum cum suis pertinenciis quondam vocatum gardinum fratrum picarum*; WAM, Muniment 17166.

PART II

The London Friars and their Friaries

10

Churches

At the heart of each friary was the church, whose east end framed the two spiritual nodes, the high altar and the choir stalls. The friary churches were not, however, static: priors and lay sponsors added to the buildings over the three centuries of mendicant life in the capital.[1] The most important distinction is between the friars' early churches of the thirteenth century and those they began to build in the following century; this distinction must surely correspond to a change in emphasis about the role and function of the friars and their priories.

Thirteenth-century churches

We lack precise evidence for the dimensions, layout and architectural detail of the seven thirteenth-century churches but, in nearly every case, there is *some* indication of size and shape – whether from archaeological excavation, documentary measurements or from cartographic information on adjacent streets and buildings. The early priors of the thirteenth century must have had in mind a model for the friary church: in nearly every case they built a relatively small, single-aisled chapel of three to six bays (Figure 64). These churches were never more than about a hundred feet long, often less, and in the case of Sack Friars, half that length. They would have had plain timber roofs, three to six windows on the long sides (presumably simple lancets or pairs of lights in an Early English style), a door at the west end and a grander window (perhaps three lancets?) at the east end. The eastern bay may have been vaulted above the high altar to mark its higher status, like the surviving mid-thirteenth-century Franciscan church in Cortona (Italy).[2] Unfortunately, no architectural fragments of these early London churches have so far been identified in

---

[1] The plural term 'priors' includes the Franciscan head, more correctly termed a guardian.
[2] The Franciscan Constitutions of Narbonne of 1260 specified that vaults and stained glass were only permitted in the east end of the order's churches: Caroline Bruzelius, *Preaching, Building,*

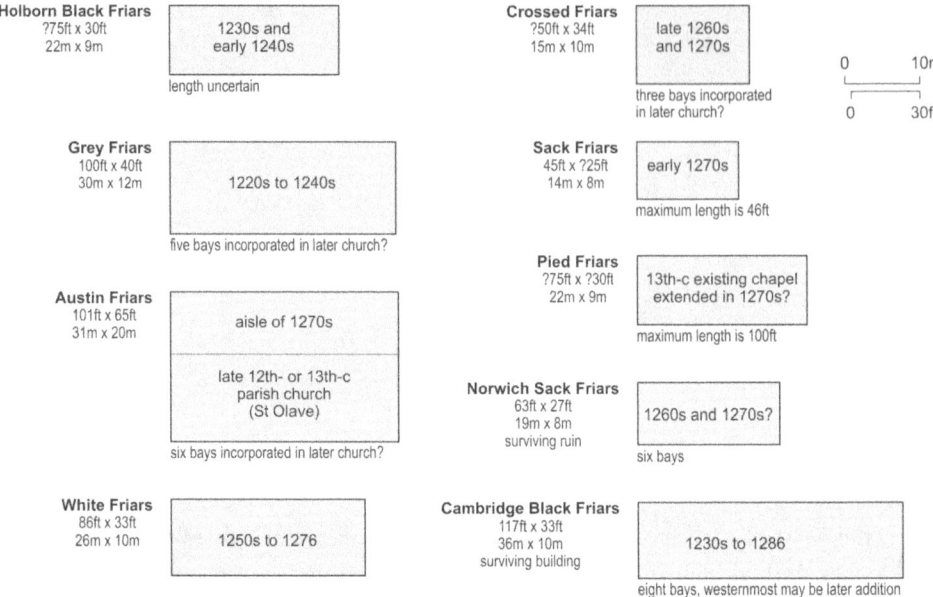

fig. 64. Plans of the seven thirteenth-century friars' churches; the partly surviving churches of the Cambridge Dominicans and Norwich Sack friars are also shown (scale: 1:1000).

archaeological excavations, although the surviving window arch of the late thirteenth-century chapter house undercroft at the (second) Black Friars gives an indication of the plain architectural taste of the early mendicants (Figure 65). Documentary evidence gives us occasional glimpses of the early chapels of the London friaries; for example, Edward I spent over 10 marks on Purbeck marble to finish off the Carmelites' church in 1273, for use in the high altar.[3] Remembering the stern instructions of the thirteenth-century Franciscan provincial prior to remove the excessive ornament from the ceiling of Grey Friars, one should probably picture these thirteenth-century interiors with little sculpture and painted decoration (Chapter 4: Grey Friars, 'Conclusion').

Part of the church of the Cambridge Dominicans survives (as the hall and parlour of Emmanuel College) and this may be the best surviving English example of a thirteenth-century friary church. The Cambridge church was begun in the 1230s and dedicated in 1286. It was a single-aisled building divided into seven or eight bays. The church was 26ft wide internally and 112ft long, perhaps originally about 90ft long if one of the bays is a later enlargement (Figure 64; 36m (or 27m) × 10m).[4] The English architectural models that the

and Burying: Friars in the Medieval City (New Haven and London: Yale University Press, 2014), pp. 33, 37–8.

[3] TNA, C 62/49, m. 4: 5 marks for the stone plus 5 marks 4 shillings transport.

[4] Deirdre O'Sullivan, In the Company of the Preachers: The Archaeology of Medieval Friaries in England and Wales, Leicester Archaeology Monographs, 23 (University of Leicester, 2013), pp. 79–81.

Fig. 65. Photograph of the simple late thirteenth-century window arch from the chapter house of the second Black Friars (moved in the early twentieth century to the grounds of what is now Selsdon Park Hotel).

thirteenth-century friars had in mind were not the large aisled Benedictine abbeys that had sprung up all over England in the late eleventh and twelfth centuries, nor the cruciform churches with transepts built by the twelfth-century Augustinian canons. The mendicants chose instead the style of the plain chapels of nuns and canonesses, or those of the early Carthusian monks. The twelfth-century Cistercian nunnery of Kirklees (Yorkshire), for example, was a simple chapel, lacking aisles or transepts; the early thirteenth-century Carthusian priory of Hinton (Somerset) had a similar plain church.[5]

These thirteenth-century churches were essentially small monastic chapels: the spiritual heart of the friary where the friars performed the spoken and sung rituals of the seven daily offices (at their choir stalls) and the midday mass (at the high altar: Chapter 16: Spiritual Life and Education in the London Friaries). The early friars went out into the town to preach, of course, but lay people rarely came into the friaries, at least, not into the first friaries of the thirteenth century. There are two exceptions to this (exceptions that were to become increasingly important): townsfolk came into open spaces within early friaries to attend public preaching, and wealthier burgesses began to request burial in the friary churches.[6] The early (and aristocratic) stages of this burial fashion can be observed at Black Friars where the founder (Hubert de Burgh, earl of Kent), his wife and his sister-in-law (Margaret, countess of Kent, and Isabel, countess of Norfolk) were all buried in the chapel. The chapel may also have been the first resting place of the former heir to the throne – Edward I's son Alphonso who died at the age of ten in 1284 (Chapter 1: The First Black Friars in Holborn).

The grandest of the early friary churches was probably the Austin Friars. Rather unusually, the friars had taken over a twelfth- or thirteenth-century parish church (St Olave Broad Street) and – in effect – closed its doors to parishioners. Even this church was probably no architectural marvel but it is worth noting that the first prior (probably William de Clare) undertook works to enlarge the church in the 1270s; the archaeological evidence, although rather slim, suggests that he added an aisle on the north side (Chapter 6: Austin Friars). Of course, by adding an aisle a more dramatic environment is created: an arcade that separates and defines two spaces, columns and capitals that hold up those arcade arches, and a new location for tombs, altars and statues. This aisle (if it is not pushing the slim evidence too far) was presumably the first London mendicant church that was lit by windows in the new style, later termed Geometric, with proper stone tracery drawing out patterns of plain or foliated circles over arches within each window.

The later friary churches

In the fourth quarter of the thirteenth century some of the priors of the London friaries started to develop new plans for their churches. It is impossible, of course, to pin down exactly what happened and when, but one can speculate that in about 1274 an extraordinary meeting was held at the first Black Friars in Holborn, attended by the Dominican

---

[5] Glyn Coppack, *Abbeys and Priories* (Stroud: Tempus, 2006), pp. 44–60.

[6] Michael Robson, 'The Franciscan Custody of York in the Thirteenth Century', in *The Friars in Medieval Britain: Proceedings of the 2007 Harlaxton Symposium*, ed. N. Rogers, Harlaxton Medieval Studies, 19 (Donington: Shaun Tyas, 2010), pp. 1–24 (pp. 11–12, 14–15); Bruzelius, *Preaching, Building, and Burying*, pp. ix–xi, 1–17, 46–51, 86–7.

prior John of Darlington, the archbishop of Canterbury Robert Kilwardby (a Dominican himself), the mayor Henry le Waleys and a representative of Edward I (Chapter 2: The Second Black Friars). In addition to agenda items such as 'move city wall of London to make space for new priory', the participants may have discussed the design of a completely new type of friary church. This church would have a proper choir and presbytery that could seat a hundred friars, and a large nave in which Londoners – perhaps in their hundreds – could stand in order to listen to the friars' sermons.

John of Darlington and his obedientiaries at Black Friars would probably have turned for inspiration to recent and ongoing examples of major cathedral and abbey construction, such as Salisbury cathedral (completed c. 1275) and Ely cathedral (new choir built in second quarter of thirteenth century). Closer to home, they would surely have been very familiar with the works at Westminster Abbey (the extensive rebuilding of the east end and part of the nave in the third quarter of thirteenth century) and at St Paul's cathedral (the 'New Work' of the enlarged east end in the second half of the century).[7] And they could count on the particular experience of mayor le Waleys, who was managing the building works at Westminster Abbey and who was soon to be involved with extensive redevelopment of the civic buildings at Guildhall.[8]

This new abbatial form of friary church was begun at Black Friars (the friars' second site in the south-west corner of the adjusted city walls) in about 1280. Construction began at the east end and moved westwards, finishing the basic choir in the 1290s and then turning to the preaching nave in the 1310s; the church seems to have been complete by the middle of the fourteenth century (Figure 66; Figure 67; Chapter 2: The Second Black Friars). There is a sense that the London Franciscans did not wish to be upstaged by their Dominican colleagues: the Grey friars planned a new building campaign in the 1280s to replace their small chapel. If the Black Friars had the support of the king, the Grey Friars recruited the new Capetian queen, Margaret of France: the former was 'his' royal mendicant church; the latter was 'hers'.[9] The construction programme at the Grey Friars seems to have been about a decade behind the Black Friars: work began on a preaching nave in the 1290s or slightly earlier, with the old chapel being enlarged into a proper choir with aisles at the turn of the century, and construction work pushing the nave westwards in the first half of the

---

[7] Richard Morris, *Cathedrals and Abbeys of England and Wales: The Building Church, 600–1540* (London: Dent, 1979), pp. 194–218, 251, 269, 274–5; Carol D. Cragoe, 'Fabric, Tombs and Precinct, 1087–1540', in *St Paul's: The Cathedral Church of London, 604–2004*, ed. D. Keene, A. Burns and A. Saint (New Haven and London: Yale University Press, 2004), pp. 127–42 (pp. 136–9); John Schofield, *St Paul's Cathedral Before Wren* (Swindon: English Heritage, 2011), pp. 110–40.

[8] Frédérique Lachaud, 'Waleys, Henry le (d. 1302)', *ODNB*, <http://www.oxforddnb.com/view/article/28460> [accessed 9 June 2014]; David Bowsher and others, *The London Guildhall: An Archaeological History of a Neighbourhood from Early Medieval to Modern Times*, MoLAS monograph, 36, 2 vols (London: Museum of London Archaeology Service, 2007), i, 139.

[9] Christian Steer, 'Royal and Noble Commemoration in the Mendicant Houses of London, c. 1240–1540', in *Memory and Commemoration in Medieval England*, ed. C.M. Barron and C. Burgess, Harlaxton Medieval Studies, 20 (Donington: Shaun Tyas, 2010), pp. 117–42 (p. 119).

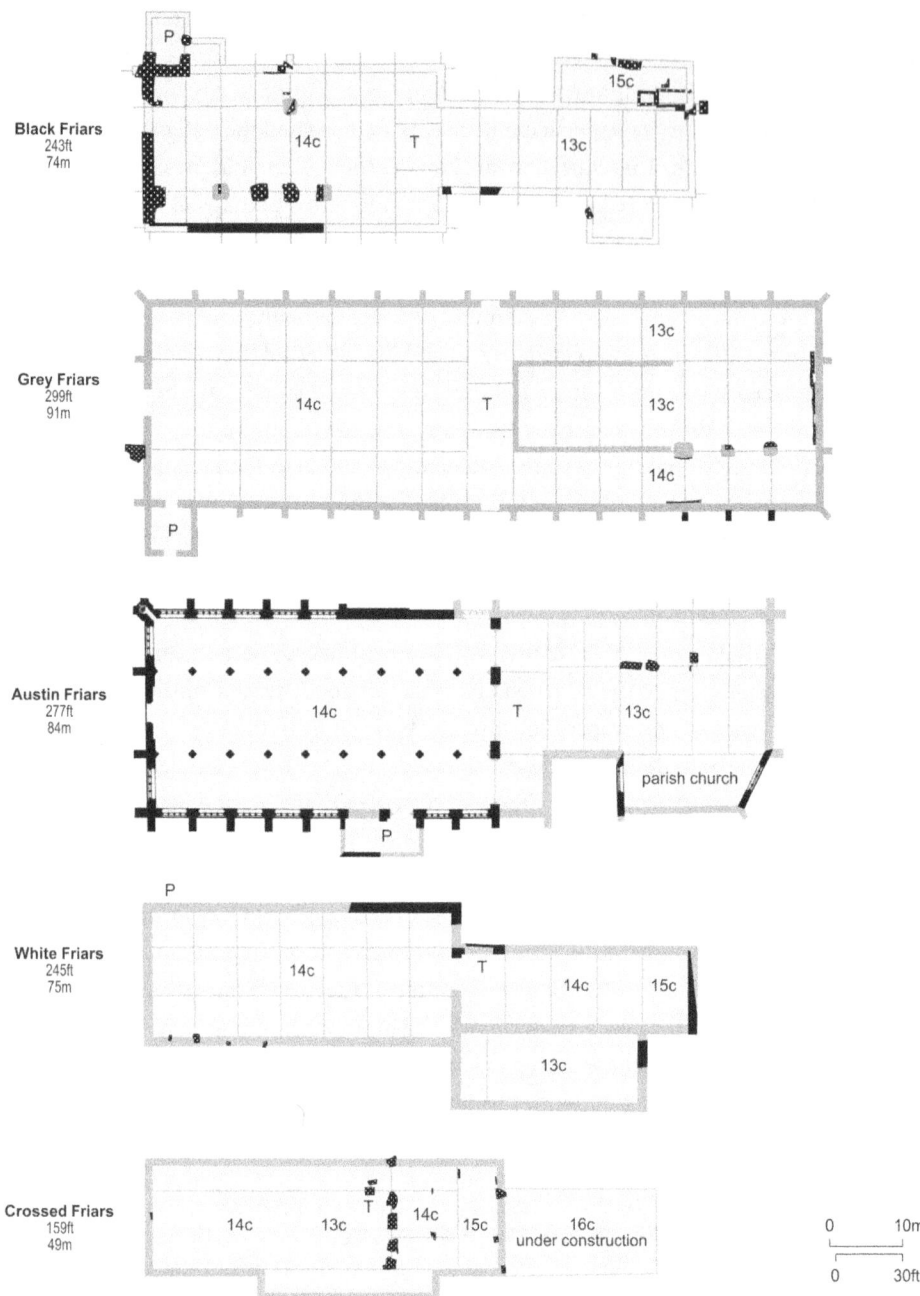

Fig. 66. Plans of the five late-medieval friars' churches ('P' indicates porch, 'T' tower; scale 1:1000)

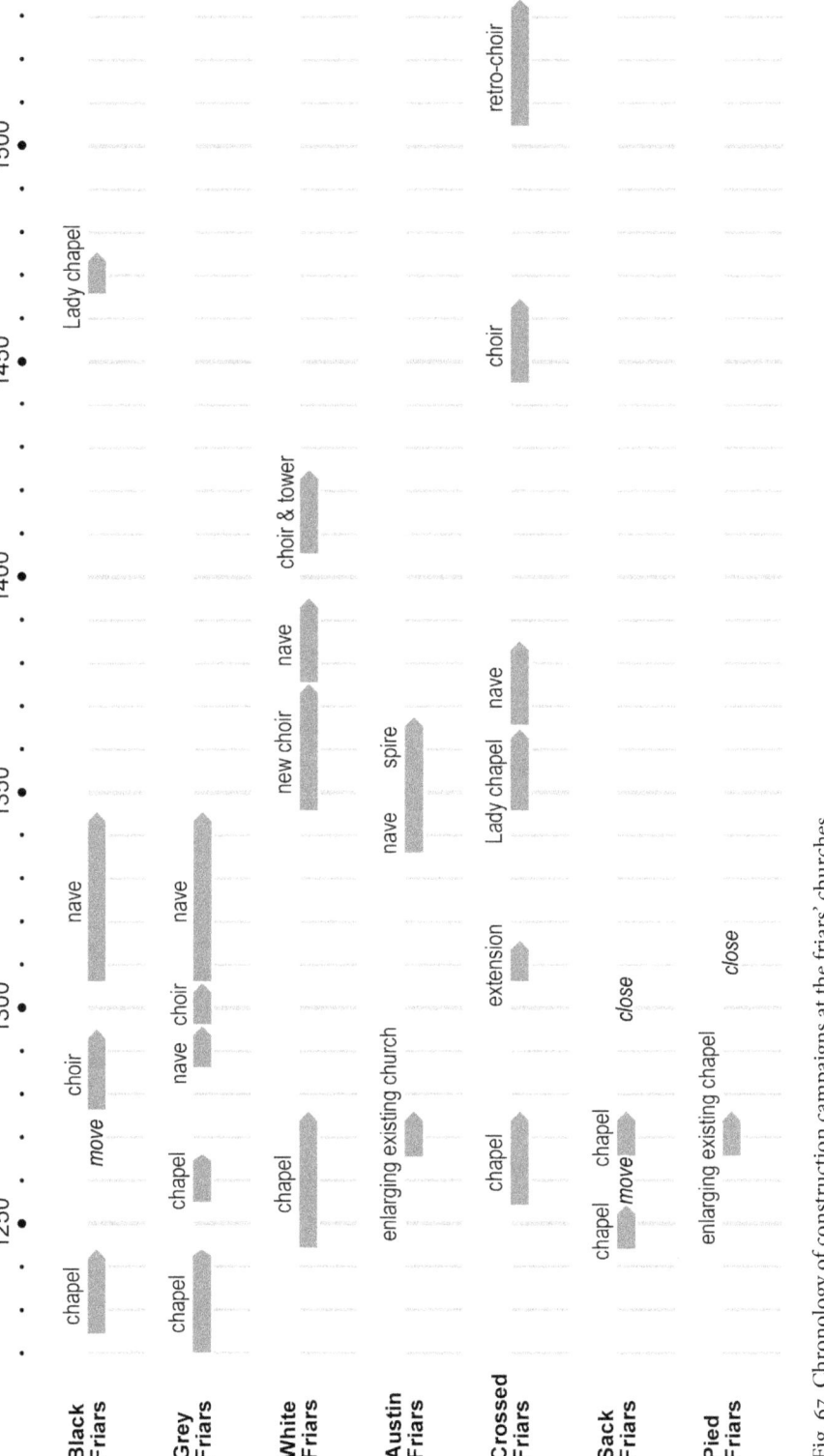

Fig. 67. Chronology of construction campaigns at the friars' churches

fourteenth century. It looks like the huge church was completed just before the Black Death with some finishing touches and the final dedication taking place in the 1350s (Figure 66; Figure 67; Chapter 4: Grey Friars). The sheer scale of these two friary churches clearly went beyond the basic need for space; they carried the bold message to Londoners 'we are here to stay'.

With the lead taken by the Dominicans and Franciscans in the late thirteenth and early fourteenth century, the other mendicants – at least, those that had survived the cull of the Second Council of Lyon – followed suit in the mid fourteenth century. The Austin friars already had a chapel with an aisle – the makings of a good choir – so they began work on a nave in the 1340s, perhaps a little earlier. It is worth noting that the Franciscans of Pisa set out the foundations for their nave decades before the main project started in order to plan carefully the spatial relationship between choir, cloister and nave; it is possible that the London Austin friars did something similar. Their finished church and cloisters are nicely dovetailed, unlike those of the London Franciscans who ended up with a narrow gap between nave and cloister (Figure 73).[10] The Augustine friars' finished church was clearly modelled on Grey Friars, although the presence of the adjacent parish chapel of St Peter Broad Street prevented the Austin friars from achieving the full three-aisled choir enjoyed by the Franciscans (Figure 66). The White friars seem to have begun a new church from scratch, beginning work on a choir shortly after the Black Death and continuing westwards with a nave in the 1380s: the Carmelite priors clearly based their new church on Black Friars (Figure 66). The Crossed friars worked on a similar timetable, first enlarging their chapel into a choir and Lady chapel, and then building a nave. However, the constraints of the site, and no doubt their budget, forced these canon-friars to build a slightly smaller church – still bigger, however, than most London parish churches.

By the end of the fourteenth century all five friary churches were effectively complete, notwithstanding further improvements and modernisations in the following century. They were very substantial buildings, all the more remarkable given that the friars had carved these huge monuments into the densely occupied London landscape, and within a century or so of their arrival. Mention has been made of the great abbeys and cathedrals that provided a model for these friary churches but, however impressive the Grey Friars church in particular might have been, the London friaries were not quite in that league. A more appropriate comparison is the slightly smaller but still impressive monastic churches of the Augustinian canons: St Mary Spital (a building campaign of the second quarter of the thirteenth century, with remodelling towards the end of the century), St Mary Overie in Southwark (a campaign lasting much of the century) or St Mary Merton in Surrey (the second and third quarters of the century).[11] The London friaries and Augustinian canons'

---

[10] Bruzelius, *Preaching, Building, and Burying*, p. 96.
[11] David Divers and others, *A New Millennium at Southwark Cathedral: Investigations into the First Two Thousand Years* (London: Pre-Construct Archaeology, 2009), pp. 41–2, 50–1, 60–2,

Table 13 Size and date of the friars' churches and other London-area churches in the fourteenth century.[a]

Church	Length	Completed
Great churches		
St Paul's (secular cathedral)	175m, 574ft	1327
Westminster (Benedictine abbey)	154m, 505ft	1269
Friaries and Augustinian priories		
St Mary Merton, Surrey (Augustinian priory)	96m, 315ft	c. 1340
Grey Friars	91m, 299ft	c. 1360
Austin Friars	84m, 277ft	c. 1370
St Mary Overie (Augustinian priory)	79m, 260ft	c. 1300
Holy Trinity (Augustinian priory)	77m, 254ft	c. 1300
Black Friars	74m, 243ft	1320s?
White Friars	68m, 220ft?[b]	1390s?
St Mary Spital (Augustinian hospital)	52m, 171ft	c. 1320
Parish churches		
St Nicholas Shambles	29m, 95ft	
St Laurence Jewry	27m, 90ft	

Notes:

[a] The lengths are the external dimension, including both nave and choir but not including buttresses. The sources for the dates and dimensions of the non-friary churches are cited in nn. 7 and 11. See also Christopher Thomas, Jane Sidell and Robert Cowie, *The Royal Palace, Abbey and Town of Westminster on Thorney Island: Archaeological Excavations (1991–8) for the London Underground Limited Jubilee Line Extension Project*, MoLAS monograph, 22 (London: Museum of London Archaeology Service, 2006), pp. 71–3; Bowsher, *Guildhall*, ii, 391–6; John Schofield, 'Excavations on the Site of St Nicholas Shambles, Newgate Street, City of London, 1975–9', *Transactions of the London and Middlesex Archaeological Society*, 48 (1997), 77–135 (pp. 96–9); Edward Hatton, *A New View of London: Or, an Ample Account of that City, in ... Eight Sections*, 2 vols (London: Chiswell and Churchill, 1708), i, 217.

[b] The length of the church in the fourteenth century (without the fifteenth-century enhancement to the choir) is uncertain.

houses thus occupy a middle rank of churches: between the ordinary parish churches and the extraordinary cathedral and Westminster Abbey (Table 13). The friary churches would certainly have dwarfed their neighbours, mere 100-foot long parish churches such as St Nicholas Shambles (next to Grey Friars) or St Andrew-by-the-Wardrobe (by Black Friars).

It is important to note that the size of the churches, and their individual components, reflects their popularity among a wealthy elite, the local topography and their date of

71–5; Christopher Thomas, Barney Sloane and Christopher Phillpotts, *Excavations at the Priory and Hospital of St Mary Spital, London*, MoLAS monograph, 1 (London: Museum of London Archaeology Service, 1997), pp. 26–35, 41; Pat Miller and David Saxby, *The Augustinian Priory of St Mary Merton, Surrey: Excavations 1976–90*, MoLAS monograph, 34 (London: Museum of London Archaeology Service, 2007), pp. 34–41.

construction, not just numbers of lay visitors or friars. The Dominicans consistently had the largest number of friars and were the wealthiest of the five friary orders, but their church was the second smallest (that of the Crossed Friars being smaller). In large part this simply reflects the date of its construction and the topography of the precinct: the large choir was begun with royal support in the 1270s but, when the nave was started in the first quarter of the fourteenth century, the overall length of the church was limited by the internal road layout and the need to allow efficient circulation within the precinct. The Grey friars had a topographical (not financial or spiritual) advantage: they had a rather long east–west precinct space in which to build their church. Conversely the Crossed friars never managed to attract the wealthiest lay supporters and so their church remained the smallest of the five London friaries, with their over-ambitious plan to extend it eastwards in the sixteenth century never realised.

The London friaries probably shared the traditional and somewhat flexible rules of circulation of monastic cathedrals, and of Continental friaries, where the nave was the main lay area but lay men were generally allowed into the aisles or ambulatory of the choir, although not into the area of the actual friars' stalls.[12] The two halves of the church – distinct but permeable – were separated by screens enclosing a lateral bay, usually described in sixteenth-century sources as a 'walking place'. This was a corridor that allowed the friars access through the church to and from their cloisters: this architectural feature was important to the itinerant friars but was not required by static communities of, for example, Benedictine monks. The rood screen (sometimes described using the Italian word 'tramezzo') would generally have formed the western wall of the walking place corridor, with stalls for the friars perhaps built up against the eastern *pulpitum* wall; both walls would have been largely built in timber but perhaps of masonry in their lower stage. A rare surviving example of this arrangement can be seen at the former Dominican friary of Guebwiller in France: the corridor still runs across the church with its open arcade wall on the nave side and solid wall on the choir side (little of the upper timber storey of the screen survives).[13] The entrances to these paired churches lay in their respective south-west or north-west corners. Thus at Black Friars, for example, the laity would arrive from the north and head for the porch in the north-west corner of the nave. In contrast, the friars would enter the choir from their cloister to the south of the church, proceeding into the walking

---

[12] Roberta Gilchrist, *Norwich Cathedral Close: The Evolution of the English Cathedral Landscape*, Studies in the History of Medieval Religion (Woodbridge: Boydell, 2005), pp. 243–6; Donal Cooper, 'Access all Areas? Spatial Divides in the Mendicant Churches of Late Medieval Tuscany', in *Ritual and Space in the Middle Ages*, ed. F. Andrews, Harlaxton Medieval Studies, 21 (Donington: Shaun Tyas, 2011), pp. 90–107; Donal Cooper and James R. Banker, 'The Church of Borgo San Sepolcro in the Late Middle Ages and Renaissance', in *Sassetta: The Borgo San Sepolcro Altarpiece*, ed. M. Israels, 2 vols (Leiden and Florence: Primavera Press/Villa I Tatti, 2009), i, 53–85, ii, 585–9 (i, 84).

[13] Joanna Cannon, *Religious Poverty, Visual Riches: Art in the Dominican Churches of Central Italy in the Thirteenth and Fourteenth Centuries* (New Haven and London: Yale University Press, 2013), pp. 29–34.

place and turning right (eastwards) into the southern aisle of the choir. The walking place bay was also the location of the tower: the huge piers required to support a central tower are best sited 'out of the way', to the east of the nave altar and to the west of the choir.

To this basic twin-church form, a variety of chapels and other screened spaces were added over the years. At first sight the friary naves – according to the simple plans we have reconstructed (Figure 66) – look like great open preaching spaces. However, the evidence of the Franciscan 'register' demonstrates the complexity of the church space, with a variety of partly screened chapels, statues and altars.[14] The naves would thus have seemed tall and narrow rather than broad, with some friaries having light flooding down from high clerestory windows. Timber screens along many of the arcades would have allowed glimpses of the colourful aisle windows, altars and statues in the aisle chapels, and framed a long view of the nave altars and rood screen at the east end. There were also additional chapels in the choir to the east. These chapels, nave and choir, were the location for the friars' commemorative services that they offered (and sold) to Londoners: daily chantry masses, trentals of masses and anniversary funeral services.[15]

It is clear that by the fourteenth century these internal arrangements of the friary churches had become a more-or-less standardised English friary plan (Figure 68). Although the London friary churches are generally larger than other English examples of their respective orders, there is not a great variation in scale and form. The greatest difference in scale between an order's London church and its other churches is for the Augustinians. With this order, the London church at 277ft long is much larger, for example, than the 165ft of the Clare Austin Friars or the 100ft of the order's Canterbury church (Figure 68). With the other mendicant orders, friary churches in large provincial English towns and cities are about the same scale as the London examples; compare, for example, the Norwich and London Black Friars, the Oxford and London Grey Friars, and the Coventry and London White Friars churches (Figure 68). The basic arrangement of fourteenth-century English friary churches (those in the larger and more prosperous towns) is usually a large three-aisled nave that is separated from a shorter and narrower choir (usually single- but sometimes double-aisled) by the walking place bay. As has been stated, most English friaries contained this relatively narrow bay in order to give the friars private access between cloister and cemetery, without disturbing a sermon in the nave or a service in the choir. And with this access bay in place, transepts were not usually needed, which, in turn, allowed more versatility in the placing of the cloister. The exceptions to this are the Coventry White Friars and the Gloucester Black Friars, which have the normal transept-crossings that one finds in other English monastic houses and in many Irish and

---

[14] BL, Cotton Vitellius F xii, ff. 274–316, printed in *The Grey Friars of London: Their History, with the Register of Their Convent and an Appendix of Documents*, ed. Charles L. Kingsford (Aberdeen: British Society of Franciscan Studies, 1915), pp. 70–133.

[15] For rare surviving contracts for the performance of chantry masses, trentals and anniversary services at Austin Friars, see TNA, LR 14/87; LR 14/91; LR 14/129; LR 14/488.

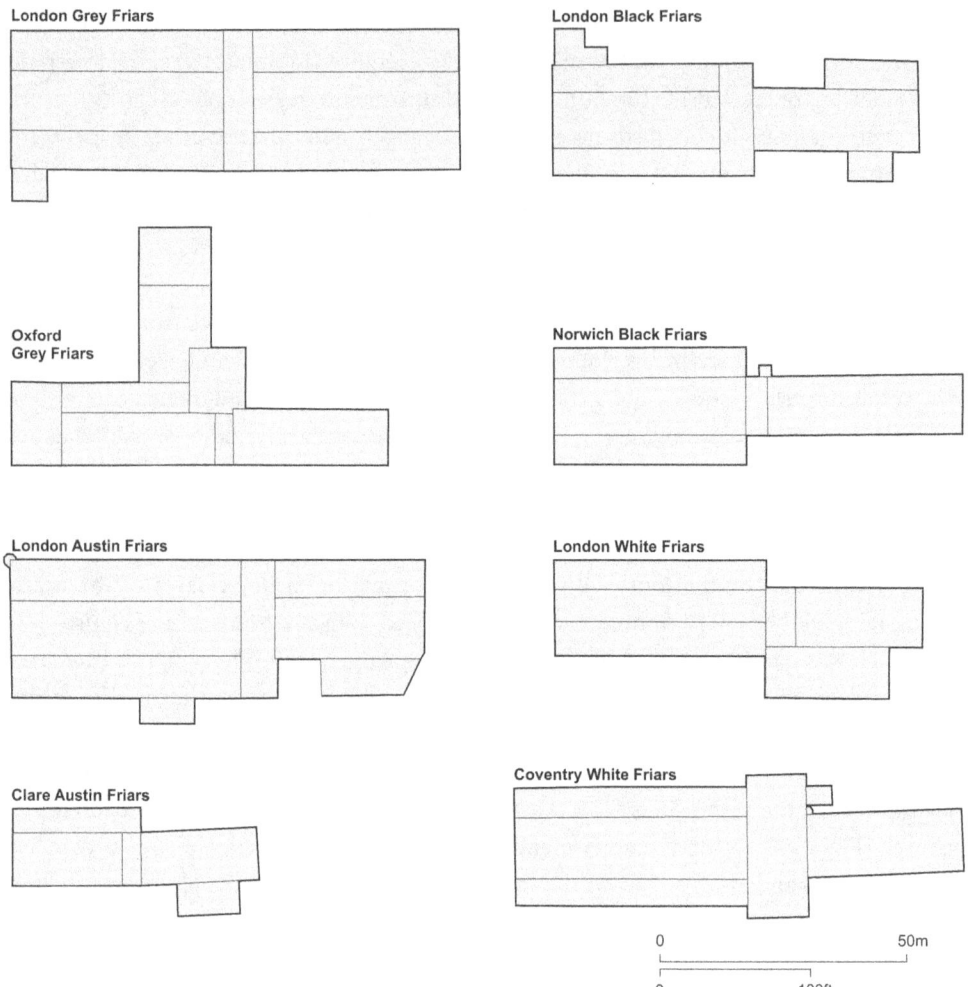

Fig. 68. Plan comparing the internal spaces of the four main London friary churches with other English mendicant churches (scale 1:1500)

Continental friaries. The larger English friary churches generally had a central tower over the walking place. The centrally positioned octagonal tower may well have been introduced to England by the friars.[16]

---

[16] Laurence Butler, 'The Houses of the Mendicant Orders in Britain: Recent Archaeological Work', in *Archaeological Papers from York Presented to M.W. Barley*, ed. P.V. Addyman and V.E. Black (York: York Archaeological Trust, 1984), pp. 123–36 (pp. 129–31); Charmian Woodfield, *The Church of Our Lady of Mount Carmel and some Conventual Buildings at the Whitefriars, Coventry* (Oxford: Archaeopress, 2005), pp. 17–20; Helen Sutermeister, *The Norwich Blackfriars: An Historical Guide to the Friary and its Buildings up to the Present Day* (Norwich: City of Norwich, 1977); O'Sullivan, *In the Company of the Preachers*, pp. 19–20, 84–6, 113–22, 144–8, 260–5, 281–3; Alfred W. Clapham, 'The Friars as Builders', in A.W. Clapham and W.H. Godfrey, *Some Famous*

The churches of Black Friars and Grey Friars must have been impressive examples of the architectural style known as Decorated. Part of a Decorated window from the choir of Grey Friars was discovered in a 1980s archaeological excavation (within the garden of the ruined seventeenth-century church; Chapter 12: Architecture and Architectural Fragments of the London Friaries; Figure 77). The seventeenth-century illustration 'The Plat of the Graye Friers' (Figure 22) shows the windows of that friary church in elevation and, although they seem at first sight to be fifteenth-century Perpendicular windows, the artist may be indicating a Decorated rose design in the upper part of the west window, with mouldings in the spandrels on either side of the rose. A fragment of the octagonal plinth for a pier of four clustered shafts was found at Black Friars, presumably deriving from the nave and dating to the first half of the fourteenth century (Chapter 12: Architecture and Architectural Fragments of the London Friaries; Figure 77). Thanks to the survival of the nave of Austin Friars until 1940, a little more is known about its early Perpendicular architecture of the mid fourteenth century. The piers of the arcade were formed by four shafts attached to a central square pillar with hollow-chamfered corners; the west window had seven lights with a six-petal rose below the apex of the arch (Figure 44; Chapter 12: Architecture and Architectural Fragments of the London Friaries).

Given the extraordinary investment in friary churches in the fourteenth century it is not surprising that the churches underwent relatively little change and reconstruction in the following century. The two significant examples of later Perpendicular friary architecture were probably the choir of White Friars (where enlargement and enhancement work was begun in the early fifteenth century) and the Lady chapel added to the choir of Black Friars in the 1430s. There is, once again, little evidence for their appearance but one should certainly expect them to have been tall and well-lit spaces with characteristic large windows divided by grid-like transoms and mullions. The Lady chapel at Black Friars may have had a spectacular fan-vaulted stone roof, given its date and the rank of its sponsor, Joan de Ingaldesthorp, who was commemorating her brother John Tiptoft, earl of Worcester, executed in 1470.[17] The London friaries almost had an example of the late flowering of the medieval Perpendicular style, at Crossed Friars, but a combination of the poor financial and administrative skills of the prior, William Bowry, and the onset of the Dissolution meant that the new choir or retro-choir of the 1520s and '30s was never completed.

As has been stated, the friary churches were really double-churches: a choir at the east end for the friars to celebrate the cycle of the daily office and a nave at the west end where they could preach to Londoners. What sort of decoration and ornament did these spaces have? If the thirteenth-century chapels were rather plain, by the fourteenth and fifteenth

---

Buildings and their Story: Being the Results of Recent Research in London and Elsewhere (London: Technical Journals, 1913), pp. 240–67 (pp. 244–6).

[17] Jens Röhrkasten, *The Mendicant Houses of Medieval London, 1221–1539*, Vita Regularis, 21 (Münster: Verlag, 2004), pp. 503–4; Benjamin G. Kohl, 'Tiptoft, John, First Earl of Worcester (1427–1470)', *ODNB*, <http://www.oxforddnb.com/view/article/27471> [accessed 11 June 2014].

centuries the choirs would have been decorated with more numerous frescoes, statues and furnishings; surviving fragments scattered in England and on the Continent hint at the richness of a typical late medieval decorative scheme. We must therefore imagine something like the fourteenth-century Thornham Parva retable with its crucifixion scene flanked by saints as the backdrop to the high altars, as it once was in the Norwich or Thetford Black Friars. We should also visualise the friars' richly decorated oak choir stalls at the west end of the choirs, like the Coventry White Friars stalls (now in the city's old Grammar School building at St John's hospital) with the arms of their lay benefactors. We could also imagine painted walls – such as the fifteenth-century fresco cycle on the life of St Catherine of Alexandria in the Franciscan church in Borgo San Sepolcro – or stained glass like the 'wyde wyndowes y-wrought y-written full thikke' satirised by the Pierce the Ploughman poet.[18] Then there are the fixed liturgical furnishings such as the piscina and sedilia, which survive in a fragmentary condition in extant friary churches such as at Brecon, Chichester or Elgin, as well as the large quantities of plate and vestments, the remnants of which were rounded up at the Dissolution.[19]

Unfortunately, even less has survived of the furnishing of mendicant naves than of choirs. The documentary evidence from the London Grey Friars – backed up by the physical evidence from East Anglia and the satirical description of a London friary by Meed the Maid in Langland's *Piers Plowman* – suggests that the aisle windows of the friaries featured the images, arms and names of lay donors almost as much as those of saints.[20] The lay donors and patrons would have been even more prominently commemorated in the floor slabs, chest tombs and wall monuments that filled the mendicant churches (nave and choir): well over 1000 people must have been buried in the Franciscan church, judging

---

[18] Nicholas Rogers, 'The Provenance of the Thornham Parva Retable', in *The Friars in Medieval Britain*, ed. N. Rogers, Harlaxton Medieval Studies, 19 (Donington: Shaun Tyas, 2010), pp. 185–93; Charles Tracy, 'Choir-Stalls from the 14th-Century Whitefriars Church in Coventry', *Journal of the British Archaeological Association*, 150 (1997), 76–95; Cooper and Banker, 'The Church of Borgo San Sepolcro'; *Pierce the Ploughmans Crede, to Which Is Appended God Spede the Plough*, ed. Walter W. Skeat, Early English Text Society, 30 (London: Paul, 1867), pp. 7–8. Note the surviving fragments of wall paintings of friars in parish churches, such as that of St Francis receiving the stigmata at Slapton in Northamptonshire: A.G. Little, *Franciscan History and Legend in English Mediaeval Art* (Manchester: Manchester University Press, 1937), p. 9.

[19] Butler, 'Houses of the Mendicant Orders in Britain', p. 131. Over 300lb of plate, along with just two mitres and a single crosier, were collected from the London friaries in November 1538: John Williams, *Account of the Monastic Treasures Confiscated at the Dissolution of the Various Houses in England*, ed. W. Turnbull (Edinburgh: Abbotsford Club, 1836), pp. 18–19.

[20] David King, 'Mendicant Glass in East Anglia', in *The Friars in Medieval Britain*, ed. N. Rogers, Harlaxton Medieval Studies, 19 (Donington: Shaun Tyas, 2010), pp. 169–84; Little, *Franciscan History and Legend in English Mediaeval Art*, pp. 27–28, 31; *Piers Plowman: A New Annotated Edition of the C-Text*, William Langland, ed. Derek A. Pearsall (Exeter: University of Exeter Press, 2008), pp. 82–3 (passus III, lines 50–76). The evidence for the London Grey Friars suggests an unusually high number of aristocratic sponsors: BL, Cotton Vitellius F xii, ff. 325–6, printed in *Grey Friars of London*, pp. 165–9.

by the 791 names recorded in the 680 tombs that were still visible in the 1530s (Chapter 17: Burial and Commemoration in the London Friaries).[21] In the absence of surviving mendicant examples in England, we must simply imagine the huge rood screen. The various chapels off the nave would have been richly decorated with a variety of sculptures, altars and hangings. There may well be some surviving embroidered or woven altar hangings from Austin Friars in a church in Genoa: in May 1542 the secretary of the Genovese ambassador in London wrote to the governor of Genoa informing him that 'tapezzerie' removed from the church (perhaps belonging to an Italian fraternity?) were being shipped back to Italy.[22] An early sixteenth-century painting known as the 'Apparition of the Virgin to the Dominicans of Utrecht' illustrates many of these features in a mendicant nave, including a vaulted timber rood screen, side altars with hangings, altar paintings (many of which are triptychs), candlesticks and a tiled floor.[23]

Using the churches

The spaces within the friary churches would have held a variety of spiritual and other meanings and uses, depending on the status and affiliation of the visitor and the time of his or her visit. On a typical day, the nave would have been busy on at least one occasion with a friar preaching to a throng of lay visitors; the choir would have seen more regular (and perhaps more static) use with the friars performing the cycle of prayer in their slightly reduced version of the standard monastic liturgical offices (Chapter 16: Spiritual Life and Education in the London Friaries).[24] The naves were also used, on occasion, for private business meetings, with deals being signed and agreed by lay people on friary premises.[25] On special days, other parts of the church would have been open to lay visitors: one can imagine that, for example, the Grey Friars chapel of St Francis was opened up to lay visitors on his saint's day of 4 October. The churches were also a meeting place for the dead, with successive family members reunited in death and commemorated by floor slabs, tomb chests or wall monuments. The financial and spiritual investment of a tomb in the choir would presumably have allowed surviving family members privileged access to the relevant aisle or chapel (Chapter 17: Burial and Commemoration in the London Friaries). Other groups such as religious fraternities and trade guilds would also have had special

---

[21] BL, Cotton Vitellius F xii, ff. 274–316, printed in *Grey Friars*, pp. 70–133.
[22] Federigo Alizeri, *Notizie dei Professori del Disegno in Liguria dalle Origini al Secolo XVI*, 6 vols (Genoa: Sambolino, 1870), ii, 485–6, 560.
[23] Susie Nash, *Northern Renaissance Art*, Oxford History of Art (Oxford: Oxford University Press, 2008), no. 168, p. 240.
[24] Frances Andrews, *The Other Friars: The Carmelite, Augustinian, Sack and Pied Friars in the Middle Ages* (Woodbridge: Boydell, 2006), pp. 124–7.
[25] Jens Röhrkasten, 'Secular Uses of the Mendicant Priories of Medieval London', in *The Use and Abuse of Sacred Places in Late Medieval Towns*, ed. M. De Smet and P. Trio, Mediaevalia Lovaniensia, series 1, 38 (Leuven: Leuven University Press, 2006), pp. 135–51 (pp. 139–40).

access to their particular sponsored chapel or altar: at Austin Friars the religious fraternity of the company of Pouchmakers maintained an altar with a 'braunche [candlestick] with five tapers of wex' on the north side of the choir, and the German fraternity of St Sebastian had an altar on the south side of the nave with a gilt 'beme and brannch' as well as 'alman ymages and tabernacles'.[26] At least seven trade guilds paid for anniversaries or chantries in the friary churches; another nine companies with religious fraternities and about twenty-five independent religious fraternities met or kept altars.[27]

Conclusion

The London churches built by the first friars in the thirteenth century were simple chapels for the friars to perform the cycle of services of the Divine Office, together with a daily mass. They seem to have been soberly decorated, single-aisled buildings, with between three and six bays. But by the end of the century the Dominicans and Franciscans were beginning to rethink and rebuild their churches. In place of the original chapels they built some of the biggest churches in the city: great double-churches with a one- or two-aisled east end for the friars in their choir and a large three-aisled nave to the west to attract Londoners to stand and listen to the friars' sermons. These new fourteenth-century churches gradually became even grander and more complex spaces, articulated with a variety of screens and altars defining chapels, and increasingly filled with the tombs and memorials of lay people. And in addition to the cries of a friar preaching in the nave, there would have been the sounds of other friars performing private chantry masses and anniversary funeral services, and of the burgesses, guildsmen and women attending these services.

---

[26] TNA, LR 15/12; LR 15/13.
[27] Numbers based on Röhrkasten, *Mendicant Houses*, pp. 472–6; Caroline M. Barron, 'The Parish Fraternities of Medieval London', in *The Church in Pre-Reformation Society: Essays in Honour of F.R.H. Du Boulay*, ed. C.M. Barron and C. Harper-Bill (Woodbridge: Boydell, 1985), pp. 13–37 (p. 23); C.M. Barron and Laura Wright, 'The London Middle English Guild Certificates of 1388–9', *Nottingham Medieval Studies*, 39 (1995), 108–45 (pp. 124–5); Henry C. Coote, 'The Ordinances of Some Secular Guilds of London, 1354 to 1496', *Transactions of the London and Middlesex Archaeological Society*, 4 (1871), 1–59; Justin Colson, 'Alien Communities and Alien Fraternities in Later Medieval London', *London Journal*, 35.2 (2010), 111–43 (pp. 117–21); *Leonis X. Pontificis Maximi Regesta*, ed. Joseph Hergenroether, 6 vols (Freiburg: Sumptibus Herder, 1884–8), v/vi, no. 13403 (p. 805). For further discussion of the guilds and fraternities meeting in friary churches, see Nick Holder, 'The Medieval Friaries of London: A Topographic and Archaeological History, before and after the Dissolution' (unpublished doctoral thesis, University of London, Royal Holloway, 2011), pp. 207–8.

11

Precincts and the Use of Space

The seven London friaries were much more than churches: at the very least the friars required food and accommodation to sustain their duties of prayer and preaching. As the numbers of friars increased (along with the ambitions of priors), they came to need other buildings: libraries and schools for study, cloisters for traditional monastic contemplation, service wings to supply the kitchen, and gardens for horticulture and leisure. And both friars and lay people required accommodation after death in cemeteries. The size and layout of these priories thus developed over time, as needs changed and as the sponsorship of Londoners and others permitted.

The early friaries in the thirteenth century

The needs of the thirteenth-century friars of London were relatively simple: a plot on which to build a church and an accommodation wing, with space for a small cemetery. The location and basic shape of the early friary precincts were to a large extent a matter of chance – the result of accepting the foundation bequest of a patron, usually in the form of a parcel of land not a purse of money. The Dominicans, Carmelites and Pied friars were given their friary plots outside the old Roman wall that defined London; the Franciscans, Austin, Sack and Crossed friars were given intramural urban plots for their priories (Figure 69). This urban/suburban distinction explains the varying size of the early friaries: the Black, White and Pied friars were given fields or closes (over 3 acres in the case of the White friars) whereas the others had smaller urban messuages (a tenth of an acre for the Sack friars: Figure 69). The varying origins of the friaries also created differences in the priors' ability to enlarge and adapt their friaries. So, during the two decades after they established their London house, the Crossed friars only managed to add one neighbouring messuage to their precinct (Figure 53; Table 11) but in the same period the Black friars acquired six additional suburban plots or closes (Figure 4; Table 3).

Although the documentary and archaeological evidence is generally lacking in detail

192   THE FRIARIES OF MEDIEVAL LONDON

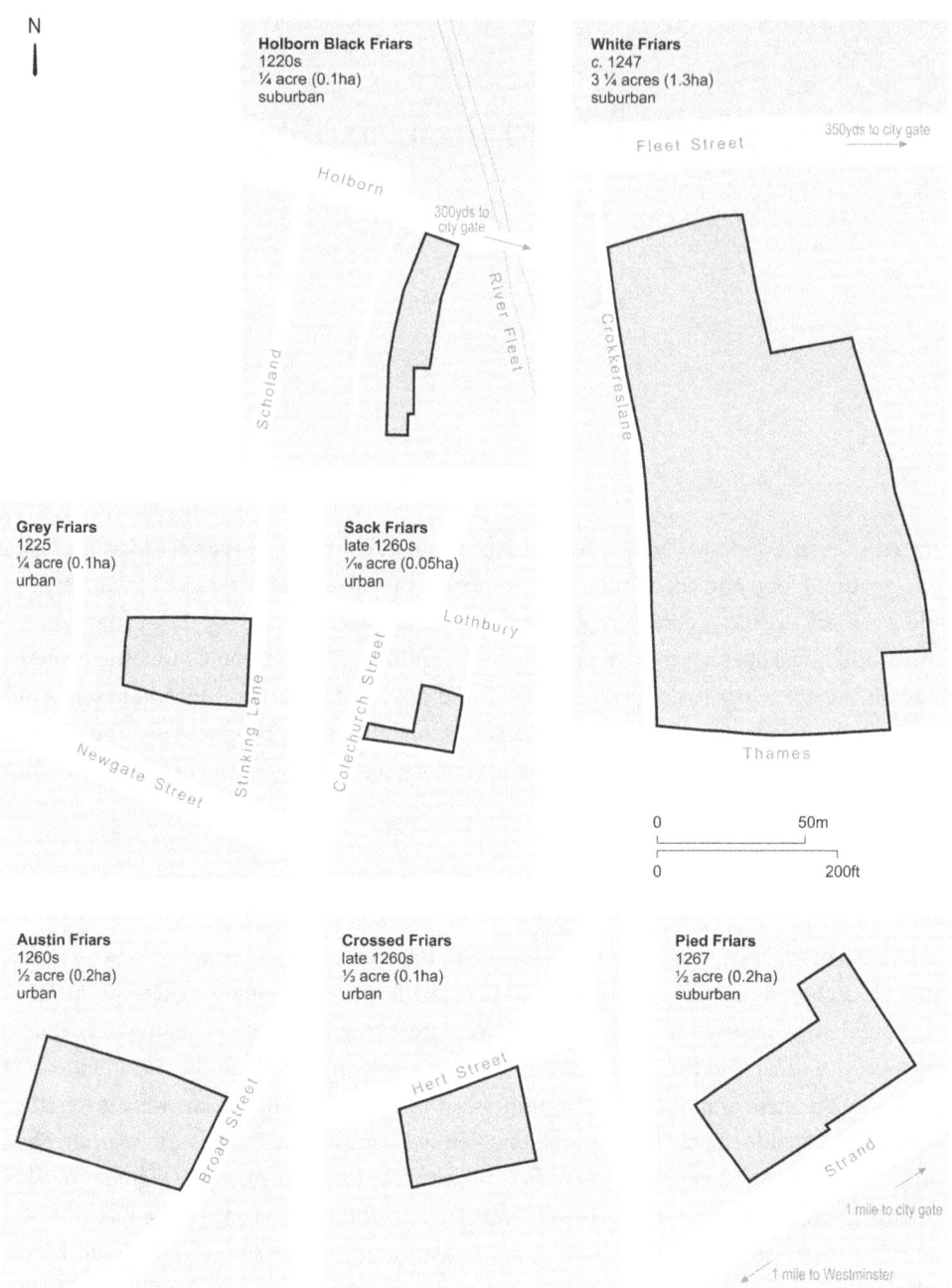

Fig. 69. Maps showing the foundation plots of the seven London friaries (scale 1:2500).

for this early period in the friars' history, the Grey Friars Register and the account of the early Franciscan Thomas of Eccleston suggest that the early guardians concentrated on building a small chapel followed by a single accommodation wing. In this case, William Joyner (a wealthy merchant in the 1220s, mayor in 1238–9, died c. 1248) gave £200 for the construction of the chapel and other buildings, and another wealthy Londoner, Peter de Helyland (active in 1220s and '30s, died c. 1239), bequeathed money for the construction of an infirmary, presumably forming part of an early accommodation wing.[1] Archaeological evidence for these early accommodation buildings is lacking but a reasonable hypothesis (one that fits with what is known of the friars' acquisition of further tenements on which to build) is that the buildings may have formed the nucleus of the east wing of the later cloister (Figure 70). The process of setting up a friary has been studied in other provinces. In Saxonia the first Franciscans looked to build a chapel and what has been termed a *domus* or 'friars' house': not a cloister but a single wing containing rooms for the refectory, chapter house and dormitory. Parts of the original thirteenth-century building survive at the friary of Salzwedel: the long, two-storey building forming a wing extending northwards from the chapel could well be the sort of building that the London Franciscans constructed.[2] The London friaries thus had, at least in their early days, a strong sense of what has been termed the 'liminality' of small monastic orders on the fringes of towns: the intramural and the suburban London priories were small sites with simple buildings that housed preacher-monks with relatively modest aspirations.[3]

If the foundation plot was too small, particularly if it lacked the east–west width required to build a church – the friars sought bequests from neighbours, or sponsors to help them buy adjacent plots. The Dominicans certainly had to do this, acquiring additional plots in the 1220s and '30s thanks to Londoners William le Veill, Alice la Brune and Richard Renger (Figure 70; tenements 2–4 on Figure 4 and in Table 3). The constraints of the urban property market make the rapid expansion of the Franciscans even more remarkable. Beginning with perhaps a quarter-acre parcel in the 1220s, the Grey friars had been able to enlarge their land holding to about 2¼ acres thanks to donations of another thirteen plots by the 1270s (Figure 69, Figure 70; Table 5). However, this was very much a precinct in the making: their plots were in three blocks, still separated by St Nicholas Lane and Stinking Lane. With the sort of neighbourly relations not envisaged by St Francis a half-century earlier, successive priors began to exert a proprietorial influence. In the 1270s the guardian was in trouble for blocking Stinking Lane, and during the London eyre of 1321 local residents complained that William de Ludgarshale had begun encroaching on another lane in about 1291, with a later guardian, Henry de Sutton, up to similar tricks in about 1306. These

---

[1] BL, Cotton Vitellius F xii, f. 322, printed in *Grey Friars*, pp. 157–8; Thomas of Eccleston, *Tractatus de Adventu Fratrum Minorum in Angliam*, ed. A.G. Little (Manchester: Manchester University Press, 1951); translated as: *The Coming of the Friars Minor to England & Germany. Being the Chronicles of . . . Thomas of Eccleston and . . . Jordan of Giano*, ed. E. Gurney Salter (London and Toronto: Dent, 1926); Röhrkasten, *Mendicant Houses*, p. 415.

[2] Leonie Silberer, 'Medieval Monastic Architecture of the Franciscan Order: Friaries as Evidence of Written and Unwritten Rules and Ideal Perceptions', in *Rules and Observance: Devising Forms of Communal Life*, ed. M. Breitenstein and others, Vita Regularis, 60 (Berlin: Verlag, 2014), pp. 281–94 (pp. 284–5, ill. 1, 2).

[3] Roberta Gilchrist, *Contemplation and Action: The Other Monasticism*, The Archaeology of Medieval Britain (London: Leicester University Press, 1995), pp. 6–7.

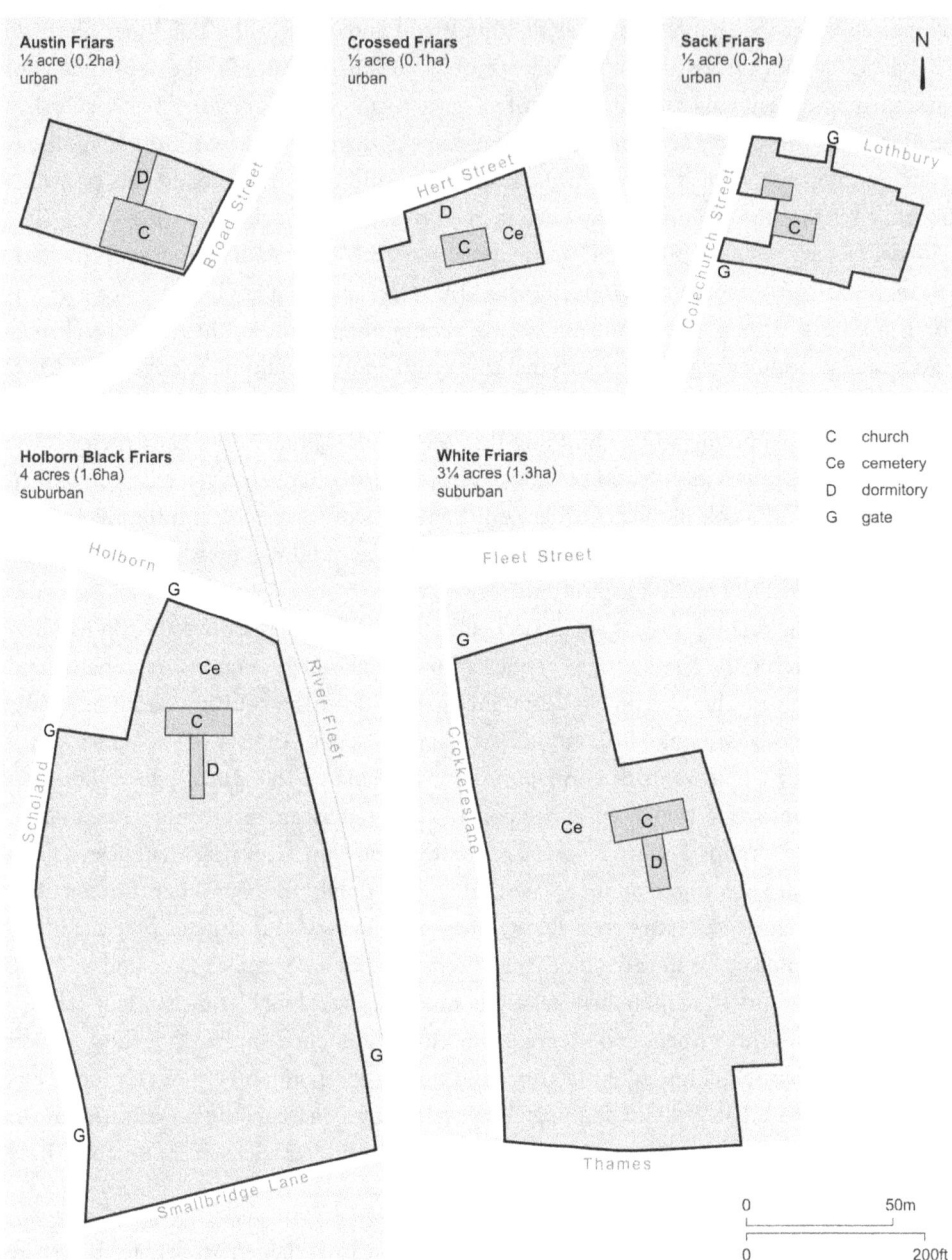

Fig. 70. Maps showing the precincts of the seven friaries in the 1270s (scale 1:2500).

tensions with neighbours only ended in the mid fourteenth century with the friars' acquisition of enough plots to form a contiguous precinct, and a royal licence to close the lanes.[4]

---

[4] TNA, JUST 1/547A, mm. 14v, 15 [eyre of 1321]; C 66/235, m. 4 [grant of 1351]; *Rotuli Hundredorum Temp. Hen. III & Edw. I. in Turr' Lond' et in Curia Receptae Scaccarij Westm. Asservati*, ed.

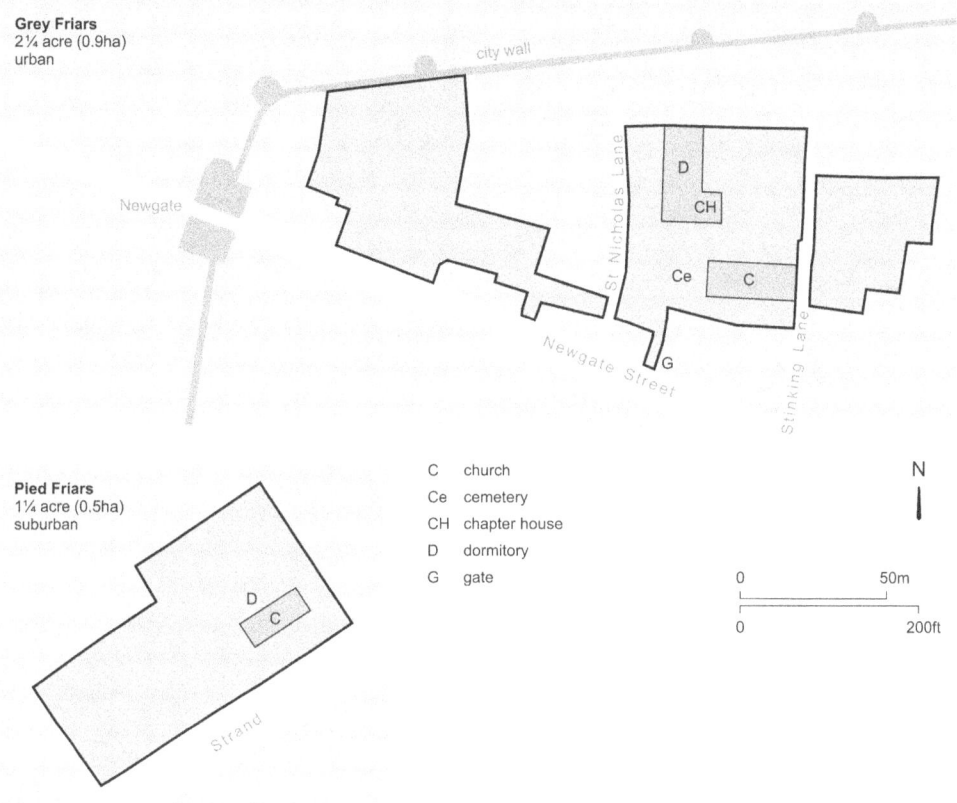

Fig. 70. (continued)

Later friary precincts

As has already been noted with regard to the friary churches, the London priors seem to have expanded their ambitions in the final quarter of the thirteenth century. This may have been related to wider changes in the Church: perhaps those mendicant groups that survived the great re-organisation of the Second Council of Lyon in 1274 decided to re-imagine themselves as more traditional monastic orders with a strong and visual local presence, a cross between the Augustinian canons (with their urban outreach) and the Cistercians (with their juxtaposition of poverty and architectural grandeur). So, towards the end of the thirteenth century the Dominican and Franciscan priors and provincial priors began planning a more traditional monastic layout of church and full cloister. The other priors soon followed suit and the five urban monasteries were formed over the next century (Figure 71, Figure 72).

William Illingworth, 2 vols (London: Eyre and Strahan, 1812), i, 404, 429; guardians from list in Caroline M. Barron and Matthew Davies, eds., *The Religious Houses of London and Middlesex* (London: Centre for Metropolitan History, 2007), p. 127.

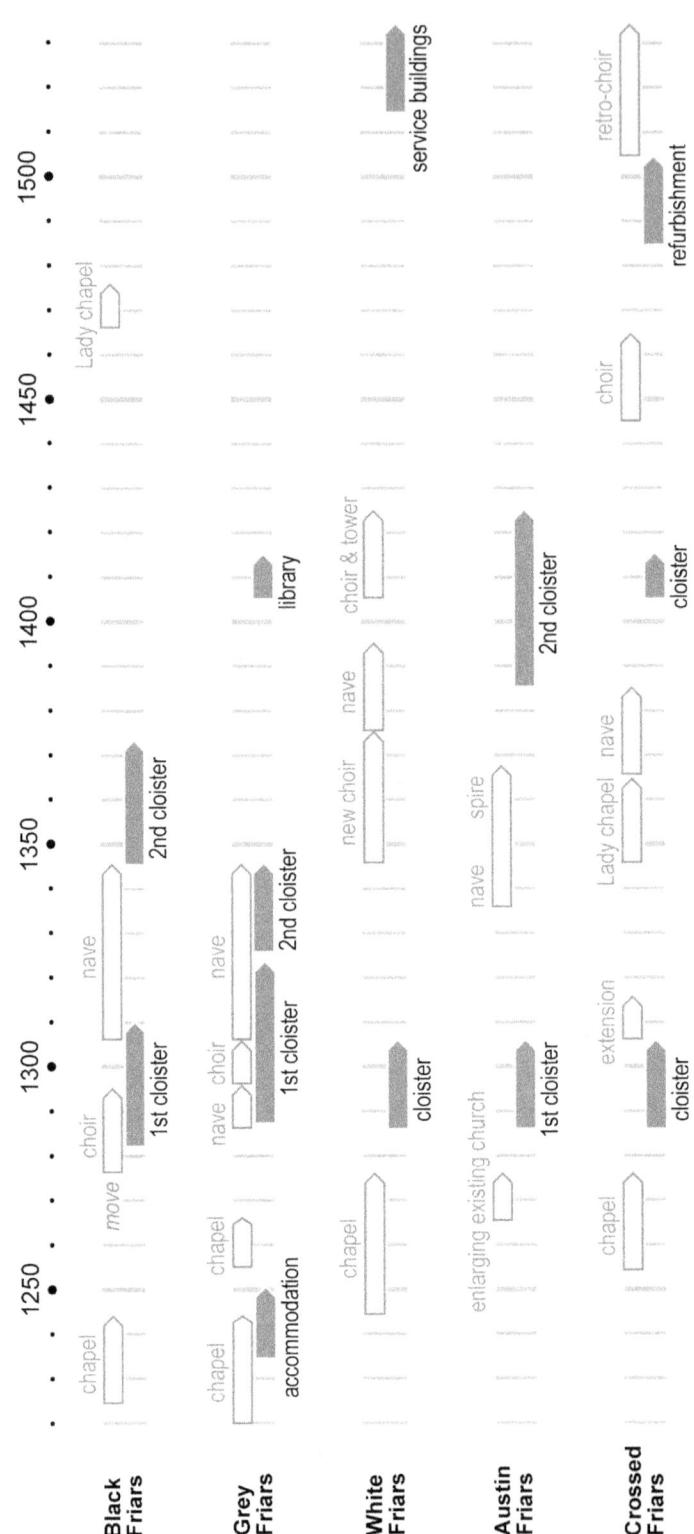

Fig. 71. Chronology of construction campaigns at the friary precincts.

Fig. 72. Plans showing the five friary precincts in the early sixteenth century (scale 1:2000).

If the Dominican prior John of Darlington started off the transition to a grander type of friary at Black Friars (Chapter 10: Churches), the unknown Franciscan guardian began work on a proper monastic cloister at about this time. It has been argued that it was the friary's acquisition of tenements along St Nicholas Lane in the 1270s, '80s and '90s that actually allowed the Franciscans to transform their accommodation

Fig. 72. (continued)

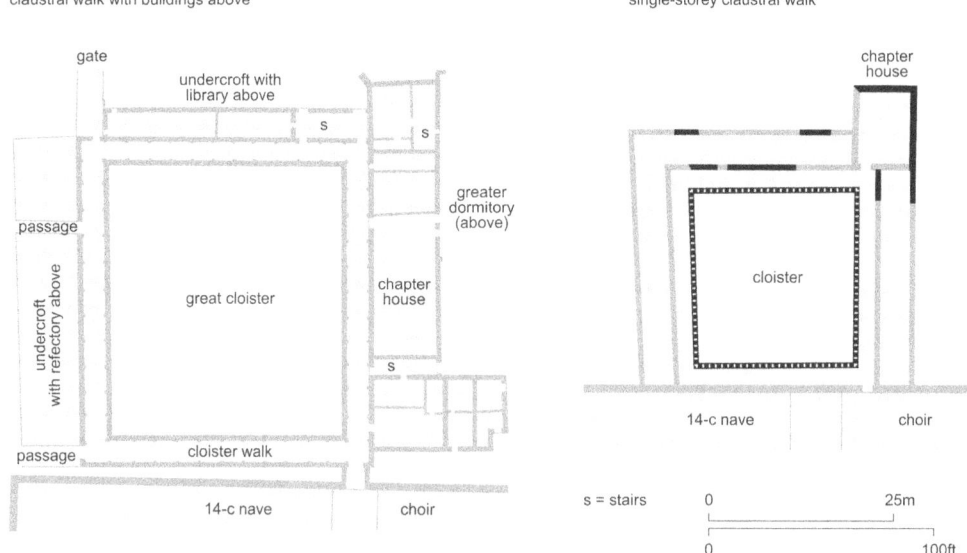

Fig. 73. Comparative plan of two late thirteenth- or early fourteenth-century cloisters: Grey Friars and Austin Friars (former largely based on plan evidence, latter on archaeological evidence; scale 1:1000).

buildings – perhaps a single wing in the mid thirteenth century – into a full four-sided cloister by the early fourteenth century. Over several decades they built what was aptly termed their 'great cloister', each side having eleven bays (plus corner bays), with the central garth a huge space some 118ft by 104ft (36.0 × 31.7m; Figure 73; Chapter 4: Grey Friars).[5] The three-light Geometric windows on the ground floor and the plainer lancets of the floor above can be seen in Figure 27 (a nineteenth-century engraving of the then-surviving cloister).[6] The priors of the other four orders seem to have been working on their own cloisters at the turn of the thirteenth and fourteenth centuries (Figure 71). Thanks to two archaeological excavations at Austin Friars (which produced *in situ* remains and some recycled architectural fragments) the first Austin Friars cloister can be reconstructed in some detail. This was smaller than that of the Grey Friars (78ft × 67ft; 23.9m × 20.5m) and probably had thirteen bays along its long sides and twelve along the short, arranged as an unglazed arcade of paired columns, perhaps commissioned by prior William de Clare (Figure 73, Figure 49; Chapter 12: Architecture

[5] The two detailed seventeenth-century surveys (Figure 22, Figure 26) clearly show *eleven* bays (plus corner bays) on each side. The engraver of the nineteenth-century view of the cloister (Figure 27) only shows *ten*; the nineteenth-century artist may have been distracted, however, by the variation between the module of the thirteenth-century lower floors and that of the fifteenth-century library floor at the top of the north wing.
[6] These windows resemble two-light windows of the late thirteenth or early fourteenth century in three parish churches; see Chapter 4: Grey Friars, n. 18.

and Architectural Fragments of the London Friaries). In the fourteenth-century poem 'Pierce the Ploughman's Crede' the narrator enters a Dominican cloister – probably the London Black Friars cloister – and praises (albeit satirically) the remarkable carved tracery and painted walls (Chapter 2: The Second Black Friars, 'The cloisters').

The late thirteenth-century priors – particularly the Dominican and Franciscan heads starting off the process – could turn to the new urban monastic precincts of the Augustinian canons for a model.[7] At Holy Trinity priory (within the city) and at the hospital and priory of St Mary Spital (beyond the walls to the north-east), thirteenth-century priors had designed a simplified urban version of the rural Benedictine cloister and precinct plan (Figure 74).[8] The position of the cloister was defined by the church: the latter needed to be reasonably close to the main adjacent road in order to create a bold architectural statement visible to townsfolk. A traditional rural cloister was sited on the south side of the church – a warmer and brighter position as the autumn and winter sun was not blocked by the church – but an urban cloister could be to the north if the lie of the land required it, for example if the main road ran along the south side of the precinct. The thirteenth-century canons' cloisters had the chapter house for daily meetings on the east side, a dormitory above (with easy access to the choir via a set of night-stairs), a refectory on the far side and the prior's accommodation and other rooms to the west. The kitchen was in a separate wing running back from the refectory (Figure 74). This basic plan was largely followed by the London friaries, with some variation in the location of the refectory (Figure 72). The Dominicans, Crossed friars and Carmelites achieved the preferred solution of a south-facing cloister, whereas the Franciscans and Augustinian friars – constrained by the relationship of precinct to main road – had to make do with a colder and darker north-facing cloister. The Dominicans and the Austin friars built a traditional single-storey cloister, a vaulted pentice abutting the claustral wings, but the other friaries had integrated cloister walks that were built over: this had the advantage of creating wider upper storeys but the disadvantage of producing narrow and dark ground-floor rooms adjacent to the cloister walk.[9]

The priors continued to develop their precincts in the fourteenth century but the construction process had to be carefully managed. The basic sequence of construction

---

[7] Roberta Gilchrist and Barney Sloane, *Requiem: The Medieval Monastic Cemetery in Britain* (London: Museum of London Archaeology Service, 2005), pp.xvii, 273; Gilchrist, *Norwich Cathedral Close*, pp.24–7.

[8] John Schofield and Richard Lea, *Holy Trinity Priory, Aldgate, City of London: An Archaeological Reconstruction and History*, MoLAS monograph, 24 (London: Museum of London Archaeology Service, 2005), pp.139–45, fig 137; Chiz Harward, Nick Holder and Christopher Thomas, *The Medieval Priory and Hospital of St Mary Spital and the Bishopsgate Suburb: Excavations at Spitalfields Market, London E1, 1991–2007*, MOLA Monograph (London: Museum of London Archaeology, forthcoming).

[9] The integrated arrangement seems to have been the norm in English friaries: Butler, 'The Houses of the Mendicant Orders in Britain', p.132. Clapham considers that this integrated cloister without a lead-covered walk was used by the friars for reasons of economy: 'The Friars as Builders', pp.247–8.

PRECINCTS AND THE USE OF SPACE   201

Fig. 74. The model for the London friaries? Two London monastic precincts of the thirteenth century: the Augustinian canons' houses of Holy Trinity and St Mary Spital (scale 1:2000). (source: MOLA digital data)

for most of the friaries seems to have been choir then cloister then nave, although this does not quite apply at Grey Friars where construction of the cloister may have preceded the enhancement of the church under the sponsorship of mayor le Waleys and Queen Margaret (Figure 71; Chapter 10: Churches). With church and cloister complete, the London priors then considered ways to improve the friary facilities, turning their attention to other monastic buildings such as a library and an infirmary. This process took place during the fourteenth century, both before and after the Black Death, and it was the Franciscans who led the way. The Grey Friars Register records that friar Richard Knotte and the London mercer William Albon gave money to pay for a guest-house or hospital (*hospicium*) by the infirmary, probably in the 1330s or '40s.[10] Evidence from post-Dissolution surveys show that the infirmary and *hospicium* formed the west side of a second cloister: this cloister was presumably being built in the second quarter of the fourteenth century (Chapter 4: Grey Friars, 'The cloisters'). The London Franciscans thus developed the thirteenth-century urban monastic plan by adding a whole additional cloister. This 'little cloister', as it was known at Grey Friars, was then emulated by the Black and Austin friars, with the former constructing an 'inner cloister' in the 1350s and '60s, and the latter building a northern cloister at the turn of the fourteenth and fifteenth centuries (Figure 71, Figure 72).[11] At Austin Friars this second cloister housed the library, infirmary and a new kitchen wing; at Black Friars it also contained a rather specialist building known as the 'parlyament Chamber', a hall that housed occasional meetings of parliament from the fourteenth century.[12] The new Black Friars library in the second cloister was visited in the 1370s by two men from Merton College, Oxford. The clerk of works John Bloxham and the mason William Humberville came to London on a fact-finding mission when the college was planning the enlargement of its own library. The Merton library (which still retains some medieval features) may, therefore, provide some clues as to the arrangement of the London friary libraries. It had hard bench seating for about fifty readers, with the books chained at desks either side of a central aisle. Narrow lancet windows lit the library wings, which were on the upper

---

[10] *Grey Friars*, pp. 132, 161, 166; Röhrkasten, *Mendicant Houses*, p. 435.
[11] The terms 'little cloister' (Grey Friars) and 'inner cloister' (Black Friars) both derive from post-Dissolution documents but they may well have been used by the friars as well: 'le greate Cloyster & le lytle Cloyster': TNA, C 66/790, m. 53 [1547]; 'le inner cloyster': TNA, E 315/212, f. 134v [1540].
[12] Irwin Smith, *Shakespeare's Blackfriars Playhouse: Its History and its Design* (London: Owen, 1966), pp. 457–8; *Blackfriars Records*, ed. Albert Feuillerat (Oxford: Malone Society, 1913), pp. 105–6. The earliest sitting of parliament at Black Friars seems to have been in 1311 – not yet in their 'parliament hall' – and it was intermittently used until the Dissolution: Enoch J. Powell and Keith Wallis, *The House of Lords in the Middle Ages: A History of the English House of Lords to 1540* (London: Weidenfeld and Nicolson, 1968), p. 276; John Roskell, Carole Rawcliffe, and Linda S. Clark, *The History of Parliament. The House of Commons 1386–1421*, 4 vols (Stroud: History of Parliament Trust and Alan Sutton, 1992), i, 150; Röhrkasten, 'Secular Uses', pp. 140–1.

floor of two sides of the cloister.¹³ This bears a strong resemblance to the design of the fifteenth-century library at Grey Friars (added as a new storey over the north wing of the late thirteenth- or early fourteenth-century cloister), funded by a donation from former mayor Richard Whittington (Figure 27).

Like their colleagues in rural monasteries, the urban friars needed a variety of ancillary buildings. Their urban mendicant status meant that the friars did not require granges to collect the harvest but they seem to have developed their catering buildings in the fourteenth or fifteenth century. The earliest mention of such a building is at Grey Friars where a bake-house is first documented in 1421.¹⁴ The ancillary buildings of bake-house, brew-house and workshops usually formed a separate court, not formally laid out as a cloister but gathered around a central yard. This court would ideally be situated as far as possible from the church (separating the domestic and the spiritual) but as close as possible to a gate and road (for ease of access and deliveries). In an urban monastery the two objectives were often in conflict and the locations of the various service courts therefore varied at the London friaries (Figure 72). At Austin Friars there was a group of buildings right in the north of the precinct with their own gate, but at Grey Friars the service buildings (including the bake-house, a brew-house and a mill, probably a horse-mill) were rather close to the church and main gate, although they probably had direct access onto the Newgate street frontage. At Black Friars and White Friars, with their Thames-side locations, the service buildings could be sited with access to both a water gate and a street gate.

The priors and the provincial priors (who were in charge of their respective order's English province) required accommodation of an appropriate standard. By the fourteenth and fifteenth centuries the priors and abbots of England's monastic houses had become important figures, with concomitant duties within secular as well as religious society. They therefore needed their own houses – small mansions – within their precincts, including space for cellarage, catering and servants. At the London friaries, and at other urban monasteries such as Norwich, these houses were generally to the east of the main cloister, approximately aligned with the choir, and had their own private garden as well.¹⁵ At Black Friars the prior and the provincial prior's separate mansions formed a little courtyard to the east of the cloister, with a private half-acre garden beyond (Figure 72). The provincial prior occupied the original thirteenth-century chapter house, which had been subdivided into three upper chambers over a vaulted undercroft, and the London prior had a 'greate dynynge Chamber', a parlour and a bedchamber on his ground floor, with a larger chamber and galleries above, as well as a private garderobe. The priors also had a separate

---

[13] Geoffrey H. Martin and J. Roger Highfield, *A History of Merton College, Oxford* (Oxford: Oxford University Press, 1997), pp. 88–91.

[14] LMA, CLA/024/01/02/51 (Plea and Memoranda Roll A 50), m. 6.

[15] Roberta Gilchrist, analysing the bishop's and prior's houses at Norwich cathedral, notes the spiritual significance of aligning the prior's house with the choir of the church, in particular the prior's chamber with the high altar: *Norwich Cathedral Close*, pp. 143–64 (p. 160).

kitchen, larder and cellar-buttery tucked in the east cloister wing.[16] An appropriate standard of dining and the ability to entertain important visitors were clearly important: an undercroft or cellar seems to be a feature of these priors' houses. The Carmelite prior had a small vaulted chamber below his mansion (surviving to this day; see Chapter 5: White Friars) and the prior of the Crossed Friars had a smaller chalk-walled cellar, revealed in recent excavations.[17] The architectural and archaeological dating evidence for the priors' houses at White and Crossed Friars suggests a construction date in the late fourteenth or early fifteenth century; this may have been when the other friaries built mansions for their leaders.

The cemeteries formed large open spaces within the friaries. These were usually sited between the church and the main road: they thus formed a reflective approach route for lay visitors walking to the nave of the church. The Black Friars cemetery was particularly large: this third of an acre space (0.1ha) ran along the whole of the north side of the church. Lay people frequently requested burial in these cemeteries, presumably a cheaper option than burial in the friary church itself (Chapter 17: Burial and Commemoration in the London Friaries). Open spaces had formed fair-weather naves for preaching in the friars' original home in Italy and the practice of outdoor preaching continued in England in the thirteenth century.[18] The Black and Austin Friars cemeteries had preaching crosses specifically for this purpose, the latter first mentioned in the early fifteenth century.[19]

One remarkable aspect of the London friaries is their huge gardens, undoubtedly the largest in the walled city. Hardly anything is known about the friars' food supply networks but it seems likely that, in addition to purchased foodstuffs, the friars grew their own fruit, vegetables, herbs and medicines, perhaps also cultivating hops and vines and keeping bees. They may well have kept small livestock such as poultry or even pigs. Perhaps surprisingly, no archaeological or documentary evidence for friary fishponds has been traced in London; fishponds seem to have been particularly popular with the Franciscans and it would be quite possible to fit a pond in one of the large gardens towards the east of the London Grey Friars.[20] The first Dominicans certainly had a large garden at their Holborn priory and this included an orchard with apple trees, pears, cherries and walnuts, as well as a close with other trees to supply firewood and timber. They also had a vineyard, perhaps the only one in a thirteenth-century London monastic house (at any

[16] Latrine pit revealed in site FRI88; documentary evidence for rooms from post-Dissolution grants: TNA, E 315/191, f. 58; C 66/749, mm. 22–3 [provincial prior's house]; TNA, C 66/814, m. 10 [prior's house].

[17] Antonietta Lerz and Nick Holder, 'Medieval Crossed Friars and its Roman to Post-Medieval Landscape: Excavations at Mariner House, in the City of London', *Transactions of the London and Middlesex Archaeological Society*, 66 (2015), 137–97.

[18] Robson, 'Franciscan Custody of York', pp. 14–15.

[19] Chapter 6: Austin Friars, n. 47.

[20] O'Sullivan, *In the Company of the Preachers*, pp. 36, 44, 50, 75, 83, 94.

rate, the only one for which there is evidence).[21] When they moved in the late thirteenth century to their new site within the city walls they could afford even larger gardens – over 3 acres (1.3ha) – including the private garden for the prior and provincial prior; we can guess that the Dominicans took a few cuttings of Holborn vines and walnut with them. Gardens are quite hard to trace with archaeological evidence but outside London the likely remains of friary orchards have been observed at Dunstable Black Friars and at Oxford White Friars.[22] At the London White Friars there were several gardens, including the prior's garden, a kitchen garden, an infirmary garden, a school garden ('the skollers gardeyne') and two convent gardens ('le covent garden' and a separate *covent garden propter Thamesiam*). There are also one or two references to orchards in the later London friaries, such as the one by the Carmelite provincial's house.[23] One of the Grey friars, Walter Roben, was the 'keper' of the friary gardens in the sixteenth century and all the friaries presumably had friars to supervise hired lay gardeners.[24] In addition to these practical considerations the gardens also provided a peaceful haven for contemplation and relaxation: in a rather charming description of White Friars in the sixteenth century, one riverside garden contained 'a littell house made upon the waters syde used for the recreation and comfort of the freers'.[25]

The friaries had a number of other buildings in their precincts such as stables (attested at all the well-documented friaries), a laundry (a laundress was cleaning the Franciscans' altar cloths and living in their gate-house in 1440) and a smithy (at Black Friars in the fourteenth and fifteenth centuries) as well as other workshops, often temporary, for stonemasons, carpenters and plumbers.[26] By the sixteenth century Grey Friars had a horse-mill in the service court to supply the bake-house (conceivably, but less likely, a windmill) and White Friars had a mill near the bake-house, quite possibly a tidal water-mill on the Thames.[27] Lay visitors needed accommodation. Black Friars had a guest hall – rather an impressive one as it was used by the emperor Charles V in 1522 – and other friaries including Austin Friars had

[21] TNA, DL 29/1/1, m. 11v. The description of the garden is from a set of accounts of the subsequent owner, but the orchard, vineyard and trees made a profit just ten years after the sale of the friary: they must surely have been planted by the friars; Chapter 1: The First Black Friars in Holborn.
[22] O'Sullivan, *In the Company of the Preachers*, pp. 134–6, 274–5.
[23] CC, MS CL/A/4/4 (Book of Deeds and Wills), p. 51; TNA, SC 6/Hen VIII/2396, f. 58v; E 315/235, f. 37v.
[24] TNA, E 321/46/51.
[25] BL, Harley charters 79.F.32.
[26] Stables: TNA, DL 29/1/1, m. 11v [Holborn Black Friars, 1296, ten years after their departure]; E 117/14/202 [Black Friars, by inner cloister, c. 1540]; C 66/686, m. 11 [Austin Friars, east of cloister near Broad Street, 1539]; BL, Topham charters 33 [Crossed Friars, 1350]; TNA, C 1/1165/34–36 [Grey Friars, near bake-house on Newgate street, 1540s]; C 66/708, m. 35 [White Friars, by eastern gate on Water Lane, 1541]. Laundress: TNA, C 146/1479, printed in *Grey Friars*, pp. 207–8. Black Friars smithy: LAA, VAL88, B. McCann, 'Fleet Valley project, interim report' (unpublished Museum of London report, 1993), pp. 72, 101, fig. 32.
[27] Mills: TNA, E 315/22, ff. 91v–92 [Grey Friars, 1540, *domu[s] molendinari[a] vocata* a milhowse]; C 66/708, m. 35 [White Friars, 1541, *dom[us] supra molendum*].

a simpler guest-house. The friaries' rented tenements and almshouses are discussed below (Chapter 18: London Friars and Londoners).

The larger English friaries seem to have shared a number of common elements in the layout of their precincts, although detailed research increasingly shows the diversity rather than the regularity of friaries.[28] Where research into other friaries has been both extensive in area and has integrated archaeological and documentary evidence, a broadly similar picture emerges. Thus, at the Coventry White Friars, the main cloister is on the south side of the church, with a pair of small 'half-cloisters' or yards further south. The chapter house and prior's accommodation were sited in wings running east off the two cloisters. The church was situated closest to the access road and the more secluded parts of the precinct had large areas of garden.[29] The Leicester Austin Friars had a similar form, although its situation in a virtual island of water meadows meant that the church had to be sited on the south, with the principal and lesser cloisters set to the north.[30] At Norwich Black Friars the cloister lay to the north, down the hill from the church, with an adjacent service court beyond.[31] The 'church and twin cloister' plan would seem, therefore, to have been the norm for the larger English friaries by the fourteenth century, although other (still quite large) friaries such as the Aylesford or Hulne White Friars managed with a single cloister complemented by more irregular wings for the lesser buildings.[32]

Using the space

The friary precincts were complex spaces, used and perceived in a variety of ways, particularly from the fourteenth century onwards when the friars built their great preaching naves (and their external counterparts, the cemeteries and preaching crosses). To the friars themselves they must have held a variety of meanings: the friaries were their home and a place of sleep and nourishment, but also their workplace, at times calm and spiritual (during services in the choir) and at times noisy and bustling (during sermons in the nave or churchyard). For lay visitors the friaries may have held quite different meanings: a place of burial for a family member, somewhere to come for spiritual instruction or, alternatively, for business meetings. Members of religious fraternities and secular guilds were also frequent visitors to the London friaries, hiring rooms and halls as meeting places (as well as having contractual entitlement to particular altars and chapels in the friary

---

[28] O'Sullivan, *In the Company of the Preachers*, pp. 7–8, 18–20.
[29] Woodfield, *Whitefriars, Coventry*, pp. 38, 489; O'Sullivan, *In the Company of the Preachers*, pp. 118–22.
[30] Jean E. Mellor and T. Pearce, *The Austin Friars, Leicester* (London: Council for British Archaeology, 1981), pp. 26–43, fig. 2; O'Sullivan, *In the Company of the Preachers*, pp. 195–7.
[31] Sutermeister, *Norwich Blackfriars*, p. 26–8 and plan; O'Sullivan, *In the Company of the Preachers*, pp. 260–5.
[32] Butler, 'Houses of the Mendicant Orders in Britain', pp. 133–4; O'Sullivan, *In the Company of the Preachers*, pp. 36–9, 166–70.

churches). The Pouchmakers used Austin Friars, the Plaisterers had a hall at Grey Friars, the French fraternity of the Immaculate Conception had their annual dinner at Black Friars and the Brabant and Lorraine fraternity of St Barbara seem to have had a hall at Crossed Friars.[33] And, members of the London clergy may, on occasion, have had access to friary libraries.

The friaries can therefore be seen as constituting an ambiguous grey area between theoretical divisions of space into lay/religious or public/private.[34] Rather than thinking of fixed areas within the friaries with clearly defined boundaries – a friars' zone, a visitors' zone – it is perhaps better to think of routes, with gates and markers to guide and control movement.[35] Black Friars is the most complex yet perhaps the most successfully mapped friary precinct and Figure 75 illustrates the likely routes taken by a variety of users in the early sixteenth century. The majority of lay visitors would have entered the friary by the northern gate, near Ludgate, and walked southwards, heading for the prominent porch in the north-west corner of the church (perhaps stopping for a drink at the well in the lane), or turning left to walk into the cemetery, perhaps to hear a sermon at the outdoor preaching cross. Lay residents would generally have come in by this gate or the north-eastern gate to get to their rented houses. Important visitors would probably have arrived by boat, going up the steps onto Water Lane and walking northwards. The king and members of parliament would have turned right, going through a courtyard and up into the parliament hall (on the west side of the southern cloister), or into the adjacent Duchy of Lancaster office. If they were also attending a service before or after the session, they would have continued up Water Lane to the church, perhaps entering by the grand west door. 'VIPs', like Emperor Charles V in 1522, stayed in the guest hall in the first floor of the west wing of the cloister (which at the time of Charles V's visit was newly connected to Henry's palace at Bridewell by a long galleried walkway over the river Fleet). The daily life of the friars themselves – when they were resident in the friary and not studying in Oxford or Cambridge or preaching in a parish church – was based around the cloister walk, which connected refectory, dormitory, chapter house and church, and also gave access to the library, infirmary and gardens beyond.

The prior and provincial prior were based beyond the cloister, around a small garden with the chapter house on its west, the prior's house to the east and the provincial prior's house to the south. A small chapel to the north led into the choir; the prior may even have had an oriel window through which to view the friars at prayer, like the one the Augustinian

---

[33] TNA, LR 15/12 [Pouchmakers]; E 315/191, f. 60 [Plaisterers]; SC 6/Hen VIII/2396, f. 63 [St Barbara]; Colson, 'Alien Communities', pp. 112, 138 [St Barbara and Immaculate Conception].

[34] For the overlap in notions of public and private urban space, see Vanessa Harding, 'Space, Property, and Propriety in Urban England', *Journal of Interdisciplinary History*, 32 (2001), 549–69. See also Chapter 18: London Friars and Londoners.

[35] Gilchrist, *Norwich Cathedral Close*, pp. 41–58, 240–48; Laurence Butler, 'The Archaeology of Urban Monasteries in Britain', in *Advances in Monastic Archaeology*, ed. R. Gilchrist and H.C. Mytum, British Archaeological Reports, 227 (Oxford: Archaeolpress, 1993), pp. 79–86 (pp. 82–3).

208 THE FRIARIES OF MEDIEVAL LONDON

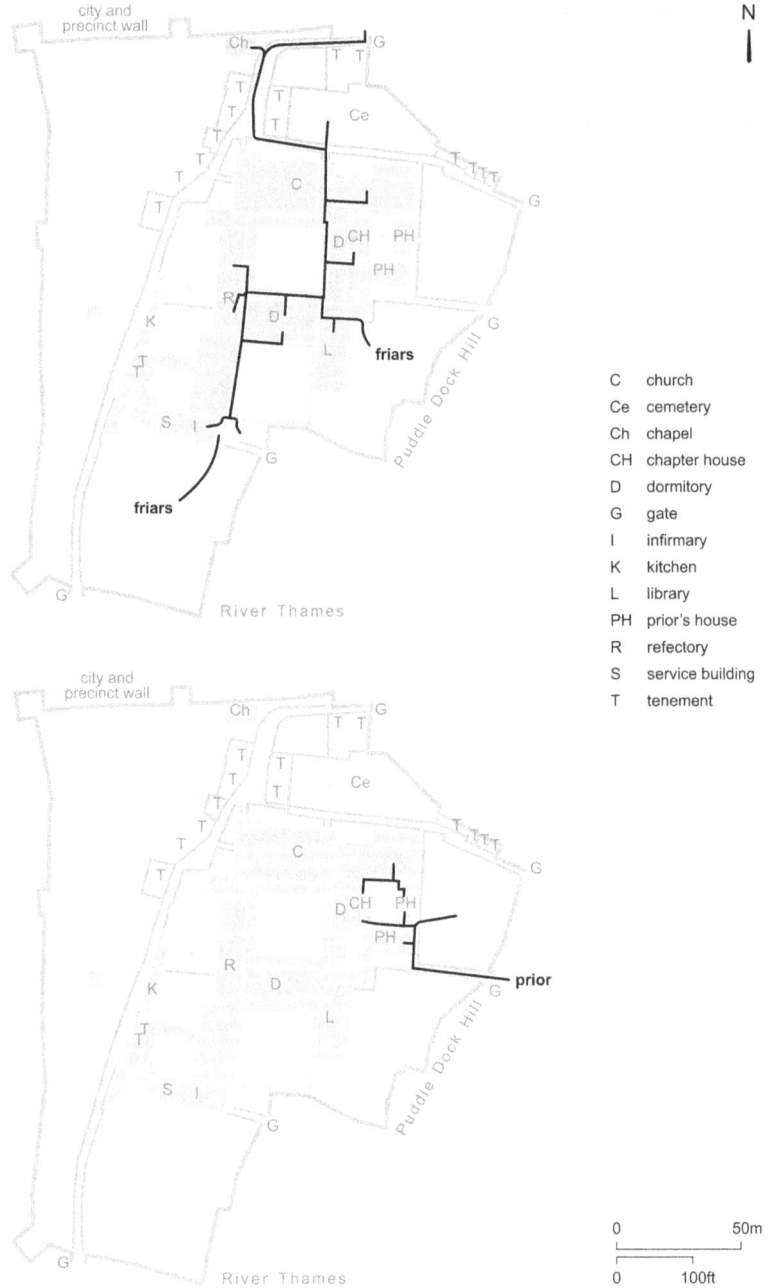

Fig. 75. Plan of Black Friars showing how friars, servants and visitors may have circulated (scale 1:3000).

PRECINCTS AND THE USE OF SPACE 209

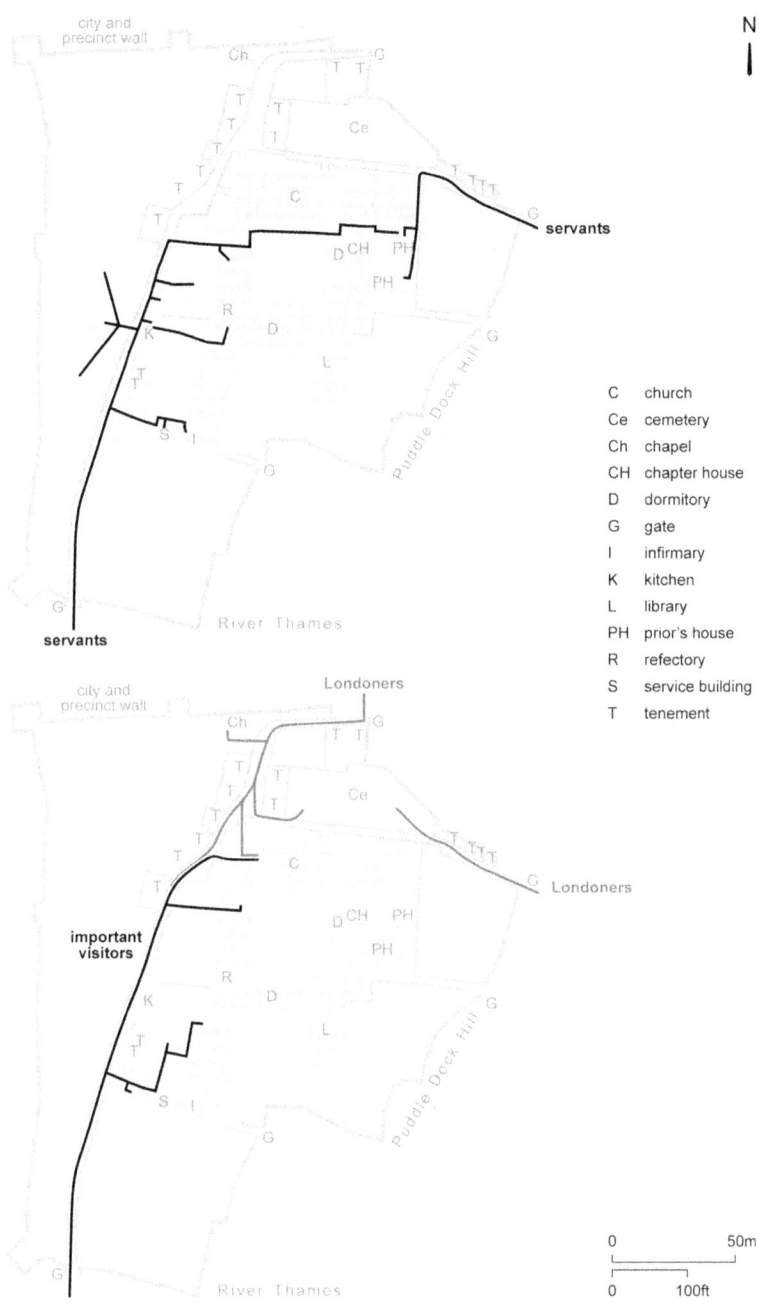

Fig. 75. (continued)

prior William Bolton had installed at St Bartholomew's in the early sixteenth century.[36] The priors and provincial priors would have come and gone through a private gate on the east of the friary. No less important to the running of the friary were the servants, whether private servants to the prior and provincial, or those working under the obedientiaries, buying and preparing the food and drink, maintaining the buildings and gardens, and washing the friars' clothes. They must also have used the main cloister, although using the northern walk as their route between the kitchen and service court in the west and the prior's court to the east. Provisions would have arrived by road and by boat and the servants would therefore have had to move all over the friary precinct (Figure 75).

Conclusion

The precincts of the thirteenth-century friaries were very much spaces in the making. Where the documentary evidence survives – for Holborn Black Friars, Grey Friars and Crossed Friars – we can see the early priors at work, patiently negotiating and assembling a jigsaw puzzle of urban and suburban properties, attempting to create a reasonably sized and appropriately shaped urban religious precinct. The initial aim of the priors seems to have been to create a space for the three key components of chapel, accommodation wing and cemetery. As we have seen for the churches, so it was for the precincts: by the late thirteenth century the ambitions of the priors had passed beyond these simple original aims. Firstly, the priors of the orders that survived the Second Council of Lyon in 1274 designed and built proper four-sided cloisters, situated on the 'private' or precinct side of the church (away from the main road) and built to house ranges of monastic buildings: refectory, dormitory and chapter house. The Franciscan guardian later came up with a new feature, a second cloister, and began work on this in the 1330s or '40s: this was to house an infirmary and guest wing. Other London priors followed suit, adding second cloisters that also included library and kitchen wings. By the turn of the fourteenth and fifteenth centuries, most of the London friaries had large urban precincts, with double-church and double-cloister, large garden and cemetery spaces, and mansions for the prior or priors (including, in some cases, the provincial prior, the head of the whole English province of that order). Within a century or two of their arrival in London the friars had thus stamped their mark on the London landscape, financed by the donations of living and dead Londoners, and with these religious communities silently maintained by small armies of servants.

---

[36] RCHME, *Inventory of the Historical Monuments in London*, 5 vols (London: HMSO, 1924–30), iv (*The City*), 125.

12

Architecture and Architectural Fragments of the London Friaries

MARK SAMUEL

THE study of architectural fragments offers us the possibility of understanding – and even reconstructing – long-vanished medieval buildings. In a city such as London – where the Dissolution, the Great Fire, redevelopment and wartime bombing have taken a severe toll on the stock of medieval architecture – architectural fragments are the only surviving primary source for understanding the architectural styles and features of great lost medieval buildings, including the London friaries. More general discussion of the architecture of the friaries can be found in the friary-by-friary chapters of Part I of this book (Chapters 1 to 9), and in Chapter 10: Churches.

The architectural fragments have usually come to us through two processes: demolition and excavation. When masons were dismantling a medieval monastic building, for example in the fourteenth century in order to rebuild it or in the sixteenth century in order to destroy it, the more decorative pieces of stonework – windows, arches, door surrounds – were often recycled as rough foundation material: their particular shapes meant that they were not generally suitable for 'ordinary' recycling in new wall superstructures. Several centuries later, modern archaeologists encounter batches of this recycled 'low value' stonework in wall foundations. Sometimes this material is studied to great advantage;[1] on other occasions the architectural fragments are retained but languish unstudied in museum store rooms.[2]

---

[1] Successful examples of the analysis of monastic architectural fragments from London include studies of Augustinian canons' houses such as St Mary Spital, Holy Trinity priory and St Mary Merton, together with work on other orders including the Cluniac abbey in Bermondsey and the priory of the Knights Hospitaller: Thomas, Sloane and Phillpotts, *St Mary Spital*, pp. 91–8, 186–94; Schofield and Lea, *Holy Trinity Priory, Aldgate*, pp. 208–18; Miller and Saxby, *St Mary Merton*, pp. 176–95; Tony Dyson and others, *The Cluniac Priory and Abbey of St Saviour Bermondsey, Surrey*, MOLA monograph, 50 (London: Museum of London Archaeology, 2011), pp. 184–98; Barney Sloane and Gordon Malcolm, *Excavations at the Priory of the Order of the Hospital of St John of Jerusalem, Clerkenwell, London*, MoLAS monograph, 20 (London: Museum of London Archaeology Service, 2004), pp. 280–97.

[2] Many of the architectural fragments excavated in the 1980s by the Museum of London's Department

Table 14 Summary of useful architectural fragments from London friary sites.

Friary	Site-code	Fragments selected for analysis	Location of fragments
Black Friars	LBY85	1 (published record)	LAA
	PIC87	3	LAA
	FRI88	6	LAA
	VAL88	0[a]	LAA
	Apothecaries' Hall	decorative 'rockery'	Apothecaries' Hall
	new Dominican friary	re-sited pillar	new Dominican friary
	Selsdon Park Hotel	re-sited arch	Selsdon Park Hotel
Austin Friars	OBE96	6	LAA
	GWS89	12 (+3 paper records)	LAA
Grey Friars	CCN80	1 published record	lost?

Note:

[a] The main 'missing' group of friary fragments (known to the author) is an assemblage of a dozen fragments of fourteenth-century window tracery discovered and recorded in the late 1980s from site VAL88. Unfortunately, these could not be re-examined in 2011 due to large-scale building works taking place in the museum's Rotunda store.

About 140 architectural fragments from archaeological sites within the London friary precincts were identified at the Museum of London's archive and stores.[3] The present author then examined this material to assess its potential to yield useful information about the architecture, structure and decoration of the friary buildings. It would be misleading to talk of a 'statistically meaningful sample' in what is essentially an art-historical exercise, but a sample of about thirty items (the majority of which are window fragments) has proved useful in answering the above points (Table 14). The tradition of art-historical and archaeological study of medieval architecture means that several important pieces of friary architecture that were discovered in the early twentieth century were preserved. A pillar and an arch from the undercroft of the late thirteenth-century chapter house at Black Friars survive, the former in the new Dominican priory in Belsize Park (London) and the latter in the wooded garden of the Selsdon Park Hotel in Croydon (London and Surrey). Another

---

of Urban Archaeology have received little study. The reasons include a perennial lack of resources for the storage and study of large finds that fall outside the archaeological norm of pot, bone and 'small finds'. Furthermore, a series of moves of the museum's stores has had the unfortunate effect of eroding the inadequately secured labelling of the stones (an architectural fragment without a label stating the site and context is virtually useless). Finally, the financial near-collapse of the museum's archaeology department in 1990 (in the wake of the city of London's recession) meant that the best assemblage of friary architectural fragments (site GWS89) was still mostly unlabelled when key staff were laid off; much of the present study has been an attempt to trace the lost information in this assemblage.

[3] The museum has recently made a real effort to sort out its architectural fragment collection and to rectify some of the problems highlighted in n. 2. The authors thank Steve Tucker and Roy Stephenson of the museum's London Archaeological Archive for their help in accessing, identifying and studying this material.

group of fragments are preserved as a decorative rockery in the courtyard of Apothecaries' Hall, close to their original find-spot.[4] To this physically surviving material can be added some 'virtual' stonework, including earlier publications and worked stone records made by the Museum of London's former Department of Urban Archaeology soon after excavation.[5] The majority of the surviving architectural material derives from Black Friars, with some fragments from Austin Friars and a single published item from Grey Friars (Table 14). No useful fragments have so far been discovered from the other friary sites.

The approach used here is to examine the architectural fragments in detail and relate their designs to the typology of medieval architectural mouldings. The thirteenth and fourteenth centuries were certainly a time of great artistic fertility and rapidly changing styles: 'the period c. 1250–1400 [...] encompasses the most inventive phase in the development of medieval mouldings'. This approach has the admitted drawback that it places 'the stress on the earliest occurrence of each type of moulding, on their distribution in the various English regions, and on whether any is likely to be of Continental origin or indigenous'; although the approach introduces the same weakness as reporting 'the year's first cuckoo', it is the only practical means of analysis.[6] The emphasis is therefore on those types of moulding which can be assigned a clear 'first cuckoo' date. With few exceptions, these are traceried window fragments probably from the church or the claustral core of the complex. Other mouldings are mentioned where, exceptionally, they can be assigned a definite role and provenance. The pillar from the first chapter house of Black Friars (now in the new Dominican priory in Belsize Park) and a nave pier base fall into this category. The collective building history of the friaries can be telescoped into two basic periods: before and after the Black Death. A third and earlier period – the time of the first friaries in the thirteenth century – is, unfortunately, entirely unrepresented.

Before discussing the style and original function of the architectural fragments, we will examine the types of stone chosen by the friars, the evidence for any painted finish to those stones and the masons' use of tools.

Petrology, finishes and tools

Most of the architectural fragments from the friaries have been dressed from a Glauconitic sand/limestone probably from the Upper Greensand; they are almost certainly Reigate stone from the north Downs. This stone was used for most detailed work in London after

---

[4] Mark Samuel and Nick Holder, 'The Thirteenth-Century Chapter House of Black Friars', forthcoming.

[5] Both the physical architectural fragments and the paper records are archived at the Museum of London's LAA, organised as is usual by site code. For the published Grey Friars and Black Friars pieces, see Richard Lea, 'The Archaeology of Standing Structures in the City of London', *Popular Archaeology*, December 1985/January 1986, 22–31 (pp. 24–25); figs 6 and 8 from that article are reproduced here as Figure 77.

[6] Richard K. Morris, 'The Development of Later Gothic Mouldings in England c. 1250–1400: Part II', *Architectural History*, 22 (1979), 1–48 (p. 19).

about 1200 (with Kentish ragstone used for the basic structure of walls).[7] However, other building stones such as Packstone from Calvados bear a strong superficial resemblance and have no doubt been misidentified in the past. The stone source is only mentioned below where it is obviously *not* Reigate stone. Caen stone (also, of course, from Normandy) is the other building stone commonly used in London that can be identified with some confidence; only three instances are seen in this London friary assemblage. Ketton stone (a Lincolnshire limestone) was occasionally used for coping stones. Purbeck 'marble' was used where the onus was on display. One window was cut from intractable Kentish ragstone.

Tracery fragments from the chancel of Austin Friars (site OBE 96) had been repeatedly whitewashed, with at least five coats applied in the two centuries between construction (mid fourteenth century) and Dissolution (1538). This fondness for whitewashed church interiors rather than polychromy set in well before the Reformation, as can be seen in depictions of fifteenth-century Continental church interiors by Jan van Eyck and others, for example in his celebrated diptych or triptych panels known as *Madonna in the Church* and *The Annunciation*.

The normal tools of the late medieval period were used by the friary masons. Their work is characterised by the use of the clawtool (a 'clawed' chisel) that creates rectilinear claws on bed. Visible surfaces were highly finished with the cock's comb (a kind of multiple-bladed stone plane). 'X' marks, indicating completion, were engraved on joints (so they would be subsequently hidden). Axial lines were scribed as usual on the mullion and jamb beds.[8] Only one instance of a masons' mark was seen (see below). Two Purbeck marble columns were roughly shaped with a point tool and the marks survive on the impost surface and other joints. Once tool marks had been removed, final polishing could be carried out. Wages lists at Westminster Abbey from the 1250s indicate that this task was carried out by specialists and the same accounts record the acquisition of special hard stones for polishing marble in 1253. The *Metrical Life of St Hugh*, written in the 1220s, mentions the use of vinegar to polish marble columns and this technique was probably used here.[9] Exemplars (patterns) for elements were probably sent to the specialist marblers based in London (see below).

Friary architecture, 1270–1350

This period is represented in the assemblage by a single window mullion, a nave pier base and an undercroft column from Black Friars, and a cloister arcade at Austin Friars. A tracery fragment from Grey Friars marks the end of this period of building.

---

[7] Tim Tatton-Brown, 'The Quarrying and Distribution of Reigate Stone in the Middle Ages', *Medieval Archaeology*, 45 (2001), 189–201.

[8] For another example of this see Mark Samuel, 'The Architectural Fragments', in *St Gregory's Priory, Northgate, Canterbury: Excavations 1988–1991*, ed. M. Hicks and A. Hicks, The Archaeology of Canterbury, new series, 2 (Canterbury: Canterbury Archaeological Trust, 2001), pp. 151–82 (pp. 153–4).

[9] Jennifer S. Alexander, 'Building Stone from the East Midlands Quarries: Sources, Transportation and Usage', *Medieval Archaeology*, 39 (1995), 107–38 (pp. 118–20).

A ?Caen stone mullion (a foot, 0.305m, on its long axis) has the scale (33kg) and severity of a great church window (Figure 76a). The mullion had been reused in later adaptations to the (second) Black Friars chapter house; its original function was presumably in one of the windows of the choir of the 1280s and '90s.[10] The highly conservative plain-chamfered moulding has a rebate for timber shutters. The finish is correspondingly old-fashioned, the same finely serrated chisel being used on all surfaces, a finish used at (for example) Selborne Priory, Hampshire, and common in France. The excellent condition suggests it was soon masked by later work.

Parts of a pier base (Figure 77) have been found on a site in the north-west corner of the nave of the Dominican church.[11] A pier of four clustered shafts formed a quatrefoil moulding; the base and sub-base respected this geometry but rested on an octagonal (sub-square) plinth. A *triple-roll* base moulding shows this as conservative English work of a sort which persisted until the 1340s in East Anglia and the south-east.[12] The pier probably derives from the arcade of the nave and its date may therefore provide us with a useful *terminus ante quem* for the construction of the west end of the church.

A one-foot (0.305 m) weather moulding for a ground table, in a hard ?Magnesian stone, survives in a rockery in the courtyard of Apothecaries' Hall (not illustrated). It was almost certainly discovered during building work at the hall in the 1920s, immediately southwest of the location of the Black Friars church.[13] Although the fragment is now cemented into the twentieth-century rockery, it is still possible to discern a scroll moulding below a concave weather moulding. A date no later than the early fourteenth century is likely; it is therefore contemporary with the arcade pier. The church seems a likely provenance, given the first-rate quality of the moulding.

A Purbeck marble column survives in the refounded Dominican priory in Belsize Park, London (Figure 78a, Figure 79). The column was discovered *in situ* in a medieval undercroft during construction and archaeological works in Ireland Yard in 1900, and was removed and donated to the medieval friars' successors. The authors argue elsewhere that the undercroft is the lower storey of the original late thirteenth-century chapter house.[14]

---

[10] Site FRI88, the blocking (context [481]) of a window (context [486]). This window was part of the parish church of St Anne, which was created from the (second) chapter house at Black Friars after the Dissolution. The thirteenth-century mullion (and several counterparts) thus survived to a late date, preserved in a much later feature.

[11] Site LBY85; Lea, 'Archaeology of Standing Structures', p. 25.

[12] Richard K. Morris, 'The Development of Later Gothic Mouldings in England c. 1250–1400: Part I', *Architectural History*, 21 (1978), 21–57 (p. 26).

[13] Pers. comm. Paul Simmons (Honorary Assistant Clerk, Apothecaries' Company); see also Apothecaries' Company, 1920s photograph album (photos of archaeological and architectural features exposed during building works at Apothecaries Hall and *The Times*), inscribed 'presented Jan. 1930'.

[14] LAA, site PRG407; Alfred W. Clapham, 'On the Topography of the Dominican Priory of London', *Archaeologia*, 63 (1911), 57–84 (p. 69); Samuel and Holder, 'The Thirteenth-Century Chapter House of Black Friars, London'.

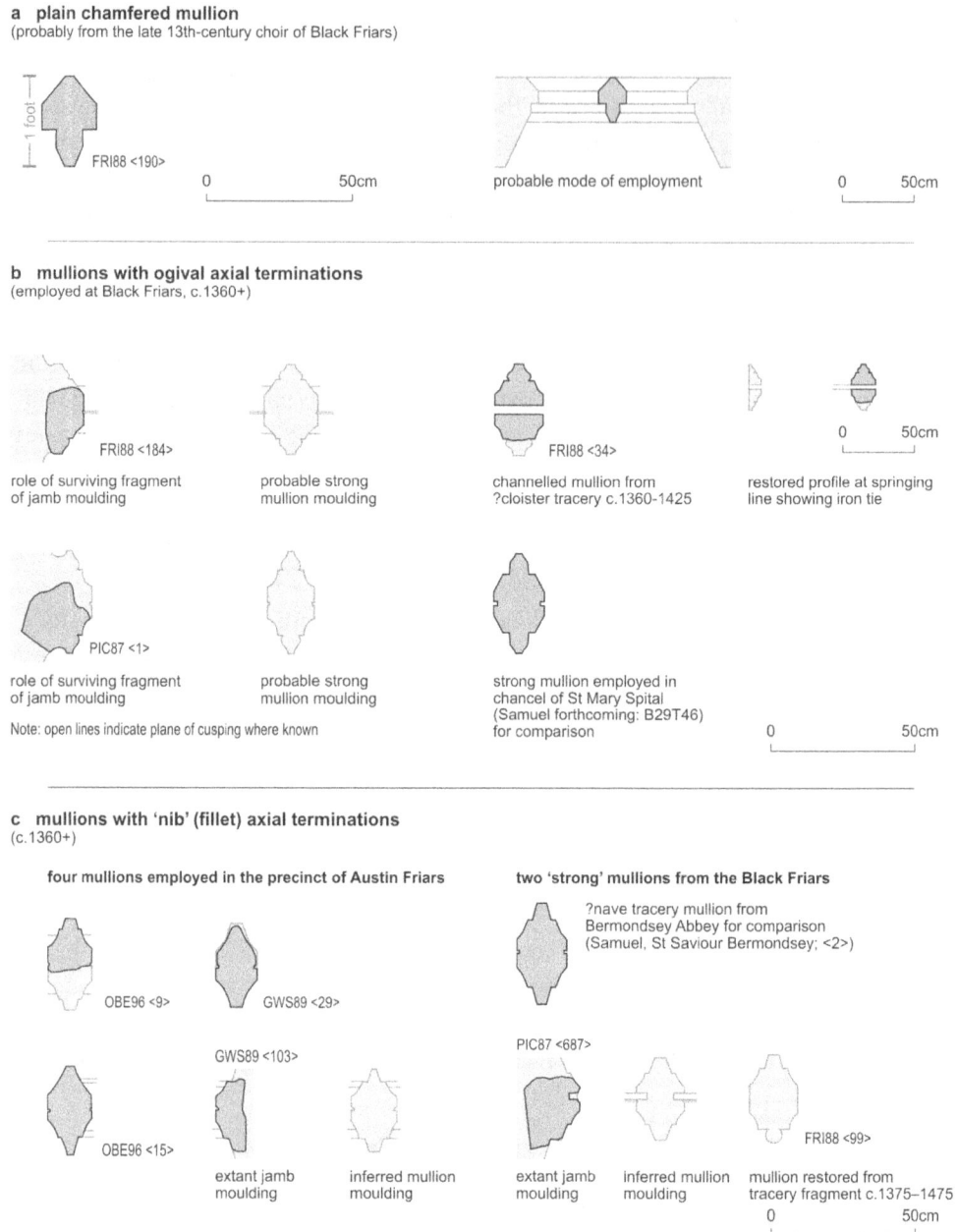

Fig. 76. A comparison of window mouldings used in the London friaries (exterior to top) (scales 1:25 and 1:50).

The column has a base typical of the Decorated period: plinths of octagonal plan with simply moulded sub-bases appeared suddenly in different parts of England in the last two decades of the thirteenth century, having developed earlier in northern France.[15] The

[15] Morris, 'Later Gothic Mouldings, Part II', p. 26.

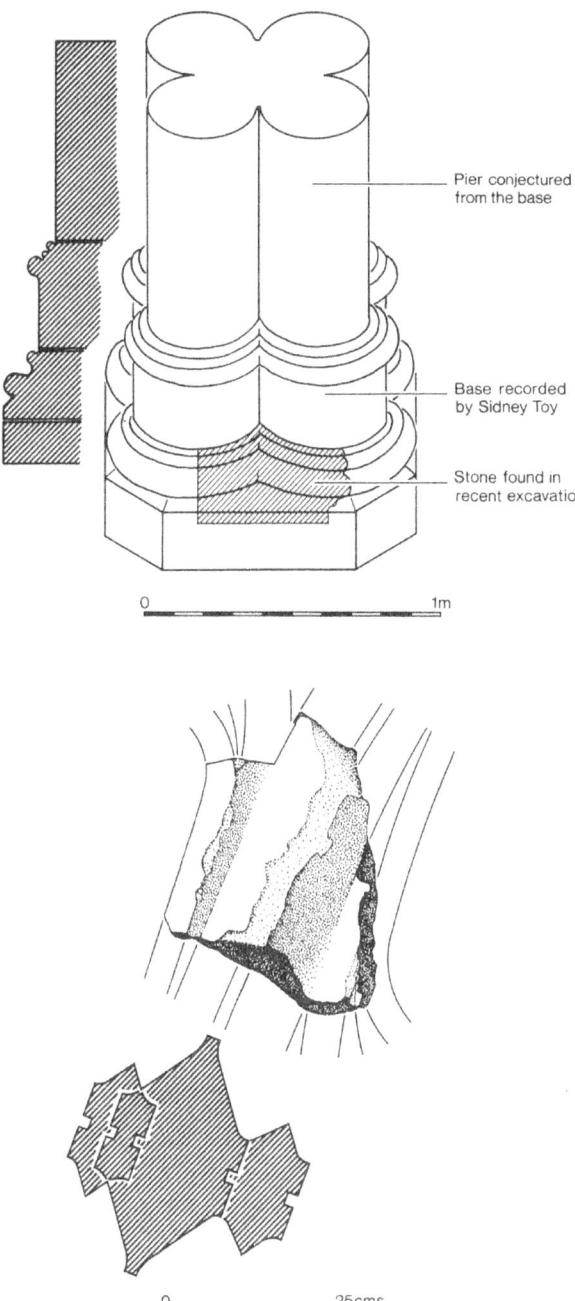

Fig. 77. Pier base from the Black Friars church, probably from the nave arcade of the first half of the fourteenth century; 'sunk chamfer' tracery (c. 1320–1340) used in a window of the Grey Friars church (scale 1:25 and 1:10; reproduced from Lea, 'Archaeology of Standing Structures', figs 6 and 8).

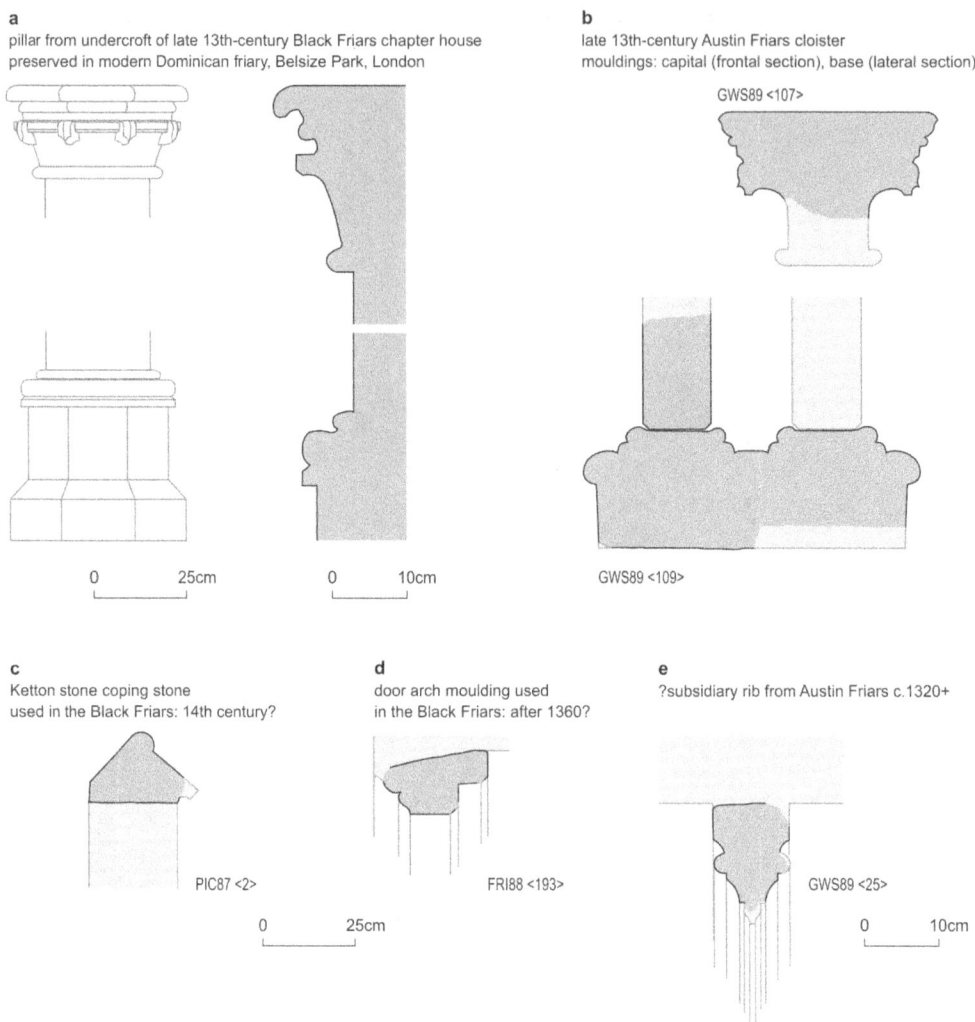

Fig. 78. Selected architectural mouldings (other than windows) from the London friaries (scales 1:10 and 1:20)

double-roll base moulding shows an unsurprising stylistic link to the corresponding part of the nave pier (see above). The rather traditional use of a round capital and distinct polygonal abacus reflects the continuing influence of Continental prototypes even after c. 1290. After that date the 'two-unit' capital appears in England.[16] The rounded drip moulding is another conservative touch, arguing for a late thirteenth-century rather than a fourteenth-century date.

Turning to the Austin Friars, the most important survival from this period were fragments of a coupled-column arcade (Figure 49). The fragments were found reused in the foundations of the late fourteenth-century northern cloister; it is argued that they were

---

[16] Morris, 'Later Gothic Mouldings, Part II', p. 22.

Fig. 79. A column from the undercroft of the late thirteenth-century chapter house of Black Friars, now in the refounded (fourth) Dominican friary in Belsize Park, London (Andy Chopping/MOLA)

originally used in the first cloister (Chapter 6: Austin Friars).[17] The cloister arcade used both Purbeck marble and Caen stone elements, with coupled bases and capitals (<107> <109> on Figure 49) alongside a shaft fragment (<112>). The Caen stone arcade arch (<102>) was trefoliated and cusped. Another example of the coupled capital was found in excavations in 1909: it is illustrated in a surviving photograph but the original fragment does not apparently survive.[18] The *concave fillet* also occurs on capitals in the chapter house of the 1290s at Wells Cathedral. The famous cloister in Mont St Michel apparently employs a similar capital (renewed) and is traditionally dated to just after 1230 on the basis of a lost inscription and sculpture of St Francis. The use of Sussex 'marble' here may suggest a slightly later date.[19]

A massive fragment of complex tracery was discovered in 1980 in an excavation on the site of the choir of Grey Friars (Figure 77).[20] It incorporated the *sunk chamfer*, a rare moulding in London only recorded at the nearby Charterhouse.[21] Mouldings in the north transept of Bromyard church, Hereford, are closely similar, and documented occurrences are restricted to c. 1320–40.[22] The original provenance of this window fragment is not certain: as has been stated, the archaeological site was in the area of the choir of the church but the art-historical date in the second quarter of the fourteenth century is just when construction works were taking place in the nave (Chapter 4: Grey Friars, 'The church'). Most unusually, a link with an individual mason can be suggested (below, 'Conclusion').

---

[17] The fragments were discovered at site GWS89: context [169] is the west wall of the east wing of the northern Austin Friars cloister. It is likely that the arcade of the original late thirteenth-century cloister was dismantled during construction works of the late fourteenth or early fifteenth century, when a new (northern) cloister was added and the original (southern) cloister remodelled. The fragments from the dismantled first cloister arcade were then recycled as foundation material for the second cloister; Nick Holder, Mark Samuel and Ian Betts, 'The Church and Cloisters of Austin Friars', *Transactions of the London and Middlesex Archaeological Society*, 64 (2013), 143–62 (pp. 152–4).

[18] Historic England Archive, Dutch Church (London), photograph of 19 March 1909: '1139e Austin Friars relics excavation – masonry'. The archaeological site from which this fragment derives, PRG1020, was re-excavated eighty years later as site GWS89. See W.A. Cater, 'The Priory of Austin Friars, London', *Journal of the British Archaeological Association*, 18 (1912), 25–44, 57–82 (pp. 27–30).

[19] Morris, 'Later Gothic Mouldings, Part II', fig. C; Jean-Luc Legros, *Le Mont-Saint-Michel: Architecture et Civilisation* (Caen, France: CRDP de Basse-Normandie, 2005), pp. 70–1. The date of c. 1230 for the Mont St Michel cloister seems a little too early given that the capitals were originally cut from 'calcaire lumachelle importé du Sussex', i.e. a Sussex 'marble'.

[20] Site CCN80; Lea, 'Archaeology of Standing Structures', fig. 6.

[21] Bruno Barber, *The London Charterhouse*, MoLAS monograph, 10 (London: Museum of London Archaeology Service, 2002), p. 48. LAA, site PPR98, Mark Samuel, 'Preacher's Court PPR98: the worked stones', (unpublished Museum of London report, 1999).

[22] Morris, 'Later Gothic Mouldings, Part I', p. 31, fig. 5c.

Later friary architecture, 1350–1450

This period of friary architecture is represented by fragments of windows from Austin and Black Friars. The Austin Friars church has the best overall evidence for this later period of friary architecture. We argue that a small parish church was converted into the friary choir in the 1270s and a large nave added in the mid fourteenth century, with construction beginning in the 1340s or a little earlier (Chapter 6: Austin Friars; Figure 67). The survival of this great nave into the twentieth century makes its destruction in October 1940 all the more regrettable. Of some compensation, therefore, is the detailed recording that took place before its destruction.[23]

The nave arcade piers were early examples of a Perpendicular stereotype where four engaged shafts meet a central square pillar with hollow-chamfered corners. This was created by the *rotated square* technique and could be easily designed with minimal equipment, as has been demonstrated at the church of St Mary Spital.[24] Records made in the 1860s (before a restoration campaign) show these piers in detail. Although the bases were unfortunately concealed by panelling and a scale is absent, the arcade moulding with its four-way symmetry is shown clearly.[25] The use of large fillets flanked by waves, rather than double-ogees, was a legacy of the Decorated style. The moulding therefore suggests a date in the mid fourteenth century, on the cusp of the Decorated and Perpendicular styles.

The most important assemblage of architectural fragments from this friary is a group of twelve fragments recovered from a post-Dissolution pit excavated on the Old Broad Street site in 1996.[26] The mouldings of these fragments have characteristics common to those of the inner court of Rotherhithe Palace (1353–61) and the windows of the chapel of Holy Trinity at St Mary Graces, Tower Hill (1349).[27] These Austin Friars fragments are almost certainly, therefore, contemporary with the arcade piers.

Hollow-chamfered mouldings with glazing grooves and filleted axial terminations (*nibs* with canted sides) are the signature of this early Perpendicular type. Four windows are represented (Figure 76c): two from the area of the friary choir (site OBE96), two

---

[23] Chapter 6: Austin Friars, n. 25.
[24] Harward, Holder and Thomas, *Excavations at Spitalfields Market*.
[25] Thomas Hugo, 'Austin Friars', *Transactions of the London and Middlesex Archaeological Society*, 2 (1864), 1–24 (figure facing p. 19).
[26] The context is OBE96 [327], the fill of a post-Dissolution pit dug in the area of the choir: LAA, site OBE96, G. Bruce, 'An archaeological excavation and watching brief on the site of 109–118 Old Broad Street, City of London EC2' (unpublished AOC report, 1997); see 'Architectural stone' section by J. Ashbee, pp. 61–3.
[27] Simon Blatherwick and Richard Bluer, *Great Houses, Moats and Mills on the South Bank of the Thames : Medieval and Tudor Southwark and Rotherhithe*, MOLA monograph, 47 (London: Museum of London Archaeology, 2009), fig. 125; Mark Samuel, 'The Architectural Fragments', in *The Cistercian Abbey of St Mary Graces, East Smithfield, London*, ed. I. Grainger and others, MOLA Monograph, 44 (London: Museum of London Archaeology, 2011), pp. 114–29 (fig 72).

from the north cloister site (GWS89). The tracery schemes were conventional, with arrayed cinquefoil archlets at the springing line separated by supermullions, but extensive reconstruction was not possible. Of the two windows probably from the Austin Friars choir, a cinquefoil archlet/supermullion (Figure 76c, OBE96 <15>) employed large single flanking hollow chamfers on the exterior and internal 'nib' axial terminations, separated from flanking hollow chamfers by short straight pieces.[28] A second window employs a similar (but incomplete) moulding with a shorter axial termination (Figure 76c, OBE96 <9>).[29] It formed the junction of symmetrical archlets with a supermullion.

From the two windows that may have been used in the cloister, there is a single fragment of a rectilinear tracery scheme, perhaps from the chapter house (Figure 76c, GWS89 <103>). The two-way symmetry of the moulding parallels tracery at Rotherhithe. The simple hollow-chamfered forms of another fragment (Figure 76c, GWS89 <29>) suggest that this is part of a window from a more domestic part of the cloister. Several mullions of this form were found including one cut from Kentish ragstone (GWS89 <101>, not illustrated). The well-preserved tooling shows drafted margins cut with a chisel, while the hollows were finished with a point. The glazing reveal has a triangular masons' mark – the only one observed from the friary assemblages. The small size of this mullion shows there were at least two distinct types of domestic window.

Among the lost but recorded stones, a vaulting rib (Figure 78e, GWS89 <25>) is of particular interest as it is exactly paralleled by one of the subsidiary ribs in the presbytery aisle of Ely which dates to shortly after 1322.[30] A 1909 photograph of the Austin Friars Square excavations also shows a lost vault boss: it formed a complex junction of four such subsidiary?lierne ribs.[31] A rose, symbolising the Virgin, covered the boss and there can be little doubt that this vaulting adorned the presbytery or chapter house.

At Black Friars there is evidence is for a number of fourteenth-century windows from different locations. There are stylistic differences to the Austin Friars windows, but not, apparently, significant variation in date. The mouldings mostly employ hollow chamfers, but the axial termination fillet is flanked by ogees rather than straight pieces. A Caen stone mullion (Figure 76b, FRI88 <34>) lacks any provision for glass and thus identifies it as part of a cloister; the broad date of this element, c. 1360–1425, suggests that it once formed part of the arcade of the second or 'inner' cloister. Documentary evidence suggests that at least part of this cloister was finished by the 1370s (Chapter 2: The Second Black Friars, 'Acquiring and developing the friary') so the cloister arcade may date to the mid fourteenth century. A groove for a continuous iron tie, one inch in scantling (254mm), marks the

---

[28] Another mullion (<8>) and ?supermullion (<20>), not illustrated, may derive from the same window.
[29] Fragments <14> and <17>, not illustrated, may derive from this window.
[30] Morris, 'Later Gothic Mouldings, Part I', fig. 14b.
[31] See n. 19.

springing-line of?three-light tracery. Surviving fragments of such ties have been recorded at the fifteenth-century London Guildhall.[32]

A fragment of glazed trefoliated Reigate stone jamb (Figure 76b, FRI88 <184>) employs a near-identical moulding. This window and a similar but larger jamb moulding (Figure 76b, PIC87 <1>) were surrounded by a typical *hollow casement*. Another glazed window jamb fragment from that site (Figure 76c, PIC87 <687>) shows, however, the 'nib' axial termination favoured at Austin Friars (see above) and a flat internal splay. Do these three window fragments also form part of the new second cloister at Black Friars, or might they instead be part of later fourteenth-century refenestration work in the thirteenth-century choir? The presbytery of Norwich Cathedral employs such a moulding in work dating to c. 1362 but the long popularity of the type in the south-east makes any precise dating hazardous.[33] The moulding type has been recorded at several London monastic houses: St Mary Graces, Holy Trinity priory and St Mary Spital. The two types of termination were sometimes employed on the same window (the 'nib' being external).

A third tracery form (Figure 76c, FRI88 <99>) derived from a shuttered and unglazed tracery scheme, perhaps one of the domestic buildings. The moulding has a roll axial termination on the interior, another common south-east English variant first seen in the later fourteenth century (Oxford New College, c. 1387).[34] A doorway arch (Figure 78d, FRI88 <193>) was adorned with an external *double ogee*; it is probably no earlier than about 1360. A coping stone (Figure 78c, PIC87 <2>) is a late medieval stereotype cut from Ketton stone, nearly indistinguishable from those employed on the Leadenhall Garner. Mass production in Northamptonshire seems likely.[35] These three architectural elements may therefore have been used on fourteenth-century domestic buildings within Black Friars such as the second cloister or the courtyard of buildings for the prior and provincial prior.

Conclusion

If we assume that the scanty survivals are genuinely representative of friary architecture, what do they say? The picture is one of *normality*. The mouldings are almost all precisely what one would expect in any London religious house of the period or, indeed, parish church.

One notable aspect is the lack of architectural fragments from the early London friaries of the thirteenth century. However, this is common to architectural assemblages from monastic houses in other wealthy south-eastern towns: there is scant evidence for

---

[32] Bowsher, *Guildhall*, i, 193–4, figs 186, 187.
[33] John Harvey, *The Perpendicular Style, 1330–1485* (London: Batsford, 1978), fig. 21.
[34] Harvey, *Perpendicular Style*, fig. 30.
[35] Mark Samuel, 'The Fifteenth-Century Garner at Leadenhall', *Antiquaries Journal*, 69 (1989), 119–53 (p. 142).

decorative architectural features before about 1280. One exception to this is in Ipswich where the Black Friars seems to have employed more tracery in the thirteenth century.[36] While the lack of thirteenth-century mouldings from London friaries (and other religious houses) may, of course, be a result of their lack of survival, there is the distinct impression that the first friary buildings of the mid thirteenth century were rather plain structures.

The significant assemblage of Austin Friars material has given us a glimpse of the friars' first cloister of the late thirteenth century: it was a late example of the open coupled-column arcade which, in Britain, was invariably replaced by glazed and shuttered arcades in the later medieval period. It is worth pointing out that the widespread trade in prefabricated English 'marble' elements is witnessed by their use in the Mont St Michel cloister.

The surviving assemblages of London friary material have a disappointing lack of pre-1350 window tracery; other evidence, such as views of the early to mid fourteenth-century Geometric tracery of the Grey Friars cloister, offers a little compensation (Figure 27). The exception to this dearth of pre-1350 material is the complex fragment of a Decorated window from Grey Friars dating to the second quarter of the fourteenth century (Figure 77). The stylistic associations of this piece with Hereford suggest a link with Walter of Hereford, the royal master craftsman who brought masons to the Grey Friars project in the first decade of the century.[37] While his death in 1309 seems to put him out of the running as the direct author, the window can be attributed to his unnamed successor, probably one of his old Hereford apprentices.

The prevalence of (well-dated) 'nibbed' and ogival axial terminations in the window mouldings of the extant London assemblages suggests that the fortunes of these religious houses recovered quickly in the second half of the fourteenth century following the Black Death. There is widespread evidence for the introduction of early Perpendicular windows into earlier walls, probably as individual acts of piety rather than any planned scheme of modernisation. At both Austin Friars and Black Friars these new windows may have been alterations to the earlier choirs. If – like the Dominican chapter house undercroft – simple lancets were originally used, these would have been obvious targets for such modernisation.

A gradual relaxation of the mendicant orders' thirteenth-century preference for a simple building style is seen across south-east England. Elaborate masonry architecture became the norm after about 1320. No detectable 'mendicant' style is apparent, other than the apparent *avoidance* of style; the impression is that masons were simply employed to work as they saw fit. The Norwich White Friars (for example) seems to have been built by

---

[36] Mark Samuel, 'Blackfriars (site code IAS 4901): appraisal report of the moulded stone' (unpublished report for Suffolk County Council Archaeological Service, 1992).

[37] *Calendar of Early Mayor's Court Rolls, A.D. 1298–1307*, ed. Arthur H. Thomas (Cambridge: Cambridge University Press, 1924), p. 251; Howard M. Colvin, *The History of the King's Works*, 6 vols (London: HMSO, 1963–82), i, 205–6; John Harvey and Arthur Oswald, *English Mediaeval Architects: A Biographical Dictionary down to 1550* (Gloucester: Sutton, 1984), pp. 24, 136–7.

masons from the Midlands or even the borders of Wales.[38] The London friaries similarly employed the local style – what might be termed a court style – where the concentration of royalty, high-ranking ecclesiastics and courtiers in the London area made this inevitable.

The importance of transport in the selection of building stone is clearly illustrated, even slight distances having sharp effects on relative prices. The evidence from friaries in southeast England also points to distinct trends in the choice of fine building stones; it should be noted that it is not always the local building stone that was chosen. So, it is interesting to contrast the relative dearth of Caen stone in London with the situation in Ipswich where nearly all the dressings employed were of this stone. This must reflect Ipswich's convenience for seaborne trade, and a lack of suitable local building stone. In Norwich, the White friars made extensive use of varieties of East Anglian oolitic limestone, to a much greater degree than their mendicant colleagues the Grey friars. A hard chalk or clunch was also an important stone type used in Norwich in a major building campaign shortly before the Black Death. Medieval Canterbury masons had long made extensive use of Caen stone; recent scientific examination shows, however, that the White friars of the city sourced much of their dressed stone from other quarries in Calvados, with two varieties of packstone identified.[39] The builders of the London friaries (and the capital's other monastic houses) tended to use Reigate stone for their dressed stone (Table 18). This leads us to an important point about stone identification: the Calvados packstone superficially resembles Reigate stone and this similarity suggests that the two have been routinely confused in the past (by the author and probably others!). The identification of Calvados packstone from medieval London is a challenge for the future.

The exception to these regional trends is Purbeck marble, whose national prestige was such that it was sent all around England regardless of expense. The London marblers were sent patterns to execute for remote abbeys in the hinterland, as a surviving contract (1287) of Walter of Hereford proves.[40] Ketton stone was also widely transported, due to its resistance to weathering: it was used at the Dominican houses in London and Cambridge as a coping stone, it being long favoured throughout the south-east for this specialist purpose.[41]

London mendicant architecture can therefore be seen to follow a pattern of localism

---

[38] Mark Samuel, 'Structural Stonework', in *Norwich Whitefriars: Medieval Friary and Baptist Burial Ground*, ed. Rachel Clarke, East Anglian Archaeology monograph (Chelmsford: East Anglian Archaeology, forthcoming).

[39] See n. 37 [Ipswich]; Samuel, 'The Fifteenth-Century Garner at Leadenhall', p. 142; Mark Samuel, 'Structural Stonework', in *Norwich Greyfriars: Pre-Conquest Town and Medieval Friary*, ed. Phillip A. Emery and Elizabeth Rutledge, East Anglian Archaeology monograph, 120 (Dereham: Norfolk Museums and Archaeology Service, 2007), p. 98; Mark Samuel, 'The Architectural Fragments', in *Excavations at the Whitefriars, Canterbury* (Canterbury: Canterbury Archaeological Trust, forthcoming).

[40] Harvey and Oswald, *English Mediaeval Architects*, p. 136.

[41] Samuel, 'The Fifteenth-Century Garner at Leadenhall', p. 142.

evident in other prosperous trading towns and cities on the eastern seaboard of England. This localism in style and in selection of stone shares, however, some wider regional characteristics. Firstly, we can note that thirteenth-century taste in the friaries was for plain buildings. Secondly, the decorative highpoint of mendicant architecture was in the fourteenth century, with important building campaigns at the London Black, Austin and Grey Friars continuing after the Black Death but finishing in the third quarter of the century. And, thirdly, we see a virtual absence of building in the fifteenth and early sixteenth centuries: by then the friaries were more or less finished.

13

Floor Tiles and Building Materials from the London Friaries

IAN BETTS

CONSIDERABLE amounts of building material have been recovered from archaeological excavations on sites within Black Friars, White Friars and Austin Friars. A fair quantity was also recovered from Crossed Friars, although much was roofing tile. There is relatively little building material from Grey Friars, a reflection of the fact that so much of the archaeological evidence of the western part of the friary was destroyed in the early twentieth century (during the construction of the new General Post Office building). This chapter concentrates on the floor tiles from the friaries; other building materials such as roof tiles are dealt with in more summary form. As is the case for most London archaeological sites, these floor tiles were found as building rubble, not as *in situ* floors. However, Londoners have usually avoided moving their unwanted earth and rubble too far and so the area where a particular tile or group of tiles was found may give a good indication of their likely original setting.

The types of floor tile are therefore tabulated by friary, archaeological site and area of friary in Table 15. The majority of these decorated floor tiles (except for unrecognisable fragments) are illustrated in a series of friary-by-friary figures (Figure 80 to Figure 84). Medieval floor tiles are usually categorised by their place of manufacture (for example, Chertsey), although the name sometimes refers to the location of their first discovery (for example, Westminster). The types of tile found in the London friaries are listed in Table 16. The tile designs are referred to by typological codes (for example, 'Westminster' tile W3 on Figure 80). These codes relate to classification systems developed for each tile type. The bibliographic references for these codes are given in Table 16. Some tile designs found at the friaries have never before been published; these are labelled T1, T2 (etc) on Figure 80 to Figure 84. The numerical fabric codes for the ceramic building material discussed in this chapter (for example, Low Countries tile fabric 2320; below, 'Black Friars') refer to a fabric reference collection held by Museum of London Archaeology, which can be consulted on request. Building stone types are discussed in this chapter; architectural fragments are discussed in Chapter 12: Architecture and Architectural Fragments of the London Friaries.

Table 15 Types of floor tile correlated by friary and area of friary.

Friary	Site code	Area of friary	Floor tile types	Floor tile dates
Black Friars	FRI88	choir, new and old chapter houses	'Westminster'	second half of 13th to early 14th C
	APO81	nave (south-west) and main cloister (north-west)	Penn	second half 14th C
	LBY85	nave (north-west)	Low Countries	late 15th to early 16th C
	VAL88	western garden of precinct	Low Countries	late 15th to early 16th C
			Dutch	early to mid 16th C
	QVS85	south-west corner of precinct	Eltham Palace	late 13th to early 14th C
			Penn	second half of 14th C
			Low Countries	late 15th to early 16th C
Grey Friars	GF73	choir (east)	'Westminster'	second half of 13th to early 14th C
			Chertsey	second half of 13th C
	CHR76	choir (south)	Chertsey	second half of 13th C
			Low Countries	late 15th to early 16th C
White Friars	BOV95	nave	Penn	second half 14th C
			Dieppe	late 14th to early 15th C
	WFT99	south of precinct (area of 14th-century land reclamation)	'Westminster'	second half of 13th to early 14th C
			Chertsey	second half of 13th C
			Penn	second half 14th C
			Low Countries	late 15th to early 16th C
Austin Friars	GWS89	refectory, chapter houses	'Westminster'	second half of 13th to early 14th C
			Eltham Palace	late 13th to early 14th C
			Penn	second half 14th C
			Dieppe	late 14th to early 15th C
	WCH95	open area north of cloisters	Low Countries	late 15th to early 16th C
Crossed Friars	MCF06	church	'Westminster'	second half of 13th to early 14th C
			Eltham Palace	late 13th to early 14th C
			painted	13th to 14th C?
			Penn	second half 14th C
	PEP89	outer precinct garden	'Westminster'	second half of 13th to early 14th C

Table 16 Explanation of the floor tile types used in the London friaries.

Floor tile type	Comments	Principal reference (including for tile design codes)	Codes used on Figures 80–84[a]
'Westminster'	made in London (probably Farringdon) during the second half of the 13th C and the first decade of the 14th C; common in London monastic houses (named after *in situ* pavements in Westminster Abbey)	Betts, *Medieval 'Westminster' Floor Tiles*	W1, W2, etc. (Betts nos)
Chertsey	high quality tiles made at Chertsey Abbey (Surrey) in the second half of the 13th C; one kiln dated to 1290s	Ward-Perkins, *London Museum Medieval Catalogue*; Eames, *Catalogue of Medieval Lead-glazed Earthenware Tiles*	Eames nos; LM61 is London Museum no.
painted	tiles with decoration painted on surface; found in certain London parish churches	Betts, 'Medieval Floor Tiles in London Churches', pp. 133–40	
Eltham Palace	late 13th or early 14th C, first recognised at Eltham Palace where they date to c. 1300–5; less common than 'Westminster' or Penn tiles	Eames, 'Tile Pavement', pp. 238–44	Eames nos
Penn	made in Penn (Buckinghamshire) in 1350–90 and extensively used in monastic buildings and parish churches in London	Hohler, 'Medieval Paving Tiles from Buckinghamshire', pp. 1–49, 99–132; Eames, *Catalogue of Medieval Lead-glazed Earthenware Tiles*; Ward-Perkins, *London Museum Medieval Catalogue*	Eames nos; P28, P48, etc. are Hohler nos; LM13 is London Museum no.
Dieppe group	probably made in Dieppe area of France in last quarter of the 14th C and very early 15th C; found on some London monastic sites	Norton, 'Export of Decorated Floor Tiles from Normandy', pp. 81–97	
Low Countries	14th to mid 16th C, plain glazed tiles imported from Low Countries and becoming fashionable in Tudor London	Eames, *Catalogue of Medieval Lead-glazed Earthenware*	Eames no.

Note:
[a] In addition to the codes listed in Table 16, tiles published here for the first time are labelled as T1, T2 etc. Several tiles from Crossed Friars were first published in Lerz and Holder, 'Medieval Crossed Friars', figs 10, 17; these tiles appear on Figure 84 as CF1, CF2, etc.

Black Friars

Five different types of floor tile have been discovered on Black Friars sites and these include both plain and decorated 'Westminster' and Penn floor tiles, a plain floor tile belonging to the Eltham Place group and a decorated tile of uncertain source. Also present are a number of Low Countries floor tiles (Table 15, Figure 80).

'Westminster' tiles were made in London during the second half of the thirteenth century, with production perhaps extending into the first decade of the fourteenth century. A tile kiln making 'Westminster' floor tiles was found at Farringdon Road in the nineteenth century. Large quantities of 'Westminster' tiles were made in London and substantial numbers have been found associated with monastic buildings and parish churches. A rare *in situ* pavement of 'Westminster' tiles dating to the late 1250s or early 1260s still survives in the Muniment Room at Westminster Abbey.[1] The first part of the choir at the new Black Friars was built in the 1280s and five designs of 'Westminster' tile (and some plain glazed tile) of this approximate date were found at the FRI88 site: these might have been used in the choir, and/or in the adjacent chapter house of similar date (Figure 80; Chapter 2: The Second Black Friars).

There is a plain brown floor tile belonging to the Eltham Palace group (from site QVS85 context [128]; not illustrated). Floor tiles belonging to the Eltham Palace group were first recognised at the palace where they date to the first decade of the fourteenth century. The tilery making these tiles is unknown, but was presumably located in the London area as tiles in this group are only known from Greater London and in west Kent near the Greater London border. Another of the Eltham Palace designs is found at Austin Friars.

Substantial quantities of Penn tiles were brought into London during the period 1350–90. They were made at a tilery located in Penn in Buckinghamshire. Most monastic buildings and many parish churches in London seem to have had areas of Penn floor tiles. At the Norman Gate, Windsor Castle, the floor comprises bands of decorated Penn tiles separated by a single line of plain glazed tiles.[2] Construction work was taking place in the Black Friars nave in the first half of the fourteenth century: five designs of Penn tile were discovered in the APO81 site in this area, although the date of the tiles (second half of the century) might mean that they were used in the second cloister a little to the south (which was built around the third quarter of the century). One of these designs has not been found before (Figure 80 T3).

Imported tiles from the Low Countries were extremely widespread in London in the Tudor period as there seems to have been few, if any, floor tiles arriving in London from

---

[1] Ian Betts, *Medieval 'Westminster' Floor Tiles*, MoLAS Monograph, 11 (London: Museum of London Archaeology Service, 2002), pp. 32–5, figs 13–19.

[2] C. Hohler, 'Medieval Paving Tiles from Buckinghamshire', *Records of Buckinghamshire*, 14 (1942), 1–49, 99–132; Ian Betts and Thomas Cromwell, 'Windsor Castle Governor's House Floor: Recording a Medieval Tiled Floor', *CFA News* (Newsletter of English Heritage, Centre for Archaeology), winter 2002, 10–11.

Fig. 80. Floor tiles from Black Friars: 'Westminster' tiles may have been used in the late thirteenth-century choir or chapter house; Penn tiles may have been used in the fourteenth-century cloister (scale 1:6).

other sources at this time. The coloured tiles would have been laid in a chequerboard pattern with green and brown glazed examples alternating with yellow glazed tiles. *In situ* pavements of this type have been found at the Chapel Royal at Greenwich Palace, dating to c. 1506, and in the cloister of the bishop of Ely's London town house, Ely Place.[3] Several plain glazed tiles imported from the Low Countries were found at Black Friars, although it is not clear which buildings they were originally used in. A Low Countries tile (fabric 2320; unillustrated) has a green coloured glaze applied above a thin layer of white slip and this is probably of medieval date, as is a plain yellow glazed example measuring 131–135mm square by 28–30mm thick. This example has been scored across the diagonal with a knife to allow it to be broken into two triangular shapes, but in this case the knife-scored line was

[3] Julian Bowsher, 'The Chapel Royal at Greenwich Palace', *The Court Historian*, 11.2 (2006), 155–62 (p. 158); Ian Betts, 'Ceramic and Other Building Material', in *Holywell Priory and the Development of Shoreditch to c. 1600: Archaeology from the London Overground East London Line*, ed. Raoul Bull and others, MOLA monograph, 53 (London: Museum of London Archaeology, 2011), pp. 149–52 (p. 151).

too shallow and it was unsnapped (Figure 80 T5). Of particularly interest are two decorated Low Countries floor tiles: one has Eames design 2732, while the other has the very edge of an unpublished design (Figure 80 T6). Decorated Low Countries floor tiles are extremely rare, making up less than 1% of the imported tiles.

There are a number of floor tiles of uncertain source, including a worn decorated tile with what appears to be an unpublished design (Figure 80 T7). This tile, which measures 123mm in breadth by 26–27mm in thickness, could be another rare Low Countries import or it may be of English origin.

Grey Friars

The mid-thirteenth-century chapel at Grey Friars was being enlarged into a proper choir around the turn of the thirteenth and fourteenth centuries (Chapter 4: Grey Friars). Archaeological excavations on two sites in the area of the choir have produced 'Westminster' and Chertsey tiles of this date, almost certainly used in the new choir (Table 15, Figure 81).

Chertsey tiles are among the best quality floor tiles used in London. Most Grey Friars tiles are decorated with Eames design 2651 and were made at a tile kiln at Chertsey Abbey in c. 1290–1300. There is also one tile with Eames design 2171 of the same date. The other Chertsey designs present are Eames design 2655 and London Museum design 61 which were made at Chertsey sometime during the second half of the thirteenth century (Figure 81). The Chertsey tile pavement at Grey Friars may have been contemporary with a similar pavement at the nunnery of St Mary Clerkenwell which also contained floor tiles with Eames design 2651. The Grey Friars floor tiles vary in size although they could still be from the same floor: different size Chertsey tiles are present, for example, in the Chapter House at Westminster Abbey, laid by 1258.[4] Tiles with design 2651 measure 189–194mm square by 22–30mm thick, tiles with London Museum no. 61 are 163mm in breadth by 23–24mm thick, while the solitary tile with design 2171 measures 143mm in breadth by 17mm in thickness.

Grey Friars also had at least one, probably more, areas of 'Westminster' type. One 'Westminster' tile from Grey Friars is decorated with an unpublished design (Figure 81 T1). Another shows the bottom left of a heraldic design similar to Betts designs W35, W36 and W37 (not illustrated).

A number of plain glazed Low Countries tiles were recovered from Grey Friars. These are mainly in silty fabrics (MOLA types 2850, 3063, 3246; not illustrated) suggesting a 1480–1600 date. As well as their fabric, plain glazed Low Countries tiles can often distinguished

---

[4] Elizabeth S. Eames, *Catalogue of Medieval Lead-Glazed Earthenware Tiles in the Department of Medieval and Later Antiquities, British Museum* (London: British Museum Publications, 1980); J. Ward Perkins, ed., *London Museum Medieval Catalogue* (London: HMSO, 1967); Ian Betts, 'Other Stone and Ceramic Building Material', in *The Augustinian Nunnery of St Mary Clerkenwell, London: Excavations 1974–96*, ed. B. Sloane, MOLA Monograph, 57 (London: Museum of London Archaeology, 1998), pp. 212–18 (p. 214); Elizabeth Eames, *English Tilers* (London: British Museum Press, 1992), p. 42.

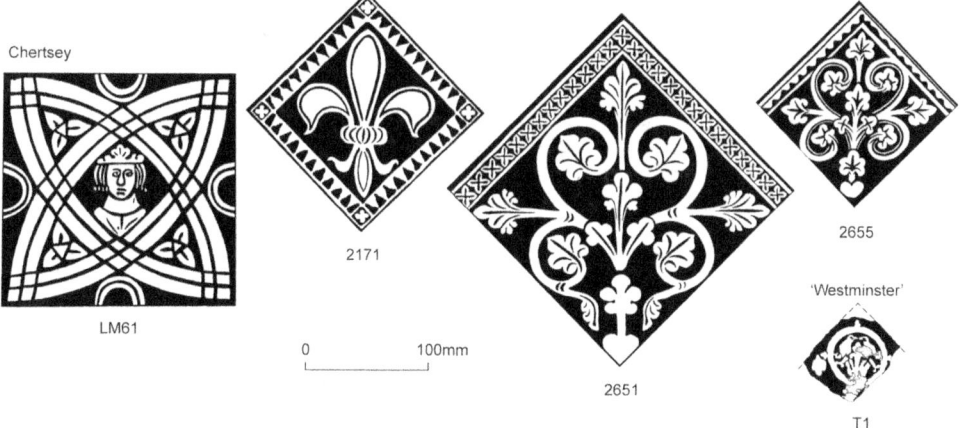

Fig. 81. Floor tiles from Grey Friars, probably from the late thirteenth- or early fourteenth-century choir (scale 1:6).

by nail holes in their top surface. These holes are the result of small nails protruding from a square wooden block which was inserted into the clay as an aid to cutting out the tiles. These holes are normally near the tile corners, although certain medieval tiles also have a central nail hole. Both square and round nail holes are visible in the top corners of the Grey Friars examples. Two sizes of tile are present: one measuring 216mm in breadth by 23–24mm thick, the other 175mm square by 25–27mm in thickness. There is also a floor tile made from a calcium carbonate-rich clay (fabric 2323; not illustrated), which could be either medieval or early post-medieval. These tiles are yellow, brown and green in colour, and the tile floors would have been of chequerboard type, with yellow glazed examples alternating with dark green, brown and occasionally black coloured tiles.

White Friars

Four types of floor tiles have been found in archaeological sites at White Friars (Table 15). The first chapel at the friary was being constructed around the third quarter of the thirteenth century and there are a small number of decorated 'Westminster' floor tiles of this approximate date. These tiles were, however, found on site WFT99 at the south of the precinct (in an area of land reclamation over 100m from the church) and were not necessarily used in the friary. The tiles are decorated with Betts designs W24, W73, W92, W128 and possibly W149 (Figure 82). Another tile which appears to be part of the 'Westminster' group, or possibly a poorly made member of the Chertsey series, has an unpublished design (Figure 82 T2). The design has certain similarities to floor tiles from Titchfield Abbey, Hampshire, although the Titchfield tiles are dated much later (c. 1396).[5]

---

[5] Eames, *Catalogue of Medieval Lead-Glazed Earthenware Tiles*, designs 2240, 2241.

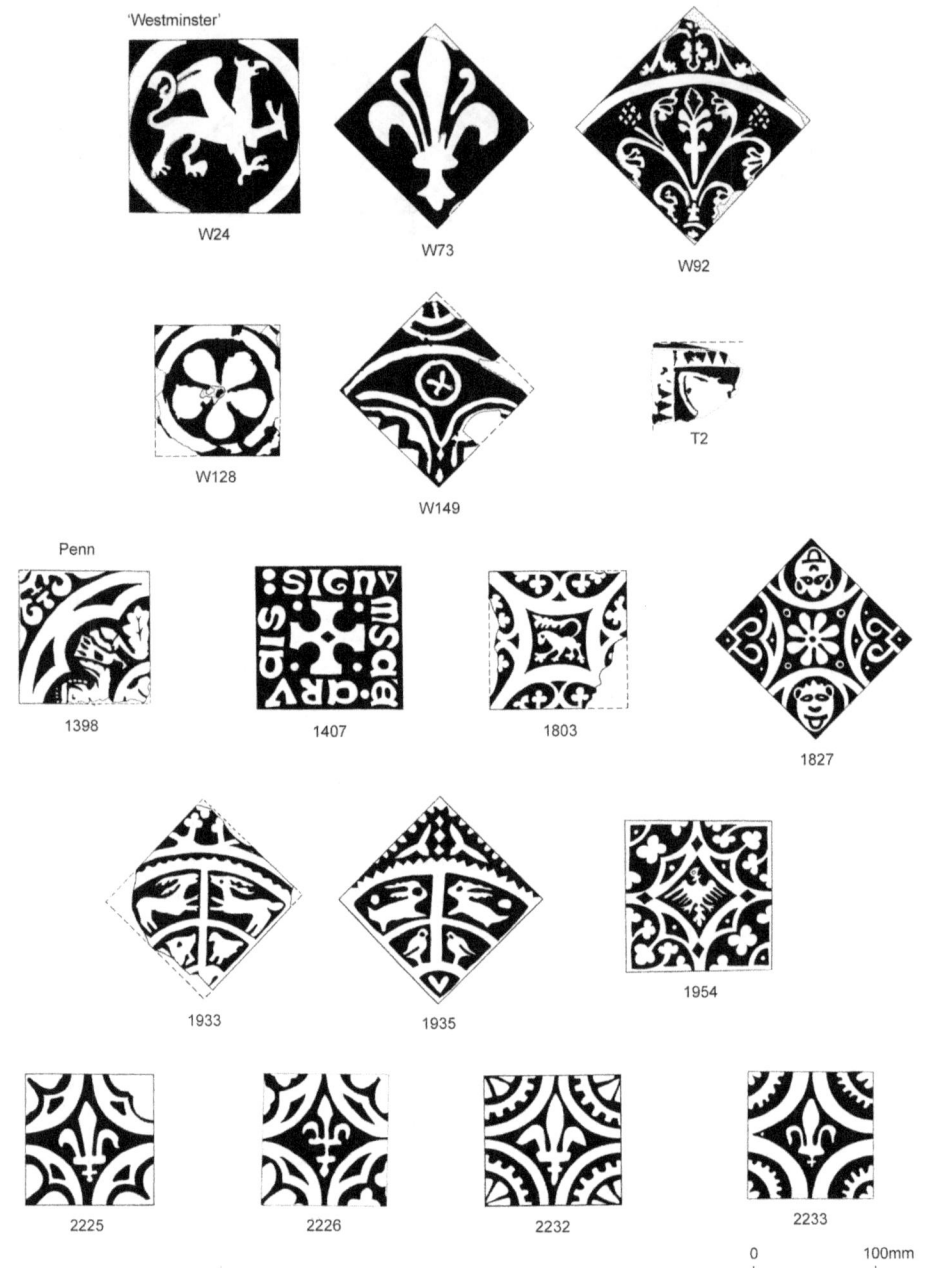

Fig. 82. Floor tiles from White Friars; Penn tiles are probably from the late fourteenth-century nave (scale 1:6)

Fig. 82. (continued)

The vast majority of the decorated floor tiles from White Friars are of Penn type. These tiles may well have been used in the floor of the nave, which was built around the fourth quarter of the fourteenth century, although some areas of the choir (third quarter of the century) could also have used the tiles. There are no fewer than twenty-seven different designs of Penn tile from the White Friars site (illustrated on Figure 82) along with a small quantity of plain glazed examples.

One decorated floor tile from White Friars was shipped into London from across the Channel. Floor tiles belonging to the same group are concentrated in the Dieppe area of France where the source tilery is presumed to have been located. They were produced in the last quarter of the fourteenth century, but production could have continued into the early years of the fifteenth century. A small number of Dieppe group tiles have been found on other monastic sites, such as the priory and abbey of St Saviour Bermondsey and the Charterhouse.[6] Unfortunately not enough survives of the White Friars example to identify which design type is present.

There are a small number of plain glazed Low Countries imports from White Friars, including some exceptionally thick (59mm) examples of probable Tudor date. A few were recovered from fourteenth-century deposits and are therefore rather early examples of this type of tile in London. The size and fabric would suggest the majority are from the period 1480–1600; some may date to after the closure of the friary.

Austin Friars

Five types of floor tile have been found on sites in Austin Friars, most of which come from the GWS89 site which investigated parts of the two cloisters (Table 15, Figure 83).[7] Other dating evidence suggests that the first cloister was built at the end of the thirteenth century, with a second cloister added to the north a century later, around the late fourteenth and early fifteenth century (Chapter 6: Austin Friars). The majority of the floor tiles found are of 'Westminster' type, dating to around 1250–1310. Although there was some work taking place in the church at this time, the location of the archaeological site would suggest that the tiles were originally used in a floor or floors in the cloister, perhaps in the chapter house. Nine design types are present (Figure 83). One rare design (W91) is of unusually large size (length/breadth 166mm). Another large 'Westminster' tile with the same design was found at St John Clerkenwell.[8]

There are two floor tiles of Eltham Palace type dating to the early fourteenth century which may have been used to repair a floor in the cloister. Only one is in a good enough condition for the design to be recognised (Figure 83 Eames design 2).

There is a single decorated floor tile made near Dieppe in northern France in the late fourteenth or early fifteenth century. This is of interest as although worn, it is not illustrated

---

[6] Christopher Norton, 'The Export of Decorated Floor Tiles from Normandy', in *Medieval Art, Architecture and Archaeology at Rouen*, ed. J. Stratford, British Archaeological Association conference transactions, 12 (London, 1993), pp. 81–97 (p. 85); Ian Betts, 'The Building Materials', in *The Cluniac Priory and Abbey of St Saviour Bermondsey, Surrey*, ed. T. Dyson and others, MOLA monograph, 50 (London: Museum of London Archaeology, 2011), pp. 201–14 (p. 209, fig. 148); Ian Betts, 'Ceramic and Stone Building Material', in *The London Charterhouse*, ed. B. Barber and C. Thomas, MoLAS monograph, 10 (London: Museum of London Archaeology Service, 2002), pp. 97–9 (p. 97, fig. 94).

[7] Holder, Samuel and Betts, 'Church and Cloisters of Austin Friars', pp. 154–8, fig. 11.

[8] Sue Pringle and Terence p. Smith, 'Other Stone and Ceramic Building Material', in *Excavations at the Priory of the Order of the Hospital of St John of Jerusalem, Clerkenwell, London*, ed. B. Sloane and G. Malcolm, MoLAS Monograph, 20 (London: Museum of London Archaeology Service, 2004), pp. 321–30 (p. 322, fig. 50).

Fig. 83. Floor tiles from Austin Friars; the 'Westminster' tiles may be from the late thirteenth-century chapter house (scale 1:6).

in the design types published by Norton (Figure 83 T4).[9] There are two Penn tiles from Austin Friars but both have had their top removed through wear so it is not certain if these were plain glazed or decorated. The Dieppe and Penn tiles may have been used in the second cloister of the late fourteenth and fifteenth centuries. Also present are a number of Low Countries tiles: these have yellow and brown glaze and are probably of 1480–1600 date.

Crossed Friars

Three types of 'Westminster' tile and four types of Eltham Palace tile were found on site MCF06, where parts of the medieval friary church were excavated (Figure 84).[10] Both types of tile date to the later thirteenth or early fourteenth century: the church was first built in the third quarter of the thirteenth century with further works taking place

[9] Norton, 'Export of Decorated Floor Tiles from Normandy', p. 85.
[10] Lerz and Holder, 'Medieval Crossed Friars', pp. 153–5, 167, figs 10, 17.

Fig. 84. Floor tiles from Crossed Friars; most were probably used in the church (scale 1:6).

in the early fourteenth century (Chapter 7: Crossed Friars). Several Penn tiles dating to the second quarter of the fourteenth century were also found on the site: they may have been used in repairs or further building works in the church. More unusual are two rare hand-painted tiles of possible thirteenth- or fourteenth-century date (Figure 84 CF27 CF28). They were found in the area of the church. Their place of manufacture is uncertain although other hand-painted tiles have been found in London parish churches.[11]

Other building material from the friaries

The roofs of the friary churches and many of the cloister buildings were covered in lead: this valuable material is rarely found in archaeological excavations but surveyors of the 1540s usually noted it and estimated the quantity, before stripping it from the roofs (Table 17). Black Friars in particular was rich in lead: the surveyor estimated 129

---

[11] Ian Betts, 'Medieval Floor Tiles in London Churches', in J. Schofield, 'Saxon and Medieval Parish Churches in the City of London: A Review', *Transactions of the London and Middlesex Archaeological Society*, 45 (1994), 23–146 (pp. 133–40).

Fig. 84. (continued)

fothers (loads) of lead on the roof of the church, the single-storey cloister pentices and the refectory.[12]

The majority of the friary buildings were covered with roofs of peg tile. Vast numbers of peg roofing tiles were made by London tilemakers from the late twelfth century onwards. These were predominantly of the two round nail-holes type, with a splash glaze or a more uniform covering of glaze over the upper surface of the bottom third of the tile. Peg tiles

[12] TNA, C 66/831, mm. 32–3, printed in Smith, *Shakespeare's Blackfriars Playhouse*, pp. 435–8; *Blackfriars Records*, pp. 8–12.

Table 17 Documentary evidence for the use of lead as a roofing material in the London friaries.

Friary	Buildings	Weight estimated in 1540s	Approximate building surface area[a]	Documentary reference
Black Friars	church (including steeple and porch), cloister pentices, refectory, water cistern	129 fothers (123 tonnes)	3460m²	TNA, C 66/831, mm. 32–3; E 351/3329; SHC, LM/347/10
Grey Friars	church, east side of cloister and laver			SBH, HC 3, m. 4; HC 19, ff. 4v–5v
White Friars	church (including porch and steeple), library, a chapel	48 or 54 fothers (46 or 51 tonnes)	1290m² or 1450m²	TNA, E 314/54 ['London and Middlesex: Whitefriars, lead at']; E 314/69 no. 29
Austin Friars	cloister	partial estimate of 2¼ fothers (2 tonnes)	60m²	TNA, E 318/13/577
Crossed Friars	church			TNA, C 66/694, m. 14

Note:

[a] A sixteenth-century estimate of lead sheet coverage (employed by a Court of Augmentations surveyor on the White Friars site) is that a ground-level building footprint of about 32 square yards produces one fother of lead when the lead sheet of the roof covering is melted. This works out at about 35.5kg of roofing lead per square metre of building footprint. Note that this is, of course, an *estimate*; it does not take into account factors such as the slope of the roof or the thickness of the lead sheet; TNA, E 314/54 ('London and Middlesex: Whitefriars, lead at').

of this type were found at all five of the major London friaries. Some of the peg holes on the tiles from Grey Friars and White Friars have not been punched all the way through, a feature noted on other peg roofing tiles found in London. Peg roofing tiles made from c. 1480 until the Dissolution are not normally glazed and can have a variety of nail-hole shapes in addition to those of round shape. Some of the peg tiles from White Friars and Black Friars have two square and two diamond nail holes.

A number of complete and partially complete peg roofing tiles were recovered from Black Friars. Those of medieval date measure (in length, breadth and thickness) 295mm × 139–172mm × 9–19mm (most up to 13mm), while those made between c. 1480 and the Dissolution measure 266–267mm × 152–166mm × 12–15mm. A number of peg tiles from Black Friars have a diagonal finger mark in the top right corner, while a White Friars peg tile has a horizontal line parallel to the top edge. Part of a finger mark was also noted on a peg tile from Austin Friars. These marks, which are fairly common on London-made medieval peg roofing tiles, are believed to be batch marks added during manufacture. One Black Friars peg tile has what appears to be rain splashes on the upper surface. The lack of such marks on other peg tiles suggests most were laid out to dry under cover prior to being fired. They also seem to have been raised from the ground as few roofing tiles have animal or other accidental marks present.

A small number of peg tiles are imports from outside the London area. These include a white and cream speckled red peg tile (fabric 3201) from Austin Friars and a yellow coloured tile from Black Friars (fabric 2278), both of which probably came from tileries situated in north Kent. Another peg tile from Black Friars has common thin cream silty and red clay bands (fabric 3204). This too is almost certainly an import although the source tilery is unknown. These roofing tiles may have been brought into London to cater for a sudden upsurge in demand which could not be met by London tilemakers, such as major roof damage after a storm.

Covering the top of peg tiled roofs would have been curved ridge tiles, some of which were also glazed. Examples have been found at all five major friaries. Part of what appears to be a decorated ridge tile, or finial, was recovered from Black Friars. If it is a ridge tile it is a rare find as most ridge tiles made from the twelfth century onwards lack decoration. Also set on the top of London roofs were decorative finials, which due to their round shape seem to have been made by potters rather than tilemakers. A glazed finial was found at Black Friars and there is a further possible example from White Friars. Similar decorative features were present on the roofs of other monastic buildings. Two finials were found at the priory and abbey of St Saviour, Bermondsey and there is a possible finial (or louver) from Holywell priory.[13] Occasional curved fragments of tile could have been used as guttering, although such tiles are extremely rare in London as most guttering would have been of wood. Black Friars produced a possible gutter tile and further possible examples are known from the priory of St John Clerkenwell and the nunnery of St Mary Clerkenwell.[14]

Bricks began to be imported to London in the fourteenth century. Yellow medieval bricks (fabric 3031) imported from the Low Countries during the fourteenth to the late fifteenth century have been found on a number of monastic sites in London, such as Holywell priory, Charterhouse and the priory and later abbey of St Saviour Bermondsey. Bricks of this type are also known from Canterbury and various sites in Essex.[15] They were also used at White Friars and Black Friars where there are incomplete examples

---

[13] Betts, 'The Building Materials', *St Saviour Bermondsey*, p. 213, fig. 152; Betts, 'Ceramic and Other Building Material', *Holywell Priory*, p. 151.

[14] Pringle and Smith, 'Other Stone and Ceramic Building Material', *St John of Jerusalem*, p. 327; Betts, 'Other Stone and Ceramic Building Material', *St Mary Clerkenwell*.

[15] Betts, 'Ceramic and Other Building Material', *Holywell Priory*, p. 151; Betts, 'Ceramic and Stone Building Material', *London Charterhouse*, p. 99; Betts, 'The Building Materials', *St Saviour Bermondsey*, p. 213; Pat Ryan, *Brick in Essex from the Roman Conquest to the Reformation* (Midhurst: Middleton Press, 1996), p. 94.

measuring 86–98mm in breadth by 42–59mm in thickness. A few pale pink and red bricks (fabric 3042) were found at White Friars and they are probably of similar medieval date to the yellow bricks (fabric 3031). Another probable Low Countries import is a type whose colour can be cream or red, fired from an estuarine silt (fabric 3043). Bricks of this type were first identified in Essex. At Black Friars these bricks, which measure 80–93mm (breadth) × 40–43mm (thickness), are probably fourteenth to late fifteenth century in date. Bricks in the same fabric were used in the priory and hospital of St Mary Spital sometime between 1400 and 1538 and similar bricks are known from the priory of St John Clerkenwell.[16]

London-made red and orange bricks dating from the later fifteenth to the mid sixteenth century were used at White Friars, Austin Friars and Black Friars (fabrics 3033, 3046). It is not entirely certain whether they were used before the Dissolution or shortly after when various monastic buildings were adapted for secular use. What is certain is that increasing amounts of brick was being used in London from the late fifteenth century and that these bricks were used on many monastic sites before the Dissolution, including at St Mary Graces, the priory and abbey of St Saviour Bermondsey and Charterhouse where Washhouse Court, a brick structure of c. 1531, still stands.[17] More complete examples of these London-made red and orange bricks from the three friaries measure 211–234mm in length by 98–116mm in breadth by 46–58mm in thickness. The Austin Friars brick assemblage includes a burnt grey header, possibly used in a decorative diaper pattern, and what may be a worn paving brick. One Black Friars brick is unusual in being pierced by a diagonal hole.

A wide variety of building stone types have been identified at the London friaries. The majority of types used are the normal stones brought into medieval London: chalk for foundations, Kentish ragstone for basic wall fabric, Reigate and Caen stone for ashlar and architectural details, with Purbeck marble used for decorative features such as pillars and paving (Table 18).

More unusual discoveries included thin slabs of what appear to be fine- and medium-grained sandstone roofing. These were found in late thirteenth- to early fourteenth-century land reclamation dumps at Black Friars: the slabs may represent the remains of roofing used at the friary, but they could of course have been brought in as building rubble from elsewhere. Sandstone roofing is certainly believed to have covered at least one building at Bermondsey Abbey at the time of the Dissolution. Some small fragments of slate from

---

[16] Ryan, *Brick in Essex*, p. 34; Naomi Crowley, 'Ceramic Building Material', in *Excavations at the Priory and Hospital of St Mary Spital, London*, ed. C. Thomas and others, MoLAS Monograph, 1 (London: Museum of London Archaeology Service, 1997), pp. 195–201 (p. 200); Pringle and Smith, 'Other Stone and Ceramic Building Material', *St John of Jerusalem*, p. 327.

[17] Naomi Crowley, 'Bricks', in *The Cistercian Abbey of St Mary Graces, East Smithfield, London*, ed. I. Grainger and others, MOLA Monograph, 44 (London: Museum of London Archaeology, 2011), pp. 133–4; Betts, 'The Building Materials', *St Saviour Bermondsey*, p. 213; Barber, *Charterhouse*, p. 38.

Table 18 Types of building stone identified at the London friaries.

Friary	Walls	Ashlar	Architectural	Roofing	Paving
Black Friars	ragstone, chalk, Hassock	Reigate	Caen, hard ?Magnesian, Purbeck marble, Reigate, Ketton	fine- and medium-grained sandstone, slate	fine- and medium-grained sandstone, limestone
Grey Friars	ragstone, chalk		Purbeck marble		
White Friars	ragstone, chalk, Hassock, septaria nodules	Caen	Purbeck marble		
Austin Friars	ragstone, chalk		Purbeck marble, Caen, ragstone, Barnack		Purbeck marble
Crossed Friars	ragstone, chalk	Reigate	Caen, Reigate		

Black Friars (from archaeological contexts dating to 1230–1350) may have been used for roofing at the new friary although (again) they may be from elsewhere. Although rare in London before the eighteenth century, there is firm evidence for the use of slate roofing at Bermondsey Abbey and St Mary Clerkenwell.[18] The fine- and medium-grained sandstone may also have been used at Black Friars for paving: a flagstone with a bevelled edge measured 432mm × 308mm × 67mm. The site also produced some possible limestone paving slabs, one of which measures 420+mm × 405mm × 54mm. A drawing of 1523 shows the parliament hall building at Black Friars with a chequered floor that might have employed these slabs in conjunction with darker Purbeck marble (or Noir Belge?) slabs.[19]

A few fragments of grey and white plaster of probable medieval date were recovered from Black Friars. A few scraps of medieval wall plaster also survive from the priory and abbey of St Saviour Bermondsey, the nunnery of St Mary Clerkenwell and Charterhouse.[20]

Conclusion

Although different quantities were collected on the various archaeological sites it is clear that similar stone and ceramic building materials were used for construction at most of

---

[18] Betts, 'The Building Materials', *St Saviour Bermondsey*, p. 202; Betts, 'Other Stone and Ceramic Building Material', *St Mary Clerkenwell*.

[19] David Dean, 'Image and Ritual in the Tudor Parliaments', in *Tudor Political Culture*, ed. D. Hoak (Cambridge: Cambridge University Press, 1995), pp. 243–71 (plate 57).

[20] Betts, 'The Building Materials', *St Saviour Bermondsey*, p. 214, fig. 154; Betts, 'Other Stone and Ceramic Building Material', *St Mary Clerkenwell*; Barber, *Charterhouse*, pp. 58–9, fig. 59.

the friaries. These are also closely similar to the stone and tile types used by other religious orders based in London, as well as the building materials used in parish churches, royal palaces and other high status buildings.

Most of the sites provide a good record of the different types of plain and decorated floor tiles used at each friary. Most comprise the three principal floor tile types found in London: 'Westminster', Penn and Low Countries. It is clear the tiled floors formed an important component of each friary: although none of these tiles were found *in situ*, the locations of the sites suggest that these floor tiles were usually laid in the church or in claustral buildings such as the chapter house. The presence of 'Westminster' tiles dating to the second half of the thirteenth century is not unexpected. It was during this period that White Friars, Austin Friars and Cross Friars were founded, while the Black friars moved to their second site in the 1280s. The considerable quantities of Penn tiles at White Friars may relate to the construction of the nave in the third quarter of the fourteenth century. During the fourteenth to late fifteenth century Low Countries floor tiles were used on four of the friary sites; they may have been shipped into London with Low Countries bricks. These variously coloured floor tiles and bricks are in different fabric types and so would appear to be from different production sources. Their presence on the friary sites is not unexpected as such bricks are known from a number of other monastic buildings in London. More unusual are the high quality Chertsey tiles from Grey Friars (probably the choir) which are rarely found in London, although at least one pavement of such tiles was installed in the priory and hospital of St Mary Spital and the nunnery of St Mary Clerkenwell.

There is also ample evidence for the use of ceramic peg and ridge roofing tile. At Black Friars stone roofing may also have been used in addition to ceramic roofing tile. The increasing use of bricks in the later medieval period seen on other London monastic buildings seems to be paralleled on the friary sites. Our hypothesis is that these bricks may have been used in some of the rented tenements built at the friaries in the fifteenth and sixteenth centuries, and perhaps in chimneys added to the claustral buildings (such as the guest wings or the priors' houses) at this time.

Much rarer is the evidence for internal plaster such as that found at Black Friars. There is likely to have been extensive use of plain and decorated plaster in friary church buildings so it is puzzling that so little has survived. The same is true of London monastic buildings generally.

14

Water Supply

In the second half of the twelfth century several English monastic houses installed their own water supply systems. The spread of the idea and the technology was done by Benedictine houses such as Christchurch Canterbury and by the newer offshoot order, the Cistercians, for example at Fountains Abbey. Identifying and enclosing freshwater springs was not, of course, a new idea; the technological novelty was the construction of a conduit-head near the spring or springs to provide a constant head of water, and the ability to cast and shape lead into long, narrow-bore pipes to transport the water from conduit-head to abbey. In the developing monastic tradition, monks required sweet and clean water at regular intervals for spiritual and physical cleansing – before celebrating the services of the Divine Office – as well as for drinking.[1] In the second quarter of the thirteenth century, several such piped water supplies were being developed in and around London. The Augustinian canons at Waltham Abbey were planning and installing one in the 1220s and '30s and the City authorities were installing a civic system between the 1230s and 1250s.[2] The London Franciscans and Dominicans planned and installed their systems around this time too, beginning with the Franciscans in the 1240s and the Dominicans a decade later. It seems very likely that there was some cooperation and shared technical expertise in the creation of these four systems in and around London.[3]

---

[1] C. James Bond, 'Water Management in the Urban Monastery', in *Advances in Monastic Archaeology*, ed. R. Gilchrist and H.C. Mytum, British Archaeological Reports, 227 (Oxford: Tempus Reparatum, 1993), pp. 43–78; Coppack, *Abbeys and Priories*, pp. 143–66.

[2] Bond, 'Water Management in the Urban Monastery', p. 57; David Lewis, '"For the Poor to Drink and the Rich to Dress Their Meat": The First London Water Conduit', *Transactions of the London and Middlesex Archaeological Society*, 55 (2004), 39–68.

[3] Barron and Davies, *Religious Houses*, pp. 20–1.

The Grey Friars water supply

The four larger London friaries – Grey Friars, Black Friars, White Friars and Austin Friars – established their own water systems, of which by far the best documented is the Franciscan system. Here, a rare combination of archaeological excavation, medieval documents and a surviving medieval conduit-head building allow us to reconstruct the water supply network. Taking the accounts of the donation and the course of the water supply given in the sixteenth-century Grey Friars Register, the early twentieth-century archaeologist Philip Norman carried out a remarkable investigation, mapping the probable course of the underground pipe network and discovering the remains of the two conduit-heads that fed the piped system.[4]

In the second quarter of the thirteenth century, probably in the 1240s, William Taylour granted the Franciscans a spring in rural Bloomsbury, nearly a mile to the north-west of the friary. Henry III and three London citizens then paid for the construction of a conduit-head and the underground piping to carry the water to Newgate. The original charter document may have specified the bore of the pipe: the 1247 grant of a water supply by the bishop of Ossory to the Dominicans of Kilkenny has a copper ring attached as a 'seal', a specification of the size of pipe to be used.[5] The archaeological discoveries in Bloomsbury show that this conduit-head was a partially subterranean building that measured about 9ft by 6ft (2.7m × 1.8m) internally, and was built of Reigate stone with a barrel-vaulted chalk roof. The cistern must have been fed by nearby wells and it held about 2000 gallons (8500 litres) of water. There was a slightly deeper settling tank in the base of the cistern to remove impurities and the water then passed into a lead pipe, pumped by the pressure of the head of water in the cistern. The likely course of the piped system is shown on Figure 85.

In the first quarter of the fourteenth century the system was improved thanks to the donations of Geoffrey de Camera and three other citizens who arranged for a second conduit-head to be built, situated a quarter-mile further west in Bloomsbury. This underground vaulted cistern was built almost entirely of Reigate stone and was significantly larger, measuring 10½ft square (3.2m) and having a capacity of nearly 4000 gallons (17,000 litres). Like the original cistern, this conduit was fed by a series of wells whose locations are indicated on a seventeenth-century plan of the water-system drawn for the Franciscans' successors, Christ's Hospital.[6] A lead pipe, inscribed with the date 1578, must mark the original piped outlet of the cistern. The fall in ground level between the fourteenth-century

[4] BL, Cotton Vitellius F xii, f. 322v, printed in *Grey Friars*, pp. 158–61; Philip Norman, 'On an Ancient Conduit-Head in Queen Square, Bloomsbury', *Archaeologia*, 56 (1899), 251–66; Philip Norman and Ernest A. Mann, 'On the White Conduit, Chapel Street, Bloomsbury, and its Connexion with the Grey Friars' Water System', *Archaeologia*, 61 (1909), 347–56; Philip Norman, 'Recent Discoveries of Medieval Remains in London', *Archaeologia*, 67 (1916), 18–26.

[5] Colman Ó Clabaigh, *The Friars in Ireland, 1224–1540* (Dublin: Four Courts, 2012), p. 210, plate 13.

[6] Not all of these wells are necessarily medieval; a retracing of the plan is reproduced in Norman and Mann, 'White Conduit', plan between pp. 352–3.

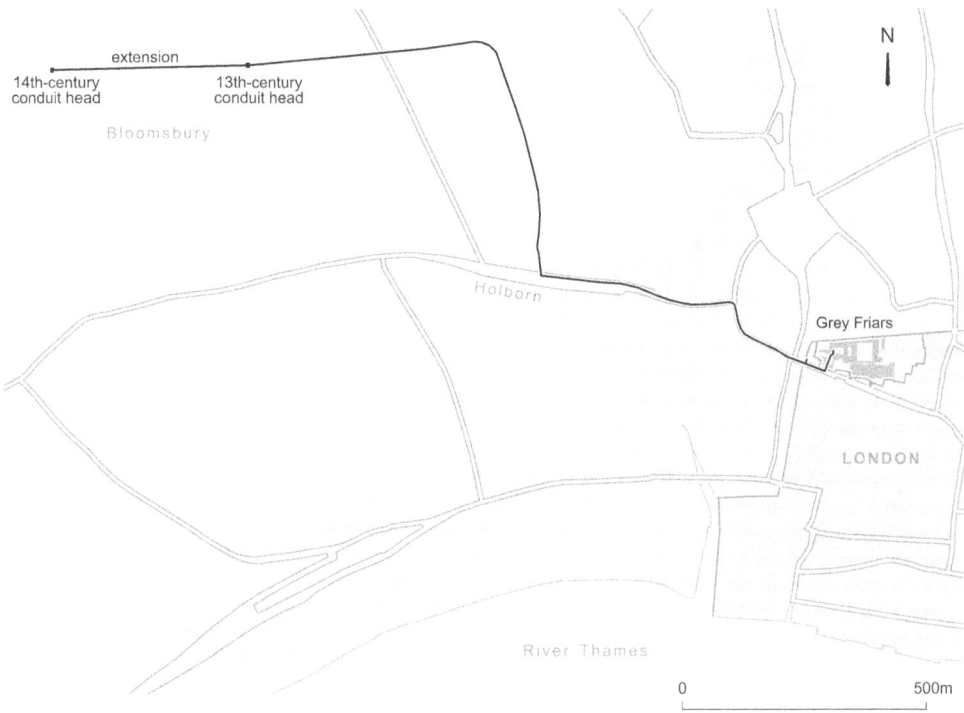

Fig. 85. Map showing the Grey Friars water supply (source: Norman and Mann, 'White Conduit') (scale 1:15,000).

water outlet in Bloomsbury and the friary is approximately 31ft (9.5m), which would have provided a reasonable pressure head to pipe the water along the 1¼ miles (2.1km) to the friary, through a system of pipes that was presumably less than perfectly sealed.[7] The surviving conduit-head was dismantled in 1911 and re-erected in 1927 in the remaining part of the seventeenth-century Round Pond reservoir in Clerkenwell, by this time the rear yard of the Metropolitan Water Board's New River Head building (Figure 86).[8]

The long pipe fed a conduit-house just south-west of the Franciscans' precinct by Newgate ('cundyt yarde' on Figure 22) and passed from there to the laver in the great cloister, where the friars washed before entering their church. The laver seems to have been installed in the early fourteenth century and had to be restored in 1422 at a cost of some £27

---

[7] The variation in elevation between the fourteenth-century conduit-head and the friary would give a rough pressure head of about 13 pounds per square inch or 1 bar (although the presence of *two* conduit-heads, thirteenth- and fourteenth-century, makes for a difficult calculation); modern water pressure in twenty-first century London is at least double this, about 2 to 4 bars.

[8] The conduit is the Grade II listed building known as the New River Head chimney conduit or devil's conduit (listing no. 1208516); Historic England listed buildings website, < https://historicengland.org.uk/listing/the-list/list-entry/1208516> (accessed 12 February 2016); Philip Temple, ed., *Northern Clerkenwell and Pentonville*, Survey of London, 48 (New Haven and London: Yale University Press, 2008), p. 184.

Fig. 86. The Grey friars' fourteenth-century conduit-head in Bloomsbury, re-erected in 1927 at the rear of the Metropolitan Water Board's New River Head building in Clerkenwell. (Andy Chopping/MOLA)

9s 1½d, paid for by friar Robert Zougg.[9] The friars chose a Cistercian model for their laver, a long and narrow basin in the cloister walk, rather than the circular Benedictine laver that usually stood in the cloister itself.[10] The sixteenth-century surveyors from the Court of Augmentations noted the details of the Grey friars' laver in the south-west corner of their cloister walk: it was a trough about 18ft long and 2ft deep, made of copper and lined with lead, and had 'in' and 'out' stopcocks fed by lead pipes.[11] The water supply continued from the laver to other parts of the friary, including the church porch (where lay worshippers could wash before entering the church), and – it is likely – to the infirmary.

Other friary water supplies

Rather less is known of the other friaries' water supplies. The Dominicans followed the Franciscans' example and between October 1259 and March 1261 Henry III made a number of gifts of lead to help the Dominicans set up their water supply; the source of this supply was probably in Clerkenwell, half a mile to the north of their Holborn friary (Table 4; Chapter 1: The First Black Friars in Holborn). The Dominicans probably kept their spring and installed a new piped extension when they moved to their second site by the Thames.[12] They also had a well, situated so that visitors would pass it when walking by the churchyard to the porch that led into the nave (Figure 10). The Franciscan chronicler Donatus Mooney described the special properties of an Irish well (in Kilkenny Grey Friars) and one can imagine the words ringing true to medieval Londoners coming to Black Friars: '[people] come from distant places to drink of its water, or to carry it to others, who, through illness, are unable to make the journey – many of whom have been restored to health'.[13] The second Black Friars had a conduit-house with a lead-lined cistern in the kitchen garden towards the west of the precinct. The various pipes of the monastic system were still functioning in the second half of the sixteenth century when rights of access to the system were frequently mentioned in letters and leases.[14] The Augustinians too had a piped system, from which

---

[9] The dating is not specific but the installation of the laver probably dates to an intermediary phase of works on the water supply, after the initial laying out in the mid thirteenth century and before the extension later in the fourteenth century: BL, Cotton Vitellius F xii, f. 322v, printed in *Grey Friars*, pp. 158–9.

[10] Coppack, *Abbeys and Priories*, pp. 149–54.

[11] In the 1546 survey it is described as 'one laver of copper ... lynd with leade, the cocks and parte of the pipes taken away'; the exact location is slightly ambiguous, either the western end of the southern cloister walk or the southern end of the western walk: SBH, HC 19, ff. 5v, 27.

[12] Bond, 'Water Management in the Urban Monastery', p. 61. The move to the new site would have entailed a 500m extension to the 750m pipe that led from Clerkenwell to their original Holborn friary.

[13] Donatus Mooney, quoted in Ó Clabaigh, *The Friars in Ireland*, p. 209.

[14] TNA, E 318/8/293, m. 3; C 66/774, mm. 31-3 [post-Dissolution particulars and grant of 1546]; C 66/831, mm. 32-3 [1550 survey]. For later sixteenth-century references to the water supply see, for example, Smith, *Shakespeare's Blackfriars Playhouse*, pp. 453–56; *Blackfriars Records*, pp. 19–26;

Thomas Cromwell (just before the Dissolution) and William Paulet (just after) obtained water for their mansions and gardens; the Augustinian friars also had a 'comen well' in the prior's garden.[15] At White Friars some lead pipes on the north side of the church (valued in c. 1545 by a surveyor from the Court of Augmentations) must have been part of their supply, as was a water pump in the yard of the infirmary building.[16]

Conclusion

Several institutions in and around London were installing the new water-supply technology in the first half of the thirteenth century. The Franciscans' system is the best documented: laid out in the 1240s and extended in the early fourteenth century, it had a laver in the main cloister and several ancillary distribution points around the friary. The whole system was fed by a network of wells and two cistern-heads in rural Bloomsbury, and a mile and a quarter of lead piping to bring the water into the city friary. One can, perhaps, view this water system as another fully monastic characteristic of the urban friars who, by the late thirteenth century, were institutionally wealthy preacher-monks, no longer the poor preachers of the days of Francis and Dominic.

Loseley letter 6729/9/90, calendared on 'Exploring Surrey's Past' web database, <http://www.exploringsurreyspast.org.uk/GetRecord/SHLOS_1058>, accessed 16 June 2009.

[15] TNA, C 66/727, m. 19; DC, charter X [piped supply to Cromwell's house]; TNA, LR 14/86 [well].

[16] TNA, E 314/54 ('London and Middlesex: Whitefriars, lead at'); E 317/Middx/15 [water pump].

15

Economy

If the prime purpose of every monastic order was prayer – with the additional component of preaching in the case of the friars – there had to be an economic infrastructure to support this. Even St Francis could not pray and preach on an empty stomach with no shelter for the night; this latter aspect was even more important in late medieval England than on a warm night in thirteenth-century Umbria.

If we were studying a Benedictine monastic house we would naturally seek records of the monastic officers who administered the kitchen, the church or the guest wing. These obedientiaries' accounts are particularly well preserved at Benedictine houses that were also cathedrals, such as Norwich or Durham, or in monasteries that converted to a cathedral after the Dissolution, such as Peterborough or Westminster.[1] Unfortunately no such records survive from English friaries; indeed, it is uncertain to what extent friaries even had such officers. However, the rather scattered sources certainly do make mention of friars with administrative roles, even if the structure was not quite as formally organised as at a large Benedictine institution. At Grey Friars, for example, there were friars who served as a physician (Eric de Vedica, specified as an 'obediencer' of the priory), a gardener (Walter Roben) and a butler (Geoffrey Turner), as well as an almoner and an infirmarer.[2]

---

[1] H.W. Saunders, *An Introduction to the Obedientiary & Manor Rolls of the Norwich Cathedral Priory* (Norwich: Jarrold, 1930); Philip Slavin, *Bread and Ale for the Brethren: The Provisioning of Norwich Cathedral Priory, 1260–1536* (Hatfield: University of Hertfordshire Press, 2012); *The Durham Household Book: Or, the Accounts of the Bursar of the Monastery of Durham*, ed. James Raine, Surtees Society, 18 (London: Nichols, 1844); *Extracts from the Account Rolls of the Abbey of Durham*, ed. Canon Fowler, 3 vols, Surtees Society, 99, 100, 103 (Durham: Andrews, 1898–1900); *Account Rolls of the Obedientiaries of Peterborough*, ed. Joan Greatrex, Northamptonshire Record Society, 33 (Northampton: Northamptonshire Record Society, 1984); Barbara F. Harvey, *Living and Dying in England, 1100–1540: The Monastic Experience* (Oxford: Clarendon Press, 1993).

[2] Physician: TNA, C 1/66/397, printed in Charles L. Kingsford, 'Additional Material for the History of the Grey Friars, London', in *Collectanea Franciscana II*, British Society of Franciscan Studies, 10 (Manchester: Manchester University Press, 1922), pp. 61–156 (pp. 147–9); gardener: E 321/46/51;

Reconstructing the finances of Austin Friars

Given the lack of any surviving obedientiaries' rolls for English friaries – if indeed this sort of record was kept – one must make do with the sources that do survive.[3] The starting point chosen here is the chance survival of a summary account showing money paid by the English province of the Austin Friars to the order's headquarters in Rome. The document of 1522 records money paid by the prior of the London Austin Friars, Edmund Bellond, to an Italian agent, Raphael Maruffus, for transfer to the papal Curia at Rome.[4] The financial transfer seems to have been the result of a special fundraising exercise by Bellond, who had obtained a papal indulgence in order to raise money for a building project (probably not at the London house).[5] The document records two categories of income raised, a proportion of which was to be transferred to Rome: money from confessional fees (*pro confessionalibus*) and from other income, the majority of which was presumably alms (*de pecuniis omnibus et singulis receptis*). The sums raised and transferred are for the whole English province: the contributions of the individual houses are not specified. Using this document as a base, one can start to piece together rather hypothetical (and somewhat anachronistic) summary accounts for the London house: a statement of income and expenditure (Table 19).

Beginning with the income of the London friars, the figure for alms can be estimated using our fragmentary account of 1522. The average annual sum given in alms to the whole English province (for the years covered, 1517–21) was about £458. The money was presumably not raised evenly by the thirty-five English friaries and one might guess that the London house raised at least a tenth of this (rather than a thirty-fifth), given its large and wealthy population. The resulting guess of £46 is rounded up to £50 in Table 19, although it is possible that these five years may have seen higher than average fundraising thanks to the papal indulgence. The figure of £50 does, however, roughly correspond to the sum raised by the Cambridge Franciscans in the fourteenth century, according to another fragment of surviving mendicant accounts.[6]

---

butler: E 36/120, f. 42; almoner and infirmarer: SP 1/86, f. 91, no. 91. De Vedica served as physician in the late fifteenth century, the others in the early sixteenth century. I am grateful to Peter Murray Jones for information about de Vedica.

[3] Jens Röhrkasten has paid particular attention to the economies of the London friaries, examining the evidence for both income and expenditure: *Mendicant Houses*, pp. 221–78, 561–7; Jens Röhrkasten, 'L'Economie des Couvents Mendiants de Londres à la Fin du Moyen Âge, d'après l'Etude des Documents d'Archives et des Testaments', in *Economie et Religion: L'Expérience des Ordres Mendiants (XIIIe–XVe Siècle)*, ed. N. Bériou and J. Chiffoleau, Collection d'Histoire et d'Archéologie Médiévale, 21 (Lyon: Presses Universitaires de Lyon, 2009), pp. 211–45.

[4] TNA, SP 1/24, f. 126, no. 85.

[5] Francis Roth, *The English Austin Friars, 1249–1538*, 2 vols (New York: Augustinian Historical Institute, 1961), ii, no. 1032.

[6] John R.H. Moorman, *The Grey Friars in Cambridge, 1225–1538* (Cambridge: Cambridge University Press, 1952), pp. 74, 242–5.

Table 19 Estimated annual income and expenditure at the London Austin Friars in the early sixteenth century (for sources, see text).

Income	
alms	£ 50
confession	£ 9
will bequests	£ 24
anniversaries	£ 22
rents	£ 59
burial fees	£ 5
guilds	£ 2
total	**£ 171**

Expenditure	
food	£ 70
expenses	£ 15
servants	£ 25
repairs	£ 14
quitrents	£ 1
subvention to Rome	£ 25
alms	£ 5
total	**£ 155**

Confessions given to lay people were clearly charged for, at least on occasion, and the average annual sum for the province was £88, giving an estimated figure of about £9 at the London house (assuming, once again, that they accounted for about a tenth of provincial income). This income from confessions may be the result of occasional donations to senior mendicant confessors by wealthy lay people, rather than the putative sum of hundreds of small payments by ordinary townsmen and women: these salary-earning friars have been termed an 'elite corps' within the mendicants.[7]

The wealthier townsmen and women of late medieval England compiled written wills to guide their executors: donations to friars constitute a standard part of the wishes or duties of these testators.[8] The bequests of London testators to the Austin friars form another substantial part of the income of the house and in the early sixteenth century the average annual income (based on the surviving written wills) was about £24 a year.[9]

---

[7] Maureen Jurkowski, 'Were Friars Paid Salaries? Evidence from Clerical Taxation Records', *The Fifteenth Century*, 13 (Woodbridge: Boydell, 2014), pp. 131–51 (p. 138).

[8] Clive Burgess, 'Friars and the Parish in Late Medieval Bristol: Observations and Possibilities', in *The Friars in Medieval Britain: Proceedings of the 2007 Harlaxton Symposium*, ed. N. Rogers, Harlaxton Medieval Studies, 19 (Donington: Shaun Tyas, 2010), pp. 73–96.

[9] The figure of £24 is an annual median average for the first three decades of the sixteenth century: Röhrkasten, *Mendicant Houses*, pp. 563–4; Röhrkasten, 'L'économie des Couvents', p. 236. The figure is an increase on the median average for the last quarter of the fifteenth century, £18: Röhrkasten, *Mendicant Houses*, pp. 272–3.

These bequests were, of course, a form of spiritual investment: the testator was usually paying for the attendance of a friar or friars at the funeral procession and service, and, if funds allowed, for chantry masses or anniversary funeral services at a later date. Wealthier testators could pay for a permanent series of masses and anniversary services, usually by setting aside future rental income, although this could also be paid for by a large one-off payment.[10] The accounting material collated by the Court of Augmentations demonstrates that at the time of the Dissolution there were still six active annual payments for anniversary funeral services, worth £22 a year.[11]

Like the majority of London's monastic houses, the Augustinian friars owned and rented out property. In common with the other London mendicants, the rental portfolio was on a small scale and was almost entirely limited to a row of tenements on the edge of their precinct, with a few tenants or corrodians living within the precinct itself (Chapter 18: London Friars and Londoners). The Augustinian friars seem to have acquired a rental portfolio quite soon after their arrival in London: at an inquisition in the early fourteenth century they were found to have acquired a messuage in the parish of St Benet Fink before the Statute of Mortmain, presumably therefore in the 1260s or 1270s.[12] By 1533 their rental income was about £59, although this had dropped to about £40 by the time of the Dissolution after they sold some tenements.[13]

Executors paid burial fees to the friary for the right to bury lay people in the church or cemetery. An agreement concerning tithes was reached with the neighbouring parish of St Peter in 1349 and other such agreements with London friaries usually include burial fees as well.[14] This type of financial arrangement between friary and parish had been allowed for and regulated in a papal bull of 1300.[15] No account of this or another London friary's income from burial fees has been traced but it could well have raised a few pounds a year. The fees for burial in a London parish church in the early sixteenth century were at the very least 6s 8d, more if the burial was at the east end or in a separate chapel.[16]

---

[10] An example of the latter can be found in 1490 when William Berkeley, marquess of Berkeley, paid £100 to the friary for two daily chantry masses and an annual anniversary service (in perpetuity) for his late wife, their deceased children, other family members and, in due course, for his own soul: TNA, LR 14/87.

[11] TNA, SC 6/HenVIII/2396, m. 60v; LR 2/262, f. 10; SC 11/436.

[12] Roth, *English Austin Friars*, ii, no. 40.

[13] Holder, 'Medieval Friaries of London', table 19, pp. 264–5.

[14] Roth, *English Austin Friars*, ii, no. 381. The Sack friars paid 40s a year to the vicar of St Botolph to compensate him for lost revenue from burial fees: LMA, GL MS 25121/592; Röhrkasten, *Mendicant Houses*, p. 58.

[15] Andrew G. Little, *Studies in English Franciscan History* (Manchester: Manchester University Press, 1917), pp. 114–15.

[16] Vanessa Harding, 'Burial Choice and Burial Location in Later Medieval London', in *Death in Towns: Urban Responses to the Dying and the Dead, 100–1600*, ed. S. Bassett (Leicester: Leicester University Press, 1992), pp. 119–35 (pp. 129–31); Susan Brigden, *London and the Reformation* (Oxford: Clarendon Press, 1989), pp. 50–1. It is quite possible that some of the simple bequests for

Finally, several guilds and religious fraternities had financial arrangements with the friary, for example the Pouchmakers' guild and the German fraternity of St Sebastian. In 1482 the Pouchmakers paid the friary an annual fee of 3s 4d (as well as a one-off payment of £10) for the use of a room and a series of masses and other spiritual services. The fraternity of St Sebastian maintained their own (eponymous) altar at the friary church and in 1496 agreed to pay 5s to have deceased members buried in the cloister, plus 2s 6d for each funeral service.[17] In York this type of agreement with local guilds and fraternities raised at least £1 a year for the Franciscans and it is likely that the London friars' houses received significantly more than this; a conservative figure of £2 has been assumed in Table 19.[18]

Turning now to expenditure, the greatest cost was probably food. When the king gave special subsidies to English friaries he paid a penny per friar and this might represent a rough daily board and lodging expense.[19] With about thirty friars in the early sixteenth century, this would suggest an annual food bill of about £45. By way of comparison, Yarmouth priory (a Benedictine cell of the wealthy Norwich cathedral priory) spent just over £39 on food in 1496–7, catering for about seven monks and priests, while even the poor nunnery of St Radegund in Cambridge spent nearly £19 in 1481–2, for about eleven nuns and five priests.[20] If the London Austin friars were really eating as modestly as the poor Cambridge nuns, an annual cost of about £45 is possible (converting the St Radegund figure for the increased numbers of London friars gives £35). While it may be an exaggeration to assume that the friars were dining in Benedictine style (which would have cost about £165 a year), it does seem likely that the £45 figure is an underestimate, particularly given the lack of 'free' food from granges and estates (although the friars may have received food as alms). The slightly higher figure of £70 is suggested here, double the cost of the Cambridge nuns (Table 19).

Other expenses on supplies such as clothing, heating, candle wax, books and stabling then have to be estimated. At Yarmouth priory they spent over £13 and at St Radegund nearly £6 on these items; the sum of £15 seems like a conservative estimate for the London friars. If there were about thirty friars in the early sixteenth century then there would

---

sums such as 6s 8d given in the wills examined by Röhrkasten (see n. 9) might be for payment of these burial fees, in which case there is a danger of 'double-counting' this income.

[17] TNA, LR 15/12; LR 15/13.

[18] J.S. Purvis, 'A York Account Roll for A.D. 1537–1538', *Yorkshire Archaeological Journal*, 42 (1971), 52–3; R. Barrie Dobson, 'Mendicant Ideal and Practice in Late Medieval York', in *Archaeological Papers from York Presented to M.W. Barley*, ed. P.V. Addyman and V.E. Black (York: York Archaeological Trust, 1984), pp. 109–22 (p. 110). The fragment of accounts (printed by Purvis and identified by Dobson) does not cover a full year.

[19] Röhrkasten, *Mendicant Houses*, p. 32; Röhrkasten, 'L'économie des Couvents', p. 220.

[20] Accounts of St Radegund for 1481–2 and Yarmouth priory for 1496–7 printed in Martin Heale, *Monasticism in Late Medieval England, c. 1300–1535* (Manchester: Manchester University Press, 2009), pp. 92–101. The figures in the St Radegund account have been corrected to give an estimate for a full calendar year. For approximate numbers of religious, see VCH, *Cambridge*, ii, 218–19; VCH, *Norfolk*, ii, 330.

probably have been as many servants, including cooks, butlers, gardeners, a washerwoman, a brewer and a baker. Some of these may have received free or subsidised accommodation, as at Grey Friars where a married washerwoman received an apartment in return for her services.[21] An annual wage bill of at least £25 is a reasonable guess given that the Benedictines at Yarmouth were paying about £17 and the nuns at Cambridge about £10.

The annual repair bill for the year following the Dissolution is £13 12s 6d and this is perhaps a surprisingly high amount given that at Yarmouth they spent just over £4 and at St Radegund just over £3. The London figure may of course reflect increased investment in the portfolio of rented tenements, the prime function of the newly dissolved house but, if it overestimates the medieval expenditure on repairs to tenements it must underestimate that expenditure on the religious buildings. An account by the clerk of St Paul's for 1539 reveals that the friary had been paying a 13s 4d quitrent that was still due on a property and there were certainly a few others.[22]

The Austin Friars account document of 1522 suggests that half of the sums raised through alms and confession payments had to be handed over to the order's general chapter in Rome, although it is not clear if this was the standard obligation. If this was the normal state of affairs then about £25 would have to have been transferred. The final category to consider is alms. Just as the friars received alms from Londoners they would probably have made some payments to deserving causes: the wealthy cell of Yarmouth priory gave away nearly £7, although the friars, as receivers of alms, would probably have paid out less.

Although the figures are approximate – outright guesses in one or two cases – they seem to suggest quite a precarious state of financial affairs, with an annual income of approximately £170 only just exceeding expenditure of about £155.

Conclusion

The Black friars were probably the most financially stable of the London mendicants: they certainly had the largest priory and they received an annual royal subvention of £20 (as did their colleagues, and the Franciscans, of Oxford and Cambridge).[23] The London Austin Friars was a more typical friary of the sixteenth century: prior Bellond seems to have managed the finances effectively, but the small annual surplus – perhaps £15 – would have provided little slack in the event of crisis or mismanagement. These urban friars could no longer live purely on alms as they once had in the early thirteenth century: there were

---

[21] TNA, C 146/1479, printed in *Grey Friars*, pp. 207–8. The only reference to servants at Austin Friars occurs in the alien 'subsidy' assessment of 1483, which lists two male servants of Saxon origin in the friary: James L. Bolton, *The Alien Communities of London in the Fifteenth Century: The Subsidy Rolls of 1440 and 1483–4* (Stamford: Richard III Society & Yorkist History Trust in association with P. Watkins, 1998), pp. 17 (n. 12), 29.

[22] TNA, E 101/474/11, f. 4. Röhrkasten notes quitrents of 3s 6d in addition to the 13s 4d just cited: 'L'économie des Couvents', p. 221.

[23] Röhrkasten, *Mendicant Houses*, pp. 260–1.

simply too many regular cash costs. And, any form of major expenditure on construction or repair could bankrupt a mendicant house, as the Crossed Friars found out in the sixteenth century when they overstretched themselves when enlarging their church. From the first decade of the century, Prior Bowry seems to have been planning and building a retrochoir or Lady chapel that extended the friary church further eastwards (Chapter 7: Crossed Friars, 'The church'). This rebuilding campaign seems to have ruined the friary financially: there are several recorded Chancery cases of the 1520s and '30s concerning unpaid bonds and loans given to the priory, as well as correspondence relating to the disputed property rights of corrodians and other benefactors.[24]

Although the friars were nominally mendicant, it is clear that by the sixteenth century they could not function without their rental income, even if their rental portfolios were smaller and more localised than those of other monastic houses. These rents – in most cases a row of houses on the fringe of the precinct – brought in reliable annual income, ranging from £23 (paid to the Grey friars) to £116 (to the Black friars; Chapter 18: London friars and Londoners, Table 20). The friars did not have rural manors and granges to run, nor is there much evidence for industrial activity within their precincts (beyond in-house milling, brewing and baking), but the friars' tenements meant that they had to be involved in the local and business affairs of the secular world just like London's other religious orders.

---

[24] Chancery cases: TNA, C 1/486, no. 4 [1525?]; C 1/534, nos 4 and 5 [refer to bond of 1526]; C 1/767, no. 6; C 1/832, no. 19 [refer to loan of 1534]. Other evidence: TNA, SP 1/89, f. 134, no. 114 [refers to corrody-type gift of money in 1518]; BL, Additional charter 24490 [bond of 1527].

16

Spiritual Life and Education in the London Friaries

JENS RÖHRKASTEN

LONDON'S role as a centre of Christian worship can be traced back to the foundation of the diocese in 604, if not to the late Roman period.[1] In addition to the cathedral and the monastery dedicated to St Peter to the west, a number of other religious institutions were founded which enhanced the religious importance of a political and economic capital that benefited significantly from the demographic and economic expansion which characterised the development of western Europe between the tenth and thirteenth centuries, allowing William FitzStephen to mention thirteen major convent churches in the City and its suburbs in the late twelfth century.[2] The mendicant houses which were established in the city from 1221 onwards were the last great contribution to this rich heritage in the middle ages. They contributed to the change of the city's topography, and the bigger convents, the Dominicans, Franciscans, Carmelites and Austin Friars, which were part of London's religious landscape for about three centuries, became important cultural centres.

Spiritual life

Although the mendicants introduced important differences to the traditional orders, notably the absence of *stabilitas loci*, the duty to remain in the convent after profession, they did retain core elements of older monasticism. In addition to the vows of chastity and poverty these included a regular performance of the liturgy. The Dominicans came to London before they had established their Constitutions (1228) and it may be assumed

---

[1] Pamela Taylor, 'Foundation and Endowment: St Paul's and the English Kingdoms, 604–1087', in *St Paul's: The Cathedral Church of London 604–2004*, ed. D. Keene, A. Burns and A. Saint (New Haven and London: Yale University Press, 2004), pp. 5–16; Alan Thacker, 'The Cult of Saints and the Liturgy', in *St Paul's: The Cathedral Church*, pp. 113–22; Barron and Davies, *Religious Houses*, pp. 27–50; Thomas Tanner, *Notitia Monastica: Or, an Account of all the Abbies, Priories and Houses of Friers, Heretofore in England and Wales* (London: William Bowyer, 1744), pp. 287–92.

[2] John Stow, *Survey of London*, ed. Charles L. Kingsford, 2 vols (Oxford: Clarendon, 1908), ii, 219.

that they were following the liturgy of the Augustinians because technically they were Augustinian canons. This consisted of prayers and the recitation of psalms and hymns at fixed times *horis et temporibus constitutes*[3] – Psalms 62, 5 and 89 for matins, a psalm with two antiphones, a reading and complet at terce, sext and at noon, a psalm with four antiphones, another psalm, a reading and complet in the evening and further services at night. In November, December, January and February these consisted of twelve antiphones, six psalms and three readings; in March, April, September and October ten antiphones, five psalms and three readings, and in the remaining months when the night hours were still shorter a reduced load of eight antiphones, four psalms and two readings.[4] This will have been the pattern for the Austin Friars as well. From 1228 the Dominican service began with matins which consisted of a service of the Virgin. Then the friars entered the choir of their church, bowing before the altar, to take their seats after a genuflection. This was followed by a Pater noster and the Creed, prayers and hymns.[5] By the time of their arrival in London, the Franciscans had already received a papal confirmation of the final version of their rule. The clauses concerning the liturgy in this *Regula bullata* catered for friars in priests' orders as well as for those who had remained members of the laity. The priests were to perform a slightly shortened version of the Roman liturgy, for which they were allowed to have a breviary, while the lay friars were to recite twenty-four Pater nosters for matins, five for lauds, seven each for prime, terce, sext and noon, for vespers twelve and another seven at night. In addition they were expected to offer prayers for the dead. The English minister general Haymo of Faversham introduced a modified liturgy in 1243.[6] This contained detailed instructions for the celebrating priest, defining ritual gestures and the acts surrounding transubstantiation. The Carmelite rule made it mandatory for all friars to celebrate the Eucharist every day, early in the morning; a detail in the fourteenth-century missal owned by the London house shows friars celebrating mass (Figure 87). Liturgies varied depending on the day and the time of year in which they were performed. Specific saints' days were marked by modifications in the liturgy to mark the occasion. The lists of such days included the major feasts of the Church, the feasts of saints from the ranks of the friars and also of those whose relics were preserved in local churches. The ways in which such feasts were marked could be modified over time, e.g. by including the vigils or the octaves or by declaring a double feast. Divine service was celebrated at all canonical hours by the Carmelites, at least after their 1281 general chapter, convened at London. The feast days of saints were

---

[3] *La Règle de Saint Augustin*, ed. Luc Verheijen, 2 vols, Études Augustiniennes (Antiquité), 29–30 (Paris: Brepols, 1967), i, 420.

[4] *Règle de Saint Augustin*, i, 148–9.

[5] *De Oudste Constituties van de Dominicanen*, ed. Antoninus H. Thomas, Bibliothèque de la Revue d'Histoire Ecclésiastique, 42 (Leuven, 1965), p. 313.

[6] *Sources of the Modern Roman Liturgy*, ed. Stephen J.P. Van Dijk, 2 vols, Studia et Documenta Franciscana, 1–2 (Leiden: Brill, 1963), i, 3–14.

Fig. 87. The fourteenth-century missal owned by the London White Friars, detail showing Carmelite friars celebrating mass on Holy Saturday. (© The British Library Board, Add. MS 29704, f. 6v)

marked by elaborate liturgical celebrations which changed and developed from the late thirteenth to the late fifteenth century.[7]

Education

London had well-established schools of apparently high standard well before the arrival of the mendicants. In the late twelfth century the three privileged schools located at the major churches of St Paul's, St Martin-le-Grand and Holy Trinity Aldgate were described as famous and of venerable antiquity and there were other similar institutions.[8] Among the subjects taught were Latin grammar and philosophy. When the first friars came to England they were in a position to benefit from an existing education system, and in the case of the Dominicans the potential for recruiting students at Oxford may have been an important attraction in the first place.

---

[7] *Fontes Liturgiae Carmelitanae. Investigatio in decreta, codices et proprium sanctorum*, ed. Paschalis Kallenberg (Rome: Institutum Carmelitanum, 1962), pp. 22, 72–7.

[8] Stow, *Survey of London*, ii, 221.

The four major mendicant convents in the City – the Dominicans, Franciscans, Carmelites and Austin Friars – became important centres of learning. The Carmelites even established a *studium generale* in their Fleet Street convent, while the schools in the other convents were important provincial centres. A number of important scholars taught and studied here, drawing on the resources of extensive libraries, parts of which can still be traced.[9] However, the origins of these schools are unknown.

Given London's importance it is likely that the mendicant houses of the four main orders developed schools as soon as their orders generated study systems, and it is this process which needs to be addressed first. Upon their arrival in England, the Dominicans, like the Franciscans, saw Oxford as one of their main destinations, undoubtedly because of its role as a centre of learning.[10] For the Franciscans, who developed a first study centre at Bologna during their founder's lifetime, Oxford was also the *studium principale*. However, from early on the London convent was remarkable not only because of its size and buildings but also because of its books.[11] Friar Vincent of Coventry was the first lector in the city's Franciscan convent in c. 1236.[12] The school of the London Grey Friars, one of the earliest Franciscan study centres, was a *studium particulare*, offering courses on Latin grammar, the liberal arts, philosophy and theology, rather than a general study like the one at Paris.[13] By the late thirteenth century, when each of the seven custodies forming the order's English province had a study centre of their own, the London convent held this role in the London custody.[14] As part of Pope Benedict XII's reforms of 1336, twenty-one provincial study centres were established in the order, and London and Norwich were among them. In the fifteenth century the school in the city's Grey Friars had the status of a *studium generale* although it was not linked to a university and could not confer academic degrees.[15]

Although the London Dominican priory predates the order's 1228 Constitutions, which laid down that no new house was to be founded *sine priore et doctore* by at least four years, it is likely that education was one of its core activities from the beginning.[16] When Jordan of Saxony, the Dominicans' second master general, visited England early in 1230, where God gave him high hopes of *bonae capturae* – of finding suitable friars for the order's purposes

---

[9] Neil Ker, *Medieval Libraries of Great Britain: A List of Surviving Books* (London: Royal Historical Society, 1964), pp. 123–5; Andrew Watson and Neil Ker, *Medieval Libraries of Great Britain. A List of Surviving Books. Supplement to the Second Edition*, Guides and Handbooks, 15 (London: Royal Historical Society, 1987), pp. 47–8.
[10] Eccleston, *Tractatus*, p. 9.
[11] Hilarin Felder, *Geschichte der wissenschaftlichen Studien im Franziskanerorden bis um die Mitte des 13. Jahrhunderts* (Freiburg: Herder, 1904), pp. 127–35; Bert Roest, *A History of Franciscan Education (c. 1210–1517)*, Education and Society in the Middle Ages and the Renaissance, 2 (Leiden: Brill, 2000), p. 6.
[12] Eccleston, *Tractatus*, pp. 21, 48, 49.
[13] Röhrkasten, *Mendicant Houses*, p. 491.
[14] Roest, *History of Franciscan Education*, p. 72.
[15] Roest, *History of Franciscan Education*, p. 41.
[16] *De Oudste Constituties van de Dominicanen*, p. 358.

– he came to London as well.[17] The Dominican Constitutions allowed a high degree of flexibility for friars, who were regarded as particularly suited for learning, and all friars were required to attend regular lectures on theology.[18] The London Dominican priory is likely to have had its own school from early on but a building dedicated to this purpose was only constructed in the early 1260s (Chapter 1: The First Black Friars in Holborn, c. 1223–1286).[19] By the early fourteenth century the theology school of the London Black Friars seems to have ranked after the general studies at Oxford and Cambridge.[20]

The city's two other large mendicant houses, the Carmelites in Fleet Street and the Austin Friars in Broad Street, were early foundations in the history of their respective orders and both probably predate the creation of a formal study system. The Austin friars, who purchased their study house in Paris in 1259, developed their own educational system in the 1280s.[21] Their London convent later housed a *studium generale provinciae*, while the order's international study centres in England were located in Oxford and Cambridge.[22] The London house of the Carmelites obtained an even higher status in their order as a *studium generale*, which was also attended by a large number of foreign Carmelite students from the early fourteenth into the sixteenth century, while the significance of the Oxford convent was restricted to the provincial level.[23]

Scholarship

Education and scholarship played a central role in the London convents of the four major mendicant orders. The names and even the works of some of their teaching staff are known and parts of their library collections have survived. Even though this information is very

---

[17] *Die Briefe Jordans von Sachsen, des zweiten Dominikanergenerals (1222–37)*, ed. Berthold Altaner (Leipzig: Harrassowitz, 1925), pp. 20, 118.

[18] Andrew G. Little, 'Educational Organisation of the Mendicant Friars in England', *Transactions of the Royal Historical Society*, new series, 8 (1894), 49–70 (p. 50).

[19] William A. Hinnebusch, *The Early English Friars Preachers*, Dissertationes Historicae, 14 (Rome: Institutum Historicum Fratrum Praedicatorum, 1951), p. 28.

[20] Hinnebusch, *Early English Friars Preachers*, p. 340; Maura O'Carroll, 'The Educational Organisation of the Dominicans in England and Wales 1221–1348: A Multidisciplinary Approach', *Archivum Fratrum Praedicatorum*, 50 (1980), 23–62 (p. 49).

[21] Eelcko Ypma, *La Formation des Professeurs chez les Ermites de Saint Augustin de 1256 à 1354* (Paris: Centre d'Etudes des Augustins, 1956), pp. 6–13; Balbino Rano, 'Agostiniani', in *Dizionario degli Istituti di Perfezione*, ed. G. Pelliccia and G. Rocca, 10 vols (Rome: Paoline 1974–2003), i, col. 278–381 (349–50).

[22] Ypma, *Formation des Professeurs*, p. 50; Adolar Zumkeller, 'Die Augustinerschule des Mittelalters: Vertreter und philosophisch-theologische Lehre', *Analecta Augustiniana*, 27 (1964), 167–262 (p. 195); Röhrkasten, *Mendicant Houses*, p. 493.

[23] Franz-Bernard Lickteig, *The German Carmelites at the Medieval Universities*, Textus et Studia Historica Carmelitana (Rome: Institutum Carmelitanum, 1981), pp. 514–18; William J. Courtenay, 'The London Studia in the Fourteenth Century', *Medievalia et Humanistica*, new series, 13 (1985), 127–41 (p. 129).

fragmentary, it shows how the study systems of the London friaries were connected with other centres of learning and that distinguished scholars were active in London over long periods of time. Vincent of Coventry, who taught at the London Grey Friars in c. 1236, later moved to Cambridge where he was the first lector. In the sixteenth century the Carmelite John Bale attributed two treatises to him, *Expositorium missae* and *Repetitiones lectionum*.[24] One of Vincent of Coventry's near contemporaries, brother Hugh, appears to have been guardian of the London Grey Friars before he became a student at Cambridge.[25] Of a later generation was Thomas Rondel, who was buried in the London convent and may have been lector there in 1309. Before that time his academic career had taken him to Oxford and Paris.[26] One of the great English Franciscans of the fourteenth century, William of Ockham, probably began his education at the London Grey Friars before moving on to Oxford. Between 1321 and 1324 Ockham wrote some of his most important works, among them a discussion of Aristotle's *Physics* (*Expositio in libros physicorum*) and his treatise on logic (*Summa logicae*). It is quite possible that he wrote them in the London convent although his time in Oxford was at least as important for his education and career.[27] In 1324 Ockham followed a summons to Avignon where he remained until 1328 when he fled and joined the German emperor Ludwig of Bavaria. During the time Ockham is thought to have resided in the London Grey Friars, he very likely coincided there with two other important Franciscan philosophers, Walter de Chatton, who was lecturer in the convent before he moved to Avignon, probably in 1333, where he was involved in the examination of a suspect treatise by the Dominican Thomas Waleys, and Adam Wodeham.[28] Chatton, who is known to have also studied at Oxford where he later became Franciscan regent master, also travelled to Assisi and to Avignon.[29] A treatise on evangelical poverty, a reaction to Pope John XXII's bull *Ad conditorem canonum*, may have been written in London. Chatton's readings on the 'Sentences' show influences from Ockham and may also have been written when the two friars were together in London.[30] Wodeham, who is usually seen as a pupil of Ockham, lectured at Norwich and London before he went to Oxford.[31]

---

[24] Alfred B. Emden, *A Biographical Register of the University of Cambridge to 1500* (Cambridge: Cambridge University Press, 1963), p. 164.
[25] Emden, *Biographical Register . . . Cambridge*, p. 319.
[26] Alfred B. Emden, *A Biographical Register of the University of Oxford to A.D. 1500*, 3 vols. (Oxford: Oxford University Press, 1957), iii, 1588–9.
[27] William J. Courtenay, 'Ockham, William of (c. 1287–1347)', *ODNB*, <http://www.oxforddnb.com/view/article/20493> (accessed 24 May 2016); William J. Courtenay, 'Ockham, Chatton, and the London *Studium*: Observations on Recent Changes in Ockham's Biography', in *Die Gegenwart Ockhams*, ed. W. Vossenkuhl and R. Schönberger (Weinheim: VCH Acta Humaniora, 1990), pp. 327–37 (p. 327).
[28] Emden, *Biographical Register . . . Oxford*, i, 395–6.
[29] Peter Biller, 'Chatton, Walter (d. 1343/4)', *ODNB*, <http://www.oxforddnb.com/view/article/4904> (accessed 24 May 2016).
[30] Courtenay, 'Ockham, Chatton, and the London *Studium*', p. 329.
[31] William J. Courtenay, 'Wodeham [Woodham, Goddam], Adam (c. 1295–1358)', *ODNB*, <http://www.oxforddnb.com/view/article/10854> (accessed 8 June 2016).

Another prominent Franciscan scholar was William Woodford, who joined the order at the London convent in c. 1350.[32] Woodford studied at Oxford and he is known to have travelled abroad, to Cologne and perhaps to Zurich. However, he always returned to the London Grey Friars, although his activities, which included the role of confessor to the countess of Norfolk, extended beyond the city. Woodford, who is known to have enjoyed the privilege of private property and his own quarters in the convent near Newgate, lectured against John Wyclif's teachings on the Eucharist.[33] He also defended the theology of apostolic poverty against the attacks by Richard FitzRalph, archbishop of Armagh, continuing the efforts by another London friar, Roger Conway, who had already obtained his Oxford doctorate and the position of minister of the English Franciscan province in 1355, while Woodford was still at the beginning of his career.[34] Among Conway's works is a treatise on the poverty of Christ, a subject which had been the cause of a rift between the Franciscans and Pope John XXII in the 1320s. However, Conway's arguments have to be seen in a wider context – the general attack on the mendicant orders – and he also wrote a *Defensio religionis mendicantium*. When he went to Avignon in 1358 he was part of a mendicant delegation including the Dominican provincial prior John Tatenhall.[35]

In addition to the small elite of Franciscan intellectuals who could boast international fame, there was a significantly larger number of university graduates, lectors and scholars who lived and worked in the London friary. Among them were Thomas Canynge, forty-eighth lector at Cambridge, and Giraldus de Pisario (Paquerii), doctor of theology, who may have retired in the London convent and who were both buried there.[36] William Querle, the convent's guardian in 1330, owned books worth £70 and John atte Welle, who taught theology in London in the second half of the fourteenth century, also acted as royal ambassador to the Curia.[37] A century after Querle, one of his successors, Robert Chamberleyn, travelled to Paris to purchase books there.[38]

The routine teaching staff only become visible in the fifteenth century. William Thorpe is the convent's first known 'cursor theologie' (1468); James Furnes and Henry Sedbar acted in the same role in the 1480s and their successors were Ambrose Kell and John Person

---

[32] Jeremy Catto, 'Woodford, William (d. in or after 1397)', *ODNB*, <http://www.oxforddnb.com/view/article/29919> (accessed 10 June 2016).

[33] Little, *Studies in English Franciscan History*, p. 77.

[34] Andrew G. Little, *The Grey Friars of Oxford*, Oxford Historical Society, 20 (Oxford, 1892), pp. 239–41; Katherine Walsh, *A Fourteenth-Century Scholar and Primate – Richard FitzRalph in Oxford, Avignon and Armagh* (Oxford: Clarendon, 1981), pp. 413, 417.

[35] Katherine Walsh, 'Conway, Roger (d. c. 1360)', *ODNB*, <http://www.oxforddnb.com/view/article/6124> (accessed 8 June 2016).

[36] Moorman, *Grey Friars in Cambridge*, p. 161; *Grey Friars*, pp. 65, 67, 84, 101; John R.H. Moorman, 'The Foreign Element among the English Franciscans', *English Historical Review*, 62 (1947), 289–303 (p. 296).

[37] *Grey Friars*, pp. 18, 19, 22, 56, 67, 69; Little, *Grey Friars of Oxford*, pp. 78, 145, 311–12; Emden, *Biographical Register... Oxford*, iii, 2008; TNA, E 403/468, m. 12.

[38] *Grey Friars*, p. 57.

in the sixteenth century.³⁹ There was a 'magister novitiorum' in 1492 and an 'informator iuvenum' in 1526.⁴⁰ They focused on formation and basic education, while the 'lector', Gilbert Mylbourn in the early sixteenth century, dealt with philosophy and probably theology, which were taught to the convent as a whole.⁴¹ More advanced studies were supervised by the 'magister regens', William Toly in 1500 and Robert Burton in 1522.⁴²

The Dominicans had equally distinguished friars in the city. John of Darlington, prior of the Holborn convent in the 1260s and royal confessor, was also a scholar working on concordances. Nicholas Trivet, the son of one of Henry III's itinerant justices, studied at Oxford and Paris, and travelled to Avignon and Italy. He may have joined the order in London and was living in the city's Black Friars in 1324. Trivet's theological and historical works, among them a treatise on the poverty controversy, are thought to have been written at Oxford, but towards the end of his career he became a teacher in the London priory.⁴³ William Cambrei may have joined the order in Chelmsford but he later went to London where he was ordained deacon and priest. In 1376 the order's general chapter ordered him to lecture on the 'Sentences' in Cambridge.⁴⁴ A time in the London priory can also be assumed for the Dominican artist John Sifrewast.⁴⁵ Less is known about the Dominicans' London teaching staff. Andrew Yakislei was lector in the convent on 1390 but this is the only information on the priory's teachers.⁴⁶ There were close contacts between the Oxford priory and Black Friars London and individual friars had their own libraries. A well-known example is William Swadell, prior in 1521.⁴⁷

The Carmelite convent in Fleet Street was an important centre of education which attracted foreign friars between the fourteenth and sixteenth centuries. More than 240 students from the German lands studied here between 1314 and 1527.⁴⁸ John Baconthorpe may have been buried here⁴⁹ but Bale's 'doctor resolutus' is known to have spent much time

---

³⁹ *Grey Friars*, pp. 22, 60, 66, 67, 103; Little, *Grey Friars of Oxford*, p. 270; Moorman, *Grey Friars in Cambridge*, pp. 21–2, n. 6.
⁴⁰ *Grey Friars*, pp. 65, 67, 92.
⁴¹ Moorman, *Grey Friars in Cambridge*, pp. 21–2, n. 6, 196; LMA, GL MS 9531/10, ff. 152v, 154.
⁴² *Grey Friars*, pp. 22, 65, 68, 79, 243; Moorman, *Grey Friars in Cambridge*, pp. 92, 159, 216; Emden, *Biographical Register... Oxford*, i, 320; Emden, *Biographical Register... Cambridge*, p. 590.
⁴³ Hinnebusch, *Early English Friars Preachers*, p. 63 [John of Darlington]; Emden, *Biographical Register... Oxford*, iii, 1902–3; Antonia Gransden, *Historical Writing in England*, 2 vols (London: Routledge, 1974–82), i, 501–7; James G. Clark, 'Trevet, Nicholas (b. 1257x65, d. in or after 1334)', ODNB, <http://www.oxforddnb.com/view/article/27744> (accessed 8 June 2016).
⁴⁴ Emden, *Biographical Register... Cambridge*, p. 118; Alfred B. Emden, *A Survey of Dominicans in England Based on the Ordination Lists in Episcopal Registers (1268–1538)*, Dissertationes Historicae, 18 (Rome: Sabina, 1967), p. 299.
⁴⁵ LMA, GL MS 9531/3, f. 5; Janet Backhouse, *The Sherborne Missall* (London: British Library, 1999).
⁴⁶ BL, MS Add. 32446, f. 2a.
⁴⁷ Dennis E. Rhodes, 'William Swadell, English Dominican: his Friends and his Books', *Archivum Fratrum Praedicatorum*, 49 (1979), 519–22.
⁴⁸ Lickteig, *The German Carmelites*, pp. 514–18.
⁴⁹ Patrick R. McCaffrey, *The White Friars: An Outline Carmelite History with Special Reference to the English-Speaking Province* (Dublin: Gill, 1926), p. 167; BL, MS Harl. 1819, f. 13.

in Oxford, Cambridge and Paris. A less well known Carmelite scholar, Osbert Pickingham, who had probably joined the order in Lynn and later graduated from Oxford, was prior of the London White Friars while Baconthorpe was prior of the English province.[50] In the second half of the fourteenth century Thomas Brome was one of the lecturers at the London Carmelite *studium*. He had joined the order in the city and later graduated from Cambridge. As provincial prior he attended general chapters and he went to the papal court at Avignon in 1375.[51] For part of Brome's time as provincial prior, John Elm was prior of the White Friars in London. Elm had studied in Cambridge where he received a doctorate in 1347.[52] He is credited with the authorship of four treatises, among them a commentary on the Apocalypse. A successor to Elm was John Wrotham, who seems to have joined the order in London before moving to Oxford.[53] Wrotham returned to London and he is credited with six treatises, among them four collections of sermons. From the 1380s onwards English Carmelite friars with a London connection were involved in the investigation of John Wyclif's teachings and some were prominent in countering them. Among these friars were John Loney, who was a member of the committee of twelve appointed by the chancellor of Oxford university for the examination of the theological opinions of Wyclif and who as prior of the London White Friars attended all sessions of the Blackfriars Council,[54] Stephen Patrington, who also attended this council in 1382,[55] and Thomas Netter, whose major work *Doctrinale Fidei Ecclesiae* was written with 'the declared purpose of combatting the errors of Wyclif and his followers'.[56] With friars like Patrington and Netter, the English Carmelite province had reached the highest point of its intellectual development, although John Sowle (Souley), author of two treatises (*Divisiones thematum epistolarum et evangeliorum de temporali pro circuitu anni* and *Conciones de tempore et de sanctis*) was a noted preacher in the city and a friend of the humanist John Colet.[57] A theological dispute about religious poverty begun by a sermon delivered by a young friar in 1464 revealed weaknesses in the intellectual foundations of the argument. The approach, an attack on the secular clergy, led to counter arguments and two senior members of the White Friars came to be involved, Thomas Halden, the convent's senior academic teacher, and the prior, John Milverton, who was also the order's provincial prior. The debate became so heated that Milverton was summoned to Rome and imprisoned in the Castel Sant'Angelo until

---

[50] Emden, *Biographical Register... Oxford*, iii, 1481.
[51] Richard Copsey, 'Brome, Thomas (d. c. 1380)', ODNB, <http://www.oxforddnb.com/view/article/3504> (accessed 8 June 2016).
[52] Emden, *Biographical Register... Cambridge*, p. 208.
[53] Emden, *Biographical Register... Oxford*, iii, 2096.
[54] Emden, *Biographical Register... Oxford*, ii, 1159.
[55] Emden, *Biographical Register... Oxford*, iii, 1435–6; Aubrey Gwynn, *The English Austin Friars in the Time of Wyclif* (Oxford: Oxford University Press, 1940), p. 234; Catto, 'Woodford, William'.
[56] Kevin Alban, *The Teaching and Impact of the Doctrinale of Thomas Netter of Walden*, Medieval Church Studies, 7 (Turnhout: Brepols, 2010), p. 1.
[57] Emden, *Biographical Register... Oxford*, iii, 1736; Emden, *Biographical Register... Cambridge*, pp. 542–3.

1468.[58] However, this episode did not put into question the convent's role as a major study centre. German Carmelites continued to be sent there. Among the teaching staff were John Blysse, 'informator philosophie' and 'magister novitiorum'[59] and John Gybbes, lector and last prior of the London convent.

The convent of the Austin Friars near Broad Street also developed into an important centre of learning. Theologians from this priory were also involved in the controversy about Wyclif's teachings; however, the Oxford scholar found supporters among them. One of these supporters was John Bankyn who suggested to the parliament of 1371 that ecclesiastical property should be part confiscated. Among his supporters was Thomas Ashbourn, who nevertheless was later considered suitable to be 'Magister regens' of the order's London *studium*.[60] Unlike Ashbourne and Bankyn, who participated in the Blackfriars Council of 1382, their confrère Peter Patteshull joined the Lollards and broke with the order.[61] In contrast, John Lowe, prior of the London house in c. 1423 and later bishop of Rochester, defended orthodoxy and was involved in the prosecution of heresy.[62] Other lectors at the time, Walter Chaddesby and the Italian friar Louis of Modena, do not seem to have been involved in the dispute.[63] As in the case of the Carmelites, there was an international presence in the London Austin Friars in the later middle ages. With Thomas Burwell, Henry of Colchester, John de Columberiis and Christian de Monte, English as well as foreign friars were present in the convent.[64] While other lectors at the time, John Clerk, John Multon, John Stocton or William Gormechestre,[65] were less prominent, one of the pupils, John Capgrave, who was 'cursor' in London and later 'lector' in Cambridge, became significant as a historian.[66] While Capgrave was in London at the beginning of his career, the theologian Thomas Penketh, who had studied in Oxford and obtained his doctorate in theology in Cambridge, spent the last years of his life in the city. Penketh went to Padua and became lector at the university there in 1474. After his return to England he became a supporter of Richard III, notably in a sermon at Easter 1484. His role was still remembered in the time of Shakespeare: he is mentioned as 'Friar Penker' in *Richard III*, Act III scene 5.[67] Members

---

[58] F.R.H. Du Boulay, 'The Quarrel between the Carmelite Friars and the Secular Clergy of London, 1464–68', *Journal of Ecclesiastical History*, 6 (1955), 156–74.

[59] LMA, GL MS 9531/9, ff. 192v–3v.

[60] Gwynn, *The English Austin Friars*, p. 214; Roth, *English Austin Friars*, ii, no. 607.

[61] Emden, *Biographical Register... Oxford*, iii, 1434.

[62] Virginia Davis, 'Lowe, John (c. 1385–1467)', *ODNB*, <http://www.oxforddnb.com/view/article/17083> (accessed 8 June 2016).

[63] Emden, *Biographical Register... Cambridge*, p. 408.

[64] Emden, *Biographical Register... Oxford*, i, 471; Roth, *English Austin Friars*, ii, nos. 588, 591, 713, 1167.

[65] Roth, *English Austin Friars*, ii, nos. 557, 713, 748, 779, 805, 1419.

[66] Emden, *Biographical Register... Cambridge*, pp. 121–2; Roth, *English Austin Friars*, ii, no. 720; Peter J. Lucas, 'Capgrave, John (1393–1464)', *ODNB*, <http://www.oxforddnb.com/view/article/4591> (accessed 28 June 2016).

[67] Jeremy Catto, 'Penketh, Thomas (d. 1487)', *ODNB*, <http://www.oxforddnb.com/view/article/21844> (accessed 8 June 2016).

of the convent's study system in the sixteenth century were friar Ricardus, Robert Holan, 'magister novitiorum' in 1521, and John Verney.[68]

Ministry and spiritual services

Mendicant education was not an end in itself but an indispensable precondition for the friars' main objective: the ministry. The core elements, preaching and the hearing of confessions, were soon joined by another activity which established a strong link between the friars and sections of the laity: the celebration of obituary masses. London friars appear as preachers in various locations and on different occasions, in their own churches, at St Paul's Cross and also at the royal court.[69] These were routine activities for those friars who had been chosen by their order and licensed by the bishop. Sermons delivered at the royal court to celebrate high ecclesiastical feasts were remunerated separately. Examples of this are the Austin friar Roger de Holcote who preached before Queen Isabella at Hertford in December 1357, the Carmelite Richard Lemster who preached before Henry IV and the Franciscan William Goddard who addressed Henry VI at Easter 1451.[70] Thomas Penketh, who had worked as a theologian at the university of Padua following his education at Oxford and Cambridge, praised Richard III in a sermon when he had moved to the London Austin Friars after his return to England. While there is little direct information on friars as confessors, the indirect sources abound because numerous testators remembered their spiritual directors in their wills. John Cutler, guardian of the London Grey Friars between 1514 and 1518, was mentioned in the wills of six testators, having acted as confessor for one of them for twelve years.[71] Cutler is just one among many mendicant friars who remained in London for a long period of time, being at the centre of a circle of laypeople who trusted them and accepted their guidance. Such links between friars and members of the laity also existed within a family context. Family relationships, which were sometimes mentioned in wills, could also be a basis for the arrangement of memorial services or prayers to be performed by a relative who had joined a mendicant order. The draper John Godeston entrusted his son Richard, a Franciscan friar, with the prayers for his soul in 1377.[72]

A number of London gilds established links with the mendicant convents, probably in the thirteenth century, although the co-operation only becomes visible in the sources later on. The Company of Pewterers met in the Franciscan church at Easter, Christmas and on the feast of the Assumption, keeping anniversaries in the same church, where they were

---

[68] Roth, *English Austin Friars*, ii, no. 1012; LMA, GL MS 9531/9, f. 194; MS 9531/10, f. 153v.
[69] Röhrkasten, *Mendicant Houses*, pp. 451–5.
[70] BL, MS Cotton Galba E XIV, m. 33 [de Holcote]; TNA, E 101/404/21, ff. 35v, 36v [Lemster]; TNA, E 101/410/6, f. 34v [Goddard].
[71] LMA, GL MS 9171/9, ff. 35, 175–6, 177v–178, 181v; *Grey Friars*, p. 61; *Letters and Papers*, i(3), no. 3107 (40).
[72] *Calendar of Wills Proved and Enrolled in the Court of Husting, 1258–1688*, ed. Reginald R. Sharpe, 2 vols (London: Francis, 1889–90), i, 685–6.

joined by the Tailors and Drapers. The Vintners and Fishmongers had anniversaries celebrated by the Dominicans and the Clothworkers by the Austin Friars. Some city companies institutionalised these links by founding a fraternity in a mendicant church. The Curriers and Tanners had fraternities in the Carmelite church; the latter perhaps made a pragmatic decision because of their physical proximity.[73] The Shearmen and Waterbearers established fraternities at the Austin Friars and there were similar associations in the churches of the Franciscans.[74] The membership of other fraternities, e.g. those of St Clement and St John who met in the church of the Minoresses, or those of St Augustine, St James or the Visitation of the Blessed Virgin Mary, does not appear to have been determined by affiliation to a gild.[75]

While the city's population was integrated into a parish structure with well over a hundred churches, allowing a choice between the spiritual provisions of the secular Church and those of the mendicants or a combination of both, the situation was different for the foreign merchants, their servants and other 'aliens', notably artisans, who remained in London for lengthy periods of time during their visits. Italian and German visitors had the opportunity to meet Italian or German friars, usually students at Oxford, Cambridge or in one of the London mendicant schools, who were given tasks in the ministry during the vacations, probably because of their linguistic background. Examples are the Venetian Austin Friar Francis Paul and his confrère and contemporary Theoderich of Erfurt, both Oxford students, who were to preach and hear confessions in London in 1390 and 1391.[76] Support could also be provided for foreign merchants who fell ill or died abroad. Numerous Hanseatic merchants made bequests to one or more or the London friaries.[77] There were even some associations of foreigners attached to some of the mendicant churches. Among them was a fraternity of the Holy Trinity attached to the Black Friars and a fraternity of St Catherine in the church of the Austin Friars.[78]

Mendicant priests also acted as confessors to nuns of London convents. Franciscans friars were attached to the Minoresses and mendicants probably had this role in other houses of female religious.[79] The Franciscan Thomas Lynwood *quondam janitor huius loci confessor monialium de Berkyng* acted in this capacity in the late fifteenth and early sixteenth century.[80] The mendicant ministry extended beyond the ordinary population of the city to include members of the nobility and gentry; many of the former had townhouses

---

[73] Barron, 'Parish Fraternities', p. 16.
[74] Röhrkasten, *Mendicant Houses*, pp. 471–4.
[75] Röhrkasten, *Mendicant Houses*, p. 475.
[76] Roth, *English Austin Friars*, ii, nos. 605, 1167.
[77] Stuart Jenks, 'Hansische Vermächtnisse in London: ca. 1363–1483', *Hansische Geschichtsblätter*, 104 (1986), 35–111.
[78] Röhrkasten, *Mendicant Houses*, pp. 475–6.
[79] Catherine Paxton, 'The Nunneries of London and its Environs in the Later Middle Ages' (unpublished doctoral thesis, University of Oxford, 1993), p. 64.
[80] *Grey Friars*, pp. 67, 99.

in London.[81] This connection is indicated by the members of high-ranking families buried in one of the city's mendicant churches and it is also expressed in wills. The Dominican Thomas de Berkles was named as executor in the will of Sir Roger Swyllyngton and he was also commissioned to celebrate masses for his soul in 1417.[82] Geoffrey of Aylesham may have been confessor to Gilbert de Clare, earl of Gloucester; he certainly facilitated the transfer of the earl's contribution towards the construction of the new Franciscan church.[83] Margaret Marshal, duchess of Norfolk, also had a Franciscan confessor, the theologian William Woodford.[84] The Carmelite magister William Morin was mentioned as confessor in the will of Marie de Seintpol, countess of Pembroke, in 1376.[85] Such friars may have had only tenuous links with their respective orders' London houses and the same is true for the royal confessors, men like Luke of Woodford, confessor to Edward I, Robert de Duffeld, confessor to Edward II in 1320, or Nicholas de Herle, who was sent to the Dominican general chapter in 1335 to request prayer for the king and his family.[86] Like the Carmelites, who were the Dominicans' successors as royal confessors in the early fifteenth century, notably Thomas Netter and Stephen Patrington,[87] they were members of the royal household and could even be entrusted with administrative tasks or sent out as ambassadors. In addition they were sometimes chosen for leading positions by their order, as conventual or even provincial prior, like the Dominican William Syward.[88] Almost invariably such friars had multiple links with the London mendicant houses, lodging in a London convent or even retiring there. Others, like Richard II's Carmelite confessor Richard Lavenham, prior of the London White Friars, or John Malberthorp, Queen Philippa's Franciscan confessor, were more formally linked to the London house.[89] This proximity to the royal family – further enhanced by the fact that some London friars were on occasion invited to deliver sermons at court – gave a special status to the London convents of the Dominicans, Franciscans and Carmelites. The Austin Friars were not affected to the same degree, although they too had access to the court. John Fekenham preached before Richard II on several occasions, and he and his fellow friars buried the body of the executed earl of Arundel in 1397.[90]

---

[81] Caroline M. Barron, 'Centres of Conspicuous Consumption: The Aristocratic Town Houses in London 1200–1550', *London Journal*, 20 (1995), 1–16.
[82] TNA, PROB 11/2, f. 300; VCH, *London*, p. 502.
[83] *Grey Friars*, p. 163.
[84] VCH, *London*, pp. 504, 509; Emden, *Biographical Register... Oxford*, iii, 2081–2.
[85] *Calendar of Wills Proved and Enrolled in the Court of Husting*, ii, 194.
[86] Society of Antiquaries, London, MS 120, f. 11v; TNA, E 101/369/16, m. 2; E 403/191, m. 5; Bede Jarrett, *The English Dominicans* (London: Burns, Oates & Washbourne, 1921), p. 115.
[87] Emden, *A Biographical Register... Oxford*, ii, 1343–4; iii, 1435–6.
[88] TNA, E 403/462, mm. 1314; E 403/471, m. 3; Jarrett, *The English Dominicans*, p. 222.
[89] *Grey Friars*, pp. 19, 56, 67; Emden, *Biographical Register... Cambridge*, p. 383; Emden, *Biographical Register... Oxford*, ii, 1109–10; LMA, GL MS 9531/3, f. 53.
[90] BL, MS Add. 35115, f. 34; TNA, E 101/402/10, f. 34; Roth, *English Austin Friars*, ii, no. 643; *The Chronicle of England by John Capgrave*, ed. Francis C. Hingeston, Rolls series, 1 (London: Longman, 1858), p. 265.

Conclusion

The proximity of the royal court and the administration, the role of the city as an economic centre and the size of its population placed the London mendicant convents in an unusual environment. They became important cultural centres with their own schools and libraries. Their ministry had to cater for a wide social range of people and at least some of them enjoyed close proximity to the royal court. With the introduction of the Franciscan Observants into England in the 1480s, two further mendicant convents were constructed in the region, at Greenwich and Richmond. Although both of them had close contacts to the royal court and were also in close physical proximity to a royal palace, London citizens showed their interest and appreciation in the form of donations and bequests. When the question of the royal divorce was raised in the 1520s, and when the issue of royal supremacy emerged in the following decade, the Observant Franciscans offered resistance. The old convents, especially the Austin Friars under George Browne and the Dominicans under John Hilsey, became active participants in the Reformation.[91]

---

[91] David Knowles, *The Religious Orders in England*, 3 vols (Cambridge: Cambridge University Press, 1948–59), iii, 177–8.

17

Burial and Commemoration in the London Friaries

CHRISTIAN STEER

ON 24 October 1500 John Smith, gentleman of Coventry, made his will in which he asked to be buried in the Coventry Grey Friars:

> I will that a lyke tombe of marbull be made and sett in the Wall there as my wif lyeth, lyke to a tombe in the Greyfreres of London made and sett there for William Maryner and his wiff wt lyke scripture and ymages as there is in every thing and according to suche covenants as [has] been specified in a peyre of Indentures not yet sealed whereof the oon parte of them is in my stody at London and the other parte remayneth wt the marbeler in Poules churche yerde and with more *here lyeth John Smyth of Coventre gentleman and Johanne and Isabell his wiffes* and so forth as is conteyned in the seid endenture.[1]

Smith specified a monument 'lyke to a tombe' he had already seen during an earlier visit to the Franciscan convent in London. The Maryner tomb was, we know, a *tumba elevata*, that is a raised tomb.[2] This probably consisted of a canopied tomb chest which contained a brass effigy of Maryner and his two wives, Agnes and Juliana, accompanied by an inscription. Smith had seen this, liked it and commissioned a London marbler to make one just like it to go over his own grave in Coventry. Within forty years almost all of the tombs from London's mendicant houses were destroyed but it is still possible to gain some impression

---

[1] TNA, PROB 11/13, ff. 47v–48v. I am grateful to Nigel Saul for drawing my attention to this will and also to Les Smith for information received. It is noteworthy that at the time John Smith drew up his will in 1500, William Maryner was still alive and he did not die until 1512. In his will, Smith was evidently a Warwickshire man with a number of bequests to the religious orders of Coventry for prayers and intercessory services. There is no other reference to his town house in London although he makes detailed provision for the distribution of his Warwickshire property.

[2] *Grey Friars*, p. 119.

of the lost landscape of these houses and to learn who chose to be buried in the five friaries of the city.

There are a number of written accounts which record London's lost tombs. The earliest manuscript was written c. 1500 and is now College of Arms MS CGY 647.[3] The Tudor herald Sir Thomas Wriothesley, Garter King of Arms, later came to illustrate some of the tombs from London's mendicant houses and his account survives in British Library Add. MS 45131. This is known as the 'Book of Funerals' and was made during the 1520s. In it Wriothesley illustrated the tombs of William, Viscount Beaumont (died 1507) and of Richard Beauchamp, Lord St Amand (d. 1508) who were buried in the London Black Friars, and also the tomb of Sir Stephen Jenyns, a former mayor of London (d. 1523) buried in the London Grey Friars (Figures 88a–c).

Shortly after Wriothesley completed his account, Thomas Hawley, Carlisle Herald at Arms, visited a number of parish churches and religious houses in the city of London during 1530 and recorded several monuments which were of interest to him. Four years later, his colleague Thomas Benolt, Clarenceaux King of Arms, also undertook a visitation and recorded other tombs.[4] Several of these accounts were seen by John Stow (1525–1605) who included records of the city's burials and tombs in his *Survey of London*, first published in 1598. By this date, almost all of the monuments from London's mendicant houses (along with many others from the religious houses and some parish churches) had been lost, a loss Stow deplored in the *Survey*. Writing about the Austin Friars, Stow criticised the actions of William Paulet, marquis of Winchester (d. 1572), who had: 'sold the monuments of noble men there buried in great numbers, the paving stone, and whatsoever (which cost many thousands) for one hundred pounds, and in place thereof made fayre stabling for horses'.[5] There is a sense here of Stow's moralistic outrage, not only at the loss of the monuments but also at the ignominious reuse of the church space where many remained interred.

Stow's distress at the loss of a large part of London's commemorative heritage led to his criticism of Sir Martin Bowes (d. 1566), alderman, who sold off the monuments from the London Grey Friars 'for 50 pounds, or thereabouts'.[6] Fortunately, an important record of the burials and monuments from the Grey Friars has survived in the form of a Register which contains transcripts of a number of documents relating to the foundation of the London house and also a list of 682 monuments of the dead. This burial list, which was

---

[3] A second manuscript at the College of Arms, A17 of c. 1505, records many monuments from London's parish churches and religious houses, but the former is the fuller version.

[4] Sir Anthony R. Wagner, *Heralds and Heraldry in the Middle Ages* (Oxford: Oxford University Press, 1939), pp. 139–46. Later lists of tombs were made including BL, MS 6033 which is a copy of College of Arms, MS CGY 647.

[5] Stow, *Survey of London*, i, 177. It is perhaps ironic that at the time these monuments were being sold off by Paulet, he was making arrangements for his and other family memorials in the church of St Mary, Basing, in Hampshire: Nikolaus Pevsner and David Lloyd, *Hampshire and the Isle of Wight*, The Buildings of England (New Haven and London: Yale University Press, 2002), p. 89.

[6] Stow, *Survey of London*, i, 322.

Fig. 88. Tombs of: a) William, Viscount Beaumont (d. 1507), Black Friars; b) Richard Beauchamp, Lord St Amand (d. 1508), Black Friars; c) Sir Stephen Jenyns (d. 1523), Grey Friars. (© The British Library Board, Add. MS 45131, ff. 88v, 82, 86)

Fig. 88. (continued): b) Richard Beauchamp, Lord St Amand (d. 1508), Black Friars

276　THE FRIARIES OF MEDIEVAL LONDON

Fig. 88. (continued): c) Sir Stephen Jenyns (d. 1523), Grey Friars

made about 1525, was probably intended to be of practical use and a means to identify available grave space for later burials in the convent.[7] This is an important – and remarkable – document for there is nothing comparable for any other London religious house.[8] The list recorded the exact location of many of the monuments within the Grey Friars convent, sometimes in relation to the position of other tombs. The tomb chest of William Maryner, for example (the one that John Smith asked to copy), was recorded in a list of memorials located in the north aisle. The compiler of the Register sometimes recorded a description of the monument, such as *tumba elevata* (raised tomb) for Maryner, and also details from the inscription:

> ... in tumba elevate jacet Willelmus Mariner, civis et salter Londonie, Agnes et Juliana uxores eius: qui W[illiam] obit 9 die mensis Aprilis, A. dni. 1512: Agnes obit 27 die mensis Maii A. domi 1500 et Juliana ... die mensis ... A. dni. 15 ... .[9]

Juliana outlived her husband and died in 1517. Although she requested burial in the Grey Friars, she was either buried elsewhere or her executors overlooked adding her date of death to the Maryner memorial.[10]

At the Austin Friars, material evidence survived in the form of indents from lost brasses. These indents are impressions left in the marble showing the outline of the brass. Those from the Austin Friars were unfortunately lost during the Blitz (the church was destroyed by an incendiary bomb in October 1940) but a record of them had been made by Frank Greenhill in 1923 when he visited the Dutch Church, which occupied the medieval nave of the friary (Chapter 6: Austin Friars). He recorded forty indents most of which he dated to the late fifteenth and early sixteenth centuries, based on their design and composition.[11] It is noteworthy that many of the early fifteenth-century indents were for inscription brasses without an accompanying effigy of the deceased. By the end of the fifteenth and early sixteenth centuries, figure brasses had become more affordable and popular, hence the sixteen indents recorded from the Austin Friars; three examples are illustrated in Figure 89.

Elsewhere, palimpsests, that is reused brasses where the reverse bears an earlier composition, provide further information on lost memorials from London's mendicant houses: for

---

[7] BL, Cotton Vitellius F xii, ff. 274–316, printed in *Grey Friars*, pp. 70–177. This record of tombs and monuments has been used to create a burial map, see Ernest B.S. Shepherd, 'The Church of the Friars Minor in London', *Archaeological Journal*, 59 (1902), 239–87, plate 1.

[8] A similar document also survives for the Coventry Grey Friars in BL, Harley 6033, ff. 17–19 which records a list of burials and tombs from c. 1270 until c. 1400. This list is printed in Iain Soden, *Coventry: The Hidden History* (Stroud: Tempus, 2005), pp. 67–71, and discussed in Peter Coss, *The Foundations of Gentry Life: The Multons of Frampton and their World, 1270–1370* (Oxford: Oxford University Press, 2010), pp. 154–63.

[9] *Grey Friars*, p. 119.

[10] LMA, GL MS 9171/9, f. 37.

[11] F.A. Greenhill, 'Austin Friars, London', *Transactions of the Monumental Brass Society*, 8.1 (1949), 330–41.

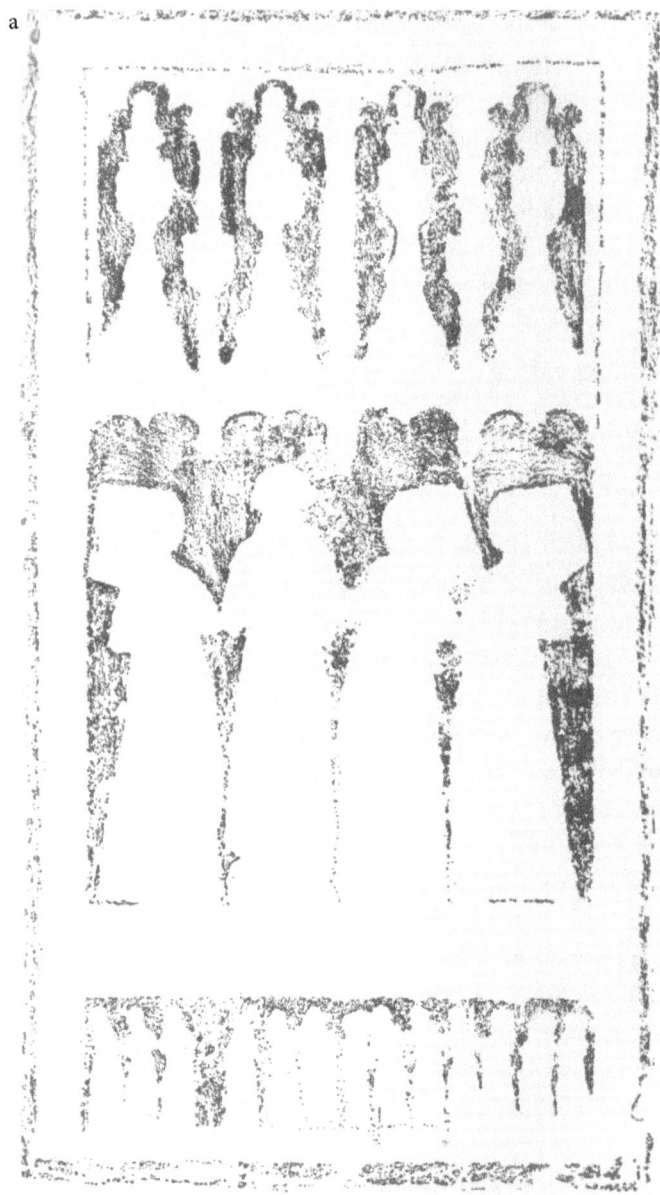

Fig. 89. Indents of memorial brasses from Austin Friars: a) a civilian with three wives, c. 1480; b) a civilian, c. 1480; c) a civilian kneeling at a prie-dieu, early sixteenth century. (rubbing by F.A. Greenhill, reproduced from Greenhill, 'Austin Friars, London', with permission from the Monumental Brass Society)

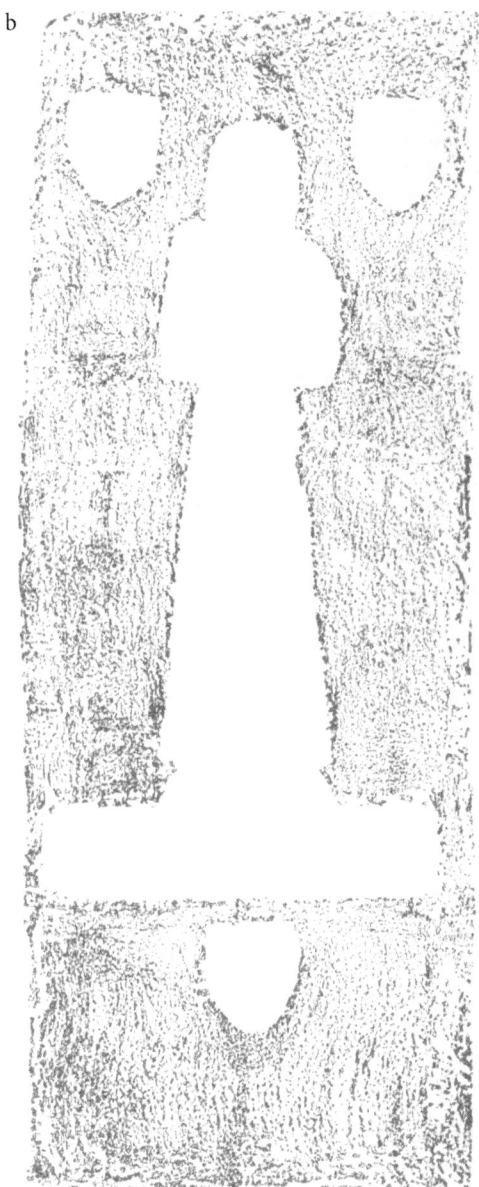

Fig. 89. (continued)

example, at Magdalen College, Oxford, there is an inscription brass for Margery (d. 1432) the wife of William Chamberlain which had been taken from the Grey Friars;[12] at Holy Trinity, Blatherwyck (Northamptonshire), the reverse of a brass dated 1548 contains an inscription to

[12] John Page-Phillips, *Palimpsests: The Backs of Monumental Brasses*, 2 vols (London: Monumental Brass Society, 1980), i, 56; *Grey Friars*, p. 87.

Fig. 89. (continued)

Katherine Strangeways (d. 1504) and her brother Jasper Fylioll and his wife Joan (who died c. 1536) which had been taken from the Black Friars;[13] and at St Mary, Standon (Hertfordshire), there is another palimpsest of 1557 with the coat of arms from the tomb of Sir Richard Empson (d. 1510) which had been removed from the White Friars.[14] In all three cases the

---

[13] TNA, PROB 11/14, f. 168v (an extract of which was printed in Raymund Palmer, 'Burials at the Priories of the Black Friars', *The Antiquary*, 23 (1891), 122–5; vol. 24 (1891), pp. 28–30, 76–9, 117–20 (vol. 24, p. 76); Page-Phillips, *Palimpsests*, i, 49. For Jasper Fylioll see, Sir John Baker, *The Men of Court 1450–1550: A Prosopography of the Inns of Court and Chancery and the Courts of Law*, 2 vols (London, 2012), i, 720.

[14] Page-Phillips, *Palimpsests*, i, 55; William Lack, H. Martin Stuchfield and Philip Whittemore, *The Monumental Brasses of Hertfordshire* (Stratford St Mary: Intercity Print, 2009), p. 594.

brasses were removed after the Dissolution and reused. But some monuments were moved and reassembled elsewhere in an effort to maintain their commemorative function. In the parish church of St Mary, Tilty (Essex), for example, there is a brass effigy for Gerard Danet (d.1520), gentleman, which appears to have been removed from the Black Friars (Figure 90). The inscription on the brass at Tilty includes the name of Danet's widow, Mary (d. 1558), but not her date of death. It seems likely that after the surrender of the London Black Friars, Mary arranged for the removal of their joint monumental brass (and perhaps Danet's body) to St Mary's church in Tilty where she owned property.[15] This was not unusual: Dame Joan Milbourne (d. 1545), another London widow, made similar arrangements to move the body and tomb of her husband, the former mayor Sir John Milbourne (d. 1536), from the Crossed Friars to the parish church of St Edmund Lombard Street, where it was noted by John Stow.[16] The sculptured effigy for Sir Richard Cholmeley (d. 1521) and his wife Dame Elizabeth was also moved from the Crossed Friars following the house's surrender in 1538 (Figure 57). In his will, Sir Richard asked to be buried in St Mary's Chapel, in the parish church of All Hallows Barking by the Tower, 'on thoderside against where Sir John Rysley knyght lyeth buried'. If the master and wardens of the chapel did not agree then he requested burial within the Crossed Friars before the image of St Mary the Virgin.[17] There is no evidence that Sir Richard's request for burial by the tomb of Sir John was fulfilled and he was instead buried in his second choice, the Crossed Friars, only to be exhumed and transplanted with his monument to the Chapel of St Peter ad Vincula in the Tower of London.

Together these various sources record over a thousand lost tombs from the churches of London's mendicant houses. There were probably many other earlier monuments which had been worn away or removed by the time the various written accounts were made. One such known loss was the tombstone of Bernat de Jambe (d. c. 1270–90) from the Grey Friars. This tomb was not recorded in the Register, but the indent was found on the site in c. 1835 and it is likely that it had been removed from the convent during the rebuilding work of the early fourteenth century.[18] There were almost certainly many other tombs which were lost in the medieval period through rebuilding and reordering works, or through natural wear and tear.

Of the known tombs in London's mendicant houses, 684 were at the Grey Friars (Franciscans), 130 at the Black Friars (Dominicans), 94 at the Austin Friars, 86 at the White

---

[15] TNA, PROB 11/42A, ff. 125v–127v; Palmer, 'Burials at the Priories of the Black Friars', vol. 24, p. 79; William Lack, H. Martin Stuchfield and Philip Whittemore, *The Monumental Brasses of Essex*, 2 vols (London: Intercity Print, 2003), ii, 714, 716. One of the late medieval emptied tombs found by archaeologists at Black Friars might have belonged to Danet: Chapter 19: Dissolution.

[16] Stow, *Survey of London*, i, 202–3. This was destroyed in the fire of 1666 and is discussed further in Christian Steer, '"Better in Remembrance": Medieval Commemoration at the Crutched Friars, London', *Journal of the Church Monuments Society*, 25 (2010), pp. 36–57.

[17] TNA, PROB 11/20, ff. 175v–176v.

[18] Bruce Watson and Christopher Thomas, 'The Mendicant Houses of Medieval London: An Archaeological Review', in *The Friars in Medieval Britain*, ed. N. Rogers, Harlaxton Medieval Studies, 19 (Donington: Shaun Tyas, 2010), pp. 265–97 (p. 273).

Fig. 90. Monumental brass of Gerard Danet (d. 1520), St Mary's church, Tilty, Essex, probably moved from the London Black Friars Church at the Dissolution. (reproduced from Lack et al., *The Monumental Brasses of Essex*, with permission)

Friars (Carmelites) and 27 at the Crossed or Crutched Friars. Since these tombs often contained wives and children as well as the (usually male) principal occupant, we know from their lost inscriptions of at least a further 193 burials within the London mendicant churches. With the exception of the Crossed Friars – the 'little brother' of the London orders – there were sufficiently large numbers of burials in London's mendicant houses to make them rich in funeral monuments. Some of these tombs were spectacular and would have been visible and eye-catching to visitors as well as to the friars themselves. However, it should be borne in mind that much of the evidence (with the exception of the Grey Friars) has come from heralds' visitations and as a consequence the records are biased towards royal, aristocratic and knightly burials which displayed elaborate coats of arms; women and the friars themselves are almost certainly under-represented.[19] There is little archaeological or documentary evidence for tombs and markers to commemorate the hundreds of ordinary Londoners buried in the external cemeteries of the London friaries.[20]

Monuments for royalty

Following Henry III's great thirteenth-century building campaign, Westminster Abbey became the principal mausoleum of English kings. But if the royal family wanted an alternative place of burial in London, they selected either the Grey Friars or the Black Friars.[21] Queen Margaret (d. 1318), consort of Edward I, and Queen Isabella (d. 1358), wife of Edward II, were buried before the high altar of the Grey Friars and commemorated with sculptured effigies.[22] Queen Isabella's tomb also contained the heart of her murdered husband. The queen's tomb was based on a contract made during her lifetime and constructed immediately after her death in 1358–9. Two payments totalling £106 18s 11d were made to the workshop of Agnes de Ramsay, daughter of the royal mason William de Ramsay (d. 1349). An iron grille that surrounded the tomb was constructed by Andrew Faber who was paid £110 and the masonry work was carried out by Robert de Burton who was paid £10. These payments had been settled by February 1359. Cadet members of the English royal family were also buried at the Grey Friars. These included Joan, queen of Scotland (d. 1362), and, Isabella, countess of Bedford (d. 1379), wife of Ingelram de Coucy, respectively daughter and granddaughter of Queen Isabella. Both were buried next to Isabella's tomb in the choir.[23] The heart of Queen Eleanor (d. 1290) was buried at the Black Friars, probably at the request of

---

[19] For tombs of friars see Christian Steer, 'The Franciscans and their Graves' in *St Francis and his Followers: Studies on the Medieval English Franciscan Province and Beyond*, ed. M. Robson and P. Zutshi (forthcoming).

[20] See Chapter 2: The Second Black Friars, 1275–1538, 'The precinct', for a discussion of the churchyard at Black Friars.

[21] Steer, 'Royal and Noble Commemoration'.

[22] *Grey Friars*, pp. 70 (Queen Margaret) and 74 (Queen Isabella).

[23] F.D. Blackley, 'The Tomb of Isabella of France, Wife of Edward II of England', *International Society for the Study of Church Monuments*, Bulletin 8 (1983), pp. 161–4.

her husband Edward I, and this formed part of a larger commemorative strategy for the dead queen: her body at Westminster Abbey, her viscera at Lincoln Cathedral and twelve crosses – the Eleanor Crosses – at the sites where her funeral cortege stopped. Edward had already demonstrated his particular devotion to the Dominicans by choosing their first priory in Holborn as the burial site for the hearts of his son and heir Prince Alphonso (d. 1284) and the king's young cousins Margaret (d. 1276) and William (d. 1277) de Valence (Chapter 1: The First Black Friars in Holborn). Edward was also the principal benefactor of the refoundation of the Black Friars in the 1280s and during these construction works the remains of the three children and their monuments were moved to the refounded church (Chapter 2: The Second Black Friars).[24] Nothing is known about the appearance of their monuments but they probably consisted of small caskets similar to the one used to commemorate the heart of Queen Eleanor.[25] There were no royal burials at the other mendicant houses, probably because the royal family had not been involved in their foundation. There were also no royal burials in the London houses after the mid fourteenth century when royalty chose burial in Westminster Abbey or in their foundations elsewhere in the kingdom.[26]

Aristocratic commemoration

The English nobility, like royalty, played a key role in the foundation of London's mendicant houses. And as founders and benefactors, the aristocracy were also buried in these houses, including, for example, Humphrey de Bohun (d. 1361), earl of Hereford and Essex, who had contributed to the rebuilding of the Austin Friars church.[27] He was also a descendant of the founder, another Humphrey, and the earl seems to have maintained his ancestor's patronage and support of the convent when he decided to be buried in the middle of its choir and probably before the high altar. His tomb is not described in any of the sources but it is likely to have been of some craftsmanship and magnificence, as befitted the benefactor and the location. It may have been a sculptured effigy set onto a tomb chest with the earl posed in prayer, similar to the tombs for the queens at the Grey Friars. There is some evidence to suggest that these mendicant houses became the preferred place of burial for the family of founders or patrons if they happened to die in London. Hugh Courtenay, earl of Devon (d. 1377), had sponsored works in the choir of the Carmelite house in Fleet Street, for example, and the church was used as a place of burial for the earl's grandson and heir Sir Hugh Courtenay (d. 1374) and also the earl's second son Sir Edward, who predeceased

---

[24] On royal children's monuments see, Sally Badham and Sophie Oosterwijk, 'The Tomb Monument of Katherine, Daughter of Henry III and Eleanor of Provence (1253–7)', *Antiquaries Journal*, 92 (2012), 169–96.

[25] Colvin, *King's Works*, i, 482–3.

[26] David Palliser, 'Royal Mausolea in the Long Fourteenth Century (1272–1422)', *Fourteenth Century England*, 3 (Woodbridge: Boydell, 2004), 1–15.

[27] Stow, *Survey of London*, i, 178.

his father (dying between 1364 and 1372).[28] The White Friars also contained several tombs of members of the Grey family – descendants of Sir Richard Grey (d. after 1265) – including John, Lord Grey (d. 1418, son of Reginald, Lord Grey of Wilton), and Richard Grey, earl of Kent (d. 1524), in whose tomb his widow Margaret requested burial in her will of 1540.[29] None of them is known to have been a benefactor of the London house but they evidently wished to retain the Grey association with the Carmelites by choosing burial there.

A mausoleum for Elizabeth Botiller, baroness de Wemme (d. 1411), and several members of her immediate family seems to have been set up at the Crossed Friars on the instructions of the baroness. In her will, Lady Wemme arranged for monuments for her third husband Sir Thomas de Molington (d. 1408), her son Robert Ferers (d. 1396) and his wife Elizabeth and their son Lionel. There is no reference to the baroness's own tomb in her will but given that her family had predeceased her it seems very likely that she oversaw the production of these tombs in the Lady chapel during her own lifetime. The only other known tomb for a member of the nobility in this house was that for Henry the son of William, Lord Lovell (d. 1455).[30]

Aristocratic mausoleums in London were rare because the nobility usually only visited the city and were rarely long-term residents. They had alternative – and more permanent – places for burial near their country seats. It was not until the creation of a 'new' nobility in the late fifteenth century that any effort was made to secure a long-term familial centre of aristocratic commemoration in London's friaries. The first to attempt this were members of the Blount family (the lords Mountjoy) who created a mausoleum for themselves in the chapel of the Apostles at the Grey Friars.[31] This contained the tombs of Walter, first Lord Mountjoy, his grandson and successor Edward, John (third Lord Mountjoy) and various members of the Blount family, including the first lord's heir, Sir William, who was killed at the battle of Barnet in 1471. The importance of this mausoleum was such that in his will of 1534, William, fourth Lord Mountjoy, set out a series of instructions to rebuild several of his family's monuments.[32] By this date there were at least seven Blount family monuments in the chapel, which must have been highly impressive, if rather cluttered. Once the Blount family had claimed this chapel as 'their space' there were very few burials for non-Blounts recorded within it.[33]

---

[28] Stow, *Survey of London*, ii, 46–7.

[29] Stow, *Survey of London*, ii, 46 (John, Lord Grey) and TNA, PROB 11/28, ff. 152–3 (Margaret, countess of Kent, in which she requested her burial in the tomb of her late husband, Richard, earl of Kent).

[30] Steer, 'Better in remembrance', p. 45; Lord Lovell chose to be buried in the Oxford Grey Friars; Little, *Grey Friars of Oxford*, p. 26.

[31] *Grey Friars*, pp. 88–9.

[32] TNA, PROB 11/25, f. 243; Steer, 'Royal and Noble Commemoration', pp. 137–41.

[33] After their appropriation of the chapel, there were only four non-Blount burials in this chapel, namely for the respected friars William Goddard (d. 1485) and Robert Brayns (d. 1492); Thurstan Hatfield (d. 1491), sergeant to Edward IV and who possibly served with the Blounts; and Robert Bradbery about whom nothing further is known.

Not all members of the nobility died peacefully and many of those who were executed were buried in the mendicant houses. This was partly because of the tradition of aristocratic interment in these houses but is also a reflection on their status, and the friars' convenient neutrality. Richard Fitzalan, earl of Arundel (executed 1397), John de Vere, earl of Oxford and his son Sir Aubrey (both ex. 1462) and Edward Stafford, duke of Buckingham (ex. 1522), were all buried at the Austin Friars.[34] The remains of James Fiennes, lord Saye and Sele, beheaded during Cade's revolt of 1450, were buried at the Grey Friars, and at the Black Friars the executed remains of 'the Butcher of England', John Tiptoft, earl of Worcester (ex. 1470), and James Tutchet, Lord Audley (ex. 1497), were interred.[35] Strangely there were no tombs of executed nobles at the Crossed Friars in spite of its proximity to Tower Green; perhaps this was because few aristocrats had been buried there and so this was not considered a sufficiently prestigious location for the last resting place of members of the nobility.

Military knights and their tombs

Perhaps the most striking feature of burial and commemoration in London's friaries is the high number of tombs recorded for knights. Of these a minority were for civic knights, that is those who had been knighted for service in the city as alderman or mayor (below: 'Memorials for Londoners'). Others were what can best be described as civil servants who had been rewarded for their service to the Crown by a knighthood. But the majority of knightly burials were for military men who had served the state in warfare and were buried in London. One of the most famous of this band of brothers was Sir Robert Knolles (d. 1407) who was a major benefactor of the London White Friars where his wife Constance was buried c. 1389.[36] Sir Robert died in 1407, and following his death at his manor at Sculthorpe (Norfolk) his body was brought to London to be buried with his wife in a joint tomb. In 1530 Thomas Hawley, Carlisle Herald of Arms, described Sir Robert and Lady Constance as 'lying in Pykter of Alyblaster on a Towme of Marbyll', which suggests that these were alabaster effigies set on to a tomb chest.[37] Such a monument would have been in keeping for a man of Sir Robert's wealth and status, and for such a major benefactor of the convent.

Sir Robert Knolles had evidently wanted to be buried with his wife in the church of the White Friars to which he had contributed substantially during the rebuilding of the 1380s and 1390s (Chapter 5: White Friars, c. 1247–1538, 'Acquiring and developing the friary'). Other military knights seem to have been buried in the friaries for different reasons,

---

[34] Stow, *Survey of London*, i, 178–9.
[35] *Grey Friars*, p. 76 (Saye and Sele); Stow, *Survey of London*, i, 341 (Worcester and Audley).
[36] Michael Jones, 'Knolles, Sir Robert (d. 1407)', *ODNB*, <http://www.oxforddnb.com/view/article/15758> [accessed 13 May 2015].
[37] Wagner, *Heralds and Heraldry*, p. 141.

probably out of convenience when they died unexpectedly while in London. Sir Andrew Sackville, for example, was buried at the Grey Friars in 1369 having died while away from his Sussex estates.[38] The wives and children of country knights might also die away from home: Lady Cradock, wife of Sir David Cradock of Nuneaton (Cheshire), was buried in the Austin Friars rather in their parish church of St Mary in Nuneaton where her husband was to be buried c. 1384.[39]

The popularity of knightly burial in an urban centre is not surprising given that the fourteenth and fifteenth centuries saw a great deal of military mobility and campaigning, and included a civil war. During the Wars of the Roses many knights were buried in London's mendicant houses. Some, such as Sir William Blount, killed at Barnet (1471), enjoyed the privileges of nobility in death; he was buried within his family's mausoleum at the Grey Friars. Others, such as Sir Thomas Tuddenham who was executed in 1462 for his part in the assassination plot to kill Edward IV, were buried in the Austin Friars; Tuddenham was interred alongside his fellow conspirators, the earl of Oxford and his son Sir Aubrey.[40] There is some uncertainty about the monument Stow recorded at the Austin Friars for 'the lorde Barons slaine at Barnet' for there were few noble casualties from this particular battle during the Wars of the Roses and none who can readily be identified as 'Lord Barons'. It is possible that this was a cenotaph memorial whose commemorative function dovetailed with the chapel dedicated to St Blaise on the battlefield. A more intriguing possibility is that this was the original monument for Sir Humphrey Bourchier, son and heir of Lord Berners, who was killed during the battle. His burial on the south side of the choir in the Austin Friars was recorded on Easter Monday, 1471.[41] Sir Humphrey was evidently exhumed later during the Yorkist reigns and transplanted to Westminster Abbey where in c. 1500 the herald Thomas Benolt identified him on his tomb as 'lord barnes'.[42] The political turmoil endured into the reign of Henry VII when others, less fortunate at manoeuvring themselves through the complex web of political alliances, fell victim through their support for the wrong candidate. Sir James Tyrell (ex. 1502) was buried in the Austin Friars following his alleged allegiance to Edmund de la Pole, earl of Suffolk, the Yorkist heir.[43] Executed knights, like the nobility who were the victims of political conflict, were also buried in London's mendicant houses.

---

[38] *Grey Friars*, p. 128.
[39] Stow, *Survey of London*, i, 178.
[40] Stow, *Survey of London*, i, 178.
[41] Stow, *Survey of London*, i, 178; Christian Steer, 'The Lorde Barons Slaine at Barnet Field', *Ricardian*, 26 (2016), 87–98. For a list of those of knightly and noble rank who died at Barnet, see Livia Visser-Fuchs, 'A Ricardian Riddle: The Casualty List of the Battle of Barnet', *Ricardian*, 8(100), 1988, 9–12.
[42] College of Arms, MS CGY 647 f. 2v. Sir Humphrey's father John Bourchier, Lord Berners, died in 1474 and was buried in Chertsey Abbey, Surrey; Steer, 'Lorde Barons Slaine at Barnet Field'.
[43] Stow, *Survey of London*, i, 179.

Alien burials

One of the distinctive features of London's mendicant houses is the burials of aliens, that is those who died while visiting from overseas. The various written sources record thirty-nine instances of aliens who chose to be buried in and commemorated by a tomb in a city convent. Very few aliens were recorded as buried elsewhere in the city, and there were hardly any in the parish churches. There were also no alien burials recorded at either the White Friars or at the Crossed Friars. It is particularly surprising that there were none at the Crossed Friars given that the fraternity of the Holy Blood of Wilsnack was founded in the church in 1459, together with the Brotherhood of St Catherine established the same year. Both were established for the 'Doche' (i.e. German- and Dutch-speaking) community with a large Flemish membership.[44] It is possible that the relative poverty of the alien craftsmen explains their lack of tombs, although the fire here in 1490 or '91 may have destroyed several older monuments, including some for the alien community (Chapter 7: Crossed Friars, 'Acquiring and developing the friary').

Of the thirty-nine recorded tombs, ten were for alien members of the nobility who had died in London. At the Austin Friars, for example, were the burials of Guy de Châtillon, count of St Pol (d. 1317), in the choir and of Guy d'Angle (d. 1380), who had been created earl of Huntingdon by his former pupil Richard II and whose burial was recorded in the 'west wing' of the convent.[45] In St John's chapel at the Austin Friars, two French lords, Angleur and Tremayle, were buried although nothing further is known of them.[46] They were possibly captives from the Hundred Years War who died as prisoners of war while their ransom was being arranged. There were also two aristocratic tombs at the Black Friars, of John de Bermingham, earl of Louth and justiciar of Ireland (d. 1329), and Robert of Artois, count of Beaumont (d. 1342).[47] Their choice to be interred in London's friaries may reflect the fact that their English counterparts had already made the London convents a natural place of burial when dying away from home.

Although it is known that the Italian community in London were particularly associated with the Austin Friars, none of their inscriptions were recorded with the exception of one for Lucia Visconti, countess of Kent (d. 1424).[48] This was copied down by Thomas Benolt in c. 1500, probably from a hanging board adjacent to her tomb which recorded (in translation):

---

[44] Colson, 'Alien Communities'; Steer, 'Better in Remembrance', pp. 40–2.
[45] Stow, *Survey of London*, i, 178 (St Pol) and 179 (Huntingdon).
[46] College of Arms, MS CGY 647, f. 16. Neither was recorded by Stow.
[47] Stow, *Survey of London*, i, 340.
[48] Helen Bradley, 'Italian Merchants in London 1350–1450' (unpublished doctoral thesis, University of London, Royal Holloway, 1992), pp. 13–62; Helen Bradley, 'Lucia Visconti, Countess of Kent (d. 1424)', in *Medieval London Widows, 1300–1500*, ed. C.M. Barron and A.F. Sutton (London: Hambledon, 1994), 77–84. I thank David Moncur for his assistance in translating this complicated and muddled epitaph.

Here lies Lucia daughter of Bernabo the Magnificent
most celebrated scion of the Lord of Milan
two of her sisters were queens of Cyprus
three were Duchesses of Bavaria, a fourth of Austria
a fifth holds the rich dukedom of Milan;
[there was] also a Countess of Wurtemburg, one too who was Mantua's
worthy mistress. A niece was that [worthy] queen
of France, her great-niece a famous queen
of England. Thus her fame flew to the four corners of the earth
through her virtues, the charm of her manners and her beauty.
What now does such great honour, what now do earthly delights
profit her since they have not the strength to ward off such a great thing [i.e. death]?

Given the extent of the genealogical information, and the rarity of such a text, it is perhaps not surprising that the herald chose to write it down. This reflects the interests of the heralds who only copied out what was of importance to them rather than compiling a complete account. The survival of the Register of the Grey Friars, however, shows that men such as Andrew de Maneriis (d. 1390), a merchant from Florence, and Peter de Balby (d. 1430) from Venice chose to be buried and commemorated in the chapel of St Francis. The Register also shows that members of the Bardi company chose burial there, including Dinus Forceti (or Forcinetti/Forsetti) (d. about 1349) and Philip Bardi (d. 1362). Both were buried in the ambulatory. None of these tombs was recorded by the heralds and it seems very likely that many of the Italian burials at the Austin Friars may well have had a commemorative tomb but one that was not sufficiently impressive to attract the interests of the heralds.

Memorials for Londoners

There were comparatively few monuments for Londoners themselves in the city convents. The lists of burials and tombs from the Austin and White Friars, for example, show very few instances of Londoners enjoying commemoration in either place. This is again perhaps because of the bias of the heraldic visitations. The Black Friars appears to have been rather more popular with Londoners as a place for burial and commemoration compared with the Austin and White Friars: for example, the citizen and grocer William Hanwell (d. 1446) was buried at Black Friars where he had already arranged his marble stone,[49] but this was not recorded in the written accounts. Neither was the brass for John Gulle, citizen and spurrier (d. 1465), which he had requested his executors to commission following his burial in the Dominican church.[50] This is not to say that their tombs were not made; it is quite possible that neither memorial was considered to be worth noting when the heralds visited.

[49] LMA, GL MS 9171/4, f. 189.
[50] LMA, GL MS 9171/5, f. 368v.

There is considerably more evidence for Londoners' monuments in the Grey Friars. In part this is because the Register provides such a full account but it is also explained by the early enthusiasm which greeted the Grey Friars on their arrival in the city around 1225. It was not until almost eighty years later that royalty took an active interest in the house, which in turn acted as a trigger for the nobility to follow their lead with their own gifts. Yet Londoners continued to give generously during the rebuilding projects at the Grey Friars and this is seen in their financing, both as individuals and also later as the companies, of the glazing of the church. For instance, the alderman Simon Parys (d. 1324) and his wife Rose, and the former sheriff Walter Mordon (d. 1351) with his wife Christina, contributed towards the costs of glazing as did the Vintners' Company (between 1313 and 1336) and the Drapers' Company (before 1350).[51] In spite of their role as benefactors, it seems that many Londoners did not seriously consider the Grey Friars as a place of burial until the 1370s. One of the earliest burials was that of Sir John Philipot (d. 1384), a former mayor, who in his will requested burial next to his wife Joan (d. 1374) who had been interred in the Grey Friars ten years earlier.[52] The Register records their monument in the chapel of the Apostles and, from this description, the tomb seems to have been a flat (perhaps Purbeck) marble stone with a monumental brass which recorded their dates of death, together with a second brass recording the burial there of Joan's son Master John Sampford, also fixed on the stone. Immediately to the left of their memorial were the remains of Sir John's associate and brother-in-law Sir Nicholas Brembre, who was executed in 1388.[53] He too was buried under a large stone (*magno lapide*). It is striking that Brembre was buried next to Sir John, almost certainly a deliberate choice.

There appear to have been very few Londoners buried in the Grey Friars during the first half of the fifteenth century. John Vyaunde, a grocer (d. 1410), was one example who wished to be buried in the chapel of All Hallows;[54] elsewhere the brewer John Basset was buried in the nave in 1424;[55] a little later, Thomas Berow, a vintner (d. 1433), was buried in the south aisle.[56] The absence of large numbers of memorials for Londoners in this period at the Grey Friars may stem from the fact that the early fifteenth century saw a greater choice of burial places in London as a result of the substantial rebuilding work taking place in many of the parish churches, such as at St Bride and St Dionis Backchurch.[57] This gave a wider choice of where to be buried, with new grave space now available within the parish churches. Elsewhere there were the initiatives of men such as John Neel, master of the Hospital of St Thomas of Acre (1420–63), who not only encouraged donations and gifts to

---

[51] *Grey Friars*, pp. 165, 167–8.
[52] *Grey Friars*, p. 91.
[53] *Grey Friars*, p. 91.
[54] *Grey Friars*, p. 78.
[55] *Grey Friars*, p. 115.
[56] *Grey Friars*, p. 124.
[57] John Schofield, 'Saxon and Medieval Parish Churches in the City of London: A Review', *Transactions of the London and Middlesex Archaeological Society*, 45 (1994), 23–146 (pp. 98–101).

his fundraising activities but also prompted an increase in the number of Londoners who chose to be buried in the hospital (especially mercers).[58] It is perhaps significant that after Sir John Philipot and Sir Nicholas Brembre were buried in the Grey Friars there were no other recorded civic office holders commemorated there for more than a hundred years, until the former mayor Sir Stephen Jenyns (d. 1523) elected to be buried here rather than in his parish church of St Andrew Cornhill (Undershaft).[59] The civic elite had evidently been attracted by other burial places and in particular by their own parish churches.

The smallest London house was the Crossed Friars where there are very few records of burials until the second half of the fifteenth century.[60] In the 1470s some Londoners, such as the skinner William Narborough (d. 1470) and his wife Elizabeth (d. 1483), chose to be buried in their Lady chapel.[61] But it was not until after the disastrous fire of 1490/1 that Londoners began in earnest to leave large sums to the Crossed friars and, increasingly, to choose this convent as their place of burial. There were Londoners from the whole social spectrum. Former office holders such as John Rest, grocer and former mayor (d. 1523), Sir John Skevington, merchant tailor and a former sheriff (d. 1525), and Sir John Milbourne, draper and former mayor (d. 1536), were all buried and commemorated in the Crossed Friars.[62] Other London men and women similarly wished to be buried here, including the widow Isabel Edwarde (d. 1490; she preferred burial on her own here rather than with her late husband William Edwarde, grocer and mayor, at the Austin Friars), the mercer Hugh Brown (d. 1500) and Oliver Turner (d. 1520), a porter at the Tower of London.[63] In the years immediately preceding the Dissolution, the London Crossed Friars had clearly become a popular place of burial for Londoners of all backgrounds.

Conclusion

This chapter has attempted to show the different patterns of commemoration in the mendicant houses of medieval London. The larger – and oldest – houses, the Grey Friars and the Black Friars, were popular places of burial for the royal consorts and cadet members of the royal family until the mid fourteenth century. Their evident enthusiasm for the mendicants led the aristocracy to follow this lead and to become benefactors themselves and, likewise, to adopt these friaries as places of burial and remembrance. There seems to

---

[58] Anne F. Sutton, 'The Hospital of St Thomas of Acre of London: The Search for Patronage, Liturgical Improvement, and a School, under Master John Neel, 1420–63', in *The Late Medieval English College and its Context*, ed. C. Burgess and M. Heale (York: York Medieval Press, 2008), pp. 199–229.
[59] TNA, PROB 11/21, ff. 60v–61.
[60] Stow, *Survey of London*, i, 147; Steer, 'Better in Remembrance'.
[61] LMA, GL MS 9171/6, f. 50 [William]; TNA, PROB 11/7, ff. 52v–53 [Elizabeth].
[62] Stow, *Survey of London*, i, 147.
[63] Stow, *Survey of London*, i, 147 [Edwarde]; TNA, PROB 11/13, ff. 223v–225; Wagner, *Heralds and Heraldry*, p. 145 [Turner].

be little evidence that the established nobility intended to use any of the London houses as a long-term mausoleum for their families, although there were associations between some of the houses and certain families, such as the Courtenays and the Greys with the Carmelite house, and this made the choice of burial sites for members of their families who died in London an easier one. Lady Wemme's efforts at the Crossed Friars seem to reflect the intentions of a grieving matriarch to ensure a permanent memorial for the dead males of her family. Yet this study has also shown that some newly created members of the nobility took the opportunity to promote themselves and their families through the creation of a mausoleum in a prestigious London house. The Blounts' choice of the Grey Friars was surely inspired by the desire to be associated there with the royal tombs and with other, and older, aristocratic families. Military knights evidently also considered the London houses a convenient place of burial and their need for a memorial would, naturally, have been all the greater when they died away from home, hence the large numbers of tombs recorded for the knights and their families. It is possible that in this they were adopting the custom they had observed among the aristocracy, many of whom they would have known and served. Several members of the alien aristocracy who died in London adopted the same burial practices as their English counterparts. Merchants from overseas also chose burial in mendicant houses, perhaps because they were familiar with the friars' houses in their home cities. The Londoners, on the other hand, tended not to choose the mendicant houses for burial, although it is worth noting that Londoners' wills suggest that there were more citizens' tombs at the Black Friars than those recorded by the heralds. The evidence from the Grey Friars suggests that apart from a handful of very rich Londoners in the late fourteenth century, who had served in civic office, there was little demand for burial in this house until the late fifteenth century. But in the early sixteenth century it was the tomb in the Grey Friars of a London salter, William Maryner, that a visitor from Coventry admired, and he specified that his own monument was to be 'lyke to a tombe in the Greyfreres of London'.

18

London Friars and Londoners

Traditional monks and nuns lived a static and enclosed life in their convents, following St Benedict's rule of *stabilitas loci*; friars certainly had elements of this lifestyle but had a dual focus, looking inwards at the community and outwards at the town. The friars' liturgy and in-house schools represent the inward aspect (Chapter 16: Spiritual Life and Education in the London Friaries), but other aspects of the friars' lives were outward looking: they regularly stepped outside their precincts, going out into the city and supplying what might be termed spiritual services to Londoners, whether native, foreign or alien. These same Londoners increasingly came into the friars' convents (in life and in death) to 'consume' spiritual services and to use the spaces of the convents in a number of other ways; a comparison can be drawn between the thriving mercantile economy of London and the developing 'salvation market' of debits (sin) and credits (intercession and good works).[1] The relations between friars and Londoners were therefore quite extensive and surprisingly varied. It is notable that the surviving place-names relating to the London friaries nearly all derive from the way that Londoners saw or talked about the friars outside the friaries: 'Blackfriars' describes the black cloak the Dominicans wore in the street, not the white tunic and scapular they wore in church and cloister; 'Whitefriars' the white cloak of the Carmelites rather than their undyed wool tunic.[2] And the modern street of Crutched Friars takes its name from the way that Londoners pronounced the Latin name for the Crossed friars: *cruciferi* (presumably 'crutchy-furry').

The friars' patrons

Ordinary Londoners had begun to act as founders of religious institutions in the late twelfth century when the mercer Walter Brown (Brunus) and his wife Rosia endowed

---

[1] Bruzelius, *Preaching, Building, and Burying*, p. 8.
[2] Ó Clabaigh, *The Friars in Ireland*, pp. 118–24.

the hospital and priory of St Mary Spital.³ However, to found a religious house, especially one in London, was an expensive business and the founders of most houses were higher ranking landowners and nobility. The priory of the Sack friars was founded directly by Henry III and his daughter-in-law Eleanor of Castile, and the king was certainly a prominent supporter of many English monastic houses. The Dominican, Carmelite and Augustinian friars' houses were founded by members of the English nobility (respectively, Hubert de Burgh, earl of Kent, the baron Richard de Grey and Humphrey de Bohun, earl of Hereford and Essex). The founder of the Pied Friars, William Arnald, appears to have been a Middlesex knight, perhaps with a London connection. The Londoners Ralph Hosiar and William Sabernes founded the Crossed Friars in the 1260s and their names can be traced in London deeds of the period; they were presumably part of the same wealthy mercantile class as the St Mary Spital founders Walter and Rosia Brown. In the case of the Grey Friars, another London mercer, John Iwyn, founded the house in 1225. There is a good sense of his strong spiritual motivation: he actually joined the order at this time and so his foundation bequest was part of his renunciation of worldly goods. In his foundation grant (expressively translated by the seventeenth-century historian William Dugdale) he grants 'for the Health of my Soul, in pure and perpetual Alms, all the Ground I had, with the Houses built on the same which I had, in the parish of St Nicholas in the Shambles, there to entertain the poor Friers-Minors as long as they will stay there'.⁴ A detail of this grant reveals another aspect of the relationship between the Franciscan friars and Londoners: the foundation bequest was not directly to the friars but was to the City of London Corporation, who would hold the land on behalf of the friars. The Franciscans – but not the other mendicant orders – employed the same principle of ownership on trust by local civic authorities in many other English and Continental friaries.⁵

If few Londoners had the opportunity to found a whole friary from scratch, many townsmen and women facilitated the growth of the friaries by granting messuages that were adjacent to the foundation plots. This process has been traced at the first (Holborn) Black Friars, the Grey Friars and the Crossed Friars (the relative lack of documentation makes this harder to do for the other friaries), and the complexity and sheer length of the process surely demonstrates that the early priors had long-term plans for their friaries and that they cultivated good relations with their neighbours to encourage such generosity. Over the course of a century and a quarter the Franciscans accepted a series of twenty-six donations that followed the original gift from their new member John Iwyn (Table 5; Chapter 4: Grey Friars). The majority of these benefactors were London merchants like Joce fitz-Peter and Philip le Taillour, both sheriffs of the city at times in their careers, or the goldsmith William Moday. At the turn of the thirteenth and fourteenth centuries London donors like Henry le Waleys were acting in some sort of unofficial partnership, in co-operation with the civic

---

[3] Barron and Davies, *Religious Houses*, p. 7; Thomas, *St Mary Spital*, p. 19.
[4] Dugdale, *Monasticon*, vi(3), 1516.
[5] Röhrkasten, *Mendicant Houses*, p. 44.

authorities, the friars and their new royal sponsor, Margaret of France (the second wife of Edward I).[6] The friars' benefactors also included religious men like Bartholomew, a canon of the nearby priory and hospital of St Bartholomew. The wives and daughters of merchants also acted independently, such as Eleanor de Ewelle (a widow?) or, at the Crossed Friars, Herildis, daughter of William Burgoine. These Londoners allowed successive priors of the London friaries to create their precincts. Looking again at the maps of these urban and suburban tenements (Figure 4 for the Dominicans, Figure 20 for the Franciscans, Figure 53 for the Crossed friars, Figure 59 for the Sack friars and Figure 62 for the Pied friars), one can picture the priors playing, as it were, with their long-term jigsaw puzzles for a century or more, patiently piecing together viable urban monastic precincts.

For their major architectural projects, particularly grander ones, the priors usually looked to nobles or knights for financial support. As has been seen, the Dominicans and Franciscans enjoyed royal patronage in the thirteenth and fourteenth centuries; the Carmelites and Augustinian friars received financial help from nobles such as Hugh de Courtenay, earl of Devon, who sponsored work on a new choir at White Friars in the mid fourteenth century, or the earl of Hereford and Essex, Humphrey de Bohun (the great-great-grandson of the friary's founder), who allowed the completion of the Austin Friars nave at the same time. A few Londoners were wealthy enough to sponsor major building projects at the friary, among them the merchant and mayor Richard Whittington who contributed £400 towards the new library at Grey Friars and laid the foundation stone in 1411 (the finished building lasted into the nineteenth century and can be seen in Figure 27).

Relations between friars and Londoners

The friars and the friaries were undoubtedly important to many if not most medieval Londoners. The surviving records, however, tend to illustrate the relationship between friars and Londoners at the time of their death; it is harder to find evidence of *living* Londoners engaging with the friars. The friars provided Londoners with a spiritually potent cycle of charity, penance and intercession: townsmen and women gave alms to the friars, who then brought penance to the citizens through the sacrament of confession. After death the friars could intercede on behalf of Londoners through masses and anniversary funeral services.[7] Wills, while primarily aimed at the period after death, can also illuminate the testator's life: at least six Londoners remembered John Cutler, the early sixteenth-century guardian of the Grey Friars, in their wills, specifically acknowledging his valuable role as their confessor (Chapter 16: Spiritual Life and Education in the London Friaries).

---

[6] Laura Slater, 'Defining Queenship at Greyfriars London, c. 1300–1358', *Gender and History*, 27.1 (2015), 53–76.

[7] 'The interlinking axes of charity, penance and intercession that sustained mendicancy': Burgess, 'Friars and the Parish', pp. 74, 96. Burgess also points out the same problem of understanding the relations between friars and *living* townsmen and women.

It would be good to have some more evidence of how Londoners reacted to the preaching of the friars. Those attending sermons – in one of the huge friary naves or outdoors at the cemetery preaching crosses at Black and Austin Friars – may have listened attentively to the retelling of passages from the Scriptures and the *exempla* from Classical sources; did some in the audience go as far as Margery Kempe who joined in with a friar's sermon, crying and wailing, her spiritual passion awakened?[8] Friars also delivered sermons at parish churches, the churchyard cross at St Paul's and at the royal court. Perhaps inevitably, it is the controversial sermons of the friars that tend to leave the most documentary evidence, such as when the Augustinian friar Peter Patteshull preached his support at St Christopher le Stocks for John Wyclif and the Lollards.[9]

The friars performed a special role for London's foreigners and aliens who may have remained somewhat apart from the city's tight parish structure. Austin friars like the Venetian Francis Paul or the German Theoderich of Erfurt came to London from Oxford in the late fourteenth century in order to preach to and hear confessions from their London-based compatriots (Chapter 16: Spiritual Life and Education in the London Friaries). Religious confraternities of alien merchants met at Crossed Friars and Austin Friars, and these religious clubs seem to have been particularly important for German speakers who had, for example, the fraternity of St Sebastian at Austin Friars with its 'alman ymages and tabernacles . . . set upon the seid auter of seint Sebastian'.[10]

Citizens and aliens with close links to the friars in life would have wished to maintain that important spiritual connection after death. The friars could provide personnel for the funeral procession and service (even if the service was held at a parish church), a physical place of burial and commemoration, and a range of *post mortem* spiritual services including chantry masses and anniversary funeral services. The London chronicler Henry Machyn records the Dominicans' house style at funeral services and processions, here describing the elaborate ceremony for Cecily Mansel in 1558: 'the frers song durge [the *dirige* Office of the Dead] after ther songe, and bered her after ther fasyon, with-owt clarkes or prestes'.[11] Most London testators remained loyal to their parish church and requested burial there but they frequently requested the additional presence of friars in the funeral procession to the church and at the ensuing service.[12] Although little of the friars' equipment survived

---

[8] William H. Campbell, 'Franciscan Preaching in Thirteenth-Century England: Sources, Problems and Possibilities', in *The Friars in Medieval Britain: Proceedings of the 2007 Harlaxton Symposium*, ed. N. Rogers, Harlaxton Medieval Studies, 19 (Donington: Shaun Tyas, 2010), pp. 25–40; Barry Windeatt, 'Margary Kempe and the Friars', in *The Friars in Medieval Britain*, ed. Rogers, pp. 125–41.

[9] Röhrkasten, *Mendicant Houses*, pp. 453, 531.

[10] TNA, LR 15/13

[11] *The Diary of Henry Machyn: Citizen and Merchant-Taylor of London, from A.D. 1550 to A.D. 1563*, ed. John G. Nichols, Camden Society, old series, 42 (London: Camden Society, 1848), pp. 100, 174. The passage is quoted more fully in Chapter 3: The Third Black Friars at St Bartholomew's. Even though this describes a service during Mary's reign it probably represents the traditional funerary ceremonies of medieval Dominicans.

[12] Röhrkasten, *Mendicant Houses*, pp. 462–3.

the Reformation, we can imagine a Franciscan leading such a procession, carrying a silver gilt processional cross mounted on a pole like the late fifteenth-century examples surviving from Multyfarnham and Lislaughtin (both in Ireland).[13]

As has been discussed (Chapter 17: Burial and Commemoration in the London Friaries), some members of the London merchant class, a number of knights and some clusters of the nobility with particular connections to the capital chose a London friary for their place of burial and commemoration, in preference to their local church. If the actual choirs of these churches remained more or less reserved for living friars, the naves (and the side chapels of the choirs) were filled with the tombs and memorials of those aristocrats, knights, merchants and aliens. The Grey Friars has the best documentary evidence – the Register – and this lists 710 people buried in 682 tombs; adding another fifty or so people named in other sources, and making allowance for a few more wives and children, there must have been well over a thousand lay people buried in this one friary church.[14] One must then remember those buried outside in the friary churchyards; archaeological evidence reveals this cheaper and perhaps more popular option. No friary cemetery has been fully excavated but the sixty burials found on a site in the Dominican churchyard (Carter Lane, site PIC87) suggest that the full cemetery contained about a thousand people. The presence of women and children shows that many interred here were lay Londoners not friars.[15]

The big attraction of the friars to those drawing up their wills and contemplating the forthcoming horrors of Purgatory was, of course, the mendicants' ability to perform *post mortem* masses with all their special intercessory powers. The friars probably had a market advantage over other religious orders because they had more flexible rules and less full religious service timetables, which allowed them to supply priests for commemorative services as well as for processions and funerals. And, unlike the local parish church with its limited personnel, the friaries with their large cohorts of friars could ensure a rapid and early burst of *post mortem* masses. For the sum of 2s 6d a friary would undertake to perform a trental of masses for the soul of the testator – the rather neat pricing structure meant that the spiritual investment of thirty pence netted the intercessory return of thirty masses.[16] And

---

[13] Ó Clabaigh, *The Friars in Ireland*, plates 19, 20.
[14] BL, Cotton Vitellius F xii (ff. 274–316), printed in *Grey Friars*, pp. 70–133.
[15] In the excavated sample there were nearly three times as many men as women (2.8 male:1 female) and there was a relatively low proportion (13%) of children and adolescents. Thirteen of the burials had been interred in a burial trench, a type of mass grave associated with the mid-fourteenth-century Black Death. Assuming that the density of burials found on this site was the same throughout the cemetery, and that the cemetery originally extended from the church northwards to a postulated cemetery chapel by the city wall (as the evidence of a grave and a wall arcade found at site PRG431 might suggest), there could easily have been 1000 burials here. LAA, site PRG431 in 'Post Roman Gazetteer'; site PIC87, B. Watson, 'Excavations at 54/56–66 Carter Lane, 1–3 Pilgrim Street and 25–27 Ludgate Hill (PIC87)', unpublished Museum of London report, 1990 (pp. 47–64); Gilchrist and Sloane, *Requiem*, p. 241.
[16] Röhrkasten, *Mendicant Houses*, pp. 460–2.

this *post mortem* service was available to those buried elsewhere, for example in the local parish church.

Where more detailed contracts survive one can, on occasion, glimpse the living engaged in after-death planning for the whole family. For example, in 1490 William Berkeley, marquess of Berkeley, made a donation of £100 to the Austin friars: he was purchasing two perpetual daily chantry masses and an annual anniversary funeral service for his late wife, their deceased children, other family members and his own soul (the latter element of this investment was realised just two years later). The intention expressed in this contract was that Berkeley would rejoin his wife in death and be buried at the friary, 'at the awlters of our lady and saint Jamys'.[17] Sometimes the negotiations that took place after death are revealed when executors arranged the details of a testator's wishes with a particular friary. In one such surviving contract of 1515 the executors of Nicholas Gerard promised the Austin friars the sum of £22 10s, with the prior agreeing that his friars would perform annually 'a solempe obite or anniversary with noote in the quere of theire conventuall chirche' for the soul of Nicholas and his wife Elizabeth, 'with *placebo* and *dirige* over nyght and masse of *requiem* with a noote in the next day ensuyng and with procession unto the grave or herce to be ordeynyd upon the Stone of Sepulture of the said Nicholas wyth wax and other thynges nedefull'.[18]

Living with the friars

There was another important point of contact between the members of London's religious houses and the townsfolk: many Londoners rented accommodation owned by monastic houses. For example, the moderately sized Augustinian hospital and priory of St Mary Spital owned property that provided an income of over £562, nearly half of which was derived from its London rental book. Furthermore, several of these London properties lay in a close of fourteenth- and fifteenth-century timber-framed houses inside the actual precinct, situated between the priory cemetery and the large outer precinct field.[19] Although the friars nominally followed St Francis' early example of poverty (these mendicants took their name, of course, from the Latin *mendicare*, 'to beg'), they also began to develop small property portfolios in order to provide accommodation for lay people and to bring in some more regular annual 'alms' to finance the life of prayer and preaching.

The origins of the friars' rented tenements may stretch back to the gifts of donors in

---

[17] TNA, LR 14/87.
[18] TNA, LR 14/91. It is worth noting that this TNA series preserves a number of documents from the late medieval archive of Austin Friars; more commonly this type of document – useless, of course, after Dissolution – must simply have been thrown away.
[19] Barney Sloane, 'Tenements in London's Monasteries c. 1450–1540', in *The Archaeology of Reformation 1480–1580*, ed. D. Gaimster and R. Gilchrist (Leeds: Maney, 2003), pp. 290–8; Thomas, *St Mary Spital*, p. 81; Harward, Holder and Thomas, *The Medieval Priory and Hospital of St Mary Spital*, forthcoming.

the thirteenth century: at an inquisition in the early fourteenth century the Austin friars were found to have acquired a messuage in the parish of St Benet Fink (the parish to the south of their home parish, St Peter the Poor) before the Statutes of Mortmain, presumably therefore in the 1260s or 1270s.[20] Similarly, a royal enquiry of 1349 names two shops owned by the Dominicans just outside their gate; the friars claimed that they formed part of the original land donation of the 1270s by their (re)founder, Archbishop Kilwardby.[21] The development of tenements *within* the friary precincts may have been the result of adaptation to changing circumstances after the Black Death. With a much reduced population of religious personnel, urban and rural monastic houses found themselves unbalanced in personnel and space terms: they simply had too many buildings for the numbers of religious personnel. The smaller urban houses in particular – friaries and Augustinian priories lacking huge property portfolios and rural granges – relied on bought-in food and services. The urban houses therefore experienced a double-economic impact of higher costs for purchased food and services combined with lower profits from rural estates (in the case of Augustinian canons' houses). The provision of tenements within their urban precincts to willing tenants must have seemed an attractive solution. It may therefore be significant that the earliest evidence for tenants inside a friary precinct comes in 1373 when the Dominicans were renting a house and garden in their precinct to Robert Pypot.[22]

The detailed evidence for these rented tenements is for the period right at the end of the friaries' existence. The main source is in the accounts prepared by the rather efficient men in the government department that was administering the Dissolution of the Monasteries, the Court of Augmentations. The evidence (which includes the name of the existing tenant, the rent paid and often an approximate location) shows that these London-based friars had developed a policy for their rental properties. They did not really own property beyond their precincts in the manner of normal monastic houses (like Benedictine monks or Augustinian canons), but they allowed themselves two types of rented tenement. Most of the friaries – the five that survived into the sixteenth century – owned and managed a row of rented houses by their gatehouse on the main road, with additional more scattered tenements inside the precinct. Like in the case of the canons of St Mary Spital, these detached tenements were on one or more of the internal lanes, often close to the cemetery (Table 20; the location of friary tenements is indicated by 'T' on Figure 72). Several friaries leased out individual garden plots within the friary gardens, with the Dominicans raising over £6 a year from thirteen rented gardens.

By the 1530s most of the priors had also begun renting out surplus space within the heart of the precinct. These prestigious apartments were reserved for the 'right sort' of

---

[20] Roth, *English Austin Friars*, ii, no. 40.
[21] Röhrkasten, *Mendicant Houses*, pp. 239–40; Andrew G. Little, 'A Royal Inquiry into Property Held by the Mendicant Friars in England in 1349 and 1350', in *Historical Essays in Honour of James Tait*, ed. J.G. Edwards, V.H. Galbraith and E.F. Jacob (Manchester: privately printed, 1933), pp. 79–88 (pp. 81–3).
[22] Röhrkasten, *Mendicant Houses*, p. 240.

Table 20 The friars' rental income in the early sixteenth century.[a]

		Black Friars	Grey Friars	White Friars	Austin Friars	Crossed Friars
Tenements on street by gatehouse	no.	12	0	9	6	10
	value	£26 1s 4d		£29 10s 0d	£14 13s 4d	£4 4s 0d
Tenements in precinct	no.	17	8	28	6	5
	value	£62 10s 8d	£12 4s 8d	£45 16s 8d	£22 9s 4d	£5 11s 8d
Gardens in precinct	no.	13	4	3		
	value	£6 3s 4d	£1 6s 8d	15s 0d		
Apartments in cloisters (from 1530s?)	no.	5	3		4	2
	value	£20 6s 8d	£9 9s 4d		£5 16s 8d	£1 6s 8d
Other London property	value	£1 0s 0d			£21 18s 8d	£26 4s 0d
Property outside London	value					£3 10s 4d
Total rents at Dissolution		£116 2s 0d	£23 0s 8d	£76 1s 8d	£43 14s 8d	£40 8s 8d
Estimated rent before 1530		£95	£13	£75	£59	£39

Note:

[a] This table is principally based on the rent collector's accounts (known as ministers' accounts) drawn up in the year after the Dissolution: TNA, SC 6/HenVIII/2396, mm. 54–5, 57–66. The table also includes data from a number of other sources; for fuller tabular data and notes, see Holder, 'Medieval Friaries of London', pp. 257–67. For Black Friars, the 'tenements on street' category includes nine riverside tenements with wharfs that fronted onto the 'street' of the river Thames. For White Friars, the 'tenements in precinct' category includes the Clothworkers' almshouse building set up in 1536; this rent is not included in the 'estimated rent before 1530' total. For Austin Friars, the 'total rents at Dissolution' figure is less than the sum of the subtotals above: Thomas Cromwell (and to a lesser extent Thomas Paulet) bought tenements within and without the precinct in the 1530s and these lost rents are not, therefore, included in the 'total rents at Dissolution' figure. Furthermore, the 'estimated rent before 1530' is therefore greater than the 'total rents at Dissolution' for this friary.

tenant and often commanded premium rents: the courtier Sir William Kingston paid £5 rent to the Dominicans by 1536 for the 'under lybrarye', presumably an undercroft below the library on the east side of the inner cloister. At White Friars, the London dyer Thomas Geffery and his wife Agnes were paying £2 rent for the old prior's house in 1537. One can guess that such conversion of under-utilised space in the claustral buildings was not standard practice before the sixteenth century; the priors may only have created these luxury apartments from the 1530s, a response to the rapidly changing times of that decade. (The 'estimated rent before 1530' figures in Table 20 therefore exclude the rents from these claustral apartments.)

There are some exceptions to this general pattern of rented properties. The Grey friars did not own the row of shops and houses on their street frontage: in the second half of the fourteenth century they had transferred the ownership to the Bridge House estates, the charitable trust managed by the City Corporation that funded the maintenance of London Bridge.[23] The Austin friars owned a significant number of tenements in other London parishes, which brought in over £21 a year. The Crossed friars – friar-canons rather than full mendicants – were the only London friars to have a rental portfolio beyond London: they held a manor in Suffolk, in addition to their tenements elsewhere in London.

Recent archaeological work on the site of the Augustinian canons' house of St Mary Spital has shown that from the first half of the fourteenth century successive priors developed a close of detached timber-framed tenements along an internal lane within the precinct, situated alongside the cemetery and close to the monastic church.[24] There is a lack of comparative archaeological evidence for the friaries but the documentary evidence shows that the priors of Black, White and Austin Friars followed a similar policy by the sixteenth century, quite possibly much earlier. The setting of these tenements by the cemetery and the church is probably significant. One or two friary leases specify that the tenant had special access to the friary church. Margaret, countess of Kent, signed a complicated agreement with the Carmelite prior in 1527: she gave £60 towards the construction of a new mansion on which she would pay £4 annual rent (reduced to £2 if the prior did not repay the capital) and she was to have access to divine services 'in like manner and fourme as other like tenantes of the said prior and convent', as well as having the useful right to draw water from the friary's conduit.[25] Archaeological evidence from Black Friars shows that this cemetery was used by lay people as well as friars (as noted earlier, the excavations revealed the graves of several women and children) and so the cemeteries may have been regarded as lay spaces: still, of course, holy places, but with a spiritual connection particularly close to ordinary Londoners.[26] Indeed, it is quite likely – although no direct evidence has been found – that the tenants of these precinct houses chose to live here, at least in part, in order to be close to their relatives. With some houses backing onto the graveyards, the living and the dead were close neighbours.

The best evidence for the form of these rented tenements comes from Austin Friars. Here, prior Edmund Bellond built a secluded close of two or three rather grand houses in about 1510: in a fortuitous combination of surviving evidence there is documentation concerning the construction, a written survey of 1543 and a seventeenth-century plan of the houses.[27] In a contract of 1510 the draper William Calley paid £40 to the prior to finance the new buildings. This was not a corrodian arrangement – Calley was not intending to live here at retirement – but in return for his £40 outlay he was to receive commemorative masses after his death. If Calley was to receive a spiritual reward, the

---

[23] BL, Cotton Vitellius F xii, ff. 327–9v, printed in *Grey Friars*, pp. 171–7.
[24] Harward, Holder and Thomas, *The Medieval Priory and Hospital of St Mary Spital*, forthcoming.
[25] BL, Harley charters 79.F.32.
[26] See n. 15.
[27] TNA, LR 14/129 [1510 contract concerning construction]; DC, M B 1c (Minute book), p. 759 [written survey of 1543]; DC, A XII 121 [drawn survey of c. 1620].

Austin friars were clearly aiming to increase their temporal income. The ground-floor plans of two of these houses have been redrawn as Figure 91. The new houses were not quite mansions for the city elite but they were substantial urban townhouses intended, no doubt, for wealthy tenants who could pay the £4 annual rent; the houses were adjacent to the church and churchyard, and both house and tenant would therefore need to have been of the 'right sort'. The names of the first tenants are unknown but an ambitious administrator working for Cardinal Wolsey (by the name of Thomas Cromwell) lived here by about 1522.[28]

The new houses for rent were only two-storey buildings (in order not to block light from the west front of the church across the lane), with kitchen, hall and parlour on the ground floor and heated bedchambers on the first floor (the northern house having five upper chambers and the southern house only four; Figure 91). Both houses were clearly designed with the latest facilities: fireplaces in nearly every room, kitchens equipped with a cellar, buttery and scullery ('a rowme to wasshe yn with a well and a bucket') and yards with a privy and a wood- and coal-shed. In the northern house there were probably two separate staircases, one on the service side and a second on the hall and parlour side (unfortunately the northern part of the house had been adapted by the time of the seventeenth-century survey so the evidence is not certain). The houses' plan-form seems quite new as well: the halls are relatively small with more emphasis placed on the heated parlour rooms. The northern house seems to have had a surprisingly long corridor that looks more like a modern hallway than a medieval cross-passage. It is likely that the houses were built of brick, although the internal walls and some structural walls may have been of timber (being noticeably thinner on the seventeenth-century plan).[29] The houses were well lit with large windows with stone (or brick) mullions.

One should not, of course, be surprised by all this evidence of close links between the friars and the city. Firstly, it is worth noting that late medieval monasticism in England was something of an urban phenomenon: the majority of post-Conquest religious houses were founded in towns (even if some of these 'towns' only became truly urban by the subsequent effects of accretion and attraction *to* the monastery). English monks, canons and nuns were rarely far from English townsfolk, and economic and spiritual ties tended to draw them ever closer. And of course the whole raison d'être of the friars (or at least the reason for their enthusiastic promotion by the Church hierarchy) was their ability to offer spiritual support to the ever-growing numbers of town-dwellers throughout Europe, thus buttressing the uneven coverage of the urban parishes of the secular

---

[28] Holder, 'Medieval Friaries of London', pp. 160–2; Tracy Borman, *Thomas Cromwell: The Untold Story of Henry VIII's Most Faithful Servant* (London: Hodder & Stoughton, 2014), pp. 46–8.

[29] Measuring the walls from the seventeenth-century plan, the front wall was about 0.6m or 2ft thick, i.e. two and a half London Tudor bricks (two stretchers and one header); the side walls were just less than 0.5m or 1½ft thick, i.e. two bricks. Internal walls (probably timber-framed over a brick or stone sleeper wall) were 0.3m (1ft) thick (a brick and a half).

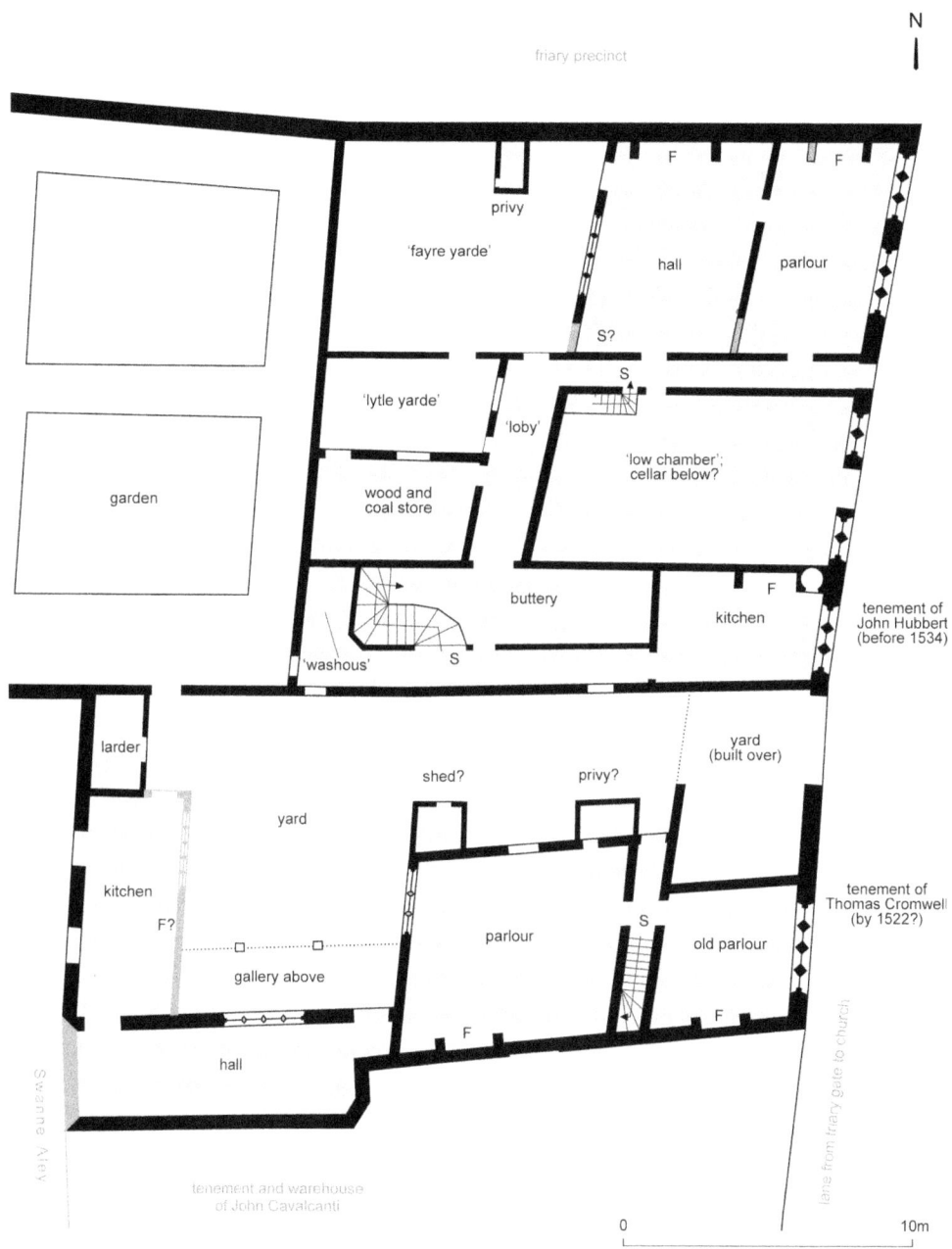

Fig. 91. Two rented tenements developed by the prior of Austin Friars in 1510 ('S' indicates stairs, 'F' fireplace; scale 1:250)

church.[30] Monastic houses were, by necessity, closely linked to their lay neighbours and the wider community in a more practical sense: they were major purchasers of food and services, and they were significant employers (quite possibly the largest single employer in many towns). Urban monastic houses, especially the Augustinian canons, were providers of what would now be termed social and even medical care: virtually all hospitals in London were run by the order. Indeed, most religious houses throughout the land provided at least basic guest accommodation for pilgrims and other travellers.[31] Many urban monasteries (not just the friaries) provided space for meetings and services of religious and craft-based fraternities, particularly in the case of less wealthy organisations who could not afford their own hall and chapel. And in London, several parish churches were physically within or adjoining monastic precincts, including St Helen Bishopsgate and St Mary Clerkenwell (the churches shared with the nunneries), St Katherine Cree (a separate parish church provided by Holy Trinity priory) and St Peter the Poor (the parish church attached to the Augustinian friary).

Conclusion

The close links between the friars and Londoners were, therefore, part of the wider picture of late medieval monasticism. They demonstrate a close relationship between the religious houses and their lay supporters, with monasteries and friaries providing tailored spiritual services of prayer, burial and commemoration to a discerning urban community, able to shop around for their preferred places of burial or commemoration. The friars would have established particularly close links with living Londoners thanks to the mendicants' role in preaching. The friars were also particularly important to aliens, with foreign-born friars able to hear confession of foreign merchants and others in their native tongue. The increasing presence of lay people within certain areas of the friaries and other urban religious houses was also mutually beneficial. The religious houses gained a regular income and a group of lay supporters, and the lay residents were able to enjoy life in a spiritually privileged gated community, in the heart of London (or close to it), but segregated from the full impact of the noise and bustle of the city.

---

[30] Butler, 'The Archaeology of Urban Monasteries in Britain', pp. 79–86; Heale, *Monasticism in Late Medieval England*, pp. 33–41, 44–46, 48, 53–64; David Palliser, 'The Topography of Monastic Houses in Yorkshire Towns', in *Advances in Monastic Archaeology*, ed. R. Gilchrist and H.C. Mytum, British Archaeological Reports, 227 (Oxford: Archaeopress, 1993), pp. 3–9; J. Patrick Greene, *Medieval Monasteries* (Leicester: Leicester University Press, 1992), pp. 162–72; Barron and Davies, *Religious Houses*, pp. 5–24.

[31] Gilchrist, *Contemplation and Action*, pp. 8–61.

19

Dissolution

It must have been quite extraordinary to live in England during that heady and dangerous decade of the 1530s. The English Reformation – a retrospective and over-neat label – was set in motion by a strange chain of events involving great men like Erasmus and Luther, and, closer to home, Henry VIII with his interleaving dynastic, personal and religious worries. The sense of unpredictability must have been particularly strong in London where close proximity to court, Church and parliament would have sent rumours and opinions flying around the city. The priors of the five London friaries must have seen the end coming in the 1530s, but exactly when they realised it was inevitable is harder to say.

The 1530s: a decade of uncertainty

Four of the London priors were closely allied with Thomas Cromwell and the rapidly evolving Crown policy (the exception seems to have been the Carmelite prior, John Gybbes). George Brown of Austin Friars had been taking precautions and making changes for a few years, even before 1534 when the king's commissioners (led by the prior of the London Dominicans, John Hilsey) were sent to investigate England's mendicant houses. In March 1531 Brown had leased a mansion and garden within the friary precinct to Thomas Paulet, brother of the courtier William Paulet. In May the following year, Brown enhanced the friary's ties to its influential tenant Thomas Cromwell (by then Henry's principal secretary) by granting him a ninety-nine-year lease on a block of houses on the edge of the precinct so that he could redevelop it as a grand urban mansion. Brown later welcomed two well-connected protégés of Cromwell as tenants, Richard Rich and Richard Morrison (in 1536 and 1538 respectively).[1] Of course, as an ally of Cromwell, Brown may have been seeking to secure his own position rather than that of his priory. The Dominican prior, John Hilsey,

---

[1] TNA, LR 14/88 [Paulet]; SP 2/L, ff. 205–10, nos 183–8; DC, A I 61 [Cromwell]; TNA, LR 14/86 [Rich]; E 318/13/577 [Morrison].

began renting out what he saw as under-used parts of his cloisters to courtiers in the early 1530s. Like the prior of Austin Friars, Hilsey was almost certainly acting to safeguard his own future. The Grey Friars guardian, Thomas Chapman, was another supporter of Cromwell, although he does not seem to have taken the same steps to bring in influential tenants. The Carmelite prior, John Gybbes, and the prior of Crossed Friars, Robert Ball, took a slightly different tack, allowing the setting up of almshouses in the mid-1530s in an attempt, perhaps, to secure their own friary's future: at the former friary this was in partnership with the countess of Kent and the Clothworkers' Company, at the latter it was with Sir John Milbourne and the Drapers' Company.[2]

The evidence from wills of the 1520s and '30s suggests that Londoners continued to support the friaries, right up to the end: citizens maintained the same level of bequests in the 1530s as in previous decades, at least up to about 1537.[3] Furthermore, Londoners continued to request burial in the friary churches, right up to 1538. Ralph Pexsall and Lady Jane Gilford both requested burial at Black Friars that year; the former's will was proved in February and the latter's in September – a few weeks before the closure of the friary – but their ultimate resting places are not clear.[4]

Some of the lay people connected with the friaries could, however, see the end coming in the late 1530s and took appropriate precautions. The founder of the Clothworkers' almshouses at White Friars, Margaret, countess of Kent, took steps to safeguard her new establishment. In July 1537 she was finalising an agreement with the company concerning the obligations of the almswomen and the company to attend obits and say daily prayers for her soul and that of her husband. He was buried in the Carmelite church and she was clearly becoming concerned for its future. She therefore inserted what might be termed an 'in the event of Dissolution' clause into the agreement:

> provided always yf yt happen or chaunce the saide house of white freers to be suppressed hereafter or yn tyme to come to be turned ynto some other use, so that the obytes of the said erle and comtesse cannot be observed and kept within the saide house, nor that the saide almes women maye not daylly resorte to the place appoynted for them whereas the saide Earle and comtesse ar buried, that then the saide master and wardeyns and their successoures shall observe kepe and maynteyne the saide obytes and all other the promisses at and within the paryshe chirche of Saynte Dunstane yn the west within the saide citie of London, or yn some other place which shalbe thought convenyent by the saide master and wardeyns for the tyme beynge, soo that the Soulles may be prayed for perpetually forever.[5]

---

[2] Holder, 'Medieval Friaries of London', pp. 128–9, 191–3.
[3] Röhrkasten, *Mendicant Houses*, pp. 561–7.
[4] Palmer, 'Burials at the Priories of the Black Friars', vol. 24, 119. Note also a request for burial at Black Friars in 1539, after it had been closed: Röhrkasten, *Mendicant Houses*, p. 562.
[5] CC, MS CL/A/4/4 (Book of Deeds and Wills), p. 69.

1538: closure

Certainty about the imminent closure of the friaries may not have come until spring 1538 when the Dominican friar Richard Ingworth, a former provincial prior and now bishop of Dover, was appointed head of the royal commission charged with securing the surrender of the English mendicant houses.[6]

In the months approaching the final closure of the friaries Richard Ingworth must have warned the priors not to sell off the friaries' property and movable goods in a reckless manner, nor to issue leases at knock-down rates. By and large the priors seem to have behaved, presumably because they were loyalists and perhaps also since they were rather under the eyes of the London-based officials of the Court of Augmentations. In November the priors must have faced the same options from Ingworth as he gave the Gloucester priors: to continue in their houses or release them to the king. Like their Gloucester counterparts, the London priors presumably gave the right answer and agreed that they were 'nott abull to contynew' as before.[7] On Thursday 10 November 1538 Thomas Legh, probably the busiest of Cromwell's crack team of monastic commissioners (or should that be decommissioners?), witnessed the signature of prior John Gibbys and eleven other Carmelites in their chapter house. Two days later he went through the same process at the houses of the Franciscans and the Austin friars, while his colleague Richard Layton witnessed the declarations of the Dominicans and the Crossed friars.[8]

The houses were now legally in the hands of the Crown and royal officials quickly took steps to secure the newly acquired properties. Of course, London's monastic houses were rather easier to secure than rural Benedictine houses: as has been noted, large numbers of lay people already lived within the precincts, including a number of influential courtiers and royal officers. In at least three cases the Court of Augmentations appointed an official guardian to safeguard the empty monastic buildings of the church and cloisters: at Black Friars the guardian was an existing resident called John Portinari, an Italian military engineer and architect who, five years earlier, had worked on Thomas Cromwell's new house at Austin Friars.[9] At the Grey Friars the caretaker was John Wyseman, a naval commander, and at Crossed Friars it was Lionel Martyn, a junior military engineer.[10] Once in

---

[6] Youings, *Dissolution of the Monasteries*, pp. 75–6; Knowles, *Religious Orders*, iii, 360–2; G.W.O. Woodward, *The Dissolution of the Monasteries* (London: Blandford, 1966), pp. 66–7, 115–18. Ingworth was appointed in February but set off in earnest in May.

[7] Knowles, *Religious Orders*, iii, 361; Youings, *Dissolution of the Monasteries*, pp. 75–6; Bernard, *King's Reformation*, pp. 452–5; *Letters and Papers*, xiii(1), no. 1484(3).

[8] *Letters and Papers*, xiii(2), nos 788, 806–9. For Legh and Layton, see Knowles, *Religious Orders*, iii, 270–2; Anthony N. Shaw, 'Legh, Sir Thomas (d. 1545)', *ODNB*, <http://www.oxforddnb.com/view/article/16363> (accessed 8 June 2016); Peter Cunich, 'Layton, Richard (c. 1498–1544)', *ODNB*, <http://www.oxforddnb.com/view/article/16226> (accessed 8 June 2016).

[9] Loseley MS printed in *Blackfriars Records*, p. 52.

[10] TNA, SC 6/HenVIII/2396, mm. 62 and 63; Bryson, 'Wallop, Sir John' [Wyseman]; *Letters and Papers*, xix(2), no. 86 [Martyn].

control of the friaries, the Crown could gather and confiscate the monastic plate and jewels: over 300lb of plate from the London friaries was collected by Cromwell's servant Thomas Thacker and delivered to the Jewel Tower on 29 November. The authorities may also have organised local sales of the more portable fixtures and fittings (although no records of such sales survive for the London friaries).[11]

Mention has been made of the 'in the event of Dissolution' clause written for Margaret, countess of Kent, when she was setting up her almshouses in the White Friars in 1537 (above). When the friary was indeed closed the following year, did Margaret have her husband's body exhumed and moved to neighbouring St Dunstan (where the almswomen were to pray after the closure of the friary)? Unfortunately, the fate of her husband Richard Grey's body and the resting place of Margaret have not been traced.[12] In fact, the evidence suggests that remarkably few relatives of lay people buried in the London friaries moved the bodies at the time of the Dissolution. At the Crossed Friars, Sir John Milbourne's body was moved to St Edmund Lombard Street by his widow Joan and it seems likely that the retired Clothworkers living in the almshouses he founded had to walk the 500 yards or so to the parish church to attend commemorative masses for his soul, at least for the remaining decade when the practice was allowed. The tomb and corpse of Sir Richard Cholmeley (died 1523) were moved from Crossed Friars after the Dissolution and – uniquely among the thousands of medieval Londoners buried in the London friaries – this tomb survives, having been re-erected in St Peter ad Vincula in the Tower, perhaps by his widow Elizabeth (Figure 57). Although this and other examples of exhumation and translation are hard to prove from the documentary evidence, it does seem that the practice was the exception in the late 1530s rather than the rule. By way of comparison, when the Dominicans built a new church in the 1280s, they brought dozens of tombs with them from their old church in Holborn.

There is also a little archaeological evidence for the translation of corpses and burial monuments during the Dissolution. Excavations in the Lady chapel of Black Friars revealed two empty brick-lined late medieval tombs, with a possible third emptied tomb discovered in the north aisle of the nave: the unknown occupants were probably exhumed around the time of the Dissolution and moved, presumably with their commemorative floor-slabs, to another London church.[13] The limited archaeological evidence for the interior of the other

---

[11] Knowles, *Religious Orders*, iii, 383–4; Williams, *Account of the Monastic Treasures*, pp. 18–19.

[12] Her will of 1540 requests burial at the late White Friars but there is no evidence that this was carried out: CC, MS CL/A/4/4 (Book of Deeds and Wills), p. 69; *Testamenta Vetusta*, ii, 691–2.

[13] Watson and Thomas, 'Mendicant Houses', pp. 269–70. The brick-lined feature in the nave is less convincingly a tomb: it is square rather than wedge-shaped and it could therefore be a post-Dissolution brick-lined pit, dug in Thomas Cawarden's new mansion rather than in its predecessor the church nave. The archaeological sites are FRI88 (Lady chapel) and LBY85 (nave). One of these tombs could perhaps be for Gerard Danet (d. 1520), whose brass effigy (and body?) was moved to the parish church of St Mary, Tilty (Essex): Chapter 17: Burial and Commemoration in the London Friaries, Figure 90.

friary churches does not, however, reveal other examples of this practice, although similar evidence has been found for one or two exhumed tombs in the Augustinian canons' church of St Mary Spital.[14]

1539: *the Crown's new income*

With trusted men appointed as caretakers, and with the friaries' tenants keen to maintain order and the status quo, the Crown did not have to rush into decisions about what to do with the churches and cloisters. In fact, the Court of Augmentations seems to have done very little about the friary precincts for over a year: its officers were no doubt rather busy just dealing with the basic transfers of land and goods from monastic houses all over the country. Nor did the Court of Augmentations rush into demolishing the friary churches: most were closed but remained standing for the next four or five years.[15] The exception might be Crossed Friars: a memorandum of Thomas Cromwell in 1539 suggested that the church stone and other materials could be reused in works at the Tower of London (although there is little evidence that this actually took place).[16]

The important task of calculating and collecting the new income from the friaries began immediately after the Dissolution in 1539. The Court of Augmentations' London rent collector was Hugh Losse – a rather ambitious and industrious worker – and surviving documents show that he collated lists of lay tenants and the rent they owed, presumably copying lists handed over by the priors, and that he collected most of the rents due in 1539. At the end of the year Thomas Spilman, the receiver of the Court of Augmentations with responsibility for London, acknowledged receipt of the money.[17] Memoranda concerning the friaries' tenants were still being exchanged between Hugh Losse and other Augmentations

---

[14] Harward, Holder and Thomas, *The Medieval Priory and Hospital of St Mary Spital*, forthcoming.

[15] A similar delay has been noted in other detailed case studies, for example at Coventry: I. Soden, 'The Conversion of Former Monastic Buildings to Secular Use: The Case of Coventry', in *The Archaeology of Reformation 1480–1580*, ed. D. Gaimster and R. Gilchrist (Leeds: Maney, 2003), pp. 280–9.

[16] TNA, SP 1/153, f. 219, no. 171. Colvin suggested that the church stone and timber might have been used in the new house for the lieutenant of the Tower, built in 1540. A recent architectural study of the house did not reveal any evidence for the reuse of earlier timbers but, intriguingly, Hollar's mid-seventeenth-century view of the Tower from the Thames shows what appears to be a medieval church window in the upper hall of this Tudor building. Was this window (perhaps 12ft or 3.5m wide) moved in 1540 from a fourteenth-century aisle of the Crossed Friars church? Colvin, *King's Works*, iii, 268; James Wright, 'Queen's House and Bell Tower' (unpublished MOLA standing building report, 2016); pers. comm. Alden Gregory, Historic Royal Palaces.

[17] Nick Holder, 'Losse, Hugh, (d. 1555), Administrator and Property Speculator', *ODNB*, <http://www.oxforddnb.com/view/article/101321> [accessed 8 June 2016]; TNA, SC 11/985 [summary of rents due]; E 314/54 ('London and Middlesex: Carmelite priory, valor') [draft list of rents due at White Friars]; SC 6/HenVIII/2427 [receiver's accounts]. The accounts of the rent collector and the receiver work on an 'Exchequer year' ending at Michaelmas (29 September).

officers the following year.[18] Losse and Spilman also drew up lists of anniversary payments due to the friary (from institutions and the executors of wills) for the performance of commemorative masses: perhaps surprisingly, these contracts remained theoretically in force, even though there were no friars left to perform the masses. They managed to collect, for example, two of the seven anniversary payments due to the Augustinian friars for a few years after the house's closure and were still collecting two or three anniversary payments due to the Dominicans as late as 1552.[19]

The fate of the friaries in the 1540s

For the four or five years following the Dissolution, Crown policy was largely to retain these (and other) dissolved monastic houses: this was property nationalisation (an anachronistic term, of course) on an unprecedented scale. Additionally, the monastic churches were useful 'quarries' of building materials such as lead, stone and timber. In 1544 and 1545 the lead was stripped from the church roofs and probably melted into ingots *in situ*; the bells would have had to be transported to specialists for re-melting at a much higher temperature.[20] Black Friars was a particularly rich quarry: a Court of Augmentations surveyor working there in 1544 estimated that the friary had 129 fothers (123 tonnes) of lead on the roofs of the church and cloister (Chapter 13: Floor Tiles and Building Materials from the London Friaries, Table 17). In 1546 stone, lead and iron was stripped from the church of Crossed Friars for reuse in building works at the Palace of Whitehall, perhaps the King Street gate.[21]

The Crown issued several leases to new tenants of the friaries, particularly for the newly available buildings of the cloisters. In several cases royal patronage could be handed out in the form of rent-free leases for life, or rental income packages (known as 'farms of rents'). With a few exceptions, the emphasis was on the curation of a valuable new property portfolio with all its long-term potential for Crown revenue.

But within a few years of the execution of the architect of the Dissolution – that promising administrator in the service of Cardinal Wolsey whom we encountered renting one of the new tenements at Austin Friars (Chapter 18: London Friars and Londoners) – the policy changed. Instead of the former friaries and the countless other monastic estates being seen

---

[18] TNA, SP 1/157, f. 174.

[19] The court successfully collected anniversary payments from parishes and city guilds, but not from individual executors or from institutions that had themselves been dissolved: TNA, SC 6/HenVIII/2396, mm. 60–61v; SC 6/EdwVI/297, mm. 12v–13v.

[20] The tightest dating evidence for the stripping of the roofs comes from White Friars: the lead was valued on 8 July 1544, payment for the property was received from the purchaser on 23 January 1545 and the lead was handed in to the Tower on 12 February: TNA, E 314/69, no. 29; E 315/105, f. 120; E 117/13/96. The evidence for the other friaries suggests that the same process took place at about this time. For the processes of melting the lead and bell-metal, see Greene, *Medieval Monasteries*, pp. 185–7.

[21] TNA, SP 4/1, f. 35, no. 73; Colvin, *King's Works*, iv, 312–13.

as a long-term investment, they were quickly sold off in 1544–5 for ready cash, largely to pay for the king's expensive wars with France and Scotland. By the mid 1540s London's five great mendicant houses – for three centuries powerhouses of prayer and preaching – were in the hands of forty-four secular landlords.[22]

Conclusion

Some Londoners, including the London priors, were responding to the rapid religious changes at quite an early date, by 1531 or 1532; this was when George Brown of the Austin friars was leasing houses within the precinct to powerful courtiers. A real sense that all the urban monasteries, including the London friaries, might actually be closed down only seems to have hit Londoners in about 1537. It was in July that the charismatic and well-married Margaret, countess of Kent, added a dissolution clause to the contract governing the running of her new almshouses: 'provided always yf yt happen or chaunce the saide house of white freers to be subpressed hereafter or yn tyme to come to be turned ynto some other use . . .'.[23] This was the month when Robert Aske was executed: he had led the Pilgrimage of Grace, the failed uprising that was intimately linked to the fate of the monasteries of Yorkshire and the north. And in London the month before, the great monastery of the Charterhouse had been closed.[24] This must surely be the time that the 'penny dropped' and English people realised exactly what Henry and Cromwell were planning.

The actual dissolution of the friaries in November 1538 seems to have been an orderly process: the Crown appointed caretakers and removed portable assets; the friars' lay tenants must have continued as before. But they were now paying their rent to a new landlord, the Crown: this was the initial result of the Dissolution – the creation of a valuable long-term property asset that would significantly boost Crown finances. This must surely have been the prime motivation behind the Dissolution for Henry's principal minister Thomas Cromwell. There is evidence for the actual friary churches being dismantled in the early 1540s – the lead, timber, iron and stone were another valuable asset and the destruction of the church would also make it harder to reverse the closure – but the rest of the precincts stayed intact. The change in policy came in 1544: the financial goal was now the short-term

---

[22] The aftermath of the Dissolution of the London friaries is recounted in more detail in Holder, 'Medieval Friaries of London', pp. 237–55. For the forty-four new landlords see table 14, pp. 242–4.

[23] Margaret was widowed on three occasions and, at least after the first two, she was able to make judicious remarriages. Before being Lady Margaret, she was Mrs Margaret Dawes and married to a Clothworker (perhaps the alderman and sheriff John Dawes); she seems to have retained her links with the company after her subsequent marriage to Richard Grey, earl of Kent. George W. Bernard, 'Grey, Richard, Third Earl of Kent (b. in or before 1478, d. 1524)', *ODNB*, <http://www.oxforddnb.com/view/article/58355> (accessed 14 October 2008); Caroline M. Barron, *London in the Later Middle Ages: Government and People, 1200–1500* (Oxford: Oxford University Press, 2004), p. 350.

[24] Rosemary O'Day, *The Routledge Companion to the Tudor Age* (Abingdon: Routledge, 2010); *Letters and Papers*, xii(2), no. 91.

income of sales rather than the long-term curation of a rental asset. Cash was urgently needed to pay for Henry's wars with Scotland and France. The friaries were therefore broken up into multiple property units in order to raise as much cash as possible: by 1546 the five priories had forty-four new secular landlords who had paid the Crown about £2800 for their new houses, lands and rents.

Conclusions

In the Introduction to this book I stated its purpose: to reconstruct the urban landscape of the seven medieval friaries of London, and to understand something of the experience of the friars and visitors who used them. Using the available evidence (800 or so documents, nearly one hundred archaeological excavations and a handful of maps: Table 2), the authors have attempted to describe and analyse these medieval friaries. Focusing for a moment on the numbers, one can note that by the sixteenth century the friars' precinct walls enclosed 20 acres of valuable urban land, about 5% of the whole walled city of London (8.1ha out of 143ha; 20 out of 353 acres), and the suburban White Friars accounted for another 5 acres (2.1ha). This simple numerical expression of the friars' footprint in the city shows just how important the friars were to the Londoners and other patrons who had paid for the friaries. The 160 or so friars living in the five friaries in the fifteenth century constituted less than 0.5% of the population of the city; put another way, this elite group of religious men had about twenty times as much space as the average Londoner.[1]

Turning to the methodology of studying these friaries (and other urban monastic houses), the present study continues the interdisciplinary academic tradition of monastic studies pioneered by late nineteenth-century archaeologist-historians such as William St John Hope.[2] If historians studying British monastic sites lack the art-historical material available to colleagues working in, say, northern Italy (think of Assisi with its surviving medieval basilica complete with Giotto's late thirteenth-century fresco cycle), we have to make the most of the evidence we have. The strand of evidence that has perhaps been undervalued, but which lies behind most of the maps and plans in this book, is the use of

---

[1] Surface area of the walled city (not including the Tower) calculated from MOLA digital map data; for the approximate number of friars in the fifteenth century, see Röhrkasten, *Mendicant Houses*, pp. 73–85. The estimated population of London in the fifteenth century is 40,000: see Caroline Barron, *London in the Later Middle Ages: Government and People, 1200–1500* (Oxford: Oxford University Press, 2004), pp. 237–42.

[2] Coppack, *Abbeys & Priories*, pp. 24–5.

historic maps and map regression (Introduction, 'The approach of this book'; Figure 2). By working backwards in time from modern maps to sixteenth-century maps, the size and some of the internal patterns of the monastic precincts can be understood. This spatial information then helps the often limited documentary and archaeological information to go a little further; we can now understand, for example, the land reclamation works of the Dominicans in the late thirteenth and early fourteenth century when they reclaimed nearly 1¾ acres of land from the Thames (6800m^2) to make a friary precinct of just under 8 acres (3.1 ha), nearly half of which was gardens (3½ acres, 1.4ha).

There are still many aspects of the London friars and friaries which elude us. Little is known of the organisational structure of the friaries, nor quite how they functioned economically. Estimating the annual income and expenditure of the London Austin friars (Chapter 15: Economy) allows one to consider the difficult financial status of the friaries: mendicant in name but living in the heart of a busy and expensive capital city, making ends meet but relying on donors to pay for major building or repair projects. Is there perhaps an obedientiary's account roll from an English friary waiting to be discovered in a regional or Continental archive?

From an archaeological perspective it would be desirable to know more about the material culture and diet of the friars. In this book we have looked at architectural fragments and floor tiles (Chapters 12 and 13) but the archaeological archive holds many other boxes of material waiting to be studied: pottery, other artefacts, animal bones and botanical evidence. An interdisciplinary study of monastic diet and provisioning – linking documentary and archaeological evidence, looking at all types of monastic house and with a wider regional coverage – would also be welcome (although such a study would probably not find much documentary evidence for the mendicants). Perhaps a future excavation will reveal more about friary outbuildings such as a mill or a workshop.

In order to understand the patterns of growth and investment in medieval London it would be useful to examine the construction projects of the friars in conjunction with other religious houses and the parish churches: how many church-building projects were being funded and executed in the early fourteenth century? With work still going on at St Paul's, with major construction taking place at the friaries, at Augustinian priories (such as St Mary Bishopsgate) and other monasteries, at St Stephen in the Palace of Westminster, and at several parish churches, this must have been a good time to be a skilled mason.

Another line of future enquiry would be to compare the London friaries with those of their Continental colleagues, perhaps in Paris, Rome or German cities. In particular, it might be instructive to study construction campaigns and the way that these urban monastic precincts were assembled and developed; a model of the development of friaries during the thirteenth century and beyond is outlined below.[3]

---

[3] This approach would build on the work done by Caroline Bruzelius who has looked at the Italian and north European friaries in a stimulating new light, combining art-historical and social history perspectives; Bruzelius, *Preaching, Building, and Burying*.

Further work might also examine British or Continental urban monasteries more generally, comparing, in particular, the Augustinian canons with the mendicants (houses of the former are usually a little earlier than those of the mendicants). The Augustinian canons and the mendicants seem to have created a new type of urban monastery (Chapter 11: Precincts and the Use of Space). Compared to rural monasteries, this type of thirteenth- and fourteenth-century urban monastery was of course rather small, lacking extensive outer courts and lands, but in urban terms they must have been remarkable and privileged spaces – green oases in grey cities. The precincts of the London Grey friars or the Augustinian canons of St Mary Bishopsgate, those of the Norwich Black friars or the canons of nearby St Giles, seem to share several common features.[4] The monastic church was sited close to the road, to attract the visits and donations of townsfolk. The cemetery was usually between the road and the church, or close to the main gate beside the church, acting, again, as a focal point for living and dead townspeople. The cloister – reserved for the friars or canons – was on the other side of the church, away from the road. Subsidiary buildings such as infirmaries or service courts were then added in the fourteenth and fifteenth centuries, perhaps forming a second cloister, or as detached wings and rows of buildings. And the walled enclosure always included large urban gardens (helping to feed the religious), as well as some form of clean water supply and waste system.

The London priors and other senior friars developed their friaries over three centuries: three parts to this story of development can be defined.

'Phase one', 1220s to 1270s: establishing an urban preaching base of chapel, accommodation wing and cemetery

'Phase two', late thirteenth century to second half of fourteenth century: creating a full urban monastery – an architectural and spiritual mark in the landscape

'Phase three', late fourteenth or early fifteenth century to Dissolution: using the spaces for worship, preaching and intercession; filling the internal church space with tombs and altars; housing lay tenants in the precincts

From the arrival of the Dominicans and Franciscans in the 1220s to about the 1270s (defined here as 'Phase one'), the friars seem to have had relatively modest ambitions, aims that were certainly in keeping with the vision of the two founders, Saints Francis and Dominic, who had set up the ideals of corporate poverty and the apostolic life of preaching. Over this half-century the priors of the seven London houses sought to enlarge their

---

[4] For St Mary Bishopsgate, see Thomas, *St Mary Spital*; Harward, Holder and Thomas, *The Medieval Priory and Hospital of St Mary Spital*, forthcoming; for the Norwich Black Friars, see Sutermeister, *Norwich Blackfriars*. The canons of the hospital and priory of St Giles Norwich were Augustinian-like secular canons: Carole Rawcliffe, *Medicine for the Soul: The Life, Death and Resurrection of an English Medieval Hospital, St Giles's, Norwich, c. 1249–1550* (Stroud: Sutton, 1999), pp. 30–1, 43 (map II), 62 (map III).

foundation plots and establish simple urban bases with a chapel and a wing or two of accommodation: the basic outlines of these foundation plots have been reconstructed in Figure 69, and the early friaries in Figure 70 (Chapter 11: Precincts and the Use of Space). The early churches were almost certainly simple unaisled halls, with plain timber roofs and any vaulting (if there was any) restricted to the easternmost bay or bays (Chapter 10: Churches, Figure 64). The lack of any identifiable architectural fragments surviving from this early period is evidence of the relative austerity of these early buildings; a surviving window arch of the undercroft of the late thirteenth-century Dominican chapter house (from the second Black Friars) gives us an example of this plain architectural taste (Chapter 12: Architecture and Architectural Fragments of the London Friaries, Figure 65).

The friars established close links with London's civic authorities, right from the time of their establishment here in the thirteenth century. The London aldermen actually owned the Franciscan site, a legal detail that ensured the friars' poverty (Chapter 4: Grey Friars). The city fathers also co-operated with the Dominicans: a partnership of king, city and friary moved the city wall to enclose the new friary in the 1270s. They thus transformed this part of the city, getting rid of the old Norman earthworks, reclaiming land from the Thames and upgrading the western defences of the city (Chapter 2: The Second Black Friars). And there was certainly some shared expertise and finance as the City was building its new water supply system at the same time as the Franciscans and Dominicans in the second quarter of the thirteenth century (Chapter 14: Water Supply).

The priors seem to have upped their ambitions in the last quarter of the thirteenth century: this second period of development of the London friaries lasted until the late fourteenth or early fifteenth century (defined here as 'Phase two'). In just over a century, the priors of the five surviving orders – the Dominicans, Franciscans, Carmelites, Austin and Crossed friars – rebuilt their friaries as full urban monasteries, complete with double church of choir and nave, a full monastic cloister (in some cases two cloisters) and large walled precincts filled with gardens and a cemetery (Chapter 10: Churches, Chapter 11: Precincts and the Use of Space). The new churches were some of the grandest in London and the friars' gardens were certainly the largest open areas within the walled city. Documentary evidence gives some indication of the variety of garden spaces: by the sixteenth century the Carmelites had several separate gardens including the prior's garden, a kitchen garden, an infirmary garden, a school garden and two further spaces known as convent gardens. The thirteenth-century Dominicans had an orchard with apple trees, pears, cherries and walnuts, as well as a vineyard – a rare feature in London. However, we need to investigate a little further what pushed the London priors in the late thirteenth century to up their game and begin building abbey-sized urban monasteries rather than the plain chapels and dormitories that had satisfied the early friars.

The founders of the two original mendicant orders, Saints Francis and Dominic, established clear aims for the new preacher-monks: they were to relive the life of preaching of Jesus' original apostles in a new *vita apostolica*. They were to sustain themselves spiritually with prayer and a simplified version of the daily monastic services (the Office), and they were to meet their physical needs by begging for food and money. But, as Dominic understood better than Francis, this apostolic life required careful organisation. The friars' ideal of 'organised destitution' was, however, rather harder to achieve in practice. This tension between the need to organise – which included building friaries as effective preaching bases – and the principle of corporate poverty kept erupting in the thirteenth-century movements. The Franciscans and the Augustinian friars both had internal factions, emphasising either poverty or organisation; there was also rivalry between the Dominicans and Franciscans over who was truer to the spirit of corporate poverty. And there was the larger institutional matter of how the Church would adapt to the growing numbers of friars and friar-movements in its ranks.[5]

Several of these issues were coming to a head around the 1270s and this might help to explain why our London priors began to change their focus. In institutional terms, the death in 1274 of the Franciscans' important minister-general, Bonaventure, allowed the 'conventual' Franciscans (who favoured efficient organisation over absolute corporate poverty) to gain ground. Further signs of the friars' successful integration in the traditional Church came when the first mendicants were appointed to the senior post of cardinal in this decade: the Dominican Peter of Tarentaise in 1273 (the future pope Innocent V) and the Franciscan Girolamo Masci in 1278 (the future Nicholas IV).

The Dominicans were also changing the way they conceived their friaries at this time. Their early leader Jordan of Saxony had embellished the friars' late evening service of Compline to include a hymn to Mary, the Salve Regina, and a procession. With its colourful associations of repelling demons and encouraging visions of the Virgin, the theatricality of the procession of robed friars and its convenient time after the working day, this service became an *event* for townsfolk to attend. The Dominican Gerard de Frachet records lay people thronging to the order's churches in southern France to watch and listen to the service in the 1250s.[6] It may be this that caused the Dominicans to think about changing their simple chapels for the celebration of the Office into double churches with naves to house the eager townspeople.

There was another significant event in the 1270s: the important Church council known as the Second Council of Lyon met in 1274 and senior mendicants like Bonaventure attended (he died in Lyon), in addition to all the bishops, cardinals and abbots. One of the decisions made at the council was to re-organise the mendicant movements: the orders of friars approved by the time of the earlier 1215 Fourth Lateran Council – essentially the Franciscans and Dominicans – were allowed to continue but the smaller orders were to be disbanded. Now, the Carmelites, Augustine and Crossed friars successfully argued that they predated 1215 (with some creative accounts of the early history of their orders), but the

---

[5] Lawrence, *The Friars*, chapters 2–5; for Lawrence's neat paradox of 'organised destitution', see pp. x, 24.

[6] Lawrence, *The Friars*, pp. 81–2; William R. Bonniwell, *A History of the Dominican Liturgy, 1215–1945*, 2nd edn (New York: Wagner, 1945), pp. 148–66.

Pied and Sack friars were no longer allowed to recruit and so they withered away over a generation. The two smaller London friaries were, therefore, never able to progress into a 'Phase two' with a full monastic plan. It seems very likely that this major event had an effect on the mentality of the senior members of the 'spared' orders: they may have consciously decided to take a safer option and become more traditionally monastic, and therefore more integrated with the conventional church. They certainly did not want to be associated with radical friars such as the *zelanti* Franciscans who were on the fringes of heresy in the mid thirteenth century, even (like Gerard of Borgo San Donnino) prophesying the end of the Church and the replacement of the corrupt clergy with holy friars.[7] In England, the mendicant archbishops of Canterbury Robert Kilwardby and John Pecham, and the priors John of Darlington and Peter of Tewkesbury, were high ranking friars who travelled widely and may have influenced the direction their orders were taking at this time.[8]

The timing of the crucial decision by the London Dominicans is easier to pin down than that of the Franciscans. In October 1273 the Dominicans were still planning construction works on their original priory in the western suburb of Holborn; in June 1275 the Dominican archbishop of Canterbury Robert Kilwardby was beginning to acquire property for a new and larger priory in the south-west of the city (Chapter 2: The Second Black Friars). It is certainly tempting to date a strategic meeting of the London chapter (or of the archbishop, provincial prior, prior and senior obedientiaries) to 1274 when news about the developments at Lyon arrived. The decision taken was a great one: the Dominicans planned to build a grand new friary on an unprecedented scale, a project which would entail moving part of London's city wall and demolishing two Norman castles! The equivalent chapter meeting of the London Franciscans may not have reached quite such a dramatic decision but in the fourth quarter of the thirteenth century they too seem to have decided to begin work on a grander friary. At the very end of the century they received the backing of Edward I's new queen, Margaret of France, but even before this they were receiving significant financial and logistical support from leading townsmen such as the sheriff Walter le Potter in the 1270s and mayor Henry le Waleys in the 1280s or '90s (Chapter 4: Grey Friars, 'Acquiring and developing the friary'). The Franciscans accepted land donations in the 1270s, '80s and '90s that enabled them to extend their friary buildings northwards and westwards: this is when they were planning the transformation of their simple chapel and accommodation wing into a great church and cloister. The Geometric windows of this cloister certainly point to a completion date in the early fourteenth century (Figure 27). Did the London Franciscans watch their Dominican rivals develop a new site (rather close to theirs) and decide to compete by building a grand church and monastic cloister?

It seems that it was the Dominicans who made the first move, and this change might also be explained by local factors. At their Holborn priory they had a church and an accommodation wing by about 1267 (Figure 5). However, there were two constraints on any plans

---

[7] Lawrence, *The Friars*, pp. 53–60, 158–9.
[8] Röhrkasten, *Mendicant Houses*, pp. 38–9, 181, 189, 307.

they might have had to enlarge their church. Firstly, the land sloped down towards the river Fleet to the east: it would therefore be hard to extend the church eastwards and build a grander choir. Secondly, the friars' precinct only extended another 30ft (9m) westwards from their church and this was hardly enough room to build a preaching nave in which to process and sing the Salve Regina hymn. Was this part of the explanation for their decision to move house? Mayor Henry le Waleys and Edward I may also have sensed an opportunity to enhance the urban defences and refurbish this corner of the city.

The Carmelites and the Austin friars followed the lead of their more influential colleagues. The Carmelites rewrote their statutes at the general chapter held in London in 1281, reconciling their internal tensions – they were now urban preacher-monks rather than mountain-dwelling hermits of the Holy Land.[9] As has been described, both the Carmelites and the Austin friars began work on grander London friaries with a full cloister and double church, with work on their respective cloisters beginning in about the 1290s.

This change in the aspirations of the London friars, who came to view their priories as urban monasteries rather than simple preaching bases, has been more widely observed among the mendicants. In the third quarter of the thirteenth century the priors and guardians of several major Italian friaries began to transform their priories. Large building projects began in the 1260s in the Dominican friaries of Vicenza, Siena, Florence, Rome and Rieti, with the Franciscans beginning works around this time in Vicenza, Pisa and Piacenza. The Dominicans of Paris also began major works at this time. This change in aspirations has been described as 'monumentalization': the friars embraced a more monastic and therefore conventual life, and sought to stamp their spiritual vision on the urban landscape.[10] The London friars were therefore following the new developments of their international orders, albeit a decade or two behind their colleagues in the heartland of the mendicant movement. Some major English houses were embarking on building projects at just this time, for example the Gloucester Dominicans who appear to have been enlarging their thirteenth-century choir and accommodation wing into a full cloister. Other English priors and guardians of houses in the larger towns and cities then followed suit at the turn of the thirteenth and fourteenth centuries. The Exeter Franciscans planned a whole new site in the 1290s, the Hereford Dominicans did the same in the 1310s, the Franciscans of Ipswich and the Augustinian friars of Leicester began their large cloisters in the first half of the fourteenth century, at the same time as the Norwich Carmelites shifted the focus of their precinct, adding a whole new church to the south side of the cloister (and retaining their thirteenth-century chapel to the north).[11]

---

[9] Lawrence, *The Friars*, p. 96.
[10] Bruzelius, *Preaching, Building, and Burying*, pp. 38–46; Philippe Lorentz and Dany Sandron, *Atlas de Paris Au Moyen Âge: Éspace Urbain, Habitat, Société, Religion, Lieux de Pouvoir* (Paris: Parigramme, 2006), pp. 147–8.
[11] O'Sullivan, *In the Company of the Preachers*, pp. 142–3, 145–8, 161–4, 178–80, 195–7, 257–60.

To achieve all this, the priors needed financial backing from several wealthy patrons as well as the 'bread and butter' financial support provided by the alms and bequests of more ordinary Londoners. The generations of priors must have had some form of long-term planning in order to develop the relatively humble urban precincts of the 1270s (Figure 70) into the finished, almost abbatial, monasteries of the fifteenth century (Figure 72). Furthermore, this planning was two-fold: the priors had to acquire the necessary plots of land as well as managing a long-running construction campaign. Where there is enough evidence to track the accumulation of real estate, it took a century and a quarter for the Franciscans (Table 5, Figure 20) and over two centuries for the less-popular Crossed friars (Table 11, Figure 53). The actual construction campaigns tended to follow a basic sequence of choir, cloister, nave then second cloister, but there were variations (Figure 71). At Grey Friars and Crossed Friars the construction of the first cloister in the late thirteenth and early fourteenth century preceded the creation of a larger nave and choir; at White Friars a new choir and nave were built in the fourteenth century, but the friars retained their original thirteenth-century chapel (perhaps a Carmelite tradition), with the church thus having adjacent 'ould quyre' and 'new quire'. A recent study of Italian friaries described this long-term development as more of a 'process' (an evolving response to the aspirations of townsfolk and the needs of the friars) than a 'project' (the patient laying out of an architectural blueprint).[12] In London the lengthy process of acquiring dozens of small tenements to create the necessary space – the Grey friars and the Crossed friars played their respective jigsaw puzzles of land acquisition for over a century – may suggest more of a planned long-term project, at least by the late thirteenth century.

The architectural style of these new cloisters and naves was significantly more ornate than that of the thirteenth-century buildings – a large fragment of one of the windows of the early fourteenth-century Grey Friars nave is a very incomplete example (Figure 77) – but a relatively restrained and certainly not innovative style. The best illustration of this is the fourteenth-century nave of Austin Friars, which survived the Dissolution and the Great Fire, only to be destroyed in 1940 (Figure 44). There is perhaps a sense of a fourteenth-century London architectural style, broadly followed by the mendicants and the Augustinian canons and influenced by the concentration of secular and ecclesiastical architectural projects in the capital (Chapter 12: Architecture and Architectural Fragments of the London Friaries). This sense of architectural style associated with the town rather than the religious order has been observed in some Italian friaries, a reflection perhaps of the importance of local support from civic authorities and patrons.[13] The London mendicants – with their royal, noble and civic patrons – may have been particularly influential in one aspect of design. In the first half of the fourteenth century the London Dominicans and Franciscans built large and relatively open naves, divided by arcades supported on slender clustered

---

[12] Bruzelius, *Preaching, Building, and Burying*, pp. 1–17.
[13] Christopher Wilson, *The Gothic Cathedral: The Architecture of the Great Church, 1130–1530* (London: Thames and Hudson, 1990), p. 261.

piers and lit by large windows: the two naves may well have influenced the design of the parish churches in the new royal towns of Winchelsea and Kingston-upon-Hull and thus changed the expectation of what a grand parish church should look like.[14]

By the third quarter of the fourteenth century, the buildings of Black Friars and Grey Friars were effectively finished. It is notable, however, that the other mendicant orders continued their construction projects in the third quarter of the fourteenth century, right through the difficult time that followed the disaster of the Black Death in the middle of the century (Figure 71). The Carmelite, Austin and Crossed friars were all carrying out works on their churches, with the Carmelites boldly beginning work on a new choir in 1349 with the sponsorship of Hugh de Courtenay, earl of Devon, and the Crossed friars collecting alms for their new Lady chapel the following year. Even in the more or less completed Black Friars, window fragments from the second half of the fourteenth century show that individual donors paid for new windows, perhaps replacing outdated lancets with newer Perpendicular designs with all their associated opportunities for painted glass (Chapter 12: Architecture and Architectural Fragments of the London Friaries). The wide sense of loss experienced by the survivors of the Black Death sharpened the need for commemoration and intercession; the friars could provide Londoners with both these services.

The priors of the Carmelites and Austin friars achieved a satisfactory precinct by the turn of the fourteenth and fifteenth centuries; the less well endowed Crossed friars were still enlarging their choir in the second half of the fifteenth century. In our postulated 'Phase three' of the friaries, once the priors had completed the friary buildings they simply got on with the important business: performing the daily liturgy, educating the friars, preaching to and hearing confession from the living, assisting with the funerals of the recently deceased, and curating the spiritual health of deceased benefactors by means of chantry masses and anniversary funeral services. This sense of the completion of the London friaries is in contrast to the houses in the Italian peninsula, which were characterised instead by 'endemic incompletion': Italian fundraising and building campaigns continued to add wings and chapels, and to refurbish older spaces in the fifteenth and sixteenth centuries.[15] But in London, the friary building campaigns had largely stopped by the early fifteenth century or before (Figure 71); Londoners continued to support their friaries and invest in the friars' spiritual services but were now turning their fundraising towards rebuilding their parish churches.[16]

This 'Phase three' of the London friaries should not be seen as stagnation. There were still construction works going on: as we have seen, individual sponsors probably paid for new windows to replace old lancets at Black Friars in the years following the Black Death. And the Dominicans were later able to add a Lady chapel onto the north side of the choir in

---

[14] Clapham, 'The Friars as Builders', pp. 250–5; Nicola Coldstream, *The Decorated Style: Architecture and Ornament, 1240–1360* (London: British Museum, 1994), pp. 63–4, 149.

[15] Bruzelius, *Preaching, Building, and Burying*, pp. 1–17, 46–51, 104.

[16] Schofield, 'Saxon and Medieval Parish Churches in the City of London', pp. 76–8, table 1.

the 1470s, sponsored by Joan de Ingaldesthorp and intended to commemorate her brother John Tiptoft, earl of Worcester, who was executed in 1470 for his support for the Yorkist side in the Wars of the Roses. At Crossed Friars the ambitious prior William Bowry was planning another such grand architectural statement, either a Lady chapel or a retro-choir that would extend the church eastwards.

The sounds and atmosphere of the friary precincts were also changing. In our 'Phase two', priors built great friary churches in order to attract lay people to come and hear the friars' sermons; in our 'Phase three', the priors invited lay people into the precincts *to live*, at a price, of course. The first tenants were probably welcomed after the Black Death and their rents may have allowed the priors to weather the economic difficulties of those years. By the late medieval period there were about twenty-four households within the Black Friars (not counting the riverside properties the friars owned, or the claustral apartments converted in the 1530s) and a similar number at the White Friars. The mendicant friars thus became secular landlords, albeit on a smaller scale than other monastic orders. The tenants of these gated communities appreciated their privileged access to the friary churches, and many residents may also have chosen to live in these tenements – many of which were sited by the friary cemetery – to be close to deceased relatives (Chapter 18: London Friars and Londoners).

The friars established remarkable links with many other Londoners: for some citizens, and for many foreigners and aliens, the friaries were cross-boundary parish churches, where the living could hear preaching and the dead could rest. Many members of the wealthier merchant class of London supported the friars in life although surprisingly few chose to be buried here, preferring their London parish churches or their 'home' churches in their place of origin (Chapter 17: Burial and Commemoration in the London Friaries). An exception is the former mayor Sir Stephen Jenyns who died in 1523 and chose burial in the London Grey Friars; a rare illustration of his tomb survives, drawn by the Tudor herald Sir Thomas Wriothesley, Garter King of Arms (Figure 88c). But the friars' growing role in the city also brought tensions: agreements over burial fees had to be sought with the secular clergy in their parishes and some lay neighbours saw the friars' works as an irritant rather than an opportunity for salvation.[17]

By the second half of the fourteenth century the friars were a powerful spiritual force in London and throughout much of Europe. At the risk of reducing them to a checklist, they ticked so many boxes of medieval religion, even if some of these were verging on the contradictory. They were poor, so their prayers were particularly efficacious; however, many individual friaries were, in reality if not in principle, wealthy so the priors could build grand statements of religious devotion and effectively manage the spiritual services they offered. Friars were useful at funerary and civic processions, they celebrated masses for the dead (the sheer numbers of friars made them particularly good at delivering trentals, rapid bursts of thirty masses after death), they specialised of course in preaching, confession and

---

[17] For negotiations concerning tithes and burial fees, see Chapter 15: Economy, n. 14; for complaints by the Franciscans' neighbours, see Chapter 11: Precincts and the Use of Space, n. 4.

penance, they celebrated the liturgical sequence of services known as the Divine Office, and they ably turned their minds to academia and royal service. The London friars established close working relations with the highest patrons in the land, Henry III and his successors; for a while the royal family used the Black and Grey Friars as subsidiary mausoleums, as did one or two aristocratic patrons of the White Friars and Austin Friars (Chapter 17: Burial and Commemoration in the London Friaries). The London friars, like the movement as a whole, took academic study very seriously – study was the route to successful preaching – and several celebrated teachers and writers, including the Franciscan William of Ockham (he of the metaphorical razor), spent time here (Chapter 16: Spiritual Life and Education in the London Friaries).

What did the friars lack? The London friars did not own any important relics, unlike the Franciscans and Crossed friars of Paris who had fragments of the True Cross. A few English friaries had relics, including the York Dominicans who had the right hand of Mary Magdalene.[18] The English friars did not generally provide hospice care (this was the job of the Augustinian canons), nor education for lay people or other religious (their highly effective education system was largely internal), nor did they directly compete with the parish priests who provided masses for the living.[19]

When the draper William Calley paid £40 to the prior of Austin Friars in 1510 for a trental of masses to be performed every year, he was expecting this third phase of the friary to continue for ever; the merchant tailor John Skevyngton similarly expected his 1517 arrangement of daily masses at the Crossed Friars to be perpetual.[20] And so it might have been, had it not been for the curious chain of events set off by Erasmus, Luther and Henry VIII, the latter with his particularly complicated marital, dynastic and religious affairs. One of the early outcomes of England's long and unpredictable Reformation was, of course, the Dissolution of the Monasteries – including the friaries – at the end of the 1530s. The evidence discussed in Chapter 19: Dissolution suggests that it was only in 1537 that Londoners finally realised that their friaries and the other monasteries were doomed. The end came in November 1538 when monastic commissioners Thomas Legh and Richard Layton knocked on the friary doors and the priors and their friars signed the surrender documents.

But this was not quite the end: the early death of Edward VI in 1553 and the failure of the plot to install 'Queen Jane' on the throne allowed Mary to return the country to traditional religious practice. The brief re-establishment of the London Dominicans at Smithfield – one of only six monastic refoundations in her reign – gives us a fleeting taste of a counterfactual 'what if' history of a Catholic late Tudor England (Chapter 3: The Third Black Friars at St Bartholomew's, 1556–9).

---

[18] Ibid., p. 359; Michael Hayden, *Crutched Friars and Croisiers: The Canons Regular of the Order of the Holy Cross in England and France* (Rome: Crosier Generalate, 2013), p. 152.

[19] In Ireland it was the tertiary order of Franciscan laymen and women who ran schools for children; England had no tertiary friars: Ó Clabaigh, *The Friars in Ireland*, pp. 305–17.

[20] TNA, LR 14/129; CRO, DCH/X/13/2.

The seven orders of friars arrived in England in the thirteenth century imbued with the simple yet powerful ideas of Saints Francis and Dominic, with their emphasis on poverty and preaching. In the final quarter of the thirteenth century the Church was realigning these ideals and fixing the friars in a more traditional monastic structure centred on the celebration of Divine Office in church, in an urban context. The London priors rose to this challenge and built five remarkable friaries, with two more, the Sack Friars and Pied Friars, falling by the wayside in the re-organisation of the Church. The friars changed the physical and spiritual landscape of London in the thirteenth and fourteenth centuries. Their urban monasteries became remarkable centres of prayer, preaching and scholarship for the friars; they were also important spiritual poles of attraction for living and dead Londoners.

Timeline

Reign	Major events	London friaries
Henry III (1216–72)	1205–17 creation of Franciscan and Dominican orders in Europe	
		c. 1223 foundation of first Black Friars (in Holborn)
		1225 foundation of Grey Friars
	1245 Henry begins his great rebuilding of Westminster Abbey, foremost project in his sponsorship of the English Church	c. 1247 foundation of White Friars
	1264–7 Second Barons' War in southern England	c. 1265 foundation of Austin Friars
		1267 foundation of Pied Friars
		c. 1268 foundation of Crossed Friars
		1270 foundation of Sack Friars
Edward I (1272–1307)	1274 Second Council of Lyon: lesser orders of friars not allowed to continue	
		1286 refoundation of second Black Friars
		1305 closure of Sack Friars
Edward II (1307–27)		1317 closure of Pied Friars
	1310s and '20s rebellion and civil war	1326 murder of Edward's *custos* of London, Bishop Stapeldon, and his temporary burial at Pied Friars
Edward III (1327–77)	1337 Hundred Years War with France begins	
	1348–9 plague in England	1350s completion of church and double cloister at Grey Friars
		1360s completion of church and double cloister at Black Friars
Richard II (1377–99)	1381 Peasants' Revolt	1382 church synod at Black Friars condemns heresy of John Wyclif

326 TIMELINE

Reign	Major events	London friaries
Henry IV (1399–1413)	1400 Henry has Richard's body buried in the Black Friars at Kings Langley	1410s completion of White Friars church and cloister
Henry V (1413–22)	1415–22 campaigns in France	
Henry VI (1422–61)	1453 end of Hundred Years War	1440s completion of Austin Friars church and double cloister
	1455 beginning of Wars of Roses	
Edward IV (1461–83)	1470–1 temporary re-accession of Henry VI	1460s completion of Crossed Friars church and cloister
Richard III (1483–5)	1485 burial of Richard at Leicester Grey Friars following his defeat at Battle of Bosworth	
Henry VII (1485–1509)	1485 (or 1487) end of Wars of Roses	1490 or 1491 fire at Crossed Friars
Henry VIII (1509–47)	1517 beginning of Lutheran Reformation in Holy Roman Empire	c. 1522 Thomas Cromwell moves to a house in Austin Friars
	1529–34 Reformation Parliament; creation of independent (but Catholic) Church of England and divorce of Henry and Catherine of Aragon	1529 Cardinal Campeggio holds legatine court at Black Friars to investigate the legality of Henry's marriage to Catherine
	1536–41 Dissolution of the Monasteries	1538 closure and nationalisation of London friaries
		1544–5 sale of friary properties by Crown
Edward VI (1547–53)	Church of England becomes Protestant	
Mary (1553–58)	English church becomes Catholic once more	1556 refoundation of third Black Friars (in St Bartholomew's)
Elizabeth I (1558–1603)	re-establishment of Protestant Church of England	1559 closure of third Black Friars

Bibliography

Primary sources

Apothecaries' Company, London

'Secondary sources' files (archivists' notes and papers)
1920s photograph album (photos of archaeological and architectural features exposed during building works at Apothecaries' Hall and *The Times* building, inscribed 'presented Jan. 1930')

Ashmolean Museum, Oxford

WA1950.206   Panorama of London by Anton van den Wyngaerde

Bodleian Library, Oxford

MS Laud misc. 625   Register of Leicester Abbey

British Library, London (BL)

Department of Manuscripts

Additional MSS 5415.art.56, 7966A, 29704, 45131
Additional Charter 24490
Cotton Vitellius F xii
Harley charter 79.F.32
Harley MS 6033

Department of Maps

Crace Collection

Department of Rare Books

IA.55480 (incunable)

Centre for Metropolitan History (CMH), Institute of Historical Research, London

SESML   card index, maps etc. of 'Social and Economic Study of Medieval London, c. 1100–1666' project

328 BIBLIOGRAPHY

Cheshire Record Office, Chester (CRO)

DCH/O/, DCH/X/   Cholmondeley collection

Clothworkers' Company, London (CC)

CL/A/4/4   Book of deeds and wills
CL/G/7/1   Plan book
Uncatalogued manuscripts

College of Arms, London

MS CGY 647   Herald's list of tombs

Drapers' Company, London (DC)

A I   deeds and leases
A VII   deeds and leases
A XII   plans
Charter X
M B 1   Minute book
Plan Book

Folger Shakespeare Library, Washington DC, USA (FSL)

Loseley MSS (consulted on microfilm at Surrey History Centre; microfilms Z/407/2 and /3)

Guildhall Library, London (GL)

Guildhall Library manuscripts now accessed at London Metropolitan Archives

Historic England, London

'Registered files' (notes and records of London sites investigated by architectural historians at Historic England and its predecessors)

Historic England Archive, Swindon

RCHME investigators' field notes (research archive for Royal Commission on Historical Monuments (England) *Inventory* publications, including for *London* volumes of 1920s)
Photographic collection

London Archaeological Archive, London (LAA; part of Museum of London)

Archaeological site archives (sixty-two site archives consulted; archived by alphanumeric site code)

Dyson and Taylor archive (card-index of medieval property transactions created by Tony Dyson and Colin Taylor, primarily derived from Court of Husting enrolments, ordered by property. The archive thus functions as a property-based index to the Husting rolls in the LMA.)

'Post-Roman Gazetteer' (C. Harding, 1986 with later additions; typescript, three files, card index and maps); archaeological sites with 'PRG' prefix refer to this document

London Metropolitan Archives, London (LMA)

ACC/1360	Clitherow archive
CLA/007/FN/02/	Bridge wardens' accounts
CLA/008/EM/02/01/	City Lands grant books
CLA/023/DW/01/	Husting rolls (usually viewed on microfilm X109)
CLA/024/01/02/	Plea and Memoranda rolls of Mayor's Court
COL/CA/01/01/	Repertory books
COLLAGE	former Guildhall Library Print Room collections (now indexed and ordered via LMA COLLAGE number)
GL MSS	former Guildhall Library manuscripts (now accessed at LMA)

Museum of London

'copperplate' map	two plates of 1550s map; impression of third surviving plate (plate in Anhalt Art Gallery, Dessau, Germany)

Museum of London Archaeology, London (MOLA; now separate from Museum of London)

Unpublished reports (archived by site code and project code)
Digital data (archived by site code and project code)

The National Archives, London (TNA)

C 1	Court of Chancery cases
C 143	Inquisitions ad quod damnum
C 146	'ancient deeds', series C
C 54	close rolls
C 66	patent rolls
E 36	Treasury of the Receipt, miscellaneous books
E 40	'ancient deeds', series A
E 101	King's Remembrancer accounts
E 117	Exchequer, Church goods inventories and miscellanea
E 303	Court of Augmentations, conventual leases
E 310	Court of Augmentations, particulars for leases
E 314	Court of Augmentations, miscellaneous documents
E 315	Court of Augmentations, miscellaneous books
E 317	Parliamentary (Civil War) surveys
E 318	Court of Augmentations, particulars for grants

330 BIBLIOGRAPHY

E 321	Court of Augmentations, legal proceedings
E 326	'ancient deeds', series B
E 328	'ancient deeds', series BB
E 351	Pipe Office accounts
E 403	liberate rolls
JUST 1	Justices in eyre
LR 2	Auditors of Land Revenue, miscellaneous books
LR 14 and LR 15	Court of Augmentations, conventual deeds and documents
SC 6	Court of Augmentations, accounts
SC 11, SC 12	Court of Augmentations, rentals, surveys and valors
SP 1, SP 4	State Papers (viewed on 'State Papers Online')[1]

Nomura, Nomura House, St Martin-le-Grand, London (private collection)

Framed documents (on display on ninth floor)
Loose documents (kept in document store)

St Bartholomew's Hospital archive, London (SBH)

HC 1/	deeds and leases
HC 3	particulars for grant of St Bartholomew's Hospital and Grey Friars, 1546
HC 19	plan book

Society of Antiquaries, London

| MS 120 | Account book of the Wardrobe |

Surrey History Centre, Woking, Surrey (SHC)

| LM 346/, 347/ | Loseley collection |
| Microfilm Z/407/2 and /3 | copies of Folger Shakespeare Library, Loseley collection |

Victoria and Albert Museum, London

Department of Prints, Drawings and Paintings, D.1291–1907 (record of archaeological excavation at Blackfriars)

Westminster Abbey Muniments (WAM), London

Muniment book
Muniments
Register books

---

[1] References are given in the form TNA, SP 1/95, f. 71, no. 63, where 'f.' refers to the manuscript folio number and 'no.' refers to the former microfilm frame number; confusingly, only the latter element is used in 'State Papers Online' citations, abbreviated as f[rame] number. (The 'State Papers Online' reference for the above item is therefore 'TNA, SP 1/95, f. 63'.)

Printed primary sources

Account Rolls of the Obedientiaries of Peterborough, ed. Joan Greatrex, Northamptonshire Record Society, 33 (Northampton: NRS, 1984)

Blackfriars Records, ed. Albert Feuillerat (Oxford: Malone Society, 1913)

Die Briefe Jordans von Sachsen, des Zweiten Dominikanergenerals (1222–37), ed. Berthold Altaner (Leipzig: Harrassowitz, 1925)

Calendar of the Charter Rolls Preserved in the Public Record Office [*CChR*], 6 vols (London: HMSO, 1903–20)

Calendar of the Close Rolls Preserved in the Public Record Office [*CCR*], 61 vols (London: HMSO, 1892–1975)

Calendar of Early Mayor's Court Rolls: Preserved among the Archives of the Corporation of the City of London at the Guildhall, A.D. 1298–1307, ed. Arthur H. Thomas (Cambridge: Cambridge University Press, 1924) [series continues as *Calendar of Plea and Memoranda Rolls*]

Calendar of Inquisitions Miscellaneous, Chancery, Preserved in the Public Record Office, 8 vols (various publishers, 1916–2003)

Calendar of Letter-Books Preserved among the Archives of the Corporation of the City of London at the Guildhall, ed. Reginald R. Sharpe, 11 vols (London: Francis, 1899–1912)

Calendar of the Liberate Rolls Preserved in the Public Record Office [*CLR*], ed. William H. Stevenson, 6 vols (London: HMSO, 1916–64)

Calendar of Papal Letters [alternative title of some vols: *Calendar of Entries in the Papal Registers Relating to Great Britain and Ireland*], 20 vols (various publishers, 1893–)

Calendar of Patent Rolls Preserved in the Public Record Office [*CPR*], 36 vols (various publishers, 1893–)

Calendar of Plea and Memoranda Rolls Preserved among the Archives of the Corporation of the City of London at the Guildhall, ed. Arthur H. Thomas and P.E. Jones, 6 vols (Cambridge: Cambridge University Press, 1926–61)

Calendar of Wills Proved and Enrolled in the Court of Husting, 1258–1688, ed. Reginald R. Sharpe, 2 vols (London: Corporation of London, 1889–90)

Capgrave, John, *The Chronicle of England by John Capgrave*, ed. Francis C. Hingeston, Rolls series, 1 (London: Longman, 1858)

Cartulary of Holy Trinity Aldgate, ed. Gerald A.J. Hodgett, London Record Society, 7 (London: LRS, 1971)

Cartulary of St Bartholomew's Hospital, Founded 1123, ed. Nellie J.M. Kerling (London: St Bartholomew's Hospital, 1973)

Chronicon Angliae, ab Anno Domini 1328 usque ad Annum 1388, Auctore Monacho Quodam Sancti Albani, Rolls series, 64 (London: Longman, 1874)

Dugdale, William, *Monasticon Anglicanum: A History of the Abbies and Other Monasteries, Hospitals, Frieries, and Cathedral and Collegiate Churches, with their Dependencies, in England and Wales*, ed. J. Caley and others, 6 vols (London: Longman, 1817–30)

Durham Household Book: Or, the Accounts of the Bursar of the Monastery of Durham. From Pentecost 1530 to Pentecost 1534, ed. James Raine, Surtees Society, 18 (London: Nichols, 1844)

Eccleston, Thomas of, *Tractatus de Adventu Fratrum Minorum in Angliam*, ed. Andrew G. Little (Manchester: Manchester University Press, 1951)

_____, *The Coming of the Friars Minor to England & Germany: Being the Chronicles of . . . Thomas of Eccleston and . . . Jordan of Giano*, ed. E. Gurney Salter (London and Toronto: Dent, 1926)

Excerpta Historica: Or Illustrations of English History, ed. Samuel Bentley (London: privately printed, 1831)

Extracts from the Account Rolls of the Abbey of Durham, ed. Canon Fowler, 3 vols, Surtees Society, 99, 100, 103 (Durham: Andrews, 1898–1900)

Eyre of London, 14 Edward II, A.D. 1321, ed. Helen M. Cam, 2 vols, Selden Society, 85–6 (London, 1968)

Fitz-Thedmar, Arnold, *Chronicles of the Mayors and Sheriffs of London: A.D. 1188 to A.D. 1274*, ed. Henry T. Riley (London: Trübner, 1863)

Fontes Liturgiae Carmelitanae. Investigatio in decreta, codices et proprium sanctorum, ed. Paschalis Kallenberg (Rome: Institutum Carmelitanum, 1962)

Grey Friars of London: Their History, with the Register of Their Convent and an Appendix of Documents, ed. Charles L. Kingsford (Aberdeen: British Society of Franciscan Studies, 1915)

Hatton, Edward, *A New View of London: Or, an Ample Account of that City, in . . . Eight Sections*, 2 vols (London: Chiswell and Churchill, 1708)

Howes, John, *John Howes' MS., 1582: Being 'a Brief Note of the Order and Manner of the Proceedings in the First Erection Of' the Three Royal Hospitals of Christ, Bridewell & St Thomas the Apostle*, ed. William Lempriere (London: privately printed, 1904)

Knighton, Henry, *Knighton's Chronicle, 1337–1396*, ed. Geoffrey H. Martin, Oxford Medieval Texts (Oxford: Clarendon, 1995)

Langland, William, *Piers Plowman: A New Annotated Edition of the C-Text*, ed. Derek A. Pearsall (Exeter: University of Exeter Press, 2008)

Leland, John, *Antiquarii de Rebus Britannicis Collectanea*, ed. Thomas Hearne, 6 vols (London: Richardson, 1770)

Leonis X. Pontificis Maximi Regesta, ed. Joseph A. G. Hergenroether, 6 vols (Freiburg: Sumptibus Herder, 1884–8)

Letters and Papers, Foreign and Domestic, of the Reign of Henry VIII, ed. John S. Brewer, James Gairdner and Robert H. Brodie, 22 vols (London: Longman, 1862–1932)

London Viewers and Their Certificates, 1508–1558: Certificates of the Sworn Viewers of the City of London, ed. Janet S. Loengard, London Record Society publications, 26 (London: LRS, 1989)

Machyn, Henry, *The Diary of Henry Machyn: Citizen and Merchant-Taylor of London, from A.D. 1550 to A.D. 1563*, ed. John G. Nichols, Camden Society, old series, 42 (London: Camden Society, 1848)

Manners and Household Expenses of England in the Thirteenth and Fifteenth Centuries: Illustrated by Original Records, ed. Beriah Botfield (London: Nicol, 1841)

Mills, Peter, and John Oliver *The Survey of Building Sites in the City of London after the Great Fire of 1666*, 5 vols, London Topographical Society, 97–9, 101, 103 (London: LTS, 1962–7)

Monumenta Franciscana, ed. John S. Brewer, 2 vols (London: Longman, 1858)

De Oudste Constituties van de Dominicanen, ed. Antoninus H. Thomas, Bibliothèque de la Revue d'Histoire Ecclésiastique, 42 (Leuven, 1965)

Paris, Matthew, *Chronica Majora*, ed. H.R. Luard, Rolls series, 57, 7 vols (London: Longman, 1872–83)

Parliament Rolls of Medieval England, 1275–1504, ed. Chris Given-Wilson and others, 16 vols (Woodbridge: Boydell, 2005)

Pierce the Ploughmans Crede, to Which Is Appended God Spede the Plough, ed. Walter W. Skeat, Early English Text Society, 30 (London: Paul, 1867)

Pio, Giovanni M., *Delle Vite de gli Huomini Illustri de S. Domenico* (Bologna: Bellagamba, 1607)

Records of St Bartholomew's Priory and of the Church and Parish of St. Bartholomew the Great, West Smithfield, ed. Edward A. Webb, 2 vols (Oxford: Oxford University Press, 1921)

Records of the Worshipful Company of Carpenters, ed. Bower Marsh, 7 vols (Oxford: Oxford University Press, 1913–68)

La Règle de Saint Augustin, ed. Luc Verheijen, 2 vols, Études Augustiniennes (Antiquité), 29–30 (Paris: Brepols, 1967)

Report of the Deputy Keeper of the Public Records, 120 vols (London: HMSO, 1865–)

Rotuli Hundredorum Temp. Hen. III & Edw. I. in Turr' Lond' et in Curia Receptae Scaccarij Westm. Asservati, ed. William Illingworth, 2 vols (London: Eyre and Strahan, 1812)

Royal Commission on Historic Monuments, England (RCHME), *Inventory of the Historical Monuments in London*, 5 vols (London: HMSO, 1924–30),

Sources of the Modern Roman Liturgy, ed. Stephen J.P. Van Dijk, 2 vols, Studia et Documenta Franciscana, 1–2 (Leiden: Brill, 1963)

Statutes of the Realm: From Original Records, etc. (1101–1713), ed. A. Luders and others, 11 vols (London, 1810–28)

Stow, John, *A Survey of London*, ed. Charles L. Kingsford, 2 vols (Oxford: Clarendon, 1908)

Tanner, Thomas, *Notitia Monastica: Or, an Account of All the Abbies, Priories and Houses of Friers, Heretofore in England and Wales*, (London: William Bowyer, 1744)

Testamenta Vetusta: Being Illustrations from Wills, of Manners, Customs, &c. as Well as of the Descents and Possessions of Many Distinguished Families, ed. Nicholas H. Nicolas, 2 vols (London: Nichols, 1826)

Three Chapters of Letters Relating to the Suppression of Monasteries, ed. Thomas Wright Camden Society, old series, 26 (London: Camden Society, 1843)

Walsingham, Thomas, *Historia Anglicana: Thomæ Walsingham, Quondam Monachi S. Albani*, ed. Henry T. Riley, Rolls series, 28, 2 vols (London: Longman, 1863)

Williams, John, *Account of the Monastic Treasures Confiscated at the Dissolution of the Various Houses in England*, ed. W. Turnbull (Edinburgh: Abbotsford Club, 1836)

Wriothesley, Charles, *A Chronicle of England during the Reigns of the Tudors, from A.D. 1485 to 1559*, ed. William D. Hamilton, Camden Society, new series, 11, 20, 2 vols (London: Camden Society, 1875)

Maps and plans

In chronological order

Wyngaerde's panorama of 1540s (Figure 12, Figure 23, Figure 47, Figure 51) Ashmolean Museum WA1950.206, printed in *Panorama of London by Antonis Van der Wyngaerde Circa 1544*, ed. H. Colvin and S. Foister, London Topographical Society publication, 151 (London: LTS, 1996)

'copperplate' map of 1550s (Figure 24, Figure 40)
   two plates in Museum of London, third plate in Anhalt Art Gallery, Dessau; printed in *Tudor London: A Map and a View*, ed. A. Saunders and J. Schofield, London Topographical Society, 159 (London: LTS in association with the Museum of London, 2001)
'Agas' woodcut map of 1560s
   printed in *A Collection of Early Maps of London, 1553-1667* (Lympne Castle, Kent: H. Margary in association with Guildhall Library, 1981)
Haiward & Gascoyne plan of 1597
   various versions printed in *The Elizabethan Tower of London: The Haiward and Gascoyne Plan of 1597*, ed. A. Keay, London Topographical Society, 158 (London: LTS, 2001)
seventeenth-century plans of Greyfriars (Figure 22, Figure 26, Figure 29)
   GL, MS 22637/02 (c. 1660); LMA, COLLAGE 21718 (1656); Nomura, unnumbered loose plan (1639?); SBH, HC 19, f. 59 (1616); printed in Dorian Gerhold, *London Plotted: Plans of London Buildings c. 1450-1720*, London Topographical Society, 178 (London: LTS, 2016), pp. 206-7, plan 119, fig. 247 [GL plan]; pp. 85-6, plan 26, fig. 86 [LMA plan]; pp. 213-14, plan 125, fig. 256 [Nomura plan]; pp. 69-71, plan 20, fig. 63 [SBH plan]
seventeenth-century plans of Whitefriars (Figure 37)
   BL, Maps Crace Portfolio 8 104 (19th-century copy of plan of c. 1630); CC; CL/G/7/1 (Plan Book), f. 42 (alternative numbering: f. 59) (plan of c. 1658); latter printed in Gerhold, *London Plotted*, pp. 86-8, plan 27, fig. 88
seventeenth-century plan of part of Austin Friars
   DC, A XII 121 (c. 1620); printed in Gerhold, *London Plotted*, pp. 78-82, plan 24, figs 77, 82
Leake survey of 1666
   BL, Add. MS 5415.art.56 (formerly Add. MS 5415.E.1)
Ogilby & Morgan map of 1676 (Figure 52)
   printed in *A Large and Accurate Map of the City of London* (Lympne Castle, Kent: H. Margary in association with Guildhall Library, 1976)
Rocque map of 1746
   printed in *A Plan of the Cities of London and Westminster, and Borough of Southwark* (Lympne Castle, Kent: H. Margary in association with Guildhall Library, 1971)
Ordnance Survey maps of 1870s
   1:1056 maps printed (at reduced scale) in *Godfrey Edition* series (Consett: A. Godfrey Maps)
Ordnance Survey digital mapping (2008 update)
   1:1250 digital 'MasterMap' series (Southampton: Ordnance Survey)

Secondary sources

Includes unpublished reports [archival location in square brackets where appropriate]

Alban, Kevin, *The Teaching and Impact of the Doctrinale of Thomas Netter of Walden*, Medieval Church Studies, 7 (Turnhout: Brepols, 2010)

Alexander, Jennifer S., 'Building Stone from the East Midlands Quarries: Sources, Transportation and Usage', *Medieval Archaeology*, 39 (1995), 107-38

Alizeri, Federigo, *Notizie dei Professori del Disegno in Liguria dalle Origini al Secolo XVI*, 6 vols (Genoa: Sambolino, 1870)

Andrews, Frances, *The Other Friars: The Carmelite, Augustinian, Sack and Pied Friars in the Middle Ages* (Woodbridge: Boydell, 2006)

Backhouse, Janet, *The Sherborne Missal* (London: British Library, 1999)

Badham, Sally, and Sophie Oosterwijk, 'The Tomb Monument of Katherine, Daughter of Henry III and Eleanor of Provence (1253–7)', *Antiquaries Journal*, 92 (2012), 169–96

Baker, John H., *The Men of Court 1450-1550: A Prosopography of the Inns of Court and Chancery and the Courts of Law*, 2 vols (London: Selden Society, 2012)

____, 'Rede, Sir Robert (d. 1519)', *ODNB* (Oxford: Oxford University Press, 2004) <http://www.oxforddnb.com/view/article/23247> [accessed 14 May 2015]

Barber, Bruno, '10 Bouverie Street, London EC4, an archaeological excavation and watching brief', (unpublished Museum of London report, 1997) [LAA, BOV95]

____, *The London Charterhouse*, MoLAS Monograph, 10 (London: Museum of London Archaeology Service, 2002)

Barron, Caroline M., 'Centres of Conspicuous Consumption: The Aristocratic Town Houses in London 1200–1550', *London Journal*, 20 (1995), 1–16

____, *London in the Later Middle Ages: Government and People, 1200–1500* (Oxford: Oxford University Press, 2004)

____, 'The Parish Fraternities of Medieval London', in *The Church in Pre-Reformation Society: Essays in Honour of F.R.H. Du Boulay*, ed. C.M. Barron and C. Harper-Bill (Woodbridge: Boydell, 1985), pp. 13–37

Barron, Caroline M., and Matthew Davies, eds, *The Religious Houses of London and Middlesex* (London: Centre for Metropolitan History, 2007)

Barron, Caroline M., and Vanessa Harding, 'London', in *English County Histories: A Guide. A Tribute to C.R. Elrington* (Stroud: Alan Sutton, 1994), pp. 258–69

Barron, Caroline M., with Penelope Hunting and Jane Roscoe, *The Parish of St Andrew Holborn* (London: Diamond Trading Company, 1979)

Barron, Caroline M., and Laura Wright, 'The London Middle English Guild Certificates of 1388–9', *Nottingham Medieval Studies*, 39 (1995), 108–45

Bernard, George W., 'Grey, Richard, Third Earl of Kent (b. in or before 1478, d. 1524)', *ODNB* (Oxford: Oxford University Press, 2004) <http://www.oxforddnb.com/view/article/58355> [accessed 14 October 2008]

____, *The King's Reformation: Henry VIII and the Remaking of the English Church* (New Haven and London: Yale University Press, 2005)

Betts, Ian, 'The Building Materials', in *The Cluniac Priory and Abbey of St Saviour Bermondsey, Surrey*, ed. T. Dyson and others, MOLA Monograph, 50 (London: Museum of London Archaeology, 2011), pp. 201–14

____, 'Ceramic and Other Building Material', in *Holywell Priory and the Development of Shoreditch to c. 1600: Archaeology from the London Overground East London Line*, ed. R. Bull and others, MOLA Monograph, 53 (London: Museum of London Archaeology, 2011), pp. 149–52

____, 'Ceramic and Stone Building Material', in *The London Charterhouse*, ed. B. Barber and C. Thomas, MoLAS Monograph, 10 (London: Museum of London Archaeology Service, 2002), pp. 97–9

____, 'Medieval Floor Tiles in London Churches', in J. Schofield, 'Saxon and Medieval Parish Churches in the City of London: A Review', *Transactions of the London and Middlesex Archaeological Society*, 45 (1994), 23–146 (pp. 133–40)

____, *Medieval 'Westminster' Floor Tiles*, MoLAS Monograph, 11 (London: Museum of London Archaeology Service, 2002)

____, 'Other Stone and Ceramic Building Material', in *The Augustinian Nunnery of St Mary Clerkenwell, London: Excavations 1974-96*, ed. B. Sloane, MOLA Monograph, 57 (London: Museum of London Archaeology, 2013), pp. 212-18

Betts, Ian, and Thomas Cromwell, 'Windsor Castle Governor's House Floor: Recording a Medieval Tiled Floor', *CFA News* (newsletter of English Heritage, Centre for Archaeology), Winter 2002, 10-11

Biller, Peter, 'Chatton, Walter (d. 1343/4)', *ODNB* (Oxford: Oxford University Press, 2004) <http://www.oxforddnb.com/view/article/4904> [accessed 24 May 2016]

Blackley, F.D., 'The Tomb of Isabella of France, Wife of Edward II of England', *International Society for the Study of Church Monuments*, Bulletin 8 (1983), 161-4

Blatherwick, Simon, and Richard Bluer, *Great Houses, Moats and Mills on the South Bank of the Thames: Medieval and Tudor Southwark and Rotherhithe*, MOLA Monograph, 47 (London: Museum of London Archaeology, 2009)

Bluer, Richard, and Patrick Allen, 'A watching brief at Apothecaries Hall, 20-26 Blackfriars Lane, EC4' (unpublished Museum of London report, 1985) [LAA, site APO81]

Bolton, James L., *The Alien Communities of London in the Fifteenth Century: The Subsidy Rolls of 1440 and 1483-4* (Stamford: Richard III & Yorkist History Trust in association with P. Watkins, 1998)

Bond, C. James, 'Water Management in the Urban Monastery', in *Advances in Monastic Archaeology*, ed. R. Gilchrist and H.C. Mytum, British Archaeological Reports, 227 (Oxford: Tempus Reparatum, 1993), pp. 43-78

Bonniwell, William Raymond, *A History of the Dominican Liturgy, 1215-1945*, 2nd edn (New York: Wagner, 1945)

Borman, Tracy, *Thomas Cromwell: The Untold Story of Henry VIII's Most Faithful Servant* (London: Hodder & Stoughton, 2014)

Bowsher, David, Nick Holder, Tony Dyson and Isca Howell, *The London Guildhall: An Archaeological History of a Neighbourhood from Early Medieval to Modern Times*, MoLAS Monograph, 36, 2 vols (London: Museum of London Archaeology Service, 2007)

Bowsher, Julian, 'The Chapel Royal at Greenwich Palace', *The Court Historian*, 11 (2006), 155-62

Bradley, Helen L., 'Italian Merchants in London 1350-1450' (unpublished doctoral thesis, University of London, Royal Holloway, 1992) [Institute of Historical Research library]

____, 'Lucia Visconti, Countess of Kent (d. 1424)', in *Medieval London Widows, 1300-1500*, ed. C.M. Barron and A.F. Sutton (London: Hambledon, 1994), pp. 77-84

Bradley, Simon, and Nikolaus Pevsner, *London 1: The City of London*, The Buildings of England (New Haven and London: Yale University Press, 2002)

Brigden, Susan, *London and the Reformation* (Oxford: Clarendon Press, 1989)

Bruce, Graham, 'An archaeological excavation and watching brief on the site of 109-118 Old Broad Street, City of London EC2' (unpublished AOC Archaeology report, 1997) [LAA, site OBE96]

Bruzelius, Caroline, *Preaching, Building, and Burying: Friars in the Medieval City* (New Haven and London: Yale University Press, 2014)

Bryson, Alan, 'Wallop, Sir John (b. before 1492, d. 1551)', *ODNB* (Oxford: Oxford University Press, 2008) <http://www.oxforddnb.com/view/article/28581> [accessed 28 June 2016]

Buck, Mark C., 'Stapeldon, Walter (b. in or before 1265, d. 1326)', *ODNB* (Oxford: Oxford University Press, 2004) <http://www.oxforddnb.com/view/article/26296> [accessed 11 May 2015]

Burgess, Clive, 'Friars and the Parish in Late Medieval Bristol: Observations and Possibilities', in *The Friars in Medieval Britain: Proceedings of the 2007 Harlaxton Symposium*, ed. N. Rogers, Harlaxton Medieval Studies, 19 (Donington: Shaun Tyas, 2010), pp. 73–96

Butler, Laurence, 'The Archaeology of Urban Monasteries in Britain', in *Advances in Monastic Archaeology*, ed. R. Gilchrist and H.C. Mytum, British Archaeological Reports, 227 (Oxford: Archaeopress, 1993), pp. 79–86

——, 'The Houses of the Mendicant Orders in Britain: Recent Archaeological Work', in *Archaeological Papers from York Presented to M. W. Barley*, ed. P.V. Addyman and V.E. Black (York: York Archaeological Trust, 1984), pp. 123–36

Campbell, William H., 'Franciscan Preaching in Thirteenth-Century England: Sources, Problems and Possibilities', in *The Friars in Medieval Britain: Proceedings of the 2007 Harlaxton Symposium*, ed. N. Rogers, Harlaxton Medieval Studies, 19 (Donington: Shaun Tyas, 2010), pp. 25–40

Cannon, Joanna, *Religious Poverty, Visual Riches: Art in the Dominican Churches of Central Italy in the Thirteenth and Fourteenth Centuries* (New Haven and London: Yale University Press, 2013)

Carlin, Martha, and Derek Keene, 'Historical Gazetteer of London before the Great Fire. St Botolph Aldgate: Minories, East Side; the Abbey of St Clare; Holy Trinity Minories' (unpublished typescript, London: University of London, Institute of Historical Research, 1987) [Institute of Historical Research library]

Carter, P.R.N., 'Rich, Richard, First Baron Rich (1496/7–1567)', *ODNB* (Oxford: Oxford University Press, 2004) <http://www.oxforddnb.com/view/article/23491> [accessed 28 May 2014]

Cater, William A., 'Further Notes on the Austin Friary of London', *Journal of the British Archaeological Association*, 21 (1915), 205–30

——, 'The Priory of Austin Friars, London', *Journal of the British Archaeological Association*, 18 (1912), 25–44, 57–82

Catto, Jeremy, 'Patrington, Stephen (d. 1417)', *ODNB* (Oxford: Oxford University Press, 2004) <http://www.oxforddnb.com/view/article/21569> [accessed 10 June 2016]

——, 'Penketh, Thomas (d. 1487)', *ODNB* (Oxford: Oxford University Press, 2004) <http://www.oxforddnb.com/view/article/21844> [accessed 10 June 2016]

——, 'Woodford, William (d. in or after 1397)', *ODNB* (Oxford: Oxford University Press, 2004) <http://www.oxforddnb.com/view/article/29919> [accessed 10 June 2016)]

Clapham, Alfred W., 'The Friars as Builders', in A.W. Clapham and W.H. Godfrey, *Some Famous Buildings and their Story: Being the Results of Recent Research in London and Elsewhere* (London: Technical Journals, 1913), pp. 240–67

——, 'The Topography of the Carmelite Priory of London', *Journal of the British Archaeological Association*, 17 (1910), 15–31

——, 'On the Topography of the Dominican Priory of London', *Archaeologia*, 63 (1911), 57–84

Clark, James G., 'Trevet, Nicholas (b. 1257×65, d. in or after 1334)', *ODNB* (Oxford: Oxford University Press, 2004) <http://www.oxforddnb.com/view/article/27744> [accessed 8 June 2016]

Clarke, Rachel, ed., *Norwich White Friars*, East Anglian Archaeology Monograph (Chelmsford: East Anglian Archaeology, forthcoming)

Clay, Rotha Mary, *The Hermits and Anchorities of England* (London: Methuen, 1914)

Coldstream, Nicola, *The Decorated Style: Architecture and Ornament, 1240–1360* (London: British Museum, 1994)

Colson, Justin, 'Alien Communities and Alien Fraternities in Later Medieval London', *London Journal*, 35(2) (2010), 111–43

Colvin, Howard M., *The History of the King's Works*, 6 vols (London: HMSO, 1963–82)

Cooper, Donal, 'Access all Areas? Spatial Divides in the Mendicant Churches of Late Medieval Tuscany', in *Ritual and Space in the Middle Ages*, ed. F. Andrews, Harlaxton Medieval Studies, 21 (Donington: Shaun Tyas, 2011), pp. 90–107

Cooper, Donal, and James R. Banker, 'The Church of Borgo San Sepolcro in the Late Middle Ages and Renaissance', in *Sassetta: The Borgo San Sepolcro Altarpiece*, ed. M. Israels, 2 vols (Leiden and Florence: Primavera Press/Villa I Tatti, 2009), i, 53–85; ii, 585–9

Coote, Henry C., 'The Ordinances of Some Secular Guilds of London, 1354 to 1496', *Transactions of the London and Middlesex Archaeological Society*, 4 (1871), 1–59

Coppack, Glyn, *Abbeys and Priories* (Stroud: Tempus, 2006)

Copsey, Richard, 'Brome, Thomas (d. c. 1380)', *ODNB* (Oxford: Oxford University Press) <http://www.oxforddnb.com/view/article/3504> [accessed 8 June 2016]

____, 'The Medieval Carmelite Priory at London, a Chronology' (unpublished typescript, 2008), <http://www.carmelite.org/> [accessed 13 May 2015]

Coss, Peter, *The Foundations of Gentry Life: The Multons of Frampton and their World, 1270–1370* (Oxford: Oxford University Press, 2010)

Courtenay, William J. 'The London Studia in the Fourteenth Century', *Medievalia et Humanistica*, new series, 13 (1985), 127–41

____, 'Ockham, Chatton, and the London *Studium*: Observations on Recent Changes in Ockham's Biography', in *Die Gegenwart Ockhams*, ed. W. Vossenkuhl and R. Schönberger (Weinheim: VCH Acta Humaniora, 1990), pp. 327–37

____, 'Ockham, William of (c. 1287–1347)', *ODNB* (Oxford: Oxford University Press, 2004) <http://www.oxforddnb.com/view/article/20493> [accessed 24 May 2016]

____, 'Wodeham [Woodham, Goddam], Adam (c. 1295–1358)', *ODNB* (Oxford: Oxford University Press, 2004) <http://www.oxforddnb.com/view/article/10854> [accessed 8 June 2016]

Cowie, Robert, 'The Priory and Manor of Hounslow: Excavations at Hounslow Police Station, Montague Road, Hounslow', *Transactions of the London and Middlesex Archaeological Society*, 46 (1995), 125–35

Cragoe, Carol D., 'Fabric, Tombs and Precinct, 1087–1540', in *St Paul's: The Cathedral Church of London, 604–2004*, ed. D. Keene, A. Burns and A. Saint (New Haven and London: Yale University Press, 2004), pp. 127–42

Crowley, Naomi, 'Bricks', in *The Cistercian Abbey of St Mary Graces, East Smithfield, London*, ed. I. Grainger, C. Phillpotts and p. Mills, MOLA Monograph, 44 (London: Museum of London Archaeology, 2011), pp. 133–4

____, 'Ceramic Building Material', in *Excavations at the Priory and Hospital of St Mary*

Spital, London, ed. C. Thomas, B. Sloane and C. Phillpotts, MoLAS Monograph, 1 (London: Museum of London Archaeology Service, 1997), pp. 195–201

Cunich, Peter, 'Layton, Richard (c. 1498–1544)', *ODNB* (Oxford: Oxford University Press, 2008) <http://www.oxforddnb.com/view/article/16226> [accessed 28 June 2016]

Davies, Richard G., 'Mascall, Robert (d. 1416)', *ODNB* (Oxford: Oxford University Press, 2004) <http://www.oxforddnb.com/view/article/18257> [accessed 14 May 2015]

Davis, Virginia, 'Lowe, John (c. 1385–1467)', *ODNB* (Oxford: Oxford University Press, 2004) <http://www.oxforddnb.com/view/article/17083> [accessed 8 June 2016]

____, 'Mendicants in London in the Reign of Richard II', *London Journal*, 25(2) (2000), 1–12

D'Avray, David L., *The Preaching of the Friars: Sermons Diffused from Paris before 1300* (Oxford: Clarendon Press, 1985)

De Belsunce, François-Xavier, *L'Antiquité de l'Église de Marseille et la Succession de ses Évêques*, 3 vols (Marseilles: Brébion, 1747)

Dean, David, 'Image and Ritual in the Tudor Parliaments', in *Tudor Political Culture*, ed. D. Hoak (Cambridge: Cambridge University Press, 1995), pp. 243–71

Divers, David, Chris Mayo, Nathalie Cohen and Chris Jarrett, *A New Millennium at Southwark Cathedral: Investigations into the First Two Thousand Years* (London: Pre-Construct Archaeology, 2009)

Dobson, R. Barrie, 'Mendicant Ideal and Practice in Late Medieval York', in *Archaeological Papers from York Presented to M.W. Barley*, ed. P.V. Addyman and V.E. Black (York: York Archaeological Trust, 1984), pp. 109–22

Du Boulay, F.R.H., 'The Quarrel between the Carmelite Friars and the Secular Clergy of London, 1464–68', *Journal of Ecclesiastical History*, 6 (1955), 156–74

Duffy, Eamon, *The Stripping of the Altars: Traditional Religion in England, c. 1400–c. 1580* (New Haven and London: Yale University Press, 2005), 2nd edn

Dyson, T., and others, *The Cluniac Priory and Abbey of St Saviour Bermondsey, Surrey*, MOLA Monograph, 50 (London: Museum of London Archaeology, 2011)

Eames, Elizabeth, *Catalogue of Medieval Lead-Glazed Earthenware Tiles in the Department of Medieval and Later Antiquities, British Museum* (London: British Museum Publications, 1980)

____, *English Tilers* (London: British Museum Press, 1992)

____, 'The Tile Pavement', in 'Excavations at Eltham Palace', *Transactions of the London and Middlesex Archaeological Society*, 33 (1982), 238–44

Emden, Alfred B., *A Biographical Register of the University of Cambridge to 1500* (Cambridge: Cambridge University Press, 1963)

____, *A Biographical Register of the University of Oxford to A.D. 1500*, 3 vols (Oxford: Oxford University Press, 1957)

____, *A Survey of Dominicans in England Based on the Ordination Lists in Episcopal Registers (1268–1538)*, Dissertationes Historicae, 18 (Rome: Sabina, 1967)

Emery, Phillip A., and Elizabeth Rutledge, *Norwich Greyfriars: Pre-Conquest Town and Medieval Friary* (Dereham: Norfolk Museums and Archaeology Service, 2007)

Emery, Richard, *The Friars in Medieval France: A Catalogue of French Mendicant Convents, 1200–1550* (New York: Columbia University Press, 1962)

____, 'The Friars of the Blessed Mary and the Pied Friars', *Speculum*, 24 (1949), 228–38

____, 'The Friars of the Sack', *Speculum*, 18 (1943), 323–34

Erler, Mary C., *Reading and Writing during the Dissolution: Monks, Friars, and Nuns 1530–1558* (Cambridge: Cambridge University Press, 2013)

Felder, Hilarin, *Geschichte der wissenschaftlichen Studien im Franziskanerorden bis um die Mitte des 13. Jahrhunderts* (Freiburg: Herder, 1904)

Galloway, James, Derek Keene and Margaret Murphy, 'Fuelling the City: Production and Distribution of Firewood and Fuel in London's Region, 1290–1400', *Economic History Review*, 49 (1996), 447–72

Gerhold, Dorian, *London Plotted: Plans of London Buildings c. 1450–1720*, London Topographical Society, 178 (London: LTS, 2016)

Gilchrist, Roberta, *Contemplation and Action: The Other Monasticism*, The Archaeology of Medieval Britain (London: Leicester University Press, 1995)

―――, *Norwich Cathedral Close: The Evolution of the English Cathedral Landscape* (Woodbridge: Boydell, 2005)

Gilchrist, Roberta, and Barney Sloane, *Requiem: The Medieval Monastic Cemetery in Britain* (London: Museum of London Archaeology Service, 2005)

Grainger, Ian, and others, *The Black Death Cemetery, East Smithfield, London*, MOLA Monograph, 43 (London: Museum of London Archaeology Service, 2008)

Grainger, Ian, and Christopher Phillpotts, *The Cistercian Abbey of St Mary Graces, East Smithfield, London*, MOLA Monograph, 44 (London: Museum of London Archaeology, 2011)

Gransden, Antonia, *Historical Writing in England*, 2 vols (London: Routledge, 1974–82)

Greene, J. Patrick, *Medieval Monasteries* (Leicester: Leicester University Press, 1992)

Greenhill, Frank A., 'Austin Friars, London', *Transactions of the Monumental Brass Society*, 8.1 (1949), 330–41

Grimes, William Francis, *The Excavation of Roman and Mediaeval London* (New York: Praeger, 1968)

Gwynn, Aubrey, *The English Austin Friars in the Time of Wyclif* (Oxford: Oxford University Press, 1940)

Hamilton, J.S., 'Lacy, Henry de, Fifth Earl of Lincoln (1249–1311)', *ODNB* (Oxford: Oxford University Press, 2004) <http://www.oxforddnb.com/view/article/15851> [accessed 20 December 2013]

Harding, Vanessa, 'Burial Choice and Burial Location in Later Medieval London', in *Death in Towns: Urban Responses to the Dying and the Dead, 100–1600*, ed. S. Bassett (Leicester: Leicester University Press, 1992), pp. 119–35

―――, 'Space, Property, and Propriety in Urban England', *Journal of Interdisciplinary History*, 32 (2001), 549–69

Hart, Stephen, *Medieval Church Window Tracery in England* (Woodbridge: Boydell, 2010)

Harvey, Barbara F., *Living and Dying in England, 1100–1540: The Monastic Experience* (Oxford: Clarendon Press, 1993)

Harvey, John, *The Perpendicular Style, 1330–1485* (London: Batsford, 1978)

Harvey, John, and Arthur Oswald, *English Mediaeval Architects: A Biographical Dictionary down to 1550, Including Master Masons, Carpenters, Carvers, Building Contractors and Others Responsible for Design* (Gloucester: Sutton, 1987), 2nd edn

Harward, Chiz, Nick Holder and Christopher Thomas, *The Medieval Priory and Hospital of St Mary Spital and the Bishopsgate Suburb: Excavations at Spitalfields Market,*

London E1, 1991–2007, MOLA Monograph (London: Museum of London Archaeology, forthcoming)

Hayden, Michael, *Crutched Friars and Croisiers: The Canons Regular of the Order of the Holy Cross in England and France* (Rome: Crosier Generalate, 2013)

―――, 'The Crutched Friars in England', *Clairlieu*, 47 (1989), 145–75

Heale, Martin, *Monasticism in Late Medieval England, c. 1300–1535* (Manchester: Manchester University Press, 2009)

Hillaby, Joe, 'London: The 13th-Century Jewry Revisited', *Jewish Historical Studies*, 32 (1990), 89–158

Hinnebusch, William A., *The Early English Friars Preachers*, Dissertationes Historicae, 14 (Rome: Institutum Historicum Fratrum Praedicatorum, 1951)

Hohler, C., 'Medieval Paving Tiles from Buckinghamshire', *Records of Buckinghamshire*, 14 (1942), 1–49, 99–132

Holder, Nick, 'Losse, Hugh, (d. 1555), Administrator and Property Speculator', *ODNB* (Oxford: Oxford University Press, 2012) <http://www.oxforddnb.com/view/article/101321> [accessed 28 June 2016]

―――, 'Mapping Medieval and Early Modern London: The Use of Cartographic, Documentary and Archaeological Evidence', in *'Hidden Histories and Records of Antiquity': Essays on Saxon and Medieval London for John Clark, Curator Emeritus, Museum of London*, London and Middlesex Archaeological Society special paper, 17 (London: LAMAS, 2014), pp. 26–32

―――, 'The Medieval Friaries of London: A Topographic and Archaeological History, before and after the Dissolution' (unpublished doctoral thesis, University of London, Royal Holloway, 2011) [Royal Holloway research portal: <https://pure.royalholloway.ac.uk/portal/en/publications/search.html>]

Holder, Nick, Mark Samuel and Ian Betts, 'The Church and Cloisters of Austin Friars', *Transactions of the London and Middlesex Archaeological Society*, 64 (2013), 143–62

Honeybourne, Marjorie B., 'The Extent and Value of the Property in London and Southwark Occupied by the Religious Houses (Including the Prebends of St Paul's and St Martin's-Le-Grand), the Inns of the Bishops and Abbots, and the Churches and Churchyards, before the Dissolution of the Monasteries' (unpublished Masters thesis, University of London, 1929) [Institute of Historical Research library]

―――, 'The Reconstructed Map of London under Richard II', *London Topographical Record*, 22 (1965), 29–66

Hudson, Anne, and Anthony Kenny, 'Wyclif, John (d. 1384)', *ODNB* (Oxford: Oxford University Press, 2004) <http://www.oxforddnb.com/view/article/30122> [accessed 10 June 2014]

Hugo, Thomas, 'Austin Friars', *Transactions of the London and Middlesex Archaeological Society*, 2 (1864), 1–24

Humphreys, Kenneth W., *The Friars' Libraries* (London: British Library in assoc. with British Academy, 1990)

I'Anson, Edward, 'Account of the Restoration of the Dutch Church, Austin Friars', *Papers Read at the Royal Institute of British Architects* (1866), 67–75

Jarrett, Bede, *The English Dominicans* (London: Burns, Oates & Washbourne, 1921)

Jenks, Stuart, 'Hansische Vermächtnisse in London: ca. 1363–1483', *Hansische Geschichtsblätter*, 104 (1986), 35–111

Johnstone, Hilda, 'The Chapel of St Louis, Greyfriars, London', *English Historical Review*, 56 (1941), 447–50

Jones, Michael, 'Knolles, Sir Robert (d. 1407)', *ODNB* (Oxford: Oxford University Press, 2009) <http://www.oxforddnb.com/view/article/15758> [accessed 13 May 2015]

Jurkowski, Maureen, 'Were Friars Paid Salaries? Evidence from Clerical Taxation Records', *The Fifteenth Century*, 13 (Woodbridge: Boydell, 2014), pp. 131–51

Keene, Derek, and Vanessa Harding, *A Survey of Documentary Sources for Property Holding in London before the Great Fire*, London Record Society, 22 (London: London Record Society, 1985)

Kemp, Richard, *Some Notes on the Ward of Aldgate, Its Neighbourhood and Its Ancient and Modern History* (London: Eden Fisher, 1935), 2nd edn

Ker, Neil R., *Medieval Libraries of Great Britain: A List of Surviving Books* (London: Royal Historical Society, 1964)

Killock, Douglas, 'An archaeological excavation at Whitefriars, City of London' (unpublished Pre-Construct Archaeology report, 2002) [LAA, site WFT99]

King, David, 'Mendicant Glass in East Anglia', in *The Friars in Medieval Britain*, ed. N. Rogers, Harlaxton Medieval Studies, 19 (Donington: Shaun Tyas, 2010), pp. 169–84

Kingsford, Charles L., 'Additional Material for the History of the Grey Friars, London', in *Collectanea Franciscana II*, British Society of Franciscan Studies, 10 (Manchester: Manchester University Press, 1922), pp. 61–156

Knighton, C.S., 'Westminster Abbey Restored', in *The Church of Mary Tudor*, ed. E. Duffy and D. Loades (Aldershot: Ashgate, 2006), pp. 77–123

Knowles, David, *The Religious Orders in England*, 3 vols (Cambridge: Cambridge University Press, 1948–59)

Kohl, Benjamin G., 'Tiptoft, John, First Earl of Worcester (1427–1470)', *ODNB* (Oxford: Oxford University Press, 2006) <http://www.oxforddnb.com/view/article/27471> [accessed 11 June 2014]

Lachaud, Frédérique, 'Waleys, Henry le (d. 1302)', *ODNB* (Oxford: Oxford University Press, 2004) <http://www.oxforddnb.com/view/article/28460> [accessed 9 June 2014]

Lack, William, H. Martin Stuchfield and Philip Whittemore, *The Monumental Brasses of Essex*, 2 vols (London: Intercity Print, 2003)

____, *The Monumental Brasses of Hertfordshire* (Stratford St Mary: Intercity Print, 2009)

Lawrence, C. Hugh, 'Darlington, John of (d. 1284)', *ODNB* (Oxford: Oxford University Press, 2009) <http://www.oxforddnb.com/view/article/7159> [accessed 9 June 2014]

____, *The Friars: The Impact of the Mendicant Orders on Western Society* (London: Tauris, 2013), 2nd edn

____, 'Nottingham, William of (d. 1254)', *ODNB* (Oxford: Oxford University Press, 2004) <http://www.oxforddnb.com/view/article/20373> [accessed 26 June 2014]

Lea, Richard, 'Archaeology of Standing Structures', *Popular Archaeology*, December 1985/January 1986, 22–31

Le Goff, Jacques, 'Apostolat Mendiant et Fait Urbain dans la France Médiévale: L'implantation des Ordres Mendiants', *Annales*, 23 (1968), 335–48

____, 'Ordres Mendiants et Urbanisation dans la France Médiévale', *Annales*, 25 (1970), 924–46

Legros, Jean-Luc, *Le Mont-Saint-Michel: Architecture et Civilisation* (Caen, France: CRDP de Basse-Normandie, 2005)

Lerz, Antonietta, and Nick Holder, 'Medieval Crossed Friars and its Roman to Post-Medieval Landscape: Excavations at Mariner House, in the City of London', *Transactions of the London and Middlesex Archaeological Society*, 66 (2015), 137–97

Lewis, David, '"For the Poor to Drink and the Rich to Dress their Meat": The First London Water Conduit', *Transactions of the London and Middlesex Archaeological Society*, 55 (2004), 39–68

Lickteig, Franz-Bernard, *The German Carmelites at the Medieval Universities*, Textus et Studia Historica Carmelitana (Rome: Institutum Carmelitanum, 1981)

Lindeboom, Johannes, *Austin Friars: History of the Dutch Reformed Church in London, 1550–1950*, trans. D. de Iongh (The Hague: Nijhoff, 1950)

Little, Andrew G., 'Educational Organisation of the Mendicant Friars in England', *Transactions of the Royal Historical Society*, new series, 8 (1894), 49–70

____, *Franciscan History and Legend in English Mediaeval Art* (Manchester: Manchester University Press, 1937)

____, *The Grey Friars of Oxford*, Oxford Historical Society, 20 (Oxford, 1892)

____, 'A Royal Inquiry into Property Held by the Mendicant Friars in England in 1349 and 1350', in *Historical Essays in Honour of James Tait*, ed. J.G. Edwards, V.H. Galbraith and E.F. Jacob (Manchester: privately printed, 1933), pp. 79–88

____, *Studies in English Franciscan History* (Manchester: Manchester University Press, 1917)

Lloyd, Simon, 'Longespée, Sir William (II) (c. 1209–1250)', *ODNB* (Oxford: Oxford University Press, 2004) <http://www.oxforddnb.com/view/article/16984> [accessed 20 December 2013]

Lobel, Mary D., *The City of London from Prehistoric Times to c. 1520* (Oxford: Oxford University Press, in conjunction with the Historic Towns Trust, 1989)

Lorentz, Philippe, and Dany Sandron, *Atlas de Paris Au Moyen Âge: Éspace Urbain, Habitat, Société, Religion, Lieux de Pouvoir* (Paris: Parigramme, 2006)

Lucas, Peter J., 'Capgrave, John (1393–1464)', *ODNB* (Oxford: Oxford University Press, 2004) <http://www.oxforddnb.com/view/article/4591> [accessed 28 June 2016]

McCaffrey, Patrick R., *The White Friars: An Outline Carmelite History with Special Reference to the English-Speaking Province* (Dublin: Gill, 1926)

McCann, Bill, 'Fleet Valley project, interim report' (unpublished Museum of London report, 1993) [LAA, VAL88]

MacCulloch, Diarmaid, *Reformation: Europe's House Divided 1490–1700* (Penguin, 2004)

Maggs, Frances, 'Londoners and the London House of the Greyfriars' (unpublished MA dissertation, Royal Holloway, University of London, 1996) [Guildhall Library]

Martin, A.R., *Franciscan Architecture in England* (Manchester: Manchester University Press, 1937)

Martin, Geoffrey H., and J. Roger Highfield, *A History of Merton College, Oxford* (Oxford: Oxford University Press, 1997)

Martin, William, 'Blackfriars and *The Times*', *Transactions of the London and Middlesex Archaeological Society*, 6 (1929), 205–7

____, 'The Excavation at Whitefriars, Fleet Street, 1927–8: Report of Committee', *Journal of the British Archaeological Association*, 30 (1927), 293–320

Mellor, Jean E., and Terry Pearce, *The Austin Friars, Leicester* (London: Council for British Archaeology, 1981)

Miller, Pat, and David Saxby, *The Augustinian Priory of St Mary Merton, Surrey: Excavations 1976–90*, MoLAS Monograph, 34 (London: Museum of London Archaeology Service, 2007)

Moorman, John, 'The Foreign Element among the English Franciscans', *English Historical Review*, 62 (1947), 289–303

——, *The Grey Friars in Cambridge* (Cambridge: Cambridge University Press, 1952)

——, *A History of the Franciscan Order from its Origins to the Year 1517* (Oxford: Clarendon, 1968)

Morgan, Nigel, 'The Scala Coeli Indulgence and the Royal Chapels', in *The Reign of Henry VII*, ed. B. Thompson, Harlaxton Medieval Studies, 5 (Stamford: Paul Watkins, 1995), pp. 82–103

Morris, Richard K., *Cathedrals and Abbeys of England and Wales: The Building Church, 600–1540* (London: Dent, 1979)

——, 'The Development of Later Gothic Mouldings in England c. 1250–1400: Part I', *Architectural History*, 21 (1978), 21–57

——, 'The Development of Later Gothic Mouldings in England c. 1250–1400: Part II', *Architectural History*, 22 (1979), 1–48

Museum of London Archaeology, 'Fleet Building... and Plumtree Court... London EC4A: historic environment assessment' (unpublished report, 2012) [MOLA]

Nash, Susie, *Northern Renaissance Art*, Oxford History of Art (Oxford: Oxford University Press, 2008)

Norman, Philip, 'On an Ancient Conduit-Head in Queen Square, Bloomsbury', *Archaeologia*, 56 (1899), 251–66

——, 'Recent Discoveries of Medieval Remains in London', *Archaeologia*, 67 (1916), 1–26

Norman, Philip, and Ernest A. Mann, 'On the White Conduit, Chapel Street, Bloomsbury, and its Connexion with the Grey Friars' Water System', *Archaeologia*, 61 (1909), 347–56

Norman, Philip, and Francis W. Reader, 'Further Discoveries Relating to Roman London, 1906–12', *Archaeologia*, 63 (1912), 257–344

Norton, Christopher, 'The Export of Decorated Floor Tiles from Normandy', in *Medieval Art, Architecture and Archaeology at Rouen*, ed. Jenny Stratford, British Archaeological Association conference transactions, 12 (London, 1993), pp. 81–97

O'Carroll, Maura, 'The Educational Organisation of the Dominicans in England and Wales 1221–1348: A Multidisciplinary Approach', *Archivum Fratrum Praedicatorum*, 50 (1980), 23–62

Ó Clabaigh, Colman, *The Friars in Ireland, 1224–1540* (Dublin: Four Courts, 2012)

O'Day, Rosemary, *The Routledge Companion to the Tudor Age* (Abingdon: Routledge, 2010)

Oldland, John, 'The Allocation of Merchant Capital in Early Tudor London', *Economic History Review*, 63 (2010), 1058–80

O'Sullivan, Deirdre, *In the Company of the Preachers: The Archaeology of Medieval Friaries in England and Wales*, Leicester Archaeology Monographs, 23 (University of Leicester, 2013)

Page-Phillips, John, *Palimpsests: The Backs of Monumental Brasses*, 2 vols (London: Monumental Brass Society, 1980)

Palliser, David, 'Royal Mausolea in the Long Fourteenth Century (1272–1422)', *Fourteenth Century England*, 3 (Woodbridge: Boydell, 2004), 1–15

____, 'The Topography of Monastic Houses in Yorkshire Towns', in *Advances in Monastic Archaeology*, ed. R. Gilchrist and H.C. Mytum, British Archaeological Reports, 227 (Oxford: Archaeopress, 1993), pp. 3–9

Palmer, Raymund, 'Burials at the Priories of the Black Friars', *The Antiquary*, 23 (1891), 122–6; vol. 24 (1891), 28–30, 76–9, 117–20

Parsons, John C., 'Eleanor (1241–1290)', *ODNB* (Oxford: Oxford University Press, 2006) <www.oxforddnb.com/view/article/8619> [accessed 23 November 2012]

Paxton, Catherine, 'The Nunneries of London and its Environs in the Later Middle Ages' (unpublished doctoral thesis, University of Oxford, 1993) [Institute of Historical Research library]

Payling, Simon J., 'Cornewall, John, Baron Fanhope (d. 1443)', *ODNB* (Oxford: Oxford University Press, 2004) <http://www.oxforddnb.com/view/article/54423> [accessed 22 May 2015]

Pearce, Ernest H., *Annals of Christ's Hospital* (London: Methuen, 1901)

Pevsner, Nikolaus, and David Lloyd, *Hampshire and the Isle of Wight*, The Buildings of England (New Haven and London: Yale University Press, 2002)

Powell, J. Enoch, and Keith Wallis, *The House of Lords in the Middle Ages: A History of the English House of Lords to 1540* (London: Weidenfeld and Nicolson, 1968)

Pringle, Sue, and Terence p. Smith, 'Other Stone and Ceramic Building Material', in *Excavations at the Priory of the Order of the Hospital of St John of Jerusalem, Clerkenwell, London*, ed. B. Sloane and G. Malcolm, MoLAS Monograph, 20 (London: Museum of London Archaeology Service, 2004), pp. 321–30

Purvis, J.S., 'A York Account Roll for A.D. 1537–1538', *Yorkshire Archaeological Journal*, 42 (1971), 52–3

Rackham, Oliver, *The History of the Countryside: The Classic History of Britain's Landscape, Flora and Fauna* (London: Phoenix, 2000)

Rano, Balbino, 'Agostiniani', in *Dizionario degli Istituti di Perfezione*, ed. G. Pelliccia and G. Rocca, 10 vols (Rome: Paoline 1974–2003), i, col. 278–381 (349–50)

Rawcliffe, Carole, *Medicine for the Soul: The Life, Death and Resurrection of an English Medieval Hospital, St Giles's, Norwich, c. 1249–1550* (Stroud: Sutton, 1999)

Reddan, Minnie, and Alfred W. Clapham, *The Parish of St Helen, Bishopsgate*, Survey of London, 9 (London: Survey of London and LCC, 1924)

Rex, Richard, *The Tudors* (Stroud: Tempus, 2006)

Rhodes, Dennis E., 'William Swadell, English Dominican: his Friends and his Books', *Archivum Fratrum Praedicatorum*, 49 (1979), 519–22

Richardson, Walter C., 'Records of the Court of Augmentations', *Journal of the Society of Archivists*, 1(6) (1957), 159–68

Robson, Michael, 'The Franciscan Custody of York in the Thirteenth Century', in *The Friars in Medieval Britain: Proceedings of the 2007 Harlaxton Symposium*, ed. N. Rogers, Harlaxton Medieval Studies, 19 (Donington: Shaun Tyas, 2010), pp. 1–24

Roest, Bert, *A History of Franciscan Education (c. 1210–1517)*, Education and Society in the Middle Ages and the Renaissance, 2 (Leiden: Brill, 2000)

Rogers, Nicholas, ed., *The Friars in Medieval Britain: Proceedings of the 2007 Harlaxton Symposium*, Harlaxton Medieval Studies, 19 (Donington: Shaun Tyas, 2010)

____, 'The Provenance of the Thornham Parva Retable', in *The Friars in Medieval Britain*, Harlaxton Medieval Studies, 19 (Donington: Shaun Tyas, 2010), pp. 185–93

Röhrkasten, Jens, 'L'économie des Couvents Mendiants de Londres à la Fin du Moyen Âge, d'après l'étude des Documents d'Archives et des Testaments', in *Économie et Religion: L'Expérience des Ordres Mendiants (XIIIe-XVe Siècle)*, ed. N. Bériou and J. Chiffoleau, Collection d'Histoire et d'Archéologie Médiévale, 21 (Lyon: Presses Universitaires de Lyon, 2009), pp. 211–45

____, *The Mendicant Houses of Medieval London, 1221–1539*, Vita Regularis, 21 (Münster: Verlag, 2004)

____, 'Secular Uses of the Mendicant Priories of Medieval London', in *The Use and Abuse of Sacred Places in Late Medieval Towns*, ed. M. De Smet and P. Trio, Mediaevalia Lovaniensia, series 1, 38 (Leuven: Leuven University Press, 2006), pp. 135–51

Rosborough, Catherine, 'Archaeological excavations at Pinners' Hall, 105–108 Old Broad Street and 8 Austin Friars Square' (unpublished Museum of London report, 1990) [LAA, GWS89]

Roskell, John S., Carole Rawcliffe and Linda S. Clark, *The History of Parliament: The House of Commons 1386–1421*, 4 vols (Stroud: History of Parliament Trust and Alan Sutton, 1992)

Roth, Francis, *The English Austin Friars, 1249–1538* (New York: Augustinian Historical Institute, 1961), 2 vols

Ryan, Pat, *Brick in Essex from the Roman Conquest to the Reformation* (Midhurst: Middleton Press, 1996)

Samuel, Mark, 'The Architectural Fragments', in *The Cistercian Abbey of St Mary Graces, East Smithfield, London*, ed. I. Grainger, C. Phillpotts and P. Mills, MOLA Monograph, 44 (London: Museum of London Archaeology, 2011), pp. 114–29

____, 'Architectural Fragments', in *The Cluniac Priory and Abbey of St Saviour Bermondsey, Surrey*, ed. T. Dyson and others, MOLA Monograph, 50 (London: Museum of London Archaeology, 2011), pp. 184–98

____, 'The Architectural Fragments', in *Excavations at the Whitefriars, Canterbury* (Canterbury: Canterbury Archaeological Trust, forthcoming)

____, 'The Architectural Fragments', in *St Gregory's Priory, Northgate, Canterbury: Excavations 1988–1991*, ed. M. Hicks and A. Hicks, The Archaeology of Canterbury, new series, 2 (Canterbury: Canterbury Archaeological Trust, 2001), pp. 151–82

____, 'Architectural Fragments', in *The Medieval Priory and Hospital of St Mary Spital and the Bishopsgate Suburb: Excavations at Spitalfields Market, London E1, 1991–2007*, ed. C. Harward, N. Holder and C. Thomas, MOLA Monograph (London: Museum of London Archaeology, forthcoming)

____, 'Blackfriars (site code IAS 4901): appraisal report of the moulded stone' (unpublished report for Suffolk County Council Archaeological Service, 1992) [Suffolk County Council Archaeological Service, IAS 4901]

____, 'The Fifteenth-Century Garner at Leadenhall', *Antiquaries Journal*, 69 (1989), 119–53

____, 'Preacher's Court PPR98: the worked stones' (unpublished Museum of London report, 1999) [LAA, PPR98]

____, 'Structural Stonework', in *Norwich Greyfriars: Pre-Conquest Town and Medieval Friary*, ed. P. A. Emery and E. Rutledge, East Anglian Archaeology Monograph, 120 (Dereham: Norfolk Museums and Archaeology Service, 2007)

____, 'Structural Stonework', in *Norwich Whitefriars: Medieval Friary and Baptist Burial Ground*, ed. R. Clarke, East Anglian Archaeology Monograph (Chelmsford: East Anglian Archaeology, forthcoming)

Samuel, Mark, and Nick Holder, 'The Thirteenth-Century Chapter House of Black Friars, London', forthcoming

Saunders, H.W., *An Introduction to the Obedientiary & Manor Rolls of the Norwich Cathedral Priory* (Norwich: Jarrold, 1930)

Schofield, John, 'Excavations on the Site of St Nicholas Shambles, Newgate Street, City of London, 1975-9', *Transactions of the London and Middlesex Archaeological Society*, 48 (1997), 77-135

____, *London, 1100-1600: The Archaeology of a Capital City* (Sheffield: Equinox, 2011)

____, *The London Surveys of Ralph Treswell* (London: London Topographical Society, 1987)

____, *St Paul's Cathedral Before Wren* (Swindon: English Heritage, 2011)

____, 'Saxon and Medieval Parish Churches in the City of London: A Review', *Transactions of the London and Middlesex Archaeological Society*, 45 (1994), 23-146

Schofield, John, and Richard Lea, *Holy Trinity Priory, Aldgate, City of London: An Archaeological Reconstruction and History*, MoLAS monograph, 24 (London: Museum of London Archaeology Service, 2005)

Schofield, John, and Catherine Maloney, *Archaeology in the City of London, 1907-1991: A Guide to Records of Excavations by the Museum of London and its Predecessors* (London: Museum of London, 1998)

Scott, W.W., 'Margaret, Countess of Kent (1187×95-1259)', *ODNB* (Oxford: Oxford University Press, 2004) <http://www.oxforddnb.com/view/article/49377> [accessed 19 December 2013]

Shaw, Anthony N., 'Legh, Sir Thomas (d. 1545)', *ODNB* (Oxford: Oxford University Press, 2008) <http://www.oxforddnb.com/view/article/16363> [accessed 28 June 2016]

Shepherd, Ernest B.S., 'The Church of the Friars Minors in London', *Archaeological Journal*, 59 (1902), 238-87

Sheppard, Francis H.W., *Covent Garden*, Survey of London, 36 (London: Athlone Press, 1970)

Silberer, Leonie, 'Medieval Monastic Architecture of the Franciscan Order: Friaries as Evidence of Written and Unwritten Rules and Ideal Perceptions', in *Rules and Observance: Devising Forms of Communal Life*, ed. M. Breitenstein and others, Vita Regularis, 60 (Berlin: Verlag, 2014), pp. 281-94

Simpson, W. Sparrow, 'Visitations of Certain Churches in the City of London in the Patronage of St Paul's Cathedral Church, between the Years 1138 and 1250', *Archaeologia*, 55 (1897), 283-300

Slater, Laura, 'Defining Queenship at Greyfriars London, c. 1300-1358', *Gender and History*, 27 (2015), 53-76

Slavin, Philip, *Bread and Ale for the Brethren: The Provisioning of Norwich Cathedral Priory, 1260-1536* (Hatfield: University of Hertfordshire Press, 2012)

Sloane, Barney, 'Tenements in London's Monasteries c. 1450-1540', in *The Archaeology of Reformation 1480-1580*, ed. D. Gaimster and R. Gilchrist (Leeds: Maney, 2003), pp. 290-8

Sloane, Barney, and Gordon Malcolm, *Excavations at the Priory of the Order of the Hospital of St John of Jerusalem, Clerkenwell, London*, MoLAS Monograph, 20 (London: Museum of London Archaeology Service, 2004)

Smith, Irwin, *Shakespeare's Blackfriars Playhouse: Its History and its Design* (London: Owen, 1966)

Soden, Iain, 'The Conversion of Former Monastic Buildings to Secular Use: The Case of Coventry', in *The Archaeology of Reformation 1480–1580*, ed. D. Gaimster and R. Gilchrist (Leeds: Maney, 2003), pp. 280–9

____, *Coventry: The Hidden History* (Stroud: Tempus, 2005)

Somerville, R., 'The Duchy of Lancaster Council and Court of Duchy Chamber', *Transactions of the Royal Historical Society*, 23 (1941), 159–77

Steedman, Ken, 'Queen Victoria Street Excavation', *Archaeology Today*, 8(11) (1987), 26–30

Steer, Christian, '"Better in Remembrance": Medieval Commemoration at the Crutched Friars, London', *Journal of the Church Monuments Society*, 25 (2010), 36–57

____, 'The Franciscans and their Graves' in *St Francis and his Followers: Studies on the Medieval English Franciscan Province and Beyond*, ed. M. Robson and P. Zutshi (forthcoming)

____, 'The Lorde Barons Slaine at Barnet Field', *Ricardian*, 26 (2016), 87–98

____, 'Royal and Noble Commemoration in the Mendicant Houses of London, c. 1240–1540', in *Memory and Commemoration in Medieval England*, ed. C.M. Barron and C. Burgess, Harlaxton Medieval Studies, 20 (Donington: Shaun Tyas, 2010), pp. 117–42

Strickland, Matthew, 'Longespée, William (I), Third Earl of Salisbury (b. in or before 1167, d. 1226)', *ODNB* (Oxford: Oxford University Press, 2004) <http://www.oxforddnb.com/article/16983> [accessed 25 October 2013]

Sudds, Barry, 'An Archaeological Watching Brief on a Geotechnical Investigation at One Lothbury, City of London, London EC4' (unpublished Pre-Construct Archaeology report, 2006) [LAA, OLO06]

Summerson, Henry, 'Seen through the Eyes of the Law: Judicial Records as Evidence for London's Physical Environment, 1272–1327', *London Topographical Record*, 31 (2015), 1–13

Sutermeister, Helen, *The Norwich Blackfriars: An Historical Guide to the Friary and its Buildings up to the Present Day* (Norwich: City of Norwich, 1977)

Sutton, Anne F., 'The Hospital of St Thomas of Acre of London: The Search for Patronage, Liturgical Improvement, and a School, under Master John Neel, 1420–63', in *The Late Medieval English College and its Context*, ed. C. Burgess and M. Heale (York: York Medieval Press, 2008), pp. 199–229

Tatton-Brown, Tim, 'The Quarrying and Distribution of Reigate Stone in the Middle Ages', *Medieval Archaeology*, 45 (2001), 189–201

Taylor, Colin, 'The Building of the City Wall at the Friars Preachers', in 'Fleet Valley project, interim report', ed. B. McCann (unpublished Museum of London report, 1993), pp. 87–92 [LAA, VAL88]

Taylor, Pamela, 'Foundation and Endowment: St Paul's and the English Kingdoms, 604–1087', in *St Paul's: The Cathedral Church of London 604–2004*, ed. D. Keene, A. Burns and A. Saint (New Haven and London: Yale University Press, 2004), pp. 5–16

Temple, Philip, ed., *Northern Clerkenwell and Pentonville*, Survey of London, 48 (New Haven and London: Yale University Press, 2008)

Thacker, Alan, 'The Cult of Saints and the Liturgy', in *St Paul's: The Cathedral Church of London 604–2004*, ed. D. Keene, A. Burns and A. Saint (New Haven and London: Yale University Press, 2004), 113–22

Thomas, Christopher, Jane Sidell and Robert Cowie, *The Royal Palace, Abbey and Town of Westminster on Thorney Island: Archaeological Excavations (1991–8) for the London Underground Limited Jubilee Line Extension Project*, MoLAS Monograph, 22 (London: Museum of London Archaeology Service, 2006)

Thomas, Christopher, Barney Sloane and Christopher Phillpotts, *Excavations at the Priory and Hospital of St Mary Spital, London*, MoLAS Monograph, 1 (London: Museum of London Archaeology Service, 1997)

Thompson, S., 'Hilsey, John (d. 1539)', *ODNB* (Oxford: Oxford Univesity Press, 2004) <http://www.oxforddnb.com/view/article/13325> [accessed 11 June 2014]

Toy, Sidney, *Building Report by Mr Sidney Toy, F.S.A., F.R.I.B.A., on the Excavations at Whitefriars, Fleet Street, 1927–8, London* (London: The News of the World, no date [1930s?])

____, 'The Crypt at Whitefriars, London', *Journal of the British Archaeological Association*, 37 (1932), 334–6

Tracy, Charles, 'Choir-Stalls from the 14th-Century Whitefriars Church in Coventry', *Journal of the British Archaeological Association*, 150 (1997), 76–95

Trollope, William, *A History of the Royal Foundation of Christ's Hospital: With an Account of the Plan of Education, the Internal Economy of the Institution, and Memoirs of Eminent Blues* (London: Pickering, 1834)

Tugwell, Simon, 'Kilwardby, Robert (c. 1215–1279)', *ODNB* (Oxford: Oxford University Press, 2004) <http://www.oxforddnb.com/view/article/15546> [accessed 9 June 2014]

Tyler, Kieron, 'Changing the Landscape: Excavations at Black Friar's Court, Ludgate Broadway, London EC4', *Transactions of the London and Middlesex Archaeological Society*, 53 (2002), 25–51

VCH (Victoria County History), *Cambridge and the Isle of Ely*, 10 vols (various publishers, 1938–2002)

____, *Kent*, ed. William Page, 3 vols (London: various publishers, 1908–32)

____, *London*, ed. William Page (London: University of London, 1909)

____, *Norfolk*, ed. Herbert A. Doubleday and William Page, 2 vols (London: various publishers, 1901–6)

Vincent, Nicholas, 'Bohun, Humphrey (IV) de, Second Earl of Hereford and Seventh Earl of Essex (d. 1275)', *ODNB* (Oxford: Oxford University Press, 2008) <http://www.oxforddnb.com/view/article/2775> [accessed 28 June 2016]

Visser-Fuchs, Livia, 'A Ricardian Riddle: The Casualty List of the Battle of Barnet', *Ricardian*, 8(100) (1988), 9–12

Wagner, Sir Anthony R., *Heralds and Heraldry in the Middle Ages* (Oxford: Oxford University Press, 1939)

Walsh, Katherine, 'Conway, Roger (d. c. 1360)', *ODNB* (Oxford: Oxford University Press, 2004) <http://www.oxforddnb.com/view/article/6124> [accessed 8 June 2016]

____, *A Fourteenth-Century Scholar and Primate: Richard FitzRalph in Oxford, Avignon and Armagh* (Oxford: Clarendon, 1981)

Ward, Jennifer C., 'Ela, suo jure Countess of Salisbury (b. in or after 1190, d. 1261', *ODNB* (Oxford: Oxford University Press, 2004) <http://www.oxforddnb.com/article/47205> [accessed 25 October 2013]

Ward-Perkins, J., ed., *London Museum Medieval Catalogue* (London: HMSO, 1967)

Warren, Ann K., *Anchorites and their Patrons in Medieval England* (Berkeley and London: University of California Press, 1985)

Watney, John, *Some Account of the Hospital of St Thomas of Acon, in the Cheap, London, and of the Plate of the Mercer's Company* (London: privately printed, 1892)

Watson, Andrew G., and Neil R. Ker, *Medieval Libraries of Great Britain: A List of Surviving Books. Supplement to the Second Edition*, Guides and Handbooks, 15 (London: Royal Historical Society, 1987)

Watson, Bruce, 'Excavations at 54/56–66 Carter Lane, 1–3 Pilgrim Street and 25–27 Ludgate Hill (PIC87)' (unpublished Museum of London report, 1990) [LAA, PIC87]

____, 'Excavations and Observations on the Site of the Dutch Church, Austin Friars, in the City of London', *Transactions of the London and Middlesex Archaeological Society*, 45 (1994), 13–22

____, 'The Norman Fortress on Ludgate Hill in the City of London, England, Recent Excavations 1986–1990', *Château Gaillard*, 15 (1992), 335–45

Watson, Bruce, and Christopher Thomas, 'The Mendicant Houses of Medieval London: An Archaeological Review', in *The Friars in Medieval Britain*, ed. N. Rogers, Harlaxton Medieval Studies, 19 (Donington: Shaun Tyas, 2010), pp. 265–97

West, F.J., 'Burgh, Hubert de, Earl of Kent (c. 1170–1243)', *ODNB* (Oxford: Oxford University Press, 2008) <http://www.oxforddnb.com/view/article/3991> [accessed 28 June 2016]

Williams, Elijah, *Early Holborn and the Legal Quarter of London: A Topographical Survey of the Beginnings of the District Known as Holborn and of the Inns of Court and of Chancery*, 2 vols (London: Sweet & Maxwell, 1927)

Wilson, Christopher, 'Canterbury, Michael (fl. 1275–1321)', *ODNB* (Oxford: Oxford University Press, 2004) <http://www.oxforddnb.com/view/article/37763> [accessed 11 June 2014]

____, *The Gothic Cathedral: The Architecture of the Great Church, 1130–1530* (London: Thames and Hudson, 1990)

Windeatt, Barry, 'Margary Kempe and the Friars', in *The Friars in Medieval Britain*, ed. N. Rogers, Harlaxton Medieval Studies, 19 (Donington: Shaun Tyas, 2010), pp. 125–41

Wood, Robert, 'Life and Death: A Study of the Wills and Testaments of Men and Women in London and Bury St Edmunds in the late Fourteenth and early Fifteenth Centuries' (unpublished doctoral thesis, University of London, Royal Holloway, 2013) [Royal Holloway research portal: <https://pure.royalholloway.ac.uk/portal/en/publications/search.html>]

Woodfield, Charmian, *The Church of Our Lady of Mount Carmel and Some Conventual Buildings at the Whitefriars, Coventry*, British Archaeological Reports, 389 (Oxford: Archaeopress, 2005)

Woodward, G.W.O., *The Dissolution of the Monasteries* (London: Blandford, 1966)

Wright, James, 'Queen's House and Bell Tower' (unpublished MOLA standing building report, 2016) [MOLA]

Youings, Joyce, *The Dissolution of the Monasteries* (London: Allen and Unwin, 1971)

Ypma, Eelcko, *La Formation des Professeurs chez les Ermites de Saint Augustin de 1256 à 1354* (Paris: Centre d'Études des Augustins, 1956)

Zumkeller, Adolar, 'Die Augustinerschule des Mittelalters: Vertreter und philosophisch-theologische Lehre', *Analecta Augustiniana*, 27 (1964), 167–262

Online sources

British History Online, <http://www.british-history.ac.uk/> [accessed 12 May 2016]
British Province of Carmelite Friars, <http://www.carmelite.org/> [accessed 12 May 2016]

Exploring Surrey's Past, <http://www.exploringsurreyspast.org.uk/> [accessed 13 May 2016]

Google Books, <https://books.google.co.uk/> [accessed 12 May 2016]

Historic England, listed buildings online, <https://historicengland.org.uk/listing/> [accessed 12 February 2016]

Internet Archive, < https://archive.org/> [accessed 30 June 2016]

Royal Holloway research portal, <https://pure.royalholloway.ac.uk/portal/en/publications/search.html> [accessed 30 June 2016]

State Papers Online, < http://gale.cengage.co.uk/state-papers-online-15091714.aspx> [accessed 11 July 2016]

Index

Abbreviations in index:
O. Aug.   Augustinian (Austin) friar
O. Carm. Carmelite (White) friar
OFM   Franciscan (Grey) friar
OP   Dominican (Black) friar

Abiton, John de, prior of St Mary Bishopsgate, 125n
Acton, Hugh, 85
Albon, William, OFM, 73, 202
Aldenham, William de, 170
aliens, 120, 143, 256n, 269, 288–9, 296
almshouses, 115, 154, 158, 306–7, 308
Alphonso, son of Edward I, 22, 178, 284
altars, 42–3, 83–6 (Table 6), 103–4, 110, 129–30, 132 (Table 10), 185, 190, 255
    high, 37n, 60, 84, 85, 103–4, 176, 188, 283
    altar cloths, 94, 121n, 189, 205
anchoress, 40
Angle, Guy d', earl of Huntingdon, 288
Angleur, unidentified French lord, 288
Anne, St, 42, 110, 152
anniversary funeral services, 55, 59, 109, 152, 185n, 254, 298, 310, 321
Anthony, St, 110
'Apparition of the Virgin to the Dominicans of Utrecht', 189
Aquinas, Thomas, St, 43
architectural fragments, 135–6, 137 (Fig. 49), 211–26, 316
Ardern, John de, 126
Aren, France, see Pied friars
Arnald (Arnaud), William, 169, 170, 194
Arnulphus the monk, 72
Artois, Robert of, count of Beaumont, 288
Ashbourn, Thomas, O. Aug., 267
Aske, Robert, 311
Asshe, William, 85
Assheley, Edward, 84
Assisi, Italy, Franciscans, 313
Auderuco, Egidius de, 72
Augustine, St (of Hippo), 119, 130
    rule, 160
    fraternity of, 269
Augustinian order (canons), 177, 182–3, 195, 200, 201 (Fig. 74), 211n, 259, 299, 304, 313, 323
Augustinian order (mendicant), 119, 259, 317

Aylesford, Kent, White Friars, 97, 206
Aylesham, Geoffrey de, OFM, 270

Baconthorpe, John, O. Carm., 265–6
Bailley, John, 83
bake-house, monastic, 52, 93–4, 116, 138n, 139, 203, 205
Balby, Peter de, 289
Bale, John, 97, 110, 263
Ball, Robert, prior of Crossed Friars, 143, 306
Bankyn, John, O. Aug., 267
Barbara, St, fraternity of, 150 (Fig. 54), 157, 158, 207
Bardevyle, David, 84
Bardi, Philip, 289
Barking Abbey, Essex, 147, 148, 156
Barnack stone, 136, 243 (Table 18)
Barnes, Robert, 121
Barnet, battle of, 287
Bartholomew, canon of St Bartholomew's, 72, 295
Bartlett, Richard, 61, 63
Basing, Hants., 273n
Basset, John, 290
    Philip, 18
Bat, Gerald, 125
    Isabelle, 125
Battell, Thomas, 83
Beauchamp, Richard, Lord St Amand, 273, 275 (Fig. 88)
Beaumont, William, Viscount Beaumont, 273, 274 (Fig. 88)
beguines, 160
Belamy, Gilbert, 85
Bellond, Edmund, prior of Austin Friars, 139, 252, 301–2
Benedict XII, pope, 261
Benedictine order, 177, 200, 245, 249, 299
Benolt, Thomas, 273, 287
Berkeley, William, marquess of Berkeley, 254n, 298

Berkles, Thomas de, OP, 270
Bermingham, John de, earl of Louth, 288
Bermondsey Abbey, Surrey, 216 (Fig. 76), 241, 242, 243
Bernadine of Siena, St, 83
Bernard, St, 153
Berow, Thomas, 290
Beverley, Robert of, master mason, 48
Black Death, 53, 77, 98, 126, 143, 182, 224, 226, 297n, 299, 321, 322
Blatherwyck, Northants., 279–80
Bloomsbury, Middx, 246, 247, 248 (Fig. 86)
Blount family, 292
    Edward, lord Mountjoy, 285
    John, lord Mountjoy, 285
    Walter, lord Mountjoy, 285
    William, lord Mountjoy, 285
    Sir William, 285, 287
Bloxham, John, 202
Blysse, John, O. Carm., 267
Bocham, Galfridus de, 72
Bohun, Humphrey de (IV), earl of Hereford and Essex, 119–20, 124, 125, 126, 284, 294
    Humphrey de (VII), earl of Hereford and Essex, 126, 284
Boldero, Francis, 44n
Bologna, Italy, Franciscans, 261
Bolton, William, prior of St Bartholomew, 210
Bonaventure, St, OFM, 317
'Book of Funerals', 273
Borgo San Donnino, Gerard of, OFM, 318
Borgo San Sepolcro, Italy, Franciscans, 188
Botiller, Elizabeth, baroness de Wemme, 285, 292
Bourchier, Sir Humphrey, 287
Bowes, Sir Martin, 273
Bowry, William, prior of Crossed Friars, 143, 158, 159, 187, 257, 322
Bradbery, Robert, 285n
Bradeford, Isabelle de, 125
    John de, 125
Brayns, Robert, OFM, 285n
Brecon, Breckn., 188
Brembre, Sir Nicholas, 290
Brereton, William, 83
brew-house, monastic, 52, 93–4, 115–16, 117, 118, 139, 203, 257
bricks, 40, 53, 93, 108 (Fig. 36), 138, 158, 241–2, 244, 302, 308
Bristol, 1
Brom, Adam de, 101
Brome, Thomas, O. Carm., 266
Bromyard, Herefords., 220
Brotherton, Margaret, duchess of Norfolk, 77, 96
Brown, George, prior of Austin Friars, 120–1, 270, 305, 311
    Hugh, 291
    Rosia, 293–4
    Walter, 293–4

Brune, Alice la, 18, 25, 193
Brussels, 59
Buck, Michael, 116
Burgh, Hubert de, earl of Kent, 15, 18, 22, 178, 294
    Margaret de, countess of Kent, 22, 178
Burgoine, Herildis (Yerilda), daughter of William, 146, 147–8, 295
burials in friaries, 22, 28, 40, 53–4, 59, 61, 83–6 (Table 6), 94, 96, 104, 108 (Fig. 36), 110, 126, 133, 152, 155, 178, 188–9, 204, 272–92, 296–7, 306, 308
burial fees, 253, 254, 322
Burnell, Robert, bishop of Bath and Wells, 125
Burton, Robert de, 283
    Robert, OFM, 265
Burwell, Thomas, O. Aug., 267

Caen stone, 38, 214, 215, 220, 222, 225, 242–3
Calley, William, 301–2, 323
Cambrei, William, OP, 265
Cambridge, Austin Friars, 262
    Black Friars, 176, 225, 256
    Emmanuel College, 176
    Grey Friars, 252, 256
    Sack Friars, 161
    St Radegund nunnery, 255–6
    White Friars, 97
Camera, Geoffrey de, 246
Campeggio, Cardinal, 28, 326
Canterbury, Austin Friars, 185
    cathedral priory, 245
Canterbury, Michael, master mason, 35, 55
Canynge, Thomas, OFM, 264
Capel, Arthur, 111
Capgrave, John, O. Aug., 267, 271n
Carmelite order, 259, 317–18, 319
Carthusian order, 57, 177
cartulary, 67
Castro, Bartholomew de, 71
Catherine, St, 110, 129, 131, 188
    fraternity of, 269, 288
Cavalcanti, John, 303 (Fig. 91)
Cawarden, Thomas, 29, 43
Chaddesby, Walter, O. Aug., 267
chalk (stone), 34, 38, 76, 78, 105, 114, 151, 204, 242–3, 246
Chamberlain, Margary, 278
    William, 278
Chamberleyn, Robert, OFM, 264
chancery, court of, 40, 63, 110, 170, 172, 257
chantry masses, 55, 132, 163, 185n, 254, 268, 297, 301, 321, 322
Chapman, Thomas, guardian of Grey friars, 2n, 67, 306
Charite, William, prior of Leicester Abbey, 68n
Charles V, Holy Roman Emperor, 47, 205, 207

Châtillon, Guy de, count of St Pol, 288; see Seintpol
Chatton, Walter de, OFM, 263
Chelmsford, Essex, Black Friars, 265
Chertsey floor tiles, 228–38 (passim), 244
Chichester, Sussex, 188
chimneys, 93, 244
choir stalls, 43, 77, 86, 110, 152, 188
Cholmeley, Dame Elizabeth, 155, 281, 308
    Sir Richard, 155, 281, 308
Cholmondeley archive, 144
Christopher, St, 84, 110
Cistercian order, 195, 245, 249
Clairlieu, Belgium, 142
Clare, Suff., Austin Friars, 119, 185, 186 (Fig. 68)
Clare, Gilbert de, earl of Gloucester, 270
    Richard de, prior of Austin Friars, 124
    William de, prior of Austin Friars, 124, 126, 178, 199
Clement, St, 83
    fraternity of, 269
Clerk, John, O. Aug., 267
Clerkenwell, Middx, 25, 247, 249
Cobham, Reginald de, 125
Coefrer, Peter le, 125
Coferrer, John, 72
Colchister, John, 72
Cokayn, John, 101
Colchester, Henry of, O. Aug., 267
Colchister, John, 72
Colet, John, 266
Collyng, William, 110
Columberiis, John de, O. Aug., 267
confession, 120, 143, 252–3, 269, 295, 296, 321
Conway, Roger, OFM, 264
Cornewall, John, baron Fanhope, 54
Cortona, Italy, Franciscans, 175
Coucy, Ingelram (Enguerrand) de, 283
council (Second) of Lyon, 2, 162, 165, 167, 195, 210, 317–18
council of Blackfriars, 28, 266, 267, 325
council, Fourth Lateran, 162, 317
court of Augmentations, 10, 43, 110, 130n, 154, 240, 254, 299, 307, 309, 310
Courtenay family, 292
    Sir Edward, 284–5
    Sir Hugh, 284
    Hugh, earl of Devon, 101, 103, 104, 284, 295, 321
Coventry, Grey Friars, 271, 277n
    White Friars, 185, 186 (Fig. 68), 188, 206
Coventry, Vincent of, OFM, 261, 263
Coverdale, Miles, 121
Covyntre, Richard, 84
Cradock, Sir David, 287
    Lady, 287
Cresse, son of Moses, 163
Cromwell, Thomas, 154, 250, 305–11 (passim)

house in Austin Friars, 120, 121, 140, 300, 302, 303 (Fig. 91), 326
Crosiers, order, 142–3, 146, 317–18
Crossed friars, order, 142–3, 146, 317–18
Cruce, Richer de, 18
Cudnor, Thomas, guardian of Grey Friars, 67
Cutiler, Adam le, 18
Cutler, John, guardian of Grey Friars, 268, 295

Dagworthe, Thomas, 85
Danet, Gerard, 281, 282 (Fig. 90), 308n
    Mary, 281
Darlington, John of, prior of Black Friars, 17, 22, 27, 32, 34, 179, 197, 265, 318
Dartford, Kent, Dominican nunnery, 57
Dawes, John, 310n
    Margaret, later countess of Kent, 115, 285, 301, 306, 308, 310n
Deane, John, rector of St Bartholomew's, 61
Decorated style, 48, 55, 76, 78, 178, 187, 199, 216, 221, 224, 318
Defensio religionis mendicantium, 264
Denise, Lady, daughter of William de Munchensi, 72
Dieppe floor tiles, 228–38 (passim)
diet, monastic, 137, 156, 314
dissolution of the Monasteries, 10, 11, 273, 281, 298n, 299, 304–12, 323
Doctrinale Fidei Ecclesiae, 266
Dominic, St, 1, 15, 43, 316–17, 324
Dominican order, 15–17, 142, 160, 259, 317
    constitutions, 261–2
Dryver, John, prior of Crossed Friars, 143
Duchy of Lancaster, council of, 54–5
Dudley, John, duke of Northumberland, 58
Duffeld, Robert de, OP, 270
Dunolm, Thomas de, 126
Dunstable, Beds., Black Friars, 205
Durham Cathedral, obedientiaries' accounts, 251

Early English style, 175
Ecclestone, Thomas of, 67, 192
economy of friaries, 261–7, 298–301
Edward I, 22, 25, 103, 176, 270, 284, 319
Edward II, 72, 270, 283
Edward III, 77, 101
Edward VI, 58, 128
Edwarde, Isabel, 291
    William, 291
Ela, countess of Salisbury, 19
Eleanor of Castile, consort of Edward I, 34, 162, 283–4, 294
Elgin, Moray, 188
Elinant, Peter de, 70
Elizabeth I, 60
Elizabeth, laundress, 94

Elm, John, prior of White Friars, 102, 103, 266
Eltham Palace floor tiles, 40, 152, 228–38 (passim)
Elvedon, Joan, 84
Ely Cathedral, 179
Elyote, Margaret, 40
Empson, Sir Richard, 280
Erasmus, St, 43, 85
Erfurt, Theoderich of, O. Aug., 269, 296
Eswy, Ralph, 18
Ewelle, Eleanor de, 73, 295
Exeter, Grey Friars, 319
Expositorium missae, 263
Eyck, Jan van, 214

Faber, Andrew, 283
Fabian, St, 110
Faversham, Haymo of, OFM, 259
Fekenham, John, O. Aug., 270
Ferers, Elizabeth, 285
   Lionel, 285
   Robert, 285
Fiennes, James, lord Saye and Sele, 286
finances of friaries, 261–7, 298–301
fireplaces, 48, 89 (Fig. 28), 90, 302, 303 (Fig. 91)
FitzAlan, Richard, earl of Arundel, 270, 286
FitzPeter, Joce, 72, 294
FitzRalph, Richard, archbishop of Armagh, 264
FitzStephen, William, 258
FitzWalter, 162
floor tiles used in London buildings, 40, 135, 152, 227–44
Florence, Italy, Dominicans, 319
Forceti (Forcinetti, Forsetti), Dinus de, 289
Forest, John, OFM, 67
Foster, Katharine, 40
foundations, technique of building, 38, 73, 77, 88, 105, 150–1, 182, 211, 218, 220n, 242, 295
Fountains Abbey, Yorks., 245
Frachet, Gerard de, OP, 317
Francis, St, 1, 66, 316–17, 324
   dedication to 83, 87, 94, 188n, 189
Franciscan order, 66, 160, 259, 317
   constitutions of Narbonne, 175n
   zelanti, 318
fraternities, 83, 120, 129, 132, 139–40, 143, 157, 189–90, 206–7, 255, 269, 288, 296
Frederici, John, 120
French, John, prior of White Friars, 103
Fresnay, Gilbert de, 15
friaries, English, see Aylesford, Cambridge, Canterbury, Chelmsford, Clare, Coventry, Dunstable, Exeter, Gloucester, Greenwich, Hereford, Hulne, Ipswich, King's Langley, Leicester, London, Norwich, Oxford, Richmond, York

continental, see Assisi, Bologna, Borgo San Sepolcro, Cortona, Florence, Guebwiller, Marseilles, Paris, Piacenza, Pisa, Rieti, Rome, Siena, Utrecht, Vicenza
friars, see Augustinian, Carmelite, Crossed, Dominican, Franciscan, Observant Franciscan, Pied, Sack, Trinitarian, Williamite
friars de Areno, see Pied
friars of the Blessed Mary, see Pied
friars of Penitence of Jesus Christ, see Sack
Frowyk, Henry, 76
fuel, 21 (Table 4), 25, 160
Fulham, Adam de, 72
Furnes, James, OFM, 264
Fylioll, Jasper, 280
   Joan, 280

Garatt, John, 63
gardens, 25, 48, 53, 61, 94, 114, 115, 117, 125 (Table 9), 139, 140, 157, 163–4, 172, 203, 204–5, 207, 249, 299, 300 (Table 20), 316
Garston, Adam, 72
   Emma, 72
Gastayne, unidentified saint, 110
Gaunt, John of, 98
Gayton, John, 54
Geffery, Agnes, 300
   Thomas, 300
Genoa, Italy, 189
Geometric (Decorated) style, 71, 86, 178, 199, 224, 318
Gerard, Elizabeth, 298
   Nicholas, 298
Gilford, Lady Jane, 306
Giotto, 313
Gloucester, friaries, 307
   Black Friars, 185, 319
Goddard, William, OFM, 268, 285n
Godeston, Richard, OFM, 268
   John, 268
Gormechestre, William, O. Aug., 267
Gratian, St, 110
Greenwich, Surrey, Observant Franciscans, 3, 57, 67, 280
   palace, 231
Gresham, Paul, 44n
Grey family, 292
   John, lord Grey, 285
   Margaret, see Dawes, Margaret
   Richard de, 97, 101, 285, 294
   Richard, earl of Kent, 285, 308, 310n
Gruncestre, Peter de, 72
Guebwiller, France, Dominicans, 184
guest hall, monastic, 205–6
Gulle, John, 289
Gybbes, John, prior of White Friars, 98, 267, 305, 306, 307

Halden, Thomas, O. Carm., 266
Hallam, Richard, 84
Hamond, Thomas, prior of Austin Friars, 121
Hanseatic league, 269
Hanwell, William, 289
Hargrave, Richard, prior of Black Friars, 58, 60
Haseley, Sir Thomas, 152, 157
Hassock stone, 243
Hastings, Richard, lord Willoughby, 83
Hatfield, Thurstan, 285n
Hatton, Thomas, 83
Haudlo, John de, 125
Hawley, Thomas, 273
Helyland, Peter de, 70, 89, 193
Henry III, 20, 25, 103, 146, 160, 168, 170, 246, 249, 283, 294, 323
Henry IV, 268
Henry VI, 268
Henry VIII, 28, 47, 311
Hereford, Black Friars, 319
Hereford, John de, 125
    Walter de, master mason, 76, 79, 224, 225
Herle, Nicholas de, OP, 270
Heston, William de, prior of St Mary Bishopsgate, 125n
Hewett, Thomas, 85
Hilsey, John, prior of Black Friars, 29, 271, 305–6
Hinton, Som., 178
Holan, Robert, O. Aug., 268
Holcote, Roger de, O. Aug., 268
Holy Blood (of Wilsnack), fraternity, 143, 157, 288
Holy Trinity, fraternity, 269
Honorius III, pope, 66
horticulture, 25, 204
Hosiar, Ralph, 146, 147, 150, 294
hospitals, see London, religious houses mendicant, 323
Hoton, William, 85
Hounslow, Middx, 3
Hubbert, John, 303 (Fig. 91)
Hugh, guardian of Grey Friars, 263
Hull, Yorks., 321
Hull, Ralph de, 101
Hulne, Northumb., White Friars, 97, 98, 206
Humberville, William, 202
Hunteman, Adam, 146, 147, 148
Hurel, John le, 162
Huy, Belgium, 143n
Hythe Beds stone, 34

indulgences, 104, 149–50, 153, 252
Ingaldesthorp, Joan de, 42, 187, 322
Ingworth, Richard, OP, 307
Innocent III, pope, 66
Innocent IV, pope, 97
Innocent V, pope, 317

Ipswich, Suff., 225
    Black Friars, 224
    Grey Friars, 319
iron in monastic churches, 78, 82, 222–3, 283, 310, 311
Isabel, countess of Norfolk, 22, 178
Isabella, consort of Edward II, 67, 70, 73, 77, 95, 268, 283
Isabella, countess of Bedford, 283
Iwyn, John, OFM, 68, 72, 294

Jambe, Bernat de, 281
James, St, 85, 129, 131, 153–4
    fraternity of, 269
Jenyns, Sir Stephen, 273, 276 (Fig. 88), 291, 322
Jews, 163, 165
Joan Plantaganet, consort of David II of Scotland, 283
John the Baptist, St, 42, 131
John the Evangelist, St, 22, 25, 36
    fraternity of, 269
Johnson, Margaret, 158
    Peter, 158
Joyner, William, 70, 71, 192

Katherine, St, fraternity of, 269, 288
Kebyll, William, 84
Kell, Ambrose, OFM, 264–5
Kempe, Margary, 296
Ketton stone, 214, 223, 225, 243
Keu, Richard le, 162, 163
Kilkenny, Ireland, 246, 249
Kilwardby, Robert, archbishop of Canterbury, 17, 27, 179, 299, 318
Kings Langley, Herts., Black Friars, 326
    Dominican nunnery, 57
Kingston, Henry, 43n
    Lady Mary, 44n
    Sir William, 300
Kingston-upon-Hull, Yorks., 321
Kirklees, Yorks., 177–8
Knolles, Lady Constance, 286
    Sir Robert, 104, 105, 286
Knotte, Richard, OFM, 73, 91–2, 202
Kyngynge, Anthony, 116

Lacock Abbey, Wilts., 20
Lacok, John de, prior of White Friars, 101
Lacy, Henry de, earl of Lincoln, 17, 25
    Margaret de, 17
Lady of Grace, dedication, 43
Lady of Pity, dedication, 43, 85
Lancaster, Henry of, 77
Lasco, John à, 126
Latimer, John, O. Carm., 98
Lavenham, Richard, prior of White Friars, 270
Layton, Richard, 307, 323

lead in friaries, 21, 40, 45, 52n, 82, 93, 110, 130, 200n, 238–40 (Table 17), 245–50 (passim), 310, 311
Leake, John, 10
Legh, Thomas, 99, 307, 323
Leicester Abbey, 68n
    Austin Friars, 206, 319
    Grey Friars, 326
Leland, John, 90
Lemster, Richard, O. Carm., 268
Lethum, John, 83
Lewcas, Alice, 84
Liège, Belgium, 142
Lilleshall Abbey, Shrops., 147
Lincoln Cathedral, 284
Lislaughtin, Ireland, 297
liturgy of friars, 259–60, 316, 317, 321
Llewellyn, Martin, 77

London
    aldermen, 316
    aliens, 256n, 269
    city wall, 27, 32–4 (Fig. 9), 139, 179, 316, 319
    civic government, 179, 294, 316
    civic water supply, 245, 316
    'copperplate' map-view, 80 (Fig. 24), 116 (Fig. 40)
    diocese of, 258
    eyre (court), 138
    houses, 21, 94, 102, 103, 116, 117, 149, 244, 257, 298, 301–3 (Fig. 91)
    Leake map, 10
    Ogilby and Morgan map, 7, 8 (Fig. 2), 17, 134, 138, 139, 144, 145 (Fig. 52), 156, 157
    Rocque map, 130
    schools, 260–2
    vineyard, 25, 204–5, 316
    Wyngaerde view, 40, 41 (Fig. 12), 78, 80 (Fig. 23), 134 (Fig. 47), 144, 145 (Fig. 51), 153, 157
churches & parishes
    All Hallows Barking, 281
    Christ Church Newgate, 67, 68n, 76
    Dutch church, 121, 126, 130
    Holy Innocents, 170
    'Le Laweles Chirche', 171
    St Andrew Cornhill, 291
    St Andrew by the Wardrobe, 183
    St Anne Blackfriars, 51
    St Audoen, 68n, 74 (Fig. 20)
    St Benet Fink, 140, 254, 299
    St Botolph Aldersgate, 160, 165, 254n
    St Bride, 290
    St Christopher le Stocks, 296
    St Dionis Backchurch, 290
    St Dunstan in the West, 306
    St Edmund Lombard St, 283, 308
    St Helen Bishopsgate, 141, 304
    St John the Evangelist (Holborn), 22, 25
    St Katherine Cree, 304
    St Lawrence Jewry, 160, 183
    St Margaret the Virgin (Strand), 169
    St Margaret Lothbury, 163–4, 165
    St Martin le Grand, 260
    St Nicholas Shambles, 66, 68n, 72, 74 (Fig. 20), 183, 294
    St Olave Broad Street, 121–4
    St Olave Old Jewry, 163–4, 165
    St Paul's Cathedral, 179, 183, 256, 260, 313
    St Peter ad Vincula (Tower), 155, 281, 308
    St Peter Broad Street (the Poor), 121–4, 126, 130, 133 (Fig. 46), 138, 141, 254, 299, 304
    St Sepulchre, 68n, 74 (Fig. 20)
Companies
    Apothecaries, 47, 212–13, 215
    Clothworkers, 115, 269
        almshouses, 115, 300, 306, 308
    Curriers, 269
    Drapers, 121, 269, 290
        almshouses, 154, 158, 306
    Fishmongers, 269
    Merchant Taylors, 269
    Pewterers, 120, 139, 268–9
    Pinners, 134
    Plaisterers, 207
    Pouchmakers, 120, 131, 139, 190, 207, 255
    Shearmen, 269
    Tanners, 269
    Vintners, 269, 290
    Waterbearers, 269
fraternities
    Holy Blood (of Wilsnack), 143, 157, 288
    Holy Trinity, 269
    Immaculate Conception, 207
    St Augustine, 269
    St Barbara, 157, 158, 207
    St Catherine, 269, 288
    St Clement, 269
    St James, 269
    St John, 269
    St Sebastian, 120n, 139–40, 190, 255, 296
    Visitation of the Blessed Virgin Mary, 269
places
    Aldersgate, 161
    Baynard's Castle, 29, 31 (Fig. 8), 32
    Bell inn, 127 (Fig. 43), 140
    Blackfriars, 31 (Fig. 8), 51, 58, 266, 267, 293; see Black Friars, Water Lane
    Blackwell Hall, 4
    Bridewell Palace, 47, 207
    Bridge House estate, 70, 95, 162–3, 300–1
    Broad Street, 121, 138, 139
    Cheapside, 171
    Christ's Hospital, 57–8, 67–8, 246
    Church Entry, 38

358 INDEX

places (*cont.*)
    Colechurch Street, 161, 162, 164 (Fig. 59)
        synagogue, 163–5 (Figs 59, 60)
    Cornhill, 66
    Covent Garden, 170
    Crokkereslane, 101, 102 (Fig. 33), 103
    Crutched Friars (street), 142n, 146, 148 (Fig. 53), 293
    Ely Place, 231
    Farringdon, 135, 229, 230
    Fleet river, 15, 19, 25, 32
        quay on, 26
    Fleet Street, 101, 102, 103, 114
    Froggemerestrete, 125
    Guildhall, 4, 5, 76, 179, 223
    Hart Street, 148 (Fig. 53)
    Holborn, 21
        bridge, 19 (Fig. 4)
        suburb, 15
    Leadenhall, 4, 5, 223
    London Wall (street), 138, 139
    Lothbury, 163–4
    Ludgate, 55, 207
    Lymbrennereslan, 101, 102 (Fig. 33)
    Montfitchet's Tower, 29, 31 (Fig. 8), 32
    Newgate, 246, 247
    Newgate Street, 70, 74 (Fig. 20), 93, 95
    Old Jewry, 161
    Paul's Cross, 58, 296
    Scholand (Shoe Lane), 18, 19 (Fig. 4), 21
    Seething Lane, 148 (Fig. 53)
    Serjeants' Inn, 114
    Showell Lane, 19 (Fig. 4), 21
    Smallbridge Lane, 19 (Fig. 4), 21
    St Nicholas Lane, 71, 74 (Fig. 20), 193
    St Paul's churchyard, marbeler at, 272
    Stinking Lane, 74 (Fig. 20), 193
    Stocks market, 4
    Strand, 169 (Fig. 62)
    Swan Alley, 127 (Fig. 43), 138
    Swan inn, 127 (Fig. 43), 140
    Syvedon (Seething) Lane, 148 (Fig. 53)
    Thames, 34, 114
        reclamation of, 34, 103, 117, 118, 314, 316
        water-mill, 116–17
        wharfs, 31 (Fig. 8), 32
    Throgmorton Street, 124, 138, 140
    Tower Green, 286
    Tower Hill, 158
    Tower of London, 146
        lieutenant's house, 309n
        St Peter ad Vincula, 155, 281, 308
    Water Lane, Blackfriars, 31 (Fig. 8), 32, 35 (Fig. 10), 207
    Water Lane, Whitefriars, 106 (Fig. 34), 114, 117
    West Smithfield, 63
    Whitefriars, 8–9 (Fig. 2), 293; see White Friars, Water Lane
    Whitehall Palace, 310
    Windmill tavern, 163
    Woodruff (Woodrove) Lane, 146, 147, 148 (Fig. 53), 154, 158
religious houses
    Austin Friars, 119–41, 267–8, 319
        acquisition of land, 121–4, 294–5
        anniversary services, 310
        burials, 273, 277–80 (Fig. 89), 281–7 (passim), 288–9, 291, 298
        cemetery, 138–9
        chapter houses, 135, 222, 236–7
        church, 122–6 (passim), 128–34, 140–1, 176 (Fig. 64), 180–2, 183–90 (passim), 214, 221–2, 224
        cloister, 126, 127 (Fig. 43), 134–8, 199–200, 202, 216 (Fig. 76), 218–20, 224, 236–7, 240
        closure, 307–8
        construction campaigns, 126, 181 (Fig. 67), 196 (Fig. 71), 320, 321
        finances, 252–6, 300 (Table 20)
        floor tiles, 236–7
        foundation, 191–2, 294, 299, 315–16
        indulgence, 252
        lead, 240 (Table 17)
        library, 126
        preaching cross, 139, 296
        precinct and gardens, 138–40, 194 (Fig. 70), 196–8 (Figs 71, 72), 316
        priors' houses, 139
        prison, 139
        rented tenements, 298–303 (Fig. 91)
        school, 262
        water supply, 249–50
        priors of, see Bellond, Brown, Clare, Hamond, Lowe
    Bermondsey Abbey, see Bermondsey
    first Black Friars (Holborn), 15–26, 178, 265
        acquisition of land, 17–20, 294–5
        burials, 284, 309
        cemetery, 25
        chapter house, 23
        church, 22–24, 176 (Fig. 64)
        construction campaigns, 20–5, 181 (Fig. 67), 196 (Fig. 71)
        foundation, 191–2, 294, 315–16
        precinct and gardens, 25, 193, 194 (Fig. 70)
        royal subvention, 256
        school, 261–2
        vineyard, 25, 204–5, 316
        water supply, 25, 249, 316
    second Black Friars (Blackfriars), 27–56, 265, 318–19
        acquisition of land, 29–32
        anchoress, 40
        anniversary services, 310

burials, 280–1, 282 (Fig. 90), 283–4, 288, 289, 292, 297, 309
cemetery, 53–4, 297, 301
chapter house, 35–6, 47–51, 177 (Fig. 65), 215, 218–19 (Figs 78, 79), 224, 230, 316
church, 36–43, 179–82, 183–7 (passim), 215, 216–17 (Figs 76, 77), 223, 224, 230, 239–40, 320–1
church council at, 28, 266, 267
cloister, 43–52, 200, 202, 216 (Fig. 76), 222, 223, 239–40
closure, 307–8
construction campaigns, 34–6, 179, 181 (Fig. 67), 196 (Fig. 71), 320–1
floor tiles, 230–2
inquiry into marriage of Henry VIII, 28, 51
lead, 239–40, 310
library, 51, 202
parliament hall, 51–2, 202, 243
preaching cross, 28, 51, 296
precinct and gardens, 52–5, 196–8 (Figs 71, 72), 207–10 (Fig. 75), 314, 316
priors' houses, 48–51, 203–4, 223
refoundation, 26, 27–34, 299, 314, 316, 318–19
rented tenements, 298–302
royal subvention, 256
school, 261–2
water supply, 249
third Black Friars (St Bartholomew's), 57–65, 323
church, 60–3
gates, 63
priors of Black Friars, 208 (Fig. 75); see Darlington, Hargrave, Hilsey, Peryn, Sevenehok, Swadell, Wrotham
modern (fourth) Dominican friary (Belsize Park), 48, 212, 215
Charterhouse, 57, 220, 241, 242, 243, 311
Crossed (Crutched) Friars, 142–59, 257
acquisition of land, 146–9, 294–5, 320
cemetery, 157
chapter house, 156
church, 149, 150–5, 176 (Fig. 64), 180–2, 184, 187, 237–8, 240, 257, 309n
cloister, 149, 156, 200
closure, 307–8
construction campaigns, 149–50, 181 (Fig. 67), 196 (Fig. 71), 320, 321
floor tiles, 237–9
foundation, 191–2, 294, 315–16
kitchen, 156
lead, 240 (Table 17)
precinct and gardens, 150 (Fig. 54), 156–8, 194 (Fig. 70), 196–8 (Figs 71, 72), 316
priors' houses, 156–7, 158, 204
rented tenements, 298–302

tombs, 154 (Fig. 57), 281, 283, 285, 286, 290, 309
priors of, see Ball, Bowry, Dryver
Grey Friars, 66–96, 262–5, 318
acquisition of land, 68–70, 294–5, 318, 320
burials, 272, 273, 274–7 (Fig. 88), 279–92 (passim), 297
cartulary, 67
cemetery, 93, 94
chapter house, 86
church, 70–3, 76–82, 176 (Fig. 64), 179–82, 183–9 (passim), 217 (Fig. 77), 220, 232–3, 240, 320–1
cloister, 71–3, 82–93, 176, 193, 197–200, 202–3, 210, 240, 247–8
closure, 307–8
construction campaigns, 70–3, 179–82, 196 (Fig. 71), 320–1
floor tiles, 232–3
foundation, 191–2, 294, 315–16
gates, 93
lead, 240 (Table 17)
library, 86–90, 203
in reign of Mary, 57
obedientiaries, 251
precinct and gardens, 93–5, 193–4, 195 (Fig. 70), 196–8 (Figs 71, 72), 315, 316
register, 67
rented tenements, 298–302
royal subvention, 256
school, 67, 261, 264–5
servants, 256
water supply, 70, 240, 246–50, 316
guardians of, see Chapman, Cudnor, Cutler, Hugh, Ludgarshale, Querle, Sutton, Treviso
Holy Trinity Priory, 146, 147, 151, 183, 200, 201 (Fig. 74), 223, 260, 304
Holywell Priory, 72, 241
Hospital of St Anthony, 163
Hospital of St James, 73
Minoresses, 3, 141, 269
Pied Friars, 167–72
acquisition of land, 168–70, 294–5
cemetery, 171
church, 169–70, 176 (Fig. 64)
construction campaigns, 170, 181 (Fig. 67), 320
foundation, 191–2, 294, 315–16
precinct and gardens, 171–2, 195 (Fig. 70)
Sack Friars, 160–6
acquisition of land, 162–4, 294–5
burial fees, 254n
cemetery, 165
church, 164–5, 176 (Fig. 64)

religious houses (*cont.*)
   Sack Friars (*cont.*)
      construction campaigns, 164, 181 (Fig. 67)
      foundation, 191–2, 294, 315–16
      precinct and gardens, 164–5, 194 (Fig. 70)
   St Bartholomew's Priory, 58, 60–2, 72, 152, 210
      gatehouse, 63, 64 (Fig. 18), 65
   St Helen Bishopsgate, 141, 304
   St John Clerkenwell, 241, 242
   St Mary Bishopsgate (Spital), 182, 183, 200, 201 (Fig. 74), 223, 242, 293–4, 298, 301, 309, 313, 315
      priors of, 125; see Abiton, Heston
   St Mary Clerkenwell, 72, 232, 241, 243, 304
   St Mary Graces, 5, 221, 223, 242
   St Mary Overie (Southwark), 182, 183
   St Thomas of Acre, 290–1
   Templars, 162
      mill, 31 (Fig. 8), 32
   Westminster Abbey, see Westminster
   White Friars, 7–10, Fig. 2, 97–118, 265–7, 319
      acquisition of land, 100–3, 294–5
      almshouses, 115
      cemetery, 114
      chapter house, 110, 112
      church, 103, 104, 105–10, 176 (Fig. 64), 180–2, 183, 187, 233–5, 240, 244, 301
      cloister, 104–5, 110–14, 200, 240
      closure, 307–8
      construction campaigns, 103–5, 181 (Fig. 67), 196 (Fig. 71), 320, 321
      floor tiles, 233–6
      foundation, 191–2, 294, 315–16
      general chapter at, 103, 259, 319
      infirmary, 115
      lead, 240 (Table 17)
      library, 98, 114–15
      mill, 116–17, 118
      missal, 260 (Fig. 87)
      precinct and gardens, 114–17, 194 (Fig. 70), 196–8 (Figs 71, 72), 205, 316
      prior's house, 100 (Fig. 32), 113–14, 204
      rented tenements, 298–302
      school, 98, 115, 261–2
      tombs, 280, 281, 283, 284–5, 286, 309
      water supply, 250
      priors of, see Elm, French, Gybbes, Lacok, Lavenham, Loney, Milverton, Pickingham
Londoners, 209 (Fig. 75), 293–304, 313, 320, 321
   aliens, 120, 143, 256n, 269, 288–9, 296
   Doche, 143
   Flemish, 143
   Jews, 163
      tombs of, 289–91, 322

Loney, John, prior of White Friars, 266
Longespée, Ela de, countess of Warwick, 17, 18, 19, 72
Losse, Hugh, 130n, 309–10
Louis IX of France, St, 77, 83, 84, 160
Louvain (Leuven), Belgium, 59
Lovell, Henry, 285
   William, lord Lovell, 285
Low Countries floor tiles, 228–38 (passim), 244
Lowe, John, prior of Austin Friars, 139, 267
Ludgarshale, William de, guardian of Grey Friars, 193
Ludvig of Bavaria, emperor, 263
Lynwood, Thomas, OFM, 269

Machyn, Henry, 58, 296
Malberthorp, John, OFM, 270
Maldon, Essex, 1
Malewyn, Elizabeth, countess of Atholl, 104
Man, Katharine, 40
Maneriis, Andrew de, 289
Mansel, Cecily, 58, 296
Mansell, Edward, 77
map regression, technique of, 6–10, Fig. 2, 314
Margaret of France, consort of Edward I, 67, 70, 72, 76–77, 95, 202, 283, 295, 318
Margaret, countess of Kent, see Burgh and Dawes
Margaret, St, 169
Marseilles, France, Pied friars, 167
Marshal, Margaret, duchess of Norfolk, 270
Marshall, Robert, see Mascall
Martyn, Lionel, 307
Maruffus, Raphael, 252
Mary I, 57, 60
   counter-Reformation, 57–9
Mary Magdalene, St, 85, 323
Mary, Virgin, dedication, 42, 83, 84, 110, 129, 131, 152
   fraternity of Visitation of Blessed, 269
Maryner, Agnes, 272
   John, 272, 277, 292
   Juliana, 272, 277
Mascall, Robert, bishop of Hereford, O. Carm., 104, 105
Masci, Girolamo, OFM, 317
Melton, William de, 73
Merton Abbey, Surrey, 182, 183
Metrical Life of St Hugh, 214
Michael the Archangel, 43
Michael, St, 43, 84
Milbourne, Joan, 281, 308
   Sir John, 281, 291, 306, 308
mill, monastic, 32, 93–4, 116–17, 118, 203, 205, 257
Mills, Peter, 9, 10
Milverton, John, prior of White Friars, 266–7
Moday, William, 73, 294

Modena, Louis of, O. Aug., 267
Molington, Sir Thomas de, 285
Mont St Michel, France, 220, 224
Monte, Christian de, O. Aug., 267
Montfort, Simon de, 120
Mooney, Donatus, OFM, 249
Mordon, Christina, 290
    Walter, 77, 290
Morin, William, O. Carm., 270
Morrison, Richard, 305
Mortelak (Mortlake), Yvo de, 18
Moses of London, master, 163
Moton, Hugh, 125
moulded stone, 135–6, 137 (Fig. 49), 211–26, 316
Multon, John, O. Aug., 267
Multyfarnham, Ireland, 297
Mylbourn, Gilbert, OFM, 265

Narborough, Elizabeth, 291
    William, 291
Neel, John, master of St Thomas of Acre, 290–1
Netter, Thomas, O. Carm., 266, 270
Nicholas IV, pope, 317
Nicholas, St, 130, 131
noir Belge (stone), 243
Norwich, 1
    Black Friars, 37n, 140, 185, 186 (Fig. 68), 206, 315
    cathedral priory, 203, 223
        obedientaries' accounts, 251
    Grey Friars, 225, 261
    Pied Friars, 167
    Sack Friars, 176 (Fig. 64)
    St Giles, 315
    White Friars, 109, 224–5, 319
Norwich, Edmund de, 73
    Galfridus de, 72
Nottingham, William of, OFM, 70, 93, 95
Nuneaton, Warwicks., 287
Nutley Priory (abbey), Bucks., abbot of, 18

obedientiaries, 251, 314
Observant Franciscans, order, 67, 280
Ockham, William of, OFM, 263
Ogbourne Priory, Wilts., 29
Oliver, John, 9, 10
orchard, 25, 140, 157, 204, 205, 316
organ, 43, 82, 85
Ossory, Ireland, 246
Oxford, Austin Friars, 262
    Black Friars, 256
    Grey Friars, 185, 186 (Fig. 68), 256, 263
    Magdalen College, 278
    Merton College, 36, 202
    New College, 223
    university, 260, 261
    White Friars, 205, 262
packstone (Calvados), 214, 225

painted decoration, 45, 48, 78, 110, 143n, 152, 188n, 189, 214, 244
Paris, 1, 95, 314
    Augustine friars, 262
    Carmelites, 109
    Dominicans, 319
parliament, at Blackfriars, 51–2
Parys, Rose, 290
    Simon, 290
    William de, 125
Pateshull, Peter, O. Aug., 267, 296
Patrick, St, 43
Patrington, Stephen, O. Carm., 266, 270
Paul, Francis, O. Aug., 269, 296
Paulet, John, 130
    Thomas, 305
    William, 121, 130, 250, 273, 305
Pecham, John, archbishop of Canterbury, 318
Pembroke, earls of, 25
Pembyrton, Walter, 85
Penitence of Jesus Christ, friars of, see Sack
Penketh, Thomas, O. Aug., 267, 268
Penn floor tiles, 140, 152, 228–38 (passim), 244
Perpendicular style, 78, 88, 128, 154, 159, 187, 221, 224, 321
Person, John, OFM, 264–5
Peryn, William, prior of Black Friars, 59–65 (passim)
Peter of Milan (Verona), St, 43
Peter, St, 43
Peterborough Abbey (cathedral), obedientaries' accounts, 251
Pexsall, Ralph, 306
Philip of Spain, 57
Philipot, Joan, 290
    Sir John, 290
Philippa of Hainault, consort of Edward III, 77, 95, 270
Piacenza, Italy, Franciscans, 319
Pickingham, Osbert, prior of White Friars, 266
Pied friars, 167, 318
Pierce the Ploughman's Crede, 37, 45, 48, 188, 200
Piers Plowman, 188
pilgrimage of Grace, 311
Pisa, Italy, Franciscans, 182, 319
Pisario (Paquerii), Giraldus de, OFM, 264
Plumpton, William de, 169, 170
Pole, Edmund de la, 287
    Reginald, 57, 60
Portehors, William, O. Carm., 112–13
Portinari, John, 307
Potter, Walter (15th C), 85
Potter, Walter le (13th C), 71, 91, 318
preaching, 28, 59, 139, 178, 204, 268–70, 296
priors' houses, 47–51, 93, 100 (Fig. 32), 113–14, 136 (Fig. 48), 156–7, 203–4, 207, 208 (Fig. 75), 244
prison, monastic, 139

processions, 59, 129, 139, 296–7, 298, 317, 319, 322
pulpitum, 184
Purbeck marble, 38, 48, 52, 103, 104, 129, 135, 176, 214, 215, 220, 225, 242–3, 290
Pykering, William, 94
Pypot, Robert, 299

Querle, William, guardian of Grey Friars, 264

ragstone (Kentish), 22, 34, 38, 53, 78, 128, 156, 214, 222, 242–3
Ramsay, Agnes de, 283
　William de, master mason, 283
Rede, Robert, Sir, 109–10, 118
Reffham, John de, 73
Reigate stone, 38, 128, 213–14, 223, 225, 242–3, 246
relics, 259, 323
Renger, Richard, 18, 193
Repetitiones lectionum, 263
Rest, John, 291
Ricardus, O. Aug., 268
Rich, Richard, 58–9, 305
Richard II, 101, 270
Richmond, Surrey, Observant Franciscans, 3, 280
　palace, 3
Rieti, Italy, Dominicans, 319
Roben, Walter, OFM, 94, 205
Roche, St, 130, 131
Rokesle, Gregory de, 71
Rome, 266–7, 314
　Dominicans, 319
　S. Maria Scala Coeli, 153
Rondel, Thomas, OFM, 263
roof tiles, 239–41, 244
Roos, Thomas, 85
Rotherhithe Palace, Surrey, 221
Rysley, Sir John, 281

Sabernes (Sabarn), William, 146, 147, 150, 294
Sack friars, 160, 318
Sackville, Sir Andrew, 287
Salisbury Cathedral, Wilts., 179
Salve Regina, 317, 319
Salzwedel, Germany, 193
Sampford, John, 290
Samsun, Thomas, 58
Saxony, Jordan of, OP, 261–2, 317
scala coeli mass, 153
scholarship at friaries, 262–8
schools, mendicant, 260–2; see London, monastic houses
　for lay people, 323
Scudamore, Philip, 63
Sculthorpe, Norf., 286
Sebastian, St, 110, 130, 131, 255
　fraternity of, 120n, 139–40, 190, 255, 296
Sedbar, Henry, OFM, 264

Seintpol, Marie de, countess of Pembroke, 84, 270; see Châtillon
Selborne Priory, Hants., 214
sermons, 59, 266, 267, 268, 270, 296
servants, monastic, 94, 209–10 (Fig. 75), 253 (Table 19), 256
service courts, monastic, 93–4, 115–16, 139, 203, 205, 257, 313, 315
Sevenehok, John de, prior of Black Friars, 34
Seymour, Edward, duke of Somerset, 58
Sheen, Surrey, Carthusians, 57
Siena, Italy, Dominicans, 319
Sifrewast, John, OP, 265
Skevington, Sir John, 291, 322
Slapton, Northants., 188n
slate (roofing), 242–3
Smith, Isabelle, 272
　Joan, 272
　John, of Coventry, 272
Southwark, see London, religious houses (St Mary Overie)
Sowle (Souley), John, O. Carm., 266
Spilman, Thomas, 309–10
stables, monastic, 25, 54, 139, 157, 205
Stafford, Edward, duke of Buckingham, 286
　Eleanor, 85
　John, bishop of Bath and Wells, 101
Standon, Herts., 280
Stapeldon, Walter, bishop of Exeter, 171, 325
statutes of Mortmain, 140, 254, 299
Stocton, John, O. Aug., 267
stone, floor slabs, 242–3
　roof flags, 243, 244
　used in London buildings, 211–26 (passim), 242–3 (Table 18); see Barnack, Caen, chalk, Hassock, Hythe Beds, Ketton, packstone, Purbeck, ragstone, Reigate, slate
stonemasons' tools, 214
Storteforde, Thomas de, 72
Stow, John, 4, 97, 104, 110, 119, 133, 146, 157, 165, 273
Strangeways, Katherine, 280
Stratford, Richard de, 35, 48
Summa logicae, 263
Survey of London, 4, 273
Sutton, Henry de, guardian of Grey Friars, 77, 193
Swadell, William, prior of Black Friars, 265
Swyllyngton, Sir Roger, 270
Syon Abbey, Middx, 57
Syward, William, OP, 270

Taillour, Philip le, 72, 294
Tanner, Arnold le, 125
Tarentaise, Peter of, OP, 317
Tatenhall, John, OP, 264
Taylour, William, 246
Tegularius (Tiler), Henry, 18
　Adam, 18

Tewkesbury, Peter of, 318
Thacker, Thomas, 308
Thomas, St, 131
Thornham Parva, Suff., retable, 188
Thorpe, William, OFM, 264
Tilty, Essex, 281, 308n
timber in monastic churches, 21 (Table 4), 22, 34, 63, 70, 77n, 103, 104 (Table 8), 110, 151, 165, 184, 189, 215, 309n, 310, 311
Tiptoft, John, earl of Worcester, 42, 187, 286, 322
Titchfield Abbey, Hants., 233
Toly, William, OFM, 265
tombs, 155 (Fig. 57), 272–92
tramezzo, 184
Tremayle, unidentified French lord, 288
trental of masses, 185n, 297, 322, 323
Treviso, Henry de, guardian of Grey Friars, 70
Trinitarian friars, xvi (Table 1), 1n, 3
Trinity, dedication to, 110, 153–4
Trivet, Nicholas, OP, 265
true cross, relics, 323
Tuddenham, Sir Thomas, 287
Tudor houses, 302–3 (Fig. 91)
Turner, Oliver, 291
Turre, Hugo de, 72
    Theophania de, 72
Tutchet, James, Lord Audley, 286
Tyrell, Sir James, 287

Urmestone, Robert, 63
Uske, Nicholas, 83
Utrecht, Netherlands, Dominicans, 189

Valence, John de, 22
    Margaret de, 22, 284
    William de, earl of Pembroke, 22, 284
Veill, William le, 18, 193
Vere, John de, earl of Oxford, 286, 287
    Sir Aubrey, 286, 287
Verney, John, O. Aug., 268
Vicenza, Italy, Dominicans, 319
    Franciscans, 319
Vilagrassa, John of, OP, 58, 60
vineyard, 25, 204–5, 316
Visconti, Lucia, countess of Kent, 288
Vyaunde, John, 290

Waleys, Henry le, 27, 71, 76–7, 95, 179, 202, 294, 318, 319
    Thomas, OP, 263
walking place, 38n, 184–5
wall plaster, 243, 244
Wallop, lady Rose, 95
Wallop, see Wyseman
Waltham Abbey, Essex, 245
war with Scotland and France (1540s), 311, 312
Ware, Herts., 1

Warner, Hilary, 116, 118
water supply, 25, 245–50, 316
Welle, John atte, OFM, 264
Wells Cathedral, Som., 135, 220
Westminster Abbey, 258, 283
    chapter house, 232
    church, 179, 183
    cloisters, 136
    convent garden, 170
    muniment room, 230
    obedientaries' accounts, 251
    refoundation in 1556, 57
    sacrist, 168
    scala coeli chapel, 153
    tombs, 287
Westminster Palace, 35
    Jewel Tower, 308
    St Stephen, 314
'Westminster' floor tiles, 40, 135, 152, 228–38 (passim), 244
Whaplode, Lincs., 142
Whittington, Richard, 73, 86, 203, 295
Williamite friars, 1n
wills, bequests in, 42, 70, 83–6 (Table 6), 100, 110, 118, 126, 129, 132 (Table 10), 139, 253–4, 268, 269, 295, 306
Winchelsea, Sussex, 321
windows, stained glass, 34, 37, 40, 71, 77, 78, 86, 88, 126, 128, 152, 178, 187, 188, 199, 215–17, 220–3, 320, 321
Windsor Castle, Berks., 230
    forest, 126
Wodeham, Adam, OFM, 263
Wolsey, Thomas, 28, 302
Woodford, Luke of, OP, 270
    William, OFM, 264, 270
woodland, suburban, 25, 204
Wriothesley, Charles, 58
    Sir Thomas, 273, 322
Wrotham, John de, prior of Black Friars, 35
    John, O. Carm., 266
Wyclif, John, 264, 266, 267, 296, 325
Wynchelsey, Thomas, OFM, 77, 86
Wyngaerde, Anton van den, 40, 41 (Fig. 12), 78, 80 (Fig. 23), 134 (Fig. 47), 144, 145 (Fig. 51), 153, 157
Wyseman (Wallop), John, 307

Yakislei, Andrew, OP, 265
Yarmouth Priory, Norf., 255–6
Yonge, Margaret, 84
York, Black Friars, 323
    Grey Friars, 255
York, Hugh of, Pied friar, 167
Yorke, William de, 125

Zita, St, 43
Zougg, Robert, OFM, 249

Other volumes in
Studies in the History of Medieval Religion

I: Dedications of Monastic Houses in England and Wales 1066–1216
Alison Binns

II: The Early Charters of the Augustinian Canons of
Waltham Abbey, Essex, 1062–1230
Edited by Rosalind Ransford

III: Religious Belief and Ecclesiastical Careers in Late Medieval England
Edited by Christopher Harper-Bill

IV: The Rule of the Templars:
The French text of the Rule of the Order of the Knights Templar
Translated and introduced by J. M. Upton-Ward

V: The Collegiate Church of Wimborne Minster
Patricia H. Coulstock

VI: William Waynflete: Bishop and Educationalist
Virginia Davis

VII: Medieval Ecclesiastical Studies in honour of Dorothy M. Owen
Edited by M. J. Franklin and Christopher Harper-Bill

VIII: A Brotherhood of Canons Serving God
English Secular Cathedrals in the Later Middle Ages
David Lepine

IX: Westminster Abbey and its People c.1050–c.1216
Emma Mason

X: Gilds in the Medieval Countryside
Social and Religious Change in Cambridgeshire c.1350–1558
Virginia R. Bainbridge

XI: Monastic Revival and Regional Identity in Early Normandy
Cassandra Potts

XII: The Convent and the Community in Late Medieval England:
Female Monasteries in the Diocese of Norwich 1350–1540
Marilyn Oliva

XIII: Pilgrimage to Rome in the Middle Ages: Continuity and Change
Debra J. Birch

XIV: St Cuthbert and the Normans: the Church of Durham 1071–1153
William M. Aird

XV: The Last Generation of English Catholic Clergy:
Parish Priests in the Diocese of Coventry and Lichfield in
the Early Sixteenth Century
Tim Cooper

XVI: The Premonstratensian Order in Late Medieval England
Joseph A. Gribbin

XVII: Inward Purity and Outward Splendour:
Death and Remembrance in the Deanery of Dunwich, Suffolk, 1370–1547
Judith Middleton-Stewart

XVIII: The Religious Orders in Pre-Reformation England
Edited by James G. Clark

XIX: The Catalan Rule of the Templars:
A Critical Edition and English Translation from Barcelona,
Archito de la Corona de Aragón, 'Cartes Reales', MS 3344
Edited and translated by Judi Upton-Ward

XX: Leper Knights:
The Order of St Lazarus of Jerusalem in England, c. 1150–1544
David Marcombe

XXI: The Secular Jurisdiction of Monasteries
in Anglo-Norman and Angevin England
Kevin L. Shirley

XXII: The Dependent Priories of Medieval English Monasteries
Martin Heale

XXIII: The Cartulary of St Mary's Collegiate Church, Warwick
Edited by Charles Fonge

XXIV: Leadership in Medieval English Nunneries
Valerie G. Spear

XXV: The Art and Architecture of English Benedictine Monasteries, 1300–1540:
A Patronage History
Julian M. Luxford

XXVI: Norwich Cathedral Close: The Evolution of the
English Cathedral Landscape
Roberta Gilchrist

XXVII: The Foundations of Medieval English Ecclesiastical History
Edited by Philippa Hoskin, Christopher Brooks and Barrie Dobson

XXVIII: Thomas Becket and his Biographers
Michael Staunton

XXIX: Late Medieval Monasteries and their Patrons:
England and Wales, c.1300–1540
Karen Stöber

XXX: The Culture of Medieval English Monasticism
Edited by James G. Clark

XXXI: A History of the Abbey of Bury St Edmunds, 1182–1256:
Samson of Tottington to Edmund of Walpole
Antonia Gransden

XXXII: Monastic Hospitality:
The Benedictines in England, c.1070–c.1250
Julie Kerr

XXXIII: Religious Life in Normandy, 1050–1300:
Space, Gender and Social Pressure
Leonie V. Hicks

XXXIV: The Medieval Chantry Chapel: An Archaeology
Simon Roffey

XXXV: Monasteries and Society in the British Isles
in the Later Middle Ages
Edited by Janet Burton and Karen Stöber

XXXVI: Jocelin of Wells: Bishop, Builder, Courtier
Edited by Robert Dunning

XXXVII: War and the Making of Medieval Monastic Culture
Katherine Allen Smith

XXXVIII: Cathedrals, Communities and Conflict in the Anglo-Norman World
Edited by Paul Dalton, Charles Insley and Louise J. Wilkinson

XXXIX: English Nuns and the Law in the Middle Ages:
Cloistered Nuns and Their Lawyers, 1293–1540
Elizabeth Makowski

XL: The Nobility and Ecclesiastical Patronage in Thirteenth-Century England
Elizabeth Gemmill

XLI: Pope Gregory X and the Crusades
Philip B. Baldwin

XLII: A History of the Abbey of Bury St Edmunds, 1257–1301:
Simon of Luton and John of Northwold
Antonia Gransden

XLIII: King John and Religion
Paul Webster

XLIV: The Church and Vale of Evesham, 700–1215:
Lordship, Landscape and Prayer
David Cox

XLV: Medieval Anchorites in their Communities
Edited by Cate Gunn and Liz Herbert McAvoy

XLVI: The Friaries of Medieval London: From Foundation to Dissolution
Nick Holder

XLVII: 'The Right Ordering of Souls':
The Parish of All Saints' Bristol on the Eve of the Reformation
Clive Burgess

XLVIII: The Lateran Church in Rome and the Ark of the Covenant:
Housing the Holy Relics of Jerusalem with an edition and translation
of the *Descriptio Lateranensis Ecclesiae* (BAV Reg. Lat. 712)
Eivor Andersen Oftestad

XLIX: Apostate Nuns in the Later Middle Ages
Elizabeth Makowski

www.ingramcontent.com/pod-product-compliance
Lightning Source LLC
Chambersburg PA
CBHW060334010526
44117CB00017B/2825